4.4BSD
System Manager's Manual
(SMM)

Now in its twentieth year, the USENIX Association, the UNIX and Advanced Computing Systems professional and technical organization, is a not-for-profit membership association of individuals and institutions with an interest in UNIX and UNIX-like systems, and, by extension, C++, X windows, and other advanced tools and technologies.

USENIX and its members are dedicated to:

- fostering innovation and communicating research and technological developments,
- sharing ideas and experience relevant to UNIX, UNIX-related, and advanced computing systems, and
- providing a neutral forum for the exercise of critical thought and airing of technical issues.

USENIX publishes a journal (**Computing Systems**), a newsletter (*;login:*), Proceedings from its frequent Conferences and Symposia, and a Book Series.

SAGE, The Systems Administrators Guild, a Special Technical Group with the USENIX Association, is dedicated to the advancement of system administration as a profession.

SAGE brings together systems managers and administrators to:

- propagate knowledge of good professional practice,
- recruit talented individuals to the profession,
- recognize individuals who attain professional excellence,
- foster technical development and share solutions to technical problems, and
- communicate in an organized voice with users, management, and vendors on system administration topics.

4.4BSD
System Manager's Manual
(SMM)

Berkeley Software Distribution

April, 1994

Computer Systems Research Group
University of California at Berkeley

A USENIX Association Book
O'Reilly & Associates, Inc.
103 Morris Street, Suite A
Sebastopol, CA 94572

First Printing, 1994

This book was printed and bound in the United States of America.
Distributed by O'Reilly & Associates, Inc.

[recycle logo] This book is printed on acid-free paper with 50% recycled content, 10-13% post-consumer waste. O'Reilly & Associates is committed to using paper with the highest recycled content available consistent with high quality.

ISBN: 1-56592-080-5

Contents

Introduction

The documentation for 4.4BSD is in a format similar to the one used for the 4.2BSD and 4.3BSD manuals. It is divided into three sets; each set consists of one or more volumes. The abbreviations for the volume names are listed in square brackets; the abbreviations for the manual sections are listed in parenthesis.

- I. User's Documents
  - User's Reference Manual [URM]
    - Commands (1)
    - Games (6)
    - Macro packages and language conventions (7)
  - User's Supplementary Documents [USD]
    - Getting Started
    - Basic Utilities
    - Communicating with the World
    - Text Editing
    - Document Preparation
    - Amusements
- II. Programmer's Documents
  - Programmer's Reference Manual [PRM]
    - System calls (2)
    - Subroutines (3)
    - Special files (4)
    - File formats and conventions (5)
  - Programmer's Supplementary Documents [PSD]
    - Documents of Historic Interest
    - Languages in common use
    - Programming Tools
    - Programming Libraries
    - General Reference
- III. System Manager's Manual [SMM]
  - Maintenance commands (8)
  - System Installation and Administration

References to individual documents are given as ''volume:document'', thus USD:1 refers to the first document in the ''User's Supplementary Documents''. References to manual pages are given as ''*name*(section)'' thus *sh*(1) refers to the shell manual entry in section 1.

The manual pages give descriptions of the features of the 4.4BSD system, as developed at the University of California at Berkeley. They do not attempt to provide perspective or tutorial information about the 4.4BSD operating system, its facilities, or its implementation. Various documents on those topics are contained in the ''UNIX User's Supplementary Documents'' (USD), the ''UNIX Programmer's Supplementary Documents'' (PSD), and ''UNIX System Manager's Manual'' (SMM). In particular, for an overview see ''The UNIX Time-Sharing System'' (PSD:1) by Ritchie and Thompson; for a tutorial see ''UNIX for Beginners'' (USD:1) by Kernighan, and for an guide to the new features of this latest version, see ''Berkeley Software Architecture Manual (4.4 Edition)'' (PSD:5).

Within the area it surveys, this volume attempts to be timely, complete and concise. Where the latter two objectives conflict, the obvious is often left unsaid in favor of brevity. It is intended that each program be described as it is, not as it should be. Inevitably, this means that various sections will soon be out of date.

Commands are programs intended to be invoked directly by the user, in contrast to subroutines, that are intended to be called by the user's programs. User commands are described in URM section 1. Commands generally reside in directory */bin* (for *bin* ary programs). Some programs also reside in */usr/bin,* to save space in */bin.* These directories are searched automatically by the command interpreters. Additional directories that may be of interest include */usr/contrib/bin,* which has contributed software */usr/old/bin,* which has old but sometimes still useful software and */usr/local/bin,* which contains software local to your site.

Games have been relegated to URM section 6 and */usr/games,* to keep them from contaminating the more staid information of URM section 1.

Miscellaneous collection of information necessary for writing in various specialized languages such as character codes, macro packages for typesetting, etc is contained in URM section 7.

System calls are entries into the BSD kernel. The system call interface is identical to a C language procedure call; the equivalent C procedures are described in PRM section 2.

An assortment of subroutines is available; they are described in PRM section 3. The primary libraries in which they are kept are described in *intro*(3). The functions are described in terms of C.

PRM section 4 discusses the characteristics of each system "file" that refers to an I/O device. The names in this section refer to the HP300 device names for the hardware, instead of the names of the special files themselves.

The file formats and conventions (PRM section 5) documents the structure of particular kinds of files; for example, the form of the output of the loader and assembler is given. Excluded are files used by only one command, for example the assembler's intermediate files.

Commands and procedures intended for use primarily by the system administrator are described in SMM section 8. The files described here are almost all kept in the directory */etc.* The system administration binaries reside in */sbin,* and */usr/sbin.*

Each section consists of independent entries of a page or so each. The name of the entry is in the upper corners of its pages, together with the section number. Entries within each section are alphabetized. The page numbers of each entry start at 1; it is infeasible to number consecutively the pages of a document like this that is republished in many variant forms.

All entries are based on a common format; not all subsections always appear.

> The *name* subsection lists the exact names of the commands and subroutines covered under the entry and gives a short description of their purpose.
>
> The *synopsis* summarizes the use of the program being described. A few conventions are used, particularly in the Commands subsection:
>
> > **Boldface** words are considered literals, and are typed just as they appear.
> >
> > Square brackets [ ] around an argument show that the argument is optional. When an argument is given as "name", it always refers to a file name.
> >
> > Ellipses "..." are used to show that the previous argument-prototype may be repeated.
> >
> > A final convention is used by the commands themselves. An argument beginning with a minus sign "–" usually means that it is an option-specifying argument, even if it appears in a position where a file name could appear. Therefore, it is unwise to have files whose names begin with "–".
>
> The *description* subsection discusses in detail the subject at hand.
>
> The *files* subsection gives the names of files that are built into the program.
>
> A *see also* subsection gives pointers to related information.
>
> A *diagnostics* subsection discusses the diagnostic indications that may be produced. Messages that are intended to be self-explanatory are not listed.
>
> The *bugs* subsection gives known bugs and sometimes deficiencies. Occasionally the suggested fix is also described.

At the beginning of URM, PRM, and SSM is a List of Manual Pages, organized by section and alphabetically within each section, and a Permuted Index derived from that List. Within each index entry, the title of the writeup to which it refers is followed by the appropriate section number in parentheses. This fact is important because there is considerable name duplication among the sections, arising principally from commands that exist only to exercise a particular system call. Finally, there is a list of documents on the inside back cover of each volume.

List of Manual Pages

1. Commands and Application Programs

2. System Calls

3. C Library Subroutines

4. Special Files

5. File Formats

6. Games

7. Miscellaneous

8. System Maintenance

Permuted Index

Section 8

System Maintenance

NAME

intro – introduction to system maintenance and operation commands

DESCRIPTION

This section contains information related to system operation and maintenance. It describes commands used to create new file systems, 'newfs', verify the integrity of the file systems, 'fsck', control disk usage, 'edquota', maintain system backups, 'dump', and recover files when disks die an untimely death, 'restore'. The 'format' manual for the specific architecture the system is running on should be consulted when formatting disks and tapes. Network related services like 'inetd' and 'ftpd' are also described. The section 'crash' should be consulted to understand how to interpret system crash dumps.

HISTORY

The **intro** section manual page appeared in 4.2BSD.

M8

NAME

ac – display connect time accounting

SYNOPSIS

ac [**-d**] [**-p**] [**-w** *file*] [*users ...*]

DESCRIPTION

If the file /var/log/wtmp exists, a record of individual login and logout times are written to it by init(8) and login(8) respectively. The program **ac** examines these records and writes the accumulated connect time for all logins to the standard output.

Options available:

-d Display the connect times in 24 hour chunks.

-p Display individual user totals.

-w *file*
Read raw connect time data from *file* instead of the default file /var/log/wtmp.

users ...
Display totals for the given individuals only.

If no arguments are given, **ac** displays the total amount of login time for all active accounts on the system.

The default wtmp file is an infinitely increasing file unless frequently truncated. This is normally done by the daily daemon scripts scheduled by cron(8) which rename and rotate the wtmp files before truncating them (and keeping about a weeks worth on hand). No login times are collected however, if the file does not exist.

FILES

/var/log/wtmp
/var/log/wtmp.[0-7] rotated files

SEE ALSO

init(8), sa(8), login(1), utmp(5).

HISTORY

A **ac** command appeared in Version 6 AT&T UNIX.

M8

NAME

acucntrl – turn around tty line between dialin and dialout

SYNOPSIS

/usr/lib/uucp/acucntrl keyword ttyline

DESCRIPTION

Acucntrl turns around the terminal line, enabling it to be used for both dialin and dialout. On dialin a terminal line is assumed to have modem control enabled and a getty process in existence waiting for logins. On dialout modem control is disabled and there is no getty process.

This program must be run setuid to root.

keyword is chosen from the list: *disable* or *dialout*, to condition a line for dialout; and *enable* or *dialin*, to condition a line for dialin.

When the line is conditioned for dialing out, the login name of the real uid of the process is placed in /etc/utmp in capitals. This declares that the line is in use and acts as an additional locking mechanism. *Acucntrl* will refuse to act if the /etc/utmp entry for the line is not null, is not the the user's login name (capitalized or not), and if the process is not running as the superuser. The last condition is to allow the superuser to clear the state of the line.

Turning modem control on or off is handled by poking into /dev/kmem. It is currently implemented for dz, dh, and dmf lines.

Under 4.2 BSD the program will also refuse to disable a line if carrier is sensed on it. This is to avoid the dead period where someone has just dialed in and made the connection but has not yet logged in.

Ttyline can be either of the form tty* or /dev/tty*. Enabling/disabling a line whose name does not begin with ttyd? is prohibited unless the real uid of the process is 0 or if the login name corresponding to the real uid is uucp. This is a security precaution.

Steps taken when disabling (*i.e.* setup for dialing out)

1) check input arguments
2) look in /etc/utmp to check that the line is not in use by another user
3) disable modem control on line
4) check for carrier on device
5) change owner of device to real uid
6) edit /etc/ttys, changing the first character of the appropriate line to 0
7) send a hangup to process 1 to poke init to disable getty
8) post uid name in capitals in /etc/utmp to let world know device has been grabbed
9) make sure that DTR is on

Steps taken when enabling (*i.e.* setup for dialing in)

1) check input arguments
2) look in /etc/utmp to check that the line is not in use by another user
3) make sure modem control on line is disabled
4) turn off DTR to make sure line is hung up
5) condition line: clear exclusive use and set hangup on close modes
6) turn on modem control
7) edit /etc/ttys, changing the first character of the appropriate line to 1
8) send a hangup to process 1 to poke init to enable getty

NAME

acucntrl – turn around tty line between dialin and dialout

SYNOPSIS

/usr/lib/uucp/acucntrl keyword ttyline

DESCRIPTION

Acucntrl turns around the terminal line, enabling it to be used for both dialin and dialout. On dialin a terminal line is assumed to have modem control enabled and a getty process in existence waiting for logins. On dialout modem control is disabled and there is no getty process.

This program must be run setuid to root.

keyword is chosen from the list: *disable* or *dialout*, to condition a line for dialout; and *enable* or *dialin*, to condition a line for dialin.

When the line is conditioned for dialing out, the login name of the real uid of the process is placed in /etc/utmp in capitals. This declares that the line is in use and acts as an additional locking mechanism. *Acucntrl* will refuse to act if the /etc/utmp entry for the line is not null, is not the the user's login name (capitalized or not), and if the process is not running as the superuser. The last condition is to allow the superuser to clear the state of the line.

Turning modem control on or off is handled by poking into /dev/kmem. It is currently implemented for dz, dh, and dmf lines.

Under 4.2 BSD the program will also refuse to disable a line if carrier is sensed on it. This is to avoid the dead period where someone has just dialed in and made the connection but has not yet logged in.

Ttyline can be either of the form tty* or /dev/tty*. Enabling/disabling a line whose name does not begin with ttyd? is prohibited unless the real uid of the process is 0 or if the login name corresponding to the real uid is uucp. This is a security precaution.

Steps taken when disabling (*i.e.* setup for dialing out)

1) check input arguments
2) look in /etc/utmp to check that the line is not in use by another user
3) disable modem control on line
4) check for carrier on device
5) change owner of device to real uid
6) edit /etc/ttys, changing the first character of the appropriate line to 0
7) send a hangup to process 1 to poke init to disable getty
8) post uid name in capitals in /etc/utmp to let world know device has been grabbed
9) make sure that DTR is on

Steps taken when enabling (*i.e.* setup for dialing in)

1) check input arguments
2) look in /etc/utmp to check that the line is not in use by another user
3) make sure modem control on line is disabled
4) turn off DTR to make sure line is hung up
5) condition line: clear exclusive use and set hangup on close modes
6) turn on modem control
7) edit /etc/ttys, changing the first character of the appropriate line to 1

8) send a hangup to process 1 to poke init to enable getty

9) clear uid name for /etc/utmp

HISTORY

First written by Allan Wilkes (fisher!allan)

Modified June 8,1983 by W.Sebok (astrovax!wls) to poke the kernel rather than use a kernel hack to turn on/off modem control, using a subroutine stolen from a program written by Tsutomu Shimomura {astrovax,escher}!tsutomu

Worked over many times by W.Sebok (*i.e.* hacked to death)

FILES

/dev/kmem, /vmunix, /etc/ttys, /etc/utmp, /dev/tty*

BUGS

Sensing carrier requires the 4.2 BSD TIOCMGET ioctl call. Unfortunately this ioctl is not implemented in the vanilla 4.2 BSD dh driver even though the dz and dmf drivers use an emulation of the DH11's modem control bits. This has been fixed here.

Some time (currently 2 seconds) is required between disabling modem control and opening the device. This is probably because of a race with getty whose open is finally being allowed to complete. This time interval may not be enough on a loaded system. Because of this problem and the above problem with the dh driver there is deliberately no error message given when the TIOCMGET ioctl fails.

Previously there were similar synchronization problems with the init process. When dialins are disabled the capitalized name of the process cannot be posted into /etc/utmp until init has finished clearing /etc/utmp. However one does not know how long that will take, and, on a loaded system, it can take quite a while. This was solved by the strategy of 1) posting the name, 2) poking init, 3) going into a loop where the process repeatedly waits a second and checks whether the entry has been cleared from /etc/utmp, and 4) posting the name again.

NAME

amd – automatically mount file systems

SYNOPSIS

amd [**-nprv**] [**-a** *mount_point*] [**-c** *duration*] [**-d** *domain*] [**-k** *kernel-arch*] [**-l** *logfile*] [**-t** *interval.interval*] [**-w** *interval*] [**-x** *log-option*] [**-y** *YP-domain*] [**-C** *cluster-name*] [**-D** *option*] [*directory mapname* [**-map-options**]] ...

DESCRIPTION

Amd is a daemon that automatically mounts filesystems whenever a file or directory within that filesystem is accessed. Filesystems are automatically unmounted when they appear to be quiescent.

Amd operates by attaching itself as an NFS server to each of the specified *directories*. Lookups within the specified directories are handled by **amd**, which uses the map defined by *mapname* to determine how to resolve the lookup. Generally, this will be a host name, some filesystem information and some mount options for the given filesystem.

OPTIONS

-a *temporary-directory*
Specify an alternative location for the real mount points. The default is /a.

-c *duration*
Specify a *duration*, in seconds, that a looked up name remains cached when not in use. The default is 5 minutes.

-d *domain*
Specify the local domain name. If this option is not given the domain name is determined from the hostname.

-k *kernel-arch*
Specifies the kernel architecture. This is used solely to set the ${karch} selector.

-l *logfile*
Specify a logfile in which to record mount and unmount events. If *logfile* is the string *syslog*, the log messages will be sent to the system log daemon by syslog(3).

-n Normalize hostnames. The name referred to by ${rhost} is normalized relative to the host database before being used. The effect is to translate aliases into ''official'' names.

-p Print *PID*. Outputs the process-id of **amd** to standard output where it can be saved into a file.

-r Restart existing mounts. **Amd** will scan the mount file table to determine which filesystems are currently mounted. Whenever one of these would have been auto-mounted, **amd** *inherits* it.

-t *interval.interval*
Specify the *interval*, in tenths of a second, between NFS/RPC/UDP retries. The default is 0.8 seconds. The second values alters the retransmit counter. Useful defaults are supplied if either or both values are missing.

-v Version. Displays version and configuration information on standard error.

-w *interval*
Specify an *interval*, in seconds, between attempts to dismount filesystems that have exceeded their cached times. The default is 2 minutes.

-y *domain*
Specify an alternative NIS domain from which to fetch the NIS maps. The default is the system domain name. This option is ignored if NIS support is not available.

-x *options*
Specify run-time logging options. The options are a comma separated list chosen from: fatal, error, user, warn, info, map, stats, all.

-D *option*
Select from a variety of debug options. Prefixing an option with the string *no* reverses the effect of that option. Options are cumulative. The most useful option is *all*.

Since **-D** is only used for debugging other options are not documented here: the current supported set of options is listed by the **-v** option and a fuller description is available in the program source.

FILES

/a directory under which filesystems are dynamically mounted

CAVEATS

Some care may be required when creating a mount map.

Symbolic links on an NFS filesystem can be incredibly inefficient. In most implementations of NFS, their interpolations are not cached by the kernel and each time a symbolic link is encountered during a *lookuppn* translation it costs an RPC call to the NFS server. A large improvement in real-time performance could be gained by adding a cache somewhere. Replacing symlinks(2) with a suitable incarnation of the automounter results in a large real-time speedup, but also causes a large number of process context switches.

A weird imagination is most useful to gain full advantage of all the features.

SEE ALSO

amq(8), hostname(1), mount(8), umount(8),

Amd – The 4.4 BSD Automounter.

AUTHOR

Jan-Simon Pendry <jsp@doc.ic.ac.uk>, Department of Computing, Imperial College, London, UK.

HISTORY

The **amd** utility first appeared in 4.4BSD.

NAME

amq – automounter query tool

SYNOPSIS

amq [**-f**] [**-h** *hostname*] [**-M** *mountmap_entry*] [**-m**] [**-s**] [**-u**] [**-v**] [*directory*] ...

DESCRIPTION

Amq provides a simple way of determining the current state of the amd(8) program. Communication is by RPC. Three modes of operation are supported by the current protocol. By default a list of mount points and auto-mounted filesystems is output. An alternative host can be specified using the **-h** option.

If directory names are given, as output by default, then per-filesystem information is displayed.

OPTIONS

-f Request automounter to flush the internal caches.

-h *hostname*
Query alternate host *hostname*. By default the local host is used. In an HP-UX cluster, the root server is queried by default, since that is the system on which the automounter is normally run.

-m Request the automounter to provide a list of mounted filesystems, including the number of references to each filesystem and any error which occurred while mounting.

-s Request the automounter to provide system-wide mount statistics.

-u Request the automounter to unmount the named filesystems instead of providing information about them. Unmounts are requested, not forced. They merely cause the mounted filesystem to timeout, which will be picked up by amd's main scheduler thus causing the normal timeout action to be taken.

-v Request the automounter to provide version information. This is a subset of the information provided by amd's **-v** option.

-M Request automounter to add the given map entry to the root map and then trigger a mount request for it.

FILES

amq.x RPC protocol description.

CAVEATS

Amq uses a Sun registered RPC program number (300019 decimal) which may not be in the /etc/rpc database.

SEE ALSO

amd(8)

AUTHOR

Jan-Simon Pendry <jsp@doc.ic.ac.uk>, Department of Computing, Imperial College, London, UK.

HISTORY

Amq AT&T UNIX

M8

NAME

arp – address resolution display and control

SYNOPSIS

arp *hostname*
arp -a
arp -d *hostname*
arp -s *hostname ether_addr* [*temp*] [*pub*] [*trail*]
arp -f *filename*

DESCRIPTION

The **arp** program displays and modifies the Internet-to-Ethernet address translation tables used by the address resolution protocol (arp(4)). With no flags, the program displays the current ARP entry for *hostname*. The host may be specified by name or by number, using Internet dot notation.

Available options:

-a The program displays all of the current ARP entries.

-d A super-user may delete an entry for the host called *hostname* with the **-d** flag.

-s *hostname ether_addr*
Create an ARP entry for the host called *hostname* with the Ethernet address *ether_addr*. The Ethernet address is given as six hex bytes separated by colons. The entry will be permanent unless the word *temp* is given in the command. If the word *pub* is given, the entry will be "published"; i.e., this system will act as an ARP server, responding to requests for *hostname* even though the host address is not its own. The word *trail* indicates that trailer encapsulations may be sent to this host.

-f Causes the file *filename* to be read and multiple entries to be set in the ARP tables. Entries in the file should be of the form

hostname ether_addr [*temp*] [*pub*] [*trail*]

with argument meanings as given above.

SEE ALSO

inet(3), arp(4), ifconfig(8)

HISTORY

The **arp** command appeared in 4.3BSD.

NAME

bad144 – read/write dec standard 144 bad sector information

SYNOPSIS

bad144 [**−c**] [**−f**] [**−v**] *disk* [*sno* [*bad* ...]]
bad144 **−a** [**−c**] [**−f**] [**−v**] *disk* [*bad* ...]

DESCRIPTION

Bad144 can be used to inspect the information stored on a disk that is used by the disk drivers to implement bad sector forwarding.

Available options:

−a The argument list consists of new bad sectors to be added to an existing list. The new sectors are sorted into the list, which must have been in order. Replacement sectors are moved to accommodate the additions; the new replacement sectors are cleared.

−c Forces an attempt to copy the old sector to the replacement, and may be useful when replacing an unreliable sector.

−f For a RP06, RM03, RM05, Fujitsu Eagle, or SMD disk on a Massbus, the **−f** option may be used to mark the new bad sectors as "bad" by reformatting them as unusable sectors. This option is *required unless* the sectors have already been marked bad, or the system will not be notified that it should use the replacement sector. This option may be used while running multiuser; it is no longer necessary to perform format operations while running single-user.

−v The entire process is described as it happens in gory detail if **−v** (verbose) is given.

The format of the information is specified by DEC standard 144, as follows. The bad sector information is located in the first 5 even numbered sectors of the last track of the disk pack. There are five identical copies of the information, described by the *dkbad* structure.

Replacement sectors are allocated starting with the first sector before the bad sector information and working backwards towards the beginning of the disk. A maximum of 126 bad sectors are supported. The position of the bad sector in the bad sector table determines the replacement sector to which it corresponds. The bad sectors must be listed in ascending order.

The bad sector information and replacement sectors are conventionally only accessible through the "c" file system partition of the disk. If that partition is used for a file system, the user is responsible for making sure that it does not overlap the bad sector information or any replacement sectors. Thus, one track plus 126 sectors must be reserved to allow use of all of the possible bad sector replacements.

The bad sector structure is as follows:

```
struct dkbad {
        long     bt_csn;          /* cartridge serial number */
        u_short  bt_mbz;          /* unused; should be 0 */
        u_short  bt_flag;         /* -1 => alignment cartridge */
        struct bt_bad {
              u_short bt_cyl;     /* bad sector cylinder number */
              u_short bt_trksec;  /* track and sector number */
        } bt_bad[126];
};
```

Unused slots in the *bt_bad* array are filled with all bits set, a putatively illegal value.

Bad144 is invoked by giving a device name (e.g. hk0, hp1, etc.). With no optional arguments it reads the first sector of the last track of the corresponding disk and prints out the bad sector information. It issues a warning if the bad sectors are out of order. **Bad144** may also be invoked with a serial number for the pack and a list of bad sectors. It will write the supplied information into all copies of the bad-sector file, replacing any previous information. Note, however, that **bad144** does not arrange for the specified sectors to be marked bad in this case. This procedure should only be used to restore known bad sector information which was destroyed.

It is no longer necessary to reboot to allow the kernel to reread the bad-sector table from the drive.

SEE ALSO

badsect(8), format(8)

BUGS

It should be possible to format disks on-line under UNIX.

It should be possible to mark bad sectors on drives of all type.

On an 11/750, the standard bootstrap drivers used to boot the system do not understand bad sectors, handle ECC errors, or the special SSE (skip sector) errors of RM80-type disks. This means that none of these errors can occur when reading the file /vmunix to boot. Sectors 0-15 of the disk drive must also not have any of these errors.

The drivers which write a system core image on disk after a crash do not handle errors; thus the crash dump area must be free of errors and bad sectors.

HISTORY

The **bad144** command appeared in 4.1BSD.

M8

NAME

badsect – create files to contain bad sectors

SYNOPSIS

/etc/badsect *bbdir sector ...*

DESCRIPTION

Badsect makes a file to contain a bad sector. Normally, bad sectors are made inaccessible by the standard formatter, which provides a forwarding table for bad sectors to the driver; see bad144(8) for details. If a driver supports the bad blocking standard it is much preferable to use that method to isolate bad blocks, since the bad block forwarding makes the pack appear perfect, and such packs can then be copied with dd(1). The technique used by this program is also less general than bad block forwarding, as **badsect** can't make amends for bad blocks in the i-list of file systems or in swap areas.

On some disks, adding a sector which is suddenly bad to the bad sector table currently requires the running of the standard DEC formatter. Thus to deal with a newly bad block or on disks where the drivers do not support the bad-blocking standard **badsect** may be used to good effect.

Badsect is used on a quiet file system in the following way: First mount the file system, and change to its root directory. Make a directory BAD there. Run **badsect** giving as argument the *BAD* directory followed by all the bad sectors you wish to add. (The sector numbers must be relative to the beginning of the file system, but this is not hard as the system reports relative sector numbers in its console error messages.) Then change back to the root directory, unmount the file system and run fsck(8) on the file system. The bad sectors should show up in two files or in the bad sector files and the free list. Have fsck remove files containing the offending bad sectors, but *do not* have it remove the BAD/*nnnnn* files. This will leave the bad sectors in only the BAD files.

Badsect works by giving the specified sector numbers in a mknod(2) system call, creating an illegal file whose first block address is the block containing bad sector and whose name is the bad sector number. When it is discovered by fsck it will ask "HOLD BAD BLOCK ?" A positive response will cause fsck to convert the inode to a regular file containing the bad block.

SEE ALSO

bad144(8), fsck(8), format(8)

DIAGNOSTICS

Badsect refuses to attach a block that resides in a critical area or is out of range of the file system. A warning is issued if the block is already in use.

BUGS

If more than one sector which comprise a file system fragment are bad, you should specify only one of them to **badsect**, as the blocks in the bad sector files actually cover all the sectors in a file system fragment.

HISTORY

The **badsect** command appeared in 4.1BSD.

M8

NAME

boot – system bootstrapping procedures

DESCRIPTION

Power fail and crash recovery. Normally, the system will reboot itself at power-up or after crashes. An automatic consistency check of the file systems will be performed, and unless this fails, the system will resume multi-user operations.

Cold starts. On an HP300, the boot procedure uses the boot ROM to load a boot program from an LIF format directory at the beginning of an attached disk. The /usr/mdec directory contains a disk boot programs which should be placed in a new pack automatically by newfs(8) when the "a" partition file system on the pack is created.

This *boot* program finds the corresponding file on the given device (*vmunix* by default), loads that file into memory, and starts the program at the entry address specified in the program header.

The boot program can be interrupted by typing '^C' (ctrl-C). This will force the boot program to interactively prompt for a system to boot. If not interrupted, it will boot from the device from which the boot program itself was loaded.

The file specifications used for an interactive boot are of the form:

```
device(unit, minor)
```

where *device* is the type of the device to be searched, *unit* is 8 * the hpib number plus the unit number of the disk or tape, and *minor* is the disk partition or tape file number. Normal line editing characters can be used when typing the file specification. Currently, "rd" and "sd" are the only valid *device* specifiers.

For example, to boot from the 'a' file system of unit 0 on HP-IB 2, type rd(16, 0)vmunix to the boot prompt. For tapes, the minor device number gives a file offset.

In an emergency, the bootstrap methods described in the paper *Installing 4.3bsd on the HP300* can be used to boot from a distribution tape.

FILES

/vmunix	system code
/usr/mdec/bootrd	LIF format boot block
/usr/mdec/installboot	program to install boot blocks

SEE ALSO

halt(8), reboot(8), shutdown(8)

NAME

`reboot` – UNIX bootstrapping procedures

SYNOPSIS

`reboot [-n] [-q]`

DESCRIPTION

Power fail and crash recovery. Normally, the system will reboot itself at power-up or after crashes. An automatic consistency check of the file systems will be performed as described in `fsck`(8). and unless this fails, the system will resume multi-user operations.

Cold starts The SPARC system currently uses the SunOS bootstrap loaders. This will be changed in a future version of the system. The SunOS boot will attempt to load `vmunix` from partition A of the boot device, which must currently be an ''sd'' disk.

The [`-s`] flag to the SunOS boot loader will being the system up in single-user mode. The [`-d`] flag to the SunOS boot loader will bring the system up in debug mode. Here it waits for a kernel debugger connect; see `kgdb`(8). Other flags are currently ignored.

FILES

`/vmunix`	system code
`/boot`	system bootstrap

SEE ALSO

`crash`(8), `disklabel`(8), `fsck`(8), `halt`(8), `init`(8), `rc`(8), `shutdown`(8), `syslogd`(8)

BUGS

The use of Sun disk labels, without the ability to write them, is problematic.

M8

NAME

bugfiler – file bug reports in folders automatically

SYNOPSIS

bugfiler [**-ar**] [**-v** *version*]

DESCRIPTION

Bugfiler is a program to automatically intercept, acknowledge, redistribute and store bug reports. **Bugfiler** is normally invoked by the mail delivery program with a line similar to the following in /etc/aliases.

```
bugs:    "|bugfiler"
```

It should be noted that the login "bugs" must exist for the bugfiler to run. Unless otherwise noted all paths used by **bugfiler** are relative to the home directory of this login. **Bugfiler** also expects all of its files and directories to be owned by "bugs".

Available options.

-a Do not send automatic mail acknowledgement to the bug report filer. (The default is to send the acknowledgement with the file ~bugs/version/bug:ack appended).

-r Do not redistribute.

-v *version*
Override the *version* provided within the bug report itself.

For the bug report to be correctly filed, it must contain a line in the following format:

Index: *folder* *version*

The directories ~bugs/*version* and ~bugs/*version/folder* must exist before **bugfiler** attempts to store the bug report. Bug reports will be stored in files named by the concatenation of *version*, *folder*, and sequential numbers, i.e. if *version* is "4.3 BSD" and *folder* is "ucb" the first bug report will be placed in ~bugs/4.3BSD/ucb/1. If *folder* contains more than one component only the first one will be used, e.g. if *folder* is "bin/from.c" or "bin/adb/con.c" it will be treated as if it were simply "bin".

If the **-r** flag is not supplied, redistribution of the bug reports is done as specified in the file ~bugs/version/bug:redist. This file is in the format of the aliases(5) file, including comments and entries requiring multiple lines, with the single exception that the *folder* component of the "Index:" line replaces the name to alias. The special folder "all:" receives a redistribution of all bug reports sent to this *version*. For example, the bug:redist file

```
#       bigbug gets a copy of everything
all:    bigbug
#       ucb folder redistribution list
ucb:    karels, kjd@coke.berkeley.edu
        ra@beno.css.gov
```

will send copies of all bug reports with "ucb" as the *folder* to bigbug, karels, kjd, and ra.

Reports that cannot be filed, due to an invalid "Index:" line or some other error, are placed in the directory ~bugs/errors. The **bugfiler** maintainer should correct these bug reports and then run **bugfiler**, with the corrected report as its standard input, as bug reports with errors are neither acknowledged or redistributed. All reports that **bugfiler** handles are logged in ~bugs/log.

Valid bugs are also logged in the file `~bugs/version/summary`. This file has an entry for each bug report for *version* in the format:

```
Filename        Date
     Subject:
     Index:
     Owner:     Bugs Bunny
     Status:    Received
```

`Filename` is the concatenation of *version*, *folder*, and a number as described above. `Date` is the date as reported by the system clock, using ctime(3). The `Subject:` and `Index:` lines are copies of the "Subject:" and "index:" lines contained in the bug report. The `Owner` and `Status` fields are intended to provide a rudimentary method of tracking the status of bug reports.

The file `~bugs/bug:lock` is the focus of all locking for **bugfiler**. If you wish to manipulate any of the log or error files, rename or remove it and **bugfiler** will treat all bug reports that it receives as if they were incorrectly formatted, i.e. it will place them in the directory `~bugs/errors`, for later recovery by the **bugfiler** maintainer. Obviously, this file must be created when you first install **bugfiler**.

All errors that occur before `~bugs/log` is found are logged into the system log file, using syslog(8).

FILES

`~bugs/bug:ack`	the acknowledgement message
`~bugs/bug:redist`	the redistribution list
`~bugs/bug:lock`	the locking file
`~bugs/errors/BUG_??????`	bug reports with format errors
`~bugs/log`	the log file
`~bugs/folder/summary`	the summary files
`/usr/sbin/sendmail`	the mail delivery program
`/usr/share/misc/bugformat`	a sample bug report format

SEE ALSO

sendbug(1), aliases(5), syslog(8)

BUGS

Since mail can be forwarded in a number of different ways, **bugfiler** does not recognize forwarded mail and will acknowledge to the forwarder instead of the original sender unless there is a "Reply-To" field in the header.

This version of **bugfiler** is not compatible with the version released with 4.3BSD in that it doesn't complain to the sender about incorrectly formatted bug reports. Frankly, we got tired of the profanity, not to mention the extended conversations **bugfiler** was holding with vacation(1).

HISTORY

The **bugfiler** command appeared in 4.2BSD.

M8

NAME

chown – change file owner and group

SYNOPSIS

chown [**-R** [**-H** | **-L** | **-P**]] [**-f**] *owner* [*:group*] *file* ...
chown [**-R** [**-H** | **-L** | **-P**]] [**-f**] *:group file* ...

DESCRIPTION

Chown sets the user ID and/or the group ID of the specified files.

The options are as follows:

- **-H** If the **-R** option is specified, symbolic links on the command line are followed. (Symbolic links encountered in the tree traversal are not followed.)
- **-L** If the **-R** option is specified, all symbolic links are followed.
- **-P** If the **-R** option is specified, no symbolic links are followed.
- **-R** Change the user ID and/or the group ID for the file hierarchies rooted in the files instead of just the files themselves.
- **-f** Don't report any failure to change file owner or group, nor modify the exit status to reflect such failures.

Symbolic links don't have owners, so unless the **-H** or **-L** option is set, **chown** on a symbolic link always succeeds and has no effect. The **-H**, **-L** and **-P** options are ignored unless the **-R** option is specified. In addition, these options override each other and the command's actions are determined by the last one specified.

The *owner* and *group* operands are both optional, however, one must be specified. If the *group* operand is specified, it must be preceded by a colon (":") character.

The *owner* may be either a numeric user ID or a user name. If a user name is also a numeric user ID, the operand is used as a user name. The *group* may be either a numeric group ID or a group name. If a group name is also a numeric group ID, the operand is used as a group name.

The ownership of a file may only be altered by a super-user for obvious security reasons.

The **chown** utility exits 0 on success, and >0 if an error occurs.

COMPATIBILITY

Previous versions of the **chown** utility used the dot (".") character to distinguish the group name. This has been changed to be a colon (":") character so that user and group names may contain the dot character.

Previous versions of the **chown** utility changed the owner of symbolic links specified on the command line. In this system, symbolic links do not have owners.

SEE ALSO

chgrp(1), find(1), chown(2), fts(3), symlink(7)

STANDARDS

The **chown** command is expected to be POSIX 1003.2 compliant.

M8

NAME

chroot – change root directory

SYNOPSIS

chroot *newroot* [*command*]

DESCRIPTION

The **chroot** command changes its root directory to the supplied directory *newroot* and exec's *command*, if supplied, or an interactive copy of your shell.

Note, *command* or the shell are run as your real-user-id.

ENVIRONMENT

The following environment variable is referenced by **chroot**:

SHELL If set, the string specified by SHELL is interpreted as the name of the shell to exec. If the variable SHELL is not set, /bin/sh is used.

SEE ALSO

chdir(2), chroot(2), environ(7)

HISTORY

The **chroot** utility first appeared in 4.4BSD.

M8

NAME

`clri` – clear an inode

SYNOPSIS

`clri` *special_device inode_number ...*

DESCRIPTION

`Clri` is obsoleted for normal file system repair work by `fsck`(8).

`Clri` zeros out the inodes with the specified inode number(s) on the filesystem residing on the given *special_device*. The `fsck`(8) utility is usually run after `clri` to reclaim the zero'ed inode(s) and the blocks previously claimed by those inode(s). Both read and write permission are required on the specified *special_device*.

The primary purpose of this routine is to remove a file which for some reason is not being properly handled by `fsck`(8). Once removed, it is anticipated that `fsck`(8) will be able to clean up the resulting mess.

SEE ALSO

`fsck`(8), `fsdb`(8), `icheck`(8), `ncheck`(8)

BUGS

If the file is open, the work of `clri` will be lost when the inode is written back to disk from the inode cache.

M8

NAME

`comsat` – biff server

SYNOPSIS

`comsat`

DESCRIPTION

`Comsat` is the server process which receives reports of incoming mail and notifies users if they have requested this service. `Comsat` receives messages on a datagram port associated with the "biff" service specification (see `services`(5) and `inetd`(8)). The one line messages are of the form:

```
user@mailbox-offset
```

If the *user* specified is logged in to the system and the associated terminal has the owner execute bit turned on (by a "`biff y`"), the *offset* is used as a seek offset into the appropriate mailbox file and the first 7 lines or 560 characters of the message are printed on the user's terminal. Lines which appear to be part of the message header other than the "From", "To", "Date", or "Subject" lines are not included in the displayed message.

FILES

`/var/run/utmp` to find out who's logged on and on what terminals

SEE ALSO

`biff`(1), `inetd`(8)

BUGS

The message header filtering is prone to error. The density of the information presented is near the theoretical minimum.

Users should be notified of mail which arrives on other machines than the one to which they are currently logged in.

The notification should appear in a separate window so it does not mess up the screen.

HISTORY

The `comsat` command appeared in 4.2BSD.

M8

NAME

config – build system configuration files

SYNOPSIS

config [**-p**] *system_name*

DESCRIPTION

This is the old version of the **config** program. It understands the old autoconfiguration scheme used on the HP300, DECstation, and derivative platforms. The new version of config is used with the SPARC and i386 platforms. Only the version of **config** applicable to the architecture that you are running will be installed on your machine.

Config builds a set of system configuration files from the file *SYSTEM_NAME* which describes the system to configure. A second file tells **config** what files are needed to generate a system and can be augmented by configuration specific set of files that give alternate files for a specific machine. (see the FILES section below)

Available option and operand:

-p If the **-p** option is supplied, **config** will configure a system for profiling; for example, kgmon(8) and gprof(1).

SYSTEM_NAME specifies the name of the system configuration file containing device specifications, configuration options and other system parameters for one system configuration.

Config should be run from the conf subdirectory of the system source (usually /sys/conf). **Config** assumes the directory ../SYSTEM_NAME exists and places all output files there. The output of **config** consists of a number of files; for the VAX, they are: ioconf.c, a description of what I/O devices are attached to the system; ubglue.s, a set of interrupt service routines for devices attached to the UNIBUS; ubvec.s, offsets into a structure used for counting per-device interrupts; Makefile, used by make(1) in building the system; header files, definitions of the number of various devices that will be compiled into the system; swap configuration files, definitions for the disk areas to be used for swapping, the root file system, argument processing, and system dumps.

After running **config**, it is necessary to run "make depend" in the directory where the new makefile was created. **Config** prints a reminder of this when it completes.

If any other error messages are produced by **config**, the problems in the configuration file should be corrected and **config** should be run again. Attempts to compile a system that had configuration errors are likely to fail.

FILES

/sys/conf/Makefile.vax	generic makefile for the VAX
/sys/conf/files	list of common files system is built from
/sys/conf/files.vax	list of VAX specific files
/sys/conf/devices.vax	name to major device mapping file for the VAX
/sys/conf/files.*ERNIE*	list of files specific to *ERNIE* system

SEE ALSO

The SYNOPSIS portion of each device in section 4.

Building 4.3 BSD UNIX System with Config.

config.new(8)

BUGS

The line numbers reported in error messages are usually off by one.

HISTORY

The `config` command appeared in 4.1BSD.

NAME

config.new – build kernel compilation directories

SYNOPSIS

config [**-p**] *system-name*

DESCRIPTION

This is the new version of the **config** program. It understands the more modern autoconfiguration scheme used on the SPARC and i386 platforms. The old version of config is still used with the HP300, DECstation, and derivative platforms. Only the version of **config** applicable to the architecture that you are running will be installed on your machine.

Config builds a set of configuration files from the file *system-name*, which describes the system to configure.

Config should run from the conf subdirectory of the top-level machine-specific directory of the system source (usually /sys/MACHINE/conf, where MACHINE is one of vax, tahoe, hp300, and so forth). **Config** assumes the directory ../../compile exists; it places all output files in a subdirectory there, creating the subdirectory if necessary. The subdirectory name is taken from the *system-name*; thus, configuring with "config PICKLE" will use the directory ../../compile/PICKLE.

If the **-p** option is supplied, .PROF is appended to the compilation directory name, and **config** acts as if the lines "makeoptions PROF="-pg"" and "options GPROF" appeared in the configuration file. This will build a system that includes profiling code; see kgmon(8) and gprof(1). The **-p** flag is expected to be used for "one-shot" profiles of existing systems; for regular profiling, it is probably wiser to make a separate configuration containing the makeoptions line.

The old undocumented **-g** flag is no longer supported. Instead, use "makeoptions DEBUG="-g"" and (typically) "options KGDB".

The output of **config** consists of a number of files, principally ioconf.c, a description of I/O devices that may be attached to the system; and a Makefile, used by make(1) in building the kernel.

After running **config**, it is wise to run "make depend" in the directory where the new makefile was created. **Config** prints a reminder of this when it completes.

If **config** stops due to errors, the problems reported should be corrected and **config** should be run again. **Config** attempts to avoid changing the compilation directory if there are configuration errors, but this code is not well-tested, and some problems (such as running out of disk space) are unrecoverable.

SEE ALSO

The SYNOPSIS portion of each device in section 4.

Building 4.4 BSD Systems with Config.

config(8)

HISTORY

The **config.new** command appeared in 4.1BSD. It was completely revised in 4.4BSD.

NAME

crash – UNIX system failures

DESCRIPTION

This section explains a bit about system crashes and (very briefly) how to analyze crash dumps.

When the system crashes voluntarily it prints a message of the form

> panic: why i gave up the ghost

on the console, takes a dump on a mass storage peripheral, and then invokes an automatic reboot procedure as described in `reboot`(8). Unless some unexpected inconsistency is encountered in the state of the file systems due to hardware or software failure, the system will then resume multi-user operations.

The system has a large number of internal consistency checks; if one of these fails, then it will panic with a very short message indicating which one failed. In many instances, this will be the name of the routine which detected the error, or a two-word description of the inconsistency. A full understanding of most panic messages requires perusal of the source code for the system.

The most common cause of system failures is hardware failure, which can reflect itself in different ways. Here are the messages which are most likely, with some hints as to causes. Left unstated in all cases is the possibility that hardware or software error produced the message in some unexpected way.

iinit This cryptic panic message results from a failure to mount the root filesystem during the bootstrap process. Either the root filesystem has been corrupted, or the system is attempting to use the wrong device as root filesystem. Usually, an alternate copy of the system binary or an alternate root filesystem can be used to bring up the system to investigate.

Can't exec /etc/init
: This is not a panic message, as reboots are likely to be futile. Late in the bootstrap procedure, the system was unable to locate and execute the initialization process, `init`(8). The root filesystem is incorrect or has been corrupted, or the mode or type of `/etc/init` forbids execution.

IO err in push
hard IO err in swap
: The system encountered an error trying to write to the paging device or an error in reading critical information from a disk drive. The offending disk should be fixed if it is broken or unreliable.

realloccg: bad optim
ialloc: dup alloc
alloccgblk:cyl groups corrupted
ialloccg: map corrupted
free: freeing free block
free: freeing free frag
ifree: freeing free inode
alloccg: map corrupted
: These panic messages are among those that may be produced when filesystem inconsistencies are detected. The problem generally results from a failure to repair damaged filesystems after a crash, hardware failures, or other condition that should not normally occur. A filesystem check will normally correct the problem.

timeout table overflow
: This really shouldn't be a panic, but until the data structure involved is made to be extensible, running out of entries causes a crash. If this happens, make the timeout table bigger.

trap type %d, code = %x, v = %x

An unexpected trap has occurred within the system; the trap types are:

0	bus error
1	address error
2	illegal instruction
3	divide by zero
4	*chk* instruction
5	*trapv* instruction
6	privileged instruction
7	trace trap
8	MMU fault
9	simulated software interrupt
10	format error
11	FP coprocessor fault
12	coprocessor fault
13	simulated AST

The favorite trap type in system crashes is trap type 8, indicating a wild reference. ''code'' (hex) is the concatenation of the MMU status register (see <hp300/cpu.h>) in the high 16 bits and the 68020 special status word (see the 68020 manual, page 6-17) in the low 16. ''v'' (hex) is the virtual address which caused the fault. Additionally, the kernel will dump about a screenful of semi-useful information. ''pid'' (decimal) is the process id of the process running at the time of the exception. Note that if we panic in an interrupt routine, this process may not be related to the panic. ''ps'' (hex) is the 68020 processor status register ''ps''. ''pc'' (hex) is the value of the program counter saved on the hardware exception frame. It may *not* be the PC of the instruction causing the fault. ''sfc'' and ''dfc'' (hex) are the 68020 source/destination function codes. They should always be one. ''p0'' and ''p1'' are the VAX-like region registers. They are of the form:

<length> '@' <kernel VA>

where both are in hex. Following these values are a dump of the processor registers (hex). Finally, is a dump of the stack (user/kernel) at the time of the offense.

init died

The system initialization process has exited. This is bad news, as no new users will then be able to log in. Rebooting is the only fix, so the system just does it right away.

out of mbufs: map full

The network has exhausted its private page map for network buffers. This usually indicates that buffers are being lost, and rather than allow the system to slowly degrade, it reboots immediately. The map may be made larger if necessary.

That completes the list of panic types you are likely to see.

When the system crashes it writes (or at least attempts to write) an image of memory into the back end of the dump device, usually the same as the primary swap area. After the system is rebooted, the program `savecore`(8) runs and preserves a copy of this core image and the current system in a specified directory for later perusal. See `savecore`(8) for details.

To analyze a dump you should begin by running `adb`(1) with the **−k** flag on the system load image and core dump. If the core image is the result of a panic, the panic message is printed. Normally the command ''$c'' will provide a stack trace from the point of the crash and this will provide a clue as to what went wrong. For more details consult *Using ADB to Debug the UNIX Kernel.*

SEE ALSO

adb(1), reboot(8)

MC68020 32-bit Microprocessor User's Manual.

Using ADB to Debug the UNIX Kernel.

4.3BSD for the HP300.

HISTORY

A `crash` man page appeared in Version 6 AT&T UNIX.

M8

NAME

cron – clock daemon

SYNOPSIS

cron

DESCRIPTION

Cron executes commands at specified dates and times according to the instructions in the files /etc/crontab and /etc/crontab.local. None, either one, or both of these files may be present. Since *cron* never exits, it should only be executed once. This is best done by running *cron* from the initialization process through the file /etc/rc; see *init*(8).

The crontab files consist of lines of seven fields each. The fields are separated by spaces or tabs. The first five are integer patterns to specify:

- minute (0-59)
- hour (0-23)
- day of the month (1-31)
- month of the year (1-12)
- day of the week (1-7 with 1 = Monday)

Each of these patterns may contain:

- a number in the range above
- two numbers separated by a minus meaning a range inclusive
- a list of numbers separated by commas meaning any of the numbers
- an asterisk meaning all legal values

The sixth field is a user name: the command will be run with that user's uid and permissions. The seventh field consists of all the text on a line following the sixth field, including spaces and tabs; this text is treated as a command which is executed by the Shell at the specified times. A percent character (''%'') in this field is translated to a new-line character.

Both crontab files are checked by *cron* every minute, on the minute.

FILES

/etc/crontab
/etc/crontab.local

NAME

dev_mkdb – create /dev database

SYNOPSIS

dev_mkdb

DESCRIPTION

The **dev_mkdb** command creates a db(3) hash access method database in "/var/run/dev.db" which contains the names of all of the character and block special files in the "/dev" directory, using the file type and the *st_rdev* field as the key.

Keys are a structure containing a mode_t followed by a dev_t, with any padding zero'd out. The former is the type of the file (st_mode & S_IFMT), the latter is the st_rdev field.

FILES

/dev	Device directory.
/var/run/dev.db	Database file.

SEE ALSO

ps(1), stat(2), db(3), devname(3), kvm_nlist(3), ttyname(3), kvm_mkdb(8)

HISTORY

The **dev_mkdb** command appeared in 4.4BSD.

M8

NAME

disklabel – read and write disk pack label

SYNOPSIS

disklabel [**-r**] *disk*
disklabel -w [**-r**] *disk disktype* [*packid*]
disklabel -e [**-r**] *disk*
disklabel -R [**-r**] *disk protofile*
disklabel [**-NW**] *disk*

disklabel -B [**-b** *boot1* [**-s** *boot2*]] *disk* [*disktype*]
disklabel -w -B [**-b** *boot1* [**-s** *boot2*]] *disk disktype* [*packid*]
disklabel -R -B [**-b** *boot1* [**-s** *boot2*]] *disk protofile* [*disktype*]

DESCRIPTION

Disklabel can be used to install, examine or modify the label on a disk drive or pack. When writing the label, it can be used to change the drive identification, the disk partitions on the drive, or to replace a damaged label. On some systems, **disklabel** can be used to install bootstrap code as well. There are several forms of the command that read (display), install or edit the label on a disk. Each form has an additional option, **-r**, which causes the label to be read from or written to the disk directly, rather than going through the system's in-core copy of the label. This option may allow a label to be installed on a disk without kernel support for a label, such as when labels are first installed on a system; it must be used when first installing a label on a disk. The specific effect of **-r** is described under each command. The read and install forms also support the **-B** option to install bootstrap code. These variants are described later.

The first form of the command (read) is used to examine the label on the named disk drive (e.g. sd0 or /dev/rsd0c). It will display all of the parameters associated with the drive and its partition layout. Unless the **-r** flag is given, the kernel's in-core copy of the label is displayed; if the disk has no label, or the partition types on the disk are incorrect, the kernel may have constructed or modified the label. If the **-r** flag is given, the label from the raw disk will be displayed rather than the in-core label.

The second form of the command, with the **-w** flag, is used to write a standard label on the designated drive. The required arguments to **disklabel** are the drive to be labelled (e.g. sd0), and the drive type as described in the disktab(5) file. The drive parameters and partitions are taken from that file. If different disks of the same physical type are to have different partitions, it will be necessary to have separate disktab entries describing each, or to edit the label after installation as described below. The optional argument is a pack identification string, up to 16 characters long. The pack id must be quoted if it contains blanks. If the **-r** flag is given, the disk sectors containing the label and bootstrap will be written directly. A side-effect of this is that any existing bootstrap code will be overwritten and the disk rendered unbootable. If **-r** is not specified, the existing label will be updated via the in-core copy and any bootstrap code will be unaffected. If the disk does not already have a label, the **-r** flag must be used. In either case, the kernel's in-core label is replaced.

An existing disk label may be edited by using the **-e** flag. The label is read from the in-core kernel copy, or directly from the disk if the **-r** flag is also given. The label is formatted and then supplied to an editor for changes. If no editor is specified in an EDITOR environment variable, vi(1) is used. When the editor terminates, the formatted label is reread and used to rewrite the disk label. Existing bootstrap code is unchanged regardless of whether **-r** was specified.

With the **-R** flag, **disklabel** is capable of restoring a disk label that was formatted in a prior operation and saved in an ascii file. The prototype file used to create the label should be in the same format as that produced when reading or editing a label. Comments are delimited by # and newline. As with **-w**, any existing bootstrap code will be clobbered if **-r** is specified and will be unaffected otherwise.

The **-NW** flags for **disklabel** explicitly disallow and allow, respectively, writing of the pack label area on the selected disk.

The final three forms of **disklabel** are used to install boostrap code on machines where the bootstrap is part of the label. The bootstrap code is comprised of one or two boot programs depending on the machine. The **-B** option is used to denote that bootstrap code is to be installed. The **-r** flag is implied by **-B** and never needs to be specified. The name of the boot program(s) to be installed can be selected in a variety of ways. First, the names can be specified explicitly via the **-b** and **-s** flags. On machines with only a single level of boot program, **-b** is the name of that program. For machines with a two-level bootstrap, **-b** indicates the primary boot program and **-s** the secondary boot program. If the names are not explicitly given, standard boot programs will be used. The boot programs are located in `/usr/mdec`. The names of the programs are taken from the "b0" and "b1" parameters of the `disktab(5)` entry for the disk if *disktype* was given and its disktab entry exists and includes those parameters. Otherwise, boot program names are derived from the name of the disk. These names are of the form `basename`boot for the primary (or only) bootstrap, and boot`basename` for the secondary bootstrap; for example, `/usr/mdec/sdboot` and `/usr/mdec/bootsd` if the disk device is *sd0*.

The first of the three boot-installation forms is used to install bootstrap code without changing the existing label. It is essentially a read command with respect to the disk label itself and all options are related to the specification of the boot program as described previously. The final two forms are analogous to the basic write and restore versions except that they will install bootstrap code in addition to a new label.

FILES

`/etc/disktab`
`/usr/mdec/`*xx*`boot`
`/usr/mdec/boot`*xx*

EXAMPLES

```
disklabel sd0
```

Display the in-core label for sd0 as obtained via `/dev/rsd0c`.

```
disklabel -w -r /dev/rsd0c sd2212 foo
```

Create a label for sd0 based on information for "sd2212" found in `/etc/disktab`. Any existing bootstrap code will be clobbered.

```
disklabel -e -r sd0
```

Read the on-disk label for sd0, edit it and reinstall in-core as well as on-disk. Existing bootstrap code is unaffected.

```
disklabel -R sd0 mylabel
```

Restore the on-disk and in-core label for sd0 from information in `mylabel`. Existing bootstrap code is unaffected.

```
disklabel -B sd0
```

Install a new bootstrap on sd0. The boot code comes from `/usr/mdec/sdboot` and possibly `/usr/mdec/bootsd`. On-disk and in-core labels are unchanged.

```
disklabel -w -B /dev/rsd0c -b newboot sd2212
```

Install a new label and bootstrap. The label is derived from disktab information for "sd2212" and installed both in-core and on-disk. The bootstrap code comes from the file `/usr/mdec/newboot`.

M8

SEE ALSO

disktab(5), disklabel(5)

DIAGNOSTICS

The kernel device drivers will not allow the size of a disk partition to be decreased or the offset of a partition to be changed while it is open. Some device drivers create a label containing only a single large partition if a disk is unlabeled; thus, the label must be written to the ''a'' partition of the disk while it is open. This sometimes requires the desired label to be set in two steps, the first one creating at least one other partition, and the second setting the label on the new partition while shrinking the ''a'' partition.

On some machines the bootstrap code may not fit entirely in the area allocated for it by some filesystems. As a result, it may not be possible to have filesystems on some partitions of a ''bootable'' disk. When installing bootstrap code, **disklabel** checks for these cases. If the installed boot code would overlap a partition of type FS_UNUSED it is marked as type FS_BOOT. The newfs(8) utility will disallow creation of filesystems on FS_BOOT partitions. Conversely, if a partition has a type other than FS_UNUSED or FS_BOOT, **disklabel** will not install bootstrap code that overlaps it.

BUGS

When a disk name is given without a full pathname, the constructed device name uses the ''a'' partition on the tahoe, the ''c'' partition on all others.

M8

NAME

diskpart – calculate default disk partition sizes

SYNOPSIS

diskpart [**-p**] [**-d**] [**-s** *size*] *disk-type*

DESCRIPTION

Diskpart is used to calculate the disk partition sizes based on the default rules used at Berkeley.

Available options and operands:

-p Tables suitable for inclusion in a device driver are produced.

-d An entry suitable for inclusion in the disk description file /etc/disktab is generated; for example, disktab(5).

-s *size* The size of the disk may be limited to *size* with the **-s** option.

On disks that use bad144(8) type of bad-sector forwarding, space is normally left in the last partition on the disk for a bad sector forwarding table, although this space is not reflected in the tables produced. The space reserved is one track for the replicated copies of the table and sufficient tracks to hold a pool of 126 sectors to which bad sectors are mapped. For more information, see bad144(8). The **-s** option is intended for other controllers which reserve some space at the end of the disk for bad-sector replacements or other control areas, even if not a multiple of cylinders.

The disk partition sizes are based on the total amount of space on the disk as given in the table below (all values are supplied in units of sectors). The 'c' partition is, by convention, used to access the entire physical disk. The device driver tables include the space reserved for the bad sector forwarding table in the 'c' partition; those used in the disktab and default formats exclude reserved tracks. In normal operation, either the 'g' partition is used, or the 'd', 'e', and 'f' partitions are used. The 'g' and 'f' partitions are variable-sized, occupying whatever space remains after allocation of the fixed sized partitions. If the disk is smaller than 20 Megabytes, then **diskpart** aborts with the message "disk too small, calculate by hand".

Partition	20-60 MB	61-205 MB	206-355 MB	356+ MB
a	15884	15884	15884	15884
b	10032	33440	33440	66880
d	15884	15884	15884	15884
e	unused	55936	55936	307200
h	unused	unused	291346	291346

If an unknown disk type is specified, **diskpart** will prompt for the required disk geometry information.

SEE ALSO

disktab(5), bad144(8)

BUGS

Most default partition sizes are based on historical artifacts (like the RP06), and may result in unsatisfactory layouts.

When using the **-d** flag, alternate disk names are not included in the output.

HISTORY

The **diskpart** command appeared in 4.2BSD.

NAME

dm – dungeon master

SYNOPSIS

ln -s dm *game*

DESCRIPTION

Dm is a program used to regulate game playing. **Dm** expects to be invoked with the name of a game that a user wishes to play. This is done by creating symbolic links to **dm**, in the directory /usr/games for all of the regulated games. The actual binaries for these games should be placed in a "hidden" directory, /usr/games/hide, that may only be accessed by the **dm** program. **Dm** determines if the requested game is available and, if so, runs it. The file /etc/dm.conf controls the conditions under which games may be run.

The file /etc/nogames may be used to "turn off" game playing. If the file exists, no game playing is allowed; the contents of the file will be displayed to any user requesting a game.

FILES

/etc/dm.conf	configuration file
/etc/nogames	turns off game playing
/usr/games/hide	directory of "real" binaries
/var/log/games.log	game logging file

SEE ALSO

dm.conf(5)

BUGS

Two problems result from **dm** running the games setuid "games". First, all games that allow users to run UNIX commands should carefully set both the real and effective user id's immediately before executing those commands. Probably more important is that **dm** never be setuid anything but "games" so that compromising a game will result only in the user's ability to play games at will. Secondly, games which previously had no reason to run setuid and which accessed user files may have to be modified.

HISTORY

The **dm** command appeared in 4.3BSD–Tahoe.

NAME

dmesg – display the system message buffer

SYNOPSIS

dmesg [**-M** *core*] [**-N** *system*]

DESCRIPTION

Dmesg displays the contents of the system message buffer.

The options are as follows:

-M Extract values associated with the name list from the specified core instead of the default "/dev/kmem".

-N Extract the name list from the specified system instead of the default "/vmunix".

SEE ALSO

syslogd(8)

HISTORY

The **dmesg** command appeared in 4.0BSD.

M8

NAME

dump – filesystem backup

SYNOPSIS

dump [**0123456789BbhfusTdWn** [*argument ...*]] [*filesystem*]

DESCRIPTION

Dump examines files on a filesystem and determines which files need to be backed up. These files are copied to the given disk, tape or other storage medium for safe keeping (see the **f** option below for doing remote backups). A dump that is larger than the output medium is broken into multiple volumes. On most media the size is determined by writing until an end-of-media indication is returned. On media that cannot reliably return an end-of-media indication (such as some cartridge tape drives) each volume is of a fixed size; the actual size is determined by the tape size and density and/or block count options below. By default, the same output file name is used for each volume after prompting the operator to change media.

The following options are supported by **dump**:

0–9 Dump levels. A level 0, full backup, guarantees the entire file system is copied (but see also the **h** option below). A level number above 0, incremental backup, tells dump to copy all files new or modified since the last dump of the same or lower level. The default level is 9.

B *records*
The number of dump records per volume. This option overrides the calculation of tape size based on length and density.

b *blocksize*
The number of kilobytes per dump record.

h *level*
Honor the user ''nodump'' flag only for dumps at or above the given *level*. The default honor level is 1, so that incremental backups omit such files but full backups retain them.

f *file*
Write the backup to *file*; *file* may be a special device file like /dev/rmt12 (a tape drive), /dev/rsd1c (a disk drive), an ordinary file, or '–' (the standard output). Multiple file names may be given as a single argument separated by commas. Each file will be used for one dump volume in the order listed; if the dump requires more volumes than the number of names given, the last file name will used for all remaining volumes after prompting for media changes. If the name of the file is of the form ''host:file'', or ''user@host:file'', **dump** writes to the named file on the remote host using rmt(8).

d *density*
Set tape density to *density*. The default is 1600BPI.

n Whenever **dump** requires operator attention, notify all operators in the group ''operator'' by means similar to a wall(1).

s *feet*
Attempt to calculate the amount of tape needed at a particular density. If this amount is exceeded, **dump** prompts for a new tape. It is recommended to be a bit conservative on this option. The default tape length is 2300 feet.

u Update the file `/etc/dumpdates` after a successful dump. The format of `/etc/dumpdates` is readable by people, consisting of one free format record per line: filesystem name, increment level and `ctime`(3) format dump date. There may be only one entry per filesystem at each level. The file `/etc/dumpdates` may be edited to change any of the fields, if necessary.

T *date*
Use the specified date as the starting time for the dump instead of the time determined from looking in `/etc/dumpdates`. The format of date is the same as that of `ctime`(3). This option is useful for automated dump scripts that wish to dump over a specific period of time. The **T** option is mutually exclusive from the **u** option.

W **Dump** tells the operator what file systems need to be dumped. This information is gleaned from the files `/etc/dumpdates` and `/etc/fstab`. The **W** option causes **dump** to print out, for each file system in `/etc/dumpdates` the most recent dump date and level, and highlights those file systems that should be dumped. If the **W** option is set, all other options are ignored, and **dump** exits immediately.

w Is like W, but prints only those filesystems which need to be dumped.

Dump requires operator intervention on these conditions: end of tape, end of dump, tape write error, tape open error or disk read error (if there are more than a threshold of 32). In addition to alerting all operators implied by the **n** key, **dump** interacts with the operator on *dump's* control terminal at times when **dump** can no longer proceed, or if something is grossly wrong. All questions **dump** poses *must* be answered by typing "yes" or "no", appropriately.

Since making a dump involves a lot of time and effort for full dumps, **dump** checkpoints itself at the start of each tape volume. If writing that volume fails for some reason, **dump** will, with operator permission, restart itself from the checkpoint after the old tape has been rewound and removed, and a new tape has been mounted.

Dump tells the operator what is going on at periodic intervals, including usually low estimates of the number of blocks to write, the number of tapes it will take, the time to completion, and the time to the tape change. The output is verbose, so that others know that the terminal controlling **dump** is busy, and will be for some time.

In the event of a catastrophic disk event, the time required to restore all the necessary backup tapes or files to disk can be kept to a minimum by staggering the incremental dumps. An efficient method of staggering incremental dumps to minimize the number of tapes follows:

- Always start with a level 0 backup, for example:

  ```
  /etc/dump 0uf /dev/nrstl /usr/src
  ```

  This should be done at set intervals, say once a month or once every two months, and on a set of fresh tapes that is saved forever.

- After a level 0, dumps of active file systems are taken on a daily basis, using a modified Tower of Hanoi algorithm, with this sequence of dump levels:

  ```
  3 2 5 4 7 6 9 8 9 9 ...
  ```

  For the daily dumps, it should be possible to use a fixed number of tapes for each day, used on a weekly basis. Each week, a level 1 dump is taken, and the daily Hanoi sequence repeats beginning with 3. For weekly dumps, another fixed set of tapes per dumped file system is used, also on a cyclical basis.

After several months or so, the daily and weekly tapes should get rotated out of the dump cycle and fresh tapes brought in.

FILES

`/dev/rmt8`	default tape unit to dump to
`/etc/dumpdates`	dump date records
`/etc/fstab`	dump table: file systems and frequency
`/etc/group`	to find group *operator*

SEE ALSO

`restore`(8), `rmt`(8), `dump`(5), `fstab`(5)

DIAGNOSTICS

Many, and verbose.

Dump exits with zero status on success. Startup errors are indicated with an exit code of 1; abnormal termination is indicated with an exit code of 3.

BUGS

Fewer than 32 read errors on the filesystem are ignored. Each reel requires a new process, so parent processes for reels already written just hang around until the entire tape is written.

Dump with the **W** or **w** options does not report filesystems that have never been recorded in `/etc/dumpdates`, even if listed in `/etc/fstab`.

It would be nice if **dump** knew about the dump sequence, kept track of the tapes scribbled on, told the operator which tape to mount when, and provided more assistance for the operator running `restore`.

HISTORY

A **dump** command appeared in Version 6 AT&T UNIX.

NAME

dumpfs – dump file system information

SYNOPSIS

dumpfs [*filesys* | *device*]

DESCRIPTION

Dumpfs prints out the super block and cylinder group information for the file system or special device specified. The listing is very long and detailed. This command is useful mostly for finding out certain file system information such as the file system block size and minimum free space percentage.

SEE ALSO

fs(5), disktab(5), disklabel(8), tunefs(8), newfs(8), fsck(8)

HISTORY

The **dumpfs** command appeared in 4.2BSD.

M8

NAME

dumplfs – dump file system information

SYNOPSIS

dumplfs [*filesys* | *device*]

DESCRIPTION

Dumplfs prints out the file system layout information for the LFS file system or special device specified. The listing is very long and detailed. This command is useful mostly for finding out certain file system information such as the file system block size.

SEE ALSO

fs(5), disktab(5), disklabel(8), newlfs(8),

HISTORY

The **dumplfs** command appeared in 4.4BSD.

NAME

edquota – edit user quotas

SYNOPSIS

edquota [*–u*] [*–p* proto-username] username ...
edquota *–g* [*–p* proto-groupname] groupname ...
edquota *-t* [*-u*]
edquota *-t -g*

DESCRIPTION

Edquota is a quota editor. By default, or if the *-u* flag is specified, one or more users may be specified on the command line. For each user a temporary file is created with an ASCII representation of the current disk quotas for that user. The list of filesystems with user quotas is determined from */etc/fstab*. An editor is invoked on the ASCII file. The editor invoked is *vi*(1) unless the environment variable EDITOR specifies otherwise.

The quotas may then be modified, new quotas added, etc. Setting a quota to zero indicates that no quota should be imposed. Setting a hard limit to one indicates that no allocations should be permitted. Setting a soft limit to one with a hard limit of zero indicates that allocations should be permitted on only a temporary basis (see *-t* below). The current usage information in the file is for informational purposes; only the hard and soft limits can be changed.

On leaving the editor, *edquota* reads the temporary file and modifies the binary quota files to reflect the changes made.

If the **–p** option is specified, *edquota* will duplicate the quotas of the prototypical user specified for each user specified. This is the normal mechanism used to initialize quotas for groups of users.

If the *-g* flag is specified, *edquota* is invoked to edit the quotas of one or more groups specified on the command line. The *-p* flag can be specified in conjunction with the *-g* flag to specify a prototypical group to be duplicated among the listed set of groups.

Users are permitted to exceed their soft limits for a grace period that may be specified per filesystem. Once the grace period has expired, the soft limit is enforced as a hard limit. The default grace period for a filesystem is specified in */usr/include/ufs/quota.h*. The *-t* flag can be used to change the grace period. By default, or when invoked with the *-u* flag, the grace period is set for all the filesystems with user quotas specified in */etc/fstab*. When invoked with the *-g* flag the grace period is set for all the filesystems with group quotas specified in */etc/fstab*. The grace period may be specified in days, hours, minutes, or seconds. Setting a grace period to zero indicates that the default grace period should be imposed. Setting a grace period to one second indicates that no grace period should be granted.

Only the super-user may edit quotas.

FILES

quota.user	at the filesystem root with user quotas
quota.group	at the filesystem root with group quotas
/etc/fstab	to find filesystem names and locations

SEE ALSO

quota(1), quotactl(2), fstab(5), quotacheck(8), quotaon(8), repquota(8)

DIAGNOSTICS

Various messages about inaccessible files; self-explanatory.

M8

NAME

eeprom – openprom control utility

SYNOPSIS

eeprom [*name ...*] [*name=value ...*]

DESCRIPTION

The **eeprom** utility is used to display and modify options fields in the SPARCstation openprom.

When invoked with no arguments, **eeprom** display the values of all options. Otherwise, fields are displayed or set (in the order specified on the command line).

FILES

/dev/openprom the openprom device

SEE ALSO

openprom(4)

HISTORY

The **eeprom** utility first appeared in 4.4BSD.

NAME

ext_srvtab – extract service key files from Kerberos key distribution center database

SYNOPSIS

ext_srvtab [**–n**] [**–r realm**] [**hostname ...**]

DESCRIPTION

ext_srvtab extracts service key files from the Kerberos key distribution center (KDC) database.

Upon execution, it prompts the user to enter the master key string for the database. If the **–n** option is specified, the master key is instead fetched from the master key cache file.

For each *hostname* specified on the command line, *ext_srvtab* creates the service key file *hostname*-new-srvtab, containing all the entries in the database with an instance field of *hostname*. This new file contains all the keys registered for Kerberos-mediated service providing programs which use the *krb_get_phost*(3) principal and instance conventions to run on the host *hostname*. If the **–r** option is specified, the realm fields in the extracted file will match the given realm rather than the local realm.

DIAGNOSTICS

"verify_master_key: Invalid master key, does not match database."
The master key string entered was incorrect.

FILES

hostname-new-srvtab　Service key file generated for *hostname*

/etc/kerberosIV/principal.pag, /etc/kerberosIV/principal.dir
DBM files containing database

/etc/kerberosIV/master_key
Master key cache file.

SEE ALSO

read_service_key(3), krb_get_phost(3)

M8

NAME

fastboot, **fasthalt** – reboot/halt the system without checking the disks

SYNOPSIS

fastboot [*boot-options*]
fasthalt [*halt-options*]

DESCRIPTION

Fastboot and **fasthalt** are shell scripts which reboot and halt the system without checking the file systems. This is done by creating a file /fastboot, then invoking the reboot program. The system startup script, /etc/rc, looks for this file and, if present, skips the normal invocation of fsck(8).

SEE ALSO

halt(8), reboot(8), rc(8)

HISTORY

The **fastboot** command appeared in 4.2BSD.

Section 8

System Maintenance

M8

NAME

NAME

fingerd – remote user information server

SYNOPSIS

fingerd [**-s**] [**-l**] [**-p** *filename*]

DESCRIPTION

Fingerd is a simple protocol based on *RFC1196* that provides an interface to the Name and Finger programs at several network sites. The program is supposed to return a friendly, human-oriented status report on either the system at the moment or a particular person in depth. There is no required format and the protocol consists mostly of specifying a single "command line".

Fingerd listens for TCP requests at port 79. Once connected it reads a single command line terminated by a <CRLF> which is passed to finger(1). **Fingerd** closes its connections as soon as the output is finished.

If the line is null (i.e. just a <CRLF> is sent) then finger returns a "default" report that lists all people logged into the system at that moment.

If a user name is specified (e.g. eric<CRLF>) then the response lists more extended information for only that particular user, whether logged in or not. Allowable "names" in the command line include both "login names" and "user names". If a name is ambiguous, all possible derivations are returned.

The following options may be passed to **fingerd** as server program arguments in /etc/inetd.conf:

- **-s** Enable secure mode. Queries without a user name are rejected and forwarding of queries to other remote hosts is denied.
- **-l** Enable logging. The name of the host originating the query is reported via syslog(3) at LOG_NOTICE priority.
- **-p** Use an alternate program as the local information provider. The default local program executed by **fingerd** is finger(1). By specifying a customized local server, this option allows a system manager to have more control over what information is provided to remote sites.

SEE ALSO

finger(1)

BUGS

Connecting directly to the server from a TIP or an equally narrow-minded TELNET–protocol user program can result in meaningless attempts at option negotiation being sent to the server, which will foul up the command line interpretation. **Fingerd** should be taught to filter out IAC's and perhaps even respond negatively (IAC WON'T) to all option commands received.

HISTORY

The **fingerd** command appeared in 4.3BSD.

NAME

format – how to format disks and tapes

DESCRIPTION

Currently, there are no ''native'' BSD media formatting utilities. Formatting of both disks and cartridge tapes must be done either standalone or under HP-UX using the *mediainit* utility distributed by HP. Note that HP-brand cartridge tapes come pre-formatted, and HP disks are supposed to.

HISTORY

The **format** utility first appeared in 4.4BSD.

NAME

fsck – filesystem consistency check and interactive repair

SYNOPSIS

fsck -p [**-m** *mode*]
fsck [**-b** *block#*] [**-c** *level*] [**-l** *maxparallel*] [**-y**] [**-n**] [**-m** *mode*] [*filesystem*]
...

DESCRIPTION

The first form of **fsck** preens a standard set of filesystems or the specified filesystems. It is normally used in the script /etc/rc during automatic reboot. Here **fsck** reads the table /etc/fstab to determine which filesystems to check. Only partitions in fstab that are mounted "rw," "rq" or "ro" and that have non-zero pass number are checked. Filesystems with pass number 1 (normally just the root filesystem) are checked one at a time. When pass 1 completes, all remaining filesystems are checked, running one process per disk drive. The disk drive containing each filesystem is inferred from the longest prefix of the device name that ends in a digit; the remaining characters are assumed to be the partition designator.

The kernel takes care that only a restricted class of innocuous filesystem inconsistencies can happen unless hardware or software failures intervene. These are limited to the following:
Unreferenced inodes
Link counts in inodes too large
Missing blocks in the free map
Blocks in the free map also in files
Counts in the super-block wrong

These are the only inconsistencies that **fsck** with the **-p** option will correct; if it encounters other inconsistencies, it exits with an abnormal return status and an automatic reboot will then fail. For each corrected inconsistency one or more lines will be printed identifying the filesystem on which the correction will take place, and the nature of the correction. After successfully correcting a filesystem, **fsck** will print the number of files on that filesystem, the number of used and free blocks, and the percentage of fragmentation.

If sent a QUIT signal, **fsck** will finish the filesystem checks, then exit with an abnormal return status that causes an automatic reboot to fail. This is useful when you want to finish the filesystem checks during an automatic reboot, but do not want the machine to come up multiuser after the checks complete.

Without the **-p** option, **fsck** audits and interactively repairs inconsistent conditions for filesystems. If the filesystem is inconsistent the operator is prompted for concurrence before each correction is attempted. It should be noted that some of the corrective actions which are not correctable under the **-p** option will result in some loss of data. The amount and severity of data lost may be determined from the diagnostic output. The default action for each consistency correction is to wait for the operator to respond yes or no. If the operator does not have write permission on the filesystem **fsck** will default to a **-n** action.

Fsck has more consistency checks than its predecessors *check*, *dcheck*, *fcheck*, and *icheck* combined.

The following flags are interpreted by **fsck**.

-b Use the block specified immediately after the flag as the super block for the filesystem. Block 32 is usually an alternate super block.

-l Limit the number of parallel checks to the number specified in the following argument. By default, the limit is the number of disks, running one process per disk. If a smaller limit is given, the disks are checked round-robin, one filesystem at a time.

-m Use the mode specified in octal immediately after the flag as the permission bits to use when creating the lost+found directory rather than the default 1777. In particular, systems that do not

M8

wish to have lost files accessible by all users on the system should use a more restrictive set of permissions such as 700.

-y Assume a yes response to all questions asked by **fsck**; this should be used with great caution as this is a free license to continue after essentially unlimited trouble has been encountered.

-n Assume a no response to all questions asked by **fsck** except for `CONTINUE?`, which is assumed to be affirmative; do not open the filesystem for writing.

-c Convert the filesystem to the specified level. Note that the level of a filesystem can only be raised. There are currently three levels defined:

0 The filesystem is in the old (static table) format.

1 The filesystem is in the new (dynamic table) format.

2 The filesystem supports 32-bit uid's and gid's, short symbolic links are stored in the inode, and directories have an added field showing the file type.

In interactive mode, **fsck** will list the conversion to be made and ask whether the conversion should be done. If a negative answer is given, no further operations are done on the filesystem. In preen mode, the conversion is listed and done if possible without user interaction. Conversion in preen mode is best used when all the filesystems are being converted at once. The format of a filesystem can be determined from the first line of output from `dumpfs`(8).

If no filesystems are given to **fsck** then a default list of filesystems is read from the file `/etc/fstab`.

Inconsistencies checked are as follows:

1. Blocks claimed by more than one inode or the free map.
2. Blocks claimed by an inode outside the range of the filesystem.
3. Incorrect link counts.
4. Size checks:
   Directory size not a multiple of DIRBLKSIZ.
   Partially truncated file.
5. Bad inode format.
6. Blocks not accounted for anywhere.
7. Directory checks:
   File pointing to unallocated inode.
   Inode number out of range.
   Dot or dot-dot not the first two entries of a directory or having the wrong inode number.
8. Super Block checks:
   More blocks for inodes than there are in the filesystem.
   Bad free block map format.
   Total free block and/or free inode count incorrect.

Orphaned files and directories (allocated but unreferenced) are, with the operator's concurrence, reconnected by placing them in the `lost+found` directory. The name assigned is the inode number. If the `lost+found` directory does not exist, it is created. If there is insufficient space its size is increased.

Because of inconsistencies between the block device and the buffer cache, the raw device should always be used.

FILES

`/etc/fstab` contains default list of filesystems to check.

M8

DIAGNOSTICS

The diagnostics produced by `fsck` are fully enumerated and explained in Appendix A of *Fsck – The UNIX File System Check Program.*

SEE ALSO

fstab(5), fs(5), fsdb(8), newfs(8), mkfs(8), reboot(8)

M8

NAME

fsdb – file system debugger

SYNOPSIS

fsdb [options] special

OPTIONS

The options available to *fsdb* are:

-?	display usage
-o	override some error conditions
-p'string'	set prompt to string
-w	open for write

DESCRIPTION

Since *fsdb* reads the disk raw, it is able to circumvent normal file system security. Extreme caution is advised in determining its availability on the system. Suggested permissions are 600 and owned by bin.

Fsdb can be used to patch up a damaged file system after a crash. It has conversions to translate block and i-numbers into their corresponding disk addresses. Also included are mnemonic offsets to access different parts of an inode. These greatly simplify the process of correcting control block entries or descending the file system tree.

Fsdb contains several error-checking routines to verify inode and block addresses. These can be disabled if necessary by invoking *fsdb* with the *–o* option or by the use of the *o* command.

Fsdb reads a block at a time and will therefore work with raw as well as block I/O. A buffer management routine is used to retain commonly used blocks of data in order to reduce the number of read system calls. All assignment operations result in an immediate write-through of the corresponding block. Note that in order to modify any portion of the disk, *fsdb* must be invoked with the *-w* option.

Wherever possible, *adb-*like syntax was adopted to promote the use of *fsdb* through familiarity.

Numbers are considered hexadecimal by default. However, the user has control over how data is to be displayed or accepted. The *base* command will display or set the input/output base. Once set, all input will default to this base and all output will be shown in this base. The base can be overridden temporarily for input by preceding hexadecimal numbers with '0x', preceding decimal numbers with '0t', or octal numbers with '0'. Hexadecimal numbers beginning with a-f or A-F must be preceded with '0x' to distinguish them from commands.

Disk addressing by *fsdb* is at the byte level. However, *fsdb* offers many commands to convert a desired inode, directory entry, block, superblock etc. to a byte address. Once the address has been calculated, *fsdb* will record the result in *dot* (see next paragraph).

Several global values are maintained by *fsdb*: the current base (referred to as *base*), the current address (referred to as *dot*), the current inode (referred to as *inode*), the current count (referred to as *count*), and the current type (referred to as *type*). Most commands use the preset value of *dot* in their execution. For example,

```
> 2:inode
```

will first set the value of *dot* to 2, ':' will alert the start of a command, and the *inode* command will set *inode* to 2. A count is specified after a ','. Once set, *count* will remain at this value until a new command is encountered which will then reset the value back to 1 (the default). So, if

```
> 2000,400/X
```

is typed, 400 hex longs are listed from 2000, and when completed, the value of *dot* will be 2000 + 400 * sizeof (long). If a carriage-return is then typed, the output routine will use the current values of *dot*, *count*, and *type* and display 400 more hex longs. A '*' will cause the entire block to be displayed.

End of fragment, block and file are maintained by *fsdb*. When displaying data as fragments or blocks, an error message will be displayed when the end of fragment or block is reached. When displaying data using the *db, ib, directory,* or *file* commands an error message is displayed if the end of file is reached. This is mainly needed to avoid passing the end of a directory or file and getting unknown and unwanted results.

An example showing several commands and the use of carriage-return would be:

> 2:ino; 0:dir?d
or
> 2:ino; 0:db:block?d

The two examples are synonymous for getting to the first directory entry of the root of the file system. Once there, subsequent carriage-returns (or +, -) will advance to subsequent entries. Note that

> 2:inode; :ls
or
> :ls /

is again synonymous.

EXPRESSIONS

The symbols recognized by *fsdb* are:

carriage-return
update the value of *dot* by the current value of *type* and display using the current value of *count*.

\# numeric expressions may be composed of +, -, *, and % operators (evaluated left to right) and may use parentheses. Once evaluated, the value of *dot* is updated.

, *count* count indicator. The global value of *count* will be updated to *count*. The value of *count* will remain until a new command is run. A count specifier of '*' will attempt to show a *block's* worth of information. The default for *count* is 1.

? *f* display in structured style with format specifier *f* (see FORMATTED OUTPUT section).

/ *f* display in unstructured style with format specifier *f* (see FORMATTED OUTPUT section).

. the value of *dot*.

+*e* increment the value of *dot* by the expression *e*. The amount actually incremented is dependent on the size of *type*:
dot = dot + e * sizeof (type)
The default for *e* is 1.

-*e* decrement the value of *dot* by the expression *e* (see +).

**e* multiply the value of *dot* by the expression *e*. Multiplication and division don't use *type*. In the above calculation of *dot*, consider the sizeof (*type*) to be 1.

%*e* divide the value of *dot* by the expression *e* (see *).

< *name* restore an address saved in register *name*. *name* must be a single letter or digit.

> *name* save an address in register *name*. *name* must be a single letter or digit.

= *f* display indicator. If *f* is a legitimate format specifier (see FORMATTED OUTPUT section), then the value of *dot* is displayed using format specifier *f*. Otherwise, assignment is assumed (see next item).

= *[s] [e]*
assignment indicator. The address pointed to by *dot* has its contents changed to the value of the expression *e* or to the *ASCII* representation of the quoted (") string *s*. This may be useful for changing directory names or *ASCII* file information.

=+ *e* incremental assignment. The address pointed to by *dot* has its contents incremented by expression *e*.

=- *e* decremental assignment. The address pointed to by *dot* has its contents decremented by expression *e*.

COMMANDS

A command must be prefixed by a ':' character. Only enough letters of the command to uniquely distinguish it are needed. Multiple commands may be entered on one line by separating them by a space, tab or ';'.

In order to view a potentially unmounted disk in a reasonable manner, *fsdb* offers the *cd*, *pwd*, *ls* and *find* commands. The functionality of these commands substantially matches those of its *UNIX* counterparts (see individual command for details). The '*', '?', and '[-]' wild card characters are available.

base=b display or set base. As stated above, all input and output is governed by the current *base*. If the '=b' is left off, the current *base* is displayed. Otherwise, the current *base* is set to *b*. Note that this is interpreted using the old value of *base*, so to ensure correctness use the '0', '0t', or '0x' prefix when changing the *base*. The default for *base* is hexadecimal.

block convert the value of *dot* to a block address.

cd dir change the current directory to directory *dir*. The current values of *inode* and *dot* are also updated. If no *dir* is specified, then change directories to inode 2 ("/").

cg convert the value of *dot* to a cylinder group.

directory
If the current *inode* is a directory, then the value of *dot* is converted to a directory slot offset in that directory and *dot* now points to this entry.

file the value of *dot* is taken as a relative block count from the beginning of the file. The value of *dot* is updated to the first byte of this block.

find *dir [-name n] [-inum i]*
find files by name or i-number. *find* recursively searches directory *dir* and below for filenames whose i-number matches *i* or whose name matches pattern *n*. Note that only one of the two options (-name or -inum) may be used at one time. Also, the -print is not needed or accepted.

fill=*p* fill an area of disk with pattern *p*. The area of disk is delimited by *dot* and *count*.

fragment
convert the value of *dot* to a fragment address. The only difference between the *fragment* command and the *block* command is the amount that is able to be displayed.

inode convert the value of *dot* to an inode address. If successful, the current value of *inode* will be updated as well as the value of *dot*. As a convenient shorthand, if ':inode' appears at the beginning of the line, the value of *dot* is set to the current *inode* and that inode is displayed in inode format.

ls *[-R] [-l] pat1 pat2 ...*
list directories or files. If no file is specified, the current directory is assumed. Either or both of the options may be used (but, if used, *must* be specified before the filename specifiers). Also, as stated above, wild card characters are available and multiple arguments may be given. The long listing shows only the i-number and the name; use the *inode* command with '?i' to get more information.

override
toggle the value of override. Some error conditions may be overridden if override is toggled on.

prompt *p*
change the fsdb prompt to *p*. *p* must be surrounded by (")s.

pwd display the current working directory.

quit quit *fsdb*.

sb the value of *dot* is taken as a cylinder group number and then converted to the address of the superblock in that cylinder group. As a shorthand, ':sb' at the beginning of a line will set the value of *dot* to *the* superblock and display it in superblock format.

! escape to shell

INODE COMMANDS

In addition to the above commands, there are several commands that deal with inode fields and operate directly on the current *inode* (they still require the ':'). They may be used to more easily display or change the particular fields. The value of *dot* is only used by the ':db' and ':ib' commands. Upon completion of the command, the value of *dot* is changed to point to that particular field. For example,

```
> :ln=+1
```

would increment the link count of the current *inode* and set the value of *dot* to the address of the link count field.

at access time.

bs block size.

ct creation time.

db use the current value of *dot* as a direct block index, where direct blocks number from 0 - 11. In order to display the block itself, you need to 'pipe' this result into the *block* or *fragment* command. For example,

```
> 1:db:block,20/X
```

would get the contents of data block field 1 from the inode and convert it to a block address. 20 longs are then displayed in hexadecimal (see FORMATTED OUTPUT section).

gid group id.

ib use the current value of *dot* as an indirect block index where indirect blocks number from 0 - 2. This will only get the indirect block itself (the block containing the pointers to the actual blocks). Use the *file* command and start at block 12 to get to the actual blocks.

ln link count.

mt modification time.

md mode.

maj major device number.

min minor device number.

nm although listed here, this command actually operates on the directory name field. Once poised at the desired directory entry (using the *directory* command), this command will allow you to change or display the directory name. For example,

```
> 7:dir:nm="foo"
```

will get the 7th directory entry of the current *inode* and change its name to foo. Note that names cannot be made larger than the field is set up for. If an attempt is made, the string is truncated to fit and a warning message to this effect is displayed.

sz file size.

uid user id.

FORMATTED OUTPUT

There are two styles and many format types. The two styles are structured and unstructured. Structured output is used to display inodes, directories, superblocks and the like. Unstructured just displays raw data. The following table shows the different ways of displaying:

?

c display as cylinder groups

i	display as inodes
d	display as directories
s	display as superblocks

/

b	display as bytes
c	display as characters
o O	display as octal shorts or longs
d D	display as decimal shorts or longs
x X	display as hexadecimal shorts or longs

The format specifier immediately follows the '/' or '?' character. The values displayed by '/b' and all '?' formats are displayed in the current *base*. Also, *type* is appropriately updated upon completion.

EXAMPLES

> 2000+400%(20+20)=D
will display 2010 in decimal (use of *fsdb* as a calculator for complex arithmetic).

> 386:ino?i — display i-number 386 in an inode format. This now becomes the current *inode*.

> :ln=4 — changes the link count for the current *inode* to 4.

> :ln=+1 — increments the link count by 1.

> :ct=X — display the creation time as a hexadecimal long.

> :mt=t — display the modification time in time format.

> 0:file/c — displays, in *ASCII*, block zero of the file associated with the current *inode*.

> 2:ino,*?d — displays the first blocks worth of directory entries for the root inode of this file system. It will stop prematurely if the eof is reached.

> 5:dir:inode; 0:file,*/c
changes the current inode to that associated with the 5th directory entry (numbered from zero) of the current *inode*. The first logical block of the file is then displayed in *ASCII*.

> :sb — displays the superblock of this file system.

> 1:cg?c — displays cylinder group information and summary for cylinder group 1.

> 2:inode; 7:dir=3 — changes the i-number for the seventh directory slot in the root directory to 3.

> 7:dir:nm="name"
changes the name field in the directory slot to *name*.

> 2:db:block,*?d — displays the third block of the current *inode* as directory entries.

> 3c3:fragment,20:fill=0x20
get fragment 3c3 and fill 20 *type* elements with 0x20.

> 2050=0xffff — set the contents of address 2050 to 0xffffffff. 0xffffffff may be truncated depending on the current *type*.

> 1c92434="this is some text"
will place the *ASCII* for the string at 1c92434.

SEE ALSO

fsck(8), dir(4), fs(5).

NAME

fsinfo – co-ordinate site-wide filesystem information

SYNOPSIS

fsinfo [**-v**] [**-a** *autodir*] [**-b** *bootparams*] [**-d** *dumpsets*] [**-e** *exports*] [**-f** *fstabs*] [**-h** *hostname*] [**-m** *automounts*] [**-I** *dir*] [**-D** *string[=string]*]] [**-U** *string[=string]*]] *config ...*

DESCRIPTION

The **fsinfo** utility takes a set of system configuration information, and generates a co-ordinated set of amd, mount and mountd configuration files.

The **fsinfo** command is fully described in the document *Amd - The 4.4BSD Automounter*

SEE ALSO

amd(8), mount(8), mountd(8).

HISTORY

The **fsinfo** command first appeared in 4.4BSD.

M8

NAME

ftpd – Internet File Transfer Protocol server

SYNOPSIS

ftpd [**–dl**] [**–T** *maxtimeout*] [**–t** *timeout*]

DESCRIPTION

Ftpd is the Internet File Transfer Protocol server process. The server uses the TCP protocol and listens at the port specified in the "ftp" service specification; see services(5).

Available options:

–d Debugging information is written to the syslog using LOG_FTP.

–l Each successful and failed ftp(1) session is logged using syslog with a facility of LOG_FTP. If this option is specified twice, the retrieve (get), store (put), append, delete, make directory, remove directory and rename operations and their filename arguments are also logged.

–T A client may also request a different timeout period; the maximum period allowed may be set to *timeout* seconds with the **–T** option. The default limit is 2 hours.

–t The inactivity timeout period is set to *timeout* seconds (the default is 15 minutes).

The file /etc/nologin can be used to disable ftp access. If the file exists, **ftpd** displays it and exits. If the file /etc/ftpwelcome exists, **ftpd** prints it before issuing the "ready" message. If the file /etc/motd exists, **ftpd** prints it after a successful login.

The ftp server currently supports the following ftp requests. The case of the requests is ignored.

Request	Description
ABOR	abort previous command
ACCT	specify account (ignored)
ALLO	allocate storage (vacuously)
APPE	append to a file
CDUP	change to parent of current working directory
CWD	change working directory
DELE	delete a file
HELP	give help information
LIST	give list files in a directory ("ls -lgA")
MKD	make a directory
MDTM	show last modification time of file
MODE	specify data transfer *mode*
NLST	give name list of files in directory
NOOP	do nothing
PASS	specify password
PASV	prepare for server-to-server transfer
PORT	specify data connection port
PWD	print the current working directory
QUIT	terminate session
REST	restart incomplete transfer
RETR	retrieve a file
RMD	remove a directory

RNFR	specify rename-from file name
RNTO	specify rename-to file name
SITE	non-standard commands (see next section)
SIZE	return size of file
STAT	return status of server
STOR	store a file
STOU	store a file with a unique name
STRU	specify data transfer *structure*
SYST	show operating system type of server system
TYPE	specify data transfer *type*
USER	specify user name
XCUP	change to parent of current working directory (deprecated)
XCWD	change working directory (deprecated)
XMKD	make a directory (deprecated)
XPWD	print the current working directory (deprecated)
XRMD	remove a directory (deprecated)

The following non-standard or UNIX specific commands are supported by the SITE request.

Request	**Description**
UMASK	change umask, e.g. ‘‘SITE UMASK 002’’
IDLE	set idle-timer, e.g. ‘‘SITE IDLE 60’’
CHMOD	change mode of a file, e.g. ‘‘SITE
HELP	give help information.

The remaining ftp requests specified in Internet RFC 959 are recognized, but not implemented. MDTM and SIZE are not specified in RFC 959, but will appear in the next updated FTP RFC.

The ftp server will abort an active file transfer only when the ABOR command is preceded by a Telnet "Interrupt Process" (IP) signal and a Telnet "Synch" signal in the command Telnet stream, as described in Internet RFC 959. If a STAT command is received during a data transfer, preceded by a Telnet IP and Synch, transfer status will be returned.

Ftpd interprets file names according to the ‘‘globbing’’ conventions used by `csh`(1). This allows users to utilize the metacharacters ‘‘*? [ ] { } ~’’.

Ftpd authenticates users according to three rules.

1. The login name must be in the password data base, `/etc/passwd`, and not have a null password. In this case a password must be provided by the client before any file operations may be performed.
2. The login name must not appear in the file `/etc/ftpusers`.
3. The user must have a standard shell returned by `getusershell`(3).
4. If the user name is ‘‘anonymous’’ or ‘‘ftp’’, an anonymous ftp account must be present in the password file (user ‘‘ftp’’). In this case the user is allowed to log in by specifying any password (by convention an email address for the user should be used as the password).

In the last case, **ftpd** takes special measures to restrict the client's access privileges. The server performs a `chroot`(2) to the home directory of the ‘‘ftp’’ user. In order that system security is not breached, it is recommended that the ‘‘ftp’’ subtree be constructed with care, following these rules:

`~ftp` Make the home directory owned by ‘‘root’’ and unwritable by anyone.

~ftp/bin Make this directory owned by "root" and unwritable by anyone (mode 555). The program ls(1) must be present to support the list command. This program should be mode 111.

~ftp/etc Make this directory owned by "root" and unwritable by anyone (mode 555). The files passwd(5) and group(5) must be present for the ls command to be able to produce owner names rather than numbers. The password field in passwd is not used, and should not contain real passwords. The file motd, if present, will be printed after a successful login. These files should be mode 444.

~ftp/pub Make this directory mode 777 and owned by "ftp". Guests can then place files which are to be accessible via the anonymous account in this directory.

FILES

/etc/ftpusers	List of unwelcome/restricted users.
/etc/ftpwelcome	Welcome notice.
/etc/motd	Welcome notice after login.
/etc/nologin	Displayed and access refused.

SEE ALSO

ftp(1), getusershell(3), syslogd(8)

BUGS

The server must run as the super-user to create sockets with privileged port numbers. It maintains an effective user id of the logged in user, reverting to the super-user only when binding addresses to sockets. The possible security holes have been extensively scrutinized, but are possibly incomplete.

HISTORY

The **ftpd** command appeared in 4.2BSD.

NAME

getty – set terminal mode

SYNOPSIS

getty [*type* [*tty*]]

DESCRIPTION

The **getty** program is called by init(8) to open and initialize the tty line, read a login name, and invoke login(1).

The argument *tty* is the special device file in /dev to open for the terminal (for example, ''ttyh0''). If there is no argument or the argument is '–', the tty line is assumed to be open as file descriptor 0.

The *type* argument can be used to make **getty** treat the terminal line specially. This argument is used as an index into the **gettytab 5** database, to determine the characteristics of the line. If there is no argument, or there is no such table, the *default* table is used. If there is no /etc/gettytab a set of system defaults is used. If indicated by the table located, **getty** will clear the terminal screen, print a banner heading, and prompt for a login name. Usually either the banner or the login prompt will include the system hostname.

Most of the default actions of **getty** can be circumvented, or modified, by a suitable **gettytab** table.

The **getty** program can be set to timeout after some interval, which will cause dial up lines to hang up if the login name is not entered reasonably quickly.

DIAGNOSTICS

ttyxx: No such device or address.
ttyxx: No such file or address. A terminal which is turned on in the ttys file cannot be opened, likely because the requisite lines are either not configured into the system, the associated device was not attached during boot-time system configuration, or the special file in /dev does not exist.

FILES

/etc/gettytab

SEE ALSO

gettytab(5), init(8), login(1), ioctl(2), tty(4), ttys(5)

HISTORY

A **getty** program appeared in Version 6 AT&T UNIX.

M8

NAME

icheck – file system storage consistency check

SYNOPSIS

icheck [**–b** numbers] [filesystem]

DESCRIPTION

N.B.: *Icheck* is obsoleted for normal consistency checking by *fsck*(8).

Icheck examines a file system, builds a bit map of used blocks, and compares this bit map against the free map maintained on the file system. If the file system is not specified, a set of default file systems is checked. The normal output of *icheck* includes a report of

The total number of files and the numbers of regular, directory, block special and character special files.

The total number of blocks in use and the numbers of single-, double-, and triple-indirect blocks and directory blocks.

The number of free blocks.

The number of blocks missing; i.e. not in any file nor in any free map.

Following the **–b** option is a list of block numbers; whenever any of the named blocks turns up in a file, a diagnostic is produced.

Icheck is faster if the raw version of the special file is used, since it reads the i-list many blocks at a time.

FILES

Default file systems vary with installation.

SEE ALSO

fsck(8), dcheck(8), ncheck(8), fs(5), clri(8)

DIAGNOSTICS

For duplicate blocks and bad blocks (which lie outside the file system) *icheck* announces the difficulty, the i-number, and the kind of block involved. If a read error is encountered, the block number of the bad block is printed and *icheck* considers it to contain 0.

BUGS

Since *icheck* is inherently two-pass in nature, extraneous diagnostics may be produced if applied to active file systems.

It believes even preposterous super-blocks and consequently can get core images.

M8

NAME

ifconfig – configure network interface parameters

SYNOPSIS

ifconfig *interface address_family* [*address* [*dest_address*]] [*parameters*]
ifconfig *interface* [*protocol_family*]

DESCRIPTION

Ifconfig is used to assign an address to a network interface and/or configure network interface parameters. **Ifconfig** must be used at boot time to define the network address of each interface present on a machine; it may also be used at a later time to redefine an interface's address or other operating parameters.

Available operands for **ifconfig:**

Address
For the DARPA-Internet family, the address is either a host name present in the host name data base, hosts(5), or a DARPA Internet address expressed in the Internet standard ''dot notation''. For the Xerox Network Systems(tm) family, addresses are *net:a.b.c.d.e.f*, where *net* is the assigned network number (in decimal), and each of the six bytes of the host number, *a* through *f*, are specified in hexadecimal. The host number may be omitted on 10Mb/s Ethernet interfaces, which use the hardware physical address, and on interfaces other than the first. For the ISO family, addresses are specified as a long hexadecimal string, as in the Xerox family. However, two consecutive dots imply a zero byte, and the dots are optional, if the user wishes to (carefully) count out long strings of digits in network byte order.

address_family
Specifies the *address family* which affects interpretation of the remaining parameters. Since an interface can receive transmissions in differing protocols with different naming schemes, specifying the address family is recommeded. The address or protocol families currently supported are ''inet'', ''iso'', and ''ns''.

Interface
The *interface* parameter is a string of the form ''name unit'', for example, ''en0''

The following parameters may be set with **ifconfig**:

alias Establish an additional network address for this interface. This is sometimes useful when changing network numbers, and one wishes to accept packets addressed to the old interface.

arp Enable the use of the Address Resolution Protocol in mapping between network level addresses and link level addresses (default). This is currently implemented for mapping between DARPA Internet addresses and 10Mb/s Ethernet addresses.

–arp Disable the use of the Address Resolution Protocol.

broadcast (Inet only) Specify the address to use to represent broadcasts to the network. The default broadcast address is the address with a host part of all 1's.

debug Enable driver dependent debugging code; usually, this turns on extra console error logging.

–debug Disable driver dependent debugging code.

delete Remove the network address specified. This would be used if you incorrectly specified an alias, or it was no longer needed. If you have incorrectly set an NS address having the side effect of specifying the host portion, removing all NS addresses will allow you to respecify the host portion.

dest_address Specify the address of the correspondent on the other end of a point to point link.

down Mark an interface "down". When an interface is marked "down", the system will not attempt to transmit messages through that interface. If possible, the interface will be reset to disable reception as well. This action does not automatically disable routes using the interface.

ipdst This is used to specify an Internet host who is willing to receive ip packets encapsulating NS packets bound for a remote network. An apparent point to point link is constructed, and the address specified will be taken as the NS address and network of the destination. IP encapsulation of CLNP packets is done differently.

metric *n* Set the routing metric of the interface to *n*, default 0. The routing metric is used by the routing protocol (`routed`(8)). Higher metrics have the effect of making a route less favorable; metrics are counted as addition hops to the destination network or host.

netmask *mask* (Inet and ISO) Specify how much of the address to reserve for subdividing networks into sub-networks. The mask includes the network part of the local address and the subnet part, which is taken from the host field of the address. The mask can be specified as a single hexadecimal number with a leading 0x, with a dot-notation Internet address, or with a pseudo-network name listed in the network table `networks`(5). The mask contains 1's for the bit positions in the 32-bit address which are to be used for the network and subnet parts, and 0's for the host part. The mask should contain at least the standard network portion, and the subnet field should be contiguous with the network portion.

nsellength *n* (ISO only) This specifies a trailing number of bytes for a received NSAP used for local identification, the remaining leading part of which is taken to be the NET (Network Entity Title). The default value is 1, which is conformant to US GOSIP. When an ISO address is set in an ifconfig command, it is really the NSAP which is being specified. For example, in US GOSIP, 20 hex digits should be specified in the ISO NSAP to be assigned to the interface. There is some evidence that a number different from 1 may be useful for AFI 37 type addresses.

trailers Request the use of a "trailer" link level encapsulation when sending (default). If a network interface supports **trailers**, the system will, when possible, encapsulate outgoing messages in a manner which minimizes the number of memory to memory copy operations performed by the receiver. On networks that support the Address Resolution Protocol (see `arp`(4); currently, only 10 Mb/s Ethernet), this flag indicates that the system should request that other systems use trailers when sending to this host. Similarly, trailer encapsulations will be sent to other hosts that have made such requests. Currently used by Internet protocols only.

-trailers Disable the use of a "trailer" link level encapsulation.

link[0-2] Enable special processing of the link level of the interface. These three options are interface specific in actual effect, however, they are in general used to select special modes of operation. An example of this is to enable SLIP compression. Currently, only used by SLIP.

-link[0-2] Disable special processing at the link level with the specified interface.

up Mark an interface ''up''. This may be used to enable an interface after an ''ifconfig down.'' It happens automatically when setting the first address on an interface. If the interface was reset when previously marked down, the hardware will be re-initialized.

Ifconfig displays the current configuration for a network interface when no optional parameters are supplied. If a protocol family is specified, Ifconfig will report only the details specific to that protocol family.

Only the super-user may modify the configuration of a network interface.

DIAGNOSTICS

Messages indicating the specified interface does not exit, the requested address is unknown, or the user is not privileged and tried to alter an interface's configuration.

SEE ALSO

netstat(1), netintro(4), rc(8), routed(8),

HISTORY

The **ifconfig** command appeared in 4.2BSD.

M8

NAME

inetd – internet "super-server"

SYNOPSIS

inetd [**–d**] [**–R** *rate*] [*configuration file*]

DESCRIPTION

The **inetd** program should be run at boot time by /etc/rc (see rc(8)). It then listens for connections on certain internet sockets. When a connection is found on one of its sockets, it decides what service the socket corresponds to, and invokes a program to service the request. The server program is invoked with the service socket as its standard input, output and error descriptors. After the program is finished, **inetd** continues to listen on the socket (except in some cases which will be described below). Essentially, **inetd** allows running one daemon to invoke several others, reducing load on the system.

The options available for **inetd:**

–d Turns on debugging.

–R *rate*
Specifies the maximum number of times a service can be invoked in one minute; the default is 1000.

Upon execution, **inetd** reads its configuration information from a configuration file which, by default, is /etc/inetd.conf. There must be an entry for each field of the configuration file, with entries for each field separated by a tab or a space. Comments are denoted by a "#" at the beginning of a line. There must be an entry for each field. The fields of the configuration file are as follows:

service name
socket type
protocol
wait/nowait
user
server program
server program arguments

There are two types of services that **inetd** can start: standard and TCPMUX. A standard service has a well-known port assigned to it; it may be a service that implements an official Internet standard or is a BSD-specific service. As described in RFC 1078, TCPMUX services are nonstandard services that do not have a well-known port assigned to them. They are invoked from **inetd** when a program connects to the "tcpmux" well-known port and specifies the service name. This feature is useful for adding locally-developed servers.

The *service-name* entry is the name of a valid service in the file /etc/services. For "internal" services (discussed below), the service name *must* be the official name of the service (that is, the first entry in /etc/services). For TCPMUX services, the value of the *service-name* field consists of the string "tcpmux" followed by a slash and the locally-chosen service name. The service names listed in /etc/services and the name "help" are reserved. Try to choose unique names for your TCPMUX services by prefixing them with your organization's name and suffixing them with a version number.

The *socket-type* should be one of "stream", "dgram", "raw", "rdm", or "seqpacket", depending on whether the socket is a stream, datagram, raw, reliably delivered message, or sequenced packet socket. TCPMUX services must use "stream".

The *protocol* must be a valid protocol as given in /etc/protocols. Examples might be "tcp" or "udp". TCPMUX services must use "tcp".

The *wait/nowait* entry specifies whether the server that is invoked by inetd will take over the socket associated with the service access point, and thus whether **inetd** should wait for the server to exit before listening for new service requests. Datagram servers must use ''wait'', as they are always invoked with the original datagram socket bound to the specified service address. These servers must read at least one datagram from the socket before exiting. If a datagram server connects to its peer, freeing the socket so **inetd** can received further messages on the socket, it is said to be a ''multi-threaded'' server; it should read one datagram from the socket and create a new socket connected to the peer. It should fork, and the parent should then exit to allow **inetd** to check for new service requests to spawn new servers. Datagram servers which process all incoming datagrams on a socket and eventually time out are said to be ''single-threaded''. `Comsat`(8), (`biff`(1)) and `talkd`(8) are both examples of the latter type of datagram server. `Tftpd`(8) is an example of a multi-threaded datagram server.

Servers using stream sockets generally are multi-threaded and use the ''nowait'' entry. Connection requests for these services are accepted by **inetd**, and the server is given only the newly-accepted socket connected to a client of the service. Most stream-based services operate in this manner. Stream-based servers that use ''wait'' are started with the listening service socket, and must accept at least one connection request before exiting. Such a server would normally accept and process incoming connection requests until a timeout. TCPMUX services must use ''nowait''.

The *user* entry should contain the user name of the user as whom the server should run. This allows for servers to be given less permission than root.

The *server-program* entry should contain the pathname of the program which is to be executed by **inetd** when a request is found on its socket. If **inetd** provides this service internally, this entry should be ''internal''.

The *server program arguments* should be just as arguments normally are, starting with argv[0], which is the name of the program. If the service is provided internally, the word ''internal'' should take the place of this entry.

The **inetd** program provides several ''trivial'' services internally by use of routines within itself. These services are ''echo'', ''discard'', ''chargen'' (character generator), ''daytime'' (human readable time), and ''time'' (machine readable time, in the form of the number of seconds since midnight, January 1, 1900). All of these services are tcp based. For details of these services, consult the appropriate RFC from the Network Information Center.

The **inetd** program rereads its configuration file when it receives a hangup signal, `SIGHUP`. Services may be added, deleted or modified when the configuration file is reread.

TCPMUX

RFC 1078 describes the TCPMUX protocol: ''A TCP client connects to a foreign host on TCP port 1. It sends the service name followed by a carriage-return line-feed <CRLF>. The service name is never case sensitive. The server replies with a single character indicating positive (+) or negative (–) acknowledgment, immediately followed by an optional message of explanation, terminated with a <CRLF>. If the reply was positive, the selected protocol begins; otherwise the connection is closed.'' The program is passed the TCP connection as file descriptors 0 and 1.

If the TCPMUX service name begins with a ''+'', **inetd** returns the positive reply for the program. This allows you to invoke programs that use stdin/stdout without putting any special server code in them.

The special service name ''help'' causes **inetd** to list TCPMUX services in `inetd.conf`.

M8

EXAMPLES

Here are several example service entries for the various types of services:

```
ftp             stream  tcp    nowait root  /usr/libexec/ftpd       ftpd -l
ntalk           dgram   udp    wait   root  /usr/libexec/ntalkd     ntalkd
tcpmux/+date    stream  tcp    nowait guest /bin/date               date
tcpmux/phonebook stream tcp nowait guest /usr/local/bin/phonebook phonebook
```

ERROR MESSAGES

The **inetd** server logs error messages using `syslog`(3). Important error messages and their explanations are:

service/protocol `server failing (looping), service terminated.`
The number of requests for the specified service in the past minute exceeded the limit. The limit exists to prevent a broken program or a malicious user from swamping the system. This message may occur for several reasons: 1) there are lots of hosts requesting the service within a short time period, 2) a 'broken' client program is requesting the service too frequently, 3) a malicious user is running a program to invoke the service in a 'denial of service' attack, or 4) the invoked service program has an error that causes clients to retry quickly. Use the [**−R**] option, as described above, to change the rate limit. Once the limit is reached, the service will be reenabled automatically in 10 minutes.

service/protocol: `No such user` *'user'*, `service ignored`
service/protocol: `getpwnam:` *user*: `No such user`
No entry for *user* exists in the `passwd` file. The first message occurs when **inetd** (re)reads the configuration file. The second message occurs when the service is invoked.

service: `can't set uid` *number*
service: `can't set gid` *number*
The user or group ID for the entry's *user* is invalid.

SEE ALSO

`comsat`(8), `fingerd`(8), `ftpd`(8), `rexecd`(8), `rlogind`(8), `rshd`(8), `telnetd`(8), `tftpd`(8)

HISTORY

The **inetd** command appeared in 4.3BSD. TCPMUX is based on code and documentation by Mark Lottor.

M8

NAME

init – process control initialization

SYNOPSIS

init

DESCRIPTION

The **init** program is the last stage of the boot process. It normally runs the automatic reboot sequence as described in `reboot(8)`, and if this succeeds, begins multi-user operation. If the reboot scripts fail, **init** commences single user operation by giving the super-user a shell on the console. The **init** program may be passed parameters from the boot program to prevent the system from going multi-user and to instead execute a single user shell without starting the normal daemons. The system is then quiescent for maintenance work and may later be made to go to multi-user by exiting the single-user shell (with ^D). This causes **init** to run the `/etc/rc` start up command file in fastboot mode (skipping disk checks).

If the **console** entry in the `ttys(5)` file is marked "insecure", then **init** will require that the superuser password be entered before the system will start a single-user shell. The password check is skipped if the **console** is marked as "secure".

The kernel runs with four different levels of security. Any superuser process can raise the security level, but only **init** can lower it. Security levels are defined as follows:

- **-1** Permanently insecure mode – always run system in level 0 mode.
- **0** Insecure mode – immutable and append-only flags may be turned off. All devices may be read or written subject to their permissions.
- **1** Secure mode – immutable and append-only flags may not be changed; disks for mounted filesystems, `/dev/mem`, and `/dev/kmem` are read-only.
- **2** Highly secure mode – same as secure mode, plus disks are always read-only whether mounted or not. This level precludes tampering with filesystems by unmounting them, but also inhibits running `newfs(8)` while the system is multi-user.

Normally, the system runs in level 0 mode while single user and in level 1 mode while multiuser. If the level 2 mode is desired while running multiuser, it can be set in the startup script `/etc/rc` using `sysctl(8)`. If it is desired to run the system in level 0 mode while multiuser, the administrator must build a kernel with the variable **securelevel** defined in the file `/sys/compile/MACHINE/param.c` and initialize it to -1.

In multi-user operation, **init** maintains processes for the terminal ports found in the file `ttys(5)`. **Init** reads this file, and executes the command found in the second field. This command is usually `getty(8)`; `getty` opens and initializes the tty line and executes the `login` program. The `login` program, when a valid user logs in, executes a shell for that user. When this shell dies, either because the user logged out or an abnormal termination occurred (a signal), the **init** program wakes up, deletes the user from the `utmp(5)` file of current users and records the logout in the `wtmp` file. The cycle is then restarted by **init** executing a new `getty` for the line.

Line status (on, off, secure, getty, or window information) may be changed in the `ttys` file without a reboot by sending the signal `SIGHUP` to **init** with the command "`kill -HUP 1`". On receipt of this signal, **init** re-reads the `ttys` file. When a line is turned off in `ttys`, **init** will send a SIGHUP signal to the controlling process for the session associated with the line. For any lines that were previously turned off in the `ttys` file and are now on, **init** executes a new `getty` to enable a new login. If the getty or window field for a line is changed, the change takes effect at the end of the current login session (e.g., the next time **init** starts a process on the line). If a line is commented out or deleted from `ttys`, **init** will not do anything at all to that line. However, it will complain that the relationship between lines in the `ttys` file and records in the `utmp` file is out of sync, so this practice is not recommended.

M8

`Init` will terminate multi-user operations and resume single-user mode if sent a terminate (`TERM`) signal, for example, "`kill -TERM 1`". If there are processes outstanding that are deadlocked (because of hardware or software failure), `init` will not wait for them all to die (which might take forever), but will time out after 30 seconds and print a warning message.

`Init` will cease creating new `getty`'s and allow the system to slowly die away, if it is sent a terminal stop (`TSTP`) signal, i.e. "`kill -TSTP 1`". A later hangup will resume full multi-user operations, or a terminate will start a single user shell. This hook is used by `reboot`(8) and `halt`(8).

The role of **`init`** is so critical that if it dies, the system will reboot itself automatically. If, at bootstrap time, the `init` process cannot be located, the system will panic with the message "panic: "init died (signal %d, exit %d)".

DIAGNOSTICS

getty repeating too quickly on port %s, sleeping A process being started to service a line is exiting quickly each time it is started. This is often caused by a ringing or noisy terminal line. *Init will sleep for 10 seconds, then continue trying to start the process.*

some processes would not die; ps axl advised. A process is hung and could not be killed when the system was shutting down. This condition is usually caused by a process that is stuck in a device driver because of a persistent device error condition.

FILES

`/dev/console`	System console device.
`/dev/tty*`	Terminal ports found in `ttys`.
`/var/run/utmp`	Record of Current users on the system.
`/var/log/wtmp`	Record of all logins and logouts.
`/etc/ttys`	The terminal initialization information file.
`/etc/rc`	System startup commands.

SEE ALSO

`login`(1), `kill`(1), `sh`(1), `ttys`(5), `crash`(8), `getty`(8), `rc`(8), `reboot`(8), `halt`(8), `shutdown`(8)

HISTORY

A **`init`** command appeared in Version 6 AT&T UNIX.

BUGS

Systems without `sysctl` behave as though they have security level −1.

NAME

iostat – report I/O statistics

SYNOPSIS

iostat [**–c** *count*] [**–M** *core*] [**–N** *system*] [**–w** *wait*] [*drives*]

DESCRIPTION

Iostat displays kernel I/O statistics on terminal, disk and cpu operations.

The options are as follows:

–c Repeat the display *count* times. The first display is for the time since a reboot and each subsequent report is for the time period since the last display. If no *wait* interval is specified, the default is 1 second.

–M Extract values associated with the name list from the specified core instead of the default "/dev/kmem".

–N Extract the name list from the specified system instead of the default "/vmunix".

–w Pause *wait* seconds between each display. If no repeat *count* is specified, the default is infinity.

Iostat displays its information in the following format:

tty

tin	characters read from terminals
tout	characters written to terminals

disks Disk operations (this field is system dependent). The header of the field is the disk name and unit number. If more than four disk drives are configured in the system, **iostat** displays only the first four drives. To force **iostat** to display specific drives, their names may be supplied on the command line.

sps	sectors transferred per second
tps	transfers per second
msps	milliseconds per average seek (including implied seeks and rotational latency)

cpu

us	% of cpu time in user mode
ni	% of cpu time in user mode running niced processes
sy	% of cpu time in system mode
id	% of cpu time in idle mode

FILES

/vmunix Default kernel namelist.
/dev/kmem Default memory file.

SEE ALSO

fstat(1), netstat(1), nfsstat(1), ps(1), systat(1), vmstat(1), pstat(8)

The sections starting with "Interpreting system activity" in *Installing and Operating 4.3BSD*.

M8

NAME

kdb_destroy – destroy Kerberos key distribution center database

SYNOPSIS

kdb_destroy

DESCRIPTION

kdb_destroy deletes a Kerberos key distribution center database.

The user is prompted to verify that the database should be destroyed. A response beginning with 'y' or 'Y' confirms deletion. Any other response aborts deletion.

DIAGNOSTICS

"Database cannot be deleted at /etc/kerberosIV/principal"
The attempt to delete the database failed (probably due to a system or access permission error).

"Database not deleted." The user aborted the deletion.

FILES

/etc/kerberosIV/principal.pag, /etc/kerberosIV/principal.dir
DBM files containing database

SEE ALSO

kdb_init(8)

NAME

kdb_edit – Kerberos key distribution center database editing utility

SYNOPSIS

kdb_edit [**–n**]

DESCRIPTION

kdb_edit is used to create or change principals stored in the Kerberos key distribution center (KDC) database.

When executed, *kdb_edit* prompts for the master key string and verifies that it matches the master key stored in the database. If the **–n** option is specified, the master key is instead fetched from the master key cache file.

Once the master key has been verified, *kdb_edit* begins a prompt loop. The user is prompted for the principal and instance to be modified. If the entry is not found the user may create it. Once an entry is found or created, the user may set the password, expiration date, maximum ticket lifetime, and attributes. Default expiration dates, maximum ticket lifetimes, and attributes are presented in brackets; if the user presses return the default is selected. There is no default password. The password RANDOM is interpreted specially, and if entered the user may have the program select a random DES key for the principal.

Upon successfully creating or changing the entry, ''Edit O.K.'' is printed.

DIAGNOSTICS

"verify_master_key: Invalid master key, does not match database."
: The master key string entered was incorrect.

FILES

/etc/kerberosIV/principal.pag, /etc/kerberosIV/principal.dir
: DBM files containing database

/etc/kerberosIV/master_key
: Master key cache file.

M8

NAME

kdb_init – initialize Kerberos key distribution center database

SYNOPSIS

kdb_init [**realm**]

DESCRIPTION

kdb_init initializes a Kerberos key distribution center database, creating the necessary principals.

If the optional *realm* argument is not present, *kdb_init* prompts for a realm name (defaulting to the definition in /usr/include/krb.h). After determining the realm to be created, it prompts for a master key password. The master key password is used to encrypt every encryption key stored in the database.

DIAGNOSTICS

"/etc/kerberosIV/principal: File exists"
: An attempt was made to create a database on a machine which already had an existing database.

FILES

/etc/kerberosIV/principal.pag, /etc/kerberosIV/principal.dir
: DBM files containing database

/usr/include/kerberosIV/krb.h
: Include file defining default realm

SEE ALSO

kdb_destroy(8)

NAME

kdb_util – Kerberos key distribution center database utility

SYNOPSIS

kdb_util **operation filename**

DESCRIPTION

kdb_util allows the Kerberos key distribution center (KDC) database administrator to perform utility functions on the database.

Operation must be one of the following:

load initializes the KDC database with the records described by the text contained in the file *filename*. Any existing database is overwritten.

dump dumps the KDC database into a text representation in the file *filename*.

slave_dump
performs a database dump like the *dump* operation, and additionally creates a semaphore file signaling the propagation software that an update is available for distribution to slave KDC databases.

new_master_key
prompts for the old and new master key strings, and then dumps the KDC database into a text representation in the file *filename*. The keys in the text representation are encrypted in the new master key.

convert_old_db
prompts for the master key string, and then dumps the KDC database into a text representation in the file *filename*. The existing database is assumed to be encrypted using the old format (encrypted by the key schedule of the master key); the dumped database is encrypted using the new format (encrypted directly with master key).

DIAGNOSTICS

"verify_master_key: Invalid master key, does not match database."
The master key string entered was incorrect.

FILES

/etc/kerberosIV/principal.pag, /etc/kerberosIV/principal.dir
DBM files containing database

filename.ok semaphore file created by *slave_dump*.

M8

NAME

kgmon – generate a dump of the operating system's profile buffers

SYNOPSIS

kgmon [**-bhpr**] [**-M** *core*] [**-N** *system*]

DESCRIPTION

Kgmon is a tool used when profiling the operating system. When no arguments are supplied, **kgmon** indicates the state of operating system profiling as running, off, or not configured. (see `config`(8)) If the **-p** flag is specified, **kgmon** extracts profile data from the operating system and produces a `gmon.out` file suitable for later analysis by `gprof`(1).

The options are as follows:

-b Resume the collection of profile data.

-h Stop the collection of profile data.

-p Dump the contents of the profile buffers into a `gmon.out` file.

-r Reset all the profile buffers. If the **-p** flag is also specified, the `gmon.out` file is generated before the buffers are reset.

-M Extract values associated with the name list from the specified core instead of the default ''/dev/kmem''.

-N Extract the name list from the specified system instead of the default ''/vmunix''.

If neither **-b** nor **-h** is specified, the state of profiling collection remains unchanged. For example, if the **-p** flag is specified and profile data is being collected, profiling will be momentarily suspended, the operating system profile buffers will be dumped, and profiling will be immediately resumed.

FILES

`/vmunix` the default system
`/dev/kmem` the default memory

SEE ALSO

`gprof`(1), `config`(8)

DIAGNOSTICS

Users with only read permission on `/dev/kmem` cannot change the state of profiling collection. They can get a `gmon.out` file with the warning that the data may be inconsistent if profiling is in progress.

HISTORY

The **kgmon** command appeared in 4.2BSD.

NAME

kpasswdd – Kerberos password changing daemon

SYNOPSIS

kpasswdd

DESCRIPTION

Kpasswdd is the server for the passwd(1) program. The server provides a remote password changing facility with Kerberos authentication. A user must provide the old Kerberos password, encrypted in a random session key, to the server. **Kpasswdd** runs only on the Kerberos server, as it directly updates the Kerberos database.

SEE ALSO

kerberos(1), passwd(1)

HISTORY

The **kpasswdd** utility first appeared in 4.4BSD.

M8

NAME

kstash – stash Kerberos key distribution center database master key

SYNOPSIS

kstash

DESCRIPTION

kstash saves the Kerberos key distribution center (KDC) database master key in the master key cache file.

The user is prompted to enter the key, to verify the authenticity of the key and the authorization to store the key in the file.

DIAGNOSTICS

"verify_master_key: Invalid master key, does not match database."
: The master key string entered was incorrect.

"kstash: Unable to open master key file"
: The attempt to open the cache file for writing failed (probably due to a system or access permission error).

"kstash: Write I/O error on master key file"
: The **write**(2) system call returned an error while *kstash* was attempting to write the key to the file.

FILES

/etc/kerberosIV/principal.pag, /etc/kerberosIV/principal.dir
: DBM files containing database

/etc/kerberosIV/master_key
: Master key cache file.

NAME

kvm_mkdb – create kernel database

SYNOPSIS

kvm_mkdb [file]

DESCRIPTION

Kvm_mkdb creates a database in /var/db containing information about the specified file. If no file is specified, /vmunix is used by default. The file is named ''kvm_filename.db'', where ''filename'' is the name of the file read. Various library routines consult this database. The only information currently stored is the kernel namelist, which is used by the kvm_nlist(3) function, however, in the future the database may contain other static information about the current system.

FILES

/vmunix
/var/db/kvm_vmunix.db

SEE ALSO

kvm_nlist(3)

HISTORY

The **kvm_mkdb** utility first appeared in 4.4BSD.

NAME

`lfs_cleanerd` – garbage collect a log-structured file system

SYNOPSIS

`lfs_cleanerd [-ds] node`

DESCRIPTION

The `lfs_cleanerd` command starts a daemon process which garbage-collects the log-structured file system residing at the point named by *node* in the global file system namespace. This command is normally executed by `mount_lfs`(8) when the log-structured file system is mounted. The daemon will exit within a few minutes of when the file system it was cleaning is unmounted.

Garbage collection on a log-structured file system is done by scanning the file system's segments for active, i.e. referenced, data and copying it to new segments. When all of the active data in a given segment has been copied to a new segment that segment can be marked as empty, thus reclaiming the space taken by the inactive data which was in it.

The following options are available:

-d Run in debug mode. Do not become a daemon process, and print debugging information.

-s When cleaning the file system, read data in small chunks.

SEE ALSO

`mount_lfs`(8)

HISTORY

The `lfs_cleanerd` utility first appeared in 4.4BSD.

M8

NAME

lpc – line printer control program

SYNOPSIS

lpc [*command* [*argument* ...]]

DESCRIPTION

Lpc is used by the system administrator to control the operation of the line printer system. For each line printer configured in /etc/printcap, **lpc** may be used to:

- disable or enable a printer,
- disable or enable a printer's spooling queue,
- rearrange the order of jobs in a spooling queue,
- find the status of printers, and their associated spooling queues and printer daemons.

Without any arguments, **lpc** will prompt for commands from the standard input. If arguments are supplied, **lpc** interprets the first argument as a command and the remaining arguments as parameters to the command. The standard input may be redirected causing **lpc** to read commands from file. Commands may be abbreviated; the following is the list of recognized commands.

? [command ...]
help [command ...]
: Print a short description of each command specified in the argument list, or, if no argument is given, a list of the recognized commands.

abort { all | printer }
: Terminate an active spooling daemon on the local host immediately and then disable printing (preventing new daemons from being started by lpr) for the specified printers.

clean { all | printer }
: Remove any temporary files, data files, and control files that cannot be printed (i.e., do not form a complete printer job) from the specified printer queue(s) on the local machine.

disable { all | printer }
: Turn the specified printer queues off. This prevents new printer jobs from being entered into the queue by lpr.

down { all | printer } message ...
: Turn the specified printer queue off, disable printing and put *message* in the printer status file. The message doesn't need to be quoted, the remaining arguments are treated like echo(1). This is normally used to take a printer down and let others know why lpq(1) will indicate the printer is down and print the status message).

enable { all | printer }
: Enable spooling on the local queue for the listed printers. This will allow lpr(1) to put new jobs in the spool queue.

exit
quit Exit from lpc.

`restart` { all | printer }
: Attempt to start a new printer daemon. This is useful when some abnormal condition causes the daemon to die unexpectedly, leaving jobs in the queue. `Lpq` will report that there is no daemon present when this condition occurs. If the user is the super-user, try to abort the current daemon first (i.e., kill and restart a stuck daemon).

`start` { all | printer }
: Enable printing and start a spooling daemon for the listed printers.

`status` { all | printer }
: Display the status of daemons and queues on the local machine.

`stop` { all | printer }
: Stop a spooling daemon after the current job completes and disable printing.

`topq` printer [jobnum ...] [user ...]
: Place the jobs in the order listed at the top of the printer queue.

`up` { all | printer }
: Enable everything and start a new printer daemon. Undoes the effects of **down**.

FILES

`/etc/printcap`	printer description file
`/var/spool/*`	spool directories
`/var/spool/*/lock`	lock file for queue control

SEE ALSO

`lpd`(8), `lpr`(1), `lpq`(1), `lprm`(1), `printcap`(5)

DIAGNOSTICS

?Ambiguous command
: abbreviation matches more than one command

?Invalid command
: no match was found

?Privileged command
: command can be executed by root only

HISTORY

The `lpc` command appeared in 4.2BSD.

M8

NAME

lpd – line printer spooler daemon

SYNOPSIS

lpd [**-l**] [*port#*]

DESCRIPTION

Lpd is the line printer daemon (spool area handler) and is normally invoked at boot time from the rc(8) file. It makes a single pass through the printcap(5) file to find out about the existing printers and prints any files left after a crash. It then uses the system calls listen(2) and accept(2) to receive requests to print files in the queue, transfer files to the spooling area, display the queue, or remove jobs from the queue. In each case, it forks a child to handle the request so the parent can continue to listen for more requests.

Available options:

-l The **-l** flag causes **lpd** to log valid requests received from the network. This can be useful for debugging purposes.

port# The Internet port number used to rendezvous with other processes is normally obtained with getservbyname(3) but can be changed with the *port#* argument.

Access control is provided by two means. First, all requests must come from one of the machines listed in the file /etc/hosts.equiv or /etc/hosts.lpd. Second, if the rs capability is specified in the printcap entry for the printer being accessed, *lpr* requests will only be honored for those users with accounts on the machine with the printer.

The file *minfree* in each spool directory contains the number of disk blocks to leave free so that the line printer queue won't completely fill the disk. The *minfree* file can be edited with your favorite text editor.

The daemon begins processing files after it has successfully set the lock for exclusive access (described a bit later), and scans the spool directory for files beginning with *cf*. Lines in each *cf* file specify files to be printed or non-printing actions to be performed. Each such line begins with a key character to specify what to do with the remainder of the line.

J Job Name. String to be used for the job name on the burst page.

C Classification. String to be used for the classification line on the burst page.

L Literal. The line contains identification info from the password file and causes the banner page to be printed.

T Title. String to be used as the title for pr(1).

H Host Name. Name of the machine where lpr was invoked.

P Person. Login name of the person who invoked lpr. This is used to verify ownership by lprm.

M Send mail to the specified user when the current print job completes.

f Formatted File. Name of a file to print which is already formatted.

l Like "f" but passes control characters and does not make page breaks.

p Name of a file to print using pr(1) as a filter.

t Troff File. The file contains troff(1) output (cat phototypesetter commands).

M8

n	Ditroff File. The file contains device independent troff output.
r	DVI File. The file contains Tex l output DVI format from Standford.
g	Graph File. The file contains data produced by `plot`(3).
c	Cifplot File. The file contains data produced by *cifplot*.
v	The file contains a raster image.
r	The file contains text data with FORTRAN carriage control characters.
1	Troff Font R. Name of the font file to use instead of the default.
2	Troff Font I. Name of the font file to use instead of the default.
3	Troff Font B. Name of the font file to use instead of the default.
4	Troff Font S. Name of the font file to use instead of the default.
W	Width. Changes the page width (in characters) used by `pr`(1) and the text filters.
I	Indent. The number of characters to indent the output by (in ascii).
U	Unlink. Name of file to remove upon completion of printing.
N	File name. The name of the file which is being printed, or a blank for the standard input (when `lpr` is invoked in a pipeline).

If a file cannot be opened, a message will be logged via `syslog`(3) using the *LOG_LPR* facility. **Lpd** will try up to 20 times to reopen a file it expects to be there, after which it will skip the file to be printed.

Lpd uses `flock`(2) to provide exclusive access to the lock file and to prevent multiple daemons from becoming active simultaneously. If the daemon should be killed or die unexpectedly, the lock file need not be removed. The lock file is kept in a readable ASCII form and contains two lines. The first is the process id of the daemon and the second is the control file name of the current job being printed. The second line is updated to reflect the current status of **lpd** for the programs `lpq`(1) and `lprm`(1).

FILES

`/etc/printcap`	printer description file
`/var/spool/*`	spool directories
`/var/spool/*/minfree`	minimum free space to leave
`/dev/lp*`	line printer devices
`/dev/printer`	socket for local requests
`/etc/hosts.equiv`	lists machine names allowed printer access
`/etc/hosts.lpd`	lists machine names allowed printer access, but not under same administrative control.

SEE ALSO

`lpc`(8), `pac`(1), `lpr`(1), `lpq`(1), `lprm`(1), `syslog`(3), `printcap`(5)

4.2 BSD Line Printer Spooler Manual.

HISTORY

An **lpd** daemon appeared in Version 6 AT&T UNIX.

M8

NAME

mail.local – store mail in a mailbox

SYNOPSIS

mail.local [**-f** *from*] *user ...*

DESCRIPTION

Mail.local reads the standard input up to an end-of-file and appends it to each *user's* mail file. The *user* must be a valid user name.

The options are as follows:

-f *from*
Specify the sender's name.

Individual mail messages in the mailbox are delimited by an empty line followed by a line beginning with the string ''From ''. A line containing the string ''From '', the sender's name and a time stamp is prepended to each delivered mail message. A blank line is appended to each message. A greater-than character (''>'') is prepended to any line in the message which could be mistaken for a ''From '' delimiter line.

The mail files are exclusively locked with flock(2) while mail is appended.

If the ''biff'' service is returned by getservbyname(3), the biff server is notified of delivered mail.

The **mail.local** utility exits 0 on success, and >0 if an error occurs.

ENVIRONMENT

TZ Used to set the appropriate time zone on the timestamp.

FILES

/tmp/local.XXXXXX temporary files
/var/mail/user user's mailbox directory

SEE ALSO

mail(1), xsend(1), flock(2), getservbyname(3), comsat(8), sendmail(8)

HISTORY

A superset of **mail.local** (handling mailbox reading as well as mail delivery) appeared in Version 7 AT&T UNIX. as the program **mail**.

M8

NAME

make_keypair – generate Kerberos host key pair

SYNOPSIS

make_keypair *hostname* [*hostname* ...]

DESCRIPTION

The **make_keypair** command is used to create pairs of DES keys for each *hostname*. The keys are used by privileged programs such as register(1) to make remote updates to the Kerberos database without having to have first acquired a Kerberos ticket granting ticket (TGT). The keys created by **make_keypair** are placed (by hand) in the filesystems of the kerberos server in /etc/kerberosIV/register_keys, and in the root directory of the clients. For example, the file /.update.key128.32.130.3 would contain a copy of the key of the client with IP address 128.32.130.3. These keys provide a shared secret which may be used to establish a secure channel between the client hosts and the Kerberos server.

FILES

/.update.keyxx.xx.xx.xx	shared DES key with server
/etc/kerberosIV/register_keys	server's key storage directory

SEE ALSO

register(1), registerd(8), kerberos(1)

HISTORY

The **make_keypair** utility first appeared in 4.4BSD.

NAME

makedev – make system special files

SYNOPSIS

MAKEDEV *device ...*

DESCRIPTION

MAKEDEV is a shell script normally used to install special files. It resides in the /dev directory, as this is the normal location of special files. Arguments to **MAKEDEV** are usually of the form *device-name*? where *device-name* is one of the supported devices listed in section 4 of the manual and "?" is a logical unit number (0-9). A few special arguments create assorted collections of devices and are listed below.

std Create the *standard* devices for the system; for example the standard UNIX devices /dev/console and /dev/tty; the standard hardware dependent devices, for example in the VAX family the VAX-11/780 console floppy device, /dev/floppy, and VAX-11/750 and VAX-11/730 console cassette device(s), /dev/tu? devices would be made for the appropriate system.

local Create those devices specific to the local site. This request causes the shell file /dev/MAKEDEV.local to be executed. Site specific commands, such as those used to setup dialup lines as ttyd? should be included in this file.

Since all devices are created using mknod(8), this shell script is useful only to the super-user.

DIAGNOSTICS

Either self-explanatory, or generated by one of the programs called from the script. Use 'sh -x MAKEDEV' in case of trouble.

SEE ALSO

intro(4), config(8), mknod(8)

HISTORY

The **makedev** command appeared in 4.2BSD.

NAME

MAKEDEV – create system and device special files

SYNOPSIS

MAKEDEV *device_name ...*

DESCRIPTION

The shell script **MAKEDEV**, found in the /dev directory, is used to create the common special files. See special(8) for a more complete discussion of special files.

MAKEDEV takes any number of device names as arguments, where the names are the common abbreviation for the device. There are two special devices, *std* and *local*. The former creates the standard devices for the architecture. The latter is for devices specific to the local site, and executes the shell file MAKEDEV.local.

The HP300 supports the following devices. Where a device name is followed by a hash sign '#', the hash sign must be replaced by a unit number.

- *std* the standard devices (*console*, *drum*, *fd/**, *klog*, *kmem*, *mem*, *null*, *stderr*, *stdin*, *stdout*, *tty*).
- *local* configuration specific devices.
- *ct#* HP300 HP-IB cartridge tape.
- *cd#* "concatenated" pseudo-disks.
- *rd#* HP300 HP-IB disks
- *sd#* HP300 SCSI disks.
- *vnd#* "file" pseudo-disks.
- *dca#* HP200/300 single port serial interface.
- *dcm#* HP200/300 4 port serial mux interface.
- *pty#* set of 16 master and slave pseudo terminals.
- *flog#* kernel logging device.
- *grf#* raw interface to HP300 graphics devices.
- *ite#* terminal emulator interface to HP300 graphics devices.
- *hil* HP300 HIL input devices.

FILES

/dev The special file directory.

SEE ALSO

mknod(1), intro(4), config(8), special(8)

NAME

makekey – make encrypted keys or passwords

SYNOPSIS

makekey

DESCRIPTION

Makekey encrypts a key and salt which it reads from the standard input and writes the result to the standard output. The key is expected to be ten bytes; the salt is expected to be two bytes. See `crypt(3)` for more information on what characters the key and salt can contain and how the encrypted value is calculated.

SEE ALSO

`login(1)`, `crypt(1)`, `crypt(3)`

HISTORY

A **makekey** command appeared in Version 7 AT&T UNIX.

M8

NAME

makemap – create database maps for sendmail

SYNOPSIS

makemap [**-N**] [**-f**] [**-o**] [**-r**] [**-v**] *maptype mapname*

DESCRIPTION

makemap creates the database maps used by the keyed map lookups in sendmail(8). It reads input from the standard input and outputs them to the indicated *mapname*.

Depending on how it is compiled, **makemap** handles up to three different database formats, selected using the *maptype* parameter. They may be

dbm — DBM format maps. This requires the ndbm(3) library.

btree — B-Tree format maps. This requires the new Berkeley db(3) library.

hash — Hash format maps. This also requires the db(3) library.

In all cases, **makemap** reads lines from the standard input consisting of two words separated by white space. The first is the database key, the second is the value. The value may contain "%*n*" strings to indicated parameter substitution. Literal parentheses should be doubled ("%%"). Blank lines and lines beginning with "#" are ignored.

Flags

-N — Include the null byte that terminates strings in the map. This must match the –N flag in the sendmail.cf "K" line.

-f — Normally all upper case letters in the key are folded to lower case. This flag disables that behaviour. This is intended to mesh with the –f flag in the **K** line in sendmail.cf. The value is never case folded.

-o — Append to an old file. This allows you to augment an existing file.

-r — Allow replacement of existing keys. Normally **makemap** complains if you repeat a key, and does not do the insert.

-v — Verbosely print what it is doing.

SEE ALSO

sendmail(8)

HISTORY

The **makemap** command appeared in 4.4BSD.

NAME

mh-gen – generating the MH system

READ THIS

This documentation describes how to configure, generate, and install the UCI version of the RAND *MH* system. **Be certain** to read this document completely before you begin. You probably will also want to familiarize yourself with the *MH* Administrator's Guide before you install *MH*. A copy can be found in the file **doc/ADMIN.doc** is the *MH* sources.

DISCLAIMER

Although the *MH* system was originally developed by the RAND Corporation, and is now in the public domain, the RAND Corporation assumes no responsibility for *MH* or this particular modification of *MH*.

In addition, the Regents of the University of California issue the following **disclaimer** in regard to the UCI version of *MH*:

> ''Although each program has been tested by its contributor, no warranty, express or implied, is made by the contributor or the University of California, as to the accuracy and functioning of the program and related program material, nor shall the fact of distribution constitute any such warranty, and no responsibility is assumed by the contributor or the University of California in connection herewith.''

This version of *MH* is in the public domain, and as such, there are no real restrictions on its use. The *MH* source code and documentation have no licensing restrictions whatsoever. As a courtesy, the authors ask only that you provide appropriate credit to the RAND Corporation and the University of California for having developed the software.

GETTING HELP

MH is a software package that is neither supported by the RAND Corporation nor the University of California. However, since we do use the software ourselves and plan to continue using (and improving) *MH*, bug reports and their associated fixes should be reported back to us so that we may include them in future releases. The current computer mailbox for *MH* is **Bug–MH@ICS.UCI.EDU** (in the ARPA Internet), and **...!ucbvax!ucivax!bug–mh** (UUCP).

Presently, there are two Internet discussion groups, **MH–Users@ICS.UCI.EDU** and **MH–Workers@ICS.UCI.EDU**. **MH–Workers** is for people discussing code changes to *MH*. **MH-Users** is for general discussion about how to use *MH*. **MH–Users** is bi-directionally gatewayed into USENET as **comp.mail.mh.**

HOW TO GET MH

Since you probably already have *MH*, you may not need to read this unless you suspect you have an old version. There are two ways to get the latest release:

1. If you can FTP to the ARPA Internet, use anonymous FTP to ftp.ics.uci.edu [128.195.1.1] and retrieve the file pub/mh/mh-6.8.tar.Z. This is a tar image after being run through the compress program (approximately 1.8MB). There should also be a **README** file in that directory which tells what the current release of *MH* is, and how to get updates.

This tar file is also available on louie.udel.edu [128.175.1.3] in portal/mh-6.8.tar.Z. You may also find MH on various other hosts; to make sure you get the latest version and don't waste your time re-fixing bugs, it's best to get it from either ftp.ics.uci.edu or louie.udel.edu.

2. You can send $75 US to the address below. This covers the cost of a 6250 BPI 9-track magtape, handling, and shipping. In addition, you'll get a laser-printed hard-copy of the entire MH documentation set. Be sure to include your USPS address with your check. Checks must be drawn on U.S. funds and should be made payable to:

Regents of the University of California

The distribution address is:

Univeristy of California at Irvine
Office of Academic Computing
360 Computer Science
Irvine, CA 92717 USA

+1 714 856 5153

Sadly, if you just want the hard-copies of the documentation, you still have to pay the $75. The tar image has the documentation source (the manual is in roff format, but the rest are in TeX format). Postscript formatted versions of the TeX papers are available, as are crude tty-conversions of those papers.

SYNOPSIS

MAKE

DESCRIPTION

This is a description of how one can bring up an *MH* system. It is assumed that you have super-user privileges in order to (re–)install *MH*. Super-user privileges are not required to configure or generate *MH*.

Become the super-user and cd to /usr/src/local/ (or whatever you keep your local sources). The distribution tape contains the hierarchy for the mh.6-8/ directory. Bring the sources on-line:

```
# cd /usr/src/local
% tar xv
% cd mh-6.8
```

CONFIGURATION

First, go to the conf/ directory.

```
% cd conf/
```

This directory contains files that will produce source files tailored for your choice of *MH* configuration. You should edit only the file **MH**. This file contains configuration directives. These configuration directives are read by the *mhconfig* program to produce customized files.

For examples of various configurations, look in the directory **conf/examples/**. The file **MH** provided in **conf/** is a reasonable default. Lines beginning with '#' are comments, and are not otherwise interpreted.

Here are the *MH* configuration directives available. Be sure to read through this list completely before attempting to decide what directives are appropriate for your system.

More information on some of these options is available in the the *Administrator's Guide*. If you do not have a printed copy, you should configure your system with the default configuration file, **MH**, then generate and print a copy of the guide (as described below).

Installation paths

bin: /usr/local
: The directory where user–invoked programs go (see manual section 1).

etc: /usr/local/lib/mh
: The directory where pgm–invoked programs go (see manual section 8).

mail: /usr/spool/mail
: The directory where the maildrops are stored. If this pathname is absolute (i.e., begins with a **/**), then the user's maildrop is a file called **$USER** in this directory. If the pathname is not absolute, then the user's maildrop is in the user's home directory under the given name.

mandir: /usr/man

The parent directory of the manual entries.

manuals: standard

Where manual entries should be installed, relative to the directory given with ''mandir''. Either ''local'' to install manual entries under **manl/**, or ''new'' to install manual entries under **mann/**, or ''old'' to install manual entries under **mano/**, or ''standard'' to install manual entries under **man?/**, or ''bsd44'' to install manual entries as **man?/***page*.**0**, or ''gen'' to generate but not install them, or ''none'' to neither generate nor install them.

Any of these values may have the suffix ''/cat'' appended to it. In that case, the manual entries will be formatted with ''nroff -man'' and they will be installed in the corresponding ''cat?'' directories.

For example, to install manual entries under **/usr/man/u_man/man?**, use ''standard'' and **/usr/man/u_man** for ''mandir''. To install formatted manual entires under **/usr/contrib/man/cat?**, use ''standard/cat'' and **/usr/contrib/man** for ''mandir''. To install formatted manual entries using the BSD44 convention, use ''bsd44/cat''.

chown: /etc/chown

The location of the *chown* (8) on your system. If *chown* is in your search path, just use the value of ''chown''. On SYS5 systems, this should probably be ''/bin/chown''.

cp: cp

The command to copy files when installing, if not ''cp''. (Some sites use ''cp –p''.)

ln: ln

The command to link files together in the source tree, if not ''ln''. If you're using something like **lndir** to keep your compile tree separate from your source tree, set this to ''ln –s'' or ''cp''.

remove: mv –f

How *MH* should make backup copies of existing files when installing new files. To simply remove the old files, use ''rm –f''.

Compiler/loader

cc: cc

The name of your C compiler, if not ''cc''.

ccoptions: –O

Options given directly to *cc* (1). The most common is ''–M'' if you're running *MH* on an ALTOS. This defaults to ''–O''. If you define this and want to keep ''–O'', be sure to include it explicitly. If you're using the *GNU* C compiler, it should include '–traditional'. See ''options:'' for '–D' options.

curses: –lcurses –ltermlib

This should be the loader option required to load the *termcap* (3) and *curses* (3) libraries on your system. On SYS5 systems, it probably should be just ''–lcurses''. Some sites have reported that both ''–lcurses'' and ''–ltermlib'' are necessary.

ldoptions: –s

Options given directly to *ld* (1) (via *cc*) at the beginning of the command line. Useful for machines which require arguments to tell *ld* to increase the stack space (e.g. the Gould, which uses ''–m 8''). Usually, ''–s'' is a good choice in any event.

ldoptlibs:

Options given directly to *ld*(1) (via *cc*) at the end of the command line. The two most common are: ''–ldbm'' if you're running MMDF with the *dbm* package; and, ''–lndir'' if you are generating *MH* on a system which does not load the new directory access mechanism by default (e.g., 4.1BSD, SYS5). If you don't have *libndir* on your system, the sources are in **miscellany/libndir/**.

lex: lex –nt

Alternative version of *lex*. Used in **zotnet/tws/**.

oldload: off

This controls how *MH* will try to process library object files to eliminate local symbols. Support for the ALTOS loader if ''on''. Support for loaders not handling '–x –r' correctly if ''none''.

ranlib: on

Support for systems with *ranlib*(1). For SYSTEM 5 systems, this should be ''off'' which tells *MH* to use *lorder* and *tsort* instead. Some SYSTEM 5 sites reported that running this isn't always sufficient. If this is the case, then you should edit **conf/makefiles/uip** to include **../sbr/libmh.a** and **../zotnet/libzot.a** twice in the LIBES variable.

Message Transport System

mts: sendmail

Which message transport system to use. Either ''mmdf'' to use *MMDF* as the transport system, ''mmdf2'' to use *MMDF–II* as the transport system, ''sendmail'' to have *SendMail* as the transport system, ''zmailer'' to have *ZMAILER* as the transport system, or, ''mh'' to have *MH* as the transport system.

On UNIX systems supporting TCP/IP networking via sockets you can add the suffix ''/smtp'' to the mts setting. This often yields a superior interface as *MH* will post mail with the local *SMTP* server instead of interacting directly with *MMDF* or *SendMail*. Hence, for TCP/IP UNIX systems, the ''/smtp'' suffix to either ''sendmail'' or ''mmdf2'' is the preferred MTS configuration. The ''/smtp'' suffix is described in detail in the *Administrator's Guide*; be sure to set ''servers:'' as described in *mh–tailor*(8) if you use this option.

mf: off

Support for mail filtering on those systems in which the message transport system isn't integrated with *UUCP* This option is strictly for an *MH* system using either *MMDF–I* as its transport system or one using ''stand–alone delivery''.

UCI BBoards Facility

bboards: off

If ''on'', include support for the UCI BBoards facility. BBoards may be enabled with any mts setting. If ''off'', the BBoard reading program *bbc* will not be installed. If ''nntp'', include support for the UCI BBoards facility to read the Network News via the NNTP. If ''pop'' (formerly ''popbboards: on''), include support for the UCI BBoards facility via the POP3 service; this setting requires ''pop: on''.

bbdelivery: off

If ''off'', the BBoards delivery agent and library files will not be installed. If ''on'', and you set ''bboards:'' to something besides ''off'', then the BBoards delivery agent and library files will be installed in the *bbhome* directory (see below). To read remote BBoards, the usual configuration would have *bbc* talk to a *POP3* or *NNTP* server. However, it may be useful to set this to ''off'' if you NFS mount the *bbhome* directory from another host and want to use *bbc* to read those files directly.

bbhome: /usr/spool/bboards

The home directory for the BBoards user.

Post Office Protocol

pop: off

Support for POP service. This allows local delivery for non–local users (a major win). See **support/pop/pop.rfc** for more information on the POP. This option currently works only on UNIX systems with TCP/IP sockets. (It doesn't hurt to enable this option regardless of whether or not you intend to use POP.) See also ''bboards: pop'' to enable reading bboards with the POP.

popdir: /usr/etc

The directory where the POP daemon (**popd**) will be installed.

options:

'–D' options to *cc* (1).

APOP='''/etc/pop.auth'''

This option indicates that the POP daemon will support the non-standard **APOP** command, and specifies the name of **APOP** authorization database. The **APOP** command provides a challenge-based authentication system using the **MD5** message digest algorithm. This facility is documented in *The Internet Message* (ISBN 0–13–092941–7), a book by Marshall T. Rose.

This option also causes the **popauth** program to be installed, which allows the administrator to manipulate the **APOP** authorization database. For more details, see **support/pop/pop-more.txt** and the *Administrator's Guide.*

DPOP

This option indicates that POP subscribers do not have entries in the *passwd* (5) file, and instead have their own separate database (a win).

KPOP

Support for KERBEROS with POP. This code builds *popd, inc* and *msgchk* to support only the ''kpop'' protocol. This code is still experimental, but is available for those sites wishing to test it.

MPOP

This option indicates that the POP daemon will support the non-standard **XTND SCAN** command which provides performance enhancements when using the POP over low-speed connections. This option also causes an interactive POP client program, **popi**, to be compiled and installed. A man page for the **popi** program is also provided.

These extensions are described in *The Internet Message*, a book by Marshall T. Rose. For more details, see **support/pop/pop-more.txt**. **Note:** this option requires ''bboards: pop''.

POP2

Have the POP daemon understand the older POP2 protocol as well as the *MH* POP3 protocol – a major win. The POP daemon auto-magically determines which POP protocol your client is using. If you're enabling POP service, there's no reason not to enable this option as well. See also *POPSERVICE.*

POPSERVICE

The port name the *MH* POP will use. For historical reasons, this defaults to ''pop''.

In 1987, the *MH* POP protocol (POP version 3) was published as RFC1081 and was assigned its own port number (110), which differs from the original POP (version 1 and 2) port number (109).

To have *MH* POP use the new assigned port number, set POPSERVICE='''pop3''', and be sure that this service name is listed in your **/etc/services** file on both POP client and server hosts as ''110/tcp''. If you enable *POP2*, you can safely leave *POPSERVICE* undefined unless you are using POP3 clients besides *MH*.

RPOP

This option indicates that support for the UNIX variant of POP, RPOP, which uses privileged sockets for authentication be enabled. This peacefully co-exists with the standard POP.

SHADOW

Indicates that the **popd** POP server can find encrypted passwords in the **/etc/shadow** file (and not in the **/etc/passwd** file). It should be used only for some (newer) SYSTEM 5 systems.

The ''APOP'' and ''MPOP'' non-standard POP facilities are documented in *The Internet Message* (ISBN 0–13–092941–7), a book by Marshall T. Rose. For more details, see **support/pop/pop-more.txt**. The ''APOP'' option peacefully co-exists with the standard POP. The ''MPOP'' option requires ''bboards: pop''.

Shared libraries

sharedlib: off

If ''sun4'', makes libmh.a into a SunOS 4.0 (and later) shared library. If you enable this, be sure to also use ''options SUN40''. If ''sys5'', makes libmh.a into a SYS5 R4 (and later) shared library. If you enable this, be sure to also use ''options SVR4''.

slflags: –pic

The compiler flags to produce position independent code.

slibdir: /usr/local/lib

The directory where the *MH* shared library should go.

Under SunOS (sun4)

Since some *MH* programs are setuid, they'll only look for the library in ''trusted'' locations. Putting the library somewhere besides **/usr/lib** or **/usr/local/lib** is not advisable.

If you **must** do this, be sure that you add the path given by **slibdir** to the compiler's library search list (e.g., ''ldoptions: –L/usr/mh/lib'') and make sure the path starts with a leading '/'.

You may need to run *ldconfig* (8) manually whenever a new shared object is installed on the system. See *ld* (1) for more information about using shared libraries.

Under Solaris 2.0 (and newer)

The above instructions for SunOS apply, except you should set the run-time library search path using '–R' instead of '–L' (e.g., ''ldoptions: –R/usr/mh/lib'').

General System Dependencies

You should include the following directives which are appropriate for your version of UNIX. If you don't know what an option does, it probably doesn't apply to you.

mailgroup: off

If set, *inc* is made set-group-id to this group name. Some SYS5 systems want this to be set to ''mail''. Set this if your **/usr/spool/mail** is not world-writeable.

Note that **slocal** doesn't know how to deal with this, and will not work under these systems; just making it set-group-id will open a security hole. If you're using ''mailgroup'', you should remove **slocal** (and its man page) from your system.

signal: int

The base type (int or void) of the function parameter/return value of *signal* (2). The default is **int**. Set ''signal void'' on systems which use this type (e.g., SYSTEM 5 V3.0 and later or Sun OS 4.0 and later).

sprintf: char *

The return value of the *sprintf* library routine. This defaults to ''char *''. Set this to ''int'' if you have an older version of SYSTEM 5 which has this routine return an ''int'' type.

options:

'–D' options to *cc* (1).

ALTOS

Use on XENIX/v7 systems. Also, be sure to use ''options V7''.

ATTVIBUG

This option causes *MH* to return to the ''What now?'' prompt if your initial editor is **vi** and it exits with non-zero status. Use on Sun OS 4.1 and other systems where the **/usr/ucb/vi** editor was changed to exit with its status equal to the number of pseudo-''errors'' encountered during the edit. This causes a problem for programs that test the exit status of their editor and abort if the status is non-zero. (This includes *MH* and programs like **/usr/etc/vipw**).

AUX

Use with AUX systems.

BIND

If you are running with the BIND code on UNIX systems with TCP/IP sockets (e.g. 4.{2,3}BSD), be sure to define this.

BSD41A

Use on 4.1a Berkeley UNIX systems.

BSD42

Use on Berkeley UNIX systems on or after 4.2BSD.

BSD43

Use on 4.3 Berkeley UNIX systems. Also, be sure to use ''options BSD42''. If *openlog* (3) (see ''man 3 syslog'') takes three arguments instead of two, and your *write* (1) command is set–group–id to group ''tty'', use this option. If only one of these conditions is true, you lose.

BSD44
: Use on Berkeley UNIX systems on or after 4.4BSD. Also, be sure to use ``options BSD43'' and ``options BSD42''.

DBMPWD
: Use this option if your *getpwent* (3) routines read a dbm database (such as with Yellow Pages) instead of doing a sequential read of **/etc/passwd**. Without DBMPWD the entire passwd file is read into memory one entry at a time for alias expansion. This is a performance improvement when reading a standard **/etc/passwd** file, but is *very* slow on systems with a dbm database. At one site that runs YP on a large passwd file, it showed a 6:1 performance improvement.

GCOS_HACK
: The so-called ``gcos'' field of the password file is used as a last resort to find the user's full name (see *mh-profile* (5) for details). Enable this option if your *passwd* (5) man page notes that the '&' character in the ``gcos'' field stands for the login name.

FCNTL
: Directs *MH* to use the **fcntl()** system call for kernel-level locking. If you're using a SYS5 system, you may want this option. (See also 'FLOCK' and 'LOCKF').

FLOCK
: Directs *MH* to use the **flock()** system call for kernel-level locking. If you're on a BSD42 system, and you're not using NFS to read or write maildrops, you should enable this option. (See also 'FCNTL' and 'LOCKF').

HESIOD
: Support for HESIOD. This code was contributed, and included no documentation.

LOCKF
: Directs *MH* to use the **lockf()** system call for kernel-level locking. If you're using NFS to read or write maildrops, you should enable this option. (See also 'FLOCK' and 'FCNTL').

locname
: Hard-wires the local name for the host *MH* is running on. For example, locname=```PICKLE'''. It's probably better to either let UNIX tell *MH* this information, or to put the information in the host specific **mtstailor** file.

MORE
: Defines the location of the *more* (1) program. On ALTOS and DUAL systems, set MORE=```/usr/bin/more'''. The default is ``/usr/ucb/more''.

NDIR
: For non-Berkeley UNIX systems, this *MH* will try to find the new directory access mechanism by looking in **<ndir.h>** if this option is given. Otherwise, *MH* will try **<dir.h>**. If you still can't get this to work on your system, edit **h/local.h** as appropriate. (See also 'SYS5DIR'.)

NFS
: Tells *MH* to hack around a problem in the NFS C library. If you get an undefined symbol ``ruserpass'' when compiling *MH*, you probably need this option. If, however, you include this option and get an undefined symbol ``__ruserpass'' when compiling, then you should omit this option. (See also 'NORUSERPASS'.)

NOIOCTLH

Tells *MH* not to include the file **<sys/ioctl.h>**. To be used on systems where this file is not present.

NORUSERPASS

Tells *MH* that your system doesn't have the *ruserpass* (3) routine; *MH* will include its own copy of this routine in its library. (See also 'NFS'.)

NTOHLSWAP

Tells *MH* to use the **ntohl()** macro when processing *msh* binary map files. *MH* can use this macro on systems with the include file **netinet/in.h**, to byte-swap the binary information in these map files. If you're using the same map files on machines of different architectures, enable this option.

RENAME

Include this option if your system has a **rename()** library call. This is true on BSD42 and newer and some SYS5 systems.

SENDMAILBUG

Causes SMTP reply code 451 (failure) to be considered the same as code 250 (OK). Since this might cause problems, only enable this if you are certain that your SendMail will return this code even when it doesn't mean to indicate a failure.

SOCKETS

Indicates the availability of a socket interface for TCP/IP networking that is compatible with 4.{2,3}BSD UNIX. It is not necessary to define this when BSD42 is already defined, but it might be useful for SYSTEM 5 or HPUX systems with TCP/IP sockets.

SUN40

Use on Sun OS 4.0 (and later?) systems. You also will need "options BSD42", "options BSD43", and "signal void".

If you're using Sun's brain-damaged approach to offering Domain Name Service through NIS, be sure to include "options BIND" and "ldoptions –lresolv" to work around some NIS/DNS bugs.

SYS5

Use on AT&T SYSTEM 5 R3 (and newer?) UNIX systems. See also *mailgroup.*

SYS5DIR

Define this if your system uses "struct dirent" instead of "struct direct". This is true of System V Release 3.0 and later. Uses include file **<dirent.h>** and the routines *mkdir, rmdir* and *getcwd.*

SVR4

Use on AT&T SYSTEM 5 R4 (and newer?) UNIX systems. You should also include "options SYS5" and "options SYS5DIR". See also *mailgroup.* You will also need to include "oldload none" if your **ld** doesn't handle '–x –r' correctly.

TERMINFO

Define TERMINFO if you have it. You get it automatically if you're running SYS5, and you don't get it if you're not. (If you're not SYS5, you probably have termcap.)

TZNAME
Use time zone names from the *tzname* variable, set via *tzset*. Only applicable on SYSTEM 5 systems and only effective when you have asked for alpha–timezones (see the ATZ option). See also ZONEINFO.

UNISTD
Include this option if your system has the file **<unistd.h>**. If not specified, the LOCKF option will include **<sys/fcntl.h>**.

V7
Use on V7 UNIX systems. Also, be sure to use ''options void=int''.

VSPRINTF
Include this option if your system has the *vsprintf*(3) library routine; otherwise, *_doprnt*(3) will be used.

WAITINT
BSD42 based systems call the *wait*(2) system routine with a pointer to type *union wait*. Include this option if you included ''options BSD42'', but your system calls the *wait*(2) system routine with a pointer to type *int* (the non-BSD42 default).

ZONEINFO
Specify this if you have a BSD43 based system that keeps time zone information /etc/zoneinfo or /usr/lib/zoneinfo (SunOS), and where the *struct tm* returned by *localtime*(3) contains a *tm_gmtoff* element (see **/usr/include/time.h**). With this fix the GMT offset specified in outgoing mail will be corrected when the TZ enviornment variable is set to a different time zone. See also TZNAME.

Site Preferences

These options change the default behavior of *MH* or enable optional features. Add the options which are appropriate for your configuration or your site preferences.

editor: prompter
The default editor for *MH*.

options:
'–D' options to *cc*(1).

ATZ
Directs *MH* to use alpha–timezones whenever possible. You should not use this option if you are on the Internet, since it will make your host non-compliant with RFC-1123 (Requirements for Internet Hosts).

ATHENA
Makes *repl* '–nocc all' the default instead of '–cc all'. You may want to enable this if you're using *xmh*.

BANG
Directs *MH* to favor '!' over '@' in addressing.

BERK
Optional for for 4.{2,3}BSD sites running SendMail. Disables nearly all of the RFC822 address and header-parsing routines in favor of recognizing such formats as ASCnet, and so

on. If you don't need to disable the parser for this reason, you probably want to use ''options DUMB'' instead.

COMPAT

If you previously ran a version of *MH* earlier than mh.4 use this option. After a short grace period, remove it and re-{configure,generate,install} everything.

DUMB

Directs *MH* not to try and rewrite addresses to their ''official'' form.

FOLDPROT

Defines the octal value for default folder-protection. For example, FOLDPROT='''0700'''. The default is ''0711''.

ISI

When using ''repl –ccme'', only ''cc:'' the first address found which belongs to the user; any other *Alternate-Mailboxes* do not receive ''cc:''s.

LINK

Defines the filename for alternate file name for *dist* and *repl*. For example, LINK='''\\043''' to use the pound–sign character. The default is ''@''.

MHE

Enables crude support for Brien Reid's MHE interface. Recommended for use with the GNU Emacs mh-e package.

MHRC

Enables *MH* to recognize the *CShell*'s '~'–construct. This is useful for sites that run with a ~/.mhrc for their users.

MIME

Enables support for multi-media messages, as specified in RFC 1341 — a major win. This allows you to include things like audio, graphics, and the like, in your mail messages. Several *MH* commands are extended to support these multi-media messages, and the *mhn* command is provided to encode and decode **MIME** messages. For more details, see **miscellany/multi-media/READ-ME** and *mhn* (1).

MSGID

Enables **slocal** to detect and surpress duplicate messages received. This code uses the **<ndbm.h>** library, and requires ''options BSD42'' since it uses the *flock* (2) system call for locking. (Note that this means its database locking does not work over NFS.) It has only been tested under SUN40.

MSGPROT

Defines the octal value for default folder-protection. For example, MSGPROT='''0600'''. The default is ''0644''.

NOMHSEQ

Directs *MH* to make private sequences the default.

OVERHEAD

Enable *MH* commands to read profile/context from open fd:s without doing an open(); see *mh-profile* (5) for the details.

RPATHS

Directs *inc* to note UNIX ''From '' lines as Return-Path: info.

SBACKUP

Defines the prefix string for backup file names. For example, SBACKUP='''\\043'''. The default is '','.

TMA

Support for the TTI *trusted mail agent* (TMA). Although the TTI TMA is **not** in the public domain, the *MH* support for the TTI TMA **is** in the public domain. You should enable this option only if you are licensed to run the TMA software (otherwise, you don't have the software in your *MH* source tree).

TTYD

Support for TTYD. This is no longer in wide use, and is not recommended.

UCI

First, ''_'' and ''#'' are recognized as the prefixes for scratch files. Second, support for the UCI group–leadership mechanism is enabled in *conflict.* Third, the first line of the file file **$HOME/.signature** is used as the *Full Name* part of your ''From:'' header. This may conflict with the interpretation of this file by *News.* If you're not at UCI, you probably don't want this option.

UK

Directs the *scan* program to generate UK-style dates by default.

WHATNOW

Enable certain *MH* commands to act differently when $mhdraft set.

YEARMOD

This option makes the *mh-format* **%(year)** function always return a value less than 100. Enable this option if you have local *mh-format*(5) files which cannot handle 4-digit years. You should convert these files to use a 4-character field width, or use the **%(modulo 100)** function to obtain a 2-digit year value. After a short grace period, remove 'YEARMOD' and re-{configure,generate,install} everything.

Testing/debugging

debug: off

Support for debug mode of *MH*. Don't use this unless you know what you're doing, which isn't likely if you're reading this document!

regtest: off

Set this to ''on'' if you are doing regression testing among different compilations of *MH*, and you do not want the hostname and compile date included in *MH* binaries.

Now edit **conf/config/mtstailor**, depending on your choice of the setting for mts in the *MH* configuration file. for an mts setting of ''mh'', look at the file **conf/tailor/mhmts**; for an mts setting of ''sendmail'', ''sendmail/smtp'', ''mmdf/smtp'', or ''mmdf2/smtp'', look at the file **conf/tailor/sendmts**; and, for an mts setting of ''mmdf'', or ''mmdf2'', look at the file **conf/tailor/mmdf.**

Now install the configured files into the source areas. (On SYS5 systems, or other systems where you get complaints about ''_index'' and ''_rindex'' being undefined, you should use ''make sys5'' to compile mhconfig.)

```
% make
% ./mhconfig MH
```

Before proceeding, you should familiarize yourself with the *Administrator's Guide*. To generate an *nroff* version, go to the doc/ directory and type:

```
% (cd ../doc/; make ADMIN.doc)
```

If you're already running *MH* at your site, you should also read the *mh* changes document **CHANGES**. The source is in **papers/changes/**.

After reading the *Administrator's Guide*, you may decide to change your MH configuration. If so, cd back to the **conf/** directory, re-edit the files **MH** and **conf/config/mtstailor**, and re-run *mhconfig*.

You now proceed based on your choice of a transport system (the setting for mts above). The best interface is achieved with ''sendmail'' followed by ''mmdf'' or (''mmdf2''), and then ''mh'' (stand–alone delivery, not recommended).

SENDMAIL

If you have not enabled BBoards or POP then no further MTS–specific action is required on your part!

If you have enabled POP, but you want to let *SendMail* deliver mail POP mail using its standard delivery program **/bin/mail**, then, again, no further MTS–specific action is required on your part!

Otherwise, go to the mts/sendmail/ directory.

```
% cd ../mts/sendmail/
```

This directory contains files whose definitions correspond to the configuration of your *SendMail* system. If you have enabled BBoards or POP service, then you will need to re–configure *SendMail*. First, in the ''local info'' section of your site's *SendMail* configuration file, choose a free macro/class (B is used in this distribution), and add these lines:

```
# BBoards support
DBbboards
CBbboards
```

Second, immediately after the inclusion of the zerobase file, in the ''machine dependent part of ruleset zero'' section, add these lines:

```
# resolve names for the BBoards system
R$+<@$=B>	$#bboards$@$2$:$1	topic@bboards
```

Be sure to use tabs when separating these fields. Third, add the line

```
include(bboardsMH.m4)
```

after the line

```
include(localm.m4)
```

in your site's *SendMail* configuration file. Finally, you should link the file **mts/sendmail/bboardsMH.m4** into your *SendMail* cf/ directory and re–configure *SendMail*.

If you have enabled POP service, a similar procedure must be used on the POP service host, to re–configure *SendMail*. First, in the ''local info'' section of your site's *SendMail* configuration file, choose a free macro/class (P is used in this distribution), and add these lines:

```
# POP support
DPpop
CPpop
```

Second, immediately after the inclusion of the zerobase file, in the ''machine dependent part of ruleset zero'' section, add these lines:

```
# resolve names for the POP system
R$+<@$=P>		$#pop$@$2$:$1		subscriber@pop
```

Be sure to use tabs when separating these fields. Third, add the line

```
include(popMH.m4)
```

after the line

```
include(localm.m4)
```

in your site's *SendMail* configuration file. Finally, you should link the file **mts/sendmail/popMH.m4** into your *SendMail* cf/ directory and re–configure *SendMail.*

MMDF

If you want *MMDF* to be your transport service, and have **NOT** specified ''mmdf/smtp'' (or ''mmdf2/smtp'') as your mts setting, then go to the mmdf/ directory. (If you're using ''mmdf/smtp'' or ''mmdf2/smtp'' as your mts setting, then skip to the next section.)

```
% cd ../mts/mmdf/
```

This directory contains files whose definitions correspond to the configuration of your *MMDF* system.

If you're running *MMDF–I*, then copy the following files from wherever you keep the *MMDF* sources to this directory: mmdf/h/ch.h, mmdf/h/conf.h, utildir/conf_util.h, utildir/ll_log.h, mmdf/h/mmdf.h, utildir/util.h, mmdf/mmdf_lib.a, and utildir/util_lib.a.

If you're running *MMDF–II*, then copy the following files from where you keep the *MMDF* sources to this directory: h/ch.h, h/conf.h, h/dm.h, h/ll_log.h, h/mmdf.h, h/util.h, and lib/libmmdf.a

If you have enabled bboards, then the directories **support/bboards/mmdfI** and **support/bboards/mmdfII** contain information you'll need to put a UCI BBoards channel in your *MMDF* configuration. Similarly, if you have enabled option ''mf'' and are running *MMDF–I*, then the **zotnet/mf/mmdfI/** directory contains information you'll need to put a *UUCP* channel in your *MMDF–I* configuration. Finally, the directory **support/pop/mmdfII** contains information you'll need to put a POP channel in your *MMDF–II* configuration.

Note that *MMDF–II* is distributed with the BBoards channel, although the version in the *MH* distribution might be more current, the version in the *MMDF–II* distribution has been tested with that revision of *MMDF*.

MMDF/SMTP

If you are using ''mmdf/smtp'' as your mts setting, then no further MTS–specific action is required on your part!

MMDF2/SMTP

If you are using ''mmdf2/smtp'' as your mts setting, then no further MTS–specific action is required on your part!

STAND–ALONE DELIVERY

If, instead, you want *MH* to handle its own mail delivery, then no further MTS–specific action is required on your part!

GENERATION

Go to the *MH* top-level directory and generate the system.

% cd ../; make

This will cause a complete generation of the *MH* system. If all goes well, proceed with installation. If not, complain, as there ''should be no problems'' at this step.

INSTALLATION

If the directories you chose for the user–programs, support–programs and manuals (''bin'', ''etc'', ''pop-dir'', ''slibdir'', and ''mandir'' in the **conf/MH** file) don't exist, you should create them at this point.

Next, if you enabled support for the UCI BBoards facility, then create a login called ''bboards'' with the following characteristics: home directory is **/usr/spool/bboards/** with mode 755 (actually, use the value for ''bbhome'' given in the *MH* configuration file), login shell is **/bin/csh** (or **/bin/sh**), and, encrypted password field is ''*''. The ''bboards'' login should own the **/usr/spool/bboards/** directory. In addition to creating **/usr/spool/bboards/**, also create **/usr/spool/bboards/etc/** and **/usr/spool/bboards/archive/**. These directories should also be owned by the ''bboards'' login.

If you enabled support for POP, then on the POP service host, create a login called ''pop'' with the following characteristics: home directory is **/usr/spool/pop/** with mode 755, login shell is **/bin/csh**, and, encrypted password field is ''*''. If you don't have **/bin/csh** on your system (V7), then **/bin/sh** is just fine. The ''pop'' login should own the **/usr/spool/pop/** directory. You'll also need to add a line to the **/etc/services** file and the **/etc/rc.local** file, see the *Administrator's Guide* for more details.

If this is not the first time you have installed *MH*, these files will need particular attention:

Directory	*Files*
''etc/''	MailAliases, BBoardAliases, mtstailor
/usr/spool/bboards/	BBoards, .cshrc, .mh_profile
/usr/spool/bboards/etc/	*

The **MailAliases, BBoardAliases, mtstailor** and **BBoards** files will **NOT** be installed over existing copies; you will need to edit these by hand and merge in any changes from your previous *MH* release. The other files under **/usr/spool/bboards/** will be overwritten if they exist. You may wish to preserve your old versions of these before installing *MH*.

As the super-user, and from the mh.6/ directory, install the system.

make inst–all

This will cause the *MH* processes and files to be transferred to the appropriate areas with the appropriate attributes.

TAILORING

See the *Administrator's Guide* for information on tailoring *MH* for the MTS, BBoards, and POP.

DOCUMENTATION

In addition to this document, the *Administrator's Guide*, and the *User's Manual*, there are several documents referenced by the user's manual which may be useful. The sources for all of these can be found under the **papers/** directory.

OTHER THINGS

Consult the directory **miscellany/** for the sources to a number of things which aren't part of the mainstream *MH* distribution, but which are still quite useful.

FILES

Too numerous to mention. Really.

SEE ALSO

make(1)

BUGS

The *mhconfig* program should be smarter.

There's no way to print the *Administrator's Guide* until after you have configured the system; it is difficult to configure the system without the *Administrator's Guide*.

The Makefiles should know when *mhconfig* has been run and force ''make clean'' behavior.

NAME

mk-amd-map – create database maps for Amd

SYNOPSIS

mk-amd-map [**-p**] *mapname*

DESCRIPTION

mk-amd-map creates the database maps used by the keyed map lookups in amd(8). It reads input from the named file and outputs them to a correspondingly named hashed database.

The **-p** option prints the map on standard output instead of generating a database. This is usually used to merge continuation lines into one physical line.

SEE ALSO

amd(8)

M8

NAME

mknod – build special file

SYNOPSIS

mknod *name* [**c** | **b**] *major minor*

DESCRIPTION

The **mknod** command creates device special files. Normally the shell script /dev/MAKEDEV is used to create special files for commonly known devices; it executes **mknod** with the appropriate arguments and can make all the files required for the device.

To make nodes manually, the four required arguments are:

name Device name, for example ''sd'' for a SCSI disk on an HP300 or a ''pty'' for pseudo-devices.

b | **c** Type of device. If the device is a block type device such as a tape or disk drive which needs both cooked and raw special files, the type is **b**. All other devices are character type devices, such as terminal and pseudo devices, and are type **c**.

major The major device number is an integer number which tells the kernel which device driver entry point to use. To learn what major device number to use for a particular device, check the file /dev/MAKEDEV to see if the device is known, or check the system dependent device configuration file:

''/usr/src/sys/conf/device.*architecture*''

(for example device.hp300).

minor The minor device number tells the kernel which subunit the node corresponds to on the device; for example, a subunit may be a filesystem partition or a tty line.

SEE ALSO

mknod(2), makedev(8)

HISTORY

A **mknod** command appeared in Version 6 AT&T UNIX.

NAME

mkproto – construct a prototype file system

SYNOPSIS

mkproto *special proto*

DESCRIPTION

Mkproto is used to bootstrap a new file system. First a new file system is created using newfs(8). **Mkproto** is then used to copy files from the old file system into the new file system according to the directions found in the prototype file *proto*. The prototype file contains tokens separated by spaces or new lines. The first tokens comprise the specification for the root directory. File specifications consist of tokens giving the mode, the user-id, the group id, and the initial contents of the file. The syntax of the contents field depends on the mode.

The mode token for a file is a 6 character string. The first character specifies the type of the file. (The characters **–bcd** specify regular, block special, character special and directory files respectively.) The second character of the type is either **u** or '–' to specify set-user-id mode or not. The third is **g** or '–' for the set-group-id mode. The rest of the mode is a three digit octal number giving the owner, group, and other read, write, execute permissions, see chmod(1).

Two decimal number tokens come after the mode; they specify the user and group ID's of the owner of the file.

If the file is a regular file, the next token is a pathname whence the contents and size are copied.

If the file is a block or character special file, two decimal number tokens follow which give the major and minor device numbers.

If the file is a directory, **mkproto** makes the entries '.' and '..' and then reads a list of names and (recursively) file specifications for the entries in the directory. The scan is terminated with the token $.

A sample prototype specification follows:

```
d--777 3 1
usr     d--777 3 1
        sh      ---755 3 1 /bin/sh
        ken     d--755 6 1
                $
        b0      b--644 3 1 0 0
        c0      c--644 3 1 0 0
        $
$
```

SEE ALSO

fs(5), dir(5), fsck(8), newfs(8)

BUGS

There should be some way to specify links.

There should be some way to specify bad blocks.

Mkproto can only be run on virgin file systems. It should be possible to copy files into existent file systems.

HISTORY

The `mkproto` command appeared in 4.2BSD.

M8

NAME

mount – mount file systems

SYNOPSIS

mount [**-adfruvw**] [**-t** *ufs* | *lfs* | *external_type*]
mount [**-dfruvw**] *special* | *node*
mount [**-dfruvw**] [**-o** *options*] [**-t** *ufs* | *lfs* | *external_type*] *special node*

DESCRIPTION

The **mount** command calls the mount(2) system call to prepare and graft a *special device* or the remote node (rhost:path) on to the file system tree at the point *node*. If either *special* or *node* are not provided, the appropriate information is taken from the fstab(5) file.

The system maintains a list of currently mounted file systems. If no arguments are given to **mount**, this list is printed.

The options are as follows:

-d Causes everything to be done except for the actual system call. This option is useful in conjunction with the **-v** flag to determine what the **mount** command is trying to do.

-f Forces the revocation of write access when trying to downgrade a filesystem mount status from read-write to read-only.

-o Options are specified with a **-o** flag followed by a comma separated string of options. The following options are available:

async All I/O to the file system should be done asynchronously. This is a *dangerous* flag to set, and should not be used unless you are prepared to recreate the file system should your system crash.

force The same as **-f**; forces the revocation of write access when trying to downgrade a filesystem mount status from read-write to read-only.

nodev Do not interpret character or block special devices on the file system. This option is useful for a server that has file systems containing special devices for architectures other than its own.

noexec Do not allow execution of any binaries on the mounted file system. This option is useful for a server that has file systems containing binaries for architectures other than its own.

nosuid Do not allow set-user-identifier or set-group-identifier bits to take effect.

rdonly The same as **-r**; mount the file system read-only (even the super-user may not write it).

sync All I/O to the file system should be done synchronously.

update The same as **-u**; indicate that the status of an already mounted file system should be changed.

union Causes the namespace at the mount point to appear as the union of the mounted filesystem root and the existing directory. Lookups will be done in the mounted filesystem first. If those operations fail due to a non-existent file the underlying directory is then accessed. All creates are done in the mounted filesystem.

Any additional options specific to a filesystem type that is not one of the internally known types (see the **-t** option) may be passed as a comma separated list; these options are distinguished by a leading "-" (dash). Options that take a value are specified using the syntax -option=value. For example, the mount command:

```
mount -t mfs -o nosuid,-N,-s=4000 /dev/dk0b /tmp
```

causes **mount** to execute the equivalent of:

```
/sbin/mount_mfs -o nosuid -N -s 4000 /dev/dk0b /tmp
```

−r The file system is to be mounted read-only. Mount the file system read-only (even the super-user may not write it). The same as the ''rdonly'' argument to the **−o** option.

−t *ufs | lfs | external type*
The argument following the **−t** is used to indicate the file system type. The type *ufs* is the default. The *-t* option can be used to indicate that the actions should only be taken on filesystems of the specified type. More than one type may be specified in a comma separated list. The list of filesystem types can be prefixed with ''no'' to specify the filesystem types for which action should *not* be taken. For example, the **mount** command:

```
mount -a -t nonfs,mfs
```

mounts all filesystems except those of type NFS and MFS.

If the type is not one of the internally known types, mount will attempt to execute a program in /sbin/mount_*XXX* where *XXX* is replaced by the type name. For example, nfs filesystems are mounted by the program /sbin/mount_nfs.

−u The **−u** flag indicates that the status of an already mounted file system should be changed. Any of the options discussed above (the **−o** option) may be changed; also a file system can be changed from read-only to read-write or vice versa. An attempt to change from read-write to read-only will fail if any files on the filesystem are currently open for writing unless the **−f** flag is also specified. The set of options is determined by first extracting the options for the file system from the fstab table, then applying any options specified by the **−o** argument, and finally applying the **−r** or **−w** option.

−v Verbose mode.

−w The file system object is to be read and write.

The options specific to NFS filesystems are described in the mount_nfs(8) manual page.

FILES

/etc/fstab file system table

SEE ALSO

mount(2), fstab(5), mount_cd9660(8), mount_fdesc(8), mount_kernfs(8), mount_lfs(8), mount_lofs(8), mount_mfs(8), mount_nfs(8), mount_null(8), mount_portal(8), mount_procfs(8), mount_umap(8), mount_union(8), umount(8)

BUGS

It is possible for a corrupted file system to cause a crash.

HISTORY

A **mount** command appeared in Version 6 AT&T UNIX.

NAME

mount_cd9660 – mount an ISO-9660 filesystem

SYNOPSIS

mount_cd9660 [**-egr**] [**-o** *options*] *special* | *node*

DESCRIPTION

The **mount_cd9660** command attaches the ISO-9660 filesystem residing on the device special to the global filesystem namespace at the location indicated by node. This command is normally executed by mount(8) at boot time.

The options are as follows:

-e Enable the use of extended attributes.

-g Do not strip version numbers on files. (By default, if there are files with different version numbers on the disk, only the last one will be listed.) In either case, files may be opened without explicitly stating a version number.

-o Options are specified with a **-o** flag followed by a comma separated string of options. See the mount(8) man page for possible options and their meanings.

-r Do not use any Rockridge extensions included in the filesystem.

SEE ALSO

mount(2), unmount(2), fstab(5), mount(8)

BUGS

The cd9660 filesystem does not support the original "High Sierra" ("CDROM001") format.

POSIX device node mapping is currently not supported.

Version numbers are not stripped if Rockridge extensions are in use. In this case, accessing files that don't have Rockridge names without version numbers gets the one with the lowest version number and not the one with the highest.

There is no ECMA support.

HISTORY

The **mount_cd9660** utility first appeared 4.4BSD.

NAME

mount_fdesc – mount the file-descriptor file system

SYNOPSIS

mount_fdesc [**–o** *options*] *fdesc mount_point*

DESCRIPTION

The **mount_fdesc** command attaches an instance of the per-process file descriptor namespace to the global filesystem namespace. The conventional mount point is /dev and the filesystem should be union mounted in order to augment, rather than replace, the existing entries in /dev. This command is normally executed by mount(8) at boot time.

The options are as follows:

–o Options are specified with a **–o** flag followed by a comma separated string of options. See the mount(8) man page for possible options and their meanings.

The contents of the mount point are fd, stderr, stdin, stdout and tty.

fd is a directory whose contents appear as a list of numbered files which correspond to the open files of the process reading the directory. The files /dev/fd/0 through /dev/fd/# refer to file descriptors which can be accessed through the file system. If the file descriptor is open and the mode the file is being opened with is a subset of the mode of the existing descriptor, the call:

```
fd = open("/dev/fd/0", mode);
```

and the call:

```
fd = fcntl(0, F_DUPFD, 0);
```

are equivalent.

The files /dev/stdin, /dev/stdout and /dev/stderr appear as symlinks to the relevant entry in the /dev/fd sub-directory. Opening them is equivalent to the following calls:

```
fd = fcntl(STDIN_FILENO,  F_DUPFD, 0);
fd = fcntl(STDOUT_FILENO, F_DUPFD, 0);
fd = fcntl(STDERR_FILENO, F_DUPFD, 0);
```

Flags to the open(2) call other than O_RDONLY, O_WRONLY and O_RDWR are ignored.

The /dev/tty entry is an indirect reference to the current process's controlling terminal. It appears as a named pipe (FIFO) but behaves in exactly the same way as the real controlling terminal device.

FILES

/dev/fd/#
/dev/stdin
/dev/stdout
/dev/stderr
/dev/tty

SEE ALSO

mount(2), unmount(2), tty(4), fstab(5), mount(8)

CAVEATS

No . and . . entries appear when listing the contents of the `/dev/fd` directory. This makes sense in the context of this filesystem, but is inconsistent with usual filesystem conventions. However, it is still possible to refer to both . and . . in a pathname.

This filesystem may not be NFS-exported.

HISTORY

The **mount_fdesc** utility first appeared in 4.4BSD.

M8

NAME

mount_kernfs – mount the /kern file system

SYNOPSIS

mount_kernfs [**-o** *options*] */kern mount_point*

DESCRIPTION

The **mount_kern** command attaches an instance of the kernel parameter namespace to the global filesystem namespace. The conventional mount point is /kern. This command is normally executed by mount(8) at boot time.

The filesystem includes several regular files which can be read, some of which can also be written. The contents of the files is in a machine-independent format, either a string, or an integer in decimal ASCII. Where numbers are returned, a trailing newline character is also added.

The options are as follows:

-o Options are specified with a -o flag followed by a comma separated string of options. See the mount(8) man page for possible options and their meanings.

FILES

boottime	the time at which the system was last booted (decimal ASCII).
copyright	kernel copyright message.
hostname	the hostname, with a trailing newline. The hostname can be changed by writing to this file. A trailing newline will be stripped from the hostname being written.
hz	the frequency of the system clock (decimal ASCII).
loadavg	the 1, 5 and 15 minute load average in kernel fixed-point format. The final integer is the fixpoint scaling factor. All numbers are in decimal ASCII.
pagesize	the machine pagesize (decimal ASCII).
physmem	the number of pages of physical memory in the machine (decimal ASCII).
root	the system root directory. In a chroot'ed environment, **mount_kernfs** can be used to create a new /kern mount point. /kern/root will then refer to the system global root, not the current process root.
rootdev	the root device.
rrootdev	the raw root device.
time	the second and microsecond value of the system clock. Both numbers are in decimal ASCII.
version	the kernel version string. The head line for /etc/motd can be generated by running: "**sed 1q /kern/version**"

SEE ALSO

mount(2), unmount(2), fstab(5), mount(8)

CAVEATS

This filesystem may not be NFS-exported.

HISTORY

The **mount_kernfs** utility first appeared in 4.4BSD.

NAME

mount_lfs – mount a log-structured file system

SYNOPSIS

mount_lfs [**-dns**] [**-o** *options*] *special node*

DESCRIPTION

The **mount_lfs** command attaches a log-structured file system *special* device on to the file system tree at the point *node*. In addition, the lfs_cleanerd(8) utility is invoked to clean the file system periodically.

This command is normally executed by mount(8) at boot time.

The options are as follows:

-d Run lfs_cleanerd(8) in debug mode.

-o Options are specified with a **-o** flag followed by a comma separated string of options. See the mount(8) man page for possible options and their meanings.

-n Don't start lfs_cleanerd(8) on the file system.

-s Cause lfs_cleanerd(8) to read data in small chunks when cleaning the file system.

SEE ALSO

mount(2), unmount(2), fstab(5), lfs_cleanerd(8), mount(8)

Ousterhout and Douglis, "Beating the I/O Bottleneck: A Case for Log-structured File Systems", *Operating Systems Review*, No. 1, Vol. 23, pp. 11-27, 1989, also available as Technical Report UCB/CSD 88/467.

Rosenblum and Ousterhout, "The Design and Implementation of a Log-Structured File System", *ACM SIGOPS Operating Systems Review*, No. 5, Vol. 25, 1991.

Seltzer, "File System Performance and Transaction Support", *PhD Thesis, University of California, Berkeley*, 1992, also available as Technical Report UCB/ERL M92.

Seltzer, Bostic, McKusick and Staelin, "An Implementation of a Log-Structured File System for UNIX", *Proc. of the Winter 1993 USENIX Conf.*, pp. 315-331, 1993.

HISTORY

The **mount_lfs** function first appeared in 4.4BSD.

NAME

mount_nfs – mount nfs file systems

SYNOPSIS

mount_nfs [**-KMPTbcdiklqs**] [**-D** *deadthresh*] [**-L** *leaseterm*] [**-R** *retrycnt*] [**-a** *maxreadahead*] [**-g** *maxgroups*] [**-m** *realm*] [**-o** *options*] [**-r** *readsize*] [**-t** *timeout*] [**-w** *writesize*] [**-x** *retrans*] *rhost:path node*

DESCRIPTION

The **mount_nfs** command calls the mount(2) system call to prepare and graft a remote nfs file system (rhost:path) on to the file system tree at the point *node*. This command is normally executed by mount(8). It implements the mount protocol as described in RFC 1094, Appendix A.

The options are:

-D Used with NQNFS to set the "dead server threshold" to the specified number of round trip timeout intervals. After a "dead server threshold" of retransmit timeouts, cached data for the unresponsive server is assumed to still be valid. Values may be set in the range of 1 - 9, with 9 referring to an "infinite dead threshold" (i.e. never assume cached data still valid). This option is not generally recommended and is really an experimental feature.

-K Pass Kerberos authenticators to the server for client-to-server user-credential mapping. This may only be used over TCP mounts between 4.4BSD clients and servers.

-L Used with NQNFS to set the lease term to the specified number of seconds. Only use this argument for mounts with a large round trip delay. Values are normally in the 10-30 second range.

-M Assume that other clients are not writing a file concurrently with this client. This implements a slightly less strict consistency criteria than 4.3BSD-Reno did, that is more in line with most commercial client implementations. This is recommended for servers that do not support leasing.

-P Use a reserved socket port number. This is useful for mounting servers that require clients to use a reserved port number.

-R Set the retry count for doing the mount to the specified value.

-T Use TCP transport instead of UDP. This is recommended for servers that are not on the same LAN cable as the client. (NB: This is NOT supported by most non-BSD servers.)

-a Set the read-ahead count to the specified value. This may be in the range of 0 - 4, and determines how many blocks will be read ahead when a large file is being read sequentially. This is recommended for mounts with a large bandwidth * delay product.

-b If an initial attempt to contact the server fails, fork off a child to keep trying the mount in the background. Useful for fstab(5), where the filesystem mount is not critical to multiuser operation.

-c For UDP mount points, do not do a connect(2). This must be used for servers that do not reply to requests from the standard port number.

-d Do not estimate retransmit timeout dynamically. This may be useful for UDP mounts that exhibit high retry rates.

-g Set the maximum size of the group list for the credentials to the specified value. This should be used for mounts on old servers that cannot handle a group list size of 16, as specified in RFC 1057. Try 8, if users in a lot of groups cannot get response from the mount point.

M8

-i Make the mount interruptible, which implies that file system calls that are delayed due to an unresponsive server will fail with EINTR when a termination signal is posted for the process.

-k Used with NQNFS to specify "get a lease" for the file name being looked up. This is recommended unless the server is complaining about excessive lease load.

-l Used with NQNFS to specify that the **Readdir_and_Lookup** RPC should be used. This option reduces RPC traffic for cases such as "ls -l", but increases the lease load on the server. This is recommended unless the server is complaining about excessive lease load.

-m Set the Kerberos realm to the string argument. Used with the -K option for mounts to other realms.

-o Options are specified with a -o flag followed by a comma separated string of options. See the mount(8) man page for possible options and their meanings.

-q Use the leasing extensions to the protocol to maintain cache consistency. This protocol, referred to as Not Quite Nfs (NQNFS), is only supported by 4.4BSD servers.

-r Set the read data size to the specified value. It should be a power of 2 greater than or equal to 1024. This should be used for UDP mounts when the "fragments dropped due to timeout" value is getting large while actively using a mount point. (Use netstat(1) with the -s option to see what the "fragments dropped due to timeout" value is.) See the -w option as well.

-s A soft mount, which implies that file system calls will fail after **Retry** round trip timeout intervals.

-t Set the initial retransmit timeout to the specified value. May be useful for fine tuning UDP mounts over internetworks with high packet loss rates or an overloaded server. Try increasing the interval if nfsstat(1) shows high retransmit rates while the file system is active or reducing the value if there is a low retransmit rate but long response delay observed.

-w Set the write data size to the specified value. Ditto the comments w.r.t. the -r option, but using the "fragments dropped due to timeout" value on the server instead of the client. Note that both the -r and -w options should only be used as a last ditch effort at improving performance when mounting servers that do not support TCP mounts.

-x Set the retransmit timeout count for soft mounts to the specified value.

SEE ALSO

mount(2), unmount(2), fstab(5), mount(8)

BUGS

Due to the way that Sun RPC is implemented on top of UDP (unreliable datagram) transport, tuning such mounts is really a black art that can only be expected to have limited success. For clients mounting servers that are not on the same LAN cable or that tend to be overloaded, TCP transport is strongly recommended, but unfortunately this is restricted to mostly 4.4BSD servers.

NAME

mount_null – demonstrate the use of a null file system layer

SYNOPSIS

mount_null [**-o** *options*] *target mount-point*

DESCRIPTION

The **mount_null** command creates a null layer, duplicating a sub-tree of the file system name space under another part of the global file system namespace. In this respect, it is similar to the loopback file system (see mount_lofs(8)). It differs from the loopback file system in two respects: it is implemented using a stackable layers techniques, and it's "null-node" s stack above all lower-layer vnodes, not just over directory vnodes.

The options are as follows:

-o Options are specified with a **-o** flag followed by a comma separated string of options. See the mount(8) man page for possible options and their meanings.

The null layer has two purposes. First, it serves as a demonstration of layering by proving a layer which does nothing. (It actually does everything the loopback file system does, which is slightly more than nothing.) Second, the null layer can serve as a prototype layer. Since it provides all necessary layer framework, new file system layers can be created very easily be starting with a null layer.

The remainder of this man page examines the null layer as a basis for constructing new layers.

INSTANTIATING NEW NULL LAYERS

New null layers are created with mount_null(8). Mount_null(8) takes two arguments, the pathname of the lower vfs (target-pn) and the pathname where the null layer will appear in the namespace (mount-point-pn). After the null layer is put into place, the contents of target-pn subtree will be aliased under mount-point-pn.

OPERATION OF A NULL LAYER

The null layer is the minimum file system layer, simply bypassing all possible operations to the lower layer for processing there. The majority of its activity centers on the bypass routine, though which nearly all vnode operations pass.

The bypass routine accepts arbitrary vnode operations for handling by the lower layer. It begins by examing vnode operation arguments and replacing any null-nodes by their lower-layer equivalents. It then invokes the operation on the lower layer. Finally, it replaces the null-nodes in the arguments and, if a vnode is returned by the operation, stacks a null-node on top of the returned vnode.

Although bypass handles most operations, *vop_getattr*, *vop_inactive*, *vop_reclaim*, and *vop_print* are not bypassed. *Vop_getattr* must change the fsid being returned. *Vop_inactive* and vop_reclaim are not bypassed so that they can handle freeing null-layer specific data. *Vop_print* is not bypassed to avoid excessive debugging information.

INSTANTIATING VNODE STACKS

Mounting associates the null layer with a lower layer, in effect stacking two VFSes. Vnode stacks are instead created on demand as files are accessed.

The initial mount creates a single vnode stack for the root of the new null layer. All other vnode stacks are created as a result of vnode operations on this or other null vnode stacks.

New vnode stacks come into existence as a result of an operation which returns a vnode. The bypass routine stacks a null-node above the new vnode before returning it to the caller.

For example, imagine mounting a null layer with

```
mount_null /usr/include /dev/layer/null
```

Changing directory to `/dev/layer/null` will assign the root null-node (which was created when the null layer was mounted). Now consider opening `sys`. A vop_lookup would be done on the root null-node. This operation would bypass through to the lower layer which would return a vnode representing the UFS `sys`. Null_bypass then builds a null-node aliasing the UFS `sys` and returns this to the caller. Later operations on the null-node `sys` will repeat this process when constructing other vnode stacks.

CREATING OTHER FILE SYSTEM LAYERS

One of the easiest ways to construct new file system layers is to make a copy of the null layer, rename all files and variables, and then begin modifyng the copy. Sed can be used to easily rename all variables.

The umap layer is an example of a layer descended from the null layer.

INVOKING OPERATIONS ON LOWER LAYERS

There are two techniques to invoke operations on a lower layer when the operation cannot be completely bypassed. Each method is appropriate in different situations. In both cases, it is the responsibility of the aliasing layer to make the operation arguments "correct" for the lower layer by mapping an vnode arguments to the lower layer.

The first approach is to call the aliasing layer's bypass routine. This method is most suitable when you wish to invoke the operation currently being handled on the lower layer. It has the advantage the the bypass routine already must do argument mapping. An example of this is *null_getattrs* in the null layer.

A second approach is to directly invoked vnode operations on the lower layer with the *VOP_OPERATIONNAME* interface. The advantage of this method is that it is easy to invoke arbitrary operations on the lower layer. The disadvantage is that vnodes arguments must be manually mapped.

SEE ALSO

`mount(8)`

UCLA Technical Report CSD-910056, *Stackable Layers: an Architecture for File System Development.*

HISTORY

The **mount_null** utility first appeared in 4.4BSD.

M8

NAME

mount_portal – mount the portal daemon

SYNOPSIS

mount_portal [**-o** *options*] */etc/portal.conf mount_point*

DESCRIPTION

The **mount_portal** command attaches an instance of the portal daemon to the global filesystem namespace. The conventional mount point is /p. This command is normally executed by mount(8) at boot time.

The options are as follows:

-o Options are specified with a **-o** flag followed by a comma separated string of options. See the mount(8) man page for possible options and their meanings.

The portal daemon provides an *open* service. Objects opened under the portal mount point are dynamically created by the portal daemon according to rules specified in the named configuration file. Using this mechanism allows descriptors such as sockets to be made available in the filesystem namespace.

The portal daemon works by being passed the full pathname of the object being opened. The daemon creates an appropriate descriptor according to the rules in the configuration file, and then passes the descriptor back to the calling process as the result of the open system call.

NAMESPACE

By convention, the portal daemon divides the namespace into sub-namespaces, each of which handles objects of a particular type.

Currently, two sub-namespaces are implemented: tcp and fs. The tcp namespace takes a hostname and a port (slash separated) and creates an open TCP/IP connection. The fs namespace opens the named file, starting back at the root directory. This can be used to provide a controlled escape path from a chrooted environment.

CONFIGURATION FILE

The configuration file contains a list of rules. Each rule takes one line and consists of two or more whitespace separated fields. A hash ("#") character causes the remainder of a line to be ignored. Blank lines are ignored.

The first field is a pathname prefix to match against the requested pathname. If a match is found, the second field tells the daemon what type of object to create. Subsequent fields are passed to the creation function.

```
# @(#)portal.conf      5.1 (Berkeley) 7/13/92
tcp/            tcp tcp/
fs/             file fs/
```

FILES

/p/*

SEE ALSO

mount(2), unmount(2), fstab(5), mount(8)

CAVEATS

This filesystem may not be NFS-exported.

HISTORY

The **mount_portal** utility first appeared in 4.4BSD.

M8

NAME

mount_procfs – mount the process file system

SYNOPSIS

mount_procfs [**-o** *options*] /proc mount_point

DESCRIPTION

The **mount_procfs** command attaches an instance of the process namespace to the global filesystem namespace. The conventional mount point is /proc. This command is normally executed by mount(8) at boot time.

The options are as follows:

-o Options are specified with a **-o** flag followed by a comma separated string of options. See the mount(8) man page for possible options and their meanings.

The root of the process filesystem contains an entry for each active process. These processes are visible as a directory whose name is the process' pid. In addition, the special entry curproc references the current process.

Each directory contains several files.

ctl a writeonly file which supports a variety of control operations. Control commands are written as strings to the ctl file. The control commands are:

- attach stops the target process and arranges for the sending process to become the debug control process.
- detach continue execution of the target process and remove it from control by the debug process (which need not be the sending process).
- run continue running the target process until a signal is delivered, a breakpoint is hit, or the target process exits.
- step single step the target process, with no signal delivery.
- wait wait for the target process to come to a steady state ready for debugging. The target process must be in this state before any of the other commands are allowed.

The string can also be the name of a signal, lower case and without the SIG prefix, in which case that signal is delivered to the process (see sigaction(2)).

file A reference to the vnode from which the process text was read. This can be used to gain access to the process' symbol table, or to start another copy of the process.

mem The complete virtual memory image of the process. Only those address which exist in the process can be accessed. Reads and writes to this file modify the process. Writes to the text segment remain private to the process.

note Not implemented.

notepg Not implemented.

regs Allows read and write access to the process' register set. This file contains a binary data structure struct regs defined in <machine/reg.h>. regs can only be written when the process is stopped.

fpregs The floating point registers as defined by struct fpregs in <machine/reg.h>. fpregs is only implemented on machines which have distinct general purpose and floating point register sets.

status The process status. This file is readonly and returns a single line containing multiple space-separated fields as follows:

- command name
- process id
- parent process id
- process group id
- session id
- *major,minor* of the controlling terminal, or -1,-1 if there is no controlling terminal.
- a list of process flags: ctty if there is a controlling terminal, sldr if the process is a session leader, noflags if neither of the other two flags are set.
- the process start time in seconds and microseconds, comma separated.
- the user time in seconds and microseconds, comma separated.
- the system time in seconds and microseconds, comma separated.
- the wait channel message
- the process credentials consisting of the effective user id and the list of groups (whose first member is the effective group id) all comma separated.

In a normal debugging environment, where the target is fork/exec'd by the debugger, the debugger should fork and the child should stop itself (with a self-inflicted SIGSTOP for example). The parent should issue a wait and then an attach command via the appropriate ctl file. The child process will receive a SIGTRAP immediately after the call to exec (see execve(2)).

FILES

/proc/#
/proc/curproc
/proc/curproc/ctl
/proc/curproc/file
/proc/curproc/mem
/proc/curproc/note
/proc/curproc/notepg
/proc/curproc/regs
/proc/curproc/fpregs
/proc/curproc/status

SEE ALSO

sigaction(2), mount(2), unmount(2),

CAVEATS

No . and .. entries appear when listing the contents of the /proc directory. This makes sense in the context of this filesystem, but is inconsistent with usual filesystem conventions. However, it is still possible to refer to both . and .. in a pathname.

This filesystem may not be NFS-exported since most of the functionality of procfs requires that state be maintained.

HISTORY

The **mount_procfs** utility first appeared in 4.4BSD.

NAME

mount_umap – sample file system layer

SYNOPSIS

mount_umap [**-o** *options*] *target mount-point uid-mapfile gid-mapfile*

DESCRIPTION

The **mount_umap** command is used to mount a sub-tree of an existing file system that uses a different set of uids and gids than the local system. Such a file system could be mounted from a remote site via NFS or it could be a file system on removable media brought from some foreign location that uses a different password file.

The options are as follows:

-o Options are specified with a **-o** flag followed by a comma separated string of options. See the mount(8) man page for possible options and their meanings.

The **mount_umap** command uses a set of files provided by the user to make correspondences between uids and gids in the sub-tree's original environment and some other set of ids in the local environment. For instance, user smith might have uid 1000 in the original environment, while having uid 2000 in the local environment. The **mount_umap** command allows the subtree from smith's original environment to be mapped in such a way that all files with owning uid 1000 look like they are actually owned by uid 2000.

target should be the current location of the sub-tree in the local system's name space. *mount-point* should be a directory where the mapped subtree is to be placed. *uid-mapfile* and *gid-mapfile* describe the mappings to be made between identifiers. Briefly, the format of these files is a count of the number of mappings on the first line, with each subsequent line containing a single mapping. Each of these mappings consists of an id from the original environment and the corresponding id in the local environment, separated by white space. *uid-mapfile* should contain all uid mappings, and *gid-mapfile* should contain all gid mappings. Any uids not mapped in *uid-mapfile* will be treated as user NOBODY, and any gids not mapped in *gid-mapfile* will be treated as group NULLGROUP. At most 64 uids can be mapped for a given subtree, and at most 16 groups can be mapped by a given subtree.

The mapfiles can be located anywhere in the file hierarchy, but they must be owned by root, and they must be writable only by root. **mount_umap** will refuse to map the sub-tree if the ownership or permissions on these files are improper. It will also balk if the count of mappings in the first line of the map files is not correct.

The layer created by the **mount_umap** command is meant to serve as a simple example of file system layering. It is not meant for production use. The implementation is not very sophisticated.

SEE ALSO

mount(8), mount_null(8), mount_lofs(8)

HISTORY

The **mount_umap** utility first appeared in 4.4BSD.

M8

NAME

mount_union – mount union filesystems

SYNOPSIS

mount_union [**-br**] [**-o** *options*] *directory uniondir*

DESCRIPTION

The **mount_union** command attaches *directory* above *uniondir* in such a way that the contents of both directory trees remain visible. By default, *directory* becomes the *upper* layer and *uniondir* becomes the *lower* layer.

The options are as follows:

-b Invert the default position, so that *directory* becomes the lower layer and *uniondir* becomes the upper layer. However, *uniondir* remains the mount point.

-o Options are specified with a **-o** flag followed by a comma separated string of options. See the mount(8) man page for possible options and their meanings.

-r Hide the lower layer completely in the same way as mounting with mount_lofs(8) or mount_null(8).

To enforce filesystem security, the user mounting the filesystem must be superuser or else have write permission on the mounted-on directory.

Filenames are looked up in the upper layer and then in the lower layer. If a directory is found in the lower layer, and there is no entry in the upper layer, then a *shadow* directory will be created in the upper layer. It will be owned by the user who originally did the union mount, with mode ''rwxrwxrwx'' (0777) modified by the umask in effect at that time.

If a file exists in the upper layer then there is no way to access a file with the same name in the lower layer. If necessary, a combination of loopback and union mounts can be made which will still allow the lower files to be accessed by a different pathname.

Except in the case of a directory, access to an object is granted via the normal filesystem access checks. For directories, the current user must have access to both the upper and lower directories (should they both exist).

Requests to create or modify objects in *uniondir* are passed to the upper layer with the exception of a few special cases. An attempt to open for writing a file which exists in the lower layer causes a copy of the *entire* file to be made to the upper layer, and then for the upper layer copy to be opened. Similarly, an attempt to truncate a lower layer file to zero length causes an empty file to be created in the upper layer. Any other operation which would ultimately require modification to the lower layer fails with EROFS.

The union filesystem manipulates the namespace, rather than individual filesystems. The union operation applies recursively down the directory tree now rooted at *uniondir*. Thus any filesystems which are mounted under *uniondir* will take part in the union operation. This differs from the ***union*** option to mount(8) which only applies the union operation to the mount point itself, and then only for lookups.

EXAMPLES

The commands

```
mount -t cd9660 -o ro /dev/cd0a /usr/src
mount -t union -o /var/obj /usr/src
```

mount the CD-ROM drive /dev/cd0a on /usr/src and then attaches /var/obj on top. For most purposes the effect of this is to make the source tree appear writable even though it is stored on a CD-ROM.

The command

```
mount -t union -o -b /sys $HOME/sys
```

attaches the system source tree below the sys directory in the user's home directory. This allows individual users to make private changes to the source, and build new kernels, without those changes becoming visible to other users. Note that the files in the lower layer remain accessible via /sys.

SEE ALSO

intro(2), mount(2), unmount(2), fstab(5), mount(8), mount_lofs(8), mount_null(8)

BUGS

Without whiteout support from the filesystem backing the upper layer, there is no way that delete and rename operations on lower layer objects can be done. EROFS is returned for this kind of operations along with any others which would make modifications to the lower layer, such as chmod(1).

Running find(1) over a union tree has the side-effect of creating a tree of shadow directories in the upper layer.

HISTORY

The **mount_union** command first appeared in 4.4BSD.

NAME

mountd – service remote NFS mount requests

SYNOPSIS

/sbin/mountd [**–n**] [*exportsfile*]

DESCRIPTION

Mountd is the server for NFS mount requests from other client machines. Mountd listens for service requests at the port indicated in the NFS server specification; see *Network File System Protocol Specification*, RFC1094.

Options and operands available for **mountd**:

–n The **–n** option allows non-root mount requests to be served. This should only be specified if there are clients such as PC's, that require it.

exportsfile
The *exportsfile* argument specifies an alternate location for the exports file.

When mountd is started, it loads the export host addresses and options into the kernel using the mount(2) system call. After changing the exports file, a hangup signal should be sent to the mountd daemon to get it to reload the export information. After sending the SIGHUP (kill -HUP 'cat /var/run/mountd.pid'), check the syslog output to see if mountd logged any parsing errors in the exports file.

FILES

/etc/exports the list of exported filesystems
/var/run/mountd.pid the pid of the currently running mountd

SEE ALSO

nfsstat(1), exports(5), nfsd(8), portmap(8), showmount(8)

HISTORY

The **mountd** utility first appeared in 4.4BSD.

M8

NAME

mtree – map a directory hierarchy

SYNOPSIS

mtree [**-cderux**] [**-f** *spec*] [**-K** *keywords*] [**-k** *keywords*] [**-p** *path*] [**-s** *seed*]

DESCRIPTION

The utility **mtree** compares the file hierarchy rooted in the current directory against a specification read from the standard input. Messages are written to the standard output for any files whose characteristics do not match the specifications, or which are missing from either the file hierarchy or the specification.

The options are as follows:

-c Print a specification for the file hierarchy to the standard output.

-d Ignore everything except directory type files.

-e Don't complain about files that are in the file hierarchy, but not in the specification.

-f Read the specification from *file*, instead of from the standard input.

-K Add the specified (whitespace or comma separated) keywords to the current set of keywords.

-k Use the ''type'' keyword plus the specified (whitespace or comma separated) keywords instead of the current set of keywords.

-p Use the file hierarchy rooted in *path*, instead of the current directory.

-r Remove any files in the file hierarchy that are not described in the specification.

-s Display a single checksum to the standard error output that represents all of the files for which the keyword **cksum** was specified. The checksum is seeded with the specified value.

-u Modify the owner, group, and permissions of existing files to match the specification and create any missing directories. User, group, and permissions must all be specified for missing directories to be created.

-x Don't descend below mount points in the file hierarchy.

Specifications are mostly composed of ''keywords'', i.e. strings that that specify values relating to files. No keywords have default values, and if a keyword has no value set, no checks based on it are performed.

Currently supported keywords are as follows:

cksum The checksum of the file using the default algorithm specified by the cksum(1) utility.

ignore Ignore any file hierarchy below this file.

gid The file group as a numeric value.

gname The file group as a symbolic name.

mode The current file's permissions as a numeric (octal) or symbolic value.

nlink The number of hard links the file is expected to have.

uid The file owner as a numeric value.

uname The file group as a symbolic name.

size The size, in bytes, of the file.

link The file the symbolic link is expected to reference.

time The last modification time of the file.

type The type of the file; may be set to any one of the following:

block	block special device
char	character special device
dir	directory
fifo	fifo
file	regular file
link	symbolic link
socket	socket

The default set of keywords are **gid**, **mode**, **nlink**, **size**, **slink**, **time**, and **uid**.

There are four types of lines in a specification.

The first type of line sets a global value for a keyword, and consists of the string ''/set'' followed by whitespace, followed by sets of keyword/value pairs, separated by whitespace. Keyword/value pairs consist of a keyword, followed by an equals sign (''=''), followed by a value, without whitespace characters. Once a keyword has been set, its value remains unchanged until either reset or unset.

The second type of line unsets keywords and consists of the string ''/unset'', followed by whitespace, followed by one or more keywords, separated by whitespace.

The third type of line is a file specification and consists of a file name, followed by whitespace, followed by zero or more whitespace separated keyword/value pairs. The file name may be preceded by whitespace characters. The file name may contain any of the standard file name matching characters (''['', '']'', ''?'' or ''*''), in which case files in the hierarchy will be associated with the first pattern that they match.

Each of the keyword/value pairs consist of a keyword, followed by an equals sign (''=''), followed by the keyword's value, without whitespace characters. These values override, without changing, the global value of the corresponding keyword.

All paths are relative. Specifying a directory will cause subsequent files to be searched for in that directory hierarchy. Which brings us to the last type of line in a specification: a line containing only the string ''..'' causes the current directory path to ascend one level.

Empty lines and lines whose first non-whitespace character is a hash mark (''#'') are ignored.

The **mtree** utility exits with a status of 0 on success, 1 if any error occurred, and 2 if the file hierarchy did not match the specification.

EXAMPLES

To detect system binaries that have been ''trojan horsed'', it is recommended that **mtree** be run on the file systems, and a copy of the results stored on a different machine, or, at least, in encrypted form. The seed for the **-s** option should not be an obvious value and the final checksum should not be stored on-line under any circumstances! Then, periodically, **mtree** should be run against the on-line specifications and the final checksum compared with the previous value. While it is possible for the bad guys to change the on-line specifications to conform to their modified binaries, it shouldn't be possible for them to make it produce the same final checksum value. If the final checksum value changes, the off-line copies of the specification can be used to detect which of the binaries have actually been modified.

The **-d** and **-u** options can be used in combination to create directory hierarchies for distributions and other such things.

FILES

`/etc/mtree` system specification directory

SEE ALSO

chmod(1), chown(1), chgrp(1), cksum(1), stat(2), fts(3),

HISTORY

The **mtree** utility appeared in 4.3BSD–Reno.

NAME

named – Internet domain name server

SYNOPSIS

named [**–d** *debuglevel*] [**–p** *port#*] [{–b} *bootfile*] [**–q**] [**–r**]

DESCRIPTION

Named is the Internet domain name server. See RFC's 1033, 1034, and 1035 for more information on the Internet name-domain system. Without any arguments, *named* will read the default boot file */etc/named.boot*, read any initial data and listen for queries.

Options are:

–d Print debugging information. A number after the "d" determines the level of messages printed.

–p Use a different port number. The default is the standard port number as returned by getservbyname(3) for service "domain".

–b Use an alternate boot file. This is optional and allows you to specify a file with a leading dash.

–q Trace all incoming queries if *named* has been compiled with *QRYLOG* defined.

–r Turns recursion off in the server. Answers can come only from local (primary or secondary) zones. This can be used on root servers.

Any additional argument is taken as the name of the boot file. If multiple boot files are specified, only the last is used.

The boot file contains information about where the name server is to get its initial data. Lines in the boot file cannot be continued on subsequent lines. The following is a small example:

```
;
;        boot file for name server
;
directory       /usr/local/adm/named

; type    domain                source host/file          backup file

cache     .                                               root.cache
primary   Berkeley.EDU          berkeley.edu.zone
primary   32.128.IN-ADDR.ARPA   ucbhosts.rev
secondary CC.Berkeley.EDU       128.32.137.8 128.32.137.3 cc.zone.bak
secondary 6.32.128.IN-ADDR.ARPA 128.32.137.8 128.32.137.3 cc.rev.bak
primary   0.0.127.IN-ADDR.ARPA                            localhost.rev
forwarders 10.0.0.78 10.2.0.78
; slave
```

The "directory" line causes the server to change its working directory to the directory specified. This can be important for the correct processing of $INCLUDE files in primary zone files.

The "cache" line specifies that data in "root.cache" is to be placed in the backup cache. Its main use is to specify data such as locations of root domain servers. This cache is not used during normal operation, but is used as "hints" to find the current root servers. The file "root.cache" is in the same format as "berkeley.edu.zone". There can be more than one "cache" file specified. The "root.cache" file should be retrieved periodically from FTP.RS.INTERNIC.NET since it contains a list of root servers, and this list changes periodically.

The first example "primary" line states that the file "berkeley.edu.zone" contains authoritative data for the "Berkeley.EDU" zone. The file "berkeley.edu.zone" contains data in the master file format described in RFC883. All domain names are relative to the origin, in this case, "Berkeley.EDU" (see below for a more detailed description). The second "primary" line states that the file "ucbhosts.rev" contains

M8

authoritative data for the domain ''32.128.IN-ADDR.ARPA,'' which is used to translate addresses in network 128.32 to hostnames. Each master file should begin with an SOA record for the zone (see below).

The first example ''secondary'' line specifies that all authoritative data under ''CC.Berkeley.EDU'' is to be transferred from the name server at 128.32.137.8. If the transfer fails it will try 128.32.137.3 and continue trying the addresses, up to 10, listed on this line. The secondary copy is also authoritative for the specified domain. The first non-dotted-quad address on this line will be taken as a filename in which to backup the transferred zone. The name server will load the zone from this backup file if it exists when it boots, providing a complete copy even if the master servers are unreachable. Whenever a new copy of the domain is received by automatic zone transfer from one of the master servers, this file will be updated. If no file name is given, a temporary file will be used, and will be deleted after each successful zone transfer. This is not recommended since it is a needless waste of bandwidth. The second example ''secondary'' line states that the address-to-hostname mapping for the subnet 128.32.136 should be obtained from the same list of master servers as the previous zone.

The ''forwarders'' line specifies the addresses of sitewide servers that will accept recursive queries from other servers. If the boot file specifies one or more forwarders, then the server will send all queries for data not in the cache to the forwarders first. Each forwarder will be asked in turn until an answer is returned or the list is exhausted. If no answer is forthcoming from a forwarder, the server will continue as it would have without the forwarders line unless it is in ''slave'' mode. The forwarding facility is useful to cause a large sitewide cache to be generated on a master, and to reduce traffic over links to outside servers. It can also be used to allow servers to run that do not have access directly to the Internet, but wish to act as though they do.

The ''slave'' line (shown commented out) is used to put the server in slave mode. In this mode, the server will only make queries to forwarders. This option is normally used on machine that wish to run a server but for physical or administrative reasons cannot be given access to the Internet, but have access to a host that does have access.

The ''sortlist'' line can be used to indicate networks that are to be preferred over other networks Queries for host addresses from hosts on the same network as the server will receive responses with local network addresses listed first, then addresses on the sort list, then other addresses.

The ''xfrnets'' directive (not shown) can be used to implement primative access control. If this directive is given, then your name server will only answer zone transfer requests from hosts which are on networks listed in your ''xfrnets'' directives. This directive may also be given as ''tcplist'' for compatibility with older, interrim servers.

The ''include'' directive (not shown) can be used to process the contents of some other file as though they appeared in place of the ''include'' directive. This is useful if you have a lot of zones or if you have logical groupings of zones which are maintained by different people. The ''include'' directive takes one argument, that being the name of the file whose contents are to be included. No quotes are necessary around the file name.

The ''bogusns'' directive (not shown) tells BIND that no queries are to be sent to the specified name server addresses (which are specified as dotted quads, not as domain names). This is useful when you know that some popular server has bad data in a zone or cache, and you want to avoid contamination while the problem is being fixed.

The master file consists of control information and a list of resource records for objects in the zone of the forms:

```
$INCLUDE <filename> <opt_domain>
$ORIGIN <domain>
<domain> <opt_ttl> <opt_class> <type> <resource_record_data>
```

where *domain* is "." for root, "@" for the current origin, or a standard domain name. If *domain* is a standard domain name that does not end with ''.'', the current origin is appended to the domain. Domain names ending with "." are unmodified. The *opt_domain* field is used to define an origin for the data in an included file. It is equivalent to placing a $ORIGIN statement before the first line of the included file. The field is optional. Neither the *opt_domain* field nor $ORIGIN statements in the included file modify the current origin for this file. The *opt_ttl* field is an optional integer number for the time-to-live field. It defaults to zero, meaning the minimum value specified in the SOA record for the zone. The *opt_class* field is the object address type; currently only one type is supported, **IN**, for objects connected to the DARPA Internet. The *type* field contains one of the following tokens; the data expected in the *resource_record_data* field is in parentheses.

A a host address (dotted quad)

NS an authoritative name server (domain)

MX a mail exchanger (domain), preceded by a preference value (0..32767), with lower numeric values representing higher logical preferences.

CNAME the canonical name for an alias (domain)

SOA marks the start of a zone of authority (domain of originating host, domain address of maintainer, a serial number and the following parameters in seconds: refresh, retry, expire and minimum TTL (see RFC883)).

NULL a null resource record (no format or data)

RP a Responsible Person for some domain name (mailbox, TXT-referral)

PTR a domain name pointer (domain)

HINFO host information (cpu_type OS_type)

Resource records normally end at the end of a line, but may be continued across lines between opening and closing parentheses. Comments are introduced by semicolons and continue to the end of the line.

Note that there are other resource record types, not shown here. You should consult the BIND Operations Guide ("BOG") for the complete list. Some resource record types may have been standardized in newer RFC's but not yet implemented in this version of BIND.

Each master zone file should begin with an SOA record for the zone. An example SOA record is as follows:

```
@       IN      SOA     ucbvax.Berkeley.EDU. rwh.ucbvax.Berkeley.EDU. (
                                1989020501      ; serial
                                10800   ; refresh
                                3600    ; retry
                                3600000; expire
                                86400 ) ; minimum
```

The SOA specifies a serial number, which should be changed each time the master file is changed. Note that the serial number can be given as a dotted number, but this is a *very* unwise thing to do since the translation to normal integers is via concatenation rather than multiplication and addition. You can spell out the year, month, day of month, and 0..99 version number and still fit inside the unsigned 32-bit size of this field. It's true that we will have to rethink this strategy in the year 4294 (Greg.) but we're not worried about it. Secondary servers check the serial number at intervals specified by the refresh time in seconds; if the serial number changes, a zone transfer will be done to load the new data. If a master server cannot be contacted when a refresh is due, the retry time specifies the interval at which refreshes should be attempted. If a master server cannot be contacted within the interval given by the expire time, all data from the zone is discarded by secondary servers. The minimum value is the time-to-live ("TTL") used by records in the file with no explicit time-to-live value.

NOTES

The boot file directives "domain" and "suffixes" have been obsoleted by a more useful resolver-based implementation of suffixing for partially qualified domain names. The prior mechanisms could fail under a number of situations, especially when then local nameserver did not have complete information.

The following signals have the specified effect when sent to the server process using the *kill*(1) command.

SIGHUP
: Causes server to read named.boot and reload database. If the server is built with the FORCED_RELOAD compile-time option, then SIGHUP will also cause the server to check the serial number on all secondary zones. Normally the serial numbers are only checked at the SOA-specified intervals.

SIGINT Dumps current data base and cache to /var/tmp/named_dump.db

SIGIOT Dumps statistics data into /var/tmp/named.stats if the server is compiled -DSTATS. Statistics data is appended to the file.

SIGSYS
: Dumps the profiling data in /var/tmp if the server is compiled with profiling (server forks, chdirs and exits).

SIGTERM
: Dumps the primary and secondary database files. Used to save modified data on shutdown if the server is compiled with dynamic updating enabled.

SIGUSR1
: Turns on debugging; each SIGUSR1 increments debug level. (SIGEMT on older systems without SIGUSR1)

SIGUSR2
: Turns off debugging completely. (SIGFPE on older systems without SIGUSR2)

SIGWINCH
: Toggles logging of all incoming queries via syslog(8) (requires server to have been built with the QRYLOG option).

FILES

/etc/named.boot	name server configuration boot file
/etc/named.pid	the process id (/var/run/named.pid on newer systems)
/var/tmp/named.run	debug output
/var/tmp/named_dump.db	dump of the name server database
/var/tmp/named.stats	nameserver statistics data

SEE ALSO

kill(1), gethostbyname(3N), signal(3c), resolver(3), resolver(5), hostname(7), RFC 882, RFC 883, RFC 973, RFC 974, RFC 1033, RFC 1034, RFC 1035, RFC 1123, *Name Server Operations Guide for BIND*

NAME

named-xfer – ancillary agent for inbound zone transfers

SYNOPSIS

named-xfer **–z** *zone_to_transfer* **–f** *db_file* **–s** *serial_no* [**–d** *debuglevel*] [**–l** *debug_log_file*] [**–t** *trace_file*] [**–p** *port#*] [**–S**] *nameserver*

DESCRIPTION

Named-xfer is an ancillary program executed by *named*(8) to perform an inbound zone transfer. It is rarely executed directly, and only by system administrators who are trying to debug a zone transfer problem. See RFC's 1033, 1034, and 1035 for more information on the Internet name-domain system.

Options are:

–z specifies the name of the zone to be transferred.

–f specifies the name of the file into which the zone should be dumped when it is received from the primary server.

–s specifies the serial number of our current copy of this zone. If the SOA RR we get from the primary server does not have a serial number higher than this, the transfer will be aborted.

–d Print debugging information. A number after the ''d'' determines the level of messages printed.

–l Specifies a log file for debugging messages. The default is system- dependent but is usually in */var/tmp* or */usr/tmp*. Note that this only applies if *–d* is also specified.

–t Specifies a trace file which will contain a protocol trace of the zone transfer. This is probably only of interest to people debugging the name server itself.

–p Use a different port number. The default is the standard port number as returned by getservbyname(3) for service ''domain''.

–S Perform a restricted transfer of only the SOA, NS records and glue A records for the zone. The SOA record will not be loaded by named but will be used to determine when to verify the NS records. the ''stubs'' directive in *named*(8) for more information.

Additional arguments are taken as name server addresses in so-called ''dotted-quad'' syntax only; no host name are allowed here. At least one address must be specified. Any additional addresses will be tried in order if the first one fails to transfer to us successfully.

SEE ALSO

named(8), resolver(3), resolver(5), hostname(7), RFC 882, RFC 883, RFC 973, RFC 974, RFC 1033, RFC 1034, RFC 1035, RFC 1123, *Name Server Operations Guide for BIND*

NAME

named.reload – cause the name server to synchronize its database

DESCRIPTION

This command sends a SIGHUP to the running name server. This signal is documented in *named*(8).

BUGS

Does not check to see if the name server is actually running, and could use a stale PID cache file which may result in the death of an unrelated process.

SEE ALSO

named(8), named.restart(8)

NAME

named.restart – stop and restart the name server

DESCRIPTION

This command sends a SIGKILL to the running name server and then starts a new one.

BUGS

Does not check to see if the name server is actually running, and could use a stale PID cache file which may result in the death of an unrelated process.

Does not wait after killing the old server before starting a new one; since the server could take some time to die and the new one will experience a fatal error if the old one isn't gone by the time it starts, you can be left in a situation where you have no name server at all.

SEE ALSO

named(8), named.reload(8)

NAME

ncheck – generate names from i-numbers

SYNOPSIS

ncheck [–**i** numbers] [–**a**] [–**s**] filesystems ...

DESCRIPTION

N.B.: For most normal file system maintenance, the function of *ncheck* is subsumed by *fsck*(8).

Ncheck with no options generates a pathname vs. i-number list of all files on every specified filesystem. Names of directory files are followed by '/.'. The –**i** option reduces the report to only those files whose i-numbers follow. The –**a** option allows printing of the names '.' and '..', which are ordinarily suppressed. The –**s** option reduces the report to special files and files with set-user-ID mode; it is intended to discover concealed violations of security policy.

The report is in no useful order, and probably should be sorted.

SEE ALSO

sort(1), dcheck(8), fsck(8), icheck(8)

DIAGNOSTICS

When the filesystem structure is improper, '??' denotes the 'parent' of a parentless file and a pathname beginning with '...' denotes a loop.

NAME

newfs, **mfs** – construct a new file system

SYNOPSIS

newfs [**-NO**] [**-S** *sector-size*] [**-a** **-maxcontig**] [**-b** *block-size*] [**-c** *cylinders*] [**-d** *rotdelay*] [**-e** *maxbpg*] [**-f** *frag-size*] [**-i** *bytes*] [**-k** *skew*] [**-l** *interleave*] [**-m** *free space*] [**-o** *optimization*] [**-p** *sectors*] [**-r** *revolutions*] [**-s** *size*] [**-t** *tracks*] [**-u** *sectors*] [**-x** *sectors*] *special*
mount_mfs [**-N**] [**-a** **-maxcontig**] [**-b** *block-size*] [**-c** *cylinders*] [**-d** *rotdelay*] [**-e** *maxbpg*] [**-f** *frag-size*] [**-i** *bytes*] [**-m** *free space*] [**-o** *options*] [**-s** *size*] *special node*

DESCRIPTION

Newfs replaces the more obtuse mkfs(8) program. Before running **newfs** or **mount_mfs**, the disk must be labeled using disklabel(8). **Newfs** builds a file system on the specified special device basing its defaults on the information in the disk label. Typically the defaults are reasonable, however **newfs** has numerous options to allow the defaults to be selectively overridden.

Mount_mfs is used to build a file system in virtual memory and then mount it on a specified node. **Mount_mfs** exits and the contents of the file system are lost when the file system is unmounted. If **mount_mfs** is sent a signal while running, for example during system shutdown, it will attempt to unmount its corresponding file system. The parameters to **mount_mfs** are the same as those to **newfs**. The special file is only used to read the disk label which provides a set of configuration parameters for the memory based file system. The special file is typically that of the primary swap area, since that is where the file system will be backed up when free memory gets low and the memory supporting the file system has to be paged.

The following options define the general layout policies.

-N Causes the file system parameters to be printed out without really creating the file system.

-O Creates a 4.3BSD format filesystem. This options is primarily used to build root filesystems that can be understood by older boot ROMs.

-a *maxcontig*
This specifies the maximum number of contiguous blocks that will be laid out before forcing a rotational delay (see the **-d** option). The default value is one. See tunefs(8) for more details on how to set this option.

-b *block-size*
The block size of the file system, in bytes.

-c *#cylinders/group*
The number of cylinders per cylinder group in a file system. The default value is 16.

-d *rotdelay*
This specifies the expected time (in milliseconds) to service a transfer completion interrupt and initiate a new transfer on the same disk. The default is 4 milliseconds. See tunefs(8) for more details on how to set this option.

M8

-e *maxbpg*
This indicates the maximum number of blocks any single file can allocate out of a cylinder group before it is forced to begin allocating blocks from another cylinder group. The default is about one quarter of the total blocks in a cylinder group. See `tunefs`(8) for more details on how to set this option.

-f *frag-size*
The fragment size of the file system in bytes.

-i *number of bytes per inode*
This specifies the density of inodes in the file system. The default is to create an inode for each 2048 bytes of data space. If fewer inodes are desired, a larger number should be used; to create more inodes a smaller number should be given.

-m *free space %*
The percentage of space reserved from normal users; the minimum free space threshold. The default value used is 10%. See `tunefs`(8) for more details on how to set this option.

-o *optimization preference*
(''space'' or ''time'') The file system can either be instructed to try to minimize the time spent allocating blocks, or to try to minimize the space fragmentation on the disk. If the value of minfree (see above) is less than 10%, the default is to optimize for space; if the value of minfree is greater than or equal to 10%, the default is to optimize for time. See `tunefs`(8) for more details on how to set this option.

-s *size* The size of the file system in sectors.

The following options override the standard sizes for the disk geometry. Their default values are taken from the disk label. Changing these defaults is useful only when using **newfs** to build a file system whose raw image will eventually be used on a different type of disk than the one on which it is initially created (for example on a write-once disk). Note that changing any of these values from their defaults will make it impossible for `fsck` to find the alternate superblocks if the standard superblock is lost.

-S *sector-size*
The size of a sector in bytes (almost never anything but 512).

-k *sector 0 skew, per track*
Used to describe perturbations in the media format to compensate for a slow controller. Track skew is the offset of sector 0 on track N relative to sector 0 on track N-1 on the same cylinder.

-l *hardware sector interleave*
Used to describe perturbations in the media format to compensate for a slow controller. Interleave is physical sector interleave on each track, specified as the denominator of the ratio:

`sectors read/sectors passed over`

Thus an interleave of 1/1 implies contiguous layout, while 1/2 implies logical sector 0 is separated by one sector from logical sector 1.

-p *spare sectors per track*
Spare sectors (bad sector replacements) are physical sectors that occupy space at the end of each track. They are not counted as part of the sectors/track (**-u**) since they are not available to the file system for data allocation.

-r *revolutions/minute*
The speed of the disk in revolutions per minute.

−t *#tracks/cylinder*
The number of tracks/cylinder available for data allocation by the file system.

−u *sectors/track*
The number of sectors per track available for data allocation by the file system. This does not include sectors reserved at the end of each track for bad block replacement (see the **−p** option.)

−x *spare sectors per cylinder*
Spare sectors (bad sector replacements) are physical sectors that occupy space at the end of the last track in the cylinder. They are deducted from the sectors/track (**−u**) of the last track of each cylinder since they are not available to the file system for data allocation.

The options to the **mount_mfs** command are as described for the **newfs** command, except for the **−o** option.

That option is as follows:

−o Options are specified with a **−o** flag followed by a comma separated string of options. See the mount(8) man page for possible options and their meanings.

SEE ALSO

disktab(5), fs(5), dumpfs(8), disklabel(8), diskpart(8), fsck(8), format(8), mount(8), tunefs(8)

M. McKusick, W. Joy, S. Leffler, and R. Fabry, "A Fast File System for UNIX,", *ACM Transactions on Computer Systems 2*, 3, pp 181-197, August 1984, (reprinted in the BSD System Manager's Manual).

HISTORY

The **newfs** command appeared in 4.2BSD.

NAME

newlfs – construct a new LFS file system

SYNOPSIS

newlfs -L [*newlfs-options*] *special*

DESCRIPTION

Newlfs builds a log-structured file system on the specified special device basing its defaults on the information in the disk label. (Before running **newlfs** the disk must be labeled using disklabel(8).)

The following options define the general layout policies.

-B The logical segment size of the file system in bytes.

-b *block-size*
The block size of the file system in bytes.

-L Create a log-structured file system (LFS). This flag is currently required.

-m *free space %*
The percentage of space reserved from normal users; the minimum free space threshold. The default value used is 10%. See tunefs(8) for more details on how to set this option.

-s *size* The size of the file system in sectors.

SEE ALSO

disktab(5), fs(5), dumplfs(8), disklabel(8), diskpart(8), tunefs(8)

M. McKusick, W. Joy, S. Leffler, and R. Fabry, "A Fast File System for UNIX,", *ACM Transactions on Computer Systems* 2, 3, pp 181-197, August 1984, (reprinted in the BSD System Manager's Manual).

HISTORY

The **newlfs** command appeared in 4.4BSD.

NAME

nfsd – remote NFS server

SYNOPSIS

nfsd [**-rut**] [**-n** *num_servers*]

DESCRIPTION

Nfsd runs on a server machine to service NFS requests from client machines. At least one **nfsd** must be running for a machine to operate as a server.

Unless otherwise specified, four servers for UDP transport are started.

The following options are available:

-r Register the NFS service with portmap(8) without creating any servers. This option can be used along with the **-u** or **-t** options to re-register NFS if the portmap server is restarted.

-n Specifies how many servers to create.

-t Serve TCP NFS clients.

-u Serve UDP NFS clients.

For example, "`nfsd -u -t 6`" serves UDP and TCP transports using six daemons.

A server should run enough daemons to handle the maximum level of concurrency from its clients, typically four to six.

Nfsd listens for service requests at the port indicated in the NFS server specification; see *Network File System Protocol Specification*, RFC1094.

The **nfsd** utility exits 0 on success, and >0 if an error occurs.

SEE ALSO

nfsstat(1), nfssvc(2), mountd(8), portmap(8)

HISTORY

The **nfsd** utility first appeared in 4.4BSD.

M8

NAME

nfsiod – local NFS asynchronous I/O server

SYNOPSIS

nfsiod [**-n** *num_servers*]

DESCRIPTION

Nfsiod runs on an NFS client machine to service asynchronous I/O requests to its server. It improves performance but is not required for correct operation.

Unless otherwise specified, a single server is started.

The options are as follows:

-n Specify how many servers are to be started.

A client should run enough daemons to handle its maximum level of concurrency, typically four to six.

The **nfsiod** utility exits 0 on success, and >0 if an error occurs.

SEE ALSO

nfsstat(1), nfssvc(2), mountd(8), portmap(8)

HISTORY

The **nfsiod** utility first appeared in 4.4BSD.

NAME

nologin – politely refuse a login

SYNOPSIS

nologin

DESCRIPTION

Nologin displays a message that an account is not available and exits non-zero. It is intended as a replacement shell field for accounts that have been disabled.

SEE ALSO

login(1)

HISTORY

The **nologin** command appeared in 4.4BSD.

NAME

nslookup – query Internet name servers interactively

SYNOPSIS

nslookup [*–option ...*] [*host-to-find* | – [*server*]]

DESCRIPTION

Nslookup is a program to query Internet domain name servers. Nslookup has two modes: interactive and non-interactive. Interactive mode allows the user to query name servers for information about various hosts and domains or to print a list of hosts in a domain. Non-interactive mode is used to print just the name and requested information for a host or domain.

ARGUMENTS

Interactive mode is entered in the following cases:

a) when no arguments are given (the default name server will be used),

b) when the first argument is a hyphen (–) and the second argument is the host name or Internet address of a name server.

Non-interactive mode is used when the name or Internet address of the host to be looked up is given as the first argument. The optional second argument specifies the host name or address of a name server.

The options listed under the ''set'' command below can be specified in the .nslookuprc file in the user's home directory if they are listed one per line. Options can also be specified on the command line if they precede the arguments and are prefixed with a hyphen. For example, to change the default query type to host information, and the initial timeout to 10 seconds, type:

nslookup –query=hinfo –timeout=10

INTERACTIVE COMMANDS

Commands may be interrupted at any time by typing a control-C. To exit, type a control-D (EOF) or type exit. The command line length must be less than 256 characters. To treat a built-in command as a host name, precede it with an escape character (\). **N.B.** an unrecognized command will be interpreted as a host name.

host [*server*]

Look up information for *host* using the current default server or using *server* if specified. If *host* is an Internet address and the query type is A or PTR, the name of the host is returned. If *host* is a name and does not have a trailing period, the default domain name is appended to the name. (This behavior depends on the state of the **set** options **domain, srchlist, defname,** and **search**). To look up a host not in the current domain, append a period to the name.

server *domain*
lserver *domain*

Change the default server to *domain*. **Lserver** uses the initial server to look up information about *domain* while **server** uses the current default server. If an authoritative answer can't be found, the names of servers that might have the answer are returned.

root Changes the default server to the server for the root of the domain name space. Currently, the host ns.internic.net is used. (This command is a synonym for **lserver ns.internic.net.**) The name of the root server can be changed with the **set root** command.

finger [*name*] [> *filename*]
finger [*name*] [>> *filename*]

Connects with the finger server on the current host. The current host is defined when a previous lookup for a host was successful and returned address information (see the **set querytype=A** command). *Name* is optional. > and >> can be used to redirect output in the usual manner.

ls [*option*] *domain* [> *filename*]
ls [*option*] *domain* [>> *filename*]

List the information available for *domain*, optionally creating or appending to *filename*. The default output contains host names and their Internet addresses. *Option* can be one of the following:

–t *querytype*
lists all records of the specified type (see *querytype* below).

–a lists aliases of hosts in the domain. synonym for **–t CNAME**.

–d lists all records for the domain. synonym for **–t ANY**.

–h lists CPU and operating system information for the domain. synonym for **–t HINFO**.

–s lists well-known services of hosts in the domain. synonym for **–t WKS**.

When output is directed to a file, hash marks are printed for every 50 records received from the server.

view *filename*
Sorts and lists the output of previous **ls** command(s) with *more*(1).

help
? Prints a brief summary of commands.

exit Exits the program.

set *keyword*[=*value*]
This command is used to change state information that affects the lookups. Valid keywords are:

all Prints the current values of the frequently-used options to **set**. Information about the current default server and host is also printed.

class=*value*
Change the query class to one of:

IN	the Internet class.
CHAOS	the Chaos class.
HESIOD	the MIT Athena Hesiod class.
ANY	wildcard (any of the above).

The class specifies the protocol group of the information.
(Default = IN, abbreviation = cl)

[no]debug
Turn debugging mode on. A lot more information is printed about the packet sent to the server and the resulting answer.
(Default = nodebug, abbreviation = [no]deb)

[no]d2 Turn exhaustive debugging mode on. Essentially all fields of every packet are printed.
(Default = nod2)

domain=*name*
Change the default domain name to *name*. The default domain name is appended to a

M8

lookup request depending on the state of the **defname** and **search** options. The domain search list contains the parents of the default domain if it has at least two components in its name. For example, if the default domain is CC.Berkeley.EDU, the search list is CC.Berkeley.EDU and Berkeley.EDU. Use the **set srchlist** command to specify a different list. Use the **set all** command to display the list.
(Default = value from hostname, /etc/resolv.conf or LOCALDOMAIN, abbreviation = do)

srchlist=*name1/name2/...*
Change the default domain name to *name1* and the domain search list to *name1*, *name2*, etc. A maximum of 6 names separated by slashes (/) can be specified. For example,

```
set srchlist=lcs.MIT.EDU/ai.MIT.EDU/MIT.EDU
```

sets the domain to lcs.MIT.EDU and the search list to the three names. This command overrides the default domain name and search list of the **set domain** command. Use the **set all** command to display the list.
(Default = value based on hostname, /etc/resolv.conf or LOCALDOMAIN, abbreviation = srchl)

[no]defname
If set, append the default domain name to a single-component lookup request (i.e., one that does not contain a period).
(Default = defname, abbreviation = [no]def)

[no]search
If the lookup request contains at least one period but doesn't end with a trailing period, append the domain names in the domain search list to the request until an answer is received.
(Default = search, abbreviation = [no]sea)

port=*value*
Change the default TCP/UDP name server port to *value*.
(Default = 53, abbreviation = po)

querytype=*value*
type=*value*
Change the type of information query to one of:

A	the host's Internet address.
CNAME	the canonical name for an alias.
HINFO	the host CPU and operating system type.
MINFO	the mailbox or mail list information.
MX	the mail exchanger.
NS	the name server for the named zone.
PTR	the host name if the query is an Internet address, otherwise the pointer to other information.
SOA	the domain's "start-of-authority" information.
TXT	the text information.
UINFO	the user information.
WKS	the supported well-known services.

Other types (ANY, AXFR, MB, MD, MF, NULL) are described in the RFC-1035 document.
(Default = A, abbreviations = q, ty)

[no]recurse
Tell the name server to query other servers if it does not have the information.
(Default = recurse, abbreviation = [no]rec)

retry=*number*
Set the number of retries to *number*. When a reply to a request is not received within a certain amount of time (changed with **set timeout**), the timeout period is doubled and the request is resent. The retry value controls how many times a request is resent before giving up.
(Default = 4, abbreviation = ret)

root=*host*
Change the name of the root server to *host*. This affects the **root** command.
(Default = ns.internic.net., abbreviation = ro)

timeout=*number*
Change the initial timeout interval for waiting for a reply to *number* seconds. Each retry doubles the timeout period.
(Default = 5 seconds, abbreviation = ti)

[no]vc Always use a virtual circuit when sending requests to the server.
(Default = novc, abbreviation = [no]v)

[no]ignoretc
Ignore packet truncation errors.
(Default = noignoretc, abbreviation = [no]ig)

DIAGNOSTICS

If the lookup request was not successful, an error message is printed. Possible errors are:

Timed out
The server did not respond to a request after a certain amount of time (changed with **set timeout=***value*) and a certain number of retries (changed with **set retry=***value*).

No response from server
No name server is running on the server machine.

No records
The server does not have resource records of the current query type for the host, although the host name is valid. The query type is specified with the **set querytype** command.

Non-existent domain
The host or domain name does not exist.

Connection refused
Network is unreachable
The connection to the name or finger server could not be made at the current time. This error commonly occurs with **ls** and **finger** requests.

Server failure
The name server found an internal inconsistency in its database and could not return a valid answer.

Refused
The name server refused to service the request.

Format error
The name server found that the request packet was not in the proper format. It may indicate an error in *nslookup*.

FILES

/etc/resolv.conf initial domain name and name server addresses.

$HOME/.nslookuprc	user's initial options.
/usr/share/misc/nslookup.help	summary of commands.

ENVIRONMENT

HOSTALIASES	file containing host aliases.
LOCALDOMAIN	overrides default domain.

SEE ALSO

resolver(3), resolver(5), named(8),
RFC-1034 ''Domain Names – Concepts and Facilities''
RFC-1035 ''Domain Names – Implementation and Specification''

AUTHOR

Andrew Cherenson

NAME

pac – printer/plotter accounting information

SYNOPSIS

pac [**-P***printer*] [**-c**] [**-m**] [**-p***price*] [**-s**] [**-r**] [*name ...*]

DESCRIPTION

Pac reads the printer/plotter accounting files, accumulating the number of pages (the usual case) or feet (for raster devices) of paper consumed by each user, and printing out how much each user consumed in pages or feet and dollars.

Options and operands available:

-P*printer*
: Accounting is done for the named printer. Normally, accounting is done for the default printer (site dependent) or the value of the environment variable `PRINTER` is used.

-c
: flag causes the output to be sorted by cost; usually the output is sorted alphabetically by name.

-m
: flag causes the host name to be ignored in the accounting file. This allows for a user on multiple machines to have all of his printing charges grouped together.

-p*price*
: The value *price* is used for the cost in dollars instead of the default value of 0.02 or the price specified in `/etc/printcap`.

-r
: Reverse the sorting order.

-s
: Accounting information is summarized on the summary accounting file; this summarization is necessary since on a busy system, the accounting file can grow by several lines per day.

names
: Statistics are only printed for user(s) *name*; usually, statistics are printed for every user who has used any paper.

FILES

`/var/account/?acct` raw accounting files
`/var/account/?_sum` summary accounting files
`/etc/printcap` printer capability data base

SEE ALSO

printcap(5)

BUGS

The relationship between the computed price and reality is as yet unknown.

HISTORY

The **pac** command appeared in 4.0BSD.

M8

NAME

ping – send ICMP ECHO_REQUEST packets to network hosts

SYNOPSIS

ping [**-dfnqrvR**] [**-c** *count*] [**-i** *wait*] [**-l** *preload*] [**-p** *pattern*] [**-s** *packetsize*]

DESCRIPTION

Ping uses the ICMP protocol's mandatory ECHO_REQUEST datagram to elicit an ICMP ECHO_RESPONSE from a host or gateway. ECHO_REQUEST datagrams (''pings'') have an IP and ICMP header, followed by a ''struct timeval'' and then an arbitrary number of ''pad'' bytes used to fill out the packet. The options are as follows:

-c *count*
: Stop after sending (and receiving) *count* ECHO_RESPONSE packets.

-d
: Set the SO_DEBUG option on the socket being used.

-f
: Flood ping. Outputs packets as fast as they come back or one hundred times per second, whichever is more. For every ECHO_REQUEST sent a period ''.'' is printed, while for every ECHO_REPLY received a backspace is printed. This provides a rapid display of how many packets are being dropped. Only the super-user may use this option. *This can be very hard on a network and should be used with caution.*

-i *wait*
: Wait *wait* seconds *between sending each packet*. The default is to wait for one second between each packet. This option is incompatible with the **-f** option.

-l *preload*
: If *preload* is specified, **ping** sends that many packets as fast as possible before falling into its normal mode of behavior.

-n
: Numeric output only. No attempt will be made to lookup symbolic names for host addresses.

-p *pattern*
: You may specify up to 16 ''pad'' bytes to fill out the packet you send. This is useful for diagnosing data-dependent problems in a network. For example, ''-p ff'' will cause the sent packet to be filled with all ones.

-q
: Quiet output. Nothing is displayed except the summary lines at startup time and when finished.

-R
: Record route. Includes the RECORD_ROUTE option in the ECHO_REQUEST packet and displays the route buffer on returned packets. Note that the IP header is only large enough for nine such routes. Many hosts ignore or discard this option.

-r
: Bypass the normal routing tables and send directly to a host on an attached network. If the host is not on a directly-attached network, an error is returned. This option can be used to ping a local host through an interface that has no route through it (e.g., after the interface was dropped by routed(8)).

-s *packetsize*
: Specifies the number of data bytes to be sent. The default is 56, which translates into 64 ICMP data bytes when combined with the 8 bytes of ICMP header data.

-v
: Verbose output. ICMP packets other than ECHO_RESPONSE that are received are listed.

When using **ping** for fault isolation, it should first be run on the local host, to verify that the local network interface is up and running. Then, hosts and gateways further and further away should be ''pinged''.

Round-trip times and packet loss statistics are computed. If duplicate packets are received, they are not included in the packet loss calculation, although the round trip time of these packets is used in calculating the minimum/average/maximum round-trip time numbers. When the specified number of packets have been sent (and received) or if the program is terminated with a `SIGINT`, a brief summary is displayed.

This program is intended for use in network testing, measurement and management. Because of the load it can impose on the network, it is unwise to use **ping** during normal operations or from automated scripts.

ICMP PACKET DETAILS

An IP header without options is 20 bytes. An ICMP ECHO_REQUEST packet contains an additional 8 bytes worth of ICMP header followed by an arbitrary amount of data. When a *packetsize* is given, this indicated the size of this extra piece of data (the default is 56). Thus the amount of data received inside of an IP packet of type ICMP ECHO_REPLY will always be 8 bytes more than the requested data space (the ICMP header).

If the data space is at least eight bytes large, **ping** uses the first eight bytes of this space to include a timestamp which it uses in the computation of round trip times. If less than eight bytes of pad are specified, no round trip times are given.

DUPLICATE AND DAMAGED PACKETS

Ping will report duplicate and damaged packets. Duplicate packets should never occur, and seem to be caused by inappropriate link-level retransmissions. Duplicates may occur in many situations and are rarely (if ever) a good sign, although the presence of low levels of duplicates may not always be cause for alarm.

Damaged packets are obviously serious cause for alarm and often indicate broken hardware somewhere in the **ping** packet's path (in the network or in the hosts).

TRYING DIFFERENT DATA PATTERNS

The (inter)network layer should never treat packets differently depending on the data contained in the data portion. Unfortunately, data-dependent problems have been known to sneak into networks and remain undetected for long periods of time. In many cases the particular pattern that will have problems is something that doesn't have sufficient ''transitions'', such as all ones or all zeros, or a pattern right at the edge, such as almost all zeros. It isn't necessarily enough to specify a data pattern of all zeros (for example) on the command line because the pattern that is of interest is at the data link level, and the relationship between what you type and what the controllers transmit can be complicated.

This means that if you have a data-dependent problem you will probably have to do a lot of testing to find it. If you are lucky, you may manage to find a file that either can't be sent across your network or that takes much longer to transfer than other similar length files. You can then examine this file for repeated patterns that you can test using the **−p** option of **ping**.

TTL DETAILS

The TTL value of an IP packet represents the maximum number of IP routers that the packet can go through before being thrown away. In current practice you can expect each router in the Internet to decrement the TTL field by exactly one.

The TCP/IP specification states that the TTL field for TCP packets should be set to 60, but many systems use smaller values (4.3 BSD uses 30, 4.2 used 15).

The maximum possible value of this field is 255, and most Unix systems set the TTL field of ICMP ECHO_REQUEST packets to 255. This is why you will find you can ''ping'' some hosts, but not reach them with `telnet`(1) or `ftp`(1).

In normal operation ping prints the ttl value from the packet it receives. When a remote system receives a ping packet, it can do one of three things with the TTL field in its response:

- Not change it; this is what Berkeley Unix systems did before the 4.3BSD–Tahoe release. In this case the TTL value in the received packet will be 255 minus the number of routers in the round-trip path.
- Set it to 255; this is what current Berkeley Unix systems do. In this case the TTL value in the received packet will be 255 minus the number of routers in the path `from` the remote system *to* the **ping***ing* host.
- Set it to some other value. Some machines use the same value for ICMP packets that they use for TCP packets, for example either 30 or 60. Others may use completely wild values.

BUGS

Many Hosts and Gateways ignore the RECORD_ROUTE option.

The maximum IP header length is too small for options like RECORD_ROUTE to be completely useful. There's not much that that can be done about this, however.

Flood pinging is not recommended in general, and flood pinging the broadcast address should only be done under very controlled conditions.

SEE ALSO

`netstat(1)`, `ifconfig(8)`, `routed(8)`

HISTORY

The **ping** command appeared in 4.3BSD.

NAME

portmap – DARPA port to RPC program number mapper

SYNOPSIS

portmap [**−d**]

DESCRIPTION

Portmap is a server that converts RPC program numbers into DARPA protocol port numbers. It must be running in order to make RPC calls.

When an RPC server is started, it will tell **portmap** what port number it is listening to, and what RPC program numbers it is prepared to serve. When a client wishes to make an RPC call to a given program number, it will first contact **portmap** on the server machine to determine the port number where RPC packets should be sent.

Portmap must be started before any RPC servers are invoked.

Normally **portmap** forks and dissociates itself from the terminal like any other daemon. **Portmap** then logs errors using syslog(3).

Option available:

−d (debug) prevents **portmap** from running as a daemon, and causes errors and debugging information to be printed to the standard error output.

SEE ALSO

inetd.conf(5), rpcinfo(8), inetd(8)

BUGS

If **portmap** crashes, all servers must be restarted.

HISTORY

The **portmap** command appeared in 4.3BSD

M8

NAME

pstat – display system data structures

SYNOPSIS

pstat [**-Tfnstv**] [**-M** *core*] [**-N** *system*]

DESCRIPTION

Pstat displays open file entry, swap space utilization, terminal state, and vnode data structures. If *corefile* is given, the information is sought there, otherwise in /dev/kmem. The required namelist is taken from /vmunix unless *system* is specified. The **-n** option specifies that devices should be printed out by major/minor number rather than by name.

Options are

-T Prints the number of used and free slots in the several system tables and is useful for checking to see how large system tables have become if the system is under heavy load.

-f Print the open file table with these headings:

LOC The core location of this table entry.

TYPE The type of object the file table entry points to.

FLG Miscellaneous state variables encoded thus:

R open for reading

W open for writing

A open for appending

S shared lock present

X exclusive lock present

I signal pgrp when data ready

CNT Number of processes that know this open file.

MSG Number of messages outstanding for this file.

DATA The location of the vnode table entry or socket structure for this file.

OFFSET The file offset (see lseek(2)).

-s Print information about swap space usage on all the swap areas compiled into the kernel. The first column is the device name of the partition. The next column is the total space available in the partition. The *Used* column indicates the total blocks used so far; the *Available* column indicates how much space is remaining on each partition. The *Capacity* reports the percentage of space used.

If more than one partition is configured into the system, totals for all of the statistics will be reported in the final line of the report.

-t Print table for terminals with these headings:

RAW Number of characters in raw input queue.

CAN Number of characters in canonicalized input queue.

M8

OUT Number of characters in putput queue.

MODE See `tty`(4).

ADDR Physical device address.

DEL Number of delimiters (newlines) in canonicalized input queue.

COL Calculated column position of terminal.

STATE Miscellaneous state variables encoded thus:

T	delay timeout in progress
W	waiting for open to complete
O	open
F	outq has been flushed during DMA
C	carrier is on
B	busy doing output
A	process is awaiting output
X	open for exclusive use
S	output stopped
H	hangup on close

PGRP Process group for which this is controlling terminal.

DISC Line discipline; blank is old tty OTTYDISC or `new tty` for NTTYDISC or `net` for NETLDISC (see `bk`(4)).

−v Print the active vnodes. Each group of vnodes corresponding to a particular filesystem is preceded by a two line header. The first line consists of the following:

*** MOUNT *fstype from* on *on fsflags*

where *fstype* is one of *ufs, nfs, mfs, or pc*; *from* is the filesystem is mounted from; *on* is the directory the filesystem is mounted on; and *fsflags* is a list of optional flags applied to the mount (see `mount`(8)). the first part of which are fixed, and the second part are filesystem type specific. The headers common to all vnodes are:

ADDR Location of this vnode.

TYP File type.

VFLAG

A list of letters representing vnode flags:

R	– VROOT
T	– VTEXT
L	– VXLOCK
W	– VXWANT
E	– VEXLOCK

S – VSHLOCK

T – VLWAIT

A – VALIASED

B – VBWAIT

USE The number of references to this vnode.

HOLD The number of I/O buffers held by this vnode.

FILEID The vnode fileid. In the case of *ufs* this is the inode number.

IFLAG Miscellaneous filesystem specific state variables encoded thus:

For ufs:

L	locked
U	update time (fs(5)) must be corrected
A	access time must be corrected
W	wanted by another process (L flag is on)
C	changed time must be corrected
S	shared lock applied
E	exclusive lock applied
Z	someone waiting for a lock
M	contains modifications
R	has a rename in progress

For nfs:

W	waiting for I/O buffer flush to complete
P	I/O buffers being flushed
M	locally modified data exists
E	an earlier write failed
X	non-cacheable lease (nqnfs)
O	write lease (nqnfs)
G	lease was evicted (nqnfs)

SIZ/RDEV
Number of bytes in an ordinary file, or major and minor device of special file.

FILES

`/vmunix` namelist
`/dev/kmem` default source of tables

SEE ALSO

iostat(1), ps(1), systat(1), vmstat(1), stat(2), fs(5),

BUGS

Swap statistics are reported for all swap partitions compiled into the kernel, regardless of whether those partitions are being used.

Does not understand NFS swap servers.

HISTORY

The **pstat** command appeared in 4.0BSD.

M8

NAME

pwd_mkdb – generate the password databases

SYNOPSIS

pwd_mkdb [**-p**] *file*

DESCRIPTION

Pwd_mkdb creates db(3) style secure and insecure databases for the specified file. These databases are then installed into "/etc/spwd.db" and "/etc/pwd.db" respectively. The file is installed into "/etc/master.passwd". The file must be in the correct format (see passwd(5)). It is important to note that the format used in this system is different from the historic Version 7 style format.

The options are as follows:

-p Create a Version 7 style password file and install it into "/etc/passwd".

The two databases differ in that the secure version contains the user's encrypted password and the insecure version has an asterisk ("*")

The databases are used by the C library password routines (see getpwent(3)).

Pwd_mkdb exits zero on success, non-zero on failure.

FILES

/var/db/pwd.db	The insecure password database file.
/var/db/pwd.db.tmp	A temporary file.
/var/db/spwd.db	The secure password database file.
/var/db/spwd.db.tmp	A temporary file.
/etc/master.passwd	The current password file.
/etc/passwd	A Version 7 format password file.

BUGS

Because of the necessity for atomic update of the password files, **pwd_mkdb** uses rename(2) to install them. This, however, requires that the file specified on the command line live on the same file system as the "/etc" directory.

There are the obvious races with multiple people running **pwd_mkdb** on different password files at the same time. The front-ends to **pwd_mkdb**, chpass(1), passwd(1) and vipw(8), handle the locking necessary to avoid this problem.

COMPATIBILITY

Previous versions of the system had a program similar to **pwd_mkdb**, mkpasswd(8), which built dbm(3) style databases for the password file but depended on the calling programs to install them. The program was renamed in order that previous users of the program not be surprised by the changes in functionality.

SEE ALSO

chpass(1), passwd(1), db(3), getpwent(3), passwd(5), vipw(8)

M8

NAME

quot – display total block usage per user for a file

SYNOPSIS

quot [**-ncf**] [*filesystem ...*]

DESCRIPTION

The **quot** command displays the total count of blocks owned by a user for the filesystem *filesystem*. If the filesystem option *filesystem* is not specified, the file systems listed in /etc/fstab are used. The following options are available:

-c Display information on file size and block usage. The file sizes are listed in the first column, the second column contains a count of how many files of that size were found and the third column lists the cumulative block usage for the displayed size and all smaller files.

-f For each user, the number of files (inodes) owned is displayed in addition to the block usage.

-n A list sorted by block usage is displayed. This is the result of **quot** executing the following command:

```
ncheck filesystem | sort +0n | quot -n filesystem
```

SEE ALSO

ls(1), du(1)

HISTORY

The **quot** command appeared in Version 32V AT&T UNIX.

NAME

quotacheck – filesystem quota consistency checker

SYNOPSIS

quotacheck [**–g**] [**–u**] [**–v**] *filesystem ...*
quotacheck [**–g**] [**–u**] [**–v**] **–a**

DESCRIPTION

Quotacheck examines each filesystem, builds a table of current disk usage, and compares this table against that recorded in the disk quota file for the filesystem. If any inconsistencies are detected, both the quota file and the current system copy of the incorrect quotas are updated (the latter only occurs if an active filesystem is checked). By default both user and group quotas are checked.

Available options:

–a If the **–a** flag is supplied in place of any filesystem names, **quotacheck** will check all the filesystems indicated in /etc/fstab to be read-write with disk quotas. By default only the types of quotas listed in /etc/fstab are checked.

–g Only group quotas listed in /etc/fstab are to be checked.

–u Only user quotas listed in /etc/fstab are to be checked.

–v **quotacheck** reports discrepancies between the calculated and recorded disk quotas.

Specifying both **–g** and **–u** is equivalent to the default. Parallel passes are run on the filesystems required, using the pass numbers in /etc/fstab in an identical fashion to fsck(8).

Normally **quotacheck** operates silently.

Quotacheck expects each filesystem to be checked to have a quota files named quota.user and quota.group which are located at the root of the associated file system. These defaults may be overridden in /etc/fstab. If a file is not present, **quotacheck** will create it.

Quotacheck is normally run at boot time from the /etc/rc.local file, see rc(8), before enabling disk quotas with quotaon(8).

Quotacheck accesses the raw device in calculating the actual disk usage for each user. Thus, the filesystems checked should be quiescent while **quotacheck** is running.

FILES

quota.user at the filesystem root with user quotas
quota.group at the filesystem root with group quotas
/etc/fstab default filesystems

SEE ALSO

quota(1), quotactl(2), fstab(5), edquota(8), fsck(8), quotaon(8), repquota(8)

HISTORY

The **quotacheck** command appeared in 4.2BSD.

NAME

quotaon, **quotaoff** – turn filesystem quotas on and off

SYNOPSIS

quotaon [**–g**] [**–u**] [**–v**] *filesystem ...*
quotaon [**–g**] [**–u**] [**–v**] **–a**
quotaoff [**–g**] [**–u**] [**–v**] *filesystem ...*
quotaoff [**–g**] [**–u**] [**–v**] **–a**

DESCRIPTION

Quotaon announces to the system that disk quotas should be enabled on one or more filesystems. **Quotaoff** announces to the system that the specified filesystems should have any disk quotas diskquotas turned off. The filesystems specified must have entries in /etc/fstab and be mounted. **Quotaon** expects each filesystem to have quota files named quota.user and quota.group which are located at the root of the associated file system. These defaults may be overridden in /etc/fstab. By default both user and group quotas are enabled.

Available options:

–a If the **–a** flag is supplied in place of any filesystem names, **quotaon/quotaoff** will enable/disable all the filesystems indicated in /etc/fstab to be read-write with disk quotas. By default only the types of quotas listed in /etc/fstab are enabled.

–g Only group quotas listed in /etc/fstab should be enabled/disabled.

–u Only user quotas listed in /etc/fstab should be enabled/disabled.

–v Causes **quotaon** and **quotaoff** to print a message for each filesystem where quotas are turned on or off.

Specifying both **–g** and **–u** is equivalent to the default.

FILES

quota.user at the filesystem root with user quotas
quota.group at the filesystem root with group quotas
/etc/fstab filesystem table

SEE ALSO

quota(1), quotactl(2), fstab(5), edquota(8), quotacheck(8), repquota(8)

HISTORY

The **quotaon** command appeared in 4.2BSD.

M8

NAME

rbootd – HP remote boot server

SYNOPSIS

rbootd [**-ad**] [**-i** *interface*] [config_file]

DESCRIPTION

The **rbootd** utility services boot requests from Hewlett-Packard workstations over a local area network. All boot files must reside in the boot file directory; further, if a client supplies path information in its boot request, it will be silently stripped away before processing. By default, **rbootd** only responds to requests from machines listed in its configuration file.

The options are as follows:

-a Respond to boot requests from any machine. The configuration file is ignored if this option is specified.

-d Run **rbootd** in debug mode. Packets sent and received are displayed to the terminal.

-i *interface*
Service boot requests on specified interface. If unspecified, **rbootd** searches the system interface list for the lowest numbered, configured "up" interface (excluding loopback). Ties are broken by choosing the earliest match.

Specifying *config_file* on the command line causes **rbootd** to use a different configuration file from the default.

The configuration file is a text file where each line describes a particular machine. A line must start with a machine's Ethernet address followed by an optional list of boot file names. An Ethernet address is specified in hexadecimal with each of its six octets separated by a colon. The boot file names come from the boot file directory. The ethernet address and boot file(s) must be separated by white-space and/or comma characters. A pound sign causes the remainder of a line to be ignored.

Here is a sample configuration file:

```
#
# ethernet addr     boot file(s)          comments
#
08:00:09:0:66:ad    SYSHPBSD              # snake (4.3BSD)
08:00:09:0:59:5b                          # vandy (anything)
8::9:1:C6:75        SYSHPBSD,SYSHPUX      # jaguar (either)
```

Rbootd logs status and error messages via syslog(3). A startup message is always logged, and in the case of fatal errors (or deadly signals) a message is logged announcing the server's termination. In general, a non-fatal error is handled by ignoring the event that caused it (e.g. an invalid Ethernet address in the config file causes that line to be invalidated).

The following signals have the specified effect when sent to the server process using the kill(1) command:

SIGHUP Drop all active connections and reconfigure.

SIGUSR1 Turn on debugging, do nothing if already on.

SIGUSR2 Turn off debugging, do nothing if already off.

FILES

/dev/bpf#	packet-filter device
/etc/rbootd.conf	configuration file
/tmp/rbootd.dbg	debug output
/usr/mdec/rbootd	directory containing boot files
/var/run/rbootd.pid	process id

SEE ALSO

kill(1), socket(2), signal(3), syslog(3), rmp(4)

BUGS

If multiple servers are started on the same interface, each will receive and respond to the same boot packets.

M8

NAME

rc – command script for auto–reboot and daemons

SYNOPSIS

rc
rc.local

DESCRIPTION

Rc is the command script which controls the automatic reboot and rc.local is the script holding commands which are pertinent only to a specific site.

When an automatic reboot is in progress, rc is invoked with the argument *autoboot*. The first portion of rc runs an fsck(8) with option −p to ''preen'' all the disks of minor inconsistencies resulting from the last system shutdown and to check for serious inconsistencies caused by hardware or software failure. If this auto-check and repair succeeds, then the second part of rc is run.

The second part of rc, which is run after an auto-reboot succeeds and also if rc is invoked when a single user shell terminates (see init(8)), starts all the daemons on the system, preserves editor files and clears the scratch directory /tmp.

Rc.local is executed immediately before any other commands after a successful fsck. Normally, the first commands placed in the rc.local file define the machine's name, using hostname(1), and save any possible core image that might have been generated as a result of a system crash, with savecore(8). The latter command is included in the rc.local file because the directory in which core dumps are saved is usually site specific.

Following tradition, the startup files rc and rc.local reside in /etc.

SEE ALSO

init(8), reboot(8), savecore(8)

HISTORY

The rc command appeared in 4.0BSD.

NAME

reboot, **halt** – stopping and restarting the system

SYNOPSIS

halt [**-nq**]
reboot [**-nq**]

DESCRIPTION

The **halt** and **reboot** utilities flush the file system cache to disk, send all running processes a SIGTERM (and subsequently a SIGKILL) and, respectively, halt or restart the system. The action is logged, including entering a shutdown record into the login accounting file.

The options are as follows:

-n If the **-n** option is specified, the file system cache is not flushed. This option should probably not be used.

-q If the **-q** option is specified, the system is halted or restarted quickly and ungracefully, and only the flushing of the file system cache is performed. This option should probably not be used.

Normally, the shutdown(8) utility is used when the system needs to be halted or restarted, giving users advance warning of their impending doom.

SEE ALSO

sync(1), utmp(5), boot(8), shutdown(8)

HISTORY

A **reboot** command appeared in Version 6 AT&T UNIX.

NAME

registerd – Kerberos registration daemon

SYNOPSIS

registerd

DESCRIPTION

Act as a registration agent for a Kerberos domain.

FILES

/.update.keyxx.xx.xx.xx	shared DES key with server
/etc/kerberosIV/principal*	Kerberos database
/etc/kerberosIV/register_keys	directory containing keys for trusted hosts

SEE ALSO

registerd(8), kerberos(1)

DIAGNOSTICS

''Already exists'', if the user already exists in the Kerberos database.

''Permission Denied'', if the host on which register is being run is untrusted.

HISTORY

The **registerd** utility first appeared in 4.4BSD.

NAME

renice – alter priority of running processes

SYNOPSIS

renice *priority* [[**-p**] *pid* ...] [[**-g**] *pgrp* ...] [[**-u**] *user* ...]

DESCRIPTION

Renice alters the scheduling priority of one or more running processes. The following *who* parameters are interpreted as process ID's, process group ID's, or user names. **Renice**'ing a process group causes all processes in the process group to have their scheduling priority altered. **Renice**'ing a user causes all processes owned by the user to have their scheduling priority altered. By default, the processes to be affected are specified by their process ID's.

Options supported by **renice**:

-g Force *who* parameters to be interpreted as process group ID's.

-u Force the *who* parameters to be interpreted as user names.

-p Resets the *who* interpretation to be (the default) process ID's.

For example,

```
renice +1 987 -u daemon root -p 32
```

would change the priority of process ID's 987 and 32, and all processes owned by users daemon and root.

Users other than the super-user may only alter the priority of processes they own, and can only monotonically increase their "nice value" within the range 0 to PRIO_MAX (20). (This prevents overriding administrative fiats.) The super-user may alter the priority of any process and set the priority to any value in the range PRIO_MIN (–20) to PRIO_MAX. Useful priorities are: 20 (the affected processes will run only when nothing else in the system wants to), 0 (the "base" scheduling priority), anything negative (to make things go very fast).

FILES

/etc/passwd to map user names to user ID's

SEE ALSO

getpriority(2), setpriority(2)

BUGS

Non super-users can not increase scheduling priorities of their own processes, even if they were the ones that decreased the priorities in the first place.

HISTORY

The **renice** command appeared in 4.0BSD.

NAME

repquota – summarize quotas for a file system

SYNOPSIS

repquota [**–g**] [**–u**] [**–v**] *filesystem ...*
repquota [**–g**] [**–u**] [**–v**] **–a**

DESCRIPTION

Repquota prints a summary of the disk usage and quotas for the specified file systems.

Available options:

–a Print the quotas of all the filesystems listed in /etc/fstab.

–g Print only group quotas (the default is to print both group and user quotas if they exist).

–u Print only user quotas (the default is to print both group and user quotas if they exist).

–v Print a header line before printing each filesystem quotas.

For each user or group, the current number files and amount of space (in kilobytes) is printed, along with any quotas created with edquota(8).

Only members of the operator group or the super-user may use this command.

FILES

quota.user at the filesystem root with user quotas
quota.group at the filesystem root with group quotas
/etc/fstab for file system names and locations

SEE ALSO

quota(1), quotactl(2), fstab(5), edquota(8), quotacheck(8), quotaon(8)

DIAGNOSTICS

Various messages about inaccessible files; self-explanatory.

HISTORY

The **repquota** command appeared in 4.2BSD.

M8

NAME

restore – restore files or file systems from backups made with dump

SYNOPSIS

restore *key* [*name* ...]

DESCRIPTION

The **restore** command performs the inverse function of dump(8). A full backup of a file system may be restored and subsequent incremental backups layered on top of it. Single files and directory subtrees may be restored from full or partial backups. **Restore** works across a network; to do this see the **-f** flag described below. The actions of **restore** are controlled by the given **key**, which is a string of characters containing at most one function letter and possibly one or more function modifiers. Other arguments to the command are file or directory names specifying the files that are to be restored. Unless the **h** key is specified (see below), the appearance of a directory name refers to the files and (recursively) subdirectories of that directory.

The function portion of the key is specified by one of the following letters:

r Restore (rebuild a file system). The target file system should be made pristine with newfs(8), mounted and the user cd'd into the pristine file system before starting the restoration of the initial level 0 backup. If the level 0 restores successfully, the **r** key may be used to restore any necessary incremental backups on top of the level 0. The **r** key precludes an interactive file extraction and can be detrimental to one's health if not used carefully (not to mention the disk). An example:

```
newfs /dev/rrp0g eagle
mount /dev/rp0g /mnt
cd /mnt

restore rf /dev/rst8
```

Note that **restore** leaves a file restoresymtable in the root directory to pass information between incremental restore passes. This file should be removed when the last incremental has been restored.

Restore, in conjunction with newfs(8) and dump(8), may be used to modify file system parameters such as size or block size.

R **Restore** requests a particular tape of a multi volume set on which to restart a full restore (see the **r** key above). This is useful if the restore has been interrupted.

x The named files are read from the given media. If a named file matches a directory whose contents are on the backup and the **h** key is not specified, the directory is recursively extracted. The owner, modification time, and mode are restored (if possible). If no file argument is given, then the root directory is extracted, which results in the entire content of the backup being extracted, unless the **h** key has been specified.

t The names of the specified files are listed if they occur on the backup. If no file argument is given, then the root directory is listed, which results in the entire content of the backup being listed, unless the **h** key has been specified. Note that the **t** key replaces the function of the old dumpdir(8) program.

i This mode allows interactive restoration of files from a dump. After reading in the directory information from the dump, **restore** provides a shell like interface that allows the user to move around the directory tree selecting files to be extracted. The available commands are given below; for those commands that require an argument, the default is the current directory.

add [*arg*]
The current directory or specified argument is added to the list of files to be extracted. If a directory is specified, then it and all its descendents are added to the extraction list (unless the **h** key is specified on the command line). Files that are on the extraction list are prepended with a ''*'' when they are listed by **ls**.

cd *arg* Change the current working directory to the specified argument.

delete [*arg*]
The current directory or specified argument is deleted from the list of files to be extracted. If a directory is specified, then it and all its descendents are deleted from the extraction list (unless the **h** key is specified on the command line). The most expedient way to extract most of the files from a directory is to add the directory to the extraction list and then delete those files that are not needed.

extract All the files that are on the extraction list are extracted from the dump. **Restore** will ask which volume the user wishes to mount. The fastest way to extract a few files is to start with the last volume, and work towards the first volume.

help List a summary of the available commands.

ls [*arg*] List the current or specified directory. Entries that are directories are appended with a ''/''. Entries that have been marked for extraction are prepended with a ''*''. If the verbose key is set the inode number of each entry is also listed.

pwd Print the full pathname of the current working directory.

quit Restore immediately exits, even if the extraction list is not empty.

setmodes All the directories that have been added to the extraction list have their owner, modes, and times set; nothing is extracted from the dump. This is useful for cleaning up after a restore has been prematurely aborted.

verbose The sense of the **v** key is toggled. When set, the verbose key causes the **ls** command to list the inode numbers of all entries. It also causes **restore** to print out information about each file as it is extracted.

The following characters may be used in addition to the letter that selects the function desired.

b The next argument to **restore** is used as the block size of the media (in kilobytes). If the **-b** option is not specified, **restore** tries to determine the media block size dynamically.

f The next argument to **restore** is used as the name of the archive instead of /dev/rmt?. If the name of the file is of the form ''host:file'', **restore** reads from the named file on the remote host using rmt(8). If the name of the file is '−', **restore** reads from standard input. Thus, dump(8) and **restore** can be used in a pipeline to dump and restore a file system with the command

```
dump 0f - /usr | (cd /mnt; restore xf -)
```

h **Restore** extracts the actual directory, rather than the files that it references. This prevents hierarchical restoration of complete subtrees from the dump.

m **Restore** will extract by inode numbers rather than by file name. This is useful if only a few files are being extracted, and one wants to avoid regenerating the complete pathname to the file.

s The next argument to **restore** is a number which selects the file on a multi-file dump tape. File numbering starts at 1.

v Normally **restore** does its work silently. The **v** (verbose) key causes it to type the name of each file it treats preceded by its file type.

y **Restore** will not ask whether it should abort the restore if it gets an error. It will always try to skip over the bad block(s) and continue as best it can.

DIAGNOSTICS

Complaints about bad key characters.

Complaints if it gets a read error. If **y** has been specified, or the user responds 'y', **restore** will attempt to continue the restore.

If a backup was made using more than one tape volume, **restore** will notify the user when it is time to mount the next volume. If the **x** or **i** key has been specified, **restore** will also ask which volume the user wishes to mount. The fastest way to extract a few files is to start with the last volume, and work towards the first volume.

There are numerous consistency checks that can be listed by **restore**. Most checks are self-explanatory or can ''never happen''. Common errors are given below.

Converting to new file system format.
: A dump tape created from the old file system has been loaded. It is automatically converted to the new file system format.

<filename>: not found on tape
: The specified file name was listed in the tape directory, but was not found on the tape. This is caused by tape read errors while looking for the file, and from using a dump tape created on an active file system.

expected next file <inumber>, got <inumber>
: A file that was not listed in the directory showed up. This can occur when using a dump created on an active file system.

Incremental dump too low
: When doing incremental restore, a dump that was written before the previous incremental dump, or that has too low an incremental level has been loaded.

Incremental dump too high
: When doing incremental restore, a dump that does not begin its coverage where the previous incremental dump left off, or that has too high an incremental level has been loaded.

Tape read error while restoring <filename>
Tape read error while skipping over inode <inumber>
Tape read error while trying to resynchronize
: A tape (or other media) read error has occurred. If a file name is specified, then its contents are probably partially wrong. If an inode is being skipped or the tape is trying to resynchronize, then no extracted files have been corrupted, though files may not be found on the tape.

resync restore, skipped <num> blocks
: After a dump read error, **restore** may have to resynchronize itself. This message lists the number of blocks that were skipped over.

FILES

`/dev/rmt?`	the default tape drive
`/tmp/rstdir*`	file containing directories on the tape.
`/tmp/rstmode*`	owner, mode, and time stamps for directories.
`./restoresymtable`	information passed between incremental restores.

SEE ALSO

`dump`(8), `newfs`(8), `mount`(8), `mkfs`(8), `rmt`(8)

BUGS

Restore can get confused when doing incremental restores from dump that were made on active file systems.

A level zero dump must be done after a full restore. Because restore runs in user code, it has no control over inode allocation; thus a full restore must be done to get a new set of directories reflecting the new inode numbering, even though the contents of the files is unchanged.

HISTORY

The **restore** command appeared in 4.2BSD.

M8

NAME

rexecd – remote execution server

SYNOPSIS

rexecd

DESCRIPTION

Rexecd is the server for the `rexec(3)` routine. The server provides remote execution facilities with authentication based on user names and passwords.

Rexecd listens for service requests at the port indicated in the ''exec'' service specification; see `services(5)`. When a service request is received the following protocol is initiated:

1. The server reads characters from the socket up to a NUL ('\0') byte. The resultant string is interpreted as an ASCII number, base 10.
2. If the number received in step 1 is non-zero, it is interpreted as the port number of a secondary stream to be used for the *stderr*. A second connection is then created to the specified port on the client's machine.
3. A NUL terminated user name of at most 16 characters is retrieved on the initial socket.
4. A NUL terminated, unencrypted password of at most 16 characters is retrieved on the initial socket.
5. A NUL terminated command to be passed to a shell is retrieved on the initial socket. The length of the command is limited by the upper bound on the size of the system's argument list.
6. **Rexecd** then validates the user as is done at login time and, if the authentication was successful, changes to the user's home directory, and establishes the user and group protections of the user. If any of these steps fail the connection is aborted with a diagnostic message returned.
7. A NUL byte is returned on the initial socket and the command line is passed to the normal login shell of the user. The shell inherits the network connections established by **rexecd**.

DIAGNOSTICS

Except for the last one listed below, all diagnostic messages are returned on the initial socket, after which any network connections are closed. An error is indicated by a leading byte with a value of 1 (0 is returned in step 7 above upon successful completion of all the steps prior to the command execution).

username too long
The name is longer than 16 characters.

password too long
The password is longer than 16 characters.

command too long
The command line passed exceeds the size of the argument list (as configured into the system).

Login incorrect.
No password file entry for the user name existed.

Password incorrect.
The wrong password was supplied.

No remote directory.
The `chdir` command to the home directory failed.

Try again.
A `fork` by the server failed.

<shellname>: ...
The user's login shell could not be started. This message is returned on the connection associated with the *stderr*, and is not preceded by a flag byte.

SEE ALSO

`rexec`(3)

BUGS

Indicating ''Login incorrect'' as opposed to ''Password incorrect'' is a security breach which allows people to probe a system for users with null passwords.

A facility to allow all data and password exchanges to be encrypted should be present.

HISTORY

The **rexecd** command appeared in 4.2BSD.

NAME

rlogind – remote login server

SYNOPSIS

rlogind [**-aln**]

DESCRIPTION

Rlogind is the server for the rlogin(1) program. The server provides a remote login facility with authentication based on privileged port numbers from trusted hosts.

Options supported by **rlogind**:

-a Ask hostname for verification.

-l Prevent any authentication based on the user's ".rhosts" file, unless the user is logging in as the superuser.

-n Disable keep-alive messages.

Rlogind listens for service requests at the port indicated in the "login" service specification; see services(5). When a service request is received the following protocol is initiated:

1. The server checks the client's source port. If the port is not in the range 512-1023, the server aborts the connection.

2. The server checks the client's source address and requests the corresponding host name (see gethostbyaddr(3), hosts(5) and named(8)). If the hostname cannot be determined, the dot-notation representation of the host address is used. If the hostname is in the same domain as the server (according to the last two components of the domain name), or if the **-a** option is given, the addresses for the hostname are requested, verifying that the name and address correspond. Normal authentication is bypassed if the address verification fails.

Once the source port and address have been checked, **rlogind** proceeds with the authentication process described in rshd(8). It then allocates a pseudo terminal (see pty(4)), and manipulates file descriptors so that the slave half of the pseudo terminal becomes the *stdin*, *stdout*, and *stderr* for a login process. The login process is an instance of the login(1) program, invoked with the **-f** option if authentication has succeeded. If automatic authentication fails, the user is prompted to log in as if on a standard terminal line.

The parent of the login process manipulates the master side of the pseudo terminal, operating as an intermediary between the login process and the client instance of the rlogin program. In normal operation, the packet protocol described in pty(4) is invoked to provide ^S/^Q type facilities and propagate interrupt signals to the remote programs. The login process propagates the client terminal's baud rate and terminal type, as found in the environment variable, 'TERM'; see environ(7). The screen or window size of the terminal is requested from the client, and window size changes from the client are propagated to the pseudo terminal.

Transport-level keepalive messages are enabled unless the **-n** option is present. The use of keepalive messages allows sessions to be timed out if the client crashes or becomes unreachable.

DIAGNOSTICS

All initial diagnostic messages are indicated by a leading byte with a value of 1, after which any network connections are closed. If there are no errors before login is invoked, a null byte is returned as in indication of success.

Try again.

A fork by the server failed.

SEE ALSO

`login(1)`, `ruserok(3)`, `rshd(8)`

BUGS

The authentication procedure used here assumes the integrity of each client machine and the connecting medium. This is insecure, but is useful in an ''open'' environment.

A facility to allow all data exchanges to be encrypted should be present.

A more extensible protocol should be used.

HISTORY

The **rlogind** command appeared in 4.2BSD.

M8

NAME

rmail – handle remote mail received via uucp

SYNOPSIS

rmail *user ...*

DESCRIPTION

Rmail interprets incoming mail received via uucp(1), collapsing ''From'' lines in the form generated by mail.local(8) into a single line of the form ''return-path!sender'', and passing the processed mail on to sendmail(8).

Rmail is explicitly designed for use with uucp and sendmail.

SEE ALSO

uucp(1), mail.local(8), sendmail(8)

HISTORY

The **rmail** program appeared in 4.2BSD.

BUGS

Rmail should not reside in /bin.

M8

NAME

rmt – remote magtape protocol module

SYNOPSIS

rmt

DESCRIPTION

Rmt is a program used by the remote dump and restore programs in manipulating a magnetic tape drive through an interprocess communication connection. **Rmt** is normally started up with an `rexec(3)` or `rcmd(3)` call.

The **rmt** program accepts requests specific to the manipulation of magnetic tapes, performs the commands, then responds with a status indication. All responses are in ASCII and in one of two forms. Successful commands have responses of:

> **A***number*\n

Number is an ASCII representation of a decimal number. Unsuccessful commands are responded to with:

> **E***error-number*\n*error-message*\n

Error-number is one of the possible error numbers described in `intro(2)` and *error-message* is the corresponding error string as printed from a call to `perror(3)`. The protocol is comprised of the following commands, which are sent as indicated - no spaces are supplied between the command and its arguments, or between its arguments, and '\n' indicates that a newline should be supplied:

O*device*\n*mode*\n
: Open the specified *device* using the indicated *mode*. *Device* is a full pathname and *mode* is an ASCII representation of a decimal number suitable for passing to `open(2)`. If a device had already been opened, it is closed before a new open is performed.

C*device*\n
: Close the currently open device. The *device* specified is ignored.

L*whence*\n*offset*\n
: Perform an `lseek(2)` operation using the specified parameters. The response value is that returned from the `lseek` call.

W*count*\n
: Write data onto the open device. **Rmt** reads *count* bytes from the connection, aborting if a premature end-of-file is encountered. The response value is that returned from the `write(2)` call.

R*count*\n
: Read *count* bytes of data from the open device. If *count* exceeds the size of the data buffer (10 kilobytes), it is truncated to the data buffer size. **rmt** then performs the requested `read(2)` and responds with **A***count-read*\n if the read was successful; otherwise an error in the standard format is returned. If the read was successful, the data read is then sent.

I*operation*\n*count*\n
: Perform a `MTIOCOP` `ioctl(2)` command using the specified parameters. The parameters are interpreted as the ASCII representations of the decimal values to place in the *mt_op* and *mt_count* fields of the structure used in the `ioctl` call. The return value is the *count* parameter when the operation is successful.

S Return the status of the open device, as obtained with a `MTIOCGET` `ioctl` call. If the operation was successful, an ''ack'' is sent with the size of the status buffer, then the status buffer is sent (in binary).

Any other command causes **rmt** to exit.

DIAGNOSTICS

All responses are of the form described above.

SEE ALSO

rcmd(3), rexec(3), mtio(4), rdump(8), rrestore(8)

BUGS

People should be discouraged from using this for a remote file access protocol.

HISTORY

The **rmt** command appeared in 4.2BSD.

M8

NAME

route – manually manipulate the routing tables.

SYNOPSIS

route [**-nqv**] *command* [[*modifiers*] *args*]

DESCRIPTION

Route is a utility used to manually manipulate the network routing tables. It normally is not needed, as a system routing table management daemon such as routed(8), should tend to this task.

The **route**: utility supports a limited number of general options, but a rich command language, enabling the user to specify any arbitrary request that could be delivered via the programmatic interface discussed in route(4).

-n Bypasses attempts to print host and network names symbolically when reporting actions. (The process of translating between symbolic names and numerical equivalents can be quite time consuming, and may require correct operation of the network; thus it may be expedient to forgo this, especially when attempting to repair networking operations),

-v (verbose) Print additional details.

-q Suppress all output.

The **route**: utility provides six commands:

add Add a route.
flush Remove all routes.
delete Delete a specific route.
change Change aspects of a route (such as its gateway).
get Lookup and display the route for a destination.
monitor Continuously report any changes to the routing information base, routing lookup misses, or suspected network partitionings.

The monitor command has the syntax

route [**-n**] **monitor**

The flush command has the syntax

route [**-n**] **flush** [*family*]

If the **flush** command is specified, **route** will "flush" the routing tables of all gateway entries. When the address family may is specified by any of the **-osi**, **-xns**, or **-inet** modifiers, only routes having destinations with addresses in the delineated family will be deleted.

The other commands have the following syntax:

route [**-n**] *command* [**-net** | **-host**] *destination gateway*

where *destination* is the destination host or network, *gateway* is the next-hop intermediary via which packets should be routed. Routes to a particular host may be distinguished from those to a network by interpreting the Internet address specified as the *destination argument*. The optional modifiers **-net** and **-host** force the destination to be interpreted as a network or a host, respectively. Otherwise, if the *destination* has a "local address part" of INADDR_ANY , or if the *destination* is the symbolic name of a network, then the route is assumed to be to a network; otherwise, it is presumed to be a route to a host.

For example, `128.32` is interpreted as **-host** `128.0.0.32`; `128.32.130` is interpreted as **-host** `128.32.0.130`; **-net** `128.32` is interpreted as `128.32.0.0`; and **-net** `128.32.130` is interpreted as `128.32.130.0`.

If the destination is directly reachable via an interface requiring no intermediary system to act as a gateway, the **-interface** modifier should be specified; the gateway given is the address of this host on the common network, indicating the interface to be used for transmission.

The optional modifiers **-xns**, **-osi**, and **-link** specify that all subsequent addresses are in the XNS OSI address families, or are specified as link-level addresses, and the names must be numeric specifications rather than symbolic names.

The optional **-netmask** qualifier is intended to achieve the effect of an OSI ESIS redirect with the netmask option, or to manually add subnet routes with netmasks different from that of the implied network interface (as would otherwise be communicated using the OSPF or ISIS routing protocols). One specifies an additional ensuing address parameter (to be interpreted as a network mask). The implicit network mask generated in the AF_INET case can be overridden by making sure this option follows the destination parameter.

Routes have associated flags which influence operation of the protocols when sending to destinations matched by the routes. These flags may be set (or sometimes cleared) by indicating the following corresponding modifiers:

```
-cloning   RTF_CLONING     - generates a new route on use
-xresolve  RTF_XRESOLVE    - emit mesg on use (for external lookup)
-iface    ~RTF_GATEWAY     - destination is directly reachable
-static    RTF_STATIC      - manually added route
-nostatic ~RTF_STATIC      - pretend route added by kernel or daemon
-reject    RTF_REJECT      - emit an ICMP unreachable when matched
-blackhole RTF_BLACKHOLE   - silently discard pkts (during updates)
-proto1    RTF_PROTO1      - set protocol specific routing flag #1
-proto2    RTF_PROTO2      - set protocol specific routing flag #2
-llinfo    RTF_LLINFO      - validly translates proto addr to link addr
```

The optional modifiers **-rtt**, **-rttvar**, **-sendpipe**, **-recvpipe**, **-mtu**, **-hopcount**, **-expire**, and **-ssthresh** provide initial values to quantities maintained in the routing entry by transport level protocols, such as TCP or TP4. These may be individually locked by preceding each such modifier to be locked by the **-lock** meta-modifier, or one can specify that all ensuing metrics may be locked by the **-lockrest** meta-modifier.

In a **change** or **add** command where the destination and gateway are not sufficient to specify the route (as in the ISO case where several interfaces may have the same address), the **-ifp** or **-ifa** modifiers may be used to determine the interface or interface address.

All symbolic names specified for a *destination* or *gateway* are looked up first as a host name using `gethostbyname`(3). If this lookup fails, `getnetbyname`(3) is then used to interpret the name as that of a network.

Route uses a routing socket and the new message types RTM_ADD, RTM_DELETE, RTM_GET, and RTM_CHANGE. As such, only the super-user may modify the routing tables.

DIAGNOSTICS

add [host | network] %s: gateway %s flags %x

The specified route is being added to the tables. The values printed are from the routing table entry supplied in the `ioctl`(2) call. If the gateway address used was not the primary address of the gateway (the first one returned by `gethostbyname`(3)), the gateway address is printed numerically as well as symbolically.

delete [host &| network] %s: gateway %s flags %x

As above, but when deleting an entry.

%s %s done

When the **flush** command is specified, each routing table entry deleted is indicated with a message of this form.

Network is unreachable

An attempt to add a route failed because the gateway listed was not on a directly-connected network. The next-hop gateway must be given.

not in table

A delete operation was attempted for an entry which wasn't present in the tables.

routing table overflow

An add operation was attempted, but the system was low on resources and was unable to allocate memory to create the new entry.

SEE ALSO

`netintro`(4), `route`(4), `esis`(4), `routed`(8), `XNSrouted`(8)

HISTORY

The **route** command appeared in 4.2BSD.

BUGS

The first paragraph may have slightly exaggerated `routed`'s abilities.

NAME

routed – network routing daemon

SYNOPSIS

routed [**-d**] [**-g**] [**-q**] [**-s**] [**-t**] [*logfile*]

DESCRIPTION

Routed is invoked at boot time to manage the network routing tables. The routing daemon uses a variant of the Xerox NS Routing Information Protocol in maintaining up to date kernel routing table entries. It used a generalized protocol capable of use with multiple address types, but is currently used only for Internet routing within a cluster of networks.

In normal operation **routed** listens on the udp(4) socket for the route(8) service (see services(5)) for routing information packets. If the host is an internetwork router, it periodically supplies copies of its routing tables to any directly connected hosts and networks.

When **routed** is started, it uses the SIOCGIFCONF ioctl(2) to find those directly connected interfaces configured into the system and marked "up" (the software loopback interface is ignored). If multiple interfaces are present, it is assumed that the host will forward packets between networks. **Routed** then transmits a *request* packet on each interface (using a broadcast packet if the interface supports it) and enters a loop, listening for *request* and *response* packets from other hosts.

When a *request* packet is received, **routed** formulates a reply based on the information maintained in its internal tables. The *response* packet generated contains a list of known routes, each marked with a "hop count" metric (a count of 16, or greater, is considered "infinite"). The metric associated with each route returned provides a metric *relative to the sender*.

Response packets received by **routed** are used to update the routing tables if one of the following conditions is satisfied:

1. No routing table entry exists for the destination network or host, and the metric indicates the destination is "reachable" (i.e. the hop count is not infinite).
2. The source host of the packet is the same as the router in the existing routing table entry. That is, updated information is being received from the very internetwork router through which packets for the destination are being routed.
3. The existing entry in the routing table has not been updated for some time (defined to be 90 seconds) and the route is at least as cost effective as the current route.
4. The new route describes a shorter route to the destination than the one currently stored in the routing tables; the metric of the new route is compared against the one stored in the table to decide this.

When an update is applied, **routed** records the change in its internal tables and updates the kernel routing table. The change is reflected in the next *response* packet sent.

In addition to processing incoming packets, **routed** also periodically checks the routing table entries. If an entry has not been updated for 3 minutes, the entry's metric is set to infinity and marked for deletion. Deletions are delayed an additional 60 seconds to insure the invalidation is propagated throughout the local internet.

Hosts acting as internetwork routers gratuitously supply their routing tables every 30 seconds to all directly connected hosts and networks. The response is sent to the broadcast address on nets capable of that function, to the destination address on point-to-point links, and to the router's own address on other networks. The normal routing tables are bypassed when sending gratuitous responses. The reception of responses on each network is used to determine that the network and interface are functioning correctly. If no response is received on an interface, another route may be chosen to route around the interface, or the route may be dropped if no alternative is available.

Options supported by **routed**:

–d Enable additional debugging information to be logged, such as bad packets received.

–g This flag is used on internetwork routers to offer a route to the ''default'' destination. This is typically used on a gateway to the Internet, or on a gateway that uses another routing protocol whose routes are not reported to other local routers.

–s Supplying this option forces **routed** to supply routing information whether it is acting as an internetwork router or not. This is the default if multiple network interfaces are present, or if a point-to-point link is in use.

–q This is the opposite of the **–s** option.

–t If the **–t** option is specified, all packets sent or received are printed on the standard output. In addition, **routed** will not divorce itself from the controlling terminal so that interrupts from the keyboard will kill the process.

Any other argument supplied is interpreted as the name of file in which **routed**´s actions should be logged. This log contains information about any changes to the routing tables and, if not tracing all packets, a history of recent messages sent and received which are related to the changed route.

In addition to the facilities described above, **routed** supports the notion of ''distant'' *passive* and *active* gateways. When **routed** is started up, it reads the file /etc/gateways to find gateways which may not be located using only information from the SIOGIFCONF ioctl(2). Gateways specified in this manner should be marked passive if they are not expected to exchange routing information, while gateways marked active should be willing to exchange routing information (i.e. they should have a **routed** process running on the machine). Routes through passive gateways are installed in the kernel's routing tables once upon startup. Such routes are not included in any routing information transmitted. Active gateways are treated equally to network interfaces. Routing information is distributed to the gateway and if no routing information is received for a period of time, the associated route is deleted. Gateways marked *external* are also passive, but are not placed in the kernel routing table nor are they included in routing updates. The function of external entries is to inform **routed** that another routing process will install such a route, and that alternate routes to that destination should not be installed. Such entries are only required when both routers may learn of routes to the same destination.

The /etc/gateways is comprised of a series of lines, each in the following format:

<net | host> *name1* **gateway** *name2* **metric** *value* **<passive | active | external>**

The **net** or **host** keyword indicates if the route is to a network or specific host.

Name1 is the name of the destination network or host. This may be a symbolic name located in /etc/networks or /etc/hosts (or, if started after named(8), known to the name server), or an Internet address specified in ''dot'' notation; see inet(3).

Name2 is the name or address of the gateway to which messages should be forwarded.

Value is a metric indicating the hop count to the destination host or network.

One of the keywords **passive**, **active** or **external** indicates if the gateway should be treated as *passive* or *active* (as described above), or whether the gateway is *external* to the scope of the **routed** protocol.

Internetwork routers that are directly attached to the Arpanet or Milnet should use the Exterior Gateway Protocol (EGP) to gather routing information rather then using a static routing table of passive gateways. EGP is required in order to provide routes for local networks to the rest of the Internet system.

FILES

`/etc/gateways` for distant gateways

SEE ALSO

udp(4), icmp(4), XNSrouted(8), htable(8)

Internet Transport Protocols, XSIS 028112, Xerox System Integration Standard.

BUGS

The kernel's routing tables may not correspond to those of **routed** when redirects change or add routes. **Routed** should note any redirects received by reading the ICMP packets received via a raw socket.

Routed should incorporate other routing protocols, such as Xerox NS (XNSrouted(8)) and EGP. Using separate processes for each requires configuration options to avoid redundant or competing routes.

Routed should listen to intelligent interfaces, such as an IMP, to gather more information. It does not always detect unidirectional failures in network interfaces (e.g., when the output side fails).

HISTORY

The **routed** command appeared in 4.2BSD.

M8

NAME

rshd – remote shell server

SYNOPSIS

rshd [**-alnL**]

DESCRIPTION

The **rshd** server is the server for the rcmd(3) routine and, consequently, for the rsh(1) program. The server provides remote execution facilities with authentication based on privileged port numbers from trusted hosts.

The **rshd** server listens for service requests at the port indicated in the ''cmd'' service specification; see services(5). When a service request is received the following protocol is initiated:

1. The server checks the client's source port. If the port is not in the range 512-1023, the server aborts the connection.
2. The server reads characters from the socket up to a null ('\0') byte. The resultant string is interpreted as an ASCII number, base 10.
3. If the number received in step 2 is non-zero, it is interpreted as the port number of a secondary stream to be used for the *stderr*. A second connection is then created to the specified port on the client's machine. The source port of this second connection is also in the range 512-1023.
4. The server checks the client's source address and requests the corresponding host name (see gethostbyaddr(3), hosts(5) and named(8)). If the hostname cannot be determined, the dot-notation representation of the host address is used. If the hostname is in the same domain as the server (according to the last two components of the domain name), or if the **-a** option is given, the addresses for the hostname are requested, verifying that the name and address correspond. If address verification fails, the connection is aborted with the message, ''Host address mismatch.''
5. A null terminated user name of at most 16 characters is retrieved on the initial socket. This user name is interpreted as the user identity on the *client*'s machine.
6. A null terminated user name of at most 16 characters is retrieved on the initial socket. This user name is interpreted as a user identity to use on the **server**'s machine.
7. A null terminated command to be passed to a shell is retrieved on the initial socket. The length of the command is limited by the upper bound on the size of the system's argument list.
8. **Rshd** then validates the user using ruserok(3), which uses the file /etc/hosts.equiv and the .rhosts file found in the user's home directory. The **-l** option prevents ruserok(3) from doing any validation based on the user's ''.rhosts'' file, unless the user is the superuser.
9. If the file /etc/nologin exists and the user is not the superuser, the connection is closed.
10. A null byte is returned on the initial socket and the command line is passed to the normal login shell of the user. The shell inherits the network connections established by **rshd**.

Transport-level keepalive messages are enabled unless the **-n** option is present. The use of keepalive messages allows sessions to be timed out if the client crashes or becomes unreachable.

The **-L** option causes all successful accesses to be logged to syslogd(8) as auth.info messages.

DIAGNOSTICS

Except for the last one listed below, all diagnostic messages are returned on the initial socket, after which any network connections are closed. An error is indicated by a leading byte with a value of 1 (0 is returned in step 10 above upon successful completion of all the steps prior to the execution of the login shell).

Locuser too long.
The name of the user on the client's machine is longer than 16 characters.

Ruser too long.
The name of the user on the remote machine is longer than 16 characters.

Command too long.
The command line passed exceeds the size of the argument list (as configured into the system).

Login incorrect.
No password file entry for the user name existed.

Remote directory.
The `chdir` command to the home directory failed.

Permission denied.
The authentication procedure described above failed.

Can't make pipe.
The pipe needed for the *stderr*, wasn't created.

Can't fork; try again.
A `fork` by the server failed.

<shellname>: ...
The user's login shell could not be started. This message is returned on the connection associated with the *stderr*, and is not preceded by a flag byte.

SEE ALSO

`rsh(1)`, `rcmd(3)`, `ruserok(3)`

BUGS

The authentication procedure used here assumes the integrity of each client machine and the connecting medium. This is insecure, but is useful in an ''open'' environment.

A facility to allow all data exchanges to be encrypted should be present.

A more extensible protocol (such as Telnet) should be used.

M8

NAME

rwhod – system status server

SYNOPSIS

rwhod

DESCRIPTION

Rwhod is the server which maintains the database used by the rwho(1) and ruptime(1) programs. Its operation is predicated on the ability to *broadcast* messages on a network.

Rwhod operates as both a producer and consumer of status information. As a producer of information it periodically queries the state of the system and constructs status messages which are broadcast on a network. As a consumer of information, it listens for other **rwhod** servers' status messages, validating them, then recording them in a collection of files located in the directory /var/rwho.

The server transmits and receives messages at the port indicated in the "rwho" service specification; see services(5). The messages sent and received, are of the form:

```
struct outmp {
        char    out_line[8];            /* tty name */
        char    out_name[8];            /* user id */
        long    out_time;               /* time on */
};

struct whod {
        char    wd_vers;
        char    wd_type;
        char    wd_fill[2];
        int     wd_sendtime;
        int     wd_recvtime;
        char    wd_hostname[32];
        int     wd_loadav[3];
        int     wd_boottime;
        struct  whoent {
                struct  outmp we_utmp;
                int     we_idle;
        } wd_we[1024 / sizeof (struct whoent)];
};
```

All fields are converted to network byte order prior to transmission. The load averages are as calculated by the w(1) program, and represent load averages over the 5, 10, and 15 minute intervals prior to a server's transmission; they are multiplied by 100 for representation in an integer. The host name included is that returned by the gethostname(2) system call, with any trailing domain name omitted. The array at the end of the message contains information about the users logged in to the sending machine. This information includes the contents of the utmp(5) entry for each non-idle terminal line and a value indicating the time in seconds since a character was last received on the terminal line.

Messages received by the rwho server are discarded unless they originated at an rwho server's port. In addition, if the host's name, as specified in the message, contains any unprintable ASCII characters, the message is discarded. Valid messages received by **rwhod** are placed in files named whod.hostname in the directory /var/rwho. These files contain only the most recent message, in the format described above.

Status messages are generated approximately once every 3 minutes. **Rwhod** performs an `nlist(3)` on `/vmunix` every 30 minutes to guard against the possibility that this file is not the system image currently operating.

SEE ALSO

`rwho(1)`, `ruptime(1)`

BUGS

There should be a way to relay status information between networks. Status information should be sent only upon request rather than continuously. People often interpret the server dying or network communication failures as a machine going down.

HISTORY

The **rwhod** command appeared in 4.2BSD.

M8

NAME

sa, accton – system accounting

SYNOPSIS

sa [**–abcdDfijkKlnrstuv**] [**–S** savacctfile] [**–U** usracctfile] [file]

accton [file]

DESCRIPTION

With an argument naming an existing *file, accton* causes system accounting information for every process executed to be placed at the end of the file. If no argument is given, accounting is turned off.

Sa reports on, cleans up, and generally maintains accounting files.

Sa is able to condense the information in */var/account/acct* into a summary file */var/account/savacct* which contains a count of the number of times each command was called and the time resources consumed. This condensation is desirable because on a large system */var/account/acct* can grow by 100 blocks per day. The summary file is normally read before the accounting file, so the reports include all available information.

If a file name is given as the last argument, that file will be treated as the accounting file; */var/account/acct* is the default.

Output fields are labeled: ''cpu'' for the sum of user+system time (in minutes), ''re'' for real time (also in minutes), ''k'' for cpu-time averaged core usage (in 1k units), ''avio'' for average number of i/o operations per execution. With options fields labeled ''tio'' for total i/o operations, ''k*sec'' for cpu storage integral (kilo-core seconds), ''u'' and ''s'' for user and system cpu time alone (both in minutes) will sometimes appear.

There are near a googol of options:

a Print all command names, even those containing unprintable characters and those used only once. By default, those are placed under the name '***other.'

b Sort output by sum of user and system time divided by number of calls. Default sort is by sum of user and system times.

c Besides total user, system, and real time for each command print percentage of total time over all commands.

d Sort by average number of disk i/o operations.

D Print and sort by total number of disk i/o operations.

f Force no interactive threshold compression with –v flag.

i Don't read in summary file.

j Instead of total minutes time for each category, give seconds per call.

k Sort by cpu-time average memory usage.

K Print and sort by cpu-storage integral.

l Separate system and user time; normally they are combined.

m Print number of processes and number of CPU minutes for each user.

n Sort by number of calls.

r Reverse order of sort.

s Merge accounting file into summary file */var/account/savacct* when done.

t For each command report ratio of real time to the sum of user and system times.

u Superseding all other flags, print for each command in the accounting file the user ID and command name.

v Followed by a number *n*, types the name of each command used *n* times or fewer. Await a reply from the terminal; if it begins with 'y', add the command to the category '**junk**.' This is used to strip out garbage.

S The following filename is used as the command summary file instead of */var/account/savacct.*

U The following filename is used instead of */var/account/usracct* to accumulate the per-user statistics printed by the –m option.

FILES

/var/account/acct	raw accounting
/var/account/savacct	summary
/var/account/usracct	per-user summary

SEE ALSO

ac(8), acct(2)

BUGS

The number of options to this program is absurd.

M8

NAME

savecore – save a core dump of the operating system

SYNOPSIS

savecore -c
savecore [**-fvz**] [**-N** *system*] *directory*

DESCRIPTION

Savecore copies the currently running kernel and its associated core dump into *directory*, and enters a reboot message and information about the core dump into the system log.

The options are as follows:

-c Clears the dump, so that future invocations of **savecore** will ignore it.

-f Forces a dump to be taken even if the dump doesn't appear correct or there is insufficient disk space.

-N Use *system* as the kernel instead of the default ''/vmunix''.

-v Prints out some additional debugging information.

-z Compresses the core dump and kernel (see compress(1)).

Savecore checks the core dump in various ways to make sure that it is current and that it corresponds to the currently running system. If it passes these checks, it saves the core image in *directory*/vmcore.# and the system in *directory*/vmunix.# The ''#'' is the number from the first line of the file *directory*/bounds, and it is incremented and stored back into the file each time **savecore** successfully runs.

Savecore also checks the available disk space before attempting to make the copies. If there is insufficient disk space in the filesystem containing *directory*, or if the file *directory*/minfree exists and the number of free kilobytes (for non-superusers) in the filesystem after the copies were made would be less than the number in the first line of this file, the copies are not attempted.

If **savecore** successfully copies the kernel and the core dump, the core dump is cleared so that future invocations of **savecore** will ignore it.

Savecore is meant to be called near the end of the initialization file /etc/rc (see rc(8)).

FILES

/vmunix current UNIX

BUGS

The minfree code does not consider the effect of compression.

SEE ALSO

compress(1), syslogd(8)

HISTORY

The **savecore** command appeared in 4.1BSD.

NAME

scsiformat – format SCSI disks and show SCSI parameters

SYNOPSIS

scsiformat [**−r**] [**−p** *page-control*] *raw-device-name*

DESCRIPTION

The **scsiformat** utility can be used to format SCSI disks on systems that support on-line SCSI formatting (currently this is limited to the HP300 and SPARC ports). It will also show the various parameters set in the SCSI controller.

The options are as follows:

−p Modify how the SCSI mode sense page query is constructed. By default, **scsiformat** asks for the current settings. The page-control flag is one of:

>9n)&(XXX<99n) . nr w2 XXXu

- c gets current settings.
- d gets default settings (those provided by the disk's manufacturer).
- s gets saved settings (those that persist across power cycles).
- v shows which parameters are variable.

−r Don't format, instead display the disk parameters.

DIAGNOSTICS

These should mostly be self-explanatory. A copy of the SCSI standard (or a more readable derivative) may be useful, however.

HISTORY

The **scsiformat** utility first appeared in 4.4BSD.

M8

NAME

sendmail – send mail over the internet

SYNOPSIS

sendmail [*flags*] [*address ...*]
newaliases
mailq [**-v**]

DESCRIPTION

Sendmail sends a message to one or more *recipients*, routing the message over whatever networks are necessary. **Sendmail** does internetwork forwarding as necessary to deliver the message to the correct place.

Sendmail is not intended as a user interface routine; other programs provide user-friendly front ends; **sendmail** is used only to deliver pre-formatted messages.

With no flags, **sendmail** reads its standard input up to an end-of-file or a line consisting only of a single dot and sends a copy of the message found there to all of the addresses listed. It determines the network(s) to use based on the syntax and contents of the addresses.

Local addresses are looked up in a file and aliased appropriately. Aliasing can be prevented by preceding the address with a backslash. Normally the sender is not included in any alias expansions, e.g., if 'john' sends to 'group', and 'group' includes 'john' in the expansion, then the letter will not be delivered to 'john'.

Parameters

–B*type* Set the body type to *type*. Current legal values 7BIT or 8BITMIME.

–ba Go into ARPANET mode. All input lines must end with a CR-LF, and all messages will be generated with a CR-LF at the end. Also, the ''From:'' and ''Sender:'' fields are examined for the name of the sender.

–bd Run as a daemon. This requires Berkeley IPC. **Sendmail** will fork and run in background listening on socket 25 for incoming SMTP connections. This is normally run from /etc/rc.

–bi Initialize the alias database.

–bm Deliver mail in the usual way (default).

–bp Print a listing of the queue.

–bs Use the SMTP protocol as described in RFC821 on standard input and output. This flag implies all the operations of the **–ba** flag that are compatible with SMTP.

–bt Run in address test mode. This mode reads addresses and shows the steps in parsing; it is used for debugging configuration tables.

–bv Verify names only – do not try to collect or deliver a message. Verify mode is normally used for validating users or mailing lists.

–C*file* Use alternate configuration file. **Sendmail** refuses to run as root if an alternate configuration file is specified.

-d*X* Set debugging value to *X*.

-F*fullname*
Set the full name of the sender.

-f*name* Sets the name of the ''from'' person (i.e., the sender of the mail). **-f** can only be used by ''trusted'' users (normally *root*, *daemon*, and *network*) or if the person you are trying to become is the same as the person you are.

-h*N* Set the hop count to *N*. The hop count is incremented every time the mail is processed. When it reaches a limit, the mail is returned with an error message, the victim of an aliasing loop. If not specified, ''Received:'' lines in the message are counted.

-n Don't do aliasing.

-o*x value* Set option *x* to the specified *value*. Options are described below.

-p*protocol*
Set the name of the protocol used to receive the message. This can be a simple protocol name such as ''UUCP'' or a protocol and hostname, such as ''UUCP:ucbvax''.

-q[*time*] Processed saved messages in the queue at given intervals. If *time* is omitted, process the queue once. Time is given as a tagged number, with 's' being seconds, 'm' being minutes, 'h' being hours, 'd' being days, and 'w' being weeks. For example, -q1h30m or -q90m would both set the timeout to one hour thirty minutes. If *time* is specified, **sendmail** will run in background. This option can be used safely with **-bd**.

-r*name* An alternate and obsolete form of the **-f** flag.

-t Read message for recipients. To:, Cc:, and Bcc: lines will be scanned for recipient addresses. The Bcc: line will be deleted before transmission. Any addresses in the argument list will be suppressed, that is, they will *not* receive copies even if listed in the message header.

-v Go into verbose mode. Alias expansions will be announced, etc.

-X *logfile*
Log all traffic in and out of mailers in the indicated log file. This should only be used as a last resort for debugging mailer bugs. It will log a lot of data very quickly.

Options

There are also a number of processing options that may be set. Normally these will only be used by a system administrator. Options may be set either on the command line using the **-o** flag or in the configuration file. This is a partial list; for a complete list (and details), consult the *Sendmail Installation and Operation Guide*. The options are:

A*file* Use alternate alias file.

b*nblocks* The minimum number of free blocks needed on the spool filesystem.

c On mailers that are considered ''expensive'' to connect to, don't initiate immediate connection. This requires queueing.

C *N* Checkpoint the queue file after every *N* successful deliveries (default 10). This avoids excessive duplicate deliveries when sending to long mailing lists interrupted by system crashes.

`d`*x* Set the delivery mode to *x*. Delivery modes are '`i`' for interactive (synchronous) delivery, '`b`' for background (asynchronous) delivery, and '`q`' for queue only – i.e., actual delivery is done the next time the queue is run.

`D` Try to automatically rebuild the alias database if necessary.

`e`*x* Set error processing to mode *x*. Valid modes are '`m`' to mail back the error message, '`w`' to "write" back the error message (or mail it back if the sender is not logged in), '`p`' to print the errors on the terminal (default), '`q`' to throw away error messages (only exit status is returned), and '`e`' to do special processing for the BerkNet. If the text of the message is not mailed back by modes '`m`' or '`w`' and if the sender is local to this machine, a copy of the message is appended to the file `dead.letter` in the sender's home directory.

`f` Save UNIX–style From lines at the front of messages.

`G` Match local mail names against the GECOS portion of the password file.

`g` *N* The default group id to use when calling mailers.

`H`*file* The SMTP help file.

`h` *N* The maximum number of times a message is allowed to "hop" before we decide it is in a loop.

`i` Do not take dots on a line by themselves as a message terminator.

`j` Send error messages in MIME format.

`K`*timeout* Set connection cache timeout.

`k`*N* Set connection cache size.

`L`*n* The log level.

`l` Pay attention to the Errors-To: header.

`m` Send to "me" (the sender) also if I am in an alias expansion.

`n` Validate the right hand side of aliases during a `newaliases(1)` command.

`o` If set, this message may have old style headers. If not set, this message is guaranteed to have new style headers (i.e., commas instead of spaces between addresses). If set, an adaptive algorithm is used that will correctly determine the header format in most cases.

`Q`*queuedir*
Select the directory in which to queue messages.

`S`*file* Save statistics in the named file.

`s` Always instantiate the queue file, even under circumstances where it is not strictly necessary. This provides safety against system crashes during delivery.

`T`*time* Set the timeout on undelivered messages in the queue to the specified time. After delivery has failed (e.g., because of a host being down) for this amount of time, failed messages will be returned to the sender. The default is three days.

`t`*stz, dtz*
Set the name of the time zone.

`U`*userdatabase*
If set, a user database is consulted to get forwarding information. You can consider this an adjunct to the aliasing mechanism, except that the database is intended to be distributed; aliases

are local to a particular host. This may not be available if your sendmail does not have the USERDB option compiled in.

uN Set the default user id for mailers.

Y Fork each job during queue runs. May be convenient on memory-poor machines.

7 Strip incoming messages to seven bits.

In aliases, the first character of a name may be a vertical bar to cause interpretation of the rest of the name as a command to pipe the mail to. It may be necessary to quote the name to keep **sendmail** from suppressing the blanks from between arguments. For example, a common alias is:

```
msgs: "|/usr/bin/msgs -s"
```

Aliases may also have the syntax ":include:*filename*" to ask sendmail to read the named file for a list of recipients. For example, an alias such as:

```
poets: ":include:/usr/local/lib/poets.list"
```

would read /usr/local/lib/poets.list for the list of addresses making up the group.

Sendmail returns an exit status describing what it did. The codes are defined in <sysexits.h>:

EX_OK	Successful completion on all addresses.
EX_NOUSER	User name not recognized.
EX_UNAVAILABLE	Catchall meaning necessary resources were not available.
EX_SYNTAX	Syntax error in address.
EX_SOFTWARE	Internal software error, including bad arguments.
EX_OSERR	Temporary operating system error, such as "cannot fork".
EX_NOHOST	Host name not recognized.
EX_TEMPFAIL	Message could not be sent immediately, but was queued.

If invoked as **newaliases**, **sendmail** will rebuild the alias database. If invoked as **mailq**, **sendmail** will print the contents of the mail queue.

FILES

Except for the file /etc/sendmail.cf itself, the following pathnames are all specified in /etc/sendmail.cf. Thus, these values are only approximations.

/etc/aliases	raw data for alias names
/etc/aliases.db	data base of alias names
/etc/sendmail.cf	configuration file
/etc/sendmail.hf	help file
/var/log/sendmail.st	collected statistics
/var/spool/mqueue/*	temp files
/var/run/sendmail.pid	The process id of the daemon

SEE ALSO

binmail(1), mail(1), rmail(1), syslog(3), aliases(5), mailaddr(7), rc(8);

DARPA Internet Request For Comments *RFC819*, *RFC821*, *RFC822*.

Sendmail – An Internetwork Mail Router, No. 9, SMM.

Sendmail Installation and Operation Guide, No. 8, SMM.

HISTORY

The `sendmail` command appeared in 4.2BSD.

NAME

showmount – show remote nfs mounts on host

SYNOPSIS

showmount [**-ade**] [*host*]

DESCRIPTION

Showmount shows status information about the NFS server on *host*. By default it prints the names of all hosts that have NFS file systems mounted on the host. See *NFS: Network File System Protocol Specification*, RFC 1094, Appendix A , for a detailed description of the protocol.

-a List all mount points in the form: *host*:*dirpath*

-d List directory paths of mount points instead of hosts

-e Show the *host*'s exports list

SEE ALSO

mount(1), mountd(8)

BUGS

The mount daemon running on the server only has an idea of the actual mounts, since the NFS server is stateless. **Showmount** will only display the information as accurately as the mount daemon reports it.

HISTORY

The **showmount** utility first appeared in 4.4BSD.

M8

NAME

shutdown – close down the system at a given time

SYNOPSIS

shutdown [–] [**–fhkrn**] *time* [*warning-message ...*]

DESCRIPTION

Shutdown provides an automated shutdown procedure for super-users to nicely notify users when the system is shutting down, saving them from system administrators, hackers, and gurus, who would otherwise not bother with such niceties.

Available friendlinesses:

–f **Shutdown** arranges, in the manner of fastboot(8), for the file systems *not to be* checked on reboot.

–h The system is halted at the specified *time* when **shutdown** execs halt(8).

–k Kick every body off. The **–k** option does not actually halt the system, but leaves the system multiuser with logins disabled (for all but super-user).

–n Prevent the normal sync(2) before stopping.

–r **Shutdown** execs reboot(8) at the specified *time*.

time *Time* is the time at which **shutdown** will bring the system down and may be the word *now* (indicating an immediate shutdown) or specify a future time in one of two formats: *+number*, or *yymmddhhmm*, where the year, month, and day may be defaulted to the current system values. The first form brings the system down in *number* minutes and the second at the absolute time specified.

warning-message
Any other arguments comprise the warning message that is broadcast to users currently logged into the system.

– If '–' is supplied as an option, the warning message is read from the standard input.

At intervals, becoming more frequent as apocalypse approaches and starting at ten hours before shutdown, warning messages are displayed on the terminals of all users logged in. Five minutes before shutdown, or immediately if shutdown is in less than 5 minutes, logins are disabled by creating /etc/nologin and copying the warning message there. If this file exists when a user attempts to log in, login(1) prints its contents and exits. The file is removed just before **shutdown** exits.

At shutdown time a message is written in the system log, containing the time of shutdown, who initiated the shutdown and the reason. A terminate signal is then sent to init to bring the system down to single-user state (depending on above options). The time of the shutdown and the warning message are placed in /etc/nologin and should be used to inform the users about when the system will be back up and why it is going down (or anything else).

FILES

/etc/nologin tells login not to let anyone log in
/fastboot tells rc(8) not to run fsck when rebooting

SEE ALSO

login(1), wall(1), fastboot(8), halt(8), reboot(8)

BACKWARD COMPATIBILITY

The hours and minutes in the second time format may be separated by a colon (``:'') for backward compatibility.

HISTORY

The **shutdown** command appeared in 4.0BSD.

M8

NAME

slattach – attach serial lines as network interfaces

SYNOPSIS

Slattach *ttyname* [*baudrate*]

DESCRIPTION

Slattach is used to assign a tty line to a network interface, and to define the network source and destination addresses. The following operands are supported by **slattach**:

ttyname Specifies the name of the tty device. *Ttyname* should be a string of the form `ttyXX`, or `/dev/ttyXX`.

baudrate Specifies the speed of the connection. If not specified, the default of 9600 is used.

Only the super-user may attach a network interface.

To detach the interface, use ``ifconfig interface-name down'' after killing off the **slattach** process. *Interface-name* is the name that is shown by `netstat(1)`

EXAMPLES

```
slattach ttyh8
slattach /dev/tty01 4800
```

DIAGNOSTICS

Messages indicating the specified interface does not exit, the requested address is unknown, the user is not privileged and tried to alter an interface's configuration.

SEE ALSO

`netstat(1)`, `netintro(4)`, `ifconfig(8)`, `rc(8)`

HISTORY

The **slattach** command appeared in 4.3BSD.

M8

NAME

sliplogin – attach a serial line network interface

SYNOPSIS

sliplogin [*loginname*]

DESCRIPTION

Sliplogin is used to turn the terminal line on standard input into a Serial Line IP (SLIP) link to a remote host. To do this, the program searches the file `/etc/sliphome/slip.hosts` for an entry matching *loginname* (which defaults to the current login name if omitted). If a matching entry is found, the line is configured appropriately for slip (8-bit transparent i/o) and converted to SLIP line discipline. Then a shell script is invoked to initialize the slip interface with the appropriate local and remote IP address, netmask, etc.

The usual initialization script is `/etc/sliphome/slip.login` but, if particular hosts need special initialization, the file `/etc/sliphome/slip.login.`*loginname* will be executed instead if it exists. The script is invoked with the parameters

slipunit The unit number of the slip interface assigned to this line. E.g., **0** for **sl0**.

speed The speed of the line.

args The arguments from the `/etc/sliphome/slip.hosts` entry, in order starting with *loginname*.

Only the super-user may attach a network interface. The interface is automatically detached when the other end hangs up or the **sliplogin** process dies. If the kernel slip module has been configured for it, all routes through that interface will also disappear at the same time. If there is other processing a site would like done on hangup, the file `/etc/sliphome/slip.logout` or `/etc/sliphome/slip.logout.`*loginname* is executed if it exists. It is given the same arguments as the login script.

Format of /etc/sliphome/slip.hosts

Comments (lines starting with a '#') and blank lines are ignored. Other lines must start with a *loginname* but the remaining arguments can be whatever is appropriate for the `slip.login` file that will be executed for that name. Arguments are separated by white space and follow normal sh(1) quoting conventions (however, *loginname* cannot be quoted). Usually, lines have the form

```
loginname local-address remote-address netmask opt-args
```

where *local-address* and *remote-address* are the IP host names or addresses of the local and remote ends of the slip line and *netmask* is the appropriate IP netmask. These arguments are passed directly to `ifconfig`(8). *Opt-args* are optional arguments used to configure the line.

EXAMPLE

The normal use of **sliplogin** is to create a `/etc/passwd` entry for each legal, remote slip site with **sliplogin** as the shell for that entry. E.g.,

```
Sfoo:ikhuy6:2010:1:slip line to foo:/tmp:/usr/sbin/sliplogin
```

(Our convention is to name the account used by remote host *hostname* as *Shostname*.) Then an entry is added to `slip.hosts` that looks like:

```
Sfoo    'hostname'    foo    netmask
```

where *'hostname'* will be evaluated by sh to the local host name and *netmask* is the local host IP netmask.

Note that **sliplogin** must be setuid to root and, while not a security hole, moral defectives can use it to place terminal lines in an unusable state and/or deny access to legitimate users of a remote slip line. To prevent this, a site can create a group, say *slip*, that only the slip login accounts are put in then make sure that /usr/sbin/sliplogin is in group *slip* and mode 4550 (setuid root, only group *slip* can execute binary).

DIAGNOSTICS

Sliplogin logs various information to the system log daemon, syslogd(8), with a facility code of *daemon*. The messages are listed here, grouped by severity level.

Error Severity

ioctl (TCGETS): *reason*

A TCGETS **ioctl**() to get the line parameters failed.

ioctl (TCSETS): *reason*

A TCSETS **ioctl**() to set the line parameters failed.

/etc/sliphome/slip.hosts: *reason*

The /etc/sliphome/slip.hosts file could not be opened.

access denied for *user*

No entry for *user* was found in /etc/sliphome/slip.hosts.

Notice Severity

attaching slip unit *unit* **for** *loginname*

SLIP unit *unit* was successfully attached.

SEE ALSO

slattach(8), syslogd(8)

HISTORY

The **sliplogin** command is currently in beta test.

NAME

sticky – sticky text and append-only directories

DESCRIPTION

A special file mode, called the *sticky bit* (mode S_ISVTX), is used to indicate special treatment for shareable executable files and directories. See chmod(2) or the file /usr/include/sys/stat.h for an explanation of file modes.

STICKY TEXT EXECUTABLE FILES

An executable shareable file whose sticky bit is set will not be immediately discarded from swap space after execution. The kernel will hoard the text segment of the file for future reuse and avoid having to reload the program. Shareable text segments are normally placed in a least-frequently-used cache after use, and thus the 'sticky bit' has little effect on commonly-used text images.

Sharable executable files are created with the **−n** and **−z** options of the loader ld(1).

Only the super-user can set the sticky bit on a sharable executable file.

STICKY DIRECTORIES

A directory whose 'sticky bit' is set becomes an append-only directory, or, more accurately, a directory in which the deletion of files is restricted. A file in a sticky directory may only be removed or renamed by a user if the user has write permission for the directory and the user is the owner of the file, the owner of the directory, or the super-user. This feature is usefully applied to directories such as /tmp which must be publicly writable but should deny users the license to arbitrarily delete or rename each others' files.

Any user may create a sticky directory. See chmod(1) for details about modifying file modes.

BUGS

Since the text areas of sticky text executables are stashed in the swap area, abuse of the feature can cause a system to run out of swap.

Neither open(2) nor mkdir(2) will create a file with the sticky bit set.

HISTORY

A **sticky** command appeared in Version 32V AT&T UNIX.

NAME

swapon – specify additional device for paging and swapping

SYNOPSIS

swapon -a
swapon *special_file ...*

DESCRIPTION

Swapon is used to specify additional devices on which paging and swapping are to take place. The system begins by swapping and paging on only a single device so that only one disk is required at bootstrap time. Calls to **swapon** normally occur in the system multi-user initialization file /etc/rc making all swap devices available, so that the paging and swapping activity is interleaved across several devices.

Normally, the first form is used:

-a All devices marked as "sw" swap devices in /etc/fstab are made available.

The second form gives individual block devices as given in the system swap configuration table. The call makes only this space available to the system for swap allocation.

SEE ALSO

swapon(2), fstab(8) init(8) rc(8)

FILES

/dev/[ru][pk]?b standard paging devices
/etc/fstab ascii filesystem description table

BUGS

There is no way to stop paging and swapping on a device. It is therefore not possible to make use of devices which may be dismounted during system operation.

HISTORY

The **swapon** command appeared in 4.0BSD.

M8

NAME

sync – force completion of pending disk writes (flush cache)

SYNOPSIS

sync

DESCRIPTION

Sync can be called to insure that all disk writes have been completed before the processor is halted in a way not suitably done by `reboot`(8) or `halt`(8). Generally, it is preferable to use `reboot` or `halt` to shut down the system, as they may perform additional actions such as resynchronizing the hardware clock and flushing internal caches before performing a final **sync**.

Sync utilizes the `sync`(2) function call.

SEE ALSO

`sync`(2), `fsync`(2), `halt`(8), `reboot`(8), `update`(8)

HISTORY

A **sync** command appeared in Version 6 AT&T UNIX.

M8

NAME

sysctl – get or set kernel state

SYNOPSIS

sysctl [**-n**] *name ...*
sysctl [**-n**] **-w** *name=value ...*
sysctl [**-n**] **-aA**

DESCRIPTION

The **sysctl** utility retrieves kernel state and allows processes with appropriate privilege to set kernel state. The state to be retrieved or set is described using a ''Management Information Base'' (''MIB'') style name, described as a dotted set of components. The **-a** flag can be used to list all the currently available string or integer values. The **-A** flag will list all the known MIB names including tables. Those with string or integer values will be printed as with the **-a** flag; for the table values, the name of the utility to retrieve them is given.

The **-n** flag specifies that the printing of the field name should be suppressed and that only its value should be output. This flag is useful for setting shell variables. For example, to save the pagesize in variable psize, use:

```
set psize='sysctl -n hw.pagesize'
```

If just a MIB style name is given, the corresponding value is retrieved. If a value is to be set, the **-w** flag must be specified and the MIB name followed by an equal sign and the new value to be used.

The information available from **sysctl** consists of integers, strings, and tables. The tabular information can only be retrieved by special purpose programs such as **ps**, **systat**, and **netstat**. The string and integer information is summaried below. For a detailed description of these variable see sysctl(3). The changeable column indicates whether a process with appropriate privilege can change the value.

Name	**Type**	**Changeable**
kern.ostype	string	no
kern.osrelease	string	no
kern.osrevision	integer	no
kern.version	string	no
kern.maxvnodes	integer	yes
kern.maxproc	integer	yes
kern.maxfiles	integer	yes
kern.argmax	integer	no
kern.securelevel	integer	raise only
kern.hostname	string	yes
kern.hostid	integer	yes
kern.clockrate	struct	no
kern.posix1version	integer	no
kern.ngroups	integer	no
kern.job_control	integer	no
kern.saved_ids	integer	no
kern.link_max	integer	no
kern.max_canon	integer	no
kern.max_input	integer	no
kern.name_max	integer	no

M8

kern.path_max	integer	no
kern.pipe_buf	integer	no
kern.chown_restricted	integer	no
kern.no_trunc	integer	no
kern.vdisable	integer	no
kern.boottime	struct	no
vm.loadavg	struct	no
machdep.console_device	dev_t	no
net.inet.ip.forwarding	integer	yes
net.inet.ip.redirect	integer	yes
net.inet.ip.ttl	integer	yes
net.inet.icmp.maskrepl	integer	yes
net.inet.udp.checksum	integer	yes
hw.machine	string	no
hw.model	string	no
hw.ncpu	integer	no
hw.byteorder	integer	no
hw.physmem	integer	no
hw.usermem	integer	no
hw.pagesize	integer	no
user.cs_path	string	no
user.bc_base_max	integer	no
user.bc_dim_max	integer	no
user.bc_scale_max	integer	no
user.bc_string_max	integer	no
user.coll_weights_max	integer	no
user.expr_nest_max	integer	no
user.line_max	integer	no
user.re_dup_max	integer	no
user.posix2_version	integer	no
user.posix2_c_bind	integer	no
user.posix2_c_dev	integer	no
user.posix2_char_term	integer	no
user.posix2_fort_dev	integer	no
user.posix2_fort_run	integer	no
user.posix2_localedef	integer	no
user.posix2_sw_dev	integer	no
user.posix2_upe	integer	no

EXAMPLES

For example, to retrieve the maximum number of processes allowed in the system, one would use the follow request:

```
sysctl kern.maxproc
```

To set the maximum number of processes allowed in the system to 1000, one would use the follow request:

```
sysctl -w kern.maxproc=1000
```

Information about the system clock rate may be obtained with:

```
sysctl kern.clockrate
```

Information about the load average history may be obtained with

```
sysctl vm.loadavg
```

FILES

`<sys/sysctl.h>`	definitions for top level identifiers, second level kernel and hardware identifiers, and user level identifiers
`<sys/socket.h>`	definitions for second level network identifiers
`<sys/gmon.h>`	definitions for third level profiling identifiers
`<vm/vm_param.h>`	definitions for second level virtual memory identifiers
`<netinet/in.h>`	definitions for third level Internet identifiers and fourth level IP identifiers
`<netinet/icmp_var.h>`	definitions for fourth level ICMP identifiers
`<netinet/udp_var.h>`	definitions for fourth level UDP identifiers

SEE ALSO

sysctl(3)

HISTORY

sysctl first appeared in 4.4BSD.

NAME

syslogd – log systems messages

SYNOPSIS

syslogd [**-f** *config_file*] [**-m** *mark_interval*] [**-p** *log_socket*]

DESCRIPTION

Syslogd reads and logs messages to the system console, log files, other machines and/or users as specified by its configuration file. The options are as follows:

-f Specify the pathname of an alternate configuration file; the default is `/etc/syslog.conf`.

-m Select the number of minutes between "mark" messages; the default is 20 minutes.

-p Specify the pathname of an alternate log socket; the default is `/dev/log`.

Syslogd reads its configuration file when it starts up and whenever it receives a hangup signal. For information on the format of the configuration file, see `syslog.conf`(5).

Syslogd reads messages from the UNIX domain socket `/dev/log`, from an Internet domain socket specified in `/etc/services`, and from the special device `/dev/klog` (to read kernel messages).

Syslogd creates the file `/var/run/syslog.pid`, and stores its process id there. This can be used to kill or reconfigure **syslogd**.

The message sent to **syslogd** should consist of a single line. The message can contain a priority code, which should be a preceding decimal number in angle braces, for example, '<5.>' This priority code should map into the priorities defined in the include file <`sys/syslog.h`>.

FILES

`/etc/syslog.conf`	The configuration file.
`/var/run/syslog.pid`	The process id of current **syslogd**.
`/dev/log`	Name of the UNIX domain datagram log socket.
`/dev/klog`	The kernel log device.

SEE ALSO

`logger`(1), `syslog`(3), `services`(5), `syslog.conf`(5)

HISTORY

The **syslogd** command appeared in 4.3BSD.

M8

NAME

talkd – remote user communication server

SYNOPSIS

talkd

DESCRIPTION

Talkd is the server that notifies a user that someone else wants to initiate a conversation. It acts as a repository of invitations, responding to requests by clients wishing to rendezvous to hold a conversation. In normal operation, a client, the caller, initiates a rendezvous by sending a CTL_MSG to the server of type LOOK_UP (see <protocols/talkd.h>). This causes the server to search its invitation tables to check if an invitation currently exists for the caller (to speak to the callee specified in the message). If the lookup fails, the caller then sends an ANNOUNCE message causing the server to broadcast an announcement on the callee's login ports requesting contact. When the callee responds, the local server uses the recorded invitation to respond with the appropriate rendezvous address and the caller and callee client programs establish a stream connection through which the conversation takes place.

SEE ALSO

talk(1), write(1)

HISTORY

The **talkd** command appeared in 4.3BSD.

NAME

telnetd – DARPA TELNET protocol server

SYNOPSIS

/usr/libexec/telnetd [**-BUhlkns**] [**-D** *debugmode*] [**-I***initid*] [**-S** *tos*] [**-X** *authtype*] [**-a** *authmode*] [**-edebug**] [**-r***lowpty-highpty*] [**-u** *len*] [**-debug** [*port*]]

DESCRIPTION

The **telnetd** command is a server which supports the DARPA standard TELNET virtual terminal protocol. **Telnetd** is normally invoked by the internet server (see inetd(8)) for requests to connect to the TELNET port as indicated by the /etc/services file (see services(5)). The **-debug** option may be used to start up **telnetd** manually, instead of through inetd(8). If started up this way, *port* may be specified to run **telnetd** on an alternate TCP port number.

The **telnetd** command accepts the following options:

-a *authmode*

This option may be used for specifying what mode should be used for authentication. Note that this option is only useful if **telnetd** has been compiled with support for the AUTHENTICATION option. There are several valid values for *authmode:*

debug Turns on authentication debugging code.

user Only allow connections when the remote user can provide valid authentication information to identify the remote user, and is allowed access to the specified account without providing a password.

valid Only allow connections when the remote user can provide valid authentication information to identify the remote user. The login(1) command will provide any additional user verification needed if the remote user is not allowed automatic access to the specified account.

other Only allow connections that supply some authentication information. This option is currently not supported by any of the existing authentication mechanisms, and is thus the same as specifying **-a valid**.

none This is the default state. Authentication information is not required. If no or insufficient authentication information is provided, then the login(1) program will provide the necessary user verification.

off This disables the authentication code. All user verification will happen through the login(1) program.

-B Specifies bftp server mode. In this mode, **telnetd** causes login to start a bftp(1) session rather than the user's normal shell. In bftp daemon mode normal logins are not supported, and it must be used on a port other than the normal TELNET port.

-D *debugmode*

This option may be used for debugging purposes. This allows **telnetd** to print out debugging information to the connection, allowing the user to see what **telnetd** is doing. There are several possible values for *debugmode:*

options Prints information about the negotiation of TELNET options.

report Prints the **options** information, plus some additional information about what processing is going on.

netdata Displays the data stream received by **telnetd.**

ptydata Displays data written to the pty.

exercise Has not been implemented yet.

–debug Enables debugging on each socket created by **telnetd** (see SO_DEBUG in socket(2)).

–edebug If **telnetd** has been compiled with support for data encryption, then the **–edebug** option may be used to enable encryption debugging code.

–h Disables the printing of host-specific information before login has been completed.

–I *initid* This option is only applicable to UNICOS systems prior to 7.0. It specifies the ID from /etc/inittab to use when init starts login sessions. The default ID is fe.

–k This option is only useful if **telnetd** has been compiled with both linemode and kludge linemode support. If the **–k** option is specified, then if the remote client does not support the LINEMODE option, then **telnetd** will operate in character at a time mode. It will still support kludge linemode, but will only go into kludge linemode if the remote client requests it. (This is done by by the client sending DONT SUPPRESS-GO-AHEAD and DONT ECHO.) The **–k** option is most useful when there are remote clients that do not support kludge linemode, but pass the heuristic (if they respond with WILL TIMING-MARK in response to a DO TIMING-MARK) for kludge linemode support.

–l Specifies line mode. Tries to force clients to use line- at-a-time mode. If the LINEMODE option is not supported, it will go into kludge linemode.

–n Disable TCP keep-alives. Normally **telnetd** enables the TCP keep-alive mechanism to probe connections that have been idle for some period of time to determine if the client is still there, so that idle connections from machines that have crashed or can no longer be reached may be cleaned up.

–r *lowpty-highpty*
This option is only enabled when **telnetd** is compiled for UNICOS. It specifies an inclusive range of pseudo-terminal devices to use. If the system has sysconf variable _SC_CRAY_NPTY configured, the default pty search range is 0 to _SC_CRAY_NPTY; otherwise, the default range is 0 to 128. Either *lowpty* or *highpty* may be omitted to allow changing either end of the search range. If *lowpty* is omitted, the - character is still required so that **telnetd** can differentiate *highpty* from *lowpty*.

–s This option is only enabled if **telnetd** is compiled with support for SecurID cards. It causes the **–s** option to be passed on to login(1), and thus is only useful if login(1) supports the **–s** flag to indicate that only SecurID validated logins are allowed, and is usually useful for controlling remote logins from outside of a firewall.

–S *tos*

–u *len* This option is used to specify the size of the field in the utmp structure that holds the remote host name. If the resolved host name is longer than *len*, the dotted decimal value will be used instead. This allows hosts with very long host names that overflow this field to still be uniquely identified. Specifying **–u0** indicates that only dotted decimal addresses should be put into the utmp file.

-U This option causes **telnetd** to refuse connections from addresses that cannot be mapped back into a symbolic name via the `gethostbyaddr(3)` routine.

-X *authtype*
This option is only valid if **telnetd** has been built with support for the authentication option. It disables the use of *authtype* authentication, and can be used to temporarily disable a specific authentication type without having to recompile **telnetd**.

Telnetd operates by allocating a pseudo-terminal device (see `pty(4)`) for a client, then creating a login process which has the slave side of the pseudo-terminal as `stdin`, `stdout` and `stderr`. **Telnetd** manipulates the master side of the pseudo-terminal, implementing the TELNET protocol and passing characters between the remote client and the login process.

When a TELNET session is started up, **telnetd** sends TELNET options to the client side indicating a willingness to do the following TELNET options, which are described in more detail below:

```
DO AUTHENTICATION
WILL ENCRYPT
DO TERMINAL TYPE
DO TSPEED
DO XDISPLOC
DO NEW-ENVIRON
DO ENVIRON
WILL SUPPRESS GO AHEAD
DO ECHO
DO LINEMODE
DO NAWS
WILL STATUS
DO LFLOW
DO TIMING-MARK
```

The pseudo-terminal allocated to the client is configured to operate in cooked mode, and with `XTABS and CRMOD` enabled (see `tty(4)`).

Telnetd has support for enabling locally the following TELNET options:

WILL ECHO When the `LINEMODE` option is enabled, a `WILL ECHO` or `WONT ECHO` will be sent to the client to indicate the current state of terminal echoing. When terminal echo is not desired, a `WILL ECHO` is sent to indicate that telnetd will take care of echoing any data that needs to be echoed to the terminal, and then nothing is echoed. When terminal echo is desired, a `WONT ECHO` is sent to indicate that telnetd will not be doing any terminal echoing, so the client should do any terminal echoing that is needed.

WILL BINARY Indicates that the client is willing to send a 8 bits of data, rather than the normal 7 bits of the Network Virtual Terminal.

WILL SGA Indicates that it will not be sending `IAC GA,` go ahead, commands.

WILL STATUS Indicates a willingness to send the client, upon request, of the current status of all TELNET options.

WILL TIMING-MARK Whenever a `DO TIMING-MARK` command is received, it is always responded to with a `WILL TIMING-MARK`

M8

WILL LOGOUT — When a `DO LOGOUT` is received, a `WILL LOGOUT` is sent in response, and the TELNET session is shut down.

WILL ENCRYPT — Only sent if **telnetd** is compiled with support for data encryption, and indicates a willingness to decrypt the data stream.

Telnetd has support for enabling remotely the following TELNET options:

DO BINARY — Sent to indicate that telnetd is willing to receive an 8 bit data stream.

DO LFLOW — Requests that the client handle flow control characters remotely.

DO ECHO — This is not really supported, but is sent to identify a 4.2BSD `telnet(1)` client, which will improperly respond with `WILL ECHO`. If a `WILL ECHO` is received, a `DONT ECHO` will be sent in response.

DO TERMINAL-TYPE — Indicates a desire to be able to request the name of the type of terminal that is attached to the client side of the connection.

DO SGA — Indicates that it does not need to receive `IAC GA`, the go ahead command.

DO NAWS — Requests that the client inform the server when the window (display) size changes.

DO TERMINAL-SPEED — Indicates a desire to be able to request information about the speed of the serial line to which the client is attached.

DO XDISPLOC — Indicates a desire to be able to request the name of the X windows display that is associated with the telnet client.

DO NEW-ENVIRON — Indicates a desire to be able to request environment variable information, as described in RFC 1572.

DO ENVIRON — Indicates a desire to be able to request environment variable information, as described in RFC 1408.

DO LINEMODE — Only sent if **telnetd** is compiled with support for linemode, and requests that the client do line by line processing.

DO TIMING-MARK — Only sent if **telnetd** is compiled with support for both linemode and kludge linemode, and the client responded with `WONT LINEMODE`. If the client responds with `WILL TM`, the it is assumed that the client supports kludge linemode. Note that the [**−k**] option can be used to disable this.

DO AUTHENTICATION — Only sent if **telnetd** is compiled with support for authentication, and indicates a willingness to receive authentication information for automatic login.

DO ENCRYPT — Only sent if **telnetd** is compiled with support for data encryption, and indicates a willingness to decrypt the data stream.

ENVIRONMENT

FILES

`/etc/services`
`/etc/inittab` (UNICOS systems only)
`/etc/iptos` (if supported)
`/usr/ucb/bftp` (if supported)

SEE ALSO

telnet(1), login(1), bftp(1) (if supported)

STANDARDS

RFC-854 TELNET PROTOCOL SPECIFICATION
RFC-855 TELNET OPTION SPECIFICATIONS
RFC-856 TELNET BINARY TRANSMISSION
RFC-857 TELNET ECHO OPTION
RFC-858 TELNET SUPPRESS GO AHEAD OPTION
RFC-859 TELNET STATUS OPTION
RFC-860 TELNET TIMING MARK OPTION
RFC-861 TELNET EXTENDED OPTIONS - LIST OPTION
RFC-885 TELNET END OF RECORD OPTION
RFC-1073 Telnet Window Size Option
RFC-1079 Telnet Terminal Speed Option
RFC-1091 Telnet Terminal-Type Option
RFC-1096 Telnet X Display Location Option
RFC-1123 Requirements for Internet Hosts -- Application and Support
RFC-1184 Telnet Linemode Option
RFC-1372 Telnet Remote Flow Control Option
RFC-1416 Telnet Authentication Option
RFC-1411 Telnet Authentication: Kerberos Version 4
RFC-1412 Telnet Authentication: SPX
RFC-1571 Telnet Environment Option Interoperability Issues
RFC-1572 Telnet Environment Option

BUGS

Some TELNET commands are only partially implemented.

Because of bugs in the original 4.2 BSD telnet(1), **telnetd** performs some dubious protocol exchanges to try to discover if the remote client is, in fact, a 4.2 BSD telnet(1).

Binary mode has no common interpretation except between similar operating systems (Unix in this case).

The terminal type name received from the remote client is converted to lower case.

Telnetd never sends TELNET IAC GA (go ahead) commands.

M8

NAME

tftpd – Internet Trivial File Transfer Protocol server

SYNOPSIS

tftpd [**-l**] [**-n**] [*directory ...*]

DESCRIPTION

Tftpd is a server which supports the Internet Trivial File Transfer Protocol (RFC 783). The TFTP server operates at the port indicated in the `tftp` service description; see `services`(5). The server is normally started by `inetd`(8).

The use of `tftp`(1) does not require an account or password on the remote system. Due to the lack of authentication information, **tftpd** will allow only publicly readable files to be accessed. Files containing the string "/../" are not allowed. Files may be written only if they already exist and are publicly writable. Note that this extends the concept of "public" to include all users on all hosts that can be reached through the network; this may not be appropriate on all systems, and its implications should be considered before enabling tftp service. The server should have the user ID with the lowest possible privilege.

Access to files may be restricted by invoking **tftpd** with a list of directories by including up to 20 pathnames as server program arguments in `/etc/inetd.conf`. In this case access is restricted to files whose names are prefixed by the one of the given directories. The given directories are also treated as a search path for relative filename requests.

The options are:

-l Logs all requests using `syslog`(3).

-n Suppresses negative acknowledgement of requests for nonexistent relative filenames.

SEE ALSO

`tftp`(1), `inetd`(8)

HISTORY

The **tftpd** command appeared in 4.2BSD.

NAME

timed – time server daemon

SYNOPSIS

timed [**-M**] [**-t**] [**-d**] [**-i** *network*] [**-n** *network*] [**-F** *host1 host2 ...*]

DESCRIPTION

This is a time server daemon and is normally invoked at boot time from the rc(8) file. It synchronizes the host's time with the time of other machines in a local area network running **timed 8**. These time servers will slow down the clocks of some machines and speed up the clocks of others to bring them to the average network time. The average network time is computed from measurements of clock differences using the ICMP timestamp request message.

The service provided by **timed** is based on a master-slave scheme. When **timed 8** is started on a machine, it asks the master for the network time and sets the host's clock to that time. After that, it accepts synchronization messages periodically sent by the master and calls adjtime(2) to perform the needed corrections on the host's clock.

It also communicates with date(1) in order to set the date globally, and with timedc(8), a timed control program. If the machine running the master crashes, then the slaves will elect a new master from among slaves running with the **-M** flag. A **timed** running without the **-M** or **-F** flags will remain a slave. The **-t** flag enables **timed** to trace the messages it receives in the file /var/log/timed.log. Tracing can be turned on or off by the program timedc(8). The **-d** flag is for debugging the daemon. It causes the program to not put itself into the background. Normally **timed** checks for a master time server on each network to which it is connected, except as modified by the options described below. It will request synchronization service from the first master server located. If permitted by the **-M** flag, it will provide synchronization service on any attached networks on which no current master server was detected. Such a server propagates the time computed by the top-level master. The **-n** flag, followed by the name of a network which the host is connected to (see networks(5)), overrides the default choice of the network addresses made by the program. Each time the **-n** flag appears, that network name is added to a list of valid networks. All other networks are ignored. The **-i** flag, followed by the name of a network to which the host is connected (see networks(5)), overrides the default choice of the network addresses made by the program. Each time the **-i** flag appears, that network name is added to a list of networks to ignore. All other networks are used by the time daemon. The **-n** and **-i** flags are meaningless if used together.

Timed checks for a master time server on each network to which it is connected, except as modified by the **-n** and **-i** options described above. If it finds masters on more than one network, it chooses one network on which to be a "slave," and then periodically checks the other networks to see if the masters there have disappeared.

One way to synchronize a group of machines is to use an NTP daemon to synchronize the clock of one machine to a distant standard or a radio receiver and **-F** *hostname* to tell its timed daemon to trust only itself.

Messages printed by the kernel on the system console occur with interrupts disabled. This means that the clock stops while they are printing. A machine with many disk or network hardware problems and consequent messages cannot keep good time by itself. Each message typically causes the clock to lose a dozen milliseconds. A time daemon can correct the result.

Messages in the system log about machines that failed to respond usually indicate machines that crashed or were turned off. Complaints about machines that failed to respond to initial time settings are often associated with "multi-homed" machines that looked for time masters on more than one network and eventually chose to become a slave on the other network. If two or more time daemons, whether **timed**, NTP, try to adjust the same clock, temporal chaos will result. If both **timed** and another time daemon are run on the same machine, ensure that the **-F** flag is used, so that **timed** never attempts to adjust the local clock.

The protocol is based on UDP/IP broadcasts. All machines within the range of a broadcast that are using the TSP protocol must cooperate. There cannot be more than a single administrative domain using the **-F** flag among all machines reached by a broadcast packet. Failure to follow this rule is usually indicated by complaints concerning "untrusted" machines in the system log.

FILES

`/var/log/timed.log`	tracing file for timed
`/var/log/timed.masterlog`	log file for master timed

SEE ALSO

date(1), adjtime(2), gettimeofday(2), icmp(4), timedc(8),

R. Gusella, and S. Zatti, *TSP: The Time Synchronization Protocol for UNIX 4.3BSD*.

HISTORY

The **timed** daemon appeared in 4.3BSD.

NAME

timedc – timed control program

SYNOPSIS

timedc [*command* [*argument* ...]]

DESCRIPTION

Timedc is used to control the operation of the timed(8) program. It may be used to:

- Measure the differences between machines' clocks,
- Find the location where the master time server is running,
- Enable or disable tracing of messages received by timed, and
- Perform various debugging actions.

Without any arguments, **timedc** will prompt for commands from the standard input. If arguments are supplied, **timedc** interprets the first argument as a command and the remaining arguments as parameters to the command. The standard input may be redirected causing **timedc** to read commands from a file. Commands may be abbreviated; recognized commands are:

? [*command* ...]

help [*command* ...]
Print a short description of each command specified in the argument list, or, if no arguments are given, a list of the recognized commands.

clockdiff *host* ...
Compute the differences between the clock of the host machine and the clocks of the machines given as arguments.

msite [*host* ...]
Show the master time server for specified host(s).

trace { *on* | *off* }
Enable or disable the tracing of incoming messages to timed in the file /var/log/timed.log.

election *host*
Asks the daemon on the target host to reset its "election" timers and to ensure that a time master has been elected.

quit Exit from timedc.

Other commands may be included for use in testing and debugging timed; the help command and the program source may be consulted for details.

FILES

/var/log/timed.log	tracing file for timed
/var/log/timed.masterlog	log file for master timed

SEE ALSO

date(1), adjtime(2), icmp(4), timed(8),

R. Gusella, and S. Zatti, *TSP: The Time Synchronization Protocol for UNIX 4.3BSD.*

DIAGNOSTICS

?Ambiguous command
: abbreviation matches more than one command

?Invalid command
: no match found

?Privileged command
: command can be executed by root only

HISTORY

The `timedc` command appeared in 4.3BSD.

NAME

traceroute – print the route packets take to network host

SYNOPSIS

traceroute [**-m** *max_ttl*] [**-n**] [**-p** *port*] [**-q** *nqueries*] [**-r**] [**-s** *src_addr*] [**-t** *tos*] [**-w** *waittime*] *host* [*packetsize*]

DESCRIPTION

The Internet is a large and complex aggregation of network hardware, connected together by gateways. Tracking the route one's packets follow (or finding the miscreant gateway that's discarding your packets) can be difficult. **Traceroute** utilizes the IP protocol 'time to live' field and attempts to elicit an ICMP `TIME_EXCEEDED` response from each gateway along the path to some host.

The only mandatory parameter is the destination host name or IP number. The default probe datagram length is 38 bytes, but this may be increased by specifying a packet size (in bytes) after the destination host name.

Other options are:

-m *max_ttl*
: Set the max time-to-live (max number of hops) used in outgoing probe packets. The default is 30 hops (the same default used for TCP connections).

-n
: Print hop addresses numerically rather than symbolically and numerically (saves a nameserver address-to-name lookup for each gateway found on the path).

-p *port*
: Set the base UDP *port* number used in probes (default is 33434). **Traceroute** hopes that nothing is listening on UDP ports *base* to *base+nhops-1* at the destination host (so an ICMP `PORT_UNREACHABLE` message will be returned to terminate the route tracing). If something is listening on a port in the default range, this option can be used to pick an unused port range.

-q *nqueries*
: Set the number of probes per ''ttl'' to *nqueries* (default is three probes).

-r
: Bypass the normal routing tables and send directly to a host on an attached network. If the host is not on a directly-attached network, an error is returned. This option can be used to ping a local host through an interface that has no route through it (e.g., after the interface was dropped by `routed`(8)).

-s *src_addr*
: Use the following IP address (which must be given as an IP number, not a hostname) as the source address in outgoing probe packets. On hosts with more than one IP address, this option can be used to force the source address to be something other than the IP address of the interface the probe packet is sent on. If the IP address is not one of this machine's interface addresses, an error is returned and nothing is sent.

-t *tos*
Set the *type-of-service* in probe packets to the following value (default zero). The value must be a decimal integer in the range 0 to 255. This option can be used to see if different types-of-service result in different paths. (If you are not running a 4.3BSD–Tahoe or later system, this may be academic since the normal network services like telnet and ftp don't let you control the TOS). Not all values of TOS are legal or meaningful – see the IP spec for definitions. Useful values are probably '-t 16' (low delay) and '-t 8' (high throughput).

-v Verbose output. Received ICMP packets other than TIME_EXCEEDED and UNREACHABLEs are listed.

-w Set the time (in seconds) to wait for a response to a probe (default 3 sec.).

This program attempts to trace the route an IP packet would follow to some internet host by launching UDP probe packets with a small ttl (time to live) then listening for an ICMP "time exceeded" reply from a gateway. We start our probes with a ttl of one and increase by one until we get an ICMP "port unreachable" (which means we got to "host") or hit a max (which defaults to 30 hops & can be changed with the **-m** flag). Three probes (changed with **-q** flag) are sent at each ttl setting and a line is printed showing the ttl, address of the gateway and round trip time of each probe. If the probe answers come from different gateways, the address of each responding system will be printed. If there is no response within a 3 sec. timeout interval (changed with the **-w** flag), a "*" is printed for that probe.

We don't want the destination host to process the UDP probe packets so the destination port is set to an unlikely value (if some clod on the destination is using that value, it can be changed with the **-p** flag).

A sample use and output might be:

```
[yak 71]% traceroute nis.nsf.net.
traceroute to nis.nsf.net (35.1.1.48), 30 hops max, 56 byte packet
1  helios.ee.lbl.gov (128.3.112.1)  19 ms  19 ms  0 ms
2  lilac-dmc.Berkeley.EDU (128.32.216.1)  39 ms  39 ms  19 ms
3  lilac-dmc.Berkeley.EDU (128.32.216.1)  39 ms  39 ms  19 ms
4  ccngw-ner-cc.Berkeley.EDU (128.32.136.23)  39 ms  40 ms  39 ms
5  ccn-nerif22.Berkeley.EDU (128.32.168.22)  39 ms  39 ms  39 ms
6  128.32.197.4 (128.32.197.4)  40 ms  59 ms  59 ms
7  131.119.2.5 (131.119.2.5)  59 ms  59 ms  59 ms
8  129.140.70.13 (129.140.70.13)  99 ms  99 ms  80 ms
9  129.140.71.6 (129.140.71.6)  139 ms  239 ms  319 ms
10  129.140.81.7 (129.140.81.7)  220 ms  199 ms  199 ms
11  nic.merit.edu (35.1.1.48)  239 ms  239 ms  239 ms
```

Note that lines 2 & 3 are the same. This is due to a buggy kernel on the 2nd hop system – lbl-csam.arpa – that forwards packets with a zero ttl (a bug in the distributed version of 4.3 BSD). Note that you have to guess what path the packets are taking cross-country since the NSFNet (129.140) doesn't supply address-to-name translations for its NSSes.

A more interesting example is:

```
[yak 72]% traceroute allspice.lcs.mit.edu.
traceroute to allspice.lcs.mit.edu (18.26.0.115), 30 hops max
1  helios.ee.lbl.gov (128.3.112.1)  0 ms  0 ms  0 ms
2  lilac-dmc.Berkeley.EDU (128.32.216.1)  19 ms  19 ms  19 ms
3  lilac-dmc.Berkeley.EDU (128.32.216.1)  39 ms  19 ms  19 ms
4  ccngw-ner-cc.Berkeley.EDU (128.32.136.23)  19 ms  39 ms  39 ms
5  ccn-nerif22.Berkeley.EDU (128.32.168.22)  20 ms  39 ms  39 ms
```

```
6  128.32.197.4 (128.32.197.4)  59 ms  119 ms  39 ms
7  131.119.2.5 (131.119.2.5)  59 ms  59 ms  39 ms
8  129.140.70.13 (129.140.70.13)  80 ms  79 ms  99 ms
9  129.140.71.6 (129.140.71.6)  139 ms  139 ms  159 ms
10  129.140.81.7 (129.140.81.7)  199 ms  180 ms  300 ms
11  129.140.72.17 (129.140.72.17)  300 ms  239 ms  239 ms
12  * * *
13  128.121.54.72 (128.121.54.72)  259 ms  499 ms  279 ms
14  * * *
15  * * *
16  * * *
17  * * *
18  ALLSPICE.LCS.MIT.EDU (18.26.0.115)  339 ms  279 ms  279 ms
```

Note that the gateways 12, 14, 15, 16 & 17 hops away either don't send ICMP "time exceeded" messages or send them with a ttl too small to reach us. 14 – 17 are running the MIT C Gateway code that doesn't send "time exceeded"s. God only knows what's going on with 12.

The silent gateway 12 in the above may be the result of a bug in the 4.[23] BSD network code (and its derivatives): 4.x (x <= 3) sends an unreachable message using whatever ttl remains in the original datagram. Since, for gateways, the remaining ttl is zero, the ICMP "time exceeded" is guaranteed to not make it back to us. The behavior of this bug is slightly more interesting when it appears on the destination system:

```
1  helios.ee.lbl.gov (128.3.112.1)  0 ms  0 ms  0 ms
2  lilac-dmc.Berkeley.EDU (128.32.216.1)  39 ms  19 ms  39 ms
3  lilac-dmc.Berkeley.EDU (128.32.216.1)  19 ms  39 ms  19 ms
4  ccngw-ner-cc.Berkeley.EDU (128.32.136.23)  39 ms  40 ms  19 ms
5  ccn-nerif35.Berkeley.EDU (128.32.168.35)  39 ms  39 ms  39 ms
6  csgw.Berkeley.EDU (128.32.133.254)  39 ms  59 ms  39 ms
7  * * *
8  * * *
9  * * *
10  * * *
11  * * *
12  * * *
13  rip.Berkeley.EDU (128.32.131.22)  59 ms !  39 ms !  39 ms !
```

Notice that there are 12 "gateways" (13 is the final destination) and exactly the last half of them are "missing". What's really happening is that rip (a Sun-3 running Sun OS3.5) is using the ttl from our arriving datagram as the ttl in its ICMP reply. So, the reply will time out on the return path (with no notice sent to anyone since ICMP's aren't sent for ICMP's) until we probe with a ttl that's at least twice the path length. I.e., rip is really only 7 hops away. A reply that returns with a ttl of 1 is a clue this problem exists. `Traceroute` prints a "!" after the time if the ttl is <= 1. Since vendors ship a lot of obsolete (DEC's Ultrix, Sun 3.x) or non-standard (HPUX) software, expect to see this problem frequently and/or take care picking the target host of your probes. Other possible annotations after the time are **!H**, **!N**, **!P** (got a host, network or protocol unreachable, respectively), **!S** or **!F** (source route failed or fragmentation needed – neither of these should ever occur and the associated gateway is busted if you see one). If almost all the probes result in some kind of unreachable, `traceroute` will give up and exit.

This program is intended for use in network testing, measurement and management. It should be used primarily for manual fault isolation. Because of the load it could impose on the network, it is unwise to use `traceroute` during normal operations or from automated scripts.

AUTHOR

Implemented by Van Jacobson from a suggestion by Steve Deering. Debugged by a cast of thousands with particularly cogent suggestions or fixes from C. Philip Wood, Tim Seaver and Ken Adelman.

SEE ALSO

netstat(1), ping(8)

HISTORY

The **traceroute** command is currently in beta test.

M8

NAME

trpt – transliterate protocol trace

SYNOPSIS

trpt [**–a**] [**–f**] [**–j**] [**–p** *hex-address*] [**–s**] [**–t**][*system* [*core*]]

DESCRIPTION

Trpt interrogates the buffer of TCP trace records created when a socket is marked for "debugging" (see setsockopt(2)), and prints a readable description of these records. When no options are supplied, **trpt** prints all the trace records found in the system grouped according to TCP connection protocol control block (PCB). The following options may be used to alter this behavior.

–a In addition to the normal output, print the values of the source and destination addresses for each packet recorded.

–f Follow the trace as it occurs, waiting a short time for additional records each time the end of the log is reached.

–j Just give a list of the protocol control block addresses for which there are trace records.

–p Show only trace records associated with the protocol control block at the given address *hex-address*.

–s In addition to the normal output, print a detailed description of the packet sequencing information.

–t in addition to the normal output, print the values for all timers at each point in the trace.

The recommended use of **trpt** is as follows. Isolate the problem and enable debugging on the socket(s) involved in the connection. Find the address of the protocol control blocks associated with the sockets using the **–A** option to netstat(1). Then run **trpt** with the **–p** option, supplying the associated protocol control block addresses. The **–f** option can be used to follow the trace log once the trace is located. If there are many sockets using the debugging option, the **–j** option may be useful in checking to see if any trace records are present for the socket in question.

If debugging is being performed on a system or core file other than the default, the last two arguments may be used to supplant the defaults.

FILES

/vmunix
/dev/kmem

SEE ALSO

netstat(1), setsockopt(2), trsp(8)

DIAGNOSTICS

no namelist

When the system image doesn't contain the proper symbols to find the trace buffer; others which should be self explanatory.

BUGS

Should also print the data for each input or output, but this is not saved in the race record.

The output format is inscrutable and should be described here.

HISTORY

The `trpt` command appeared in 4.2BSD.

M8

NAME

trsp – transliterate sequenced packet protocol trace

SYNOPSIS

trsp [−a] [−s] [−t] [−j] [−p *hex-address*] [*system* [*core*]]

DESCRIPTION

Trpt interrogates the buffer of SPP trace records created when a socket is marked for "debugging" (see setsockopt(2)), and prints a readable description of these records. When no options are supplied, **trsp** prints all the trace records found in the system grouped according to SPP connection protocol control block (PCB). The following options may be used to alter this behavior.

−a In addition to the normal output, print the values of the source and destination addresses for each packet recorded.

−j Just give a list of the protocol control block addresses for which there are trace records.

−p Show only trace records associated with the protocol control block at the given address, *hex-address*.

−s in addition to the normal output, print a detailed description of the packet sequencing information.

−t in addition to the normal output, print the values for all timers at each point in the trace,

The recommended use of **trsp** is as follows. Isolate the problem and enable debugging on the socket(s) involved in the connection. Find the address of the protocol control blocks associated with the sockets using the **−A** option to netstat(1). Then run **trsp** with the **−p** option, supplying the associated protocol control block addresses. If there are many sockets using the debugging option, the **−j** option may be useful in checking to see if any trace records are present for the socket in question.

If debugging is being performed on a system or core file other than the default, the last two arguments may be used to supplant the defaults.

FILES

/vmunix
/dev/kmem

SEE ALSO

netstat(1), setsockopt(2)

DIAGNOSTICS

no namelist

When the system image doesn't contain the proper symbols to find the trace buffer; others which should be self explanatory.

BUGS

Should also print the data for each input or output, but this is not saved in the race record.

The output format is inscrutable and should be described here.

HISTORY

The **trsp** command appeared in 4.3BSD.

M8

NAME

`tunefs` – tune up an existing file system

SYNOPSIS

tunefs [**-a** *maxcontig*] [**-d** *rotdelay*] [**-e** *maxbpg*] [**-m** *minfree*]
[**-o** *optimize_preference*] [*special* | *filesys*]

DESCRIPTION

Tunefs is designed to change the dynamic parameters of a file system which affect the layout policies. The parameters which are to be changed are indicated by the flags given below:

-a *maxcontig*
This specifies the maximum number of contiguous blocks that will be laid out before forcing a rotational delay (see **-d** below). The default value is one, since most device drivers require an interrupt per disk transfer. Device drivers that can chain several buffers together in a single transfer should set this to the maximum chain length.

-d *rotdelay*
This specifies the expected time (in milliseconds) to service a transfer completion interrupt and initiate a new transfer on the same disk. It is used to decide how much rotational spacing to place between successive blocks in a file.

-e *maxbpg*
This indicates the maximum number of blocks any single file can allocate out of a cylinder group before it is forced to begin allocating blocks from another cylinder group. Typically this value is set to about one quarter of the total blocks in a cylinder group. The intent is to prevent any single file from using up all the blocks in a single cylinder group, thus degrading access times for all files subsequently allocated in that cylinder group. The effect of this limit is to cause big files to do long seeks more frequently than if they were allowed to allocate all the blocks in a cylinder group before seeking elsewhere. For file systems with exclusively large files, this parameter should be set higher.

-m *minfree*
This value specifies the percentage of space held back from normal users; the minimum free space threshold. The default value used is 10%. This value can be set to zero, however up to a factor of three in throughput will be lost over the performance obtained at a 10% threshold. Note that if the value is raised above the current usage level, users will be unable to allocate files until enough files have been deleted to get under the higher threshold.

-o *optimize_preference*
The file system can either try to minimize the time spent allocating blocks, or it can attempt to minimize the space fragmentation on the disk. If the value of minfree (see above) is less than 10%, then the file system should optimize for space to avoid running out of full sized blocks. For values of minfree greater than or equal to 10%, fragmentation is unlikely to be problematical, and the file system can be optimized for time.

SEE ALSO

fs(5), dumpfs(8), newfs(8), mkfs(8)

M. McKusick, W. Joy, S. Leffler, and R. Fabry, "A Fast File System for UNIX", *ACM Transactions on Computer Systems* 2, 3, pp 181-197, August 1984, (reprinted in the BSD System Manager's Manual, SMM:5).

BUGS

This program should work on mounted and active file systems. Because the super-block is not kept in the buffer cache, the changes will only take effect if the program is run on dismounted file systems. To change the root file system, the system must be rebooted after the file system is tuned.

You can tune a file system, but you can't tune a fish.

HISTORY

The `tunefs` command appeared in 4.2BSD.

NAME

umount – unmount file systems

SYNOPSIS

umount [**–fv**] *special* | *node*
umount **–a** [**–fv**] [**–h** *host*] [**–t** *ufs* | *lfs* | *external_type*]

DESCRIPTION

The **umount** command calls the unmount(2) system call to remove a *special device* or the remote node (rhost:path) from the file system tree at the point *node*. If either *special* or *node* are not provided, the appropriate information is taken from the fstab(5) file.

The options are as follows:

–a All of the file systems described in fstab(5) are unmounted.

–f The file system is forcibly unmounted. Active special devices continue to work, but all other files return errors if further accesses are attempted. The root file system cannot be forcibly unmounted.

–h *host*
Only filesystems mounted from the specified host will be unmounted. This option is implies the **–a** option and, unless otherwise specified with the **–t** option, will only unmount NFS filesystems.

–t *ufs* | *lfs* | *external type*
Is used to indicate the actions should only be taken on filesystems of the specified type. More than one type may be specified in a comma separated list. The list of filesystem types can be prefixed with "no" to specify the filesystem types for which action should *not* be taken. For example, the **umount** command:

```
umount -a -t nfs,mfs
```

umounts all filesystems of the type NFS and MFS.

–v Verbose, additional information is printed out as each file system is unmounted.

FILES

/etc/fstab file system table

SEE ALSO

unmount(2), fstab(5), mount(8)

HISTORY

A **umount** command appeared in Version 6 AT&T UNIX.

NAME

update – flush internal filesystem caches to disk frequently

SYNOPSIS

update

DESCRIPTION

The **update** command helps protect the integrity of disk volumes by flushing volatile cached filesystem data to disk at thirty second intervals. **Update** uses the `sync(2)` function call to do the task.

Update is commonly invoked at startup time by `rc(8)` when the system goes multi-user.

SEE ALSO

`sync(2)`, `fsck(8)`, `init(8)`, `rc(8)`, `sync(8)`

BUGS

It is possible on some systems that a `sync` occurring simultaneously with a crash may cause file system damage. See `fsck(8)`.

HISTORY

An **update** command appeared in Version 6 AT&T UNIX.

M8

NAME

uucico, **uucpd** – transfer files queued by uucp or uux

SYNOPSIS

uucico [**-L**] [**-R**] [**-d***spooldir*] [**-g***grade*] [**-r***role*] [**-s***system*] [**-x***debug*]
[**-t***turnaround*]

uucpd

DESCRIPTION

Uucico performs the actual work involved in transferring files between systems. Uucp(1) and uux(1) merely queue requests for data transfer which **uucico** processes.

The following options are available.

-L Only call "local" sites. A site is considered local if the device-type field in L.sys(5) is one of LOCAL, DIR or TCP.

-R Reverse roles. When used with the **-r***1* option, this tells the remote system to begin sending its jobs first, instead of waiting for the local machine to finish.

-d*spooldir*
Use *spooldir* as the spool directory. The default is /var/spool/uucp.

-g*grade*
Only send jobs of grade *grade* or higher this transfer. The grade of a job is specified when the job is queued by uucp(1) or uux(1).

-r*role*
role is either 1 or 0; it indicates whether **uucico** is to start up in master or slave role, respectively. 1 is used when running **uucico** by hand or from cron(8). 0 is used when another system calls the local system. Slave role is the default.

-s*system*
Call only system *system*. If **-s** is not specified, and **-r***1* is specified, **uucico** will attempt to call all systems for which there is work. If **-s** is specified, a call will be made even if there is no work for that system. This is useful for polling.

-t*turnaround*
Use *turnaround* as the line turnaround time (in minutes) instead of the default 30. If *turnaround* is missing or 0, line turnaround will be disabled. After **uucico** has been running in slave role for *turnaround* minutes, it will attempt to run in master role by negotiating with the remote machine. In earlier versions of **uucico**, a transfer of many large files in one direction would hold up mail going in the other direction. With the turnaround code working, the message flow will be more bidirectional in the short term. This option only works with newer **uucico**'s and is ignored by older ones.

-x*debug*
Turn on debugging at level *debug*. Level 5 is a good start when trying to find out why a call failed. Level 9 is very detailed. Level 99 is absurdly verbose. If *role* is 1 (master), output is written to the standard error *stderr*. If *stderr* is unavailable, output is written to /var/spool/uucp/AUDIT/*system*. When *role* is 0 (slave), debugging output is always written to the AUDIT file.

If **uucico** receives a SIGFPE (see kill(1)), it will toggle the debugging on or off.

Uucpd is the server for supporting uucp connections over networks. **Uucpd** listens for service requests at the port indicated in the "uucp" service specification; see `services(5)`. The server provides login name and password authentication before starting up **uucico** for the rest of the transaction.

Uucico is commonly used either of two ways: as a daemon run periodically by `cron(8)` to call out to remote systems, and as a "shell" for remote systems who call in. For calling out periodically, a typical line in `crontab` would be:

```
0    *    *    *    *    /usr/lib/uucp/uucico -r1
```

This will run **uucico** every hour in master role. For each system that has transfer requests queued, **uucico** calls the system, logs in, and executes the transfers. The file `L.sys(5)` is consulted for information about how to log in, while `L-devices(5)` specifies available lines and modems for calling.

For remote systems to dial in, an entry in the `passwd(5)` file must be created, with a login "shell" of **uucico**. For example:

```
nuucp:Password:6:1::/var/spool/uucppublic:/usr/lib/uucp/uucico
```

The UID for UUCP remote logins is not critical, so long as it differs from the UUCP Administrative login. The latter owns the UUCP files, and assigning this UID to a remote login would be an extreme security hazard.

FILES

/usr/lib/uucp/	UUCP internal files/utilities
/usr/lib/uucp/L-devices	Local device descriptions
/usr/lib/uucp/L-dialcodes	Phone numbers and prefixes
/usr/lib/uucp/L.aliases	Hostname aliases
/usr/lib/uucp/L.cmds	Remote command permissions list
/usr/lib/uucp/L.sys	Host connection specifications
/usr/lib/uucp/USERFILE	Remote directory tree permissions list
/var/spool/uucp/	Spool directory
/var/spool/uucp/AUDIT/*	Debugging audit trails
/var/spool/uucp/C./	Control files directory
/var/spool/uucp/D./	Incoming data file directory
/var/spool/uucp/D.hostname/	Outgoing data file directory
/var/spool/uucp/D.hostnameX/	Outgoing execution file directory
/var/spool/uucp/CORRUPT/	Place for corrupted C. and D. files
/var/spool/uucp/ERRLOG	UUCP internal error log
/var/spool/uucp/LOGFILE	UUCP system activity log
/var/spool/uucp/LCK/LCK..*	Device lock files
/var/spool/uucp/	SYSLOG File transfer statistics log
/var/spool/uucp/STST/*	System status files
/var/spool/uucp/TM./	File transfer temp directory
/var/spool/uucp/X./	Incoming execution file directory
/var/spool/uucppublic	Public access directory

SEE ALSO

`uucp(1)`, `uuq(1)`, `uux(1)`, `L-devices(5)`, `L-dialcodes(5)`, `L.aliases(5)`, `L.cmds(5)`, `L.sys(5)`, `uuclean(8)`, `uupoll(8)`, `uusnap(8)`, `uuxqt(8)`

D. A. Nowitz, and M. E. Lesk, *A Dial-Up Network of UNIX Systems.*

D. A. Nowitz, *Uucp Implementation Description.*

HISTORY

The `uucico` command appeared in 4.3BSD.

NAME

uuclean – uucp spool directory clean-up

SYNOPSIS

uuclean [**-d***subdirectory*] [**-m**] [**-n***time*] [**-p***pre*]

DESCRIPTION

`Uuclean` will scan the spool directory for files with the specified prefix and delete all those which are older than the specified number of hours.

The following options are available.

-d*subdirectory*
: Only the specified subdirectory will be cleaned.

-m
: Send mail to the owner of the file when it is deleted.

-n*time*
: Files whose age is more than *time* hours will be deleted if the prefix test is satisfied. (default time is 72 hours)

-p*pre*
: Scan for files with *pre* as the file prefix. Up to 10 **-p** arguments may be specified.

This program will typically be run daily by `cron`(8).

FILES

`/var/spool/uucp` Spool directory

SEE ALSO

`uucp`(1), `uux`(1), `uucico`(8)

HISTORY

The **uuclean** command appeared in 4.2BSD.

M8

NAME

uupoll – poll a remote UUCP site

SYNOPSIS

uupoll [**-g***grade*] [**-n**] *system*

DESCRIPTION

Uupoll is used to force a poll of a remote system. It queues a null job for the remote system and then invokes uucico(8).

The following options are available:

-g*grade* Only send jobs of grade *grade* or higher on this call.

-n Queue the null job, but do not invoke uucico.

Uupoll is usually run by cron(5) or by a user who wants to hurry a job along. A typical entry in *crontab* could be:

```
0	0,8,16	*	*	*	daemon	/usr/bin/uupoll ihnp4
0	4,12,20	*	*	*	daemon	/usr/bin/uupoll ucbvax
```

This will poll *ihnp4* at midnight, 0800, and 1600, and *ucbvax* at 0400, noon, and 2000.

If the local machine is already running uucico every hour and has a limited number of outgoing modems, a more elegant approach might be:

```
0	0,8,16	*	*	*	daemon	/usr/bin/uupoll -n ihnp4
0	4,12,20	*	*	*	daemon	/usr/bin/uupoll -n ucbvax
5	*	*	*	*	daemon	/usr/lib/uucp/uucico -r1
```

This will queue null jobs for the remote sites at the top of hour; they will be processed by uucico when it runs five minutes later.

FILES

/usr/lib/uucp/UUCP internal files/utilities
/var/spool/uucp/ Spool directory

SEE ALSO

uucp(1), uux(1), uucico(8)

HISTORY

The **uupoll** command appeared in 4.3BSD.

NAME

uusnap – show snapshot of the UUCP system

SYNOPSIS

uusnap

DESCRIPTION

Uusnap displays in tabular format a synopsis of the current UUCP situation. The format of each line is as follows:

```
site    N Cmds    N Data    N Xqts    Message
```

Where "site" is the name of the site with work, "N" is a count of each of the three possible types of work (command, data, or remote execute), and "Message" is the current status message for that site as found in the STST file.

Included in "Message" may be the time left before UUCP can re-try the call, and the count of the number of times that UUCP has tried (unsuccessfully) to reach the site.

SEE ALSO

uucp(1), uux(1), uuq(1), uucico(8)

UUCP Implementation Guide.

HISTORY

The **uusnap** command appeared in 4.2BSD.

M8

NAME

uuxqt – UUCP execution file interpreter

SYNOPSIS

uuxqt [**-x** *debug*]

DESCRIPTION

Uuxqt interprets *execution files* created on a remote system via uux(1) and transferred to the local system via uucico(8). When a user uses uux to request remote command execution, it is **uuxqt** that actually executes the command.

The options are as follows:

-x*debug* Normally, **uuxqt** is forked from uucico(8) to process queued execution files; for debugging, it may also be run manually by the UUCP administrator.

Uuxqt runs in its own subdirectory /var/spool/uucp/XTMP. It copies intermediate files to this directory when necessary.

FILES

/usr/lib/uucp/L.cmds	Remote command permissions list
/usr/lib/uucp/USERFILE	Remote directory tree permissions list
/var/spool/uucp/LOGFILE	UUCP system activity log
/var/spool/uucp/LCK/LCK.XQT	**Uuxqt** lock file
/var/spool/uucp/X./	Incoming execution file directory
/var/spool/uucp/XTMP	**Uuxqt** running directory

SEE ALSO

uucp(1), uux(1), L.cmds(5), USERFILE(5), uucico(8)

HISTORY

The **uuxqt** command appeared in 4.3BSD.

NAME

vipw – edit the password file

SYNOPSIS

vipw

DESCRIPTION

vipw edits the password file after setting the appropriate locks, and does any necessary processing after the password file is unlocked. If the password file is already locked for editing by another user, **vipw** will ask you to try again later. The default editor for **vipw** is vi(1).

vipw performs a number of consistency checks on the password entries, and will not allow a password file with a ''mangled'' entry to be installed. If **vipw** rejects the new password file, the user is prompted to re-enter the edit session.

Once the information has been verified, **vipw** uses pwd_mkdb(8) to update the user database. This is run in the background, and, at very large sites could take several minutes. Until this update is completed, the password file is unavailable for other updates and the new information is not available to programs.

ENVIRONMENT

If the following environment variable exists it will be utilized by **vipw**:

EDITOR The editor specified by the string EDITOR will be invoked instead of the default editor vi(1).

SEE ALSO

chpass(1), passwd(1), passwd(5), adduser(8), pwd_mkdb(8)

HISTORY

The **vipw** command appeared in 4.0BSD.

M8

NAME

vmstat – report virtual memory statistics

SYNOPSIS

vmstat [–fimst] [–c count] [–M core] [–N system]
[–w wait] [disks]

DESCRIPTION

Vmstat reports certain kernel statistics kept about process, virtual memory, disk, trap and cpu activity.

The options are as follows:

–c Repeat the display *count* times. The first display is for the time since a reboot and each subsequent report is for the time period since the last display. If no *wait* interval is specified, the default is 1 second.

–f Report on the number *fork*(2) and *vfork*(2) system calls since system startup, and the number of pages of virtual memory involved in each.

–i Report on the number of interrupts taken by each device since system startup.

–M Extract values associated with the name list from the specified core instead of the default ''/dev/kmem''.

–N Extract the name list from the specified system instead of the default ''/vmunix''.

–m Report on the usage of kernel dynamic memory listed first by size of allocation and then by type of usage.

–s Display the contents of the *sum* structure, giving the total number of several kinds of paging related events which have occurred since system startup.

–t Report on the number of page in and page reclaims since system startup, and the amount of time required by each.

–w Pause *wait* seconds between each display. If no repeat *count* is specified, the default is infinity.

By default, *vmstat* displays the following information:

procs Information about the numbers of processes in various states.

r in run queue
b blocked for resources (i/o, paging, etc.)
w runnable or short sleeper (< 20 secs) but swapped

memory

Information about the usage of virtual and real memory. Virtual pages (reported in units of 1024 bytes) are considered active if they belong to processes which are running or have run in the last 20 seconds.

avm active virtual pages
fre size of the free list

page Information about page faults and paging activity. These are averaged each five seconds, and given in units per second.

re page reclaims (simulating reference bits)
at pages attached (found in free list)
pi pages paged in
po pages paged out
fr pages freed per second
de anticipated short term memory shortfall
sr pages scanned by clock algorithm, per-second

disks Disk operations per second (this field is system dependent). Typically paging will be split across the available drives. The header of the field is the first character of the disk name and the unit number. If more than four disk drives are configured in the system, *vmstat* displays only the first four drives. To force *vmstat* to display specific drives, their names may be supplied on the command line.

faults Trap/interrupt rate averages per second over last 5 seconds.

in	device interrupts per interval (including clock interrupts)
sy	system calls per interval
cs	cpu context switch rate (switches/interval)

cpu Breakdown of percentage usage of CPU time.

us	user time for normal and low priority processes
sy	system time
id	cpu idle

EXAMPLES

The command ``vmstat -i 5'' will print what the system is doing every five seconds; this is a good choice of printing interval since this is how often some of the statistics are sampled in the system. Others vary every second and running the output for a while will make it apparent which are recomputed every second.

FILES

/vmunix default kernel namelist
/dev/kmem default memory file

SEE ALSO

fstat(1), *netstat*(1), *nfsstat*(1), *ps*(1), *systat*(1), *iostat*(8), *pstat*(8)

The sections starting with ``Interpreting system activity'' in *Installing and Operating 4.3BSD*.

BUGS

The –c and –w options are only available with the default output.

M8

NAME

XNSrouted – NS Routing Information Protocol daemon

SYNOPSIS

XNSrouted [**–q**] [**–s**] [**–t**] [*logfile*]

DESCRIPTION

XNSrouted is invoked at boot time to manage the Xerox NS routing tables. The NS routing daemon uses the Xerox NS Routing Information Protocol in maintaining up to date kernel routing table entries.

Available options:

–q Do not supply routing information (opposite of **–s** option below).

–s Forces **XNSrouted** to supply routing information whether it is acting as an internetwork router or not.

–t All packets sent or received are printed on the standard output. In addition, **XNSrouted** will not divorce itself from the controlling terminal so that interrupts from the keyboard will kill the process.

logfile Name of file in which **XNSrouted**'s actions should be logged. This log contains information about any changes to the routing tables and a history of recent messages sent and received which are related to the changed route.

In normal operation **XNSrouted** listens for routing information packets. If the host is connected to multiple NS networks, it periodically supplies copies of its routing tables to any directly connected hosts and networks.

When **XNSrouted** is started, it uses the SIOCGIFCONF ioctl(2) to find those directly connected interfaces configured into the system and marked "up" (the software loopback interface is ignored). If multiple interfaces are present, it is assumed the host will forward packets between networks. **XNSrouted** then transmits a *request* packet on each interface (using a broadcast packet if the interface supports it) and enters a loop, listening for *request* and *response* packets from other hosts.

When a *request* packet is received, **XNSrouted** formulates a reply based on the information maintained in its internal tables. The *response* packet generated contains a list of known routes, each marked with a "hop count" metric (a count of 16, or greater, is considered "infinite"). The metric associated with each route returned provides a metric *relative to the sender*.

Response packets received by **XNSrouted** are used to update the routing tables if one of the following conditions is satisfied:

- No routing table entry exists for the destination network or host, and the metric indicates the destination is "reachable" (i.e. the hop count is not infinite).
- The source host of the packet is the same as the router in the existing routing table entry. That is, updated information is being received from the very internetwork router through which packets for the destination are being routed.
- The existing entry in the routing table has not been updated for some time (defined to be 90 seconds) and the route is at least as cost effective as the current route.
- The new route describes a shorter route to the destination than the one currently stored in the routing tables; the metric of the new route is compared against the one stored in the table to decide this.

When an update is applied, **XNSrouted** records the change in its internal tables and generates a *response* packet to all directly connected hosts and networks. Routed(8) waits a short period of time (no more than 30 seconds) before modifying the kernel's routing tables to allow possible unstable situations to settle.

In addition to processing incoming packets, **XNSrouted** also periodically checks the routing table entries. If an entry has not been updated for 3 minutes, the entry's metric is set to infinity and marked for deletion. Deletions are delayed an additional 60 seconds to insure the invalidation is propagated to other routers.

Hosts acting as internetwork routers gratuitously supply their routing tables every 30 seconds to all directly connected hosts and networks.

SEE ALSO

idp(4)

Internet Transport Protocols, XSIS 028112, Xerox System Integration Standard.

HISTORY

The **XNSrouted** command appeared in 4.3BSD.

M8

NAME

zic – time zone compiler

SYNOPSIS

zic [**–v**] [**–d** *directory*] [**–l** *localtime*] [**–p** *posixrules*] [**–L** *leapsecondfilename*] [**–s**] [*filename* ...]

DESCRIPTION

Zic reads text from the file(s) named on the command line and creates the time conversion information files specified in this input. If a *filename* is –, the standard input is read.

These options are available:

–d *directory*
: Create time conversion information files in the named directory rather than in the standard directory named below.

–l *timezone*
: Use the given time zone as local time. *Zic* will act as if the input contained a link line of the form

  Link *timezone* localtime

–p *timezone*
: Use the given time zone's rules when handling POSIX-format time zone environment variables. *Zic* will act as if the input contained a link line of the form

  Link *timezone* posixrules

–L *leapsecondfilename*
: Read leap second information from the file with the given name. If this option is not used, no leap second information appears in output files.

–v Complain if a year that appears in a data file is outside the range of years representable by *time*(2) values.

–s Limit time values stored in output files to values that are the same whether they're taken to be signed or unsigned. You can use this option to generate SVVS-compatible files.

Input lines are made up of fields. Fields are separated from one another by any number of white space characters. Leading and trailing white space on input lines is ignored. An unquoted sharp character (#) in the input introduces a comment which extends to the end of the line the sharp character appears on. White space characters and sharp characters may be enclosed in double quotes (") if they're to be used as part of a field. Any line that is blank (after comment stripping) is ignored. Non-blank lines are expected to be of one of three types: rule lines, zone lines, and link lines.

A rule line has the form

Rule NAME FROM TO TYPE IN ON AT SAVE LETTER/S

For example:

```
Rule  USA  1969  1973  –  Apr  lastSun  2:00  1:00  D
```

The fields that make up a rule line are:

NAME Gives the (arbitrary) name of the set of rules this rule is part of.

FROM Gives the first year in which the rule applies. The word **minimum** (or an abbreviation) means the minimum year with a representable time value. The word **maximum** (or an abbreviation) means the maximum year with a representable time value.

TO Gives the final year in which the rule applies. In addition to **minimum** and **maximum** (as above), the word **only** (or an abbreviation) may be used to repeat the value of the **FROM** field.

TYPE Gives the type of year in which the rule applies. If **TYPE** is – then the rule applies in all years between **FROM** and **TO** inclusive; if **TYPE** is **uspres**, the rule applies in U.S. Presidential election years; if **TYPE** is **nonpres**, the rule applies in years other than U.S. Presidential election years. If **TYPE** is something else, then *zic* executes the command

  yearistype *year type*

to check the type of a year: an exit status of zero is taken to mean that the year is of the given type; an exit status of one is taken to mean that the year is not of the given type.

IN Names the month in which the rule takes effect. Month names may be abbreviated.

ON Gives the day on which the rule takes effect. Recognized forms include:

5	the fifth of the month
lastSun	the last Sunday in the month
lastMon	the last Monday in the month
Sun>=8	first Sunday on or after the eighth
Sun<=25	last Sunday on or before the 25th

Names of days of the week may be abbreviated or spelled out in full. Note that there must be no spaces within the **ON** field.

AT Gives the time of day at which the rule takes effect. Recognized forms include:

2	time in hours
2:00	time in hours and minutes
15:00	24-hour format time (for times after noon)
1:28:14	time in hours, minutes, and seconds

Any of these forms may be followed by the letter **w** if the given time is local "wall clock" time or **s** if the given time is local "standard" time; in the absence of **w** or **s**, wall clock time is assumed.

SAVE Gives the amount of time to be added to local standard time when the rule is in effect. This field has the same format as the **AT** field (although, of course, the **w** and **s** suffixes are not used).

LETTER/S
Gives the "variable part" (for example, the "S" or "D" in "EST" or "EDT") of time zone abbreviations to be used when this rule is in effect. If this field is –, the variable part is null.

A zone line has the form

```
Zone  NAME                     GMTOFF  RULES/SAVE  FORMAT  [UNTIL]
```

For example:

```
Zone  Australia/South–west     9:30    Aus         CST     1987 Mar 15 2:00
```

The fields that make up a zone line are:

NAME The name of the time zone. This is the name used in creating the time conversion information file for the zone.

GMTOFF
The amount of time to add to GMT to get standard time in this zone. This field has the same format as the **AT** and **SAVE** fields of rule lines; begin the field with a minus sign if time must be subtracted from GMT.

RULES/SAVE
The name of the rule(s) that apply in the time zone or, alternately, an amount of time to add to local standard time. If this field is – then standard time always applies in the time zone.

FORMAT
The format for time zone abbreviations in this time zone. The pair of characters **%s** is used to show where the "variable part" of the time zone abbreviation goes.

UNTIL The time at which the GMT offset or the rule(s) change for a location. It is specified as a year, a month, a day, and a time of day. If this is specified, the time zone information is generated from the given GMT offset and rule change until the time specified.

The next line must be a "continuation" line; this has the same form as a zone line except that the string "Zone" and the name are omitted, as the continuation line will place information starting at the time specified as the **UNTIL** field in the previous line in the file used by the previous line. Continuation lines may contain an **UNTIL** field, just as zone lines do, indicating that the next line is a further continuation.

A link line has the form

```
Link   LINK-FROM   LINK-TO
```

For example:

```
Link   US/Eastern     EST5EDT
```

The **LINK-FROM** field should appear as the **NAME** field in some zone line; the **LINK-TO** field is used as an alternate name for that zone.

Except for continuation lines, lines may appear in any order in the input.

Lines in the file that describes leap seconds have the following form:
Leap YEAR MONTH DAY HH:MM:SS CORR R/S

For example:

```
Leap   1974   Dec   31   23:59:60   +   S
```

The **YEAR, MONTH, DAY,** and **HH:MM:SS** fields tell when the leap second happened. The **CORR** field should be "+" if a second was added or "-" if a second was skipped. The **R/S** field should be (an abbreviation of) "Stationary" if the leap second time given by the other fields should be interpreted as GMT or (an abbreviation of) "Rolling" if the leap second time given by the other fields should be interpreted as local wall clock time.

NOTE

For areas with more than two types of local time, you may need to use local standard time in the **AT** field of the earliest transition time's rule to ensure that the earliest transition time recorded in the compiled file is correct.

FILE

/etc/zoneinfo standard directory used for created files

SEE ALSO

newctime(3), tzfile(5), zdump(8)

System Management Documents

Installing and Operating 4.4BSD UNIX
July 27, 1993

Marshall Kirk McKusick

Keith Bostic

Michael J. Karels

Samuel J. Leffler

Computer Systems Research Group
Department of Electrical Engineering and Computer Science
University of California, Berkeley
Berkeley, California 94720
(415) 642-7780

Mike Hibler

Center for Software Science
Department of Computer Science
University of Utah
Salt Lake City, Utah 84112
(801) 581-5017

1

ABSTRACT

This document contains instructions for the installation and operation of the 4.4BSD release of UNIX as distributed by The University of California at Berkeley.

It discusses procedures for installing UNIX on a new machine, and for upgrading an existing 4.3BSD UNIX system to the new release. An explanation of how to lay out filesystems on available disks and the space requirements for various parts of the system are given. A brief overview of the major changes to the system between 4.3BSD and 4.4BSD are outlined. An explanation of how to set up terminal lines and user accounts, and how to do system-specific tailoring is provided. A description of how to install and configure the 4.4BSD networking facilities is included. Finally, the document details system operation procedures: shutdown and startup, filesystem backup procedures, resource control, performance monitoring, and procedures for recompiling and reinstalling system software.

1

Table of Contents

1

1

1. Introduction

This document explains how to install the 4.4BSD Berkeley version of UNIX on your system. The filesystem format is compatible with 4.3BSD and it will only be necessary for you to do a full bootstrap procedure if you are installing the release on a new machine. The object file formats are completely different from the System V release, so the most straightforward procedure for upgrading a System V system is to do a full bootstrap.

The full bootstrap procedure is outlined in section 2; the process starts with copying a filesystem image onto a new disk. This filesystem is then booted and used to extract the remainder of the system binaries and sources from the archives on the tape(s).

The technique for upgrading a 4.3BSD system is described in section 3 of this document. The upgrade procedure involves extracting system binaries onto new root and `/usr` filesystems and merging local configuration files into the new system. User filesystems may be upgraded in place. Most 4.3BSD binaries may be used with 4.4BSD in the course of the conversion. It is desirable to recompile local sources after the conversion, as the new compiler (GCC) provides superior code optimization. Consult section 3.5 for a description of some of the differences between 4.3BSD and 4.4BSD.

1.1. Distribution format

The distribution comes in two formats:

(3) 6250bpi 2400' 9-track magnetic tapes, or
(1) 8mm Exabyte tape

If you have the facilities, we **strongly** recommend copying the magnetic tape(s) in the distribution kit to guard against disaster. The tapes contain 10240-byte records. There are interspersed tape marks; end-of-tape is signaled by a double end-of-file. The first file on the tape is architecture dependent. Additional files on the tape(s) contain tape archive images of the system binaries and sources (see *tar*(1)[1]). See the tape label for a description of the contents and format of each individual tape.

1.2. UNIX device naming

Device names have a different syntax depending on whether you are talking to the standalone system or a running UNIX kernel. The standalone system syntax is currently architecture dependent and is described in the various architecture specific sections as applicable. When not running standalone, devices are available via files in the `/dev/` directory. The file name typically encodes the device type, its logical unit and a partition within that unit. For example, `/dev/sd2b` refers to the second partition (''b'') of SCSI (''sd'') drive number ''2'', while `/dev/rmt0` refers to the raw (''r'') interface of 9-track tape (''mt'') unit ''0''.

The mapping of physical addressing information (e.g. controller, target) to a logical unit number is dependent on the system configuration. In all simple cases, where only a single controller is present, a drive with physical unit number 0 (e.g., as determined by its unit specification, either unit plug or other selection mechanism) will be called unit 0 in its UNIX file name. This is not, however, strictly necessary, since the system has a level of indirection in this naming. If there are multiple controllers, the disk unit numbers will normally be counted sequentially across controllers. This can be taken advantage of to make the system less dependent on the interconnect topology, and to make reconfiguration after hardware failure easier.

Each UNIX physical disk is divided into at most 8 logical disk partitions, each of which may occupy any consecutive cylinder range on the physical device. The cylinders occupied by the 8 partitions for each drive type are specified initially in the disk description file `/etc/disktab` (c.f. *disktab*(5)). The partition information and description of the drive geometry are written in one of the first sectors of each disk with the *disklabel*(8) program. Each partition may be used for either a raw data area such as a paging area or to store a UNIX filesystem. It is conventional for the first partition on a disk to be used to store a root

[1] References of the form *X*(Y) mean the entry named *X* in section Y of the ''UNIX Programmer's Manual''.

filesystem, from which UNIX may be bootstrapped. The second partition is traditionally used as a paging area, and the rest of the disk is divided into spaces for additional "mounted filesystems" by use of one or more additional partitions.

1.3. UNIX devices: block and raw

UNIX makes a distinction between "block" and "raw" (character) devices. Each disk has a block device interface where the system makes the device byte addressable and you can write a single byte in the middle of the disk. The system will read out the data from the disk sector, insert the byte you gave it and put the modified data back. The disks with the names `/dev/xx0[a-h]`, etc., are block devices. There are also raw devices available. These have names like `/dev/rxx0[a-h]`, the "r" here standing for "raw". Raw devices bypass the buffer cache and use DMA directly to/from the program's I/O buffers; they are normally restricted to full-sector transfers. In the bootstrap procedures we will often suggest using the raw devices, because these tend to work faster. Raw devices are used when making new filesystems, when checking unmounted filesystems, or for copying quiescent filesystems. The block devices are used to mount filesystems.

You should be aware that it is sometimes important whether to use the character device (for efficiency) or not (because it would not work, e.g. to write a single byte in the middle of a sector). Do not change the instructions by using the wrong type of device indiscriminately.

2. Bootstrap procedure

This section explains the bootstrap procedure that can be used to get the kernel supplied with this distribution running on your machine. If you are not currently running 4.3BSD you will have to do a full bootstrap. Section 3 describes how to upgrade a 4.3BSD system. An understanding of the operations used in a full bootstrap is helpful in doing an upgrade as well. In either case, it is highly desirable to read and understand the remainder of this document before proceeding.

The distribution supports a somewhat wider set of machines than those for which we have built binaries. The architectures that are supported only in source form include:

- Intel 386/486-based machines (ISA/AT or EISA bus only)
- Sony News MIPS-based workstations
- Omron Luna 68000-based workstations

If you wish to run one of these architectures, you will have to build a cross compilation environment. Note that the distribution does **not** include the machine support for the Tahoe and VAX architectures found in previous BSD distributions. Our primary development environment is the HP9000/300 series machines. The other architectures are developed and supported by people outside the university. Consequently, we are not able to directly test or maintain these other architectures, so cannot comment on their robustness, reliability, or completeness.

2.1. Bootstrapping from the tape

The set of files on the distribution tape are as follows:

1) A *dd*(1) (HP300), *tar*(1) (DECstation), or *dump*(8) (SPARC) image of the root filesystem
2) A *tar* image of the `/var` filesystem
3) A *tar* image of the `/usr` filesystem
4) A *tar* image of `/usr/src/sys`
5) A *tar* image of `/usr/src` except sys and contrib
6) A *tar* image of `/usr/src/contrib`
7) (8mm Exabyte tape distributions only) A *tar* image of `/usr/src/X11R5`

The tape bootstrap procedure used to create a working system involves the following major steps:

1) Transfer a bootable root filesystem from the tape to a disk and get it booted and running.

2) Build and restore the `/var` and `/usr` filesystems from tape with *tar*(1).

3) Extract the system and utility source files as desired.

The following sections describe the above steps in detail. The details of the first step vary between architectures. The specific steps for the HP300, SPARC, and DECstation are given in the next three sections respectively. You should follow the instructions for your particular architecture. In all sections, commands you are expected to type are shown in italics, while that information printed by the system is shown emboldened.

2.2. Booting the HP300

2.2.1. Supported hardware

The hardware supported by 4.4BSD for the HP300/400 is as follows:

CPU's	68020 based (318, 319, 320, 330 and 350), 68030 based (340, 345, 360, 370, 375, 400) and 68040 based (380, 425, 433).
DISK's	HP-IB/CS80 (7912, 7914, 7933, 7936, 7945, 7957, 7958, 7959, 2200, 2203) and SCSI-I (including magneto-optical).
TAPE's	Low-density CS80 cartridge (7914, 7946, 9144), high-density CS80 cartridge (9145), HP SCSI DAT and SCSI Exabyte.
RS232	98644 built-in single-port, 98642 4-port and 98638 8-port interfaces.
NETWORK	98643 internal and external LAN cards.
GRAPHICS	Terminal emulation and raw frame buffer support for 98544 / 98545 / 98547 (Topcat color & monochrome), 98548 / 98549 / 98550 (Catseye color & monochrome), 98700 / 98710 (Gatorbox), 98720 / 98721 (Renaissance), 98730 / 98731 (DaVinci) and A1096A (Hyperion monochrome).
INPUT	General interface supporting all HIL devices. (e.g. keyboard, 2 and 3 button mice, ID module, ...)
MISC	Battery-backed real time clock, builtin and 98625A/B HP-IB interfaces, builtin and 98658A SCSI interfaces, serial printers and plotters on HP-IB, and SCSI autochanger device.

Major items that are not supported include the 310 and 332 CPU's, 400 series machines configured for Domain/OS, EISA and VME bus adaptors, audio, the centronics port, 1/2" tape drives (7980), CD-ROM, and the PVRX/TVRX 3D graphics displays.

2.2.2. Standalone device file naming

The standalone system device name syntax on the HP300 is of the form:

    xx(a,c,u,p)

where *xx* is the device type, *a* specifies the adaptor to use, *c* the controller, *u* the unit, and *p* a partition. The *device type* differentiates the various disks and tapes and is one of: ‘‘rd’’ for HP-IB CS80 disks, ‘‘ct’’ for HP-IB CS80 cartridge tapes, or ‘‘sd’’ for SCSI-I disks (SCSI-I tapes are currently not supported). The *adaptor* field is a logical HP-IB or SCSI bus adaptor card number. This will typically be 0 for SCSI disks, 0 for devices on the ‘‘slow’’ HP-IB interface (usually tapes) and 1 for devices on the ‘‘fast’’ HP-IB interface (usually disks). To get a complete mapping of physical (select-code) to logical card numbers just type a ^C at the standalone prompt. The *controller* field is the disk or tape's target number on the HP-IB or SCSI bus. For SCSI the range is 0 to 6 (7 is the adaptor address) and for HP-IB the range is 0 to 7. The *unit* field is unused and should be 0. The *partition* field is interpreted differently for tapes and disks: for disks it is a disk partition (in the range 0-7), and for tapes it is a file number offset on the tape. Thus, partition 2 of a SCSI disk drive at target 3 on SCSI bus 1 would be ‘‘sd(1,3,0,2)’’. If you have only one of any type bus adaptor, you may omit the adaptor and controller numbers; e.g. ‘‘sd(0,2)’’ could be used instead of ‘‘sd(0,0,0,2)’’. The following examples always use the full syntax for clarity.

2.2.3. The procedure

The basic steps involved in bringing up the HP300 are as follows:

1) Obtain a second disk and format it, if necessary.
2) Copy a root filesystem from the tape onto the beginning of the disk.
3) Boot the UNIX system on the new disk.
4) (Optional) Build a root filesystem optimized for your disk.
5) Label the disks with the *disklabel*(8) program.

2.2.3.1. Step 1: selecting and formatting a disk

For your first system you will have to obtain a formatted disk of a type given in the "supported hardware" list above. If you want to load an entire binary system (i.e., everything except `/usr/src`), on the single disk you will need a minimum of 290MB, ruling out anything smaller than a 7959B/S disk. The disklabel included in the bootstrap root image is laid out to accommodate this scenario. Note that an HP SCSI magneto-optical disk will work fine for this case. 4.4BSD will boot and run (albeit slowly) using one. If you want to load source on a single disk system, you will need at least 640MB (at least a 2213A SCSI or 2203A HP-IB disk). A disk as small as the 7945A (54MB) can be used for the bootstrap procedure but will hold only the root and primary swap partitions. If you plan to use multiple disks, refer to section 2.5 for suggestions on partitioning.

After selecting a disk, you may need to format it. Since most HP disk drives come pre-formatted (except optical media) you probably will not, but if necessary, you can format a disk under HP-UX using the *mediainit*(1m) program. Once you have 4.4BSD up and running on one machine you can use the *scsiformat*(8) program to format additional SCSI disks. Any additional HP-IB disks will have to be formatted using HP-UX.

2.2.3.2. Step 2: copying the root filesystem from tape to disk

Once you have a formatted second disk you can use the *dd*(1) command under HP-UX to copy the root filesystem image from the tape to the beginning of the second disk. For HP's, the root filesystem image is the first file on the tape. It includes a disklabel and bootblock along with the root filesystem. An example command to copy the image from tape to the beginning of a disk is:

```
dd if=/dev/rmt/0m of=/dev/rdsk/1s0 bs=20b
```

The actual special file syntax may vary depending on unit numbers and the version of HP-UX that is running. Consult the HP-UX *mt*(7) and *disk*(7) man pages for details.

Note that if you have a SCSI disk, you don't necessarily have to use HP-UX (or an HP) to create the boot disk. Any machine and operating system that will allow you to copy the raw disk image out to block 0 of the disk will do.

If you have only a single machine with a single disk, you may still be able to install and boot 4.4BSD if you have an HP-IB cartridge tape drive. If so, you can use a more difficult approach of booting a standalone copy program from the tape, and using that to copy the root filesystem image from the tape to the disk. To do this, you need to extract the first file of the distribution tape (the root image), copy it over to a machine with a cartridge drive and then copy the image onto tape. For example:

```
dd if=/dev/rst0 of=bootimage bs=20b
rcp bootimage foo:/tmp/bootimage
<login to foo>
dd if=/tmp/bootimage of=/dev/rct/0m bs=20b
```

Once this tape is created you can boot and run the standalone tape copy program from it. The copy program is loaded just as any other program would be loaded by the bootrom in "attended" mode: reset the CPU, hold down the space bar until the word "Keyboard" appears in the installed interface list, and enter the menu selection for SYS_TCOPY. Once loaded and running:

1

From: *^C* (control-C to see logical adaptor assignments)
hpib0 at sc7
scsi0 at sc14
From: *ct(0,7,0,0)* (HP-IB tape, target 7, first tape file)
To: *sd(0,0,0,2)* (SCSI disk, target 0, third partition)
Copy completed: 1728 records copied

This copy will likely take 30 minutes or more.

2.2.3.3. Step 3: booting the root filesystem

You now have a bootable root filesystem on the disk. If you were previously running with two disks, it would be best if you shut down the machine and turn off power on the HP-UX drive. It will be less confusing and it will eliminate any chance of accidentally destroying the HP-UX disk. If you used a cartridge tape for booting you should also unload the tape at this point. Whether you booted from tape or copied from disk you should now reboot the machine and do another attended boot (see previous section), this time with SYS_TBOOT. Once loaded and running the boot program will display the CPU type and prompt for a kernel file to boot:

HP433 CPU
Boot
: */vmunix*

After providing the kernel name, the machine will boot 4.4BSD with output that looks about like this:

597480+34120+139288 start 0xfe8019ec
Copyright (c) 1982, 1986, 1989, 1991, 1993
The Regents of the University of California.
Copyright (c) 1992 Hewlett-Packard Company
Copyright (c) 1992 Motorola Inc.
All rights reserved.

4.4BSD UNIX #1: Tue Jul 20 11:40:36 PDT 1993
mckusick@vangogh.CS.Berkeley.EDU:/usr/obj/sys/compile/GENERIC.hp300
HP9000/433 (33MHz MC68040 CPU+MMU+FPU, 4k on-chip physical I/D caches)
real mem = xxx
avail mem = ###
using ### buffers containing ### bytes of memory
(... information about available devices ...)
root device?

The first three numbers are printed out by the bootstrap program and are the sizes of different parts of the system (text, initialized and uninitialized data). The system also allocates several system data structures after it starts running. The sizes of these structures are based on the amount of available memory and the maximum count of active users expected, as declared in a system configuration description. This will be discussed later.

UNIX itself then runs for the first time and begins by printing out a banner identifying the release and version of the system that is in use and the date that it was compiled.

Next the *mem* messages give the amount of real (physical) memory and the memory available to user programs in bytes. For example, if your machine has 16Mb bytes of memory, then **xxx** will be 16777216.

The messages that come out next show what devices were found on the current processor. These messages are described in *autoconf*(4). The distributed system may not have found all the communications devices you have or all the mass storage peripherals you have, especially if you have more than two of anything. You will correct this when you create a description of your machine from which to configure a site-dependent version of UNIX. The messages printed at boot here contain much of the information that will be used in creating the configuration. In a correctly configured system most of the information present in the configuration description is printed out at boot time as the system verifies that each device is present.

The "root device?" prompt was printed by the system to ask you for the name of the root filesystem to use. This happens because the distribution system is a *generic* system, i.e., it can be bootstrapped on a cpu with its root device and paging area on any available disk drive. You will most likely respond to the root device question with "sd0" if you are booting from a SCSI disk, or with "rd0" if you are booting from an HP-IB disk. This response shows that the disk it is running on is drive 0 of type "sd" or "rd" respectively. If you have other disks attached to the system, it is possible that the drive you are using will not be configured as logical drive 0. Check the autoconfiguration messages printed out by the kernel to make sure. These messages will show the type of every logical drive and their associated controller and slave addresses. You will later build a system tailored to your configuration that will not prompt you for a root device when it is bootstrapped.

> **root device?** *sd0*
> **WARNING: preposterous time in filesystem — CHECK AND RESET THE DATE!**
> **erase ^?, kill ^U, intr ^C**
> **#**

The "erase ..." message is part of the `/.profile` that was executed by the root shell when it started. This message tells you about the settings of the character erase, line erase, and interrupt characters.

UNIX is now running, and the *UNIX Programmer's Manual* applies. The "#" is the prompt from the Bourne shell, and lets you know that you are the super-user, whose login name is "root".

At this point, the root filesystem is mounted read-only. Before continuing the installation, the filesystem needs to be "updated" to allow writing and device special files for the following steps need to be created. This is done as follows:

# *mount_mfs -s 1000 -T type /dev/null /tmp*	(create a writable filesystem)
(*type* is the disk type as determined from /etc/disktab)	
# *cd /tmp*	(connect to that directory)
# *../dev/MAKEDEV sd#*	(create special files for root disk)
(*sd* is the disk type, # is the unit number)	
(ignore warning from "sh")	
# *mount –uw /tmp/sd#a /*	(read-write mount root filesystem)
# *cd /dev*	(go to device directory)
# *./MAKEDEV sd#*	(create permanent special files for root disk)
(again, ignore warning from "sh")	

2.2.3.4. Step 4: (optional) restoring the root filesystem

The root filesystem that you are currently running on is complete, however it probably is not optimally laid out for the disk on which you are running. If you will be cloning copies of the system onto multiple disks for other machines, you are advised to connect one of these disks to this machine, and build and restore a properly laid out root filesystem onto it. If this is the only machine on which you will be running 4.4BSD or peak performance is not an issue, you can skip this step and proceed directly to step 5.

Connect a second disk to your machine. If you bootstrapped using the two disk method, you can overwrite your initial HP-UX disk, as it will no longer be needed (assuming you have no plans to run HP-UX again).

To really create the root filesystem on drive 1 you should first label the disk as described in step 5 below. Then run the following commands:

```
# cd /dev
# ./MAKEDEV sd1a
# newfs /dev/rsd1a
# mount /dev/sd1a /mnt
# cd /mnt
# dump 0f - /dev/rsd0a | restore xf -
```

(Note: restore will ask if you want to "set owner/mode for '.'"
to which you should reply "yes".)

When this completes, you should then shut down the system, and boot on the disk that you just created following the procedure in step (3) above.

2.2.3.5. Step 5: placing labels on the disks

For each disk on the HP300, 4.4BSD places information about the geometry of the drive and the partition layout at byte offset 1024. This information is written with *disklabel*(8).

The root image just loaded includes a "generic" label intended to allow easy installation of the root and `/usr` and may not be suitable for the actual disk on which it was installed. In particular, it may make your disk appear larger or smaller than its real size. In the former case, you lose some capacity. In the latter, some of the partitions may map non-existent sectors leading to errors if those partitions are used. It is also possible that the defined geometry will interact poorly with the filesystem code resulting in reduced performance. However, as long as you are willing to give up a little space, not use certain partitions or suffer minor performance degradation, you might want to avoid this step; especially if you do not know how to use *ed*(1).

If you choose to edit this label, you can fill in correct geometry information from `/etc/disktab`. You may also want to rework the "e" and "f" partitions used for loading `/usr` and `/var`. You should not attempt to, and *disklabel* will not let you, modify the "a", "b" and "d" partitions. To edit a label:

```
# EDITOR=ed
# export EDITOR
# disklabel -r -e /dev/rXX#d
```

where **XX** is the type and # is the logical drive number; e.g. `/dev/rsd0d` or `/dev/rrd0d`. Note the explicit use of the "d" partition. This partition includes the bootblock as does "c" and using it allows you to change the size of "c".

If you wish to label any additional disks, run the following command for each:

```
# disklabel -rw XX# type "optional_pack_name"
```

where **XX#** is the same as in the previous command and **type** is the HP300 disk device name as listed in `/etc/disktab`. The optional information may contain any descriptive name for the contents of a disk, and may be up to 16 characters long. This procedure will place the label on the disk using the information found in `/etc/disktab` for the disk type named. If you have changed the disk partition sizes, you may wish to add entries for the modified configuration in `/etc/disktab` before labeling the affected disks.

You have now completed the HP300 specific part of the installation. Now proceed to the generic part of the installation described starting in section 2.5 below. Note that where the disk name "sd" is used throughout section 2.5, you should substitute the name "rd" if you are running on an HP-IB disk. Also, if you are loading on a single disk with the default disklabel, `/var` should be restored to the "f" partition and `/usr` to the "e" partition.

2.3. Booting the SPARC

2.3.1. Supported hardware

The hardware supported by 4.4BSD for the SPARC is as follows:

CPU's	SPARCstation 1 series (1, 1+, SLC, IPC) and SPARCstation 2 series (2, IPX).
DISK's	SCSI.
TAPE's	none.
NETWORK	SPARCstation Lance (le).
GRAPHICS	bwtwo and cgthree.
INPUT	Keyboard and mouse.
MISC	Battery-backed real time clock, built-in serial devices, Sbus SCSI controller, and audio device.

Major items that are not supported include anything VME-based, the GX (cgsix) display, the floppy disk, and SCSI tapes.

2.3.2. Limitations

There are several important limitations on the 4.4BSD distribution for the SPARC:

1) You **must** have SunOS 4.1.x or Solaris to bring up 4.4BSD. There is no SPARCstation bootstrap code in this distribution. The Sun-supplied boot loader will be used to boot 4.4BSD; you must copy this from your SunOS distribution. This imposes several restrictions on the system, as detailed below.

2) The 4.4BSD SPARC kernel does not remap SCSI IDs. A SCSI disk at target 0 will become ''sd0'', where in SunOS the same disk will normally be called ''sd3''. If your existing SunOS system is diskful, it will be least painful to have SunOS running on the disk on target 0 lun 0 and put 4.4BSD on the disk on target 3 lun 0. Both systems will then think they are running on ''sd0'', and you can boot either system as needed simply by changing the EEPROM's boot device.

3) There is no SCSI tape driver. You must have another system for tape reading and backups.

4) Although the 4.4BSD SPARC kernel will handle existing SunOS shared libraries, it does not use or create them itself, and therefore requires much more disk space than SunOS does.

5) It is currently difficult (though not completely impossible) to run 4.4BSD diskless. These instructions assume you will have a local boot, swap, and root filesystem.

6) When using a serial port rather than a graphics display as the console, only port `ttya` can be used. Attempts to use port `ttyb` will fail when the kernel tries to print the boot up messages to the console.

2.3.3. The procedure

You must have a spare disk on which to place 4.4BSD. The steps involved in bootstrapping this tape are as follows:

1) Bring up SunOS (preferably SunOS 4.1.x or Solaris 1.x, although Solaris 2 may work — this is untested).

2) Attach auxiliary SCSI disk(s). Format and label using the SunOS formatting and labeling programs as needed. Note that the root filesystem currently requires at least 10 MB; 16 MB or more is recommended. The b partition will be used for swap; this should be at least 32 MB.

3) Use the SunOS *newfs* to build the root filesystem. You may also want to build other filesystems at the same time. (By default, the 4.4BSD *newfs* builds a filesystem that SunOS will not handle; if you plan to switch OSes back and forth you may want to sacrifice the performance gain from the new filesystem format for compatibility.) You can build an old-format filesystem on 4.4BSD by giving

the –O option to *newfs*(8). *Fsck*(8) can convert old format filesystems to new format filesystems, but not vice versa, so you may want to initially build old format filesystems so that they can be mounted under SunOS, and then later convert them to new format filesystems when you are satisfied that 4.4BSD is running properly. In any case, **you must build an old-style root filesystem** so that the SunOS boot program will work.

4) Mount the new root, then copy the SunOS `/boot` into place and use the SunOS ''installboot'' program to enable disk-based booting. Note that the filesystem must be mounted when you do the ''installboot'':

```
# mount /dev/sd3a /mnt
# cp /boot /mnt/boot
# cd /usr/kvm/mdec
# installboot /mnt/boot bootsd /dev/rsd3a
```

The SunOS `/boot` will load 4.4BSD kernels; there is no SPARCstation bootstrap code on the distribution. Note that the SunOS `/boot` does not handle the new 4.4BSD filesystem format.

5) Restore the contents of the 4.4BSD root filesystem.

```
# cd /mnt
# rrestore xf tapehost:/dev/nrst0
```

6) Boot the supplied kernel:

```
# halt
ok boot sd(0,3)vmunix -s        [for old proms] OR
ok boot disk3 -s            [for new proms]
... [4.4BSD boot messages]
```

To install the remaining filesystems, use the procedure described starting in section 2.5. In these instructions, `/usr` should be loaded into the ''e'' partition and `/var` in the ''f'' partition.

After completing the filesystem installation you may want to set up 4.4BSD to reboot automatically:

```
# halt
ok setenv boot-from sd(0,3)vmunix [for old proms] OR
ok setenv boot-device disk3       [for new proms]
```

If you build backwards-compatible filesystems, either with the SunOS newfs or with the 4.4BSD ''–O'' option, you can mount these under SunOS. The SunOS fsck will, however, always think that these filesystems are corrupted, as there are several new (previously unused) superblock fields that are updated in 4.4BSD. Running ''fsck –b32'' and letting it ''fix'' the superblock will take care of this.

If you wish to run SunOS binaries that use SunOS shared libraries, you simply need to copy all the dynamic linker files from an existing SunOS system:

```
# rcp sunos-host:/etc/ld.so.cache /etc/
# rcp sunos-host:'/usr/lib/*.so*' /usr/lib/
```

The SunOS compiler and linker should be able to produce SunOS binaries under 4.4BSD, but this has not been tested. If you plan to try it you will need the appropriate .sa files as well.

1

2.4. Booting the DECstation

2.4.1. Supported hardware

The hardware supported by 4.4BSD for the DECstation is as follows:

CPU's	R2000 based (3100) and R3000 based (5000/200, 5000/20, 5000/25, 5000/1xx).
DISK's	SCSI-I (tested RZ23, RZ55, RZ57, Maxtor 8760S).
TAPE's	SCSI-I (tested DEC TK50, Archive DAT, Emulex MT02).
RS232	Internal DEC dc7085 and AMD 8530 based interfaces.
NETWORK	TURBOchannel PMAD-AA and internal LANCE based interfaces.
GRAPHICS	Terminal emulation and raw frame buffer support for 3100 (color & monochrome), TURBOchannel PMAG-AA, PMAG-BA, PMAG-DV.
INPUT	Standard DEC keyboard (LK201) and mouse.
MISC	Battery-backed real time clock, internal and TURBOchannel PMAZ-AA SCSI interfaces.

Major items that are not supported include the 5000/240 (there is code but not compiled in or tested), R4000 based machines, FDDI and audio interfaces. Diskless machines are not supported but booting kernels and bootstrapping over the network is supported on the 5000 series.

2.4.2. The procedure

The first file on the distribution tape is a tar file that contains four files. The first step requires a running UNIX (or ULTRIX) system that can be used to extract the tar archive from the first file on the tape. The command:

```
tar xf /dev/rmt0
```

will extract the following four files:

A) root.image: *dd* image of the root filesystem
B) vmunix.tape: *dd* image for creating boot tapes
C) vmunix.net: file for booting over the network
D) root.dump: *dump* image of the root filesystem

There are three basic ways a system can be bootstrapped corresponding to the first three files. You may want to read the section on bootstrapping the HP300 since many of the steps are similar. A spare, formatted SCSI disk is also useful.

2.4.2.1. Procedure A: copy root filesystem to disk

This procedure is similar to the HP300. If you have an extra disk, the easiest approach is to use *dd*(1) under ULTRIX to copy the root filesystem image to the beginning of the spare disk. The root filesystem image includes a disklabel and bootblock along with the root filesystem. An example command to copy the image to the beginning of a disk is:

```
dd if=root.image of=/dev/rz1c bs=20b
```

The actual special file syntax will vary depending on unit numbers and the version of ULTRIX that is running. This system is now ready to boot. You can boot the kernel with one of the following PROM commands. If you are booting on a 3100, the disk must be SCSI id zero because of a bug.

```
DEC 3100:     boot -f rz(0,0,0)vmunix
DEC 5000:     boot 5/rz0/vmunix
```

You can then proceed to section 2.5 to create reasonable disk partitions for your machine and then install the rest of the system.

2.4.2.2. Procedure B: bootstrap from tape

If you have only a single machine with a single disk, you need to use the more difficult approach of booting a kernel and mini-root from tape or the network, and using it to restore the root filesystem.

First, you will need to create a boot tape. This can be done using *dd* as in the following example.

```
dd if=vmunix.tape of=/dev/nrmt0 bs=1b
dd if=root.dump of=/dev/nrmt0 bs=20b
```

The actual special file syntax for the tape drive will vary depending on unit numbers, tape device and the version of ULTRIX that is running.

The first file on the boot tape contains a boot header, kernel, and mini-root filesystem that the PROM can copy into memory. Installing from tape has only been tested on a 3100 and a 5000/200 using a TK50 tape drive. Here are two example PROM commands to boot from tape.

```
DEC 3100:     boot -f tz(0,5,0) m      # 5 is the SCSI id of the TK50
DEC 5000:     boot 5/tz6 m             # 6 is the SCSI id of the TK50
```

The 'm' argument tells the kernel to look for a root filesystem in memory. Next you should proceed to section 2.4.3 to build a disk-based root filesystem.

2.4.2.3. Procedure C: bootstrap over the network

You will need a host machine that is running the *bootp* server with the `vmunix.net` file installed in the default directory defined by the configuration file for *bootp*. Here are two example PROM commands to boot across the net:

```
DEC 3100:     boot -f tftp()vmunix.net m
DEC 5000:     boot 6/tftp/vmunix.net m
```

This command should load the kernel and mini-root into memory and run the same as the tape install (procedure B). The rest of the steps are the same except you will need to start the network (if you are unsure how to fill in the <name> fields below, see sections 4.4 and 5). Execute the following to start the networking:

```
# mount -uw /
# echo 127.0.0.1 localhost >> /etc/hosts
# echo <your.host.inet.number> myname.my.domain myname >> /etc/hosts
# echo <friend.host.inet.number> myfriend.my.domain myfriend >> /etc/hosts
# ifconfig le0 inet myname
```

Next you should proceed to section 2.4.3 to build a disk-based root filesystem.

2.4.3. Label disk and create the root filesystem

There are five steps to create a disk-based root filesystem.

1) Label the disk.

```
# disklabel -W /dev/rrz?c          # This enables writing the label
# disklabel -w -r -B /dev/rrz?c $DISKTYPE
# newfs /dev/rrz?a
...
# fsck /dev/rrz?a
...
```

Supported disk types are listed in `/etc/disktab`.

2) Restore the root filesystem.

```
# mount -uw /
# mount /dev/rz?a /a
# cd /a
```

If you are restoring locally (procedure B), run:

```
# mt -f /dev/nrmt0 rew
# restore -xsf 2 /dev/rmt0
```

If you are restoring across the net (procedure c), run:

```
# rrestore xf myfriend:/path/to/root.dump
```

When the restore finishes, clean up with:

```
# cd /
# sync
# umount /a
# fsck /dev/rz?a
```

3) Reset the system and initialize the PROM monitor to boot automatically.

```
DEC 3100:    setenv bootpath boot -f rz(0,?,0)vmunix
DEC 5000:    setenv bootpath 5/rz?/vmunix -a
```

4) After booting UNIX, you will need to create `/dev/mouse` to run X windows as in the following example.

```
rm /dev/mouse
ln /dev/xx /dev/mouse
```

The 'xx' should be one of the following:

pm0 raw interface to PMAX graphics devices
cfb0 raw interface to TURBOchannel PMAG-BA color frame buffer
xcfb0 raw interface to maxine graphics devices
mfb0 raw interface to mono graphics devices

You can then proceed to section 2.5 to install the rest of the system. Note that where the disk name ''sd'' is used throughout section 2.5, you should substitute the name ''rz''.

2.5. Disk configuration

All architectures now have a root filesystem up and running and proceed from this point to layout filesystems to make use of the available space and to balance disk load for better system performance.

2.5.1. Disk naming and divisions

Each physical disk drive can be divided into up to 8 partitions; UNIX typically uses only 3 or 4 partitions. For instance, the first partition, sd0a, is used for a root filesystem, a backup thereof, or a small filesystem like, `/var/tmp`; the second partition, sd0b, is used for paging and swapping; and a third partition, typically sd0e, holds a user filesystem.

The space available on a disk varies per device. Each disk typically has a paging area of 30 to 100 megabytes and a root filesystem of about 17 megabytes. The distributed system binaries occupy about 150 (180 with X11R5) megabytes while the major sources occupy another 250 (340 with X11R5) megabytes. The `/var` filesystem as delivered on the tape is only 2Mb, however it should have at least 50Mb allocated to it just for normal system activity. Usually it is allocated the last partition on the disk so that it can provide as much space as possible to the `/var/users` filesystem. See section 2.5.4 for further details on disk layouts.

Be aware that the disks have their sizes measured in disk sectors (usually 512 bytes), while the UNIX filesystem blocks are variable sized. If BLOCKSIZE=1k is set in the user's environment, all user programs report disk space in kilobytes, otherwise, disk sizes are always reported in units of 512-byte sectors[2]. The `/etc/disktab` file used in labelling disks and making filesystems specifies disk partition sizes in sectors.

2.5.2. Layout considerations

There are several considerations in deciding how to adjust the arrangement of things on your disks. The most important is making sure that there is adequate space for what is required; secondarily, throughput should be maximized. Paging space is an important parameter. The system, as distributed, sizes the configured paging areas each time the system is booted. Further, multiple paging areas of different sizes may be interleaved.

Many common system programs (C, the editor, the assembler etc.) create intermediate files in the `/tmp` directory, so the filesystem where this is stored also should be made large enough to accommodate most high-water marks. Typically, `/tmp` is constructed from a memory-based filesystem (see *mount_mfs*(8)). Programs that want their temporary files to persist across system reboots (such as editors) should use `/var/tmp`. If you plan to use a disk-based `/tmp` filesystem to avoid loss across system reboots, it makes sense to mount this in a ''root'' (i.e. first partition) filesystem on another disk. All the programs that create files in `/tmp` take care to delete them, but are not immune to rare events and can leave dregs. The directory should be examined every so often and the old files deleted.

The efficiency with which UNIX is able to use the CPU is often strongly affected by the configuration of disk controllers; it is critical for good performance to balance disk load. There are at least five components of the disk load that you can divide between the available disks:

1) The root filesystem.
2) The `/var` and `/var/tmp` filesystems.
3) The `/usr` filesystem.
4) The user filesystems.
5) The paging activity.

The following possibilities are ones we have used at times when we had 2, 3 and 4 disks:

	disks		
what	2	3	4
root	0	0	0
var	1	2	3
usr	1	1	1
paging	0+1	0+2	0+2+3
users	0	0+2	0+2
archive	x	x	3

The most important things to consider are to even out the disk load as much as possible, and to do this by decoupling filesystems (on separate arms) between which heavy copying occurs. Note that a long term average balanced load is not important; it is much more important to have an instantaneously balanced load when the system is busy.

Intelligent experimentation with a few filesystem arrangements can pay off in much improved performance. It is particularly easy to move the root, the `/var` and `/var/tmp` filesystems and the paging areas. Place the user files and the `/usr` directory as space needs dictate and experiment with the other, more easily moved filesystems.

[2] You can thank System V intransigence and POSIX duplicity for requiring that 512-byte blocks be the units that programs report.

2.5.3. Filesystem parameters

Each filesystem is parameterized according to its block size, fragment size, and the disk geometry characteristics of the medium on which it resides. Inaccurate specification of the disk characteristics or haphazard choice of the filesystem parameters can result in substantial throughput degradation or significant waste of disk space. As distributed, filesystems are configured according to the following table.

Filesystem	Block size	Fragment size
root	8 kbytes	1 kbytes
usr	8 kbytes	1 kbytes
users	4 kbytes	512 bytes

The root filesystem block size is made large to optimize bandwidth to the associated disk. The large block size is important as many of the most heavily used programs are demand paged out of the `/bin` directory. The fragment size of 1 kbyte is a ''nominal'' value to use with a filesystem. With a 1 kbyte fragment size disk space utilization is about the same as with the earlier versions of the filesystem.

The filesystems for users have a 4 kbyte block size with 512 byte fragment size. These parameters have been selected based on observations of the performance of our user filesystems. The 4 kbyte block size provides adequate bandwidth while the 512 byte fragment size provides acceptable space compaction and disk fragmentation.

Other parameters may be chosen in constructing filesystems, but the factors involved in choosing a block size and fragment size are many and interact in complex ways. Larger block sizes result in better throughput to large files in the filesystem as larger I/O requests will then be done by the system. However, consideration must be given to the average file sizes found in the filesystem and the performance of the internal system buffer cache. The system currently provides space in the inode for 12 direct block pointers, 1 single indirect block pointer, 1 double indirect block pointer, and 1 triple indirect block pointer. If a file uses only direct blocks, access time to it will be optimized by maximizing the block size. If a file spills over into an indirect block, increasing the block size of the filesystem may decrease the amount of space used by eliminating the need to allocate an indirect block. However, if the block size is increased and an indirect block is still required, then more disk space will be used by the file because indirect blocks are allocated according to the block size of the filesystem.

In selecting a fragment size for a filesystem, at least two considerations should be given. The major performance tradeoffs observed are between an 8 kbyte block filesystem and a 4 kbyte block filesystem. Because of implementation constraints, the block size versus fragment size ratio can not be greater than 8. This means that an 8 kbyte filesystem will always have a fragment size of at least 1 kbytes. If a filesystem is created with a 4 kbyte block size and a 1 kbyte fragment size, then upgraded to an 8 kbyte block size and 1 kbyte fragment size, identical space compaction will be observed. However, if a filesystem has a 4 kbyte block size and 512 byte fragment size, converting it to an 8K/1K filesystem will result in 4-8% more space being used. This implies that 4 kbyte block filesystems that might be upgraded to 8 kbyte blocks for higher performance should use fragment sizes of at least 1 kbytes to minimize the amount of work required in conversion.

A second, more important, consideration when selecting the fragment size for a filesystem is the level of fragmentation on the disk. With an 8:1 fragment to block ratio, storage fragmentation occurs much sooner, particularly with a busy filesystem running near full capacity. By comparison, the level of fragmentation in a 4:1 fragment to block ratio filesystem is one tenth as severe. This means that on filesystems where many files are created and deleted, the 512 byte fragment size is more likely to result in apparent space exhaustion because of fragmentation. That is, when the filesystem is nearly full, file expansion that requires locating a contiguous area of disk space is more likely to fail on a 512 byte filesystem than on a 1 kbyte filesystem. To minimize fragmentation problems of this sort, a parameter in the super block specifies a minimum acceptable free space threshold. When normal users (i.e. anyone but the super-user) attempt to allocate disk space and the free space threshold is exceeded, the user is returned an error as if the filesystem were really full. This parameter is nominally set to 5%; it may be changed by supplying a parameter to *newfs*(8), or by updating the super block of an existing filesystem using *tunefs*(8).

Finally, a third, less common consideration is the attributes of the disk itself. The fragment size should not be smaller than the physical sector size of the disk. As an example, the HP magneto-optical disks have 1024 byte physical sectors. Using a 512 byte fragment size on such disks will work but is extremely inefficient.

Note that the above discussion considers block sizes of up to only 8k. As of the 4.4 release, the maximum block size has been increased to 64k. This allows an entirely new set of block/fragment combinations for which there is little experience to date. In general though, unless a filesystem is to be used for a special purpose application (for example, storing image processing data), we recommend using the values supplied above. Remember that the current implementation limits the block size to at most 64 kbytes and the ratio of block size versus fragment size must be 1, 2, 4, or 8.

The disk geometry information used by the filesystem affects the block layout policies employed. The file `/etc/disktab`, as supplied, contains the data for most all drives supported by the system. Before constructing a filesystem with *newfs*(8) you should label the disk (if it has not yet been labeled, and the driver supports labels). If labels cannot be used, you must instead specify the type of disk on which the filesystem resides; *newfs* then reads `/etc/disktab` instead of the pack label. This file also contains the default filesystem partition sizes, and default block and fragment sizes. To override any of the default values you can modify the file, edit the disk label, or use an option to *newfs*.

2.5.4. Implementing a layout

To put a chosen disk layout into effect, you should use the *newfs*(8) command to create each new filesystem. Each filesystem must also be added to the file `/etc/fstab` so that it will be checked and mounted when the system is bootstrapped.

First we will consider a system with a single disk. There is little real choice on how to do the layout; the root filesystem goes in the ''a'' partition, `/usr` goes in the ''e'' partition, and `/var` fills out the remainder of the disk in the ''f'' partition. This is the organization used if you loaded the disk-image root filesystem. With the addition of a memory-based `/tmp` filesystem, its fstab entry would be as follows:

```
/dev/sd0a   /      ufs    rw                                    1  1
/dev/sd0b   none   swap   sw                                    0  0
/dev/sd0b   /tmp   mfs    rw,-s=14000,-b=8192,-f=1024,-T=sd660  0  0
/dev/sd0e   /usr   ufs    ro                                    1  2
/dev/sd0f   /var   ufs    rw                                    1  2
```

If we had a second disk, we would split the load between the drives. On the second disk, we place the `/usr` and `/var` filesystems in their usual sd1e and sd1f partitions respectively. The sd1b partition would be used as a second paging area, and the sd1a partition left as a spare root filesystem (alternatively sd1a could be used for `/var/tmp`). The first disk still holds the the root filesystem in sd0a, and the primary swap area in sd0b. The sd0e partition is used to hold home directories in `/var/users`. The sd0f partition can be used for `/usr/src` or alternately the sd0e partition can be extended to cover the rest of the disk with *disklabel*(8). As before, the `/tmp` directory is a memory-based filesystem. Note that to interleave the paging between the two disks you must build a system configuration that specifies:

```
config    vmunix    root on sd0 swap on sd0 and sd1
```

The `/etc/fstab` file would then contain

```
/dev/sd0a   /            ufs    rw                                    1  1
/dev/sd0b   none         swap   sw                                    0  0
/dev/sd1b   none         swap   sw                                    0  0
/dev/sd0b   /tmp         mfs    rw,-s=14000,-b=8192,-f=1024,-T=sd660  0  0
/dev/sd1e   /usr         ufs    ro                                    1  2
/dev/sd0f   /usr/src     ufs    rw                                    1  2
/dev/sd1f   /var         ufs    rw                                    1  2
/dev/sd0e   /var/users   ufs    rw                                    1  2
```

To make the `/var` filesystem we would do:

> *# cd /dev*
> *# MAKEDEV sd1*
> *# disklabel -wr sd1 "disk type" "disk name"*
> *# newfs sd1f*
> (information about filesystem prints out)
> *# mkdir /var*
> *# mount /dev/sd1f /var*

2.6. Installing the rest of the system

At this point you should have your disks partitioned. The next step is to extract the rest of the data from the tape. At a minimum you need to set up the `/var` and `/usr` filesystems. You may also want to extract some or all the program sources. Since not all architectures support tape drives or don't support the correct ones, you may need to extract the files indirectly using *rsh*(1). For example, for a directly connected tape drive you might do:

> *# mt -f /dev/nrmt0 fsf*
> *# tar xbpf 20 /dev/nrmt0*

The equivalent indirect procedure (where the tape drive is on machine ''foo'') is:

> *# rsh foo mt -f /dev/nrmt0 fsf*
> *# rsh foo dd if=/dev/nrmt0 bs=20b | tar xbpf 20 -*

Obviously, the target machine must be connected to the local network for this to work. To do this:

> *# echo 127.0.0.1 localhost >> /etc/hosts*
> *# echo* your.host.inet.number myname.my.domain myname >> */etc/hosts*
> *# echo* friend.host.inet.number myfriend.my.domain myfriend >> */etc/hosts*
> *# ifconfig le0 inet* myname

where the ''host.inet.number'' fields are the IP addresses for your host and the host with the tape drive and the ''my.domain'' fields are the names of your machine and the tape-hosting machine. See sections 4.4 and 5 for more information on setting up the network.

Assuming a directly connected tape drive, here is how to extract and install `/var` and `/usr`:

# mount –uw /dev/sd#a /	(read-write mount root filesystem)
# date yymmddhhmm	(set date, see *date* (1))
....	
# passwd -l root	(set password for super-user)
New password:	(password will not echo)
Retype new password:	
# passwd -l toor	(set password for super-user)
New password:	(password will not echo)
Retype new password:	
# hostname mysitename	(set your hostname)
# newfs rsd#p	(create empty user filesystem)
(*sd* is the disk type, # is the unit number, *p* is the partition; this takes a few minutes)	
# mount /dev/sd#p /var	(mount the var filesystem)
# cd /var	(make /var the current directory)
# mt -f /dev/nrmt0 fsf	(space to end of previous tape file)
# tar xbpf 20 /dev/nrmt0	(extract all of var)
(this takes a few minutes)	
# newfs rsd#p	(create empty user filesystem)
(as before *sd* is the disk type, # is the unit number,	

p is the partition)
 # mount /dev/sd#p /mnt (mount the new /usr in temporary location)
 # cd /mnt (make /mnt the current directory)
 # mt -f /dev/nrmt0 fsf (space to end of previous tape file)
 # tar xbpf 20 /dev/nrmt0 (extract all of usr except usr/src)
(this takes about 15-20 minutes)
 # cd / (make / the current directory)
 # umount /mnt (unmount from temporary mount point)
*# rm -r /usr/** (remove excess bootstrap binaries)
 # mount /dev/sd#p /usr (remount /usr)

If no disk label has been installed on the disk, the *newfs* command will require a third argument to specify the disk type, using one of the names in `/etc/disktab`. If the tape had been rewound or positioned incorrectly before the *tar*, to extract `/var` it may be repositioned by the following commands.

 # mt -f /dev/nrmt0 rew
 # mt -f /dev/nrmt0 fsf 1

The data on the second and third tape files has now been extracted. If you are using 6250bpi tapes, the first reel of the distribution is no longer needed; you should now mount the second reel instead. The installation procedure continues from this point on the 8mm tape. The next step is to extract the sources. As previously noted, `/usr/src` requires about 250-340Mb of space. Ideally sources should be in a separate filesystem; if you plan to put them into your `/usr` filesystem, it will need at least 500Mb of space. Assuming that you will be using a separate filesystem on sd0f for `/usr/src`, you will start by creating and mounting it:

 # newfs sd0f
(information about filesystem prints out)
 # mkdir /usr/src
 # mount /dev/sd0f /usr/src

First you will extract the kernel source:

 # cd /usr/src
 # mt -f /dev/nrmt0 fsf (space to end of previous tape file)
(this should only be done on Exabyte distributions)
 # tar xpbf 20 /dev/nrmt0 (extract the kernel sources)
(this takes about 15-30 minutes)

The next tar file contains the sources for the utilities. It is extracted as follows:

 # cd /usr/src
 # mt -f /dev/nrmt0 fsf (space to end of previous tape file)
 # tar xpbf 20 /dev/rmt12 (extract the utility source)
(this takes about 30-60 minutes)

If you are using 6250bpi tapes, the second reel of the distribution is no longer needed; you should now mount the third reel instead. The installation procedure continues from this point on the 8mm tape.

The next tar file contains the sources for the contributed software. It is extracted as follows:

# cd /usr/src	
# mt -f /dev/nrmt0 fsf	(space to end of previous tape file)
(this should only be done on Exabyte distributions)	
# tar xpbf 20 /dev/rmt12	(extract the contributed software source)
(this takes about 30-60 minutes)	

If you received a distribution on 8mm Exabyte tape, there is one additional tape file on the distribution tape that has not been installed to this point; it contains the sources for X11R5 in *tar*(1) format. As distributed, X11R5 should be placed in `/usr/src/X11R5`.

# cd /usr/src	
# mt -f /dev/nrmt0 fsf	(space to end of previous tape file)
# tar xpbf 20 /dev/nrmt0	(extract the X11R5 source)
(this takes about 30-60 minutes)	

Many of the X11 utilities search using the path `/usr/X11`, so be sure that you have a symbolic link that points at the location of your X11 binaries (here, X11R5).

Having now completed the extraction of the sources, you may want to verify that your `/usr/src` filesystem is consistent. To do so, you must unmount it, and run *fsck*(8); assuming that you used sd0f you would proceed as follows:

# cd /	(change directory, back to the root)
# umount /usr/src	(unmount /usr/src)
# fsck /dev/rsd0f	

The output from *fsck* should look something like:

**** /dev/rsd0f**
**** Last Mounted on /usr/src**
**** Phase 1 - Check Blocks and Sizes**
**** Phase 2 - Check Pathnames**
**** Phase 3 - Check Connectivity**
**** Phase 4 - Check Reference Counts**
**** Phase 5 - Check Cyl groups**
23000 files, 261000 used, 39000 free (2200 frags, 4600 blocks)

If there are inconsistencies in the filesystem, you may be prompted to apply corrective action; see the *fsck*(8) or *Fsck – The UNIX File System Check Program* (SMM:3) for more details.

To use the `/usr/src` filesystem, you should now remount it with:

 # mount /dev/sd0f /usr/src

or if you have made an entry for it in `/etc/fstab` you can remount it with:

 # mount /usr/src

2.7. Additional conversion information

After setting up the new 4.4BSD filesystems, you may restore the user files that were saved on tape before beginning the conversion. Note that the 4.4BSD *restore* program does its work on a mounted filesystem using normal system operations. This means that filesystem dumps may be restored even if the characteristics of the filesystem changed. To restore a dump tape for, say, the `/a` filesystem something like the following would be used:

```
# mkdir /a
# newfs sd#p
# mount /dev/sd#p /a
# cd /a
# restore x
```

1

If *tar* images were written instead of doing a dump, you should be sure to use its '−p' option when reading the files back. No matter how you restore a filesystem, be sure to unmount it and and check its integrity with *fsck*(8) when the job is complete.

3. Upgrading a 4.3BSD system

This section describes the procedure for upgrading a 4.3BSD system to 4.4BSD. This procedure may vary according to the version of the system running before conversion. If you are converting from a System V system, some of this section will still apply (in particular, the filesystem conversion). However, many of the system configuration files are different, and the executable file formats are completely incompatible.

In particular be wary when using this information to upgrade a 4.3BSD HP300 system. There are at least four different versions of ''4.3BSD'' out there:

1) HPBSD 1.x from Utah.
This was the original version of 4.3BSD for HP300s from which the other variants (and 4.4BSD) are derived. It is largely a 4.3BSD system with Sun's NFS 3.0 filesystem code and some 4.3BSD-Tahoe features (e.g. networking code). Since the filesystem code is 4.2/4.3 vintage and the filesystem hierarchy is largely 4.3BSD, most of this section should apply.

2) MORE/bsd from Mt. Xinu.
This is a 4.3BSD-Tahoe vintage system with Sun's NFS 4.0 filesystem code upgraded with Tahoe UFS features. The instructions for 4.3BSD-Tahoe should largely apply.

3) 4.3BSD-Reno from CSRG.
At least one site bootstrapped HP300 support from the Reno distribution. The Reno filesystem code was somewhere between 4.3BSD and 4.4BSD: the VFS switch had been added but many of the UFS features (e.g. ''inline'' symlinks) were missing. The filesystem hierarchy reorganization first appeared in this release. Be extremely careful following these instructions if you are upgrading from the Reno distribution.

4) HPBSD 2.0 from Utah.
As if things were not bad enough already, this release has the 4.4BSD filesystem and networking code as well as some utilities, but still has a 4.3BSD hierarchy. No filesystem conversions are necessary for this upgrade, but files will still need to be moved around.

3.1. Installation overview

If you are running 4.3BSD, upgrading your system involves replacing your kernel and system utilities. In general, there are three possible ways to install a new BSD distribution: (1) boot directly from the distribution tape, use it to load new binaries onto empty disks, and then merge or restore any existing configuration files and filesystems; (2) use an existing 4.3BSD or later system to extract the root and `/usr` filesystems from the distribution tape, boot from the new system, then merge or restore existing configuration files and filesystems; or (3) extract the sources from the distribution tape onto an existing system, and use that system to cross-compile and install 4.4BSD. For this release, the second alternative is strongly advised, with the third alternative reserved as a last resort. In general, older binaries will continue to run under 4.4BSD, but there are many exceptions that are on the critical path for getting the system running. Ideally, the new system binaries (root and `/usr` filesystems) should be installed on spare disk partitions, then site-specific files should be merged into them. Once the new system is up and fully merged, the previous root and `/usr` filesystems can be reused. Other existing filesystems can be retained and used, except that (as usual) the new *fsck* should be run before they are mounted.

It is **STRONGLY** advised that you make full dumps of each filesystem before beginning, especially any that you intend to modify in place during the merge. It is also desirable to run filesystem checks of all filesystems to be converted to 4.4BSD before shutting down. This is an excellent time to review your disk configuration for possible tuning of the layout. Most systems will need to provide a new filesystem for system use mounted on `/var` (see below). However, the `/tmp` filesystem can be an MFS virtual-memory-resident filesystem, potentially freeing an existing disk partition. (Additional swap space may be desirable as a consequence.) See *mount_mfs*(8).

1

The recommended installation procedure includes the following steps. The order of these steps will probably vary according to local needs.

- Extract root and `/usr` filesystems from the distribution tapes.
- Extract kernel and/or user-level sources from the distribution tape if space permits. This can serve as the backup documentation as needed.
- Configure and boot a kernel for the local system. This can be delayed if the generic kernel from the distribution supports enough hardware to proceed.
- Build a skeletal `/var` filesystem (see *mtree*(8)).
- Merge site-dependent configuration files from `/etc` and `/usr/lib` into the new `/etc` directory. Note that many file formats and contents have changed; see section 3.4 of this document.
- Copy or merge files from `/usr/adm`, `/usr/spool`, `/usr/preserve`, `/usr/lib`, and other locations into `/var`.
- Merge local macros, dictionaries, etc. into `/usr/share`.
- Merge and update local software to reflect the system changes.
- Take off the rest of the morning, you've earned it!

Section 3.2 lists the files to be saved as part of the conversion process. Section 3.3 describes the bootstrap process. Section 3.4 discusses the merger of the saved files back into the new system. Section 3.5 gives an overview of the major bug fixes and changes between 4.3BSD and 4.4BSD. Section 3.6 provides general hints on possible problems to be aware of when converting from 4.3BSD to 4.4BSD.

3.2. Files to save

The following list enumerates the standard set of files you will want to save and suggests directories in which site-specific files should be present. This list will likely be augmented with non-standard files you have added to your system. If you do not have enough space to create parallel filesystems, you should create a *tar* image of the following files before the new filesystems are created. The rest of this subsection describes where theses files have moved and how they have changed.

`/.cshrc`	†	root csh startup script (moves to `/root/.cshrc`)
`/.login`	†	root csh login script (moves to `/root/.login`)
`/.profile`	†	root sh startup script (moves to `/root/.profile`)
`/.rhosts`	†	for trusted machines and users (moves to `/root/.rhosts`)
`/etc/disktab`	‡	in case you changed disk partition sizes
`/etc/fstab`	*	disk configuration data
`/etc/ftpusers`	†	for local additions
`/etc/gettytab`	‡	getty database
`/etc/group`	*	group data base
`/etc/hosts`	†	for local host information
`/etc/hosts.equiv`	†	for local host equivalence information
`/etc/hosts.lpd`	†	printer access file
`/etc/inetd.conf`	*	Internet services configuration data
`/etc/named*`	†	named configuration files
`/etc/netstart`	†	network initialization
`/etc/networks`	†	for local network information
`/etc/passwd`	*	user data base

/etc/printcap	*	line printer database
/etc/protocols	‡	in case you added any local protocols
/etc/rc	*	for any local additions
/etc/rc.local	*	site specific system startup commands
/etc/remote	†	auto-dialer configuration
/etc/services	‡	for local additions
/etc/shells	‡	list of valid shells
/etc/syslog.conf	*	system logger configuration
/etc/securettys	*	merged into ttys
/etc/ttys	*	terminal line configuration data
/etc/ttytype	*	merged into ttys
/etc/termcap	‡	for any local entries that may have been added
/lib	‡	for any locally developed language processors
/usr/dict/*	‡	for local additions to words and papers
/usr/include/*	‡	for local additions
/usr/lib/aliases	*	mail forwarding data base (moves to /etc/aliases)
/usr/lib/crontab	*	cron daemon data base (moves to /etc/crontab)
/usr/lib/crontab.local	*	local cron daemon data base (moves to /etc/crontab.local)
/usr/lib/lib*.a	†	for local libraries
/usr/lib/mail.rc	†	system-wide mail(1) initialization (moves to /etc/mail.rc)
/usr/lib/sendmail.cf	*	sendmail configuration (moves to /etc/sendmail.cf)
/usr/lib/tmac/*	‡	for locally developed troff/nroff macros (moves to /usr/share/tmac/*)
/usr/lib/uucp/*	†	for local uucp configuration files
/usr/man/manl	*	for manual pages for locally developed programs (moves to /usr/local/man)
/usr/spool/*	†	for current mail, news, uucp files, etc. (moves to /var/spool)
/usr/src/local	†	for source for locally developed programs
/sys/conf/HOST	†	configuration file for your machine (moves to /sys/<arch>/conf)
/sys/conf/files.HOST	†	list of special files in your kernel (moves to /sys/<arch>/conf)
/*/quotas	*	filesystem quota files (moves to /*/quotas.user)

† Files that can be used from 4.3BSD without change.
‡ Files that need local changes merged into 4.4BSD files.
* Files that require special work to merge and are discussed in section 3.4.

3.3. Installing 4.4BSD

The next step is to build a working 4.4BSD system. This can be done by following the steps in section 2 of this document for extracting the root and /usr filesystems from the distribution tape onto unused disk partitions. For the SPARC, the root filesystem dump on the tape could also be extracted directly. For the HP300 and DECstation, the raw disk image can be copied into an unused partition and this partition can then be dumped to create an image that can be restored. The exact procedure chosen will depend on the disk configuration and the number of suitable disk partitions that may be used. It is also desirable to run filesystem checks of all filesystems to be converted to 4.4BSD before shutting down. In any case, this is an excellent time to review your disk configuration for possible tuning of the layout. Section 2.5 and *config*(8) are required reading.

The filesystem in 4.4BSD has been reorganized in an effort to meet several goals:

1) The root filesystem should be small.
2) There should be a per-architecture centrally-shareable read-only /usr filesystem.
3) Variable per-machine directories should be concentrated below a single mount point named /var.
4) Site-wide machine independent shareable text files should be separated from architecture specific binary files and should be concentrated below a single mount point named /usr/share.

These goals are realized with the following general layouts. The reorganized root filesystem has the following directories:

/etc	(config files)
/bin	(user binaries needed when single-user)
/sbin	(root binaries needed when single-user)
/local	(locally added binaries used only by this machine)
/tmp	(mount point for memory based filesystem)
/dev	(local devices)
/home	(mount point for AMD)
/var	(mount point for per-machine variable directories)
/usr	(mount point for multiuser binaries and files)

The reorganized /usr filesystem has the following directories:

/usr/bin	(user binaries)
/usr/contrib	(software contributed to 4.4BSD)
/usr/games	(binaries for games, score files in /var)
/usr/include	(standard include files)
/usr/lib	(lib*.a from old /usr/lib)
/usr/libdata	(databases from old /usr/lib)
/usr/libexec	(executables from old /usr/lib)
/usr/local	(locally added binaries used site-wide)
/usr/old	(deprecated binaries)
/usr/sbin	(root binaries)
/usr/share	(mount point for site-wide shared text)
/usr/src	(mount point for sources)

The reorganized /usr/share filesystem has the following directories:

/usr/share/calendar	(various useful calendar files)
/usr/share/dict	(dictionaries)
/usr/share/doc	(4.4BSD manual sources)
/usr/share/games	(games text files)
/usr/share/groff_font	(groff font information)
/usr/share/man	(typeset manual pages)
/usr/share/misc	(dumping ground for random text files)
/usr/share/mk	(templates for 4.4BSD makefiles)
/usr/share/skel	(template user home directory files)
/usr/share/tmac	(various groff macro packages)
/usr/share/zoneinfo	(information on time zones)

The reorganized /var filesystem has the following directories:

/var/account	(accounting files, formerly /usr/adm)
/var/at	(*at*(1) spooling area)
/var/backups	(backups of system files)
/var/crash	(crash dumps)
/var/db	(system-wide databases, e.g. tags)
/var/games	(score files)
/var/log	(log files)
/var/mail	(users mail)
/var/obj	(hierarchy to build /usr/src)
/var/preserve	(preserve area for vi)
/var/quotas	(directory to store quota files)
/var/run	(directory to store *.pid files)
/var/rwho	(rwho databases)
/var/spool/ftp	(home directory for anonymous ftp)
/var/spool/mqueue	(sendmail spooling directory)
/var/spool/news	(news spooling area)

`/var/spool/output`	(printer spooling area)
`/var/spool/uucp`	(uucp spooling area)
`/var/tmp`	(disk-based temporary directory)
`/var/users`	(root of per-machine user home directories)

The 4.4BSD bootstrap routines pass the identity of the boot device through to the kernel. The kernel then uses that device as its root filesystem. Thus, for example, if you boot from `/dev/sd1a`, the kernel will use `sd1a` as its root filesystem. If `/dev/sd1b` is configured as a swap partition, it will be used as the initial swap area, otherwise the normal primary swap area (`/dev/sd0b`) will be used. The 4.4BSD bootstrap is backward compatible with 4.3BSD, so you can replace your old bootstrap if you use it to boot your first 4.4BSD kernel. However, the 4.3BSD bootstrap cannot access 4.4BSD filesystems, so if you plan to convert your filesystems to 4.4BSD, you must install a new bootstrap *before* doing the conversion. Note that SPARC users cannot build a 4.4BSD compatible version of the bootstrap, so must *not* convert their root filesystem to the new 4.4BSD format.

Once you have extracted the 4.4BSD system and booted from it, you will have to build a kernel customized for your configuration. If you have any local device drivers, they will have to be incorporated into the new kernel. See section 4.1.3 and "Building 4.3BSD UNIX Systems with Config" (SMM:2).

If converting from 4.3BSD, your old filesystems should be converted. If you've modified the partition sizes from the original 4.3BSD ones, and are not already using the 4.4BSD disk labels, you will have to modify the default disk partition tables in the kernel. Make the necessary table changes and boot your custom kernel **BEFORE** trying to access any of your old filesystems! After doing this, if necessary, the remaining filesystems may be converted in place by running the 4.4BSD version of *fsck*(8) on each filesystem and allowing it to make the necessary corrections. The new version of *fsck* is more strict about the size of directories than the version supplied with 4.3BSD. Thus the first time that it is run on a 4.3BSD filesystem, it will produce messages of the form:

DIRECTORY ...: LENGTH xx **NOT MULTIPLE OF 512 (ADJUSTED)**

Length "xx" will be the size of the directory; it will be expanded to the next multiple of 512 bytes. The new *fsck* will also set default *interleave* and *npsect* (number of physical sectors per track) values on older filesystems, in which these fields were unused spares; this correction will produce messages of the form:

IMPOSSIBLE INTERLEAVE=0 IN SUPERBLOCK (SET TO DEFAULT)[3]
IMPOSSIBLE NPSECT=0 IN SUPERBLOCK (SET TO DEFAULT)

Filesystems that have had their interleave and npsect values set will be diagnosed by the old *fsck* as having a bad superblock; the old *fsck* will run only if given an alternate superblock (*fsck –b32*), in which case it will re-zero these fields. The 4.4BSD kernel will internally set these fields to their defaults if fsck has not done so; again, the *–b32* option may be necessary for running the old *fsck*.

In addition, 4.4BSD removes several limits on filesystem sizes that were present in 4.3BSD. The limited filesystems continue to work in 4.4BSD, but should be converted as soon as it is convenient by running *fsck* with the *–c 2* option. The sequence *fsck –p –c 2* will update them all, fix the interleave and npsect fields, fix any incorrect directory lengths, expand maximum uid's and gid's to 32-bits, place symbolic links less than 60 bytes into their inode, and fill in directory type fields all at once. The new filesystem formats are incompatible with older systems. If you wish to continue using these filesystems with the older systems you should make only the compatible changes using *fsck –c 1*.

3.4. Merging your files from 4.3BSD into 4.4BSD

When your system is booting reliably and you have the 4.4BSD root and `/usr` filesystems fully installed you will be ready to continue with the next step in the conversion process, merging your old files into the new system.

[3] The defaults are to set *interleave* to 1 and *npsect* to *nsect*. This is correct on most drives; it affects only performance (usually virtually unmeasurably).

1

If you saved the files on a *tar* tape, extract them into a scratch directory, say /usr/convert:

```
# mkdir /usr/convert
# cd /usr/convert
# tar xp
```

The data files marked in the previous table with a dagger (†) may be used without change from the previous system. Those data files marked with a double dagger (‡) have syntax changes or substantial enhancements. You should start with the 4.4BSD version and carefully integrate any local changes into the new file. Usually these local changes can be incorporated without conflict into the new file; some exceptions are noted below. The files marked with an asterisk (*) require particular attention and are discussed below.

As described in section 3.3, the most immediately obvious change in 4.4BSD is the reorganization of the system filesystems. Users of certain recent vendor releases have seen this general organization, although 4.4BSD takes the reorganization a bit further. The directories most affected are /etc, that now contains only system configuration files; /var, a new filesystem containing per-system spool and log files; and /usr/share, that contains most of the text files shareable across architectures such as documentation and macros. System administration programs formerly in /etc are now found in /sbin and /usr/sbin. Various programs and data files formerly in /usr/lib are now found in /usr/libexec and /usr/libdata, respectively. Administrative files formerly in /usr/adm are in /var/account and, similarly, log files are now in /var/log. The directory /usr/ucb has been merged into /usr/bin, and the sources for programs in /usr/bin are in /usr/src/usr.bin. Other source directories parallel the destination directories; /usr/src/etc has been greatly expanded, and /usr/src/share is new. The source for the manual pages, in general, are with the source code for the applications they document. Manual pages not closely corresponding to an application program are found in /usr/src/share/man. The locations of all man pages is listed in /usr/src/share/man/man0/man[1-8]. The manual page *hier*(7) has been updated and made more detailed; it is included in the printed documentation. You should review it to familiarize yourself with the new layout.

A new utility, *mtree*(8), is provided to build and check filesystem hierarchies with the proper contents, owners and permissions. Scripts are provided in /etc/mtree (and /usr/src/etc/mtree) for the root, /usr and /var filesystems. Once a filesystem has been made for /var, *mtree* can be used to create a directory hierarchy there or you can simply use tar to extract the prototype from the second file of the distribution tape.

3.4.1. Changes in the /etc directory

The /etc directory now contains nearly all the host-specific configuration files. Note that some file formats have changed, and those configuration files containing pathnames are nearly all affected by the reorganization. See the examples provided in /etc (installed from /usr/src/etc) as a guide. The following table lists some of the local configuration files whose locations and/or contents have changed.

4.3BSD and Earlier	4.4BSD	Comments
/etc/fstab	/etc/fstab	new format; see below
/etc/inetd.conf	/etc/inetd.conf	pathnames of executables changed
/etc/printcap	/etc/printcap	pathnames changed
/etc/syslog.conf	/etc/syslog.conf	pathnames of log files changed
/etc/ttys	/etc/ttys	pathnames of executables changed
/etc/passwd	/etc/master.passwd	new format; see below
/usr/lib/sendmail.cf	/etc/sendmail.cf	changed pathnames
/usr/lib/aliases	/etc/aliases	may contain changed pathnames
/etc/*.pid	/var/run/*.pid	

New in 4.3BSD-Tahoe	4.4BSD	Comments
`/usr/games/dm.config`	`/etc/dm.conf`	configuration for games (see *dm* (8))
`/etc/zoneinfo/localtime`	`/etc/localtime`	timezone configuration
`/etc/zoneinfo`	`/usr/share/zoneinfo`	timezone configuration

New in 4.4BSD	Comments
`/etc/aliases.db`	database version of the aliases file
`/etc/amd-home`	location database of home directories
`/etc/amd-vol`	location database of exported filesystems
`/etc/changelist`	`/etc/security` files to back up
`/etc/csh.cshrc`	system-wide csh(1) initialization file
`/etc/csh.login`	system-wide csh(1) login file
`/etc/csh.logout`	system-wide csh(1) logout file
`/etc/disklabels`	directory for saving disklabels
`/etc/exports`	NFS list of export permissions
`/etc/ftpwelcome`	message displayed for ftp users; see ftpd(8)
`/etc/kerberosIV`	Kerberos directory; see below
`/etc/man.conf`	lists directories searched by *man* (1)
`/etc/mtree`	directory for local mtree files; see mtree(8)
`/etc/netgroup`	NFS group list used in `/etc/exports`
`/etc/pwd.db`	non-secure hashed user data base file
`/etc/spwd.db`	secure hashed user data base file
`/etc/security`	daily system security checker

System security changes require adding several new ''well-known'' groups to `/etc/group`. The groups that are needed by the system as distributed are:

name	number	purpose
wheel	0	users allowed superuser privilege
daemon	1	processes that need less than wheel privilege
kmem	2	read access to kernel memory
sys	3	access to kernel sources
tty	4	access to terminals
operator	5	read access to raw disks
bin	7	group for system binaries
news	8	group for news
wsrc	9	write access to sources
games	13	access to games
staff	20	system staff
guest	31	system guests
nobody	39	the least privileged group
utmp	45	access to utmp files
dialer	117	access to remote ports and dialers

Only users in the ''wheel'' group are permitted to *su* to ''root''. Most programs that manage directories in `/var/spool` now run set-group-id to ''daemon'' so that users cannot directly access the files in the spool directories. The special files that access kernel memory, `/dev/kmem` and `/dev/mem`, are made readable only by group ''kmem''. Standard system programs that require this access are made set-group-id to that group. The group ''sys'' is intended to control access to kernel sources, and other sources belong to group ''wsrc.'' Rather than make user terminals writable by all users, they are now placed in group ''tty'' and made only group writable. Programs that should legitimately have access to write on user terminals such as *talkd* and *write* now run set-group-id to ''tty''. The ''operator'' group controls access to disks. By default, disks are readable by group ''operator'', so that programs such as *dump* can access the filesystem information without being set-user-id to ''root''. The *shutdown*(8) program is executable only by group operator and is setuid to root so that members of group operator may shut down the system without root access.

The ownership and modes of some directories have changed. The *at* programs now run set-user-id "root" instead of "daemon." Also, the uucp directory no longer needs to be publicly writable, as *tip* reverts to privileged status to remove its lock files. After copying your version of `/var/spool`, you should do:

```
# chown –R root /var/spool/at
# chown –R uucp.daemon /var/spool/uucp
# chmod –R o–w /var/spool/uucp
```


The format of the cron table, `/etc/crontab`, has been changed to specify the user-id that should be used to run a process. The userid "nobody" is frequently useful for non-privileged programs. Local changes are now put in a separate file, `/etc/crontab.local`.

Some of the commands previously in `/etc/rc.local` have been moved to `/etc/rc`; several new functions are now handled by `/etc/rc`, `/etc/netstart` and `/etc/rc.local`. You should look closely at the prototype version of these files and read the manual pages for the commands contained in it before trying to merge your local copy. Note in particular that *ifconfig* has had many changes, and that host names are now fully specified as domain-style names (e.g., vangogh.CS.Berkeley.EDU) for the benefit of the name server.

Some of the commands previously in `/etc/daily` have been moved to `/etc/security`, and several new functions have been added to `/etc/security` to do nightly security checks on the system. The script `/etc/daily` runs `/etc/security` each night, and mails the output to the super-user. Some of the checks done by `/etc/security` are:

- Syntax errors in the password and group files.
- Duplicate user and group names and id's.
- Dangerous search paths and umask values for the superuser.
- Dangerous values in various initialization files.
- Dangerous .rhosts files.
- Dangerous directory and file ownership or permissions.
- Globally exported filesystems.
- Dangerous owners or permissions for special devices.

In addition, it reports any changes to setuid and setgid files, special devices, or the files in `/etc/changelist` since the last run of `/etc/security`. Backup copies of the files are saved in `/var/backups`. Finally, the system binaries are checksummed and their permissions validated against the *mtree*(8) specifications in `/etc/mtree`.

The C-library and system binaries on the distribution tape are compiled with new versions of *gethostbyname* and *gethostbyaddr* that use the name server, *named*(8). If you have only a small network and are not connected to a large network, you can use the distributed library routines without any problems; they use a linear scan of the host table `/etc/hosts` if the name server is not running. If you are on the Internet or have a large local network, it is recommend that you set up and use the name server. For instructions on how to set up the necessary configuration files, refer to "Name Server Operations Guide for BIND" (SMM:10). Several programs rely on the host name returned by *gethostname* to determine the local domain name.

If you are using the name server, your *sendmail* configuration file will need some updates to accommodate it. See the "Sendmail Installation and Operation Guide" (SMM:8) and the sample *sendmail* configuration files in `/usr/src/usr.sbin/sendmail/cf`. The aliases file, `/etc/aliases` has also been changed to add certain well-known addresses.

3.4.2. Shadow password files

The password file format adds change and expiration fields and its location has changed to protect the encrypted passwords stored there. The actual password file is now stored in

1

`/etc/master.passwd`. The hashed dbm password files do not contain encrypted passwords, but contain the file offset to the entry with the password in `/etc/master.passwd` (that is readable only by root). Thus, the *getpwnam*() and *getpwuid*() functions will no longer return an encrypted password string to non-root callers. An old-style passwd file is created in `/etc/passwd` by the *vipw*(8) and *pwd_mkdb*(8) programs. See also *passwd*(5).

Several new users have also been added to the group of ''well-known'' users in `/etc/passwd`. The current list is:

name	number
root	0
daemon	1
operator	2
bin	3
games	7
uucp	66
nobody	32767

The ''daemon'' user is used for daemon processes that do not need root privileges. The ''operator'' user-id is used as an account for dumpers so that they can log in without having the root password. By placing them in the ''operator'' group, they can get read access to the disks. The ''uucp'' login has existed long before 4.4BSD, and is noted here just to provide a common user-id. The password entry ''nobody'' has been added to specify the user with least privilege. The ''games'' user is a pseudo-user that controls access to game programs.

After installing your updated password file, you must run *pwd_mkdb*(8) to create the password database. Note that *pwd_mkdb*(8) is run whenever *vipw*(8) is run.

3.4.3. The `/var` filesystem

The spooling directories saved on tape may be restored in their eventual resting places without too much concern. Be sure to use the '−p' option to *tar*(1) so that files are recreated with the same file modes. The following commands provide a guide for copying spool and log files from an existing system into a new `/var` filesystem. At least the following directories should already exist on `/var`: `output`, `log`, `backups` and `db`.

```
SRC=/oldroot/usr

cd $SRC; tar cf - msgs preserve | (cd /var && tar xpf -)

# copy $SRC/spool to /var
cd $SRC/spool
tar cf - at mail rwho | (cd /var && tar xpf -)
tar cf - ftp mqueue news secretmail uucp uucppublic | \
    (cd /var/spool && tar xpf -)

# everything else in spool is probably a printer area
mkdir .save
mv at ftp mail mqueue rwho secretmail uucp uucppublic .save
tar cf - * | (cd /var/spool/output && tar xpf -)
mv .save/* .
rmdir .save
```

```
cd /var/spool/mqueue
mv syslog.7 /var/log/maillog.7
mv syslog.6 /var/log/maillog.6
mv syslog.5 /var/log/maillog.5
mv syslog.4 /var/log/maillog.4
mv syslog.3 /var/log/maillog.3
mv syslog.2 /var/log/maillog.2
mv syslog.1 /var/log/maillog.1
mv syslog.0 /var/log/maillog.0
mv syslog /var/log/maillog

# move $SRC/adm to /var
cd $SRC/adm
tar cf - . | (cd /var/account && tar  xpf -)
cd /var/account
rm -f msgbuf
mv messages messages.[0-9] ../log
mv wtmp wtmp.[0-9] ../log
mv lastlog ../log
```


3.5. Bug fixes and changes between 4.3BSD and 4.4BSD

The major new facilities available in the 4.4BSD release are a new virtual memory system, the addition of ISO/OSI networking support, a new virtual filesystem interface supporting filesystem stacking, a freely redistributable implementation of NFS, a log-structured filesystem, enhancement of the local filesystems to support files and filesystems that are up to 2^63 bytes in size, enhanced security and system management support, and the conversion to and addition of the IEEE Std1003.1 (''POSIX'') facilities and many of the IEEE Std1003.2 facilities. In addition, many new utilities and additions to the C library are present as well. The kernel sources have been reorganized to collect all machine-dependent files for each architecture under one directory, and most of the machine-independent code is now free of code conditional on specific machines. The user structure and process structure have been reorganized to eliminate the statically-mapped user structure and to make most of the process resources shareable by multiple processes. The system and include files have been converted to be compatible with ANSI C, including function prototypes for most of the exported functions. There are numerous other changes throughout the system.

3.5.1. Changes to the kernel

This release includes several important structural kernel changes. The kernel uses a new internal system call convention; the use of global (''u-dot'') variables for parameters and error returns has been eliminated, and interrupted system calls no longer abort using non-local goto's (longjmp's). A new sleep interface separates signal handling from scheduling priority, returning characteristic errors to abort or restart the current system call. This sleep call also passes a string describing the process state, that is used by the ps(1) program. The old sleep interface can be used only for non-interruptible sleeps. The sleep interface (*tsleep*) can be used at any priority, but is only interruptible if the PCATCH flag is set. When interrupted, *tsleep* returns EINTR or ERESTART.

Many data structures that were previously statically allocated are now allocated dynamically. These structures include mount entries, file entries, user open file descriptors, the process entries, the vnode table, the name cache, and the quota structures.

To protect against indiscriminate reading or writing of kernel memory, all writing and most reading of kernel data structures must be done using a new ''sysctl'' interface. The information to be accessed is described through an extensible ''Management Information Base'' (MIB) style name, described as a dotted set of components. A new utility, *sysctl*(8), retrieves kernel state and allows processes with appropriate privilege to set kernel state.

3.5.2. Security

The kernel runs with four different levels of security. Any superuser process can raise the security level, but only *init*()(8) can lower it. Security levels are defined as follows:

–1 Permanently insecure mode – always run system in level 0 mode.

0 Insecure mode – immutable and append-only flags may be turned off. All devices may be read or written subject to their permissions.

1 Secure mode – immutable and append-only flags may not be cleared; disks for mounted filesystems, `/dev/mem`, and `/dev/kmem` are read-only.

2 Highly secure mode – same as secure mode, plus disks are always read-only whether mounted or not. This level precludes tampering with filesystems by unmounting them, but also inhibits running *newfs*(8) while the system is multi-user. See *chflags*(1) and the **–o** option to *ls*(1) for information on setting and displaying the immutable and append-only flags.

Normally, the system runs in level 0 mode while single user and in level 1 mode while multiuser. If the level 2 mode is desired while running multiuser, it can be set in the startup script `/etc/rc` using *sysctl*(1). If it is desired to run the system in level 0 mode while multiuser, the administrator must build a kernel with the variable `securelevel` in the kernel source file `/sys/kern/kern_sysctl.c` initialized to –1.

3.5.2.1. Virtual memory changes

The new virtual memory implementation is derived from the Mach operating system developed at Carnegie-Mellon, and was ported to the BSD kernel at the University of Utah. It is based on the 2.0 release of Mach (with some bug fixes from the 2.5 and 3.0 releases) and retains many of its essential features such as the separation of the machine dependent and independent layers (the ''pmap'' interface), efficient memory utilization using copy-on-write and other lazy-evaluation techniques, and support for large, sparse address spaces. It does not include the ''external pager'' interface instead using a primitive internal pager interface. The Mach virtual memory system call interface has been replaced with the ''mmap''-based interface described in the ''Berkeley Software Architecture Manual'' (see UNIX Programmer's Manual, Supplementary Documents, PSD:5). The interface is similar to the interfaces shipped by several commercial vendors such as Sun, USL, and Convex Computer Corp. The integration of the new virtual memory is functionally complete, but still has serious performance problems under heavy memory load. The internal kernel interfaces have not yet been completed and the memory pool and buffer cache have not been merged. Some additional caveats:

- Since the code is based on the 2.0 release of Mach, bugs and misfeatures of the BSD version should not be considered short-comings of the current Mach virtual memory system.
- Because of the disjoint virtual memory (page) and IO (buffer) caches, it is possible to see inconsistencies if using both the mmap and read/write interfaces on the same file simultaneously.
- Swap space is allocated on-demand rather than up front and no allocation checks are performed so it is possible to over-commit memory and eventually deadlock.
- The semantics of the *vfork*(2) system call are slightly different. The synchronization between parent and child is preserved, but the memory sharing aspect is not. In practice this has been enough for backward compatibility, but newer code should just use *fork*(2).

3.5.2.2. Networking additions and changes

The ISO/OSI Networking consists of a kernel implementation of transport class 4 (TP-4), connectionless networking protocol (CLNP), and 802.3-based link-level support (hardware-compatible with Ethernet[4]). We also include support for ISO Connection-Oriented Network Service, X.25, TP-0. The session and presentation layers are provided outside the kernel using the ISO Development Environment by Marshall Rose, that is available via anonymous FTP (but is not included on the distribution tape). Included

[4] Ethernet is a trademark of the Xerox Corporation.

in this development environment are file transfer and management (FTAM), virtual terminals (VT), a directory services implementation (X.500), and miscellaneous other utilities.

Kernel support for the ISO OSI protocols is enabled with the ISO option in the kernel configuration file. The *iso*(4) manual page describes the protocols and addressing; see also *clnp*(4), *tp*(4) and *cltp*(4). The OSI equivalent to ARP is ESIS (End System to Intermediate System Routing Protocol); running this protocol is mandatory, however one can manually add translations for machines that do not participate by use of the *route*(8) command. Additional information is provided in the manual page describing *esis*(4).

The command *route*(8) has a new syntax and several new capabilities: it can install routes with a specified destination and mask, and can change route characteristics such as hop count, packet size and window size.

Several important enhancements have been added to the TCP/IP protocols including TCP header prediction and serial line IP (SLIP) with header compression. The routing implementation has been completely rewritten to use a hierarchical routing tree with a mask per route to support the arbitrary levels of routing found in the ISO protocols. The routing table also stores and caches route characteristics to speed the adaptation of the throughput and congestion avoidance algorithms.

The format of the *sockaddr* structure (the structure used to describe a generic network address with an address family and family-specific data) has changed from previous releases, as have the address family-specific versions of this structure. The *sa_family* family field has been split into a length, `sa_len`, and a family, `sa_family`. System calls that pass a *sockaddr* structure into the kernel (e.g. *sendto*() and *connect*()) have a separate parameter that specifies the *sockaddr* length, and thus it is not necessary to fill in the *sa_len* field for those system calls. System calls that pass a *sockaddr* structure back from the kernel (e.g. *recvfrom*() and *accept*()) receive a completely filled-in *sockaddr* structure, thus the length field is valid. Because this would not work for old binaries, the new library uses a different system call number. Thus, most networking programs compiled under 4.4BSD are incompatible with older systems.

Although this change is mostly source and binary compatible with old programs, there are three exceptions. Programs with statically initialized *sockaddr* structures (usually the Internet form, a *sockaddr_in*) are not compatible. Generally, such programs should be changed to fill in the structure at run time, as C allows no way to initialize a structure without assuming the order and number of fields. Also, programs with use structures to describe a network packet format that contain embedded *sockaddr* structures also require change; a definition of an *osockaddr* structure is provided for this purpose. Finally, programs that use the SIOCGIFCONF ioctl to get a complete list of interface addresses need to check the *sa_len* field when iterating through the array of addresses returned, as not all the structures returned have the same length (this variance in length is nearly guaranteed by the presence of link-layer address structures).

3.5.2.3. Additions and changes to filesystems

The 4.4BSD distribution contains most of the interfaces specified in the IEEE Std1003.1 system interface standard. Filesystem additions include IEEE Std1003.1 FIFOs, byte-range file locking, and saved user and group identifiers.

A new virtual filesystem interface has been added to the kernel to support multiple filesystems. In comparison with other interfaces, the Berkeley interface has been structured for more efficient support of filesystems that maintain state (such as the local filesystem). The interface has been extended with support for stackable filesystems done at UCLA. These extensions allow for filesystems to be layered on top of each other and allow new vnode operations to be added without requiring changes to existing filesystem implementations. For example, the umap filesystem (see *mount_umap*(8)) is used to mount a sub-tree of an existing filesystem that uses a different set of uids and gids than the local system. Such a filesystem could be mounted from a remote site via NFS or it could be a filesystem on removable media brought from some foreign location that uses a different password file.

Other new filesystems that may be stacked include the loopback filesystem *mount_lofs*(8), the kernel filesystem *mount_kernfs*(8), and the portal filesystem *mount_portal*(8).

The buffer cache in the kernel is now organized as a file block cache rather than a device block cache. As a consequence, cached blocks from a file and from the corresponding block device would no longer be kept consistent. The block device thus has little remaining value. Three changes have been made for these reasons:

1) block devices may not be opened while they are mounted, and may not be mounted while open, so that the two versions of cached file blocks cannot be created,

2) filesystem checks of the root now use the raw device to access the root filesystem, and

3) the root filesystem is initially mounted read-only so that nothing can be written back to disk during or after change to the raw filesystem by *fsck*.

The root filesystem may be made writable while in single-user mode with the command:

```
mount -uw /
```

The mount command has an option to update the flags on a mounted filesystem, including the ability to upgrade a filesystem from read-only to read-write or downgrade it from read-write to read-only.

In addition to the local "fast filesystem", we have added an implementation of the network filesystem (NFS) that fully interoperates with the NFS shipped by Sun and its licensees. Because our NFS implementation was implemented by Rick Macklem of the University of Guelph using only the publicly available NFS specification, it does not require a license from Sun to use in source or binary form. By default it runs over UDP to be compatible with Sun's implementation. However, it can be configured on a per-mount basis to run over TCP. Using TCP allows it to be used quickly and efficiently through gateways and over long-haul networks. Using an extended protocol, it supports Leases to allow a limited callback mechanism that greatly reduces the network traffic necessary to maintain cache consistency between the server and its clients. Its use will be familiar to users of other implementations of NFS. See the manual pages *mount*(8), *mountd*(8), *fstab*(5), *exports*(5), *netgroup*(5), *nfsd*(8), *nfsiod*(8), and *nfssvc*(8). and the document "The 4.4BSD NFS Implementation" (SMM:6) for further information. The format of `/etc/fstab` has changed from previous BSD releases to a blank-separated format to allow colons in pathnames.

A new local filesystem, the log-structured filesystem (LFS), has been added to the system. It provides near disk-speed output and fast crash recovery. This work is based, in part, on the LFS filesystem created for the Sprite operating system at Berkeley. While the kernel implementation is almost complete, only some of the utilities to support the filesystem have been written, so we do not recommend it for production use. See *newlfs*(8), *mount_lfs*(8) and *lfs_cleanerd*(8) for more information. For a in-depth description of the implementation and performance characteristics of log-structured filesystems in general, and this one in particular, see Dr. Margo Seltzer's doctoral thesis, available from the University of California Computer Science Department.

We have also added a memory-based filesystem that runs in pageable memory, allowing large temporary filesystems without requiring dedicated physical memory.

The local "fast filesystem" has been enhanced to do clustering that allows large pieces of files to be allocated contiguously resulting in near doubling of filesystem throughput. The filesystem interface has been extended to allow files and filesystems to grow to 2^63 bytes in size. The quota system has been rewritten to support both user and group quotas (simultaneously if desired). Quota expiration is based on time rather than the previous metric of number of logins over quota. This change makes quotas more useful on fileservers onto which users seldom login.

The system security has been greatly enhanced by the addition of additional file flags that permit a file to be marked as immutable or append only. Once set, these flags can only be cleared by the super-user when the system is running in insecure mode (normally, single-user). In addition to the immutable and append-only flags, the filesystem supports a new user-settable flag "nodump". (File flags are set using the *chflags*(1) utility.) When set on a file, *dump*(8) will omit the file from incremental backups but retain them on full backups. See the "-h" flag to *dump*(8) for details on how to change this default. The "nodump" flag is usually set on core dumps, system crash dumps, and object files generated by the compiler. Note that the flag is not preserved when files are copied so that installing an object file will cause it to be preserved.

The filesystem format used in 4.4BSD has several additions. Directory entries have an additional field, d_type, that identifies the type of the entry (normally found in the st_mode field of the stat structure). This field is particularly useful for identifying directories without the need to use *stat*(2).

Short (less than sixty byte) symbolic links are now stored in the inode itself rather than in a separate data block. This saves disk space and makes access of symbolic links faster. Short symbolic links are not given a special type, so a user-level application is unaware of their special treatment. Unlike pre-4.4BSD systems, symbolic links do not have an owner, group, access mode, times, etc. Instead, these attributes are taken from the directory that contains the link. The only attributes returned from an *lstat*(2) that refer to the symbolic link itself are the file type (S_IFLNK), size, blocks, and link count (always 1).

1

An implementation of an auto-mounter daemon, *amd*, was contributed by Jan-Simon Pendry of the Imperial College of Science, Technology & Medicine. See the document ''AMD – The 4.4BSD Automounter'' (SMM:13) for further information.

The directory /dev/fd contains special files 0 through 63 that, when opened, duplicate the corresponding file descriptor. The names /dev/stdin, /dev/stdout and /dev/stderr refer to file descriptors 0, 1 and 2. See *fd*(4) and *mount_fdesc*(8) for more information.

3.5.2.4. POSIX terminal driver changes

The 4.4BSD system uses the IEEE P1003.1 (POSIX.1) terminal interface rather than the previous BSD terminal interface. The terminal driver is similar to the System V terminal driver with the addition of the necessary extensions to get the functionality previously available in the 4.3BSD terminal driver. Both the old *ioctl* calls and old options to *stty*(1) are emulated. This emulation is expected to be unavailable in many vendors releases, so conversion to the new interface is encouraged.

4.4BSD also adds the IEEE Std1003.1 job control interface, that is similar to the 4.3BSD job control interface, but adds a security model that was missing in the 4.3BSD job control implementation. A new system call, *setsid*(), creates a job-control session consisting of a single process group with one member, the caller, that becomes a session leader. Only a session leader may acquire a controlling terminal. This is done explicitly via a TIOCSCTTY *ioctl*() call, not implicitly by an *open*() call. The call fails if the terminal is in use. Programs that allocate controlling terminals (or pseudo-terminals) require change to work in this environment. The versions of *xterm* provided in the X11R5 release includes the necessary changes. New library routines are available for allocating and initializing pseudo-terminals and other terminals as controlling terminal; see /usr/src/lib/libutil/pty.c and /usr/src/lib/libutil/login_tty.c.

The POSIX job control model formalizes the previous conventions used in setting up a process group. Unfortunately, this requires that changes be made in a defined order and with some synchronization that were not necessary in the past. Older job control shells (csh, ksh) will generally not operate correctly with the new system.

Most of the other kernel interfaces have been changed to correspond with the POSIX.1 interface, although that work is not complete. See the relevant manual pages and the IEEE POSIX standard.

3.5.2.5. Native operating system compatibility

Both the HP300 and SPARC ports feature the ability to run binaries built for the native operating system (HP-UX or SunOS) by emulating their system calls. Building an HP300 kernel with the HPUXCOMPAT and COMPAT_OHPUX options or a SPARC kernel with the COMPAT_SUNOS option will enable this feature (on by default in the generic kernel provided in the root filesystem image). Though this native operating system compatibility was provided by the developers as needed for their purposes and is by no means complete, it is complete enough to run several non-trivial applications including those that require HP-UX or SunOS shared libraries. For example, the vendor supplied X11 server and windowing environment can be used on both the HP300 and SPARC.

It is important to remember that merely copying over a native binary and executing it (or executing it directly across NFS) does not imply that it will run. All but the most trivial of applications are likely to require access to auxiliary files that do not exist under 4.4BSD (e.g. /etc/ld.so.cache) or have a slightly different format (e.g. /etc/passwd). However, by using system call tracing and through creative use of symlinks, many problems can be tracked down and corrected.

The DECstation port also has code for ULTRIX emulation (kernel option ULTRIXCOMPAT, not compiled into the generic kernel) but it was used primarily for initially bootstrapping the port and has not been used since. Hence, some work may be required to make it generally useful.

3.5.3. Changes to the utilities

We have been tracking the IEEE Std1003.2 shell and utility work and have included prototypes of many of the proposed utilities based on draft 12 of the POSIX.2 Shell and Utilities document. Because most of the traditional utilities have been replaced with implementations conformant to the POSIX standards, you should realize that the utility software may not be as stable, reliable or well documented as in traditional Berkeley releases. In particular, almost the entire manual suite has been rewritten to reflect the POSIX defined interfaces, and in some instances it does not correctly reflect the current state of the software. It is also worth noting that, in rewriting this software, we have generally been rewarded with significant performance improvements. Most of the libraries and header files have been converted to be compliant with ANSI C. The shipped compiler (gcc) is a superset of ANSI C, but supports traditional C as a command-line option. The system libraries and utilities all compile with either ANSI or traditional C.

3.5.3.1. Make and Makefiles

This release uses a completely new version of the *make* program derived from the *pmake* program developed by the Sprite project at Berkeley. It supports existing makefiles, although certain incorrect makefiles may fail. The makefiles for the 4.4BSD sources make extensive use of the new facilities, especially conditionals and file inclusion, and are thus completely incompatible with older versions of *make* (but nearly all the makefiles are now trivial!). The standard include files for *make* are in /usr/share/mk. There is a bsd.README file in /usr/src/share/mk.

Another global change supported by the new *make* is designed to allow multiple architectures to share a copy of the sources. If a subdirectory named obj is present in the current directory, *make* descends into that directory and creates all object and other files there. We use this by building a directory hierarchy in /var/obj that parallels /usr/src. We then create the obj subdirectories in /usr/src as symbolic links to the corresponding directories in /var/obj. (This step is automated. The command "make obj" in /usr/src builds both the local symlink and the shadow directory, using /usr/obj, that may be a symbolic link, as the root of the shadow tree. The use of /usr/obj is for historic reasons only, and the system make configuration files in /usr/share/mk can trivially be modified to use /var/obj instead.) We have one /var/obj hierarchy on the local system, and another on each system that shares the source filesystem. All the sources in /usr/src except for /usr/src/contrib and portions of /usr/src/old have been converted to use the new make and obj subdirectories; this change allows compilation for multiple architectures from the same source tree (that may be mounted read-only).

3.5.3.2. Kerberos

The Kerberos authentication server from MIT (version 4) is included in this release. See *kerberos*(1) for a general, if MIT-specific, introduction. If it is configured, *login*(1), *passwd*(1), *rlogin*(1) and *rsh*(1) will all begin to use it automatically. The file /etc/kerberosIV/README describes the configuration. Each system needs the file /etc/kerberosIV/krb.conf to set its realm and local servers, and a private key stored in /etc/kerberosIV/srvtab (see *ext_srvtab*(8)). The Kerberos server should be set up on a single, physically secure, server machine. Users and hosts may be added to the server database manually with *kdb_edit*(8), or users on authorized hosts can add themselves and a Kerberos password after verification of their "local" (passwd-file) password using the *register*(1) program.

Note that by default the password-changing program *passwd*(1) changes the Kerberos password, that must exist. The -l option to *passwd*(1) changes the "local" password if one exists.

Note that Version 5 of Kerberos will be released soon; Version 4 should probably be replaced at that time.

3.5.3.3. Timezone support

The timezone conversion code in the C library uses data files installed in `/usr/share/zoneinfo` to convert from "GMT" to various timezones. The data file for the default timezone for the system should be copied to `/etc/localtime`. Other timezones can be selected by setting the TZ environment variable.

The data files initially installed in `/usr/share/zoneinfo` include corrections for leap seconds since the beginning of 1970. Thus, they assume that the kernel will increment the time at a constant rate during a leap second; that is, time just keeps on ticking. The conversion routines will then name a leap second 23:59:60. For purists, this effectively means that the kernel maintains TAI (International Atomic Time) rather than UTC (Coordinated Universal Time, aka GMT).

For systems that run current NTP (Network Time Protocol) implementations or that wish to conform to the letter of the POSIX.1 law, it is possible to rebuild the timezone data files so that leap seconds are not counted. (NTP causes the time to jump over a leap second, and POSIX effectively requires the clock to be reset by hand when a leap second occurs. In this mode, the kernel effectively runs UTC rather than TAI.)

The data files without leap second information are constructed from the source directory, `/usr/src/share/zoneinfo`. Change the variable REDO in Makefile from "right" to "posix", and then do

```
make obj    (if necessary)
make
make install
```

You will then need to copy the correct default zone file to `/etc/localtime`, as the old one would still have used leap seconds, and because the Makefile installs a default `/etc/localtime` each time "make install" is done.

It is possible to install both sets of timezone data files. This results in subdirectories `/usr/share/zoneinfo/right` and `/usr/share/zoneinfo/posix`. Each contain a complete set of zone files. See `/usr/src/share/zoneinfo/Makefile` for details.

3.5.3.4. Additions and changes to the libraries

Notable additions to the libraries include functions to traverse a filesystem hierarchy, database interfaces to btree and hashing functions, a new, faster implementation of stdio and a radix and merge sort functions.

The *fts*(3) functions will do either physical or logical traversal of a file hierarchy as well as handle essentially infinite depth filesystems and filesystems with cycles. All the utilities in 4.4BSD which traverse file hierarchies have been converted to use *fts*(3). The conversion has always resulted in a significant performance gain, often of four or five to one in system time.

The *dbopen*(3) functions are intended to be a family of database access methods. Currently, they consist of *hash*(3), an extensible, dynamic hashing scheme, *btree*(3), a sorted, balanced tree structure (B+tree's), and *recno*(3), a flat-file interface for fixed or variable length records referenced by logical record number. Each of the access methods stores associated key/data pairs and uses the same record oriented interface for access.

The *qsort*(3) function has been rewritten for additional performance. In addition, three new types of sorting functions, *heapsort*(3), *mergesort*(3) and *radixsort*(3) have been added to the system. The *mergesort* function is optimized for data with pre-existing order, in which case it usually significantly outperforms *qsort*. The *radixsort*(3) functions are variants of most-significant-byte radix sorting. They take time linear to the number of bytes to be sorted, usually significantly outperforming *qsort* on data that can be sorted in this fashion. An implementation of the POSIX 1003.2 standard *sort*(1), based on *radixsort*, is included in `/usr/src/contrib/sort`.

Some additional comments about the 4.4BSD C library:

- The floating point support in the C library has been replaced and is now accurate.

- The C functions specified by both ANSI C, POSIX 1003.1 and 1003.2 are now part of the C library. This includes support for file name matching, shell globbing and both basic and extended regular expressions.
- ANSI C multibyte and wide character support has been integrated. The rune functionality from the Bell Labs' Plan 9 system is provided as well.
- The *termcap*(3) functions have been generalized and replaced with a general purpose interface named *getcap*(3).
- The *stdio*(3) routines have been replaced, and are usually much faster. In addition, the *funopen*(3) interface permits applications to provide their own I/O stream function support.

The *curses*(3) library has been largely rewritten. Important additional features include support for scrolling and *termios*(3).

An application front-end editing library, named libedit, has been added to the system.

A superset implementation of the SunOS kernel memory interface library, libkvm, has been integrated into the system.

3.5.3.5. Additions and changes to other utilities

There are many new utilities, offering many new capabilities, in 4.4BSD. Skimming through the section 1 and section 8 manual pages is sure to be useful. The additions to the utility suite include greatly enhanced versions of programs that display system status information, implementations of various traditional tools described in the IEEE Std1003.2 standard, new tools not previous available on Berkeley UNIX systems, and many others. Also, with only a very few exceptions, all the utilities from 4.3BSD that included proprietary source code have been replaced, and their 4.4BSD counterparts are freely redistributable. Normally, this replacement resulted in significant performance improvements and the increase of the limits imposed on data by the utility as well.

A summary of specific additions and changes are as follows:

`amd`	An auto-mounter implementation.
`ar`	Replacement of the historic archive format with a new one.
`awk`	Replaced by gawk; see /usr/src/old/awk for the historic version.
`bdes`	Utility implementing DES modes of operation described in FIPS PUB 81.
`calendar`	Addition of an interface for system calendars.
`cap_mkdb`	Utility for building hashed versions of termcap style databases.
`cc`	Replacement of pcc with gcc suite.
`chflags`	A utility for setting the per-file user and system flags.
`chfn`	An editor based replacement for changing user information.
`chpass`	An editor based replacement for changing user information.
`chsh`	An editor based replacement for changing user information.
`cksum`	The POSIX 1003.2 checksum utility; compatible with sum.
`column`	A columnar text formatting utility.
`cp`	POSIX 1003.2 compatible, able to copy special files.
`csh`	Freely redistributable and 8-bit clean.
`date`	User specified formats added.
`dd`	New EBCDIC conversion tables, major performance improvements.
`dev_mkdb`	Hashed interface to devices.
`dm`	Dungeon master.
`find`	Several new options and primaries, major performance improvements.
`fstat`	Utility displaying information on files open on the system.
`ftpd`	Connection logging added.
`hexdump`	A binary dump utility, superseding od.
`id`	The POSIX 1003.2 user identification utility.
`inetd`	Tcpmux added.
`jot`	A text formatting utility.

kdump	A system-call tracing facility.
ktrace	A system-call tracing facility.
kvm_mkdb	Hashed interface to the kernel name list.
lam	A text formatting utility.
lex	A new, freely redistributable, significantly faster version.
locate	A database of the system files, by name, constructed weekly.
logname	The POSIX 1003.2 user identification utility.
mail.local	New local mail delivery agent, replacing mail.
make	Replaced with a new, more powerful make, supporting include files.
man	Added support for man page location configuration.
mkdep	A new utility for generating make dependency lists.
mkfifo	The POSIX 1003.2 FIFO creation utility.
mtree	A new utility for mapping file hierarchies to a file.
nfsstat	An NFS statistics utility.
nvi	A freely redistributable replacement for the ex/vi editors.
pax	The POSIX 1003.2 replacement for cpio and tar.
printf	The POSIX 1003.2 replacement for echo.
roff	Replaced by groff; see /usr/src/old/roff for the historic versions.
rs	New utility for text formatting.
shar	An archive building utility.
sysctl	MIB-style interface to system state.
tcopy	Fast tape-to-tape copying and verification.
touch	Time and file reference specifications.
tput	The POSIX 1003.2 terminal display utility.
tr	Addition of character classes.
uname	The POSIX 1003.2 system identification utility.
vis	A filter for converting and displaying non-printable characters.
xargs	The POSIX 1003.2 argument list constructor utility.
yacc	A new, freely redistributable, significantly faster version.

The new versions of *lex*(1) (''flex'') and *yacc*(1) (''zoo'') should be installed early on if attempting to cross-compile 4.4BSD on another system. Note that the new *lex* program is not completely backward compatible with historic versions of *lex*, although it is believed that all documented features are supported.

The *find* utility has two new options that are important to be aware of if you intend to use NFS. The ''fstype'' and ''prune'' options can be used together to prevent find from crossing NFS mount points. See `/etc/daily` for an example of their use.

3.6. Hints on converting from 4.3BSD to 4.4BSD

This section summarizes changes between 4.3BSD and 4.4BSD that are likely to cause difficulty in doing the conversion. It does not include changes in the network; see section 5 for information on setting up the network.

Since the stat st_size field is now 64-bits instead of 32, doing something like:

```
foo(st.st_size);
```

and then (improperly) defining foo with an ''int'' or ''long'' parameter:

```
foo(size)
     int size;
{
     ...
}
```

will fail miserably (well, it might work on a little endian machine). This problem showed up in *emacs*(1) as well as several other programs. A related problem is improperly casting (or failing to cast) the second argument to *lseek*(2), *truncate*(2), or *ftruncate*(2) ala:

```
lseek(fd, (long)off, 0);
```

or

```
lseek(fd, 0, 0);
```

The best solution is to include <unistd.h> which has prototypes that catch these types of errors.

Determining the "namelen" parameter for a *connect*(2) call on a unix domain socket should use the "SUN_LEN" macro from <sys/un.h>. One old way that was used:

```
addrlen = strlen(unaddr.sun_path) + sizeof(unaddr.sun_family);
```

no longer works as there is an additional sun_len field.

The kernel's limit on the number of open files has been increased from 20 to 64. It is now possible to change this limit almost arbitrarily. The standard I/O library autoconfigures to the kernel limit. Note that file ("_iob") entries may be allocated by *malloc* from *fopen*; this allocation has been known to cause problems with programs that use their own memory allocators. Memory allocation does not occur until after 20 files have been opened by the standard I/O library.

Select can be used with more than 32 descriptors by using arrays of **ints** for the bit fields rather than single **ints**. Programs that used *getdtablesize* as their first argument to *select* will no longer work correctly. Usually the program can be modified to correctly specify the number of bits in an **int**. Alternatively the program can be modified to use an array of **ints**. There are a set of macros available in <sys/types.h> to simplify this. See *select*(2).

Old core files will not be intelligible by the current debuggers because of numerous changes to the user structure and because the kernel stack has been enlarged. The *a.out* header that was in the user structure is no longer present. Locally-written debuggers that try to check the magic number will need to be changed.

Files may not be deleted from directories having the "sticky" (ISVTX) bit set in their modes except by the owner of the file or of the directory, or by the superuser. This is primarily to protect users' files in publicly-writable directories such as /tmp and /var/tmp. All publicly-writable directories should have their "sticky" bits set with "chmod +t."

The following two sections contain additional notes about changes in 4.4BSD that affect the installation of local files; be sure to read them as well.

4. System setup

This section describes procedures used to set up a 4.4BSD UNIX system. These procedures are used when a system is first installed or when the system configuration changes. Procedures for normal system operation are described in the next section.

4.1. Kernel configuration

This section briefly describes the layout of the kernel code and how files for devices are made. For a full discussion of configuring and building system images, consult the document "Building 4.3BSD UNIX Systems with Config" (SMM:2).

4.1.1. Kernel organization

As distributed, the kernel source is in a separate tar image. The source may be physically located anywhere within any filesystem so long as a symbolic link to the location is created for the file /sys (many files in /usr/include are normally symbolic links relative to /sys). In further discussions of the system source all path names will be given relative to /sys.

The kernel is made up of several large generic parts:

sys		main kernel header files
kern		kernel functions broken down as follows
	init	system startup, syscall dispatching, entry points

	kern	scheduling, descriptor handling and generic I/O
	sys	process management, signals
	tty	terminal handling and job control
	vfs	filesystem management
	uipc	interprocess communication (sockets)
	subr	miscellaneous support routines
vm		virtual memory management
ufs		local filesystems broken down as follows
	ufs	common local filesystem routines
	ffs	fast filesystem
	lfs	log-based filesystem
	mfs	memory based filesystem
nfs		Sun-compatible network filesystem
miscfs		miscellaneous filesystems broken down as follows
	deadfs	where rejected vnodes go to die
	fdesc	access to per-process file descriptors
	fifofs	IEEE Std1003.1 FIFOs
	kernfs	filesystem access to kernel data structures
	lofs	loopback filesystem
	nullfs	another loopback filesystem
	portal	associate processes with filesystem locations
	specfs	device special files
	umapfs	provide alternate uid/gid mappings
dev		generic device drivers (SCSI, vnode, concatenated disk)

The networking code is organized by protocol

net	routing and generic interface drivers
netinet	Internet protocols (TCP, UDP, IP, etc)
netiso	ISO protocols (TP-4, CLNP, CLTP, etc)
netns	Xerox network systems protocols (IDP, SPP, etc)
netx25	CCITT X.25 protocols (X.25 Packet Level, HDLC/LAPB)

A separate subdirectory is provided for each machine architecture

hp300	HP 9000/300 series of Motorola 68000-based machines
hp	code common to both HP 68k and (non-existent) PA-RISC ports
i386	Intel 386/486-based PC machines
luna68k	Omron 68000-based workstations
news3400	Sony News MIPS-based workstations
pmax	Digital 3100/5000 MIPS-based workstations
sparc	Sun Microsystems SPARCstation 1, 1+, and 2
tahoe	(deprecated) CCI Power 6-series machines
vax	(deprecated) Digital VAX machines

Each machine directory is subdivided by function; for example the hp300 directory contains

include	exported machine-dependent header files
hp300	machine-dependent support code and private header files
dev	device drivers
conf	configuration files
stand	machine-dependent standalone code

Other kernel related directories

compile	area to compile kernels
conf	machine-independent configuration files
stand	machine-independent standalone code

4.1.2. Devices and device drivers

Devices supported by UNIX are implemented in the kernel by drivers whose source is kept in /sys/<architecture>/dev. These drivers are loaded into the system when included in a cpu specific configuration file kept in the conf directory. Devices are accessed through special files in the filesystem, made by the *mknod*(8) program and normally kept in the /dev directory. For all the devices supported by the distribution system, the files in /dev are created by the /dev/MAKEDEV shell script.

Determine the set of devices that you have and create a new /dev directory by running the MAKEDEV script. First create a new directory /newdev, copy MAKEDEV into it, edit the file MAKEDEV.local to provide an entry for local needs, and run it to generate a /newdevdirectory. For instance,

```
# cd /
# mkdir newdev
# cp dev/MAKEDEV newdev/MAKEDEV
# cd newdev
# MAKEDEV sd0 pt0 std LOCAL
```

Note the "std" argument causes standard devices such as /dev/console, the machine console, to be created.

You can then do

```
# cd /
# mv dev olddev ; mv newdev dev
# sync
```

to install the new device directory.

4.1.3. Building new system images

The kernel configuration of each UNIX system is described by a single configuration file, stored in the /sys/<architecture>/conf directory. To learn about the format of this file and the procedure used to build system images, start by reading "Building 4.3BSD UNIX Systems with Config" (SMM:2), look at the manual pages in section 4 of the UNIX manual for the devices you have, and look at the sample configuration files in the /sys/<architecture>/conf directory.

The configured system image vmunix should be copied to the root, and then booted to try it out. It is best to name it /newvmunix so as not to destroy the working system until you are sure it does work:

```
# cp vmunix /newvmunix
# sync
```

It is also a good idea to keep the previous system around under some other name. In particular, we recommend that you save the generic distribution version of the system permanently as /genvmunix for use in emergencies. To boot the new version of the system you should follow the bootstrap procedures outlined in section 6.1. After having booted and tested the new system, it should be installed as /vmunix before going into multiuser operation. A systematic scheme for numbering and saving old versions of the system may be useful.

4.2. Configuring terminals

If UNIX is to support simultaneous access from directly-connected terminals other than the console, the file /etc/ttys (see *ttys*(5)) must be edited.

To add a new terminal device, be sure the device is configured into the system and that the special files for the device have been made by /dev/MAKEDEV. Then, enable the appropriate lines of /etc/ttys by setting the "status" field to **on** (or add new lines). Note that lines in /etc/ttys are one-for-one with entries in the file of current users (see /var/run/utmp), and therefore it is best to make changes while running in single-user mode and to add all the entries for a new device at once.

Each line in the `/etc/ttys` file is broken into four tab separated fields (comments are shown by a '#' character and extend to the end of the line). For each terminal line the four fields are: the device (without a leading `/dev`), the program `/sbin/init` should startup to service the line (or **none** if the line is to be left alone), the terminal type (found in `/usr/share/misc/termcap`), and optional status information describing if the terminal is enabled or not and if it is ''secure'' (i.e. the super user should be allowed to login on the line). If the console is marked as ''insecure'', then the root password is required to bring the machine up single-user. All fields are character strings with entries requiring embedded white space enclosed in double quotes. Thus a newly added terminal `/dev/tty00` could be added as

1

```
tty00 "/usr/libexec/getty std.9600" vt100 on secure # mike's office
```

The std.9600 parameter provided to `/usr/libexec/getty` is used in searching the file `/etc/gettytab`; it specifies a terminal's characteristics (such as baud rate). To make custom terminal types, consult *gettytab*(5) before modifying `/etc/gettytab`.

Dialup terminals should be wired so that carrier is asserted only when the phone line is dialed up. For non-dialup terminals, from which modem control is not available, you must wire back the signals so that the carrier appears to always be present. For further details, find your terminal driver in section 4 of the manual.

For network terminals (i.e. pseudo terminals), no program should be started up on the lines. Thus, the normal entry in `/etc/ttys` would look like

```
ttyp0 none network
```

(Note, the fourth field is not needed here.)

When the system is running multi-user, all terminals that are listed in `/etc/ttys` as **on** have their line enabled. If, during normal operations, you wish to disable a terminal line, you can edit the file `/etc/ttys` to change the terminal's status to **off** and then send a hangup signal to the *init* process, by doing

```
# kill -1 1
```

Terminals can similarly be enabled by changing the status field from **off** to **on** and sending a hangup signal to *init*.

Note that if a special file is inaccessible when *init* tries to create a process for it, *init* will log a message to the system error logging process (see *syslogd*(8)) and try to reopen the terminal every minute, reprinting the warning message every 10 minutes. Messages of this sort are normally printed on the console, though other actions may occur depending on the configuration information found in `/etc/syslog.conf`.

Finally note that you should change the names of any dialup terminals to ttyd? where ? is in [0-9a-zA-Z], as some programs use this property of the names to determine if a terminal is a dialup. Shell commands to do this should be put in the `/dev/MAKEDEV.local` script.

While it is possible to use truly arbitrary strings for terminal names, the accounting and noticeably the *ps*(1) command make good use of the convention that tty names (by default, and also after dialups are named as suggested above) are distinct in the last 2 characters. Change this and you may be sorry later, as the heuristic *ps*(1) uses based on these conventions will then break down and *ps* will run MUCH slower.

4.3. Adding users

The procedure for adding a new user is described in *adduser*(8). You should add accounts for the initial user community, giving each a directory and a password, and putting users who will wish to share software in the same groups.

Several guest accounts have been provided on the distribution system; these accounts are for people at Berkeley, Bell Laboratories, and others who have done major work on UNIX in the past. You can delete these accounts, or leave them on the system if you expect that these people would have occasion to login as guests on your system.

4.4. Site tailoring

All programs that require the site's name, or some similar characteristic, obtain the information through system calls or from files located in `/etc`. Aside from parts of the system related to the network, to tailor the system to your site you must simply select a site name, then edit the file

/etc/netstart

The first lines in `/etc/netstart` use a variable to set the hostname,

hostname=*mysitename*
/bin/hostname $hostname

to define the value returned by the *gethostname*(2) system call. If you are running the name server, your site name should be your fully qualified domain name. Programs such as *getty*(8), *mail*(1), *wall*(1), and *uucp*(1) use this system call so that the binary images are site independent.

You will also need to edit `/etc/netstart` to do the network interface initialization using *ifconfig*(8). If you are not sure how to do this, see sections 5.1, 5.2, and 5.3. If you are not running a routing daemon and have more than one Ethernet in your environment you will need to set up a default route; see section 5.4 for details. Before bringing your system up multiuser, you should ensure that the networking is properly configured. The network is started by running `/etc/netstart`. Once started, you should test connectivity using *ping*(8). You should first test connectivity to yourself, then another host on your Ethernet, and finally a host on another Ethernet. The *netstat*(8) program can be used to inspect and debug your routes; see section 5.4.

4.5. Setting up the line printer system

The line printer system consists of at least the following files and commands:

/usr/bin/lpq	spooling queue examination program
/usr/bin/lprm	program to delete jobs from a queue
/usr/bin/lpr	program to enter a job in a printer queue
/etc/printcap	printer configuration and capability database
/usr/sbin/lpd	line printer daemon, scans spooling queues
/usr/sbin/lpc	line printer control program
/etc/hosts.lpd	list of host allowed to use the printers

The file `/etc/printcap` is a master database describing line printers directly attached to a machine and, also, printers accessible across a network. The manual page *printcap*(5) describes the format of this database and also shows the default values for such things as the directory in which spooling is performed. The line printer system handles multiple printers, multiple spooling queues, local and remote printers, and also printers attached via serial lines that require line initialization such as the baud rate. Raster output devices such as a Varian or Versatec, and laser printers such as an Imagen, are also supported by the line printer system.

Remote spooling via the network is handled with two spooling queues, one on the local machine and one on the remote machine. When a remote printer job is started with *lpr*, the job is queued locally and a daemon process created to oversee the transfer of the job to the remote machine. If the destination machine is unreachable, the job will remain queued until it is possible to transfer the files to the spooling queue on the remote machine. The *lpq* program shows the contents of spool queues on both the local and remote machines.

To configure your line printers, consult the printcap manual page and the accompanying document, "4.3BSD Line Printer Spooler Manual" (SMM:7). A call to the *lpd* program should be present in `/etc/rc`.

4.6. Setting up the mail system

The mail system consists of the following commands:

/usr/bin/mail	UCB mail program, described in *mail*(1)
/usr/sbin/sendmail	mail routing program
/var/spool/mail	mail spooling directory
/var/spool/secretmail	secure mail directory
/usr/bin/xsend	secure mail sender
/usr/bin/xget	secure mail receiver
/etc/aliases	mail forwarding information
/usr/bin/newaliases	command to rebuild binary forwarding database
/usr/bin/biff	mail notification enabler
/usr/libexec/comsat	mail notification daemon

Mail is normally sent and received using the *mail*(1) command (found in `/usr/bin/mail`), which provides a front-end to edit the messages sent and received, and passes the messages to *sendmail*(8) for routing. The routing algorithm uses knowledge of the network name syntax, aliasing and forwarding information, and network topology, as defined in the configuration file `/usr/lib/sendmail.cf`, to process each piece of mail. Local mail is delivered by giving it to the program `/usr/libexec/mail.local` that adds it to the mailboxes in the directory `/var/spool/mail/<username>`, using a locking protocol to avoid problems with simultaneous updates. After the mail is delivered, the local mail delivery daemon `/usr/libexec/comsat` is notified, which in turn notifies users who have issued a ''*biff* y'' command that mail has arrived.

Mail queued in the directory `/var/spool/mail` is normally readable only by the recipient. To send mail that is secure against perusal (except by a code-breaker) you should use the secret mail facility, which encrypts the mail.

To set up the mail facility you should read the instructions in the file READ_ME in the directory `/usr/src/usr.sbin/sendmail` and then adjust the necessary configuration files. You should also set up the file `/etc/aliases` for your installation, creating mail groups as appropriate. For more informations see ''Sendmail Installation and Operation Guide'' (SMM:8) and ''Sendmail – An Internetwork Mail Router'' (SMM:9).

4.6.1. Setting up a UUCP connection

The version of *uucp* included in 4.4BSD has the following features:

- support for many auto call units and dialers in addition to the DEC DN11,
- breakup of the spooling area into multiple subdirectories,
- addition of an `L.cmds` file to control the set of commands that may be executed by a remote site,
- enhanced ''expect-send'' sequence capabilities when logging in to a remote site,
- new commands to be used in polling sites and obtaining snap shots of *uucp* activity,
- additional protocols for different communication media.

This section gives a brief overview of *uucp* and points out the most important steps in its installation.

To connect two UNIX machines with a *uucp* network link using modems, one site must have an automatic call unit and the other must have a dialup port. It is better if both sites have both.

You should first read the paper in the UNIX System Manager's Manual: ''Uucp Implementation Description'' (SMM:14). It describes in detail the file formats and conventions, and will give you a little context. In addition, the document ''setup.tblms'', located in the directory `/usr/src/usr.bin/uucp/UUAIDS`, may be of use in tailoring the software to your needs.

The *uucp* support is located in three major directories: `/usr/bin`, `/usr/lib/uucp`, and `/var/spool/uucp`. User commands are kept in `/usr/bin`, operational commands in

`/usr/lib/uucp`, and `/var/spool/uucp` is used as a spooling area. The commands in `/usr/bin` are:

/usr/bin/uucp	file-copy command
/usr/bin/uux	remote execution command
/usr/bin/uusend	binary file transfer using mail
/usr/bin/uuencode	binary file encoder (for *uusend*)
/usr/bin/uudecode	binary file decoder (for *uusend*)
/usr/bin/uulog	scans session log files
/usr/bin/uusnap	gives a snap-shot of *uucp* activity
/usr/bin/uupoll	polls remote system until an answer is received
/usr/bin/uuname	prints a list of known uucp hosts
/usr/bin/uuq	gives information about the queue

The important files and commands in `/usr/lib/uucp` are:

/usr/lib/uucp/L-devices	list of dialers and hard-wired lines
/usr/lib/uucp/L-dialcodes	dialcode abbreviations
/usr/lib/uucp/L.aliases	hostname aliases
/usr/lib/uucp/L.cmds	commands remote sites may execute
/usr/lib/uucp/L.sys	systems to communicate with, how to connect, and when
/usr/lib/uucp/SEQF	sequence numbering control file
/usr/lib/uucp/USERFILE	remote site pathname access specifications
/usr/lib/uucp/uucico	*uucp* protocol daemon
/usr/lib/uucp/uuclean	cleans up garbage files in spool area
/usr/lib/uucp/uuxqt	*uucp* remote execution server

while the spooling area contains the following important files and directories:

/var/spool/uucp/C.	directory for command, "C." files
/var/spool/uucp/D.	directory for data, "D.", files
/var/spool/uucp/X.	directory for command execution, "X.", files
/var/spool/uucp/D.*machine*	directory for local "D." files
/var/spool/uucp/D.*machine*X	directory for local "X." files
/var/spool/uucp/TM.	directory for temporary, "TM.", files
/var/spool/uucp/LOGFILE	log file of *uucp* activity
/var/spool/uucp/SYSLOG	log file of *uucp* file transfers

To install *uucp* on your system, start by selecting a site name (shorter than 14 characters). A *uucp* account must be created in the password file and a password set up. Then, create the appropriate spooling directories with mode 755 and owned by user *uucp*, group *daemon*.

If you have an auto-call unit, the L.sys, L-dialcodes, and L-devices files should be created. The L.sys file should contain the phone numbers and login sequences required to establish a connection with a *uucp* daemon on another machine. For example, our L.sys file looks something like:

```
adiron Any ACU 1200 out0123456789- ogin-EOT-ogin uucp
cbosg Never Slave 300
cbosgd Never Slave 300
chico Never Slave 1200 out2010123456
```

The first field is the name of a site, the second shows when the machine may be called, the third field specifies how the host is connected (through an ACU, a hard-wired line, etc.), then comes the phone number to use in connecting through an auto-call unit, and finally a login sequence. The phone number may contain common abbreviations that are defined in the L-dialcodes file. The device specification should refer to devices specified in the L-devices file. Listing only ACU causes the *uucp* daemon, *uucico*, to search for any available auto-call unit in L-devices. Our L-dialcodes file is of the form:

ucb 2
out 9%

while our L-devices file is:

ACU cul0 unused 1200 ventel

Refer to the README file in the *uucp* source directory for more information about installation.

As *uucp* operates it creates (and removes) many small files in the directories underneath `/var/spool/uucp`. Sometimes files are left undeleted; these are most easily purged with the *uuclean* program. The log files can grow without bound unless trimmed back; *uulog* maintains these files. Many useful aids in maintaining your *uucp* installation are included in a subdirectory UUAIDS beneath `/usr/src/usr.bin/uucp`. Peruse this directory and read the ''setup'' instructions also located there.

1

5. Network setup

4.4BSD provides support for the standard Internet protocols IP, ICMP, TCP, and UDP. These protocols may be used on top of a variety of hardware devices ranging from serial lines to local area network controllers for the Ethernet. Network services are split between the kernel (communication protocols) and user programs (user services such as TELNET and FTP). This section describes how to configure your system to use the Internet networking support. 4.4BSD also supports the Xerox Network Systems (NS) protocols. IDP and SPP are implemented in the kernel, and other protocols such as Courier run at the user level. 4.4BSD provides some support for the ISO OSI protocols CLNP TP4, and ESIS. User level process complete the application protocols such as X.400 and X.500.

5.1. System configuration

To configure the kernel to include the Internet communication protocols, define the INET option. Xerox NS support is enabled with the NS option. ISO OSI support is enabled with the ISO option. In either case, include the pseudo-devices ''pty'', and ''loop'' in your machine's configuration file. The ''pty'' pseudo-device forces the pseudo terminal device driver to be configured into the system, see *pty*(4), while the ''loop'' pseudo-device forces inclusion of the software loopback interface driver. The loop driver is used in network testing and also by the error logging system.

If you are planning to use the Internet network facilities on a 10Mb/s Ethernet, the pseudo-device ''ether'' should also be included in the configuration; this forces inclusion of the Address Resolution Protocol module used in mapping between 48-bit Ethernet and 32-bit Internet addresses.

Before configuring the appropriate networking hardware, you should consult the manual pages in section 4 of the Programmer's Manual selecting the appropriate interfaces for your architecture.

All network interface drivers including the loopback interface, require that their host address(es) be defined at boot time. This is done with *ifconfig*(8) commands included in the `/etc/netstart` file. Interfaces that are able to dynamically deduce the host part of an address may check that the host part of the address is correct. The manual page for each network interface describes the method used to establish a host's address. *Ifconfig*(8) can also be used to set options for the interface at boot time. Options are set independently for each interface, and apply to all packets sent using that interface. Alternatively, translations for such hosts may be set in advance or ''published'' by a 4.4BSD host by use of the *arp*(8) command. Note that the use of trailer link-level is now negotiated between 4.4BSD hosts using ARP, and it is thus no longer necessary to disable the use of trailers with *ifconfig*.

The OSI equivalent to ARP is ESIS (End System to Intermediate System Routing Protocol); running this protocol is mandatory, however one can manually add translations for machines that do not participate by use of the *route*(8) command. Additional information is provided in the manual page describing *ESIS*(4).

To use the pseudo terminals just configured, device entries must be created in the `/dev` directory. To create 32 pseudo terminals (plenty, unless you have a heavy network load) execute the following commands.

> *# cd /dev*
> *# MAKEDEV pty0 pty1*

More pseudo terminals may be made by specifying `pty2`, `pty3`, etc. The kernel normally includes support for 32 pseudo terminals unless the configuration file specifies a different number. Each pseudo terminal really consists of two files in `/dev`: a master and a slave. The master pseudo terminal file is named `/dev/ptyp?`, while the slave side is `/dev/ttyp?`. Pseudo terminals are also used by several programs not related to the network. In addition to creating the pseudo terminals, be sure to install them in the `/etc/ttys` file (with a 'none' in the second column so no *getty* is started).

5.2. Local subnets

In 4.4BSD the Internet support includes the notion of "subnets". This is a mechanism by which multiple local networks may appears as a single Internet network to off-site hosts. Subnetworks are useful because they allow a site to hide their local topology, requiring only a single route in external gateways; it also means that local network numbers may be locally administered. The standard describing this change in Internet addressing is RFC-950.

To set up local subnets one must first decide how the available address space (the Internet "host part" of the 32-bit address) is to be partitioned. Sites with a class A network number have a 24-bit host address space with which to work, sites with a class B network number have a 16-bit host address space, while sites with a class C network number have an 8-bit host address space[5]. To define local subnets you must steal some bits from the local host address space for use in extending the network portion of the Internet address. This reinterpretation of Internet addresses is done only for local networks; i.e. it is not visible to hosts off-site. For example, if your site has a class B network number, hosts on this network have an Internet address that contains the network number, 16 bits, and the host number, another 16 bits. To define 254 local subnets, each possessing at most 255 hosts, 8 bits may be taken from the local part. (The use of subnets 0 and all-1's, 255 in this example, is discouraged to avoid confusion about broadcast addresses.) These new network numbers are then constructed by concatenating the original 16-bit network number with the extra 8 bits containing the local subnet number.

The existence of local subnets is communicated to the system at the time a network interface is configured with the *netmask* option to the *ifconfig* program. A "network mask" is specified to define the portion of the Internet address that is to be considered the network part for that network. This mask normally contains the bits corresponding to the standard network part as well as the portion of the local part that has been assigned to subnets. If no mask is specified when the address is set, it will be set according to the class of the network. For example, at Berkeley (class B network 128.32) 8 bits of the local part have been reserved for defining subnets; consequently the `/etc/netstart` file contains lines of the form

```
/sbin/ifconfig le0 netmask 0xffffff00 128.32.1.7
```

This specifies that for interface "le0", the upper 24 bits of the Internet address should be used in calculating network numbers (netmask 0xffffff00), and the interface's Internet address is "128.32.1.7" (host 7 on network 128.32.1). Hosts *m* on sub-network *n* of this network would then have addresses of the form "128.32.*n*.*m*"; for example, host 99 on network 129 would have an address "128.32.129.99". For hosts with multiple interfaces, the network mask should be set for each interface, although in practice only the mask of the first interface on each network is really used.

5.3. Internet broadcast addresses

The address defined as the broadcast address for Internet networks according to RFC-919 is the address with a host part of all 1's. The address used by 4.2BSD was the address with a host part of 0. 4.4BSD uses the standard broadcast address (all 1's) by default, but allows the broadcast address to be set (with *ifconfig*) for each interface. This allows networks consisting of both 4.2BSD, 4.3BSD and 4.4BSD hosts to coexist while the upgrade process proceeds. In the presence of subnets, the broadcast address uses

[5] If you are unfamiliar with the Internet addressing structure, consult "Address Mappings", Internet RFC-796, J. Postel; available from the Internet Network Information Center at SRI.

the subnet field as for normal host addresses, with the remaining host part set to 1's (or 0's, on a network that has not yet been converted). 4.4BSD hosts recognize and accept packets sent to the logical-network broadcast address as well as those sent to the subnet broadcast address, and when using an all-1's broadcast, also recognize and receive packets sent to host 0 as a broadcast.

5.4. Routing

If your environment allows access to networks not directly attached to your host you will need to set up routing information to allow packets to be properly routed. Two schemes are supported by the system. The first scheme employs a routing table management daemon. Optimally, you should use the routing daemon *gated* available from Cornell university. We use it on our systems and it works well, especially for multi-homed hosts using Serial Line IP (SLIP). Unfortunately, we were not able to obtain permission to include it on 4.4BSD.

1

If you do not wish to or cannot obtain *gated*, the distribution does include *routed*(8) to maintain the system routing tables. The routing daemon uses a variant of the Xerox Routing Information Protocol to maintain up to date routing tables in a cluster of local area networks. By using the `/etc/gateways` file, the routing daemon can also be used to initialize static routes to distant networks (see the next section for further discussion). When the routing daemon is started up (usually from `/etc/rc`) it reads `/etc/gateways` if it exists and installs those routes defined there, then broadcasts on each local network to which the host is attached to find other instances of the routing daemon. If any responses are received, the routing daemons cooperate in maintaining a globally consistent view of routing in the local environment. This view can be extended to include remote sites also running the routing daemon by setting up suitable entries in `/etc/gateways`; consult *routed*(8) for a more thorough discussion.

The second approach is to define a default or wildcard route to a smart gateway and depend on the gateway to provide ICMP routing redirect information to dynamically create a routing data base. This is done by adding an entry of the form

```
/sbin/route add default smart-gateway 1
```

to `/etc/netstart`; see *route*(8) for more information. The default route will be used by the system as a "last resort" in routing packets to their destination. Assuming the gateway to which packets are directed is able to generate the proper routing redirect messages, the system will then add routing table entries based on the information supplied. This approach has certain advantages over the routing daemon, but is unsuitable in an environment where there are only bridges (i.e. pseudo gateways that, for instance, do not generate routing redirect messages). Further, if the smart gateway goes down there is no alternative, save manual alteration of the routing table entry, to maintaining service.

The system always listens, and processes, routing redirect information, so it is possible to combine both of the above facilities. For example, the routing table management process might be used to maintain up to date information about routes to geographically local networks, while employing the wildcard routing techniques for "distant" networks. The *netstat*(1) program may be used to display routing table contents as well as various routing oriented statistics. For example,

```
# netstat -r
```

will display the contents of the routing tables, while

```
# netstat -r -s
```

will show the number of routing table entries dynamically created as a result of routing redirect messages, etc.

5.5. Use of 4.4BSD machines as gateways

Several changes have been made in 4.4BSD in the area of gateway support (or packet forwarding, if one prefers). A new configuration option, GATEWAY, is used when configuring a machine to be used as a gateway. This option increases the size of the routing hash tables in the kernel. Unless configured with that option, hosts with only a single non-loopback interface never attempt to forward packets or to respond with ICMP error messages to misdirected packets. This change reduces the problems that may occur when different hosts on a network disagree on the network number or broadcast address. Another change is that 4.4BSD machines that forward packets back through the same interface on which they arrived will send ICMP redirects to the source host if it is on the same network. This improves the interaction of 4.4BSD gateways with hosts that configure their routes via default gateways and redirects. The generation of redirects may be disabled with the configuration option IPSENDREDIRECTS=0 or while the system is running by using the command:


```
sysctl -w net.inet.ip.redirect=0
```

in environments where it may cause difficulties.

5.6. Network databases

Several data files are used by the network library routines and server programs. Most of these files are host independent and updated only rarely.

File	Manual reference	Use
/etc/hosts	*hosts* (5)	local host names
/etc/networks	*networks* (5)	network names
/etc/services	*services* (5)	list of known services
/etc/protocols	*protocols* (5)	protocol names
/etc/hosts.equiv	*rshd* (8)	list of "trusted" hosts
/etc/netstart	*rc* (8)	command script for initializing network
/etc/rc	*rc* (8)	command script for starting standard servers
/etc/rc.local	*rc* (8)	command script for starting local servers
/etc/ftpusers	*ftpd* (8)	list of "unwelcome" ftp users
/etc/hosts.lpd	*lpd* (8)	list of hosts allowed to access printers
/etc/inetd.conf	*inetd* (8)	list of servers started by *inetd*

The files distributed are set up for Internet hosts. Local networks and hosts should be added to describe the local configuration; the Berkeley entries may serve as examples (see also the section on `/etc/hosts`). Network numbers will have to be chosen for each Ethernet. For sites connected to the Internet, the normal channels should be used for allocation of network numbers (contact hostmaster@SRI-NIC.ARPA). For other sites, these could be chosen more or less arbitrarily, but it is generally better to request official numbers to avoid conversion if a connection to the Internet (or others on the Internet) is ever established.

5.6.1. Network servers

Most network servers are automatically started up at boot time by the command file `/etc/rc` or by the Internet daemon (see below). These include the following:

Program	Server	Started by
/usr/sbin/syslogd	error logging server	/etc/rc
/usr/sbin/named	Internet name server	/etc/rc
/sbin/routed	routing table management daemon	/etc/rc
/usr/sbin/rwhod	system status daemon	/etc/rc
/usr/sbin/timed	time synchronization daemon	/etc/rc
/usr/sbin/sendmail	SMTP server	/etc/rc
/usr/libexec/rshd	shell server	inetd
/usr/libexec/rexecd	exec server	inetd
/usr/libexec/rlogind	login server	inetd
/usr/libexec/telnetd	TELNET server	inetd
/usr/libexec/ftpd	FTP server	inetd
/usr/libexec/fingerd	Finger server	inetd
/usr/libexec/tftpd	TFTP server	inetd

Consult the manual pages and accompanying documentation (particularly for named and sendmail) for details about their operation.

The use of *routed* and *rwhod* is controlled by shell variables set in /etc/netstart. By default, *routed* is used, but *rwhod* is not; they are enabled by setting the variables *routedflags* and *rwhod* to strings other than "NO." The value of *routedflags* provides host-specific options to *routed*. For example,

```
routedflags=-q
rwhod=NO
```

would run *routed -q* and would not run *rwhod*.

To have other network servers started as well, commands of the following sort should be placed in the site-dependent file /etc/rc.local.

```
if [ -f /usr/sbin/timed ]; then
    /usr/sbin/timed & echo -n ' timed'                >/dev/console
fi
```


5.6.2. Internet daemon

In 4.4BSD most of the servers for user-visible services are started up by a "super server", the Internet daemon. The Internet daemon, /usr/sbin/inetd, acts as a master server for programs specified in its configuration file, /etc/inetd.conf, listening for service requests for these servers, and starting up the appropriate program whenever a request is received. The configuration file contains lines containing a service name (as found in /etc/services), the type of socket the server expects (e.g. stream or dgram), the protocol to be used with the socket (as found in /etc/protocols), whether to wait for each server to complete before starting up another, the user name by which the server should run, the server program's name, and at most five arguments to pass to the server program. Some trivial services are implemented internally in *inetd*, and their servers are listed as "internal." For example, an entry for the file transfer protocol server would appear as

```
ftp stream   tcp nowait   root/usr/libexec/ftpd     ftpd
```

Consult *inetd*(8) for more detail on the format of the configuration file and the operation of the Internet daemon.

5.6.3. The /etc/hosts.equiv file

The remote login and shell servers use an authentication scheme based on trusted hosts. The hosts.equiv file contains a list of hosts that are considered trusted and, under a single administrative control. When a user contacts a remote login or shell server requesting service, the client process passes the user's name and the official name of the host on which the client is located. In the simple case, if the host's name is located in hosts.equiv and the user has an account on the server's machine, then service is rendered (i.e. the user is allowed to log in, or the command is executed). Users may expand this "equivalence" of machines by installing a .rhosts file in their login directory. The root login is handled specially, bypassing the hosts.equiv file, and using only the /.rhosts file.

Thus, to create a class of equivalent machines, the hosts.equiv file should contain the *official* names for those machines. If you are running the name server, you may omit the domain part of the host name for machines in your local domain. For example, four machines on our local network are considered trusted, so the hosts.equiv file is of the form:

```
vangogh.CS.Berkeley.EDU
picasso.CS.Berkeley.EDU
okeeffe.CS.Berkeley.EDU
```

5.6.4. The /etc/ftpusers file

The FTP server included in the system provides support for an anonymous FTP account. Because of the inherent security problems with such a facility you should read this section carefully if you consider providing such a service.

An anonymous account is enabled by creating a user *ftp*. When a client uses the anonymous account a *chroot*(2) system call is performed by the server to restrict the client from moving outside that part of the filesystem where the user ftp home directory is located. Because a *chroot* call is used, certain programs and files used by the server process must be placed in the ftp home directory. Further, one must be sure that all directories and executable images are unwritable. The following directory setup is recommended. The use of the *awk* commands to copy the `/etc/passwd` and `/etc/group` files are **STRONGLY** recommended.

```
# cd ~ftp
# chmod 555 .; chown ftp .; chgrp ftp .
# mkdir bin etc pub
# chown root bin etc
# chmod 555 bin etc
# chown ftp pub
# chmod 777 pub
# cd bin
# cp /bin/sh /bin/ls .
# chmod 111 sh ls
# cd ../etc
# awk -F: '{$2="*";print$1":"$2":"$3":"$4":"$5":"$6":"}' < /etc/passwd > passwd
# awk -F: '{$2="*";print$1":"$2":"}' < /etc/group > group
# chmod 444 passwd group
```

When local users wish to place files in the anonymous area, they must be placed in a subdirectory. In the setup here, the directory `~ftp/pub` is used.

Aside from the problems of directory modes and such, the ftp server may provide a loophole for interlopers if certain user accounts are allowed. The file `/etc/ftpusers` is checked on each connection. If the requested user name is located in the file, the request for service is denied. This file normally has the following names on our systems.

```
uucp
root
```

Accounts without passwords need not be listed in this file as the ftp server will refuse service to these users. Accounts with nonstandard shells (any not listed in `/etc/shells`) will also be denied access via ftp.

6. System operation

This section describes procedures used to operate a 4.4BSD UNIX system. Procedures described here are used periodically, to reboot the system, analyze error messages from devices, do disk backups, monitor system performance, recompile system software and control local changes.

6.1. Bootstrap and shutdown procedures

In a normal reboot, the system checks the disks and comes up multi-user without intervention at the console. Such a reboot can be stopped (after it prints the date) with a ^C (interrupt). This will leave the system in single-user mode, with only the console terminal active. (If the console has been marked ''insecure'' in `/etc/ttys` you must enter the root password to bring the machine to single-user mode.) It is also possible to allow the filesystem checks to complete and then to return to single-user mode by signaling *fsck*(8) with a QUIT signal (^\).

To bring the system up to a multi-user configuration from the single-user status, all you have to do is hit ^D on the console. The system will then execute `/etc/rc`, a multi-user restart script (and `/etc/rc.local`), and come up on the terminals listed as active in the file `/etc/ttys`. See *init*(8) and *ttys*(5) Note, however, that this does not cause a filesystem check to be done. Unless the system was taken down cleanly, you should run ''fsck –p'' or force a reboot with *reboot*(8) to have the disks checked.

To take the system down to a single user state you can use

 # kill 1

or use the *shutdown*(8) command (which is much more polite, if there are other users logged in) when you are running multi-user. Either command will kill all processes and give you a shell on the console, as if you had just booted. Filesystems remain mounted after the system is taken single-user. If you wish to come up multi-user again, you should do this by:

 # cd /
 # /sbin/umount -a
 # ^D

1

Each system shutdown, crash, processor halt and reboot is recorded in the system log with its cause.

6.2. Device errors and diagnostics

When serious errors occur on peripherals or in the system, the system prints a warning diagnostic on the console. These messages are collected by the system error logging process *syslogd*(8) and written into a system error log file `/var/log/messages`. Less serious errors are sent directly to *syslogd*, which may log them on the console. The error priorities that are logged and the locations to which they are logged are controlled by `/etc/syslog.conf`. See *syslogd*(8) for further details.

Error messages printed by the devices in the system are described with the drivers for the devices in section 4 of the programmer's manual. If errors occur suggesting hardware problems, you should contact your hardware support group or field service. It is a good idea to examine the error log file regularly (e.g. with the command *tail −r /var/log/messages*).

6.3. Filesystem checks, backups, and disaster recovery

Periodically (say every week or so in the absence of any problems) and always (usually automatically) after a crash, all the filesystems should be checked for consistency by *fsck*(1). The procedures of *reboot*(8) should be used to get the system to a state where a filesystem check can be done manually or automatically.

Dumping of the filesystems should be done regularly, since once the system is going it is easy to become complacent. Complete and incremental dumps are easily done with *dump*(8). You should arrange to do a towers-of-hanoi dump sequence; we tune ours so that almost all files are dumped on two tapes and kept for at least a week in most every case. We take full dumps every month (and keep these indefinitely). Operators can execute ''dump w'' at login that will tell them what needs to be dumped (based on the `/etc/fstab` information). Be sure to create a group **operator** in the file `/etc/group` so that dump can notify logged-in operators when it needs help.

More precisely, we have three sets of dump tapes: 10 daily tapes, 5 weekly sets of 2 tapes, and fresh sets of three tapes monthly. We do daily dumps circularly on the daily tapes with sequence '3 2 5 4 7 6 9 8 9 9 9 ...'. Each weekly is a level 1 and the daily dump sequence level restarts after each weekly dump. Full dumps are level 0 and the daily sequence restarts after each full dump also.

Thus a typical dump sequence would be:

tape name	level number	date	opr	size
FULL	0	Nov 24, 1992	operator	137K
D1	3	Nov 28, 1992	operator	29K
D2	2	Nov 29, 1992	operator	34K
D3	5	Nov 30, 1992	operator	19K
D4	4	Dec 1, 1992	operator	22K
W1	1	Dec 2, 1992	operator	40K
D5	3	Dec 4, 1992	operator	15K
D6	2	Dec 5, 1992	operator	25K
D7	5	Dec 6, 1992	operator	15K
D8	4	Dec 7, 1992	operator	19K

W2	1	Dec 9, 1992	operator	118K
D9	3	Dec 11, 1992	operator	15K
D10	2	Dec 12, 1992	operator	26K
D1	5	Dec 15, 1992	operator	14K
W3	1	Dec 17, 1992	operator	71K
D2	3	Dec 18, 1992	operator	13K
FULL	0	Dec 22, 1992	operator	135K

We do weekly dumps often enough that daily dumps always fit on one tape.

Dumping of files by name is best done by *tar*(1) but the amount of data that can be moved in this way is limited to a single tape. Finally if there are enough drives entire disks can be copied with *dd*(1) using the raw special files and an appropriate blocking factor; the number of sectors per track is usually a good value to use, consult `/etc/disktab`.

It is desirable that full dumps of the root filesystem be made regularly. This is especially true when only one disk is available. Then, if the root filesystem is damaged by a hardware or software failure, you can rebuild a workable disk doing a restore in the same way that the initial root filesystem was created.

Exhaustion of user-file space is certain to occur now and then; disk quotas may be imposed, or if you prefer a less fascist approach, try using the programs *du*(1), *df*(1), and *quot*(8), combined with threatening messages of the day, and personal letters.

6.4. Moving filesystem data

If you have the resources, the best way to move a filesystem is to dump it to a spare disk partition, or magtape, using *dump*(8), use *newfs*(8) to create the new filesystem, and restore the filesystem using *restore*(8). Filesystems may also be moved by piping the output of *dump* to *restore*. The *restore* program uses an ''in-place'' algorithm that allows filesystem dumps to be restored without concern for the original size of the filesystem. Further, portions of a filesystem may be selectively restored using a method similar to the tape archive program.

If you have to merge a filesystem into another, existing one, the best bet is to use *tar*(1). If you must shrink a filesystem, the best bet is to dump the original and restore it onto the new filesystem. If you are playing with the root filesystem and only have one drive, the procedure is more complicated. If the only drive is a Winchester disk, this procedure may not be used without overwriting the existing root or another partition. What you do is the following:

1. GET A SECOND PACK, OR USE ANOTHER DISK DRIVE!!!!
2. Dump the root filesystem to tape using *dump*(8).
3. Bring the system down.
4. Mount the new pack in the correct disk drive, if using removable media.
5. Load the distribution tape and install the new root filesystem as you did when first installing the system. Boot normally using the newly created disk filesystem.

Note that if you change the disk partition tables or add new disk drivers they should also be added to the standalone system in `/sys/<architecture>/stand`, and the default disk partition tables in `/etc/disktab` should be modified.

6.5. Monitoring system performance

The *systat* program provided with the system is designed to be an aid to monitoring systemwide activity. The default ''pigs'' mode shows a dynamic ''ps''. By running in the ''vmstat'' mode when the system is active you can judge the system activity in several dimensions: job distribution, virtual memory load, paging and swapping activity, device interrupts, and disk and cpu utilization. Ideally, there should be few blocked (b) jobs, there should be little paging or swapping activity, there should be available bandwidth on the disk devices (most single arms peak out at 20-30 tps in practice), and the user cpu utilization (us) should be high (above 50%).

If the system is busy, then the count of active jobs may be large, and several of these jobs may often be blocked (b). If the virtual memory is active, then the paging demon will be running (sr will be non-zero). It is healthy for the paging demon to free pages when the virtual memory gets active; it is triggered by the amount of free memory dropping below a threshold and increases its pace as free memory goes to zero.

If you run in the ''vmstat'' mode when the system is busy, you can find imbalances by noting abnormal job distributions. If many processes are blocked (b), then the disk subsystem is overloaded or imbalanced. If you have several non-dma devices or open teletype lines that are ''ringing'', or user programs that are doing high-speed non-buffered input/output, then the system time may go high (60-70% or higher). It is often possible to pin down the cause of high system time by looking to see if there is excessive context switching (cs), interrupt activity (in) and per-device interrupt counts, or system call activity (sy). Cumulatively on one of our large machines we average about 60-200 context switches and interrupts per second and about 50-500 system calls per second.

If the system is heavily loaded, or if you have little memory for your load (2M is little in most any case), then the system may be forced to swap. This is likely to be accompanied by a noticeable reduction in system performance and pregnant pauses when interactive jobs such as editors swap out. If you expect to be in a memory-poor environment for an extended period you might consider administratively limiting system load.

6.6. Recompiling and reinstalling system software

It is easy to regenerate either the entire system or a single utility, and it is a good idea to try rebuilding pieces of the system to build confidence in the procedures.

In general, there are six well-known targets supported by all the makefiles on the system:

all — This entry is the default target, the same as if no target is specified. This target builds the kernel, binary or library, as well as its associated manual pages. This target **does not** build the dependency files. Some of the utilities require that a *make depend* be done before a *make all* can succeed.

depend — Build the include file dependency file, ''.depend'', which is read by *make*. See *mkdep*(1) for further details.

install — Install the kernel, binary or library, as well as its associated manual pages. See *install*(1) for further details.

clean — Remove the kernel, binary or library, as well as any object files created when building it.

cleandir — The same as clean, except that the dependency files and formatted manual pages are removed as well.

obj — Build a shadow directory structure in the area referenced by `/usr/obj` and create a symbolic link in the current source directory to referenced it, named ''obj''. Once this shadow structure has been created, all the files created by *make* will live in the shadow structure, and `/usr/src` may be mounted read-only by multiple machines. Doing a *make obj* in `/usr/src` will build the shadow directory structure for everything on the system except for the contributed, old, and kernel software.

The system consists of three major parts: the kernel itself, found in `/usr/src/sys`, the libraries , found in `/usr/src/lib`, and the user programs (the rest of `/usr/src`).

Deprecated software, found in `/usr/src/old`, often has old style makefiles; some of it does not compile under 4.4BSD at all.

Contributed software, found in `/usr/src/contrib`, usually does not support the ''cleandir'', ''depend'', or ''obj'' targets.

The kernel does not support the ''obj'' shadow structure. All kernels are compiled in subdirectories of `/usr/src/sys/compile` which is usually abbreviated as `/sys/compile`. If you want to mount your source tree read-only, `/usr/src/sys/compile` will have to be on a separate filesystem from `/usr/src`. Separation from `/usr/src` can be done by making `/usr/src/sys/compile` a symbolic link that references `/usr/obj/sys/compile`. If it is a symbolic link, the *S* variable in the kernel Makefile must be changed from `../..` to the absolute pathname needed to locate the kernel sources, usually `/usr/src/sys`. The symbolic link created by *config*(8) for `machine` must also be manually changed to an absolute pathname. Finally, the `/usr/src/sys/libkern/obj` directory must be located in `/usr/obj/sys/libkern`.

Each of the standard utilities and libraries may be built and installed by changing directories into the correct location and doing:

```
# make
# make install
```

Note, if system include files have changed between compiles, *make* will not do the correct dependency checks if the dependency files have not been built using the ‘‘depend’’ target.

The entire library and utility suite for the system may be recompiled from scratch by changing directory to `/usr/src` and doing:

```
# make build
```

This target installs the system include files, cleans the source tree, builds and installs the libraries, and builds and installs the system utilities.

To recompile a specific program, first determine where the binary resides with the *whereis*(1) command, then change to the corresponding source directory and build it with the Makefile in the directory. For instance, to recompile ‘‘passwd’’, all one has to do is:

```
# whereis passwd
/usr/bin/passwd
# cd /usr/src/usr.bin/passwd
# make
# make install
```

this will compile and install the *passwd* utility.

If you wish to recompile and install all programs into a particular target area you can override the default path prefix by doing:

```
# make
# make DESTDIR=pathname install
```

Similarly, the mode, owner, group, and other characteristics of the installed object can be modified by changing other default make variables. See *make*(1), `/usr/src/share/mk/bsd.README`, and the ‘‘.mk’’ scripts in the `/usr/share/mk` directory for more information.

If you modify the C library or system include files, to change a system call for example, and want to rebuild and install everything, you have to be a little careful. You must ensure that the include files are installed before anything is compiled, and that the libraries are installed before the remainder of the source, otherwise the loaded images will not contain the new routine from the library. If include files have been modified, the following commands should be done first:

```
# cd /usr/src/include
# make install
```

Then, if, for example, C library files have been modified, the following commands should be executed:

```
# cd /usr/src/lib/libc
# make depend
# make
# make install
```

1

```
# cd /usr/src
# make depend
# make
# make install
```

Alternatively, the *make build* command described above will accomplish the same tasks. This takes several hours on a reasonably configured machine.

6.7. Making local modifications

The source for locally written commands is normally stored in `/usr/src/local`, and their binaries are kept in `/usr/local/bin`. This isolation of local binaries allows `/usr/bin`, and `/bin` to correspond to the distribution tape (and to the manuals that people can buy). People using local commands should be made aware that they are not in the base manual. Manual pages for local commands should be installed in `/usr/local/man/cat[1-8]`. The *man*(1) command automatically finds manual pages placed in /usr/local/man/cat[1-8] to encourage this practice (see *man.conf*(5)).

6.8. Accounting

UNIX optionally records two kinds of accounting information: connect time accounting and process resource accounting. The connect time accounting information is stored in the file `/var/log/wtmp`, which is summarized by the program *ac*(8). The process time accounting information is stored in the file `/var/account/acct` after it is enabled by *accton*(8), and is analyzed and summarized by the program *sa*(8).

If you need to recharge for computing time, you can develop procedures based on the information provided by these commands. A convenient way to do this is to give commands to the clock daemon `/usr/sbin/cron` to be executed every day at a specified time. This is done by adding lines to `/etc/crontab.local`; see *cron*(8) for details.

6.9. Resource control

Resource control in the current version of UNIX is more elaborate than in most UNIX systems. The disk quota facilities developed at the University of Melbourne have been incorporated in the system and allow control over the number of files and amount of disk space each user and/or group may use on each filesystem. In addition, the resources consumed by any single process can be limited by the mechanisms of *setrlimit*(2). As distributed, the latter mechanism is voluntary, though sites may choose to modify the login mechanism to impose limits not covered with disk quotas.

To use the disk quota facilities, the system must be configured with ''options QUOTA''. Filesystems may then be placed under the quota mechanism by creating a null file `quota.user` and/or `quota.group` at the root of the filesystem, running *quotacheck*(8), and modifying `/etc/fstab` to show that the filesystem is to run with disk quotas (options userquota and/or groupquota). The *quotaon*(8) program may then be run to enable quotas.

Individual quotas are applied by using the quota editor *edquota*(8). Users may view their quotas (but not those of other users) with the *quota*(1) program. The *repquota*(8) program may be used to summarize the quotas and current space usage on a particular filesystem or filesystems.

Quotas are enforced with *soft* and *hard* limits. When a user and/or group first reaches a soft limit on a resource, a message is generated on their terminal. If the user and/or group fails to lower the resource usage below the soft limit for longer than the time limit established for that filesystem (default seven days) the system then treats the soft limit as a *hard* limit and disallows any allocations until enough space is reclaimed to bring the user and/or group back below the soft limit. Hard limits are enforced strictly resulting in errors when a user and/or group tries to create or write a file. Each time a hard limit is exceeded the system will generate a message on the user's terminal.

Consult the auxiliary document, ''Disc Quotas in a UNIX Environment'' (SMM:4) and the appropriate manual entries for more information.

6.10. Network troubleshooting

If you have anything more than a trivial network configuration, from time to time you are bound to run into problems. Before blaming the software, first check your network connections. On networks such as the Ethernet a loose cable tap or misplaced power cable can result in severely deteriorated service. The *netstat*(1) program may be of aid in tracking down hardware malfunctions. In particular, look at the **–i** and **–s** options in the manual page.

Should you believe a communication protocol problem exists, consult the protocol specifications and attempt to isolate the problem in a packet trace. The SO_DEBUG option may be supplied before establishing a connection on a socket, in which case the system will trace all traffic and internal actions (such as timers expiring) in a circular trace buffer. This buffer may then be printed out with the *trpt*(8) program. Most of the servers distributed with the system accept a **–d** option forcing all sockets to be created with debugging turned on. Consult the appropriate manual pages for more information.

6.11. Files that need periodic attention

We conclude the discussion of system operations by listing the files that require periodic attention or are system specific:

`/etc/fstab`	how disk partitions are used
`/etc/disktab`	default disk partition sizes/labels
`/etc/printcap`	printer database
`/etc/gettytab`	terminal type definitions
`/etc/remote`	names and phone numbers of remote machines for *tip*(1)
`/etc/group`	group memberships
`/etc/motd`	message of the day
`/etc/master.passwd`	password file; each account has a line
`/etc/rc.local`	local system restart script; runs reboot; starts daemons
`/etc/inetd.conf`	local internet servers
`/etc/hosts`	local host name database
`/etc/networks`	network name database
`/etc/services`	network services database
`/etc/hosts.equiv`	hosts under same administrative control
`/etc/syslog.conf`	error log configuration for *syslogd*(8)
`/etc/ttys`	enables/disables ports
`/etc/crontab`	commands that are run periodically
`/etc/crontab.local`	local commands that are run periodically
`/etc/aliases`	mail forwarding and distribution groups
`/var/account/acct`	raw process account data
`/var/log/messages`	system error log
`/var/log/wtmp`	login session accounting

Building 4.4BSD Kernels with Config

Samuel J. Leffler and Michael J. Karels

Computer Systems Research Group
Department of Electrical Engineering and Computer Science
University of California, Berkeley
Berkeley, California 94720

2

ABSTRACT

This document describes the use of *config* (8) to configure and create bootable 4.4BSD system images. It discusses the structure of system configuration files and how to configure systems with non-standard hardware configurations. Sections describing the preferred way to add new code to the system and how the system's autoconfiguration process operates are included. An appendix contains a summary of the rules used by the system in calculating the size of system data structures, and also indicates some of the standard system size limitations (and how to change them). Other configuration options are also listed.

Revised July 5, 1993

1. INTRODUCTION

Config is a tool used in building 4.4BSD system images (the UNIX kernel). It takes a file describing a system's tunable parameters and hardware support, and generates a collection of files which are then used to build a copy of UNIX appropriate to that configuration. *Config* simplifies system maintenance by isolating system dependencies in a single, easy to understand, file.

This document describes the content and format of system configuration files and the rules which must be followed when creating these files. Example configuration files are constructed and discussed.

Later sections suggest guidelines to be used in modifying system source and explain some of the inner workings of the autoconfiguration process. Appendix D summarizes the rules used in calculating the most important system data structures and indicates some inherent system data structure size limitations (and how to go about modifying them).

2. CONFIGURATION FILE CONTENTS

A system configuration must include at least the following pieces of information:

- machine type
- cpu type
- system identification
- timezone
- maximum number of users

- location of the root file system
- available hardware

Config allows multiple system images to be generated from a single configuration description. Each system image is configured for identical hardware, but may have different locations for the root file system and, possibly, other system devices.

2.1. Machine type

The *machine type* indicates if the system is going to operate on a DEC VAX-11† computer, or some other machine on which 4.4BSD operates. The machine type is used to locate certain data files which are machine specific, and also to select rules used in constructing the resultant configuration files.

2.2. Cpu type

The *cpu type* indicates which, of possibly many, cpu's the system is to operate on. For example, if the system is being configured for a VAX-11, it could be running on a VAX 8600, VAX-11/780, VAX-11/750, VAX-11/730 or MicroVAX II. (Other VAX cpu types, including the 8650, 785 and 725, are configured using the cpu designation for compatible machines introduced earlier.) Specifying more than one cpu type implies that the system should be configured to run on any of the cpu's specified. For some types of machines this is not possible and *config* will print a diagnostic indicating such.

2.3. System identification

The *system identification* is a moniker attached to the system, and often the machine on which the system is to run. For example, at Berkeley we have machines named Ernie (Co-VAX), Kim (No-VAX), and so on. The system identifier selected is used to create a global C ''#define'' which may be used to isolate system dependent pieces of code in the kernel. For example, Ernie's Varian driver used to be special cased because its interrupt vectors were wired together. The code in the driver which understood how to handle this non-standard hardware configuration was conditionally compiled in only if the system was for Ernie.

The system identifier ''GENERIC'' is given to a system which will run on any cpu of a particular machine type; it should not otherwise be used for a system identifier.

2.4. Timezone

The timezone in which the system is to run is used to define the information returned by the *gettimeofday*(2) system call. This value is specified as the number of hours east or west of GMT. Negative numbers indicate a value east of GMT. The timezone specification may also indicate the type of daylight savings time rules to be applied.

2.5. Maximum number of users

The system allocates many system data structures at boot time based on the maximum number of users the system will support. This number is normally between 8 and 40, depending on the hardware and expected job mix. The rules used to calculate system data structures are discussed in Appendix D.

2.6. Root file system location

When the system boots it must know the location of the root of the file system tree. This location and the part(s) of the disk(s) to be used for paging and swapping must be specified in order to create a complete configuration description. *Config* uses many rules to calculate default locations for these items; these are described in Appendix B.

When a generic system is configured, the root file system is left undefined until the system is booted. In this case, the root file system need not be specified, only that the system is a generic system.

---

† DEC, VAX, UNIBUS, MASSBUS and MicroVAX are trademarks of Digital Equipment Corporation.

2.7. Hardware devices

When the system boots it goes through an *autoconfiguration* phase. During this period, the system searches for all those hardware devices which the system builder has indicated might be present. This probing sequence requires certain pieces of information such as register addresses, bus interconnects, etc. A system's hardware may be configured in a very flexible manner or be specified without any flexibility whatsoever. Most people do not configure hardware devices into the system unless they are currently present on the machine, expect them to be present in the near future, or are simply guarding against a hardware failure somewhere else at the site (it is often wise to configure in extra disks in case an emergency requires moving one off a machine which has hardware problems).

The specification of hardware devices usually occupies the majority of the configuration file. As such, a large portion of this document will be spent understanding it. Section 6.3 contains a description of the autoconfiguration process, as it applies to those planning to write, or modify existing, device drivers.

2.8. Pseudo devices

Several system facilities are configured in a manner like that used for hardware devices although they are not associated with specific hardware. These system options are configured as *pseudo-devices*. Some pseudo devices allow an optional parameter that sets the limit on the number of instances of the device that are active simultaneously.

2.9. System options

Other than the mandatory pieces of information described above, it is also possible to include various optional system facilities or to modify system behavior and/or limits. For example, 4.4BSD can be configured to support binary compatibility for programs built under 4.3BSD. Also, optional support is provided for disk quotas and tracing the performance of the virtual memory subsystem. Any optional facilities to be configured into the system are specified in the configuration file. The resultant files generated by *config* will automatically include the necessary pieces of the system.

3. SYSTEM BUILDING PROCESS

In this section we consider the steps necessary to build a bootable system image. We assume the system source is located in the ''/sys'' directory and that, initially, the system is being configured from source code.

Under normal circumstances there are 5 steps in building a system.

1) Create a configuration file for the system.
2) Make a directory for the system to be constructed in.
3) Run *config* on the configuration file to generate the files required to compile and load the system image.
4) Construct the source code interdependency rules for the configured system with *make* depend using *make*(1).
5) Compile and load the system with *make*.

Steps 1 and 2 are usually done only once. When a system configuration changes it usually suffices to just run *config* on the modified configuration file, rebuild the source code dependencies, and remake the system. Sometimes, however, configuration dependencies may not be noticed in which case it is necessary to clean out the relocatable object files saved in the system's directory; this will be discussed later.

3.1. Creating a configuration file

Configuration files normally reside in the directory ''/sys/conf''. A configuration file is most easily constructed by copying an existing configuration file and modifying it. The 4.4BSD distribution contains a number of configuration files for machines at Berkeley; one may be suitable or, in worst case, a copy of the generic configuration file may be edited.

The configuration file must have the same name as the directory in which the configured system is to be built. Further, *config* assumes this directory is located in the parent directory of the directory in which it is run. For example, the generic system has a configuration file ''/sys/conf/GENERIC'' and an accompanying directory named ''/sys/GENERIC''. Although it is not required that the system sources and configuration files reside in ''/sys,'' the configuration and compilation procedure depends on the relative locations of directories within that hierarchy, as most of the system code and the files created by *config* use pathnames of the form ''../''. If the system files are not located in ''/sys,'' it is desirable to make a symbolic link there for use in installation of other parts of the system that share files with the kernel.

When building the configuration file, be sure to include the items described in section 2. In particular, the machine type, cpu type, timezone, system identifier, maximum users, and root device must be specified. The specification of the hardware present may take a bit of work; particularly if your hardware is configured at non-standard places (e.g. device registers located at funny places or devices not supported by the system). Section 4 of this document gives a detailed description of the configuration file syntax, section 5 explains some sample configuration files, and section 6 discusses how to add new devices to the system. If the devices to be configured are not already described in one of the existing configuration files you should check the manual pages in section 4 of the UNIX Programmers Manual. For each supported device, the manual page synopsis entry gives a sample configuration line.

Once the configuration file is complete, run it through *config* and look for any errors. Never try and use a system which *config* has complained about; the results are unpredictable. For the most part, *config*'s error diagnostics are self explanatory. It may be the case that the line numbers given with the error messages are off by one.

A successful run of *config* on your configuration file will generate a number of files in the configuration directory. These files are:

- A file to be used by *make* (1) in compiling and loading the system, *Makefile*.
- One file for each possible system image for this machine, *swapxxx.c*, where *xxx* is the name of the system image, which describes where swapping, the root file system, and other miscellaneous system devices are located.
- A collection of header files, one per possible device the system supports, which define the hardware configured.
- A file containing the I/O configuration tables used by the system during its *autoconfiguration* phase, *ioconf.c*.
- An assembly language file of interrupt vectors which connect interrupts from the machine's external buses to the main system path for handling interrupts, and a file that contains counters and names for the interrupt vectors.

Unless you have reason to doubt *config*, or are curious how the system's autoconfiguration scheme works, you should never have to look at any of these files.

3.2. Constructing source code dependencies

When *config* is done generating the files needed to compile and link your system it will terminate with a message of the form ''Don't forget to run make depend''. This is a reminder that you should change over to the configuration directory for the system just configured and type ''make depend'' to build the rules used by *make* to recognize interdependencies in the system source code. This will insure that any changes to a piece of the system source code will result in the proper modules being recompiled the next time *make* is run.

This step is particularly important if your site makes changes to the system include files. The rules generated specify which source code files are dependent on which include files. Without these rules, *make* will not recognize when it must rebuild modules due to the modification of a system header file. The dependency rules are generated by a pass of the C preprocessor and reflect the global system options. This step must be repeated when the configuration file is changed and *config* is used to regenerate the system makefile.

3.3. Building the system

The makefile constructed by *config* should allow a new system to be rebuilt by simply typing ''make image-name''. For example, if you have named your bootable system image ''vmunix'', then ''make vmunix'' will generate a bootable image named ''vmunix''. Alternate system image names are used when the root file system location and/or swapping configuration is done in more than one way. The makefile which *config* creates has entry points for each system image defined in the configuration file. Thus, if you have configured ''vmunix'' to be a system with the root file system on an ''hp'' device and ''hkvmunix'' to be a system with the root file system on an ''hk'' device, then ''make vmunix hkvmunix'' will generate binary images for each. As the system will generally use the disk from which it is loaded as the root filesystem, separate system images are only required to support different swap configurations.

Note that the name of a bootable image is different from the system identifier. All bootable images are configured for the same system; only the information about the root file system and paging devices differ. (This is described in more detail in section 4.)

The last step in the system building process is to rearrange certain commonly used symbols in the symbol table of the system image; the makefile generated by *config* does this automatically for you. This is advantageous for programs such as *netstat*(1) and *vmstat*(1), which run much faster when the symbols they need are located at the front of the symbol table. Remember also that many programs expect the currently executing system to be named ''/vmunix''. If you install a new system and name it something other than ''/vmunix'', many programs are likely to give strange results.

3.4. Sharing object modules

If you have many systems which are all built on a single machine there are at least two approaches to saving time in building system images. The best way is to have a single system image which is run on all machines. This is attractive since it minimizes disk space used and time required to rebuild systems after making changes. However, it is often the case that one or more systems will require a separately configured system image. This may be due to limited memory (building a system with many unused device drivers can be expensive), or to configuration requirements (one machine may be a development machine where disk quotas are not needed, while another is a production machine where they are), etc. In these cases it is possible for common systems to share relocatable object modules which are not configuration dependent; most of the modules in the directory ''/sys/sys'' are of this sort.

To share object modules, a generic system should be built. Then, for each system configure the system as before, but before recompiling and linking the system, type ''make links'' in the system compilation directory. This will cause the system to be searched for source modules which are safe to share between systems and generate symbolic links in the current directory to the appropriate object modules in the directory ''../GENERIC''. A shell script, ''makelinks'' is generated with this request and may be checked for correctness. The file ''/sys/conf/defines'' contains a list of symbols which we believe are safe to ignore when checking the source code for modules which may be shared. Note that this list includes the definitions used to conditionally compile in the virtual memory tracing facilities, and the trace point support used only rarely (even at Berkeley). It may be necessary to modify this file to reflect local needs. Note further that interdependencies which are not directly visible in the source code are not caught. This means that if you place per-system dependencies in an include file, they will not be recognized and the shared code may be selected in an unexpected fashion.

3.5. Building profiled systems

It is simple to configure a system which will automatically collect profiling information as it operates. The profiling data may be collected with *kgmon*(8) and processed with *gprof*(1) to obtain information regarding the system's operation. Profiled systems maintain histograms of the program counter as well as the number of invocations of each routine. The *gprof* command will also generate a dynamic call graph of the executing system and propagate time spent in each routine along the arcs of the call graph (consult the *gprof* documentation for elaboration). The program counter sampling can be driven by the system clock, or if you have an alternate real time clock, this can be used. The latter is highly recommended, as use of the system clock will result in statistical anomalies, and time spent in the clock routine will not be accurately attributed.

To configure a profiled system, the **−p** option should be supplied to *config*. A profiled system is about 5-10% larger in its text space due to the calls to count the subroutine invocations. When the system executes, the profiling data is stored in a buffer which is 1.2 times the size of the text space. The overhead for running a profiled system varies; under normal load we see anywhere from 5-25% of the system time spent in the profiling code.

Note that systems configured for profiling should not be shared as described above unless all the other shared systems are also to be profiled.

4. CONFIGURATION FILE SYNTAX

In this section we consider the specific rules used in writing a configuration file. A complete grammar for the input language can be found in Appendix A and may be of use if you should have problems with syntax errors.

A configuration file is broken up into three logical pieces:

- configuration parameters global to all system images specified in the configuration file,
- parameters specific to each system image to be generated, and
- device specifications.

4.1. Global configuration parameters

The global configuration parameters are the type of machine, cpu types, options, timezone, system identifier, and maximum users. Each is specified with a separate line in the configuration file.

machine *type*

The system is to run on the machine type specified. No more than one machine type can appear in the configuration file. Legal values are **vax** and **sun.**

cpu ''*type*''

This system is to run on the cpu type specified. More than one cpu type specification can appear in a configuration file. Legal types for a **vax** machine are **VAX8600, VAX780, VAX750, VAX730** and **VAX630** (MicroVAX II). The 8650 is listed as an 8600, the 785 as a 780, and a 725 as a 730.

options *optionlist*

Compile the listed optional code into the system. Options in this list are separated by commas. Possible options are listed at the top of the generic makefile. A line of the form ''options FUNNY,HAHA'' generates global ''#define''s −DFUNNY −DHAHA in the resultant makefile. An option may be given a value by following its name with ''='', then the value enclosed in (double) quotes. The following are major options are currently in use: COMPAT (include code for compatibility with 4.1BSD binaries), INET (Internet communication protocols), NS (Xerox NS communication protocols), and QUOTA (enable disk quotas). Other kernel options controlling system sizes and limits are listed in Appendix D; options for the network are found in Appendix E. There are additional options which are associated with certain peripheral devices; those are listed in the Synopsis section of the manual page for the device.

makeoptions *optionlist*

Options that are used within the system makefile and evaluated by *make* are listed as *makeoptions*. Options are listed with their values with the form ''makeoptions name=value,name2=value2.'' The values must be enclosed in double quotes if they include numerals or begin with a dash.

timezone *number* [**dst** [*number*]]

Specifies the timezone used by the system. This is measured in the number of hours your timezone is west of GMT. EST is 5 hours west of GMT, PST is 8. Negative numbers indicate hours east of GMT. If you specify **dst**, the system will operate under daylight savings time. An optional integer or floating point number may be included to specify a particular daylight saving time correction algorithm; the default value is 1, indicating the United States. Other values are: 2 (Australian style), 3 (Western European), 4 (Middle European), and 5 (Eastern European). See *gettimeofday*(2) and *ctime*(3) for more information.

ident *name*

This system is to be known as *name*. This is usually a cute name like ERNIE (short for Ernie Co-Vax) or VAXWELL (for Vaxwell Smart). This value is defined for use in conditional compilation, and is also used to locate an optional list of source files specific to this system.

maxusers *number*

The maximum expected number of simultaneously active user on this system is *number*. This number is used to size several system data structures.

4.2. System image parameters

Multiple bootable images may be specified in a single configuration file. The systems will have the same global configuration parameters and devices, but the location of the root file system and other system specific devices may be different. A system image is specified with a ''config'' line:

config *sysname config-clauses*

The *sysname* field is the name given to the loaded system image; almost everyone names their standard system image ''vmunix''. The configuration clauses are one or more specifications indicating where the root file system is located and the number and location of paging devices. The device used by the system to process argument lists during *execve*(2) calls may also be specified, though in practice this is almost always selected by *config* using one of its rules for selecting default locations for system devices.

A configuration clause is one of the following

root [**on**] *root-device*
swap [**on**] *swap-device* [**and** *swap-device*] ...
dumps [**on**] *dump-device*
args [**on**] *arg-device*

(the ''on'' is optional.) Multiple configuration clauses are separated by white space; *config* allows specifications to be continued across multiple lines by beginning the continuation line with a tab character. The ''root'' clause specifies where the root file system is located, the ''swap'' clause indicates swapping and paging area(s), the ''dumps'' clause can be used to force system dumps to be taken on a particular device, and the ''args'' clause can be used to specify that argument list processing for *execve* should be done on a particular device.

The device names supplied in the clauses may be fully specified as a device, unit, and file system partition; or underspecified in which case *config* will use builtin rules to select default unit numbers and file system partitions. The defaulting rules are a bit complicated as they are dependent on the overall system configuration. For example, the swap area need not be specified at all if the root device is specified; in this case the swap area is placed in the ''b'' partition of the same disk where the root file system is located. Appendix B contains a complete list of the defaulting rules used in selecting system configuration devices.

The device names are translated to the appropriate major and minor device numbers on a per-machine basis. A file, ''/sys/conf/devices.machine'' (where ''machine'' is the machine type specified in the configuration file), is used to map a device name to its major block device number. The minor device number is calculated using the standard disk partitioning rules: on unit 0, partition ''a'' is minor device 0, partition ''b'' is minor device 1, and so on; for units other than 0, add 8 times the unit number to get the minor device.

If the default mapping of device name to major/minor device number is incorrect for your configuration, it can be replaced by an explicit specification of the major/minor device. This is done by substituting

major *x* **minor** *y*

where the device name would normally be found. For example,

config vmunix **root on major** 99 **minor** 1

Normally, the areas configured for swap space are sized by the system at boot time. If a non-standard size is to be used for one or more swap areas (less than the full partition), this can also be specified. To do this, the device name specified for a swap area should have a ''size'' specification appended. For example,

config vmunix **root on** hp0 **swap on** hp0b **size** 1200

would force swapping to be done in partition ''b'' of ''hp0'' and the swap partition size would be set to 1200 sectors. A swap area sized larger than the associated disk partition is trimmed to the partition size.

To create a generic configuration, only the clause ''swap generic'' should be specified; any extra clauses will cause an error.

4.3. Device specifications

Each device attached to a machine must be specified to *config* so that the system generated will know to probe for it during the autoconfiguration process carried out at boot time. Hardware specified in the configuration need not actually be present on the machine where the generated system is to be run. Only the hardware actually found at boot time will be used by the system.

2

The specification of hardware devices in the configuration file parallels the interconnection hierarchy of the machine to be configured. On the VAX, this means that a configuration file must indicate what MASSBUS and UNIBUS adapters are present, and to which *nexi* they might be connected.* Similarly, devices and controllers must be indicated as possibly being connected to one or more adapters. A device description may provide a complete definition of the possible configuration parameters or it may leave certain parameters undefined and make the system probe for all the possible values. The latter allows a single device configuration list to match many possible physical configurations. For example, a disk may be indicated as present at UNIBUS adapter 0, or at any UNIBUS adapter which the system locates at boot time. The latter scheme, termed *wildcarding*, allows more flexibility in the physical configuration of a system; if a disk must be moved around for some reason, the system will still locate it at the alternate location.

A device specification takes one of the following forms:

master *device-name device-info*
controller *device-name device-info* [*interrupt-spec*]
device *device-name device-info interrupt-spec*
disk *device-name device-info*
tape *device-name device-info*

A ''master'' is a MASSBUS tape controller; a ''controller'' is a disk controller, a UNIBUS tape controller, a MASSBUS adapter, or a UNIBUS adapter. A ''device'' is an autonomous device which connects directly to a UNIBUS adapter (as opposed to something like a disk which connects through a disk controller). ''Disk'' and ''tape'' identify disk drives and tape drives connected to a ''controller'' or ''master.''

The *device-name* is one of the standard device names, as indicated in section 4 of the UNIX Programmers Manual, concatenated with the *logical* unit number to be assigned the device (the *logical* unit number may be different than the *physical* unit number indicated on the front of something like a disk; the *logical* unit number is used to refer to the UNIX device, not the physical unit number). For example, ''hp0'' is logical unit 0 of a MASSBUS storage device, even though it might be physical unit 3 on MASSBUS adapter 1.

The *device-info* clause specifies how the hardware is connected in the interconnection hierarchy. On the VAX, UNIBUS and MASSBUS adapters are connected to the internal system bus through a *nexus*. Thus, one of the following specifications would be used:

controller	mba0	**at nexus** *x*
controller	uba0	**at nexus** *x*

To tie a controller to a specific nexus, ''x'' would be supplied as the number of that nexus; otherwise ''x'' may be specified as ''?'', in which case the system will probe all nexi present looking for the specified controller.

* While VAX-11/750's and VAX-11/730 do not actually have nexi, the system treats them as having *simulated nexi* to simplify device configuration.

The remaining interconnections on the VAX are:

- a controller may be connected to another controller (e.g. a disk controller attached to a UNIBUS adapter),
- a master is always attached to a controller (a MASSBUS adapter),
- a tape is always attached to a master (for MASSBUS tape drives),
- a disk is always attached to a controller, and
- devices are always attached to controllers (e.g. UNIBUS controllers attached to UNIBUS adapters).

The following lines give an example of each of these interconnections:

controller	hk0	**at** uba0 ...
master	ht0	**at** mba0 ...
disk	hp0	**at** mba0 ...
tape	tu0	**at** ht0 ...
disk	rk1	**at** hk0 ...
device	dz0	**at** uba0 ...

Any piece of hardware which may be connected to a specific controller may also be wildcarded across multiple controllers.

The final piece of information needed by the system to configure devices is some indication of where or how a device will interrupt. For tapes and disks, simply specifying the *slave* or *drive* number is sufficient to locate the control status register for the device. *Drive* numbers may be wildcarded on MASSBUS devices, but not on disks on a UNIBUS controller. For controllers, the control status register must be given explicitly, as well the number of interrupt vectors used and the names of the routines to which they should be bound. Thus the example lines given above might be completed as:

controller	hk0	**at** uba0 **csr** 0177440	**vector** rkintr
master	ht0	**at** mba0 **drive** 0	
disk	hp0	**at** mba0 **drive** ?	
tape	tu0	**at** ht0 **slave** 0	
disk	rk1	**at** hk0 **drive** 1	
device	dz0	**at** uba0 **csr** 0160100	**vector** dzrint dzxint

Certain device drivers require extra information passed to them at boot time to tailor their operation to the actual hardware present. The line printer driver, for example, needs to know how many columns are present on each non-standard line printer (i.e. a line printer with other than 80 columns). The drivers for the terminal multiplexors need to know which lines are attached to modem lines so that no one will be allowed to use them unless a connection is present. For this reason, one last parameter may be specified to a *device*, a *flags* field. It has the syntax

flags *number*

and is usually placed after the *csr* specification. The *number* is passed directly to the associated driver. The manual pages in section 4 should be consulted to determine how each driver uses this value (if at all). Communications interface drivers commonly use the flags to indicate whether modem control signals are in use.

The exact syntax for each specific device is given in the Synopsis section of its manual page in section 4 of the manual.

4.4. Pseudo-devices

A number of drivers and software subsystems are treated like device drivers without any associated hardware. To include any of these pieces, a ''pseudo-device'' specification must be used. A specification for a pseudo device takes the form

pseudo-device *device-name* [*howmany*]

Examples of pseudo devices are **pty**, the pseudo terminal driver (where the optional *howmany* value indicates the number of pseudo terminals to configure, 32 default), and **loop**, the software loopback network pseudo-interface. Other pseudo devices for the network include **imp** (required when a CSS or ACC imp is configured) and **ether** (used by the Address Resolution Protocol on 10 Mb/sec Ethernets). More information on configuring each of these can also be found in section 4 of the manual.

5. SAMPLE CONFIGURATION FILES

In this section we will consider how to configure a sample VAX-11/780 system on which the hardware can be reconfigured to guard against various hardware mishaps. We then study the rules needed to configure a VAX-11/750 to run in a networking environment.

5.1. VAX-11/780 System

Our VAX-11/780 is configured with hardware recommended in the document "Hints on Configuring a VAX for 4.2BSD" (this is one of the high-end configurations). Table 1 lists the pertinent hardware to be configured.

Item	Vendor	Connection	Name	Reference
cpu	DEC		VAX780	
MASSBUS controller	Emulex	nexus ?	mba0	hp(4)
disk	Fujitsu	mba0	hp0	
disk	Fujitsu	mba0	hp1	
MASSBUS controller	Emulex	nexus ?	mba1	
disk	Fujitsu	mba1	hp2	
disk	Fujitsu	mba1	hp3	
UNIBUS adapter	DEC	nexus ?		
tape controller	Emulex	uba0	tm0	tm(4)
tape drive	Kennedy	tm0	te0	
tape drive	Kennedy	tm0	te1	
terminal multiplexor	Emulex	uba0	dh0	dh(4)
terminal multiplexor	Emulex	uba0	dh1	
terminal multiplexor	Emulex	uba0	dh2	

Table 1. VAX-11/780 Hardware support.

We will call this machine ANSEL and construct a configuration file one step at a time.

The first step is to fill in the global configuration parameters. The machine is a VAX, so the *machine type* is "vax". We will assume this system will run only on this one processor, so the *cpu type* is "VAX780". The options are empty since this is going to be a "vanilla" VAX. The system identifier, as mentioned before, is "ANSEL," and the maximum number of users we plan to support is about 40. Thus the beginning of the configuration file looks like this:

```
#
# ANSEL VAX (a picture perfect machine)
#
machine         vax
cpu             VAX780
timezone        8 dst
ident           ANSEL
maxusers        40
```

To this we must then add the specifications for three system images. The first will be our standard system with the root on "hp0" and swapping on the same drive as the root. The second will have the root file system in the same location, but swap space interleaved among drives on each controller. Finally, the third will be a generic system, to allow us to boot off any of the four disk drives.

```
config          vmunix          root on hp0
config          hpvmunix        root on hp0 swap on hp0 and hp2
config          genvmunix       swap generic
```

Finally, the hardware must be specified. Let us first just try transcribing the information from Table 1.

```
controller      mba0            at nexus ?
disk            hp0             at mba0 disk 0
disk            hp1             at mba0 disk 1
controller      mba1            at nexus ?
disk            hp2             at mba1 disk 2
disk            hp3             at mba1 disk 3
controller      uba0            at nexus ?
controller      tm0             at uba0 csr 0172520     vector tmintr
tape            te0             at tm0 drive 0
tape            te1             at tm0 drive 1
device          dh0             at uba0 csr 0160020     vector dhrint dhxint
device          dm0             at uba0 csr 0170500     vector dmintr
device          dh1             at uba0 csr 0160040     vector dhrint dhxint
device          dh2             at uba0 csr 0160060     vector dhrint dhxint
```

(Oh, I forgot to mention one panel of the terminal multiplexor has modem control, thus the ''dm0'' device.)

This will suffice, but leaves us with little flexibility. Suppose our first disk controller were to break. We would like to recable the drives normally on the second controller so that all our disks could still be used without reconfiguring the system. To do this we wildcard the MASSBUS adapter connections and also the slave numbers. Further, we wildcard the UNIBUS adapter connections in case we decide some time in the future to purchase another adapter to offload the single UNIBUS we currently have. The revised device specifications would then be:

```
controller      mba0            at nexus ?
disk            hp0             at mba? disk ?
disk            hp1             at mba? disk ?
controller      mba1            at nexus ?
disk            hp2             at mba? disk ?
disk            hp3             at mba? disk ?
controller      uba0            at nexus ?
controller      tm0             at uba? csr 0172520     vector tmintr
tape            te0             at tm0 drive 0
tape            te1             at tm0 drive 1
device          dh0             at uba? csr 0160020     vector dhrint dhxint
device          dm0             at uba? csr 0170500     vector dmintr
device          dh1             at uba? csr 0160040     vector dhrint dhxint
device          dh2             at uba? csr 0160060     vector dhrint dhxint
```

The completed configuration file for ANSEL is shown in Appendix C.

5.2. VAX-11/750 with network support

Our VAX-11/750 system will be located on two 10Mb/s Ethernet local area networks and also the DARPA Internet. The system will have a MASSBUS drive for the root file system and two UNIBUS drives. Paging is interleaved among all three drives. We have sold our standard DEC terminal multiplexors since this machine will be accessed solely through the network. This machine is not intended to have a large user community, it does not have a great deal of memory. First the global parameters:

```
#
# UCBVAX (Gateway to the world)
#
machine          vax
cpu              "VAX780"
cpu              "VAX750"
ident            UCBVAX
timezone         8 dst
maxusers         32
options          INET
options          NS
```

The multiple cpu types allow us to replace UCBVAX with a more powerful cpu without reconfiguring the system. The value of 32 given for the maximum number of users is done to force the system data structures to be over-allocated. That is desirable on this machine because, while it is not expected to support many users, it is expected to perform a great deal of work. The ''INET'' indicates that we plan to use the DARPA standard Internet protocols on this machine, and ''NS'' also includes support for Xerox NS protocols. Note that unlike 4.2BSD configuration files, the network protocol options do not require corresponding pseudo devices.

The system images and disks are configured next.

```
config           vmunix           root on hp swap on hp and rk0 and rk1
config           upvmunix         root on up
config           hkvmunix         root on hk swap on rk0 and rk1

controller       mba0             at nexus ?
controller       uba0             at nexus ?
disk             hp0              at mba? drive 0
disk             hp1              at mba? drive 1
controller       sc0              at uba? csr 0176700       vector upintr
disk             up0              at sc0 drive 0
disk             up1              at sc0 drive 1
controller       hk0              at uba? csr 0177440       vector rkintr
disk             rk0              at hk0 drive 0
disk             rk1              at hk0 drive 1
```

UCBVAX requires heavy interleaving of its paging area to keep up with all the mail traffic it handles. The limiting factor on this system's performance is usually the number of disk arms, as opposed to memory or cpu cycles. The extra UNIBUS controller, ''sc0'', is in case the MASSBUS controller breaks and a spare controller must be installed (most of our old UNIBUS controllers have been replaced with the newer MASSBUS controllers, so we have a number of these around as spares).

Finally, we add in the network devices. Pseudo terminals are needed to allow users to log in across the network (remember the only hardwired terminal is the console). The software loopback device is used for on-machine communications. The connection to the Internet is through an IMP, this requires yet another *pseudo-device* (in addition to the actual hardware device used by the IMP software). And, finally, there are the two Ethernet devices. These use a special protocol, the Address Resolution Protocol (ARP), to map between Internet and Ethernet addresses. Thus, yet another *pseudo-device* is needed. The additional device specifications are show below.

```
pseudo-device    pty
pseudo-device    loop
pseudo-device    imp
device           acc0     at uba? csr 0167600    vector accrint accxint
pseudo-device    ether
device           ec0      at uba? csr 0164330    vector ecrint eccollide ecxint
device           il0      at uba? csr 0164000    vector ilrint ilcint
```

The completed configuration file for UCBVAX is shown in Appendix C.

5.3. Miscellaneous comments

It should be noted in these examples that neither system was configured to use disk quotas or the 4.1BSD compatibility mode. To use these optional facilities, and others, we would probably clean out our current configuration, reconfigure the system, then recompile and relink the system image(s). This could, of course, be avoided by figuring out which relocatable object files are affected by the reconfiguration, then reconfiguring and recompiling only those files affected by the configuration change. This technique should be used carefully.

2

6. ADDING NEW SYSTEM SOFTWARE

This section is not for the novice, it describes some of the inner workings of the configuration process as well as the pertinent parts of the system autoconfiguration process. It is intended to give those people who intend to install new device drivers and/or other system facilities sufficient information to do so in the manner which will allow others to easily share the changes.

This section is broken into four parts:

- general guidelines to be followed in modifying system code,
- how to add non-standard system facilities to 4.4BSD,
- how to add a device driver to 4.4BSD, and

6.1. Modifying system code

If you wish to make site-specific modifications to the system it is best to bracket them with

```
#ifdef SITENAME
...
#endif
```

to allow your source to be easily distributed to others, and also to simplify *diff*(1) listings. If you choose not to use a source code control system (e.g. SCCS, RCS), and perhaps even if you do, it is recommended that you save the old code with something of the form:

```
#ifndef SITENAME
...
#endif
```

We try to isolate our site-dependent code in individual files which may be configured with pseudo-device specifications.

Indicate machine-specific code with "#ifdef vax" (or other machine, as appropriate). 4.4BSD underwent extensive work to make it extremely portable to machines with similar architectures– you may someday find yourself trying to use a single copy of the source code on multiple machines.

6.2. Adding non-standard system facilities

This section considers the work needed to augment *config*'s data base files for non-standard system facilities. *Config* uses a set of files that list the source modules that may be required when building a system. The data bases are taken from the directory in which *config* is run, normally /sys/conf. Three such files may be used: *files*, *files*.machine, and *files*.ident. The first is common to all systems, the second contains files unique to a single machine type, and the third is an optional list of modules for use on a specific machine. This last file may override specifications in the first two. The format of the *files* file has grown somewhat complex over time. Entries are normally of the form

dir/source.c type option-list modifiers

for example,

vaxuba/foo.c **optional** foo **device-driver**

The *type* is one of **standard** or **optional**. Files marked as standard are included in all system configurations. Optional file specifications include a list of one or more system options that together require the inclusion of this module. The options in the list may be either names of devices that may be in the configuration file, or the names of system options that may be defined. An optional file may be listed multiple times with different options; if all of the options for any of the entries are satisfied, the module is included.

2

If a file is specified as a *device-driver*, any special compilation options for device drivers will be invoked. On the VAX this results in the use of the **–i** option for the C optimizer. This is required when pointer references are made to memory locations in the VAX I/O address space.

Two other optional keywords modify the usage of the file. *Config* understands that certain files are used especially for kernel profiling. These files are indicated in the *files* files with a *profiling-routine* keyword. For example, the current profiling subroutines are sequestered off in a separate file with the following entry:

*sys/subr_mcount.c***optional** **profiling-routine**

The *profiling-routine* keyword forces *config* not to compile the source file with the **–pg** option.

The second keyword which can be of use is the *config-dependent* keyword. This causes *config* to compile the indicated module with the global configuration parameters. This allows certain modules, such as *machdep.c* to size system data structures based on the maximum number of users configured for the system.

6.3. Adding device drivers to 4.4BSD

The I/O system and *config* have been designed to easily allow new device support to be added. The system source directories are organized as follows:

/sys/h	machine independent include files
/sys/sys	machine-independent system source files
/sys/conf	site configuration files and basic templates
/sys/net	network-protocol-independent, but network-related code
/sys/netinet	DARPA Internet code
/sys/netimp	IMP support code
/sys/netns	Xerox NS code
/sys/vax	VAX-specific mainline code
/sys/vaxif	VAX network interface code
/sys/vaxmba	VAX MASSBUS device drivers and related code
/sys/vaxuba	VAX UNIBUS device drivers and related code

Existing block and character device drivers for the VAX reside in ''/sys/vax'', ''/sys/vaxmba'', and ''/sys/vaxuba''. Network interface drivers reside in ''/sys/vaxif''. Any new device drivers should be placed in the appropriate source code directory and named so as not to conflict with existing devices. Normally, definitions for things like device registers are placed in a separate file in the same directory. For example, the ''dh'' device driver is named ''dh.c'' and its associated include file is named ''dhreg.h''.

Once the source for the device driver has been placed in a directory, the file ''/sys/conf/files.machine'', and possibly ''/sys/conf/devices.machine'' should be modified. The *files* files in the conf directory contain a line for each C source or binary-only file in the system. Those files which are machine independent are located in ''/sys/conf/files,'' while machine specific files are in

''/sys/conf/files.machine.'' The ''devices.machine'' file is used to map device names to major block device numbers. If the device driver being added provides support for a new disk you will want to modify this file (the format is obvious).

In addition to including the driver in the *files* file, it must also be added to the device configuration tables. These are located in ''/sys/vax/conf.c'', or similar for machines other than the VAX. If you don't understand what to add to this file, you should study an entry for an existing driver. Remember that the position in the device table specifies the major device number. The block major number is needed in the ''devices.machine'' file if the device is a disk.

With the configuration information in place, your configuration file appropriately modified, and a system reconfigured and rebooted you should incorporate the shell commands needed to install the special files in the file system to the file ''/dev/MAKEDEV'' or ''/dev/MAKEDEV.local''. This is discussed in the document ''Installing and Operating 4.4BSD''.

2

APPENDIX A. CONFIGURATION FILE GRAMMAR

The following grammar is a compressed form of the actual *yacc* (1) grammar used by *config* to parse configuration files. Terminal symbols are shown all in upper case, literals are emboldened; optional clauses are enclosed in brackets, ''['' and '']''; zero or more instantiations are denoted with ''*''

Configuration ::= [Spec ;]*

Spec ::= Config_spec
 | Device_spec
 | **trace**
 | /* lambda */

/* configuration specifications */

Config_spec ::= **machine** ID
 | **cpu** ID
 | **options** Opt_list
 | **ident** ID
 | System_spec
 | **timezone** [–] NUMBER [**dst** [NUMBER]]
 | **timezone** [–] FPNUMBER [**dst** [NUMBER]]
 | **maxusers** NUMBER

/* system configuration specifications */

System_spec ::= **config** ID System_parameter [System_parameter]*

System_parameter ::= swap_spec | root_spec | dump_spec | arg_spec

swap_spec ::= **swap** [**on**] swap_dev [**and** swap_dev]*

swap_dev ::= dev_spec [**size** NUMBER]

root_spec ::= **root** [**on**] dev_spec

dump_spec ::= **dumps** [**on**] dev_spec

arg_spec ::= **args** [**on**] dev_spec

dev_spec ::= dev_name | major_minor

major_minor ::= **major** NUMBER **minor** NUMBER

dev_name ::= ID [NUMBER [ID]]

/* option specifications */

Opt_list ::= Option [**,** Option]*

Option ::= ID [= Opt_value]

Opt_value ::= ID | NUMBER

Mkopt_list ::= Mkoption [**,** Mkoption]*

Mkoption ::= ID = Opt_value

/* device specifications */

Device_spec ::= **device** Dev_name Dev_info Int_spec
  | **master** Dev_name Dev_info
  | **disk** Dev_name Dev_info
  | **tape** Dev_name Dev_info
  | **controller** Dev_name Dev_info [Int_spec]
  | **pseudo-device** Dev [NUMBER]

Dev_name ::= Dev NUMBER

Dev ::= **uba** | **mba** | ID

Dev_info ::= Con_info [Info]*

Con_info ::= **at** Dev NUMBER
  | **at nexus** NUMBER

Info ::= **csr** NUMBER
  | **drive** NUMBER
  | **slave** NUMBER
  | **flags** NUMBER

Int_spec ::= **vector** ID [ID]*
  | **priority** NUMBER

Lexical Conventions

The terminal symbols are loosely defined as:

ID

One or more alphabetics, either upper or lower case, and underscore, ''_''.

NUMBER

Approximately the C language specification for an integer number. That is, a leading ''0x'' indicates a hexadecimal value, a leading ''0'' indicates an octal value, otherwise the number is expected to be a decimal value. Hexadecimal numbers may use either upper or lower case alphabetics.

FPNUMBER

A floating point number without exponent. That is a number of the form ''nnn.ddd'', where the fractional component is optional.

In special instances a question mark, ''?'', can be substituted for a ''NUMBER'' token. This is used to effect wildcarding in device interconnection specifications.

Comments in configuration files are indicated by a ''#'' character at the beginning of the line; the remainder of the line is discarded.

A specification is interpreted as a continuation of the previous line if the first character of the line is tab.

APPENDIX B. RULES FOR DEFAULTING SYSTEM DEVICES

When *config* processes a ''config'' rule which does not fully specify the location of the root file system, paging area(s), device for system dumps, and device for argument list processing it applies a set of rules to define those values left unspecified. The following list of rules are used in defaulting system devices.

1) If a root device is not specified, the swap specification must indicate a ''generic'' system is to be built.
2) If the root device does not specify a unit number, it defaults to unit 0.
3) If the root device does not include a partition specification, it defaults to the ''a'' partition.
4) If no swap area is specified, it defaults to the ''b'' partition of the root device.
5) If no device is specified for processing argument lists, the first swap partition is selected.
6) If no device is chosen for system dumps, the first swap partition is selected (see below to find out where dumps are placed within the partition).

2

The following table summarizes the default partitions selected when a device specification is incomplete, e.g. ''hp0''.

Type	Partition
root	''a''
swap	''b''
args	''b''
dumps	''b''

Multiple swap/paging areas

When multiple swap partitions are specified, the system treats the first specified as a ''primary'' swap area which is always used. The remaining partitions are then interleaved into the paging system at the time a *swapon*(2) system call is made. This is normally done at boot time with a call to *swapon*(8) from the /etc/rc file.

System dumps

System dumps are automatically taken after a system crash, provided the device driver for the ''dumps'' device supports this. The dump contains the contents of memory, but not the swap areas. Normally the dump device is a disk in which case the information is copied to a location at the back of the partition. The dump is placed in the back of the partition because the primary swap and dump device are commonly the same device and this allows the system to be rebooted without immediately overwriting the saved information. When a dump has occurred, the system variable *dumpsize* is set to a non-zero value indicating the size (in bytes) of the dump. The *savecore* (8) program then copies the information from the dump partition to a file in a ''crash'' directory and also makes a copy of the system which was running at the time of the crash (usually ''/vmunix''). The offset to the system dump is defined in the system variable *dumplo* (a sector offset from the front of the dump partition). The *savecore* program operates by reading the contents of *dumplo*, *dumpdev*, and *dumpmagic* from /dev/kmem, then comparing the value of *dumpmagic* read from /dev/kmem to that located in corresponding location in the dump area of the dump partition. If a match is found, *savecore* assumes a crash occurred and reads *dumpsize* from the dump area of the dump partition. This value is then used in copying the system dump. Refer to *savecore* (8) for more information about its operation.

The value *dumplo* is calculated to be

dumpdev-size – memsize

where *dumpdev-size* is the size of the disk partition where system dumps are to be placed, and *memsize* is the size of physical memory. If the disk partition is not large enough to hold a full dump, *dumplo* is set to 0 (the start of the partition).

APPENDIX C. SAMPLE CONFIGURATION FILES

The following configuration files are developed in section 5; they are included here for completeness.

```
#
# ANSEL VAX (a picture perfect machine)
#
machine         vax
cpu             VAX780
timezone        8 dst
ident           ANSEL
maxusers        40

config          vmunix          root on hp0
config          hpvmunix        root on hp0 swap on hp0 and hp2
config          genvmunix       swap generic

controller      mba0            at nexus ?
disk            hp0             at mba? disk ?
disk            hp1             at mba? disk ?
controller      mba1            at nexus ?
disk            hp2             at mba? disk ?
disk            hp3             at mba? disk ?
controller      uba0            at nexus ?
controller      tm0             at uba? csr 0172520     vector tmintr
tape            te0             at tm0 drive 0
tape            te1             at tm0 drive 1
device          dh0             at uba? csr 0160020     vector dhrint dhxint
device          dm0             at uba? csr 0170500     vector dmintr
device          dh1             at uba? csr 0160040     vector dhrint dhxint
device          dh2             at uba? csr 0160060     vector dhrint dhxint
```

```
#
# UCBVAX - Gateway to the world
#
machine         vax
cpu             "VAX780"
cpu             "VAX750"
ident           UCBVAX
timezone        8 dst
maxusers        32
options         INET
options         NS

config          vmunix      root on hp swap on hp and rk0 and rk1
config          upvmunix    root on up
config          hkvmunix    root on hk swap on rk0 and rk1

controller      mba0        at nexus ?
controller      uba0        at nexus ?
disk            hp0         at mba? drive 0
disk            hp1         at mba? drive 1
controller      sc0         at uba? csr 0176700     vector upintr
disk            up0         at sc0 drive 0
disk            up1         at sc0 drive 1
controller      hk0         at uba? csr 0177440     vector rkintr
disk            rk0         at hk0 drive 0
disk            rk1         at hk0 drive 1
pseudo-device   pty
pseudo-device   loop
pseudo-device   imp
device          acc0        at uba? csr 0167600     vector accrint accxint
pseudo-device   ether
device          ec0         at uba? csr 0164330     vector ecrint eccollide ecxint
device          il0         at uba? csr 0164000     vector ilrint ilcint
```

APPENDIX D. VAX KERNEL DATA STRUCTURE SIZING RULES

Certain system data structures are sized at compile time according to the maximum number of simultaneous users expected, while others are calculated at boot time based on the physical resources present, e.g. memory. This appendix lists both sets of rules and also includes some hints on changing built-in limitations on certain data structures.

Compile time rules

The file */sys/conf/param.c* contains the definitions of almost all data structures sized at compile time. This file is copied into the directory of each configured system to allow configuration-dependent rules and values to be maintained. (Each copy normally depends on the copy in /sys/conf, and global modifications cause the file to be recopied unless the makefile is modified.) The rules implied by its contents are summarized below (here MAXUSERS refers to the value defined in the configuration file in the ''maxusers'' rule). Most limits are computed at compile time and stored in global variables for use by other modules; they may generally be patched in the system binary image before rebooting to test new values.

nproc

The maximum number of processes which may be running at any time. It is referred to in other calculations as NPROC and is defined to be

20 + 8 * MAXUSERS

ntext

The maximum number of active shared text segments. The constant is intended to allow for network servers and common commands that remain in the table. It is defined as

36 + MAXUSERS.

ninode

The maximum number of files in the file system which may be active at any time. This includes files in use by users, as well as directory files being read or written by the system and files associated with bound sockets in the UNIX IPC domain. It is defined as

(NPROC + 16 + MAXUSERS) + 32

nfile

The number of ''file table'' structures. One file table structure is used for each open, unshared, file descriptor. Multiple file descriptors may reference a single file table entry when they are created through a *dup* call, or as the result of a *fork*. This is defined to be

16 * (NPROC + 16 + MAXUSERS) / 10 + 32

ncallout

The number of ''callout'' structures. One callout structure is used per internal system event handled with a timeout. Timeouts are used for terminal delays, watchdog routines in device drivers, protocol timeout processing, etc. This is defined as

16 + NPROC

nclist

The number of ''c-list'' structures. C-list structures are used in terminal I/O, and currently each holds 60 characters. Their number is defined as

60 + 12 * MAXUSERS

nmbclusters

The maximum number of pages which may be allocated by the network. This is defined as 256 (a quarter megabyte of memory) in /sys/h/mbuf.h. In practice, the network rarely uses this much memory. It starts off by allocating 8 kilobytes of memory, then requesting more as required. This value represents an upper bound.

nquota

The number of ''quota'' structures allocated. Quota structures are present only when disc quotas are configured in the system. One quota structure is kept per user. This is defined to be

(MAXUSERS * 9) / 7 + 3

ndquot

The number of ''dquot'' structures allocated. Dquot structures are present only when disc quotas are configured in the system. One dquot structure is required per user, per active file system quota. That is, when a user manipulates a file on a file system on which quotas are enabled, the information regarding the user's quotas on that file system must be in-core. This information is cached, so that not all information must be present in-core all the time. This is defined as

NINODE + (MAXUSERS * NMOUNT) / 4

where NMOUNT is the maximum number of mountable file systems.

2

In addition to the above values, the system page tables (used to map virtual memory in the kernel's address space) are sized at compile time by the SYSPTSIZE definition in the file /sys/vax/vmparam.h. This is defined to be

20 + MAXUSERS

pages of page tables. Its definition affects the size of many data structures allocated at boot time because it constrains the amount of virtual memory which may be addressed by the running system. This is often the limiting factor in the size of the buffer cache, in which case a message is printed when the system configures at boot time.

Run-time calculations

The most important data structures sized at run-time are those used in the buffer cache. Allocation is done by allocating physical memory (and system virtual memory) immediately after the system has been started up; look in the file /sys/vax/machdep.c. The amount of physical memory which may be allocated to the buffer cache is constrained by the size of the system page tables, among other things. While the system may calculate a large amount of memory to be allocated to the buffer cache, if the system page table is too small to map this physical memory into the virtual address space of the system, only as much as can be mapped will be used.

The buffer cache is comprised of a number of ''buffer headers'' and a pool of pages attached to these headers. Buffer headers are divided into two categories: those used for swapping and paging, and those used for normal file I/O. The system tries to allocate 10% of the first two megabytes and 5% of the remaining available physical memory for the buffer cache (where *available* does not count that space occupied by the system's text and data segments). If this results in fewer than 16 pages of memory allocated, then 16 pages are allocated. This value is kept in the initialized variable *bufpages* so that it may be patched in the binary image (to allow tuning without recompiling the system), or the default may be overridden with a configuration-file option. For example, the option **options BUFPAGES="3200"** causes 3200 pages (3.2M bytes) to be used by the buffer cache. A sufficient number of file I/O buffer headers are then allocated to allow each to hold 2 pages each. Each buffer maps 8K bytes. If the number of buffer pages is larger than can be mapped by the buffer headers, the number of pages is reduced. The number of buffer headers allocated is stored in the global variable *nbuf*, which may be patched before the system is booted. The system option **options NBUF="1000"** forces the allocation of 1000 buffer headers. Half as many swap I/O buffer headers as file I/O buffers are allocated, but no more than 256.

System size limitations

As distributed, the sum of the virtual sizes of the core-resident processes is limited to 256M bytes. The size of the text segment of a single process is currently limited to 6M bytes. It may be increased to no greater than the data segment size limit (see below) by redefining MAXTSIZ. This may be done with a configuration file option, e.g. **options MAXTSIZ="(10*1024*1024)"** to set the limit to 10 million bytes. Other per-process limits discussed here may be changed with similar options with names given in parentheses. Soft, user-changeable limits are set to 512K bytes for stack (DFLSSIZ) and 6M bytes for the data segment (DFLDSIZ) by default; these may be increased up to the hard limit with the *setrlimit*(2) system call. The data and stack segment size hard limits are set by a system configuration option to one of 17M, 33M or 64M bytes. One of these sizes is chosen based on the definition of MAXDSIZ; with no option, the limit is 17M bytes; with an option **options MAXDSIZ="(32*1024*1024)"** (or any value between 17M and 33M), the limit is increased to 33M bytes, and values larger than 33M result in a limit of 64M bytes. You must be careful in doing this that you have adequate paging space. As normally configured , the system has 16M or 32M bytes per paging area, depending on disk size. The best way to get more space is to provide multiple, thereby interleaved, paging areas. Increasing the virtual memory limits results in interleaving of swap space in larger sections (from 500K bytes to 1M or 2M bytes).

By default, the virtual memory system allocates enough memory for system page tables mapping user page tables to allow 256 megabytes of simultaneous active virtual memory. That is, the sum of the virtual memory sizes of all (completely- or partially-) resident processes can not exceed this limit. If the limit is exceeded, some process(es) must be swapped out. To increase the amount of resident virtual space possible, you can alter the constant USRPTSIZE (in /sys/vax/vmparam.h). Each page of system page tables allows 8 megabytes of user virtual memory.

Because the file system block numbers are stored in page table *pg_blkno* entries, the maximum size of a file system is limited to 2^24 1024 byte blocks. Thus no file system can be larger than 8 gigabytes.

The number of mountable file systems is set at 20 by the definition of NMOUNT in /sys/h/param.h. This should be sufficient; if not, the value can be increased up to 255. If you have many disks, it makes sense to make some of them single file systems, and the paging areas don't count in this total.

The limit to the number of files that a process may have open simultaneously is set to 64. This limit is set by the NOFILE definition in /sys/h/param.h. It may be increased arbitrarily, with the caveat that the user structure expands by 5 bytes for each file, and thus UPAGES (/sys/vax/machparam.h) must be increased accordingly.

The amount of physical memory is currently limited to 64 Mb by the size of the index fields in the core-map (/sys/h/cmap.h). The limit may be increased by following instructions in that file to enlarge those fields.

Fsck – The UNIX† File System Check Program

Marshall Kirk McKusick

Computer Systems Research Group
Computer Science Division
Department of Electrical Engineering and Computer Science
University of California, Berkeley
Berkeley, CA 94720

T. J. Kowalski

Bell Laboratories
Murray Hill, New Jersey 07974

ABSTRACT

This document reflects the use of *fsck* with the 4.2BSD and 4.3BSD file system organization. This is a revision of the original paper written by T. J. Kowalski.

File System Check Program (*fsck*) is an interactive file system check and repair program. *Fsck* uses the redundant structural information in the UNIX file system to perform several consistency checks. If an inconsistency is detected, it is reported to the operator, who may elect to fix or ignore each inconsistency. These inconsistencies result from the permanent interruption of the file system updates, which are performed every time a file is modified. Unless there has been a hardware failure, *fsck* is able to repair corrupted file systems using procedures based upon the order in which UNIX honors these file system update requests.

The purpose of this document is to describe the normal updating of the file system, to discuss the possible causes of file system corruption, and to present the corrective actions implemented by *fsck*. Both the program and the interaction between the program and the operator are described.

Revised July 16, 1985

3

---

†UNIX is a trademark of Bell Laboratories.

This work was done under grants from the National Science Foundation under grant MCS80-05144, and the Defense Advance Research Projects Agency (DoD) under Arpa Order No. 4031 monitored by Naval Electronic System Command under Contract No. N00039-82-C-0235.

TABLE OF CONTENTS

1. Introduction

This document reflects the use of *fsck* with the 4.2BSD and 4.3BSD file system organization. This is a revision of the original paper written by T. J. Kowalski.

When a UNIX operating system is brought up, a consistency check of the file systems should always be performed. This precautionary measure helps to insure a reliable environment for file storage on disk. If an inconsistency is discovered, corrective action must be taken. *Fsck* runs in two modes. Normally it is run non-interactively by the system after a normal boot. When running in this mode, it will only make changes to the file system that are known to always be correct. If an unexpected inconsistency is found *fsck* will exit with a non-zero exit status, leaving the system running single-user. Typically the operator then runs *fsck* interactively. When running in this mode, each problem is listed followed by a suggested corrective action. The operator must decide whether or not the suggested correction should be made.

The purpose of this memo is to dispel the mystique surrounding file system inconsistencies. It first describes the updating of the file system (the calm before the storm) and then describes file system corruption (the storm). Finally, the set of deterministic corrective actions used by *fsck* (the Coast Guard to the rescue) is presented.

2. Overview of the file system

The file system is discussed in detail in [Mckusick84]; this section gives a brief overview.

2.1. Superblock

A file system is described by its *super-block*. The super-block is built when the file system is created (*newfs*(8)) and never changes. The super-block contains the basic parameters of the file system, such as the number of data blocks it contains and a count of the maximum number of files. Because the super-block contains critical data, *newfs* replicates it to protect against catastrophic loss. The *default super block* always resides at a fixed offset from the beginning of the file system's disk partition. The *redundant super blocks* are not referenced unless a head crash or other hard disk error causes the default super-block to be unusable. The redundant blocks are sprinkled throughout the disk partition.

3

Within the file system are files. Certain files are distinguished as directories and contain collections of pointers to files that may themselves be directories. Every file has a descriptor associated with it called an *inode*. The inode contains information describing ownership of the file, time stamps indicating modification and access times for the file, and an array of indices pointing to the data blocks for the file. In this section, we assume that the first 12 blocks of the file are directly referenced by values stored in the inode structure itself†. The inode structure may also contain references to indirect blocks containing further data block indices. In a file system with a 4096 byte block size, a singly indirect block contains 1024 further block addresses, a doubly indirect block contains 1024 addresses of further single indirect blocks, and a triply indirect block contains 1024 addresses of further doubly indirect blocks (the triple indirect block is never needed in practice).

In order to create files with up to 2↑32 bytes, using only two levels of indirection, the minimum size of a file system block is 4096 bytes. The size of file system blocks can be any power of two greater than or equal to 4096. The block size of the file system is maintained in the super-block, so it is possible for file systems of different block sizes to be accessible simultaneously on the same system. The block size must be decided when *newfs* creates the file system; the block size cannot be subsequently changed without rebuilding the file system.

2.2. Summary information

Associated with the super block is non replicated *summary information*. The summary information changes as the file system is modified. The summary information contains the number of blocks, fragments, inodes and directories in the file system.

†The actual number may vary from system to system, but is usually in the range 5-13.

2.3. Cylinder groups

The file system partitions the disk into one or more areas called *cylinder groups*. A cylinder group is comprised of one or more consecutive cylinders on a disk. Each cylinder group includes inode slots for files, a *block map* describing available blocks in the cylinder group, and summary information describing the usage of data blocks within the cylinder group. A fixed number of inodes is allocated for each cylinder group when the file system is created. The current policy is to allocate one inode for each 2048 bytes of disk space; this is expected to be far more inodes than will ever be needed.

All the cylinder group bookkeeping information could be placed at the beginning of each cylinder group. However if this approach were used, all the redundant information would be on the top platter. A single hardware failure that destroyed the top platter could cause the loss of all copies of the redundant super-blocks. Thus the cylinder group bookkeeping information begins at a floating offset from the beginning of the cylinder group. The offset for the *i+1* st cylinder group is about one track further from the beginning of the cylinder group than it was for the *i* th cylinder group. In this way, the redundant information spirals down into the pack; any single track, cylinder, or platter can be lost without losing all copies of the super-blocks. Except for the first cylinder group, the space between the beginning of the cylinder group and the beginning of the cylinder group information stores data.

2.4. Fragments

3

To avoid waste in storing small files, the file system space allocator divides a single file system block into one or more *fragments*. The fragmentation of the file system is specified when the file system is created; each file system block can be optionally broken into 2, 4, or 8 addressable fragments. The lower bound on the size of these fragments is constrained by the disk sector size; typically 512 bytes is the lower bound on fragment size. The block map associated with each cylinder group records the space availability at the fragment level. Aligned fragments are examined to determine block availability.

On a file system with a block size of 4096 bytes and a fragment size of 1024 bytes, a file is represented by zero or more 4096 byte blocks of data, and possibly a single fragmented block. If a file system block must be fragmented to obtain space for a small amount of data, the remainder of the block is made available for allocation to other files. For example, consider an 11000 byte file stored on a 4096/1024 byte file system. This file uses two full size blocks and a 3072 byte fragment. If no fragments with at least 3072 bytes are available when the file is created, a full size block is split yielding the necessary 3072 byte fragment and an unused 1024 byte fragment. This remaining fragment can be allocated to another file, as needed.

2.5. Updates to the file system

Every working day hundreds of files are created, modified, and removed. Every time a file is modified, the operating system performs a series of file system updates. These updates, when written on disk, yield a consistent file system. The file system stages all modifications of critical information; modification can either be completed or cleanly backed out after a crash. Knowing the information that is first written to the file system, deterministic procedures can be developed to repair a corrupted file system. To understand this process, the order that the update requests were being honored must first be understood.

When a user program does an operation to change the file system, such as a *write*, the data to be written is copied into an internal *in-core* buffer in the kernel. Normally, the disk update is handled asynchronously; the user process is allowed to proceed even though the data has not yet been written to the disk. The data, along with the inode information reflecting the change, is eventually written out to disk. The real disk write may not happen until long after the *write* system call has returned. Thus at any given time, the file system, as it resides on the disk, lags the state of the file system represented by the in-core information.

The disk information is updated to reflect the in-core information when the buffer is required for another use, when a *sync* (2) is done (at 30 second intervals) by */etc/update* (8), or by manual operator intervention with the *sync* (8) command. If the system is halted without writing out the in-core information, the file system on the disk will be in an inconsistent state.

If all updates are done asynchronously, several serious inconsistencies can arise. One inconsistency is that a block may be claimed by two inodes. Such an inconsistency can occur when the system is halted before the pointer to the block in the old inode has been cleared in the copy of the old inode on the disk, and after the pointer to the block in the new inode has been written out to the copy of the new inode on the disk. Here, there is no deterministic method for deciding which inode should really claim the block. A similar problem can arise with a multiply claimed inode.

The problem with asynchronous inode updates can be avoided by doing all inode deallocations synchronously. Consequently, inodes and indirect blocks are written to the disk synchronously (*i.e.* the process blocks until the information is really written to disk) when they are being deallocated. Similarly inodes are kept consistent by synchronously deleting, adding, or changing directory entries.

3. Fixing corrupted file systems

A file system can become corrupted in several ways. The most common of these ways are improper shutdown procedures and hardware failures.

File systems may become corrupted during an *unclean halt*. This happens when proper shutdown procedures are not observed, physically write-protecting a mounted file system, or a mounted file system is taken off-line. The most common operator procedural failure is forgetting to *sync* the system before halting the CPU.

File systems may become further corrupted if proper startup procedures are not observed, e.g., not checking a file system for inconsistencies, and not repairing inconsistencies. Allowing a corrupted file system to be used (and, thus, to be modified further) can be disastrous.

Any piece of hardware can fail at any time. Failures can be as subtle as a bad block on a disk pack, or as blatant as a non-functional disk-controller. 3

3.1. Detecting and correcting corruption

Normally *fsck* is run non-interactively. In this mode it will only fix corruptions that are expected to occur from an unclean halt. These actions are a proper subset of the actions that *fsck* will take when it is running interactively. Throughout this paper we assume that *fsck* is being run interactively, and all possible errors can be encountered. When an inconsistency is discovered in this mode, *fsck* reports the inconsistency for the operator to chose a corrective action.

A quiescent‡ file system may be checked for structural integrity by performing consistency checks on the redundant data intrinsic to a file system. The redundant data is either read from the file system, or computed from other known values. The file system **must** be in a quiescent state when *fsck* is run, since *fsck* is a multi-pass program.

In the following sections, we discuss methods to discover inconsistencies and possible corrective actions for the cylinder group blocks, the inodes, the indirect blocks, and the data blocks containing directory entries.

3.2. Super-block checking

The most commonly corrupted item in a file system is the summary information associated with the super-block. The summary information is prone to corruption because it is modified with every change to the file system's blocks or inodes, and is usually corrupted after an unclean halt.

The super-block is checked for inconsistencies involving file-system size, number of inodes, free-block count, and the free-inode count. The file-system size must be larger than the number of blocks used by the super-block and the number of blocks used by the list of inodes. The file-system size and layout information are the most critical pieces of information for *fsck*. While there is no way to actually check these sizes, since they are statically determined by *newfs*, *fsck* can check that these sizes are within reasonable bounds. All other file system checks require that these sizes be correct. If *fsck* detects corruption in the static parameters of the default super-block, *fsck* requests the operator to specify the location of an alternate super-block.

‡ I.e., unmounted and not being written on.

3.3. Free block checking

Fsck checks that all the blocks marked as free in the cylinder group block maps are not claimed by any files. When all the blocks have been initially accounted for, *fsck* checks that the number of free blocks plus the number of blocks claimed by the inodes equals the total number of blocks in the file system.

If anything is wrong with the block allocation maps, *fsck* will rebuild them, based on the list it has computed of allocated blocks.

The summary information associated with the super-block counts the total number of free blocks within the file system. *Fsck* compares this count to the number of free blocks it found within the file system. If the two counts do not agree, then *fsck* replaces the incorrect count in the summary information by the actual free-block count.

The summary information counts the total number of free inodes within the file system. *Fsck* compares this count to the number of free inodes it found within the file system. If the two counts do not agree, then *fsck* replaces the incorrect count in the summary information by the actual free-inode count.

3.4. Checking the inode state

An individual inode is not as likely to be corrupted as the allocation information. However, because of the great number of active inodes, a few of the inodes are usually corrupted.

The list of inodes in the file system is checked sequentially starting with inode 2 (inode 0 marks unused inodes; inode 1 is saved for future generations) and progressing through the last inode in the file system. The state of each inode is checked for inconsistencies involving format and type, link count, duplicate blocks, bad blocks, and inode size.

3

Each inode contains a mode word. This mode word describes the type and state of the inode. Inodes must be one of six types: regular inode, directory inode, symbolic link inode, special block inode, special character inode, or socket inode. Inodes may be found in one of three allocation states: unallocated, allocated, and neither unallocated nor allocated. This last state suggests an incorrectly formated inode. An inode can get in this state if bad data is written into the inode list. The only possible corrective action is for *fsck* is to clear the inode.

3.5. Inode links

Each inode counts the total number of directory entries linked to the inode. *Fsck* verifies the link count of each inode by starting at the root of the file system, and descending through the directory structure. The actual link count for each inode is calculated during the descent.

If the stored link count is non-zero and the actual link count is zero, then no directory entry appears for the inode. If this happens, *fsck* will place the disconnected file in the *lost+found* directory. If the stored and actual link counts are non-zero and unequal, a directory entry may have been added or removed without the inode being updated. If this happens, *fsck* replaces the incorrect stored link count by the actual link count.

Each inode contains a list, or pointers to lists (indirect blocks), of all the blocks claimed by the inode. Since indirect blocks are owned by an inode, inconsistencies in indirect blocks directly affect the inode that owns it.

Fsck compares each block number claimed by an inode against a list of already allocated blocks. If another inode already claims a block number, then the block number is added to a list of *duplicate blocks*. Otherwise, the list of allocated blocks is updated to include the block number.

If there are any duplicate blocks, *fsck* will perform a partial second pass over the inode list to find the inode of the duplicated block. The second pass is needed, since without examining the files associated with these inodes for correct content, not enough information is available to determine which inode is corrupted and should be cleared. If this condition does arise (only hardware failure will cause it), then the inode with the earliest modify time is usually incorrect, and should be cleared. If this happens, *fsck* prompts the operator to clear both inodes. The operator must decide which one should be kept and which one should be cleared.

Fsck checks the range of each block number claimed by an inode. If the block number is lower than the first data block in the file system, or greater than the last data block, then the block number is a *bad block number*. Many bad blocks in an inode are usually caused by an indirect block that was not written to the file system, a condition which can only occur if there has been a hardware failure. If an inode contains bad block numbers, *fsck* prompts the operator to clear it.

3.6. Inode data size

Each inode contains a count of the number of data blocks that it contains. The number of actual data blocks is the sum of the allocated data blocks and the indirect blocks. *Fsck* computes the actual number of data blocks and compares that block count against the actual number of blocks the inode claims. If an inode contains an incorrect count *fsck* prompts the operator to fix it.

Each inode contains a thirty-two bit size field. The size is the number of data bytes in the file associated with the inode. The consistency of the byte size field is roughly checked by computing from the size field the maximum number of blocks that should be associated with the inode, and comparing that expected block count against the actual number of blocks the inode claims.

3.7. Checking the data associated with an inode

An inode can directly or indirectly reference three kinds of data blocks. All referenced blocks must be the same kind. The three types of data blocks are: plain data blocks, symbolic link data blocks, and directory data blocks. Plain data blocks contain the information stored in a file; symbolic link data blocks contain the path name stored in a link. Directory data blocks contain directory entries. *Fsck* can only check the validity of directory data blocks.

Each directory data block is checked for several types of inconsistencies. These inconsistencies include directory inode numbers pointing to unallocated inodes, directory inode numbers that are greater than the number of inodes in the file system, incorrect directory inode numbers for ''.'' and ''..'', and directories that are not attached to the file system. If the inode number in a directory data block references an unallocated inode, then *fsck* will remove that directory entry. Again, this condition can only arise when there has been a hardware failure.

If a directory entry inode number references outside the inode list, then *fsck* will remove that directory entry. This condition occurs if bad data is written into a directory data block.

The directory inode number entry for ''.'' must be the first entry in the directory data block. The inode number for ''.'' must reference itself; e.g., it must equal the inode number for the directory data block. The directory inode number entry for ''..'' must be the second entry in the directory data block. Its value must equal the inode number for the parent of the directory entry (or the inode number of the directory data block if the directory is the root directory). If the directory inode numbers are incorrect, *fsck* will replace them with the correct values. If there are multiple hard links to a directory, the first one encountered is considered the real parent to which ''..'' should point; *fsck* recommends deletion for the subsequently discovered names.

3.8. File system connectivity

Fsck checks the general connectivity of the file system. If directories are not linked into the file system, then *fsck* links the directory back into the file system in the *lost+found* directory. This condition only occurs when there has been a hardware failure.

Acknowledgements

I thank Bill Joy, Sam Leffler, Robert Elz and Dennis Ritchie for their suggestions and help in implementing the new file system. Thanks also to Robert Henry for his editorial input to get this document together. Finally we thank our sponsors, the National Science Foundation under grant MCS80-05144, and the Defense Advance Research Projects Agency (DoD) under Arpa Order No. 4031 monitored by Naval Electronic System Command under Contract No. N00039-82-C-0235. (Kirk McKusick, July 1983)

I would like to thank Larry A. Wehr for advice that lead to the first version of *fsck* and Rick B. Brandt for adapting *fsck* to UNIX/TS. (T. Kowalski, July 1979)

3

References

[Dolotta78] Dolotta, T. A., and Olsson, S. B. eds., *UNIX User's Manual, Edition 1.1*, January 1978.

[Joy83] Joy, W., Cooper, E., Fabry, R., Leffler, S., McKusick, M., and Mosher, D. 4.2BSD System Manual, *University of California at Berkeley*, *Computer Systems Research Group Technical Report* #4, 1982.

[McKusick84] McKusick, M., Joy, W., Leffler, S., and Fabry, R. A Fast File System for UNIX, *ACM Transactions on Computer Systems 2*, 3. pp. 181-197, August 1984.

[Ritchie78] Ritchie, D. M., and Thompson, K., The UNIX Time-Sharing System, *The Bell System Technical Journal* **57**, 6 (July-August 1978, Part 2), pp. 1905-29.

[Thompson78] Thompson, K., UNIX Implementation, *The Bell System Technical Journal* **57**, 6 (July-August 1978, Part 2), pp. 1931-46.

3

4. Appendix A – Fsck Error Conditions

4.1. Conventions

Fsck is a multi-pass file system check program. Each file system pass invokes a different Phase of the *fsck* program. After the initial setup, *fsck* performs successive Phases over each file system, checking blocks and sizes, path-names, connectivity, reference counts, and the map of free blocks, (possibly rebuilding it), and performs some cleanup.

Normally *fsck* is run non-interactively to *preen* the file systems after an unclean halt. While preen'ing a file system, it will only fix corruptions that are expected to occur from an unclean halt. These actions are a proper subset of the actions that *fsck* will take when it is running interactively. Throughout this appendix many errors have several options that the operator can take. When an inconsistency is detected, *fsck* reports the error condition to the operator. If a response is required, *fsck* prints a prompt message and waits for a response. When preen'ing most errors are fatal. For those that are expected, the response taken is noted. This appendix explains the meaning of each error condition, the possible responses, and the related error conditions.

The error conditions are organized by the *Phase* of the *fsck* program in which they can occur. The error conditions that may occur in more than one Phase will be discussed in initialization.

4.2. Initialization

Before a file system check can be performed, certain tables have to be set up and certain files opened. This section concerns itself with the opening of files and the initialization of tables. This section lists error conditions resulting from command line options, memory requests, opening of files, status of files, file system size checks, and creation of the scratch file. All the initialization errors are fatal when the file system is being preen'ed.

3

***C* option?**
C is not a legal option to *fsck*; legal options are –b, –c, –y, –n, and –p. *Fsck* terminates on this error condition. See the *fsck*(8) manual entry for further detail.

cannot alloc NNN bytes for blockmap
cannot alloc NNN bytes for freemap
cannot alloc NNN bytes for statemap
cannot alloc NNN bytes for lncntp
Fsck's request for memory for its virtual memory tables failed. This should never happen. *Fsck* terminates on this error condition. See a guru.

Can't open checklist file: *F*
The file system checklist file *F* (usually */etc/fstab*) can not be opened for reading. *Fsck* terminates on this error condition. Check access modes of *F*.

Can't stat root
Fsck's request for statistics about the root directory "/" failed. This should never happen. *Fsck* terminates on this error condition. See a guru.

Can't stat *F*
Can't make sense out of name *F*
Fsck's request for statistics about the file system *F* failed. When running manually, it ignores this file system and continues checking the next file system given. Check access modes of *F*.

Can't open *F*
Fsck's request attempt to open the file system *F* failed. When running manually, it ignores this file system and continues checking the next file system given. Check access modes of *F*.

_F_: (NO WRITE)
Either the –n flag was specified or *fsck*'s attempt to open the file system *F* for writing failed. When running manually, all the diagnostics are printed out, but no modifications are attempted to fix them.

file is not a block or character device; OK
You have given *fsck* a regular file name by mistake. Check the type of the file specified.

Possible responses to the OK prompt are:

YES ignore this error condition.

NO ignore this file system and continues checking the next file system given.

UNDEFINED OPTIMIZATION IN SUPERBLOCK (SET TO DEFAULT)
The superblock optimization parameter is neither OPT_TIME nor OPT_SPACE.

Possible responses to the SET TO DEFAULT prompt are:

YES The superblock is set to request optimization to minimize running time of the system. (If optimization to minimize disk space utilization is desired, it can be set using *tunefs*(8).)

NO ignore this error condition.

IMPOSSIBLE MINFREE=_D_ IN SUPERBLOCK (SET TO DEFAULT)
The superblock minimum space percentage is greater than 99% or less then 0%.

3

Possible responses to the SET TO DEFAULT prompt are:

YES The minfree parameter is set to 10%. (If some other percentage is desired, it can be set using *tunefs*(8).)

NO ignore this error condition.

IMPOSSIBLE INTERLEAVE=_D_ IN SUPERBLOCK (SET TO DEFAULT)
The file system interleave is less than or equal to zero.

Possible responses to the SET TO DEFAULT prompt are:

YES The interleave parameter is set to 1.

NO ignore this error condition.

IMPOSSIBLE NPSECT=_D_ IN SUPERBLOCK (SET TO DEFAULT)
The number of physical sectors per track is less than the number of usable sectors per track.

Possible responses to the SET TO DEFAULT prompt are:

YES The npsect parameter is set to the number of usable sectors per track.

NO ignore this error condition.

One of the following messages will appear:
MAGIC NUMBER WRONG
NCG OUT OF RANGE
CPG OUT OF RANGE
NCYL DOES NOT JIVE WITH NCG*CPG
SIZE PREPOSTEROUSLY LARGE
TRASHED VALUES IN SUPER BLOCK
and will be followed by the message:
_F_: BAD SUPER BLOCK: _B_
USE -b OPTION TO FSCK TO SPECIFY LOCATION OF AN ALTERNATE SUPER-BLOCK TO SUPPLY NEEDED INFORMATION; SEE fsck(8).
The super block has been corrupted. An alternative super block must be selected from among those listed

by *newfs* (8) when the file system was created. For file systems with a blocksize less than 32K, specifying –b 32 is a good first choice.

INTERNAL INCONSISTENCY: ***M***
Fsck's has had an internal panic, whose message is specified as *M*. This should never happen. See a guru.

CAN NOT SEEK: BLK ***B*** **(CONTINUE)**
Fsck's request for moving to a specified block number *B* in the file system failed. This should never happen. See a guru.

Possible responses to the CONTINUE prompt are:

YES attempt to continue to run the file system check. Often, however the problem will persist. This error condition will not allow a complete check of the file system. A second run of *fsck* should be made to re-check this file system. If the block was part of the virtual memory buffer cache, *fsck* will terminate with the message "Fatal I/O error".

NO terminate the program.

CAN NOT READ: BLK ***B*** **(CONTINUE)**
Fsck's request for reading a specified block number *B* in the file system failed. This should never happen. See a guru.

Possible responses to the CONTINUE prompt are:

YES attempt to continue to run the file system check. It will retry the read and print out the message:
THE FOLLOWING SECTORS COULD NOT BE READ: ***N***
where *N* indicates the sectors that could not be read. If *fsck* ever tries to write back one of the blocks on which the read failed it will print the message:
WRITING ZERO'ED BLOCK ***N*** **TO DISK**
where *N* indicates the sector that was written with zero's. If the disk is experiencing hardware problems, the problem will persist. This error condition will not allow a complete check of the file system. A second run of *fsck* should be made to re-check this file system. If the block was part of the virtual memory buffer cache, *fsck* will terminate with the message "Fatal I/O error".

NO terminate the program.

CAN NOT WRITE: BLK ***B*** **(CONTINUE)**
Fsck's request for writing a specified block number *B* in the file system failed. The disk is write-protected; check the write protect lock on the drive. If that is not the problem, see a guru.

Possible responses to the CONTINUE prompt are:

YES attempt to continue to run the file system check. The write operation will be retried with the failed blocks indicated by the message:
THE FOLLOWING SECTORS COULD NOT BE WRITTEN: ***N***
where *N* indicates the sectors that could not be written. If the disk is experiencing hardware problems, the problem will persist. This error condition will not allow a complete check of the file system. A second run of *fsck* should be made to re-check this file system. If the block was part of the virtual memory buffer cache, *fsck* will terminate with the message "Fatal I/O error".

NO terminate the program.

bad inode number DDD to ginode
An internal error has attempted to read non-existent inode *DDD*. This error causes *fsck* to exit. See a guru.

3

4.3. Phase 1 – Check Blocks and Sizes

This phase concerns itself with the inode list. This section lists error conditions resulting from checking inode types, setting up the zero-link-count table, examining inode block numbers for bad or duplicate blocks, checking inode size, and checking inode format. All errors in this phase except **INCORRECT BLOCK COUNT** and **PARTIALLY TRUNCATED INODE** are fatal if the file system is being preen'ed.

UNKNOWN FILE TYPE I=*I* (CLEAR)
The mode word of the inode *I* indicates that the inode is not a special block inode, special character inode, socket inode, regular inode, symbolic link, or directory inode.

Possible responses to the CLEAR prompt are:

YES de-allocate inode *I* by zeroing its contents. This will always invoke the UNALLOCATED error condition in Phase 2 for each directory entry pointing to this inode.

NO ignore this error condition.

PARTIALLY TRUNCATED INODE I=*I* (SALVAGE)
Fsck has found inode *I* whose size is shorter than the number of blocks allocated to it. This condition should only occur if the system crashes while in the midst of truncating a file. When preen'ing the file system, *fsck* completes the truncation to the specified size.

3

Possible responses to SALVAGE are:

YES complete the truncation to the size specified in the inode.

NO ignore this error condition.

LINK COUNT TABLE OVERFLOW (CONTINUE)
An internal table for *fsck* containing allocated inodes with a link count of zero cannot allocate more memory. Increase the virtual memory for *fsck*.

Possible responses to the CONTINUE prompt are:

YES continue with the program. This error condition will not allow a complete check of the file system. A second run of *fsck* should be made to re-check this file system. If another allocated inode with a zero link count is found, this error condition is repeated.

NO terminate the program.

B* BAD I=*I
Inode *I* contains block number *B* with a number lower than the number of the first data block in the file system or greater than the number of the last block in the file system. This error condition may invoke the **EXCESSIVE BAD BLKS** error condition in Phase 1 (see next paragraph) if inode *I* has too many block numbers outside the file system range. This error condition will always invoke the **BAD/DUP** error condition in Phase 2 and Phase 4.

EXCESSIVE BAD BLKS I=*I* (CONTINUE)
There is more than a tolerable number (usually 10) of blocks with a number lower than the number of the first data block in the file system or greater than the number of last block in the file system associated with inode *I*.

Possible responses to the CONTINUE prompt are:

YES ignore the rest of the blocks in this inode and continue checking with the next inode in the file system. This error condition will not allow a complete check of the file system. A second run of *fsck* should be made to re-check this file system.

NO terminate the program.

BAD STATE DDD TO BLKERR
An internal error has scrambled *fsck*'s state map to have the impossible value *DDD*. *Fsck* exits immediately. See a guru.

B* DUP I=*I
Inode *I* contains block number *B* that is already claimed by another inode. This error condition may invoke the **EXCESSIVE DUP BLKS** error condition in Phase 1 if inode *I* has too many block numbers claimed by other inodes. This error condition will always invoke Phase 1b and the **BAD/DUP** error condition in Phase 2 and Phase 4.

EXCESSIVE DUP BLKS I=*I* (CONTINUE)
There is more than a tolerable number (usually 10) of blocks claimed by other inodes.

Possible responses to the CONTINUE prompt are:

YES ignore the rest of the blocks in this inode and continue checking with the next inode in the file system. This error condition will not allow a complete check of the file system. A second run of *fsck* should be made to re-check this file system.

NO terminate the program.

DUP TABLE OVERFLOW (CONTINUE)
An internal table in *fsck* containing duplicate block numbers cannot allocate any more space. Increase the amount of virtual memory available to *fsck*.

Possible responses to the CONTINUE prompt are:

YES continue with the program. This error condition will not allow a complete check of the file system. A second run of *fsck* should be made to re-check this file system. If another duplicate block is found, this error condition will repeat.

NO terminate the program.

3

PARTIALLY ALLOCATED INODE I=*I* (CLEAR)
Inode *I* is neither allocated nor unallocated.

Possible responses to the CLEAR prompt are:

YES de-allocate inode *I* by zeroing its contents.

NO ignore this error condition.

INCORRECT BLOCK COUNT I=*I* (*X* should be *Y*) (CORRECT)
The block count for inode *I* is *X* blocks, but should be *Y* blocks. When preen'ing the count is corrected.

Possible responses to the CORRECT prompt are:

YES replace the block count of inode *I* with *Y*.

NO ignore this error condition.

4.4. Phase 1B: Rescan for More Dups

When a duplicate block is found in the file system, the file system is rescanned to find the inode that previously claimed that block. This section lists the error condition when the duplicate block is found.

B* DUP I=*I
Inode *I* contains block number *B* that is already claimed by another inode. This error condition will always invoke the **BAD/DUP** error condition in Phase 2. You can determine which inodes have overlapping blocks by examining this error condition and the DUP error condition in Phase 1.

4.5. Phase 2 – Check Pathnames

This phase concerns itself with removing directory entries pointing to error conditioned inodes from Phase 1 and Phase 1b. This section lists error conditions resulting from root inode mode and status, directory inode pointers in range, and directory entries pointing to bad inodes, and directory integrity checks. All errors in this phase are fatal if the file system is being preen'ed, except for directories not being a multiple of the blocks size and extraneous hard links.

ROOT INODE UNALLOCATED (ALLOCATE)
The root inode (usually inode number 2) has no allocate mode bits. This should never happen.

Possible responses to the ALLOCATE prompt are:

YES allocate inode 2 as the root inode. The files and directories usually found in the root will be recovered in Phase 3 and put into *lost+found*. If the attempt to allocate the root fails, *fsck* will exit with the message:
CANNOT ALLOCATE ROOT INODE.

NO *fsck* will exit.

ROOT INODE NOT DIRECTORY (REALLOCATE)
The root inode (usually inode number 2) is not directory inode type.

Possible responses to the REALLOCATE prompt are:

YES clear the existing contents of the root inode and reallocate it. The files and directories usually found in the root will be recovered in Phase 3 and put into *lost+found*. If the attempt to allocate the root fails, *fsck* will exit with the message:
CANNOT ALLOCATE ROOT INODE.

NO *fsck* will then prompt with **FIX**

Possible responses to the FIX prompt are:

YES replace the root inode's type to be a directory. If the root inode's data blocks are not directory blocks, many error conditions will be produced.

NO terminate the program.

DUPS/BAD IN ROOT INODE (REALLOCATE)
Phase 1 or Phase 1b have found duplicate blocks or bad blocks in the root inode (usually inode number 2) for the file system.

Possible responses to the REALLOCATE prompt are:

YES clear the existing contents of the root inode and reallocate it. The files and directories usually found in the root will be recovered in Phase 3 and put into *lost+found*. If the attempt to allocate the root fails, *fsck* will exit with the message:
CANNOT ALLOCATE ROOT INODE.

NO *fsck* will then prompt with **CONTINUE.**

Possible responses to the CONTINUE prompt are:

YES ignore the **DUPS/BAD** error condition in the root inode and attempt to continue to run the file system check. If the root inode is not correct, then this may result in many other error conditions.

NO terminate the program.

NAME TOO LONG *F*
An excessively long path name has been found. This usually indicates loops in the file system name space. This can occur if the super user has made circular links to directories. The offending links must be removed (by a guru).

I OUT OF RANGE I=*I* NAME=*F* (REMOVE)
A directory entry *F* has an inode number *I* that is greater than the end of the inode list.

Possible responses to the REMOVE prompt are:

YES the directory entry *F* is removed.

NO ignore this error condition.

UNALLOCATED I=*I* OWNER=*O* MODE=*M* SIZE=*S* MTIME=*T* *type=F* (REMOVE)
A directory or file entry *F* points to an unallocated inode *I*. The owner *O*, mode *M*, size *S*, modify time *T*, and name *F* are printed.

Possible responses to the REMOVE prompt are:

YES the directory entry *F* is removed.

NO ignore this error condition.

DUP/BAD I=*I* OWNER=*O* MODE=*M* SIZE=*S* MTIME=*T* *type=F* (REMOVE)
Phase 1 or Phase 1b have found duplicate blocks or bad blocks associated with directory or file entry *F*, inode *I*. The owner *O*, mode *M*, size *S*, modify time *T*, and directory name *F* are printed.

Possible responses to the REMOVE prompt are:

YES the directory entry *F* is removed.

NO ignore this error condition.

ZERO LENGTH DIRECTORY I=*I* OWNER=*O* MODE=*M* SIZE=*S* MTIME=*T* DIR=*F* (REMOVE)
A directory entry *F* has a size *S* that is zero. The owner *O*, mode *M*, size *S*, modify time *T*, and directory name *F* are printed.

Possible responses to the REMOVE prompt are:

YES the directory entry *F* is removed; this will always invoke the BAD/DUP error condition in Phase 4.

NO ignore this error condition.

DIRECTORY TOO SHORT I=*I* OWNER=*O* MODE=*M* SIZE=*S* MTIME=*T* DIR=*F* (FIX)
A directory *F* has been found whose size *S* is less than the minimum size directory. The owner *O*, mode *M*, size *S*, modify time *T*, and directory name *F* are printed.

Possible responses to the FIX prompt are:

YES increase the size of the directory to the minimum directory size.

NO ignore this directory.

DIRECTORY *F* LENGTH *S* NOT MULTIPLE OF *B* (ADJUST)
A directory *F* has been found with size *S* that is not a multiple of the directory blocksize *B*.

Possible responses to the ADJUST prompt are:

YES the length is rounded up to the appropriate block size. This error can occur on 4.2BSD file systems. Thus when preen'ing the file system only a warning is printed and the directory is adjusted.

NO ignore the error condition.

DIRECTORY CORRUPTED I=*I* OWNER=*O* MODE=*M* SIZE=*S* MTIME=*T* DIR=*F* (SALVAGE)
A directory with an inconsistent internal state has been found.

Possible responses to the FIX prompt are:

3

YES throw away all entries up to the next directory boundary (usually 512-byte) boundary. This drastic action can throw away up to 42 entries, and should be taken only after other recovery efforts have failed.

NO skip up to the next directory boundary and resume reading, but do not modify the directory.

BAD INODE NUMBER FOR '.' I=*I* OWNER=*O* MODE=*M* SIZE=*S* MTIME=*T* DIR=*F* (FIX)

A directory *I* has been found whose inode number for '.' does does not equal *I*.

Possible responses to the FIX prompt are:

YES change the inode number for '.' to be equal to *I*.

NO leave the inode number for '.' unchanged.

MISSING '.' I=*I* OWNER=*O* MODE=*M* SIZE=*S* MTIME=*T* DIR=*F* (FIX)

A directory *I* has been found whose first entry is unallocated.

Possible responses to the FIX prompt are:

YES build an entry for '.' with inode number equal to *I*.

NO leave the directory unchanged.

MISSING '.' I=*I* OWNER=*O* MODE=*M* SIZE=*S* MTIME=*T* DIR=*F*
CANNOT FIX, FIRST ENTRY IN DIRECTORY CONTAINS *F*

A directory *I* has been found whose first entry is *F*. *Fsck* cannot resolve this problem. The file system should be mounted and the offending entry *F* moved elsewhere. The file system should then be unmounted and *fsck* should be run again.

3

MISSING '.' I=*I* OWNER=*O* MODE=*M* SIZE=*S* MTIME=*T* DIR=*F*
CANNOT FIX, INSUFFICIENT SPACE TO ADD '.'

A directory *I* has been found whose first entry is not '.'. *Fsck* cannot resolve this problem as it should never happen. See a guru.

EXTRA '.' ENTRY I=*I* OWNER=*O* MODE=*M* SIZE=*S* MTIME=*T* DIR=*F* (FIX)

A directory *I* has been found that has more than one entry for '.'.

Possible responses to the FIX prompt are:

YES remove the extra entry for '.'.

NO leave the directory unchanged.

BAD INODE NUMBER FOR '..' I=*I* OWNER=*O* MODE=*M* SIZE=*S* MTIME=*T* DIR=*F* (FIX)

A directory *I* has been found whose inode number for '..' does does not equal the parent of *I*.

Possible responses to the FIX prompt are:

YES change the inode number for '..' to be equal to the parent of *I* (''**..**'' in the root inode points to itself).

NO leave the inode number for '..' unchanged.

MISSING '..' I=*I* OWNER=*O* MODE=*M* SIZE=*S* MTIME=*T* DIR=*F* (FIX)

A directory *I* has been found whose second entry is unallocated.

Possible responses to the FIX prompt are:

YES build an entry for '..' with inode number equal to the parent of *I* (''**..**'' in the root inode points to itself).

NO leave the directory unchanged.

MISSING '..' I=*I* OWNER=*O* MODE=*M* SIZE=*S* MTIME=*T* DIR=*F*
CANNOT FIX, SECOND ENTRY IN DIRECTORY CONTAINS *F*
A directory *I* has been found whose second entry is *F*. *Fsck* cannot resolve this problem. The file system should be mounted and the offending entry *F* moved elsewhere. The file system should then be unmounted and *fsck* should be run again.

MISSING '..' I=*I* OWNER=*O* MODE=*M* SIZE=*S* MTIME=*T* DIR=*F*
CANNOT FIX, INSUFFICIENT SPACE TO ADD '..'
A directory *I* has been found whose second entry is not '..'. *Fsck* cannot resolve this problem. The file system should be mounted and the second entry in the directory moved elsewhere. The file system should then be unmounted and *fsck* should be run again.

EXTRA '..' ENTRY I=*I* OWNER=*O* MODE=*M* SIZE=*S* MTIME=*T* DIR=*F* (FIX)
A directory *I* has been found that has more than one entry for '..'.

Possible responses to the FIX prompt are:

YES remove the extra entry for '..'.

NO leave the directory unchanged.

***N* IS AN EXTRANEOUS HARD LINK TO A DIRECTORY *D* (REMOVE)**
Fsck has found a hard link, *N*, to a directory, *D*. When preen'ing the extraneous links are ignored.

Possible responses to the REMOVE prompt are:

YES delete the extraneous entry, *N*.

NO ignore the error condition.

3

BAD INODE *S* TO DESCEND
An internal error has caused an impossible state *S* to be passed to the routine that descends the file system directory structure. *Fsck* exits. See a guru.

BAD RETURN STATE *S* FROM DESCEND
An internal error has caused an impossible state *S* to be returned from the routine that descends the file system directory structure. *Fsck* exits. See a guru.

BAD STATE *S* FOR ROOT INODE
An internal error has caused an impossible state *S* to be assigned to the root inode. *Fsck* exits. See a guru.

4.6. Phase 3 – Check Connectivity

This phase concerns itself with the directory connectivity seen in Phase 2. This section lists error conditions resulting from unreferenced directories, and missing or full *lost+found* directories.

UNREF DIR I=*I* OWNER=*O* MODE=*M* SIZE=*S* MTIME=*T* (RECONNECT)
The directory inode *I* was not connected to a directory entry when the file system was traversed. The owner *O*, mode *M*, size *S*, and modify time *T* of directory inode *I* are printed. When preen'ing, the directory is reconnected if its size is non-zero, otherwise it is cleared.

Possible responses to the RECONNECT prompt are:

YES reconnect directory inode *I* to the file system in the directory for lost files (usually *lost+found*). This may invoke the *lost+found* error condition in Phase 3 if there are problems connecting directory inode *I* to *lost+found*. This may also invoke the CONNECTED error condition in Phase 3 if the link was successful.

NO ignore this error condition. This will always invoke the UNREF error condition in Phase 4.

NO lost+found DIRECTORY (CREATE)

There is no *lost+found* directory in the root directory of the file system; When preen'ing *fsck* tries to create a *lost+found* directory.

Possible responses to the CREATE prompt are:

YES create a *lost+found* directory in the root of the file system. This may raise the message:
NO SPACE LEFT IN / (EXPAND)
See below for the possible responses. Inability to create a *lost+found* directory generates the message:
SORRY. CANNOT CREATE lost+found DIRECTORY
and aborts the attempt to linkup the lost inode. This will always invoke the UNREF error condition in Phase 4.

NO abort the attempt to linkup the lost inode. This will always invoke the UNREF error condition in Phase 4.

lost+found IS NOT A DIRECTORY (REALLOCATE)

The entry for *lost+found* is not a directory.

Possible responses to the REALLOCATE prompt are:

YES allocate a directory inode, and change *lost+found* to reference it. The previous inode reference by the *lost+found* name is not cleared. Thus it will either be reclaimed as an UNREF'ed inode or have its link count ADJUST'ed later in this Phase. Inability to create a *lost+found* directory generates the message:
SORRY. CANNOT CREATE lost+found DIRECTORY
and aborts the attempt to linkup the lost inode. This will always invoke the UNREF error condition in Phase 4.

NO abort the attempt to linkup the lost inode. This will always invoke the UNREF error condition in Phase 4.

3

NO SPACE LEFT IN /lost+found (EXPAND)

There is no space to add another entry to the *lost+found* directory in the root directory of the file system. When preen'ing the *lost+found* directory is expanded.

Possible responses to the EXPAND prompt are:

YES the *lost+found* directory is expanded to make room for the new entry. If the attempted expansion fails *fsck* prints the message:
SORRY. NO SPACE IN lost+found DIRECTORY
and aborts the attempt to linkup the lost inode. This will always invoke the UNREF error condition in Phase 4. Clean out unnecessary entries in *lost+found*. This error is fatal if the file system is being preen'ed.

NO abort the attempt to linkup the lost inode. This will always invoke the UNREF error condition in Phase 4.

DIR I=*I1* CONNECTED. PARENT WAS I=*I2*

This is an advisory message indicating a directory inode *I1* was successfully connected to the *lost+found* directory. The parent inode *I2* of the directory inode *I1* is replaced by the inode number of the *lost+found* directory.

DIRECTORY *F* LENGTH *S* NOT MULTIPLE OF *B* (ADJUST)

A directory *F* has been found with size *S* that is not a multiple of the directory blocksize *B* (this can reoccur in Phase 3 if it is not adjusted in Phase 2).

Possible responses to the ADJUST prompt are:

YES the length is rounded up to the appropriate block size. This error can occur on 4.2BSD file systems. Thus when preen'ing the file system only a warning is printed and the directory is adjusted.

NO ignore the error condition.

BAD INODE *S* TO DESCEND
An internal error has caused an impossible state *S* to be passed to the routine that descends the file system directory structure. *Fsck* exits. See a guru.

4.7. Phase 4 – Check Reference Counts

This phase concerns itself with the link count information seen in Phase 2 and Phase 3. This section lists error conditions resulting from unreferenced files, missing or full *lost+found* directory, incorrect link counts for files, directories, symbolic links, or special files, unreferenced files, symbolic links, and directories, and bad or duplicate blocks in files, symbolic links, and directories. All errors in this phase are correctable if the file system is being preen'ed except running out of space in the *lost+found* directory.

UNREF FILE I=*I* OWNER=*O* MODE=*M* SIZE=*S* MTIME=*T* (RECONNECT)
Inode *I* was not connected to a directory entry when the file system was traversed. The owner *O*, mode *M*, size *S*, and modify time *T* of inode *I* are printed. When preen'ing the file is cleared if either its size or its link count is zero, otherwise it is reconnected.

Possible responses to the RECONNECT prompt are:

YES reconnect inode *I* to the file system in the directory for lost files (usually *lost+found*). This may invoke the *lost+found* error condition in Phase 4 if there are problems connecting inode *I* to *lost+found*.

NO ignore this error condition. This will always invoke the CLEAR error condition in Phase 4.

3

(CLEAR)
The inode mentioned in the immediately previous error condition can not be reconnected. This cannot occur if the file system is being preen'ed, since lack of space to reconnect files is a fatal error.

Possible responses to the CLEAR prompt are:

YES de-allocate the inode mentioned in the immediately previous error condition by zeroing its contents.

NO ignore this error condition.

NO lost+found DIRECTORY (CREATE)
There is no *lost+found* directory in the root directory of the file system; When preen'ing *fsck* tries to create a *lost+found* directory.

Possible responses to the CREATE prompt are:

YES create a *lost+found* directory in the root of the file system. This may raise the message:
NO SPACE LEFT IN / (EXPAND)
See below for the possible responses. Inability to create a *lost+found* directory generates the message:
SORRY. CANNOT CREATE lost+found DIRECTORY
and aborts the attempt to linkup the lost inode. This will always invoke the UNREF error condition in Phase 4.

NO abort the attempt to linkup the lost inode. This will always invoke the UNREF error condition in Phase 4.

lost+found IS NOT A DIRECTORY (REALLOCATE)
The entry for *lost+found* is not a directory.

Possible responses to the REALLOCATE prompt are:

YES allocate a directory inode, and change *lost+found* to reference it. The previous inode reference by the *lost+found* name is not cleared. Thus it will either be reclaimed as an UNREF'ed inode or have its link count ADJUST'ed later in this Phase. Inability to create a *lost+found* directory generates the message:
SORRY. CANNOT CREATE lost+found DIRECTORY
and aborts the attempt to linkup the lost inode. This will always invoke the UNREF error condition in Phase 4.

NO abort the attempt to linkup the lost inode. This will always invoke the UNREF error condition in Phase 4.

NO SPACE LEFT IN /lost+found (EXPAND)
There is no space to add another entry to the *lost+found* directory in the root directory of the file system. When preen'ing the *lost+found* directory is expanded.

Possible responses to the EXPAND prompt are:

YES the *lost+found* directory is expanded to make room for the new entry. If the attempted expansion fails *fsck* prints the message:
SORRY. NO SPACE IN lost+found DIRECTORY
and aborts the attempt to linkup the lost inode. This will always invoke the UNREF error condition in Phase 4. Clean out unnecessary entries in *lost+found*. This error is fatal if the file system is being preen'ed.

3

NO abort the attempt to linkup the lost inode. This will always invoke the UNREF error condition in Phase 4.

LINK COUNT *type* **I=***I* **OWNER=***O* **MODE=***M* **SIZE=***S* **MTIME=***T* **COUNT=***X* **SHOULD BE** *Y* **(ADJUST)**
The link count for inode *I*, is *X* but should be *Y*. The owner *O*, mode *M*, size *S*, and modify time *T* are printed. When preen'ing the link count is adjusted unless the number of references is increasing, a condition that should never occur unless precipitated by a hardware failure. When the number of references is increasing under preen mode, *fsck* exits with the message:
LINK COUNT INCREASING

Possible responses to the ADJUST prompt are:

YES replace the link count of file inode *I* with *Y*.

NO ignore this error condition.

UNREF *type* **I=***I* **OWNER=***O* **MODE=***M* **SIZE=***S* **MTIME=***T* **(CLEAR)**
Inode *I*, was not connected to a directory entry when the file system was traversed. The owner *O*, mode *M*, size *S*, and modify time *T* of inode *I* are printed. When preen'ing, this is a file that was not connected because its size or link count was zero, hence it is cleared.

Possible responses to the CLEAR prompt are:

YES de-allocate inode *I* by zeroing its contents.

NO ignore this error condition.

BAD/DUP *type* **I=***I* **OWNER=***O* **MODE=***M* **SIZE=***S* **MTIME=***T* **(CLEAR)**
Phase 1 or Phase 1b have found duplicate blocks or bad blocks associated with inode *I*. The owner *O*, mode *M*, size *S*, and modify time *T* of inode *I* are printed. This error cannot arise when the file system is being preen'ed, as it would have caused a fatal error earlier.

Possible responses to the CLEAR prompt are:

YES de-allocate inode *I* by zeroing its contents.

NO ignore this error condition.

4.8. Phase 5 - Check Cyl groups

This phase concerns itself with the free-block and used-inode maps. This section lists error conditions resulting from allocated blocks in the free-block maps, free blocks missing from free-block maps, and the total free-block count incorrect. It also lists error conditions resulting from free inodes in the used-inode maps, allocated inodes missing from used-inode maps, and the total used-inode count incorrect.

CG *C*: BAD MAGIC NUMBER
The magic number of cylinder group *C* is wrong. This usually indicates that the cylinder group maps have been destroyed. When running manually the cylinder group is marked as needing to be reconstructed. This error is fatal if the file system is being preen'ed.

BLK(S) MISSING IN BIT MAPS (SALVAGE)
A cylinder group block map is missing some free blocks. During preen'ing the maps are reconstructed.

Possible responses to the SALVAGE prompt are:

YES reconstruct the free block map.

NO ignore this error condition.

SUMMARY INFORMATION BAD (SALVAGE)
The summary information was found to be incorrect. When preen'ing, the summary information is recomputed.

Possible responses to the SALVAGE prompt are:

YES reconstruct the summary information.

NO ignore this error condition.

FREE BLK COUNT(S) WRONG IN SUPERBLOCK (SALVAGE)
The superblock free block information was found to be incorrect. When preen'ing, the superblock free block information is recomputed.

Possible responses to the SALVAGE prompt are:

YES reconstruct the superblock free block information.

NO ignore this error condition.

4.9. Cleanup

Once a file system has been checked, a few cleanup functions are performed. This section lists advisory messages about the file system and modify status of the file system.

***V* files, *W* used, *X* free (*Y* frags, *Z* blocks)**
This is an advisory message indicating that the file system checked contained *V* files using *W* fragment sized blocks leaving *X* fragment sized blocks free in the file system. The numbers in parenthesis breaks the free count down into *Y* free fragments and *Z* free full sized blocks.

******* REBOOT UNIX *******
This is an advisory message indicating that the root file system has been modified by *fsck*. If UNIX is not rebooted immediately, the work done by *fsck* may be undone by the in-core copies of tables UNIX keeps. When preen'ing, *fsck* will exit with a code of 4. The standard auto-reboot script distributed with 4.3BSD interprets an exit code of 4 by issuing a reboot system call.

******* FILE SYSTEM WAS MODIFIED *******

This is an advisory message indicating that the current file system was modified by *fsck.* If this file system is mounted or is the current root file system, *fsck* should be halted and UNIX rebooted. If UNIX is not rebooted immediately, the work done by *fsck* may be undone by the in-core copies of tables UNIX keeps.

Disc Quotas in a UNIX[*] Environment

Robert Elz

Department of Computer Science
University of Melbourne,
Parkville,
Victoria,
Australia.

ABSTRACT

In most computing environments, disc space is not infinite. The disc quota system provides a mechanism to control usage of disc space, on an individual basis.

Quotas may be set for each individual user, on any, or all filesystems.

The quota system will warn users when they exceed their allotted limit, but allow some extra space for current work. Repeatedly remaining over quota at logout, will cause a fatal over quota condition eventually.

The quota system is an optional part of VMUNIX that may be included when the system is configured.

1. Users' view of disc quotas

To most users, disc quotas will either be of no concern, or a fact of life that cannot be avoided. The *quota* (1) command will provide information on any disc quotas that may have been imposed upon a user.

There are two individual possible quotas that may be imposed, usually if one is, both will be. A limit can be set on the amount of space a user can occupy, and there may be a limit on the number of files (inodes) he can own.

Quota provides information on the quotas that have been set by the system administrators, in each of these areas, and current usage.

There are four numbers for each limit, the current usage, soft limit (quota), hard limit, and number of remaining login warnings. The soft limit is the number of 1K blocks (or files) that the user is expected to remain below. Each time the user's usage goes past this limit, he will be warned. The hard limit cannot be exceeded. If a user's usage reaches this number, further requests for space (or attempts to create a file) will fail with an EDQUOT error, and the first time this occurs, a message will be written to the user's terminal. Only one message will be output, until space occupied is reduced below the limit, and reaches it again, in order to avoid continual noise from those programs that ignore write errors.

Whenever a user logs in with a usage greater than his soft limit, he will be warned, and his login warning count decremented. When he logs in under quota, the counter is reset to its maximum value (which is a system configuration parameter, that is typically 3). If the warning count should ever reach zero (caused by three successive logins over quota), the particular limit that has been exceeded will be treated as if the hard limit has been reached, and no more resources will be allocated to the user. The **only** way to reset this condition is to reduce usage below quota, then log in again.

* UNIX is a trademark of Bell Laboratories.

1.1. Surviving when quota limit is reached

In most cases, the only way to recover from over quota conditions, is to abort whatever activity was in progress on the filesystem that has reached its limit, remove sufficient files to bring the limit back below quota, and retry the failed program.

However, if you are in the editor and a write fails because of an over quota situation, that is not a suitable course of action, as it is most likely that initially attempting to write the file will have truncated its previous contents, so should the editor be aborted without correctly writing the file not only will the recent changes be lost, but possibly much, or even all, of the data that previously existed.

There are several possible safe exits for a user caught in this situation. He may use the editor **!** shell escape command to examine his file space, and remove surplus files. Alternatively, using *csh*, he may suspend the editor, remove some files, then resume it. A third possibility, is to write the file to some other filesystem (perhaps to a file on /tmp) where the user's quota has not been exceeded. Then after rectifying the quota situation, the file can be moved back to the filesystem it belongs on.

2. Administering the quota system

To set up and establish the disc quota system, there are several steps necessary to be performed by the system administrator.

First, the system must be configured to include the disc quota sub-system. This is done by including the line:

```
options QUOTA
```

in the system configuration file, then running *config* (8) followed by a system configuration*.

Second, a decision as to what filesystems need to have quotas applied needs to be made. Usually, only filesystems that house users' home directories, or other user files, will need to be subjected to the quota system, though it may also prove useful to also include **/usr**. If possible, **/tmp** should usually be free of quotas.

4

Having decided on which filesystems quotas need to be set upon, the administrator should then allocate the available space amongst the competing needs. How this should be done is (way) beyond the scope of this document.

Then, the *edquota* (8) command can be used to actually set the limits desired upon each user. Where a number of users are to be given the same quotas (a common occurrence) the **–p** switch to edquota will allow this to be easily accomplished.

Once the quotas are set, ready to operate, the system must be informed to enforce quotas on the desired filesystems. This is accomplished with the *quotaon* (8) command. *Quotaon* will either enable quotas for a particular filesystem, or with the **–a** switch, will enable quotas for each filesystem indicated in **/etc/fstab** as using quotas. See *fstab* (5) for details. Most sites using the quota system, will include the line

```
/etc/quotaon -a
```

in **/etc/rc.local**.

Should quotas need to be disabled, the *quotaoff*(8) command will do that, however, should the filesystem be about to be dismounted, the *umount* (8) command will disable quotas immediately before the filesystem is unmounted. This is actually an effect of the *umount* (2) system call, and it guarantees that the quota system will not be disabled if the umount would fail because the filesystem is not idle.

Periodically (certainly after each reboot, and when quotas are first enabled for a filesystem), the records retained in the quota file should be checked for consistency with the actual number of blocks and files allocated to the user. The *quotacheck* (8) command can be used to accomplish this. It is not necessary to dismount the filesystem, or disable the quota system to run this command, though on active filesystems inaccurate results may occur. This does no real harm in most cases, another run of *quotacheck* when the filesystem is idle will certainly correct any inaccuracy.

---

* See also the document "Building 4.2BSD UNIX Systems with Config".

The super-user may use the *quota* (1) command to examine the usage and quotas of any user, and the *repquota* (8) command may be used to check the usages and limits for all users on a filesystem.

3. Some implementation detail.

Disc quota usage and information is stored in a file on the filesystem that the quotas are to be applied to. Conventionally, this file is **quotas** in the root of the filesystem. While this name is not known to the system in any way, several of the user level utilities "know" it, and choosing any other name would not be wise.

The data in the file comprises an array of structures, indexed by uid, one structure for each user on the system (whether the user has a quota on this filesystem or not). If the uid space is sparse, then the file may have holes in it, which would be lost by copying, so it is best to avoid this.

The system is informed of the existence of the quota file by the *setquota* (2) system call. It then reads the quota entries for each user currently active, then for any files open owned by users who are not currently active. Each subsequent open of a file on the filesystem, will be accompanied by a pairing with its quota information. In most cases this information will be retained in core, either because the user who owns the file is running some process, because other files are open owned by the same user, or because some file (perhaps this one) was recently accessed. In memory, the quota information is kept hashed by user-id and filesystem, and retained in an LRU chain so recently released data can be easily reclaimed. Information about those users whose last process has recently terminated is also retained in this way.

Each time a block is accessed or released, and each time an inode is allocated or freed, the quota system gets told about it, and in the case of allocations, gets the opportunity to object.

Measurements have shown that the quota code uses a very small percentage of the system cpu time consumed in writing a new block to disc.

4. Acknowledgments

The current disc quota system is loosely based upon a very early scheme implemented at the University of New South Wales, and Sydney University in the mid 70's. That system implemented a single combined limit for both files and blocks on all filesystems.

A later system was implemented at the University of Melbourne by the author, but was not kept highly accurately, eg: chown's (etc) did not affect quotas, nor did i/o to a file other than one owned by the instigator.

The current system has been running (with only minor modifications) since January 82 at Melbourne. It is actually just a small part of a much broader resource control scheme, which is capable of controlling almost anything that is usually uncontrolled in unix. The rest of this is, as yet, still in a state where it is far too subject to change to be considered for distribution.

For the 4.2BSD release, much work has been done to clean up and sanely incorporate the quota code by Sam Leffler and Kirk McKusick at The University of California at Berkeley.

A Fast File System for UNIX*

Marshall Kirk McKusick, William N. Joy†,
Samuel J. Leffler‡, Robert S. Fabry

Computer Systems Research Group
Computer Science Division
Department of Electrical Engineering and Computer Science
University of California, Berkeley
Berkeley, CA 94720

ABSTRACT

A reimplementation of the UNIX file system is described. The reimplementation provides substantially higher throughput rates by using more flexible allocation policies that allow better locality of reference and can be adapted to a wide range of peripheral and processor characteristics. The new file system clusters data that is sequentially accessed and provides two block sizes to allow fast access to large files while not wasting large amounts of space for small files. File access rates of up to ten times faster than the traditional UNIX file system are experienced. Long needed enhancements to the programmers' interface are discussed. These include a mechanism to place advisory locks on files, extensions of the name space across file systems, the ability to use long file names, and provisions for administrative control of resource usage.

Revised February 18, 1984

CR Categories and Subject Descriptors: D.4.3 **[Operating Systems]**: File Systems Management – *file organization, directory structures, access methods*; D.4.2 **[Operating Systems]**: Storage Management – *allocation/deallocation strategies, secondary storage devices*; D.4.8 **[Operating Systems]**: Performance – *measurements, operational analysis*; H.3.2 **[Information Systems]**: Information Storage – *file organization*

Additional Keywords and Phrases: UNIX, file system organization, file system performance, file system design, application program interface.

General Terms: file system, measurement, performance.

5

* UNIX is a trademark of Bell Laboratories.

† William N. Joy is currently employed by: Sun Microsystems, Inc, 2550 Garcia Avenue, Mountain View, CA 94043

‡ Samuel J. Leffler is currently employed by: Lucasfilm Ltd., PO Box 2009, San Rafael, CA 94912

This work was done under grants from the National Science Foundation under grant MCS80-05144, and the Defense Advance Research Projects Agency (DoD) under ARPA Order No. 4031 monitored by Naval Electronic System Command under Contract No. N00039-82-C-0235.

TABLE OF CONTENTS

1. Introduction

This paper describes the changes from the original 512 byte UNIX file system to the new one released with the 4.2 Berkeley Software Distribution. It presents the motivations for the changes, the methods used to effect these changes, the rationale behind the design decisions, and a description of the new implementation. This discussion is followed by a summary of the results that have been obtained, directions for future work, and the additions and changes that have been made to the facilities that are available to programmers.

The original UNIX system that runs on the PDP-11† has simple and elegant file system facilities. File system input/output is buffered by the kernel; there are no alignment constraints on data transfers and all operations are made to appear synchronous. All transfers to the disk are in 512 byte blocks, which can be placed arbitrarily within the data area of the file system. Virtually no constraints other than available disk space are placed on file growth [Ritchie74], [Thompson78].*

When used on the VAX-11 together with other UNIX enhancements, the original 512 byte UNIX file system is incapable of providing the data throughput rates that many applications require. For example, applications such as VLSI design and image processing do a small amount of processing on a large quantities of data and need to have a high throughput from the file system. High throughput rates are also needed by programs that map files from the file system into large virtual address spaces. Paging data in and out of the file system is likely to occur frequently [Ferrin82b]. This requires a file system providing higher bandwidth than the original 512 byte UNIX one that provides only about two percent of the maximum disk bandwidth or about 20 kilobytes per second per arm [White80], [Smith81b].

Modifications have been made to the UNIX file system to improve its performance. Since the UNIX file system interface is well understood and not inherently slow, this development retained the abstraction and simply changed the underlying implementation to increase its throughput. Consequently, users of the system have not been faced with massive software conversion.

Problems with file system performance have been dealt with extensively in the literature; see [Smith81a] for a survey. Previous work to improve the UNIX file system performance has been done by

† DEC, PDP, VAX, MASSBUS, and UNIBUS are trademarks of Digital Equipment Corporation.
* In practice, a file's size is constrained to be less than about one gigabyte.

[Ferrin82a]. The UNIX operating system drew many of its ideas from Multics, a large, high performance operating system [Feiertag71]. Other work includes Hydra [Almes78], Spice [Thompson80], and a file system for a LISP environment [Symbolics81]. A good introduction to the physical latencies of disks is described in [Pechura83].

2. Old File System

In the file system developed at Bell Laboratories (the ''traditional'' file system), each disk drive is divided into one or more partitions. Each of these disk partitions may contain one file system. A file system never spans multiple partitions.† A file system is described by its super-block, which contains the basic parameters of the file system. These include the number of data blocks in the file system, a count of the maximum number of files, and a pointer to the *free list*, a linked list of all the free blocks in the file system.

Within the file system are files. Certain files are distinguished as directories and contain pointers to files that may themselves be directories. Every file has a descriptor associated with it called an *inode*. An inode contains information describing ownership of the file, time stamps marking last modification and access times for the file, and an array of indices that point to the data blocks for the file. For the purposes of this section, we assume that the first 8 blocks of the file are directly referenced by values stored in an inode itself*. An inode may also contain references to indirect blocks containing further data block indices. In a file system with a 512 byte block size, a singly indirect block contains 128 further block addresses, a doubly indirect block contains 128 addresses of further singly indirect blocks, and a triply indirect block contains 128 addresses of further doubly indirect blocks.

A 150 megabyte traditional UNIX file system consists of 4 megabytes of inodes followed by 146 megabytes of data. This organization segregates the inode information from the data; thus accessing a file normally incurs a long seek from the file's inode to its data. Files in a single directory are not typically allocated consecutive slots in the 4 megabytes of inodes, causing many non-consecutive blocks of inodes to be accessed when executing operations on the inodes of several files in a directory.

The allocation of data blocks to files is also suboptimum. The traditional file system never transfers more than 512 bytes per disk transaction and often finds that the next sequential data block is not on the same cylinder, forcing seeks between 512 byte transfers. The combination of the small block size, limited read-ahead in the system, and many seeks severely limits file system throughput.

The first work at Berkeley on the UNIX file system attempted to improve both reliability and throughput. The reliability was improved by staging modifications to critical file system information so that they could either be completed or repaired cleanly by a program after a crash [Kowalski78]. The file system performance was improved by a factor of more than two by changing the basic block size from 512 to 1024 bytes. The increase was because of two factors: each disk transfer accessed twice as much data, and most files could be described without need to access indirect blocks since the direct blocks contained twice as much data. The file system with these changes will henceforth be referred to as the *old file system.*

This performance improvement gave a strong indication that increasing the block size was a good method for improving throughput. Although the throughput had doubled, the old file system was still using only about four percent of the disk bandwidth. The main problem was that although the free list was initially ordered for optimal access, it quickly became scrambled as files were created and removed. Eventually the free list became entirely random, causing files to have their blocks allocated randomly over the disk. This forced a seek before every block access. Although old file systems provided transfer rates of up to 175 kilobytes per second when they were first created, this rate deteriorated to 30 kilobytes per second after a few weeks of moderate use because of this randomization of data block placement. There was no

† By ''partition'' here we refer to the subdivision of physical space on a disk drive. In the traditional file system, as in the new file system, file systems are really located in logical disk partitions that may overlap. This overlapping is made available, for example, to allow programs to copy entire disk drives containing multiple file systems.

* The actual number may vary from system to system, but is usually in the range 5-13.

way of restoring the performance of an old file system except to dump, rebuild, and restore the file system. Another possibility, as suggested by [Maruyama76], would be to have a process that periodically reorganized the data on the disk to restore locality.

3. New file system organization

In the new file system organization (as in the old file system organization), each disk drive contains one or more file systems. A file system is described by its super-block, located at the beginning of the file system's disk partition. Because the super-block contains critical data, it is replicated to protect against catastrophic loss. This is done when the file system is created; since the super-block data does not change, the copies need not be referenced unless a head crash or other hard disk error causes the default super-block to be unusable.

To insure that it is possible to create files as large as 2^{32} bytes with only two levels of indirection, the minimum size of a file system block is 4096 bytes. The size of file system blocks can be any power of two greater than or equal to 4096. The block size of a file system is recorded in the file system's super-block so it is possible for file systems with different block sizes to be simultaneously accessible on the same system. The block size must be decided at the time that the file system is created; it cannot be subsequently changed without rebuilding the file system.

The new file system organization divides a disk partition into one or more areas called *cylinder groups*. A cylinder group is comprised of one or more consecutive cylinders on a disk. Associated with each cylinder group is some bookkeeping information that includes a redundant copy of the super-block, space for inodes, a bit map describing available blocks in the cylinder group, and summary information describing the usage of data blocks within the cylinder group. The bit map of available blocks in the cylinder group replaces the traditional file system's free list. For each cylinder group a static number of inodes is allocated at file system creation time. The default policy is to allocate one inode for each 2048 bytes of space in the cylinder group, expecting this to be far more than will ever be needed.

All the cylinder group bookkeeping information could be placed at the beginning of each cylinder group. However if this approach were used, all the redundant information would be on the top platter. A single hardware failure that destroyed the top platter could cause the loss of all redundant copies of the super-block. Thus the cylinder group bookkeeping information begins at a varying offset from the beginning of the cylinder group. The offset for each successive cylinder group is calculated to be about one track further from the beginning of the cylinder group than the preceding cylinder group. In this way the redundant information spirals down into the pack so that any single track, cylinder, or platter can be lost without losing all copies of the super-block. Except for the first cylinder group, the space between the beginning of the cylinder group and the beginning of the cylinder group information is used for data blocks.†

3.1. Optimizing storage utilization

Data is laid out so that larger blocks can be transferred in a single disk transaction, greatly increasing file system throughput. As an example, consider a file in the new file system composed of 4096 byte data blocks. In the old file system this file would be composed of 1024 byte blocks. By increasing the block size, disk accesses in the new file system may transfer up to four times as much information per disk transaction. In large files, several 4096 byte blocks may be allocated from the same cylinder so that even larger data transfers are possible before requiring a seek.

† While it appears that the first cylinder group could be laid out with its super-block at the ''known'' location, this would not work for file systems with blocks sizes of 16 kilobytes or greater. This is because of a requirement that the first 8 kilobytes of the disk be reserved for a bootstrap program and a separate requirement that the cylinder group information begin on a file system block boundary. To start the cylinder group on a file system block boundary, file systems with block sizes larger than 8 kilobytes would have to leave an empty space between the end of the boot block and the beginning of the cylinder group. Without knowing the size of the file system blocks, the system would not know what roundup function to use to find the beginning of the first cylinder group.

The main problem with larger blocks is that most UNIX file systems are composed of many small files. A uniformly large block size wastes space. Table 1 shows the effect of file system block size on the amount of wasted space in the file system. The files measured to obtain these figures reside on one of our time sharing systems that has roughly 1.2 gigabytes of on-line storage. The measurements are based on the active user file systems containing about 920 megabytes of formatted space.

Space used	% waste	Organization
775.2 Mb	0.0	Data only, no separation between files
807.8 Mb	4.2	Data only, each file starts on 512 byte boundary
828.7 Mb	6.9	Data + inodes, 512 byte block UNIX file system
866.5 Mb	11.8	Data + inodes, 1024 byte block UNIX file system
948.5 Mb	22.4	Data + inodes, 2048 byte block UNIX file system
1128.3 Mb	45.6	Data + inodes, 4096 byte block UNIX file system

Table 1 – Amount of wasted space as a function of block size.

The space wasted is calculated to be the percentage of space on the disk not containing user data. As the block size on the disk increases, the waste rises quickly, to an intolerable 45.6% waste with 4096 byte file system blocks.

To be able to use large blocks without undue waste, small files must be stored in a more efficient way. The new file system accomplishes this goal by allowing the division of a single file system block into one or more *fragments*. The file system fragment size is specified at the time that the file system is created; each file system block can optionally be broken into 2, 4, or 8 fragments, each of which is addressable. The lower bound on the size of these fragments is constrained by the disk sector size, typically 512 bytes. The block map associated with each cylinder group records the space available in a cylinder group at the fragment level; to determine if a block is available, aligned fragments are examined. Figure 1 shows a piece of a map from a 4096/1024 file system.

Bits in map	XXXX	XXOO	OOXX	OOOO
Fragment numbers	0-3	4-7	8-11	12-15
Block numbers	0	1	2	3

Figure 1 – Example layout of blocks and fragments in a 4096/1024 file system.

Each bit in the map records the status of a fragment; an "X" shows that the fragment is in use, while a "O" shows that the fragment is available for allocation. In this example, fragments 0–5, 10, and 11 are in use, while fragments 6–9, and 12–15 are free. Fragments of adjoining blocks cannot be used as a full block, even if they are large enough. In this example, fragments 6–9 cannot be allocated as a full block; only fragments 12–15 can be coalesced into a full block.

On a file system with a block size of 4096 bytes and a fragment size of 1024 bytes, a file is represented by zero or more 4096 byte blocks of data, and possibly a single fragmented block. If a file system block must be fragmented to obtain space for a small amount of data, the remaining fragments of the block are made available for allocation to other files. As an example consider an 11000 byte file stored on a 4096/1024 byte file system. This file would uses two full size blocks and one three fragment portion of another block. If no block with three aligned fragments is available at the time the file is created, a full size block is split yielding the necessary fragments and a single unused fragment. This remaining fragment can be allocated to another file as needed.

Space is allocated to a file when a program does a *write* system call. Each time data is written to a file, the system checks to see if the size of the file has increased*. If the file needs to be expanded to hold the new data, one of three conditions exists:

5

* A program may be overwriting data in the middle of an existing file in which case space would already have been allocated.

1) There is enough space left in an already allocated block or fragment to hold the new data. The new data is written into the available space.

2) The file contains no fragmented blocks (and the last block in the file contains insufficient space to hold the new data). If space exists in a block already allocated, the space is filled with new data. If the remainder of the new data contains more than a full block of data, a full block is allocated and the first full block of new data is written there. This process is repeated until less than a full block of new data remains. If the remaining new data to be written will fit in less than a full block, a block with the necessary fragments is located, otherwise a full block is located. The remaining new data is written into the located space.

3) The file contains one or more fragments (and the fragments contain insufficient space to hold the new data). If the size of the new data plus the size of the data already in the fragments exceeds the size of a full block, a new block is allocated. The contents of the fragments are copied to the beginning of the block and the remainder of the block is filled with new data. The process then continues as in (2) above. Otherwise, if the new data to be written will fit in less than a full block, a block with the necessary fragments is located, otherwise a full block is located. The contents of the existing fragments appended with the new data are written into the allocated space.

The problem with expanding a file one fragment at a a time is that data may be copied many times as a fragmented block expands to a full block. Fragment reallocation can be minimized if the user program writes a full block at a time, except for a partial block at the end of the file. Since file systems with different block sizes may reside on the same system, the file system interface has been extended to provide application programs the optimal size for a read or write. For files the optimal size is the block size of the file system on which the file is being accessed. For other objects, such as pipes and sockets, the optimal size is the underlying buffer size. This feature is used by the Standard Input/Output Library, a package used by most user programs. This feature is also used by certain system utilities such as archivers and loaders that do their own input and output management and need the highest possible file system bandwidth.

The amount of wasted space in the 4096/1024 byte new file system organization is empirically observed to be about the same as in the 1024 byte old file system organization. A file system with 4096 byte blocks and 512 byte fragments has about the same amount of wasted space as the 512 byte block UNIX file system. The new file system uses less space than the 512 byte or 1024 byte file systems for indexing information for large files and the same amount of space for small files. These savings are offset by the need to use more space for keeping track of available free blocks. The net result is about the same disk utilization when a new file system's fragment size equals an old file system's block size.

In order for the layout policies to be effective, a file system cannot be kept completely full. For each file system there is a parameter, termed the free space reserve, that gives the minimum acceptable percentage of file system blocks that should be free. If the number of free blocks drops below this level only the system administrator can continue to allocate blocks. The value of this parameter may be changed at any time, even when the file system is mounted and active. The transfer rates that appear in section 4 were measured on file systems kept less than 90% full (a reserve of 10%). If the number of free blocks falls to zero, the file system throughput tends to be cut in half, because of the inability of the file system to localize blocks in a file. If a file system's performance degrades because of overfilling, it may be restored by removing files until the amount of free space once again reaches the minimum acceptable level. Access rates for files created during periods of little free space may be restored by moving their data once enough space is available. The free space reserve must be added to the percentage of waste when comparing the organizations given in Table 1. Thus, the percentage of waste in an old 1024 byte UNIX file system is roughly comparable to a new 4096/512 byte file system with the free space reserve set at 5%. (Compare 11.8% wasted with the old file system to 6.9% waste + 5% reserved space in the new file system.)

3.2. File system parameterization

Except for the initial creation of the free list, the old file system ignores the parameters of the underlying hardware. It has no information about either the physical characteristics of the mass storage device, or the hardware that interacts with it. A goal of the new file system is to parameterize the processor capabilities and mass storage characteristics so that blocks can be allocated in an optimum configuration-dependent way. Parameters used include the speed of the processor, the hardware support for mass storage transfers, and the characteristics of the mass storage devices. Disk technology is constantly improving and a given installation can have several different disk technologies running on a single processor. Each file system is parameterized so that it can be adapted to the characteristics of the disk on which it is placed.

For mass storage devices such as disks, the new file system tries to allocate new blocks on the same cylinder as the previous block in the same file. Optimally, these new blocks will also be rotationally well positioned. The distance between ''rotationally optimal'' blocks varies greatly; it can be a consecutive block or a rotationally delayed block depending on system characteristics. On a processor with an input/output channel that does not require any processor intervention between mass storage transfer requests, two consecutive disk blocks can often be accessed without suffering lost time because of an intervening disk revolution. For processors without input/output channels, the main processor must field an interrupt and prepare for a new disk transfer. The expected time to service this interrupt and schedule a new disk transfer depends on the speed of the main processor.

The physical characteristics of each disk include the number of blocks per track and the rate at which the disk spins. The allocation routines use this information to calculate the number of milliseconds required to skip over a block. The characteristics of the processor include the expected time to service an interrupt and schedule a new disk transfer. Given a block allocated to a file, the allocation routines calculate the number of blocks to skip over so that the next block in the file will come into position under the disk head in the expected amount of time that it takes to start a new disk transfer operation. For programs that sequentially access large amounts of data, this strategy minimizes the amount of time spent waiting for the disk to position itself.

To ease the calculation of finding rotationally optimal blocks, the cylinder group summary information includes a count of the available blocks in a cylinder group at different rotational positions. Eight rotational positions are distinguished, so the resolution of the summary information is 2 milliseconds for a typical 3600 revolution per minute drive. The super-block contains a vector of lists called *rotational layout tables*. The vector is indexed by rotational position. Each component of the vector lists the index into the block map for every data block contained in its rotational position. When looking for an allocatable block, the system first looks through the summary counts for a rotational position with a non-zero block count. It then uses the index of the rotational position to find the appropriate list to use to index through only the relevant parts of the block map to find a free block.

The parameter that defines the minimum number of milliseconds between the completion of a data transfer and the initiation of another data transfer on the same cylinder can be changed at any time, even when the file system is mounted and active. If a file system is parameterized to lay out blocks with a rotational separation of 2 milliseconds, and the disk pack is then moved to a system that has a processor requiring 4 milliseconds to schedule a disk operation, the throughput will drop precipitously because of lost disk revolutions on nearly every block. If the eventual target machine is known, the file system can be parameterized for it even though it is initially created on a different processor. Even if the move is not known in advance, the rotational layout delay can be reconfigured after the disk is moved so that all further allocation is done based on the characteristics of the new host.

3.3. Layout policies

The file system layout policies are divided into two distinct parts. At the top level are global policies that use file system wide summary information to make decisions regarding the placement of new inodes and data blocks. These routines are responsible for deciding the placement of new directories and files. They also calculate rotationally optimal block layouts, and decide when to force a long seek to a new cylinder group because there are insufficient blocks left in the current cylinder group to do reasonable layouts. Below the global policy routines are the local allocation routines that use a locally optimal scheme to lay out data blocks.

Two methods for improving file system performance are to increase the locality of reference to minimize seek latency as described by [Trivedi80], and to improve the layout of data to make larger transfers possible as described by [Nevalainen77]. The global layout policies try to improve performance by clustering related information. They cannot attempt to localize all data references, but must also try to spread unrelated data among different cylinder groups. If too much localization is attempted, the local cylinder group may run out of space forcing the data to be scattered to non-local cylinder groups. Taken to an extreme, total localization can result in a single huge cluster of data resembling the old file system. The global policies try to balance the two conflicting goals of localizing data that is concurrently accessed while spreading out unrelated data.

One allocatable resource is inodes. Inodes are used to describe both files and directories. Inodes of files in the same directory are frequently accessed together. For example, the ''list directory'' command often accesses the inode for each file in a directory. The layout policy tries to place all the inodes of files in a directory in the same cylinder group. To ensure that files are distributed throughout the disk, a different policy is used for directory allocation. A new directory is placed in a cylinder group that has a greater than average number of free inodes, and the smallest number of directories already in it. The intent of this policy is to allow the inode clustering policy to succeed most of the time. The allocation of inodes within a cylinder group is done using a next free strategy. Although this allocates the inodes randomly within a cylinder group, all the inodes for a particular cylinder group can be read with 8 to 16 disk transfers. (At most 16 disk transfers are required because a cylinder group may have no more than 2048 inodes.) This puts a small and constant upper bound on the number of disk transfers required to access the inodes for all the files in a directory. In contrast, the old file system typically requires one disk transfer to fetch the inode for each file in a directory.

The other major resource is data blocks. Since data blocks for a file are typically accessed together, the policy routines try to place all data blocks for a file in the same cylinder group, preferably at rotationally optimal positions in the same cylinder. The problem with allocating all the data blocks in the same cylinder group is that large files will quickly use up available space in the cylinder group, forcing a spill over to other areas. Further, using all the space in a cylinder group causes future allocations for any file in the cylinder group to also spill to other areas. Ideally none of the cylinder groups should ever become completely full. The heuristic solution chosen is to redirect block allocation to a different cylinder group when a file exceeds 48 kilobytes, and at every megabyte thereafter.* The newly chosen cylinder group is selected from those cylinder groups that have a greater than average number of free blocks left. Although big files tend to be spread out over the disk, a megabyte of data is typically accessible before a long seek must be performed, and the cost of one long seek per megabyte is small.

The global policy routines call local allocation routines with requests for specific blocks. The local allocation routines will always allocate the requested block if it is free, otherwise it allocates a free block of the requested size that is rotationally closest to the requested block. If the global layout policies had complete information, they could always request unused blocks and the allocation routines would be reduced to simple bookkeeping. However, maintaining complete information is costly; thus the implementation of the global layout policy uses heuristics that employ only partial information.

If a requested block is not available, the local allocator uses a four level allocation strategy:

1) Use the next available block rotationally closest to the requested block on the same cylinder. It is assumed here that head switching time is zero. On disk controllers where this is not the case, it may be possible to incorporate the time required to switch between disk platters when constructing the rotational layout tables. This, however, has not yet been tried.

2) If there are no blocks available on the same cylinder, use a block within the same cylinder group.

3) If that cylinder group is entirely full, quadratically hash the cylinder group number to choose another cylinder group to look for a free block.

4) Finally if the hash fails, apply an exhaustive search to all cylinder groups.

Quadratic hash is used because of its speed in finding unused slots in nearly full hash tables [Knuth75]. File systems that are parameterized to maintain at least 10% free space rarely use this strategy. File systems that are run without maintaining any free space typically have so few free blocks that almost

---

* The first spill over point at 48 kilobytes is the point at which a file on a 4096 byte block file system first requires a single indirect block. This appears to be a natural first point at which to redirect block allocation. The other spillover points are chosen with the intent of forcing block allocation to be redirected when a file has used about 25% of the data blocks in a cylinder group. In observing the new file system in day to day use, the heuristics appear to work well in minimizing the number of completely filled cylinder groups.

any allocation is random; the most important characteristic of the strategy used under such conditions is that the strategy be fast.

4. Performance

Ultimately, the proof of the effectiveness of the algorithms described in the previous section is the long term performance of the new file system.

Our empirical studies have shown that the inode layout policy has been effective. When running the "list directory" command on a large directory that itself contains many directories (to force the system to access inodes in multiple cylinder groups), the number of disk accesses for inodes is cut by a factor of two. The improvements are even more dramatic for large directories containing only files, disk accesses for inodes being cut by a factor of eight. This is most encouraging for programs such as spooling daemons that access many small files, since these programs tend to flood the disk request queue on the old file system.

Table 2 summarizes the measured throughput of the new file system. Several comments need to be made about the conditions under which these tests were run. The test programs measure the rate at which user programs can transfer data to or from a file without performing any processing on it. These programs must read and write enough data to insure that buffering in the operating system does not affect the results. They are also run at least three times in succession; the first to get the system into a known state and the second two to insure that the experiment has stabilized and is repeatable. The tests used and their results are discussed in detail in [Kridle83]†. The systems were running multi-user but were otherwise quiescent. There was no contention for either the CPU or the disk arm. The only difference between the UNIBUS and MASSBUS tests was the controller. All tests used an AMPEX Capricorn 330 megabyte Winchester disk. As Table 2 shows, all file system test runs were on a VAX 11/750. All file systems had been in production use for at least a month before being measured. The same number of system calls were performed in all tests; the basic system call overhead was a negligible portion of the total running time of the tests.

Type of File System	Processor and Bus Measured	Read		
		Speed	Bandwidth	% CPU
old 1024	750/UNIBUS	29 Kbytes/sec	29/983 3%	11%
new 4096/1024	750/UNIBUS	221 Kbytes/sec	221/983 22%	43%
new 8192/1024	750/UNIBUS	233 Kbytes/sec	233/983 24%	29%
new 4096/1024	750/MASSBUS	466 Kbytes/sec	466/983 47%	73%
new 8192/1024	750/MASSBUS	466 Kbytes/sec	466/983 47%	54%

Table 2a – Reading rates of the old and new UNIX file systems.

Type of File System	Processor and Bus Measured	Write		
		Speed	Bandwidth	% CPU
old 1024	750/UNIBUS	48 Kbytes/sec	48/983 5%	29%
new 4096/1024	750/UNIBUS	142 Kbytes/sec	142/983 14%	43%
new 8192/1024	750/UNIBUS	215 Kbytes/sec	215/983 22%	46%
new 4096/1024	750/MASSBUS	323 Kbytes/sec	323/983 33%	94%
new 8192/1024	750/MASSBUS	466 Kbytes/sec	466/983 47%	95%

Table 2b – Writing rates of the old and new UNIX file systems.

Unlike the old file system, the transfer rates for the new file system do not appear to change over time. The throughput rate is tied much more strongly to the amount of free space that is maintained. The measurements in Table 2 were based on a file system with a 10% free space reserve. Synthetic work loads suggest that throughput deteriorates to about half the rates given in Table 2 when the file systems are full.

† A UNIX command that is similar to the reading test that we used is "cp file /dev/null", where "file" is eight megabytes long.

The percentage of bandwidth given in Table 2 is a measure of the effective utilization of the disk by the file system. An upper bound on the transfer rate from the disk is calculated by multiplying the number of bytes on a track by the number of revolutions of the disk per second. The bandwidth is calculated by comparing the data rates the file system is able to achieve as a percentage of this rate. Using this metric, the old file system is only able to use about 3–5% of the disk bandwidth, while the new file system uses up to 47% of the bandwidth.

Both reads and writes are faster in the new system than in the old system. The biggest factor in this speedup is because of the larger block size used by the new file system. The overhead of allocating blocks in the new system is greater than the overhead of allocating blocks in the old system, however fewer blocks need to be allocated in the new system because they are bigger. The net effect is that the cost per byte allocated is about the same for both systems.

In the new file system, the reading rate is always at least as fast as the writing rate. This is to be expected since the kernel must do more work when allocating blocks than when simply reading them. Note that the write rates are about the same as the read rates in the 8192 byte block file system; the write rates are slower than the read rates in the 4096 byte block file system. The slower write rates occur because the kernel has to do twice as many disk allocations per second, making the processor unable to keep up with the disk transfer rate.

In contrast the old file system is about 50% faster at writing files than reading them. This is because the write system call is asynchronous and the kernel can generate disk transfer requests much faster than they can be serviced, hence disk transfers queue up in the disk buffer cache. Because the disk buffer cache is sorted by minimum seek distance, the average seek between the scheduled disk writes is much less than it would be if the data blocks were written out in the random disk order in which they are generated. However when the file is read, the read system call is processed synchronously so the disk blocks must be retrieved from the disk in the non-optimal seek order in which they are requested. This forces the disk scheduler to do long seeks resulting in a lower throughput rate.

In the new system the blocks of a file are more optimally ordered on the disk. Even though reads are still synchronous, the requests are presented to the disk in a much better order. Even though the writes are still asynchronous, they are already presented to the disk in minimum seek order so there is no gain to be had by reordering them. Hence the disk seek latencies that limited the old file system have little effect in the new file system. The cost of allocation is the factor in the new system that causes writes to be slower than reads.

The performance of the new file system is currently limited by memory to memory copy operations required to move data from disk buffers in the system's address space to data buffers in the user's address space. These copy operations account for about 40% of the time spent performing an input/output operation. If the buffers in both address spaces were properly aligned, this transfer could be performed without copying by using the VAX virtual memory management hardware. This would be especially desirable when transferring large amounts of data. We did not implement this because it would change the user interface to the file system in two major ways: user programs would be required to allocate buffers on page boundaries, and data would disappear from buffers after being written.

Greater disk throughput could be achieved by rewriting the disk drivers to chain together kernel buffers. This would allow contiguous disk blocks to be read in a single disk transaction. Many disks used with UNIX systems contain either 32 or 48 512 byte sectors per track. Each track holds exactly two or three 8192 byte file system blocks, or four or six 4096 byte file system blocks. The inability to use contiguous disk blocks effectively limits the performance on these disks to less than 50% of the available bandwidth. If the next block for a file cannot be laid out contiguously, then the minimum spacing to the next allocatable block on any platter is between a sixth and a half a revolution. The implication of this is that the best possible layout without contiguous blocks uses only half of the bandwidth of any given track. If each track contains an odd number of sectors, then it is possible to resolve the rotational delay to any number of sectors by finding a block that begins at the desired rotational position on another track. The reason that block chaining has not been implemented is because it would require rewriting all the disk drivers in the system, and the current throughput rates are already limited by the speed of the available processors.

Currently only one block is allocated to a file at a time. A technique used by the DEMOS file system when it finds that a file is growing rapidly, is to preallocate several blocks at once, releasing them when the file is closed if they remain unused. By batching up allocations, the system can reduce the overhead of allocating at each write, and it can cut down on the number of disk writes needed to keep the block pointers on the disk synchronized with the block allocation [Powell79]. This technique was not included because block allocation currently accounts for less than 10% of the time spent in a write system call and, once again, the current throughput rates are already limited by the speed of the available processors.

5. File system functional enhancements

The performance enhancements to the UNIX file system did not require any changes to the semantics or data structures visible to application programs. However, several changes had been generally desired for some time but had not been introduced because they would require users to dump and restore all their file systems. Since the new file system already required all existing file systems to be dumped and restored, these functional enhancements were introduced at this time.

5.1. Long file names

File names can now be of nearly arbitrary length. Only programs that read directories are affected by this change. To promote portability to UNIX systems that are not running the new file system, a set of directory access routines have been introduced to provide a consistent interface to directories on both old and new systems.

Directories are allocated in 512 byte units called chunks. This size is chosen so that each allocation can be transferred to disk in a single operation. Chunks are broken up into variable length records termed directory entries. A directory entry contains the information necessary to map the name of a file to its associated inode. No directory entry is allowed to span multiple chunks. The first three fields of a directory entry are fixed length and contain: an inode number, the size of the entry, and the length of the file name contained in the entry. The remainder of an entry is variable length and contains a null terminated file name, padded to a 4 byte boundary. The maximum length of a file name in a directory is currently 255 characters.

Available space in a directory is recorded by having one or more entries accumulate the free space in their entry size fields. This results in directory entries that are larger than required to hold the entry name plus fixed length fields. Space allocated to a directory should always be completely accounted for by totaling up the sizes of its entries. When an entry is deleted from a directory, its space is returned to a previous entry in the same directory chunk by increasing the size of the previous entry by the size of the deleted entry. If the first entry of a directory chunk is free, then the entry's inode number is set to zero to indicate that it is unallocated.

5.2. File locking

The old file system had no provision for locking files. Processes that needed to synchronize the updates of a file had to use a separate ''lock'' file. A process would try to create a ''lock'' file. If the creation succeeded, then the process could proceed with its update; if the creation failed, then the process would wait and try again. This mechanism had three drawbacks. Processes consumed CPU time by looping over attempts to create locks. Locks left lying around because of system crashes had to be manually removed (normally in a system startup command script). Finally, processes running as system administrator are always permitted to create files, so were forced to use a different mechanism. While it is possible to get around all these problems, the solutions are not straight forward, so a mechanism for locking files has been added.

The most general schemes allow multiple processes to concurrently update a file. Several of these techniques are discussed in [Peterson83]. A simpler technique is to serialize access to a file with locks. To attain reasonable efficiency, certain applications require the ability to lock pieces of a file. Locking down to the byte level has been implemented in the Onyx file system by [Bass81]. However, for the standard system applications, a mechanism that locks at the granularity of a file is sufficient.

Locking schemes fall into two classes, those using hard locks and those using advisory locks. The primary difference between advisory locks and hard locks is the extent of enforcement. A hard lock is always enforced when a program tries to access a file; an advisory lock is only applied when it is requested by a program. Thus advisory locks are only effective when all programs accessing a file use the locking scheme. With hard locks there must be some override policy implemented in the kernel. With advisory locks the policy is left to the user programs. In the UNIX system, programs with system administrator privilege are allowed override any protection scheme. Because many of the programs that need to use locks must also run as the system administrator, we chose to implement advisory locks rather than create an additional protection scheme that was inconsistent with the UNIX philosophy or could not be used by system administration programs.

The file locking facilities allow cooperating programs to apply advisory *shared* or *exclusive* locks on files. Only one process may have an exclusive lock on a file while multiple shared locks may be present. Both shared and exclusive locks cannot be present on a file at the same time. If any lock is requested when another process holds an exclusive lock, or an exclusive lock is requested when another process holds any lock, the lock request will block until the lock can be obtained. Because shared and exclusive locks are advisory only, even if a process has obtained a lock on a file, another process may access the file.

Locks are applied or removed only on open files. This means that locks can be manipulated without needing to close and reopen a file. This is useful, for example, when a process wishes to apply a shared lock, read some information and determine whether an update is required, then apply an exclusive lock and update the file.

A request for a lock will cause a process to block if the lock can not be immediately obtained. In certain instances this is unsatisfactory. For example, a process that wants only to check if a lock is present would require a separate mechanism to find out this information. Consequently, a process may specify that its locking request should return with an error if a lock can not be immediately obtained. Being able to conditionally request a lock is useful to ''daemon'' processes that wish to service a spooling area. If the first instance of the daemon locks the directory where spooling takes place, later daemon processes can easily check to see if an active daemon exists. Since locks exist only while the locking processes exist, lock files can never be left active after the processes exit or if the system crashes.

Almost no deadlock detection is attempted. The only deadlock detection done by the system is that the file to which a lock is applied must not already have a lock of the same type (i.e. the second of two successive calls to apply a lock of the same type will fail).

5.3. Symbolic links

The traditional UNIX file system allows multiple directory entries in the same file system to reference a single file. Each directory entry ''links'' a file's name to an inode and its contents. The link concept is fundamental; inodes do not reside in directories, but exist separately and are referenced by links. When all the links to an inode are removed, the inode is deallocated. This style of referencing an inode does not allow references across physical file systems, nor does it support inter-machine linkage. To avoid these limitations *symbolic links* similar to the scheme used by Multics [Feiertag71] have been added.

5

A symbolic link is implemented as a file that contains a pathname. When the system encounters a symbolic link while interpreting a component of a pathname, the contents of the symbolic link is prepended to the rest of the pathname, and this name is interpreted to yield the resulting pathname. In UNIX, pathnames are specified relative to the root of the file system hierarchy, or relative to a process's current working directory. Pathnames specified relative to the root are called absolute pathnames. Pathnames specified relative to the current working directory are termed relative pathnames. If a symbolic link contains an absolute pathname, the absolute pathname is used, otherwise the contents of the symbolic link is evaluated relative to the location of the link in the file hierarchy.

Normally programs do not want to be aware that there is a symbolic link in a pathname that they are using. However certain system utilities must be able to detect and manipulate symbolic links. Three new system calls provide the ability to detect, read, and write symbolic links; seven system utilities required changes to use these calls.

In future Berkeley software distributions it may be possible to reference file systems located on remote machines using pathnames. When this occurs, it will be possible to create symbolic links that span machines.

5.4. Rename

Programs that create a new version of an existing file typically create the new version as a temporary file and then rename the temporary file with the name of the target file. In the old UNIX file system renaming required three calls to the system. If a program were interrupted or the system crashed between these calls, the target file could be left with only its temporary name. To eliminate this possibility the *rename* system call has been added. The rename call does the rename operation in a fashion that guarantees the existence of the target name.

Rename works both on data files and directories. When renaming directories, the system must do special validation checks to insure that the directory tree structure is not corrupted by the creation of loops or inaccessible directories. Such corruption would occur if a parent directory were moved into one of its descendants. The validation check requires tracing the descendents of the target directory to insure that it does not include the directory being moved.

5.5. Quotas

The UNIX system has traditionally attempted to share all available resources to the greatest extent possible. Thus any single user can allocate all the available space in the file system. In certain environments this is unacceptable. Consequently, a quota mechanism has been added for restricting the amount of file system resources that a user can obtain. The quota mechanism sets limits on both the number of inodes and the number of disk blocks that a user may allocate. A separate quota can be set for each user on each file system. Resources are given both a hard and a soft limit. When a program exceeds a soft limit, a warning is printed on the users terminal; the offending program is not terminated unless it exceeds its hard limit. The idea is that users should stay below their soft limit between login sessions, but they may use more resources while they are actively working. To encourage this behavior, users are warned when logging in if they are over any of their soft limits. If users fails to correct the problem for too many login sessions, they are eventually reprimanded by having their soft limit enforced as their hard limit.

Acknowledgements

We thank Robert Elz for his ongoing interest in the new file system, and for adding disk quotas in a rational and efficient manner. We also acknowledge Dennis Ritchie for his suggestions on the appropriate modifications to the user interface. We appreciate Michael Powell's explanations on how the DEMOS file system worked; many of his ideas were used in this implementation. Special commendation goes to Peter Kessler and Robert Henry for acting like real users during the early debugging stage when file systems were less stable than they should have been. The criticisms and suggestions by the reviews contributed significantly to the coherence of the paper. Finally we thank our sponsors, the National Science Foundation under grant MCS80-05144, and the Defense Advance Research Projects Agency (DoD) under ARPA Order No. 4031 monitored by Naval Electronic System Command under Contract No. N00039-82-C-0235.

References

[Almes78] Almes, G., and Robertson, G. "An Extensible File System for Hydra" Proceedings of the Third International Conference on Software Engineering, IEEE, May 1978.

[Bass81] Bass, J. "Implementation Description for File Locking", Onyx Systems Inc, 73 E. Trimble Rd, San Jose, CA 95131 Jan 1981.

[Feiertag71] Feiertag, R. J. and Organick, E. I., "The Multics Input-Output System", Proceedings of the Third Symposium on Operating Systems Principles, ACM, Oct 1971. pp 35-41

[Ferrin82a] Ferrin, T.E., "Performance and Robustness Improvements in Version 7 UNIX", Computer Graphics Laboratory Technical Report 2, School of Pharmacy, University of California, San Francisco, January 1982. Presented at the 1982 Winter Usenix Conference, Santa Monica, California.

[Ferrin82b] Ferrin, T.E., "Performance Issuses of VMUNIX Revisited", ;login: (The Usenix Association Newsletter), Vol 7, #5, November 1982. pp 3-6

[Kridle83] Kridle, R., and McKusick, M., "Performance Effects of Disk Subsystem Choices for VAX Systems Running 4.2BSD UNIX", Computer Systems Research Group, Dept of EECS, Berkeley, CA 94720, Technical Report #8.

[Kowalski78] Kowalski, T. "FSCK - The UNIX System Check Program", Bell Laboratory, Murray Hill, NJ 07974. March 1978

[Knuth75] Kunth, D. "The Art of Computer Programming", Volume 3 - Sorting and Searching, Addison-Wesley Publishing Company Inc, Reading, Mass, 1975. pp 506-549

[Maruyama76] Maruyama, K., and Smith, S. "Optimal reorganization of Distributed Space Disk Files", CACM, 19, 11. Nov 1976. pp 634-642

[Nevalainen77] Nevalainen, O., Vesterinen, M. "Determining Blocking Factors for Sequential Files by Heuristic Methods", The Computer Journal, 20, 3. Aug 1977. pp 245-247

[Pechura83] Pechura, M., and Schoeffler, J. "Estimating File Access Time of Floppy Disks", CACM, 26, 10. Oct 1983. pp 754-763

[Peterson83] Peterson, G. "Concurrent Reading While Writing", ACM Transactions on Programming Languages and Systems, ACM, 5, 1. Jan 1983. pp 46-55

[Powell79] Powell, M. "The DEMOS File System", Proceedings of the Sixth Symposium on Operating Systems Principles, ACM, Nov 1977. pp 33-42

[Ritchie74] Ritchie, D. M. and Thompson, K., "The UNIX Time-Sharing System", CACM 17, 7. July 1974. pp 365-375

[Smith81a] Smith, A. "Input/Output Optimization and Disk Architectures: A Survey", Performance and Evaluation 1. Jan 1981. pp 104-117

[Smith81b] Smith, A. "Bibliography on File and I/O System Optimization and Related Topics", Operating Systems Review, 15, 4. Oct 1981. pp 39-54

[Symbolics81] "Symbolics File System", Symbolics Inc, 9600 DeSoto Ave, Chatsworth, CA 91311 Aug 1981.

[Thompson78] Thompson, K. "UNIX Implementation", Bell System Technical Journal, 57, 6, part 2. pp 1931-1946 July-August 1978.

[Thompson80] Thompson, M. "Spice File System", Carnegie-Mellon University, Department of Computer Science, Pittsburg, PA 15213 #CMU-CS-80, Sept 1980.

[Trivedi80] Trivedi, K. "Optimal Selection of CPU Speed, Device Capabilities, and File Assignments", Journal of the ACM, 27, 3. July 1980. pp 457-473

[White80] White, R. M. "Disk Storage Technology", Scientific American, 243(2), August 1980.

The 4.4BSD NFS Implementation

Rick Macklem
University of Guelph

ABSTRACT

The 4.4BSD implementation of the Network File System (NFS)[1] is intended to interoperate with other NFS Version 2 Protocol (RFC1094) implementations but also allows use of an alternate protocol that is hoped to provide better performance in certain environments. This paper will informally discuss these various protocol features and their use. There is a brief overview of the implementation followed by several sections on various problem areas related to NFS and some hints on how to deal with them.

Not Quite NFS (NQNFS) is an NFS like protocol designed to maintain full cache consistency between clients in a crash tolerant manner. It is an adaptation of the NFS protocol such that the server supports both NFS and NQNFS clients while maintaining full consistency between the server and NQNFS clients. It borrows heavily from work done on Spritely-NFS [Srinivasan89], but uses Leases [Gray89] to avoid the need to recover server state information after a crash.

1. NFS Implementation

The 4.4BSD implementation of NFS and the alternate protocol nicknamed Not Quite NFS (NQNFS) are kernel resident, but make use of a few system daemons. The kernel implementation does not use an RPC library, handling the RPC request and reply messages directly in *mbuf* data areas. NFS interfaces to the network using sockets via. the kernel interface available in *sys/kern/uipc_syscalls.c* as *sosend(), soreceive(),...* There are connection management routines for support of sockets for connection oriented protocols and timeout/retransmit support for datagram sockets on the client side. For connection oriented transport protocols, such as TCP/IP, there is one connection for each client to server mount point that is maintained until an umount. If the connection breaks, the client will attempt a reconnect with a new socket. The client side can operate without any daemons running, but performance will be improved by running nfsiod daemons that perform read-aheads and write-behinds. For the server side to function, the daemons portmap, mountd and nfsd must be running. The mountd daemon performs two important functions.

1) Upon startup and after a hangup signal, mountd reads the exports file and pushes the export information for each local file system down into the kernel via. the mount system call.

2) Mountd handles remote mount protocol (RFC1094, Appendix A) requests.

The nfsd master daemon forks off children that enter the kernel via. the nfssvc system call. The children normally remain kernel resident, providing a process context for the NFS RPC servers. The only exception to this is when a Kerberos [Steiner88] ticket is received and at that time the nfsd exits the kernel temporarily to verify the ticket via. the Kerberos libraries and then returns to the kernel with the results. (This only happens for Kerberos mount points as described further under Security.) Meanwhile, the master nfsd waits to accept new connections from clients using connection oriented transport protocols and passes the new sockets down into the kernel. The client side mount_nfs along with portmap and mountd are the only parts of the NFS subsystem that make any use of the Sun RPC library.

6

2. Mount Problems

There are several problems that can be encountered at the time of an NFS mount, ranging from a unresponsive NFS server (crashed, network partitioned from client, etc.) to various interoperability problems between different NFS implementations.

[1]Network File System (NFS) is believed to be a registered trademark of Sun Microsystems Inc.

On the server side, if the 4.4BSD NFS server will be handling any PC clients, mountd will require the **-n** option to enable non-root mount request servicing. Running of a pcnfsd[2] daemon will also be necessary. The server side requires that the daemons mountd and nfsd be running and that they be registered with portmap properly. If problems are encountered, the safest fix is to kill all the daemons and then restart them in the order portmap, mountd and nfsd. Other server side problems are normally caused by problems with the format of the exports file, which is covered under Security and in the exports man page.

On the client side, there are several mount options useful for dealing with server problems. In cases where a file system is not critical for system operation, the **-b** mount option may be specified so that mount_nfs will go into the background for a mount attempt on an unresponsive server. This is useful for mounts specified in *fstab(5)*, so that the system will not get hung while booting doing **mount -a** because a file server is not responsive. On the other hand, if the file system is critical to system operation, this option should not be used so that the client will wait for the server to come up before completing bootstrapping. There are also three mount options to help deal with interoperability issues with various non-BSD NFS servers. The **-P** option specifies that the NFS client use a reserved IP port number to satisfy some servers' security requirements.[3] The **-c** option stops the NFS client from doing a *connect* on the UDP socket, so that the mount works with servers that send NFS replies from port numbers other than the standard 2049.[4] Finally, the **-g=***num* option sets the maximum size of the group list in the credentials passed to an NFS server in every RPC request. Although RFC1057 specifies a maximum size of 16 for the group list, some servers can't handle that many. If a user, particularly root doing a mount, keeps getting access denied from a file server, try temporarily reducing the number of groups that user is in to less than 5 by editing /etc/group. If the user can then access the file system, slowly increase the number of groups for that user until the limit is found and then peg the limit there with the **-g=***num* option. This implies that the server will only see the first *num* groups that the user is in, which can cause some accessibility problems.

For sites that have many NFS servers, amd [Pendry93] is a useful administration tool. It also reduces the number of actual NFS mount points, alleviating problems with commands such as df(1) that hang when any of the NFS servers is unreachable.

3. Dealing with Hung Servers

There are several mount options available to help a client deal with being hung waiting for response from a crashed or unreachable[5] server. By default, a hard mount will continue to try to contact the server "forever" to complete the system call. This type of mount is appropriate when processes on the client that access files in the file system do not tolerate file I/O systems calls that return -1 with *errno == EINTR* and/or access to the file system is critical for normal system operation.

There are two other alternatives:

1) A soft mount (**-s** option) retries an RPC *n* times and then the corresponding system call returns -1 with errno set to EINTR. For TCP transport, the actual RPC request is not retransmitted, but the timeout intervals waiting for a reply from the server are done in the same manner as UDP for this purpose. The problem with this type of mount is that most applications do not expect an EINTR error return from file I/O system calls (since it never occurs for a local file system) and get confused by the error return from the I/O system call. The option **-x=***num* is used to set the RPC retry limit and if set too low, the error returns will start occurring whenever the NFS server is slow due to heavy load. Alternately, a large retry limit can result in a process hung for a long time, due to a crashed server or network partitioning.

2) An interruptible mount (**-i** option) checks to see if a termination signal is pending for the process when waiting for server response and if it is, the I/O system call posts an EINTR. Normally this results in the process being terminated by the signal when returning from the system call. This

[2] Pcnfsd is available in source form from Sun Microsystems and many anonymous ftp sites.

[3] Any security benefit of this is highly questionable and as such the BSD server does not require a client to use a reserved port number.

[4] The Encore Multimax is known to require this.

[5] Due to a network partitioning or similar.

feature allows you to ''^C'' out of processes that are hung due to unresponsive servers. The problem with this approach is that signals that are caught by a process are not recognized as termination signals and the process will remain hung.[6]

4. RPC Transport Issues

The NFS Version 2 protocol runs over UDP/IP transport by sending each Sun Remote Procedure Call (RFC1057) request/reply message in a single UDP datagram. Since UDP does not guarantee datagram delivery, the Remote Procedure Call (RPC) layer times out and retransmits an RPC request if no RPC reply has been received. Since this round trip timeout (RTO) value is for the entire RPC operation, including RPC message transmission to the server, queuing at the server for an nfsd, performing the RPC and sending the RPC reply message back to the client, it can be highly variable for even a moderately loaded NFS server. As a result, the RTO interval must be a conservation (large) estimate, in order to avoid extraneous RPC request retransmits.[7] Also, with an 8Kbyte read/write data size (the default), the read/write reply/request will be an 8+Kbyte UDP datagram that must normally be fragmented at the IP layer for transmission.[8] For IP fragments to be successfully reassembled into the IP datagram at the receive end, all fragments must be received within a fairly short ''time to live''. If one fragment is lost/damaged in transit, the entire RPC must be retransmitted and redone. This problem can be exaggerated by a network interface on the receiver that cannot handle the reception of back to back network packets. [Kent87a]

There are several tuning mount options on the client side that can prove useful when trying to alleviate performance problems related to UDP RPC transport. The options **-r=***num* and **-w=***num* specify the maximum read or write data size respectively. The size *num* should be a power of 2 (4K, 2K, 1K) and adjusted downward from the maximum of 8Kbytes whenever IP fragmentation is causing problems. The best indicator of IP fragmentation problems is a significant number of *fragments dropped after timeout* reported by the *ip:* section of a **netstat -s** command on either the client or server. Of course, if the fragments are being dropped at the server, it can be fun figuring out which client(s) are involved. The most likely candidates are clients that are not on the same local area network as the server or have network interfaces that do not receive several back to back network packets properly.

By default, the 4.4BSD NFS client dynamically estimates the retransmit timeout interval for the RPC and this appears to work reasonably well for many environments. However, the **-d** flag can be specified to turn off the dynamic estimation of retransmit timeout, so that the client will use a static initial timeout interval.[9] The **-t=***num* option can be used with **-d** to set the initial timeout interval to other than the default of 2 seconds. The best indicator that dynamic estimation should be turned off would be a significant number[10] in the *X Replies* field and a large number in the *Retries* field in the *Rpc Info:* section as reported by the **nfsstat** command. On the server, there would be significant numbers of *Inprog* recent request cache hits in the *Server Cache Stats:* section as reported by the **nfsstat** command, when run on the server.

The tradeoff is that a smaller timeout interval results in a better average RPC response time, but increases the risk of extraneous retries that in turn increase server load and the possibility of damaged files on the server. It is probably best to err on the safe side and use a large (>= 2sec) fixed timeout if the dynamic retransmit timeout estimation seems to be causing problems.

An alternative to all this fiddling is to run NFS over TCP transport instead of UDP. Since the 4.4BSD TCP implementation provides reliable delivery with congestion control, it avoids all of the above problems. It also permits the use of read and write data sizes greater than the 8Kbyte limit for UDP tran-

---

[6] Unfortunately, there are also some resource allocation situations in the BSD kernel where the termination signal will be ignored and the process will not terminate.

[7] At best, an extraneous RPC request retransmit increases the load on the server and at worst can result in damaged files on the server when non-idempotent RPCs are redone [Juszczak89].

[8] 6 IP fragments for an Ethernet, which has an maximum transmission unit of 1500bytes.

[9] After the first retransmit timeout, the initial interval is backed off exponentially.

[10] Even 0.1% of the total RPCs is probably significant.

sport.[11] NFS over TCP usually delivers comparable to significantly better performance than NFS over UDP unless the client or server processor runs at less than 5-10MIPS. For a slow processor, the extra CPU overhead of using TCP transport will become significant and TCP transport may only be useful when the client to server interconnect traverses congested gateways. The main problem with using TCP transport is that it is only supported between BSD clients and servers.[12]

5. Other Tuning Tricks

Another mount option that may improve performance over certain network interconnects is **-a=***num* which sets the number of blocks that the system will attempt to read-ahead during sequential reading of a file. The default value of 1 seems to be appropriate for most situations, but a larger value might achieve better performance for some environments, such as a mount to a server across a ''high bandwidth * round trip delay'' interconnect.

For the adventurous, playing with the size of the buffer cache can also improve performance for some environments that use NFS heavily. Under some workloads, a buffer cache of 4-6Mbytes can result in significant performance improvements over 1-2Mbytes, both in client side system call response time and reduced server RPC load. The buffer cache size defaults to 10% of physical memory, but this can be overridden by specifying the BUFPAGES option in the machine's config file.[13] When increasing the size of BUFPAGES, it is also advisable to increase the number of buffers NBUF by a corresponding amount. Note that there is a tradeoff of memory allocated to the buffer cache versus available for paging, which implies that making the buffer cache larger will increase paging rate, with possibly disastrous results.

6. Security Issues

When a machine is running an NFS server it opens up a great big security hole. For ordinary NFS, the server receives client credentials in the RPC request as a user id and a list of group ids and trusts them to be authentic! The only tool available to restrict remote access to file systems with is the exports(5) file, so file systems should be exported with great care. The exports file is read by mountd upon startup and after a hangup signal is posted for it and then as much of the access specifications as possible are pushed down into the kernel for use by the nfsd(s). The trick here is that the kernel information is stored on a per local file system mount point and client host address basis and cannot refer to individual directories within the local server file system. It is best to think of the exports file as referring to the various local file systems and not just directory paths as mount points. A local file system may be exported to a specific host, all hosts that match a subnet mask or all other hosts (the world). The latter is very dangerous and should only be used for public information. It is also strongly recommended that file systems exported to ''the world'' be exported read-only. For each host or group of hosts, the file system can be exported read-only or read/write. You can also define one of three client user id to server credential mappings to help control access. Root (user id == 0) can be mapped to some default credentials while all other user ids are accepted as given. If the default credentials for user id equal zero are root, then there is essentially no remapping. Most NFS file systems are exported this way, most commonly mapping user id == 0 to the credentials for the user nobody. Since the client user id and group id list is used unchanged on the server (except for root), this also implies that the user id and group id space must be common between the client and server. (ie. user id N on the client must refer to the same user on the server) All user ids can be mapped to a default set of credentials, typically that of the user nobody. This essentially gives world access to all users on the corresponding hosts.

There is also a non-standard BSD **-kerb** export option that requires the client provide a KerberosIV rcmd service ticket to authenticate the user on the server. If successful, the Kerberos principal is looked up in the server's password and group databases to get a set of credentials and a map of client userid to these credentials is then cached. The use of TCP transport is strongly recommended, since the scheme depends on the TCP connection to avert replay attempts. Unfortunately, this option is only usable between BSD

---

[11]Read/write data sizes greater than 8Kbytes will not normally improve performance unless the kernel constant MAXBSIZE is increased and the file system on the server has a block size greater than 8Kbytes.

[12]There are rumors of commercial NFS over TCP implementations on the horizon and these may well be worth exploring.

[13]BUFPAGES is the number of physical machine pages allocated to the buffer cache. ie. BUFPAGES * NBPG = buffer cache size in bytes

clients and servers since it is not compatible with other known ''kerberized'' NFS systems. To enable use of this Kerberos option, both mount_nfs on the client and nfsd on the server must be rebuilt with the -DKERBEROS option and linked to KerberosIV libraries. The file system is then exported to the client(s) with the **-kerb** option in the exports file on the server and the client mount specifies the **-K** and **-T** options. The **-m=***realm* mount option may be used to specify a Kerberos Realm for the ticket (it must be the Kerberos Realm of the server) that is other than the client's local Realm. To access files in a **-kerb** mount point, the user must have a valid TGT for the server's Realm, as provided by kinit or similar.

As well as the standard NFS Version 2 protocol (RFC1094) implementation, BSD systems can use a variant of the protocol called Not Quite NFS (NQNFS) that supports a variety of protocol extensions. This protocol uses 64bit file offsets and sizes, an *access rpc*, an *append* option on the write rpc and extended file attributes to support 4.4BSD file system functionality more fully. It also makes use of a variant of short term *leases* [Gray89] with delayed write client caching, in an effort to provide full cache consistency and better performance. This protocol is available between 4.4BSD systems only and is used when the **-q** mount option is specified. It can be used with any of the aforementioned options for NFS, such as TCP transport (**-T**) and KerberosIV authentication (**-K**). Although this protocol is experimental, it is recommended over NFS for mounts between 4.4BSD systems.[14]

7. Monitoring NFS Activity

The basic command for monitoring NFS activity on clients and servers is nfsstat. It reports cumulative statistics of various NFS activities, such as counts of the various different RPCs and cache hit rates on the client and server. Of particular interest on the server are the fields in the *Server Cache Stats:* section, which gives numbers for RPC retries received in the first three fields and total RPCs in the fourth. The first three fields should remain a very small percentage of the total. If not, it would indicate one or more clients doing retries too aggressively and the fix would be to isolate these clients, disable the dynamic RTO estimation on them and make their initial timeout interval a conservative (ie. large) value.

On the client side, the fields in the *Rpc Info:* section are of particular interest, as they give an overall picture of NFS activity. The *TimedOut* field is the number of I/O system calls that returned -1 for ''soft'' mounts and can be reduced by increasing the retry limit or changing the mount type to ''intr'' or ''hard''. The *Invalid* field is a count of trashed RPC replies that are received and should remain zero.[15] The *X Replies* field counts the number of repeated RPC replies received from the server and is a clear indication of a too aggressive RTO estimate. Unfortunately, a good NFS server implementation will use a ''recent request cache'' [Juszczak89] that will suppress the extraneous replies. A large value for *Retries* indicates a problem, but it could be any of:

- a too aggressive RTO estimate
- an overloaded NFS server
- IP fragments being dropped (gateway, client or server)

and requires further investigation. The *Requests* field is the total count of RPCs done on all servers.

The **netstat -s** comes in useful during investigation of RPC transport problems. The field *fragments dropped after timeout* in the *ip:* section indicates IP fragments are being lost and a significant number of these occurring indicates that the use of TCP transport or a smaller read/write data size is in order. A significant number of *bad checksums* reported in the *udp:* section would suggest network problems of a more generic sort. (cabling, transceiver or network hardware interface problems or similar)

There is a RPC activity logging facility for both the client and server side in the kernel. When logging is enabled by setting the kernel variable nfsrtton to one, the logs in the kernel structures nfsrtt (for the client side) and nfsdrt (for the server side) are updated upon the completion of each RPC in a circular manner. The pos element of the structure is the index of the next element of the log array to be updated. In

[14] I would appreciate email from anyone who can provide NFS vs. NQNFS performance measurements, particularly fast clients, many clients or over an internetwork connection with a large ''bandwidth * RTT'' product.

[15] Some NFS implementations run with UDP checksums disabled, so garbage RPC messages can be received.

other words, elements of the log array from *log*[pos] to *log*[pos - 1] are in chronological order. The include file <sys/nfsrtt.h> should be consulted for details on the fields in the two log structures.[16]

8. Diskless Client Support

The NFS client does include kernel support for diskless/dataless operation where the root file system and optionally the swap area is remote NFS mounted. A diskless/dataless client is configured using a version of the ''swapvmunix.c'' file as provided in the directory *contrib/diskless.nfs*. If the swap device == NODEV, it specifies an NFS mounted swap area and should be configured the same size as set up by diskless_setup when run on the server. This file must be put in the *sys/compile/<machine_name>* kernel build directory after the config command has been run, since config does not know about specifying NFS root and swap areas. The kernel variable mountroot must be set to nfs_mountroot instead of ffs_mountroot and the kernel structure nfs_diskless must be filled in properly. There are some primitive system administration tools in the *contrib/diskless.nfs* directory to assist in filling in the nfs_diskless structure and in setting up an NFS server for diskless/dataless clients. The tools were designed to provide a bare bones capability, to allow maximum flexibility when setting up different servers.

The tools are as follows:

- diskless_offset.c - This little program reads a ''vmunix'' object file and writes the file byte offset of the nfs_diskless structure in it to standard out. It was kept separate because it sometimes has to be compiled/linked in funny ways depending on the client architecture. (See the comment at the beginning of it.)
- diskless_setup.c - This program is run on the server and sets up files for a given client. It mostly just fills in an nfs_diskless structure and writes it out to either the "vmunix" file or a separate file called /var/diskless/setup.<official-hostname>
- diskless_boot.c - There are two functions in here that may be used by a bootstrap server such as tftpd to permit sharing of the ''vmunix'' object file for similar clients. This saves disk space on the bootstrap server and simplify organization, but are not critical for correct operation. They read the ''vmunix'' file, but optionally fill in the nfs_diskless structure from a separate "setup.<official-hostname>" file so that there is only one copy of "vmunix" for all similar (same arch etc.) clients. These functions use a text file called /var/diskless/boot.<official-hostname> to control the netboot.

The basic setup steps are:

- make a "vmunix" for the client(s) with mountroot() == nfs_mountroot() and swdevt[0].sw_dev == NODEV if it is to do nfs swapping as well (See the same swapvmunix.c file)
- run diskless_offset on the vmunix file to find out the byte offset of the nfs_diskless structure
- Run diskless_setup on the server to set up the server and fill in the nfs_diskless structure for that client. The nfs_diskless structure can either be written into the vmunix file (the -x option) or saved in /var/diskless/setup.<official-hostname>.
- Set up the bootstrap server. If the nfs_diskless structure was written into the ''vmunix'' file, any vanilla bootstrap protocol such as bootp/tftp can be used. If the bootstrap server has been modified to use the functions in diskless_boot.c, then a file called /var/diskless/boot.<official-hostname> must be created. It is simply a two line text file, where the first line is the pathname of the correct ''vmunix'' file and the second line has the pathname of the nfs_diskless structure file and its byte offset in it. For example:

  /var/diskless/vmunix.pmax
  /var/diskless/setup.rickers.cis.uoguelph.ca 642308
- Create a /var subtree for each client in an appropriate place on the server, such as /var/diskless/var/<client-hostname>/... By using the <client-hostname> to differentiate /var for each host, /etc/rc can be modified to mount the correct /var from the server.

---

[16] Unfortunately, a monitoring tool that uses these logs is still in the planning (dreaming) stage.

9. Not Quite NFS, Crash Tolerant Cache Consistency for NFS

Not Quite NFS (NQNFS) is an NFS like protocol designed to maintain full cache consistency between clients in a crash tolerant manner. It is an adaptation of the NFS protocol such that the server supports both NFS and NQNFS clients while maintaining full consistency between the server and NQNFS clients. This section borrows heavily from work done on Spritely-NFS [Srinivasan89], but uses Leases [Gray89] to avoid the need to recover server state information after a crash. The reader is strongly encouraged to read these references before trying to grasp the material presented here.

9.1. Overview

The protocol maintains cache consistency by using a somewhat Sprite [Nelson88] like protocol, but is based on short term leases[17] instead of hard state information about open files. The basic principal is that the protocol will disable client caching of a file whenever that file is write shared[18]. Whenever a client wishes to cache data for a file it must hold a valid lease. There are three types of leases: read caching, write caching and non-caching. The latter type requires that all file operations be done synchronously with the server via. RPCs. A read caching lease allows for client data caching, but no file modifications may be done. A write caching lease allows for client caching of writes, but requires that all writes be pushed to the server when the lease expires. If a client has dirty buffers[19] when a write cache lease has almost expired, it will attempt to extend the lease but is required to push the dirty buffers if extension fails. A client gets leases by either doing a **GetLease RPC** or by piggybacking a **GetLease Request** onto another RPC. Piggybacking is supported for the frequent RPCs Getattr, Setattr, Lookup, Readlink, Read, Write and Readdir in an effort to minimize the number of **GetLease RPCs** required. All leases are at the granularity of a file, since all NFS RPCs operate on individual files and NFS has no intrinsic notion of a file hierarchy. Directories, symbolic links and file attributes may be read cached but are not write cached. The exception here is the attribute file_size, which is updated during cached writing on the client to reflect a growing file.

It is the server's responsibility to ensure that consistency is maintained among the NQNFS clients by disabling client caching whenever a server file operation would cause inconsistencies. The possibility of inconsistencies occurs whenever a client has a write caching lease and any other client, or local operations on the server, tries to access the file or when a modify operation is attempted on a file being read cached by client(s). At this time, the server sends an **eviction notice** to all clients holding the lease and then waits for lease termination. Lease termination occurs when a **vacated the premises** message has been received from all the clients that have signed the lease or when the lease expires via. timeout. The message pair **eviction notice** and **vacated the premises** roughly correspond to a Sprite server→client callback, but are not implemented as an actual RPC, to avoid the server waiting indefinitely for a reply from a dead client.

Server consistency checking can be viewed as issuing intrinsic leases for a file operation for the duration of the operation only. For example, the **Create RPC** will get an intrinsic write lease on the directory in which the file is being created, disabling client read caches for that directory.

By relegating this responsibility to the server, consistency between the server and NQNFS clients is maintained when NFS clients are modifying the file system as well.[20]

The leases are issued as time intervals to avoid the requirement of time of day clock synchronization. There are three important time constants known to the server. The **maximum_lease_term** sets an upper bound on lease duration. The **clock_skew** is added to all lease terms on the server to correct for differing clock speeds between the client and server and **write_slack** is the number of seconds the server is willing to wait for a client with an expired write caching lease to push dirty writes.

The server maintains a **modify_revision** number for each file. It is defined as a unsigned quadword integer that is never zero and that must increase whenever the corresponding file is modified on the server. It is used by the client to determine whether or not cached data for the file is stale. Generating this value is

---

[17] A lease is a ticket permitting an activity that is valid until some expiry time.

[18] Write sharing occurs when at least one client is modifying a file while other client(s) are reading the file.

[19] Cached write data is not yet pushed (written) to the server.

[20] The NFS clients will continue to be *approximately* consistent with the server.

easier said than done. The current implementation uses the following technique, which is believed to be adequate. The high order longword is stored in the ufs inode and is initialized to one when an inode is first allocated. The low order longword is stored in main memory only and is initialized to zero when an inode is read in from disk. When the file is modified for the first time within a given second of wall clock time, the high order longword is incremented by one and the low order longword reset to zero. For subsequent modifications within the same second of wall clock time, the low order longword is incremented. If the low order longword wraps around to zero, the high order longword is incremented again. Since the high order longword only increments once per second and the inode is pushed to disk frequently during file modification, this implies $0 \le$ Current–Disk ≤ 5. When the inode is read in from disk, 10 is added to the high order longword, which ensures that the quadword is greater than any value it could have had before a crash. This introduces apparent modifications every time the inode falls out of the LRU inode cache, but this should only reduce the client caching performance by a (hopefully) small margin.

9.2. Crash Recovery and other Failure Scenarios

The server must maintain the state of all the current leases held by clients. The nice thing about short term leases is that maximum_lease_term seconds after the server stops issuing leases, there are no current leases left. As such, server crash recovery does not require any state recovery. After rebooting, the server refuses to service any RPCs except for writes until write_slack seconds after the last lease would have expired[21]. By then, the server would not have any outstanding leases to recover the state of and the clients have had at least write_slack seconds to push dirty writes to the server and get the server sync'd up to date. After this, the server simply services requests in a manner similar to NFS. In an effort to minimize the effect of "recovery storms" [Baker91], the server replies **try_again_later** to the RPCs it is not yet ready to service.

After a client crashes, the server may have to wait for a lease to timeout before servicing a request if write sharing of a file with a cachable lease on the client is about to occur. As for the client, it simply starts up getting any leases it now needs. Any outstanding leases for that client on the server prior to the crash will either be renewed or expire via timeout.

Certain network partitioning failures are more problematic. If a client to server network connection is severed just before a write caching lease expires, the client cannot push the dirty writes to the server. After the lease expires on the server, the server permits other clients to access the file with the potential of getting stale data. Unfortunately I believe this failure scenario is intrinsic in any delay write caching scheme unless the server is required to wait **forever** for a client to regain contact[22]. Since the write caching lease has expired on the client, it will sync up with the server as soon as the network connection has been re-established.

There is another failure condition that can occur when the server is congested. The worst case scenario would have the client pushing dirty writes to the server but a large request queue on the server delays these writes for more than **write_slack** seconds. It is hoped that a congestion control scheme using the **try_again_later** RPC reply after booting combined with the following lease termination rule for write caching leases can minimize the risk of this occurrence. A write caching lease is only terminated on the server when there are have been no writes to the file and the server has not been overloaded during the previous write_slack seconds. The server has not been overloaded is approximated by a test for sleeping nfsd(s) at the end of the write_slack period.

9.3. Server Disk Full

There is a serious unresolved problem for delayed write caching with respect to server disk space allocation. When the disk on the file server is full, delayed write RPCs can fail due to "out of space". For NFS, this occurrence results in an error return from the close system call on the file, since the dirty blocks are pushed on close. Processes writing important files can check for this error return to ensure that the file was written successfully. For NQNFS, the dirty blocks are not pushed on close and as such the client may

6

[21] The last lease expiry time may be safely estimated as "boottime+maximum_lease_term+clock_skew" for machines that cannot store it in nonvolatile RAM.

[22] Gray and Cheriton avoid this problem by using a **write through** policy.

not attempt the write RPC until after the process has done the close which implies no error return from the close. For the current prototype, the only solution is to modify programs writing important file(s) to call fsync and check for an error return from it instead of close.

9.4. Protocol Details

The protocol specification is identical to that of NFS [Sun89] except for the following changes.

- RPC Information

```
Program Number 300105
Version Number 1
```

- Readdir_and_Lookup RPC

```
struct readdirlookargs {
    fhandle file;
    nfscookie cookie;
    unsigned count;
    unsigned duration;
};

struct entry {
    unsigned cachable;
    unsigned duration;
    modifyrev rev;
    fhandle entry_fh;
    nqnfs_fattr entry_attrib;
    unsigned fileid;
    filename name;
    nfscookie cookie;
    entry *nextentry;
};

union readdirlookres switch (stat status) {
case NFS_OK:
    struct {
        entry *entries;
        bool eof;
    } readdirlookok;
default:
    void;
};

readdirlookres
NQNFSPROC_READDIRLOOK(readdirlookargs) = 18;
```

Reads entries in a directory in a manner analogous to the NFSPROC_READDIR RPC in NFS, but returns the file handle and attributes of each entry as well. This allows the attribute and lookup caches to be primed.

- Get Lease RPC

```
struct getleaseargs {
    fhandle file;
    cachetype readwrite;
    unsigned duration;
};

union getleaseres switch (stat status) {
case NFS_OK:
```

```
        bool cachable;
        unsigned duration;
        modifyrev rev;
        nqnfs_fattr attributes;
default:
        void;
};

getleaseres
NQNFSPROC_GETLEASE(getleaseargs) = 19;
```

Gets a lease for "file" valid for "duration" seconds from when the lease was issued on the server[23]. The lease permits client caching if "cachable" is true. The modify revision level and attributes for the file are also returned.

- Eviction Message

```
void
NQNFSPROC_EVICTED (fhandle) = 21;
```

This message is sent from the server to the client. When the client receives the message, it should flush data associated with the file represented by "fhandle" from its caches and then send the **Vacated Message** back to the server. Flushing includes pushing any dirty writes via. write RPCs.

- Vacated Message

```
void
NQNFSPROC_VACATED (fhandle) = 20;
```

This message is sent from the client to the server in response to the **Eviction Message**. See above.

- Access RPC

```
struct accessargs {
        fhandle file;
        bool read_access;
        bool write_access;
        bool exec_access;
};

stat
NQNFSPROC_ACCESS(accessargs) = 22;
```

The access RPC does permission checking on the server for the given type of access required by the client for the file. Use of this RPC avoids accessibility problems caused by client->server uid mapping.

- Piggybacked Get Lease Request

The piggybacked get lease request is functionally equivalent to the Get Lease RPC except that is attached to one of the other NQNFS RPC requests as follows. A getleaserequest is prepended to all of the request arguments for NQNFS and a getleaserequestres is inserted in all NFS result structures just after the "stat" field only if "stat == NFS_OK".


```
union getleaserequest switch (cachetype type) {
case NQLREAD:
case NQLWRITE:
        unsigned duration;
default:
```

[23] To be safe, the client may only assume that the lease is valid for ''duration'' seconds from when the RPC request was sent to the server.

```
        void;
};

union getleaserequestres switch (cachetype type) {
case NQLREAD:
case NQLWRITE:
        bool cachable;
        unsigned duration;
        modifyrev rev;
default:
        void;
};
```

The get lease request applies to the file that the attached RPC operates on and the file attributes remain in the same location as for the NFS RPC reply structure.

- Three additional "stat" values

  Three additional values have been added to the enumerated type "stat".

```
NQNFS_EXPIRED=500
NQNFS_TRYLATER=501
NQNFS_AUTHERR=502
```

The "expired" value indicates that a lease has expired. The "try later" value is returned by the server when it wishes the client to retry the RPC request after a short delay. It is used during crash recovery (Section 2) and may also be useful for server congestion control. The "authetication error" value is returned for kerberized mount points to indicate that there is no cached authentication mapping and a Kerberos ticket for the principal is required.

9.5. Data Types

- cachetype

```
enum cachetype {
        NQLNONE = 0,
        NQLREAD = 1,
        NQLWRITE = 2
};
```

  Type of lease requested. NQLNONE is used to indicate no piggybacked lease request.

- modifyrev

```
typedef unsigned hyper modifyrev;
```

  The "modifyrev" is a unsigned quadword integer value that is never zero and increases every time the corresponding file is modified on the server.

- nqnfs_time

```
struct nqnfs_time {
        unsigned seconds;
        unsigned nano_seconds;
};
```

  For NQNFS times are handled at nano second resolution instead of micro second resolution for NFS.

- nqnfs_fattr

```
struct nqnfs_fattr {
        ftype type;
        unsigned mode;
        unsigned nlink;
        unsigned uid;
        unsigned gid;
        unsigned hyper size;
```

6

```
        unsigned blocksize;
        unsigned rdev;
        unsigned hyper bytes;
        unsigned fsid;
        unsigned fileid;
        nqnfs_time atime;
        nqnfs_time mtime;
        nqnfs_time ctime;
        unsigned flags;
        unsigned generation;
        modifyrev rev;
};
```

The nqnfs_fattr structure is modified from the NFS fattr so that it stores the file size as a 64bit quantity and the storage occupied as a 64bit number of bytes. It also has fields added for the 4.4BSD va_flags and va_gen fields as well as the file's modify rev level.

- nqnfs_sattr

```
struct nqnfs_sattr {
        unsigned mode;
        unsigned uid;
        unsigned gid;
        unsigned hyper size;
        nqnfs_time atime;
        nqnfs_time mtime;
        unsigned flags;
        unsigned rdev;
};
```

The nqnfs_sattr structure is modified from the NFS sattr structure in the same manner as fattr.

The arguments to several of the NFS RPCs have been modified as well. Mostly, these are minor changes to use 64bit file offsets or similar. The modified argument structures follow.

- Lookup RPC

```
struct lookup_diropargs {
        unsigned duration;
        fhandle dir;
        filename name;
};

union lookup_diropres switch (stat status) {
case NFS_OK:
        struct {
                union getleaserequestres lookup_lease;
                fhandle file;
                nqnfs_fattr attributes;
        } lookup_diropok;
default:
        void;
};
```

The additional "duration" argument tells the server to get a lease for the name being looked up if it is non-zero and the lease is specified in "lookup_lease".

- Read RPC

```
struct nqnfs_readargs {
        fhandle file;
        unsigned hyper offset;
```

6

```
unsigned count;
};
```

- Write RPC

```
struct nqnfs_writeargs {
     fhandle file;
     unsigned hyper offset;
     bool append;
     nfsdata data;
};
```

The "append" argument is true for apeend only write operations.

- Get Filesystem Attributes RPC

```
union nqnfs_statfsres (stat status) {
case NFS_OK:
     struct {
          unsigned tsize;
          unsigned bsize;
          unsigned blocks;
          unsigned bfree;
          unsigned bavail;
          unsigned files;
          unsigned files_free;
     } info;
default:
     void;
};
```

The "files" field is the number of files in the file system and the "files_free" is the number of additional files that can be created.

10. Summary

The configuration and tuning of an NFS environment tends to be a bit of a mystic art, but hopefully this paper along with the man pages and other reading will be helpful. Good Luck.

11. Bibliography

[Baker91] Mary Baker and John Ousterhout, Availability in the Sprite Distributed File System, In *Operating System Review*, (25)2, pg. 95-98, April 1991.

[Baker91a] Mary Baker, Private Email Communication, May 1991.

[Burrows88] Michael Burrows, Efficient Data Sharing, Technical Report #153, Computer Laboratory, University of Cambridge, Dec. 1988.

[Gray89] Cary G. Gray and David R. Cheriton, Leases: An Efficient Fault-Tolerant Mechanism for Distributed File Cache Consistency, In *Proc. of the Twelfth ACM Symposium on Operating Systems Principals*, Litchfield Park, AZ, Dec. 1989.

[Howard88] John H. Howard, Michael L. Kazar, Sherri G. Menees, David A. Nichols, M. Satyanarayanan, Robert N. Sidebotham and Michael J. West, Scale and Performance in a Distributed File System, *ACM Trans. on Computer Systems*, (6)1, pg 51-81, Feb. 1988.

[Juszczak89] Chet Juszczak, Improving the Performance and Correctness of an NFS Server, In *Proc. Winter 1989 USENIX Conference,* pg. 53-63, San Diego, CA, January 1989.

[Keith90] Bruce E. Keith, Perspectives on NFS File Server Performance Characterization, In *Proc. Summer 1990 USENIX Conference*, pg. 267-277, Anaheim, CA, June 1990.

[Kent87] Christopher. A. Kent, *Cache Coherence in Distributed Systems*, Research Report 87/4, Digital Equipment Corporation Western Research Laboratory, April 1987.

[Kent87a] Christopher. A. Kent and Jeffrey C. Mogul, *Fragmentation Considered Harmful*, Research Report 87/3, Digital Equipment Corporation Western Research Laboratory, Dec. 1987.

[Macklem91] Rick Macklem, Lessons Learned Tuning the 4.3BSD Reno Implementation of the NFS Protocol, In *Proc. Winter USENIX Conference*, pg. 53-64, Dallas, TX, January 1991.

[Nelson88] Michael N. Nelson, Brent B. Welch, and John K. Ousterhout, Caching in the Sprite Network File System, *ACM Transactions on Computer Systems* (6)1 pg. 134-154, February 1988.

[Nowicki89] Bill Nowicki, Transport Issues in the Network File System, In *Computer Communication Review*, pg. 16-20, Vol. 19, Number 2, April 1989.

[Ousterhout90] John K. Ousterhout, Why Aren't Operating Systems Getting Faster As Fast as Hardware? In *Proc. Summer 1990 USENIX Conference*, pg. 247-256, Anaheim, CA, June 1990.

[Pendry93] Jan-Simon Pendry, 4.4 BSD Automounter Reference Manual, In *src/usr.sbin/amd/doc directory of 4.4 BSD distribution tape*.

[Reid90] Jim Reid, N(e)FS: the Protocol is the Problem, In *Proc. Summer 1990 UKUUG Conference*, London, England, July 1990.

[Sandberg85] Russel Sandberg, David Goldberg, Steve Kleiman, Dan Walsh, and Bob Lyon, Design and Implementation of the Sun Network filesystem, In *Proc. Summer 1985 USENIX Conference*, pages 119-130, Portland, OR, June 1985.

[Schroeder85] Michael D. Schroeder, David K. Gifford and Roger M. Needham, A Caching File System For A Programmer's Workstation, In *Proc. of the Tenth ACM Symposium on Operating Systems Principals*, pg. 25-34, Orcas Island, WA, Dec. 1985.

[Srinivasan89] V. Srinivasan and Jeffrey. C. Mogul, *Spritely NFS: Implementation and Performance of Cache-Consistency Protocols*, Research Report 89/5, Digital Equipment Corporation Western Research Laboratory, May 1989.

[Steiner88] Jennifer G. Steiner, Clifford Neuman and Jeffrey I. Schiller, Kerberos: An Authentication Service for Open Network Systems, In *Proc. Winter 1988 USENIX Conference*, Dallas, TX, February 1988.

[Stern] Hal Stern, *Managing NFS and NIS*, O'Reilly and Associates, ISBN 0-937175-75-7.

[Sun87] Sun Microsystems Inc., *XDR: External Data Representation Standard*, RFC1014, Network Information Center, SRI International, June 1987.

[Sun88] Sun Microsystems Inc., *RPC: Remote Procedure Call Protocol Specification Version 2*, RFC1057, Network Information Center, SRI International, June 1988.

[Sun89] Sun Microsystems Inc., *NFS: Network File System Protocol Specification*, ARPANET Working Group Requests for Comment, DDN Network Information Center, SRI International, Menlo Park, CA, March 1989, RFC-1094.

4.3BSD Line Printer Spooler Manual

Ralph Campbell

Computer Systems Research Group
Computer Science Division
Department of Electrical Engineering and Computer Science
University of California, Berkeley
Berkeley, CA 94720

ABSTRACT

This document describes the structure and installation procedure for the line printer spooling system developed for the 4.3BSD version of the UNIX* operating system.

Revised June 8, 1993

1. Overview

The line printer system supports:

- multiple printers,
- multiple spooling queues,
- both local and remote printers, and
- printers attached via serial lines that require line initialization such as the baud rate.

Raster output devices such as a Varian or Versatec, and laser printers such as an Imagen, are also supported by the line printer system.

The line printer system consists mainly of the following files and commands:

/etc/printcap	printer configuration and capability data base
/usr/lib/lpd	line printer daemon, does all the real work
/usr/ucb/lpr	program to enter a job in a printer queue
/usr/ucb/lpq	spooling queue examination program
/usr/ucb/lprm	program to delete jobs from a queue
/etc/lpc	program to administer printers and spooling queues
/dev/printer	socket on which lpd listens

The file /etc/printcap is a master data base describing line printers directly attached to a machine and, also, printers accessible across a network. The manual page entry *printcap*(5) provides the authoritative definition of the format of this data base, as well as specifying default values for important items such as the directory in which spooling is performed. This document introduces some of the information that may be placed *printcap*.

---

* UNIX is a trademark of Bell Laboratories.

2. Commands

2.1. lpd – line printer daemon

The program *lpd*(8), usually invoked at boot time from the /etc/rc file, acts as a master server for coordinating and controlling the spooling queues configured in the printcap file. When *lpd* is started it makes a single pass through the *printcap* database restarting any printers that have jobs. In normal operation *lpd* listens for service requests on multiple sockets, one in the UNIX domain (named ''/dev/printer'') for local requests, and one in the Internet domain (under the ''printer'' service specification) for requests for printer access from off machine; see *socket*(2) and *services*(5) for more information on sockets and service specifications, respectively. *Lpd* spawns a copy of itself to process the request; the master daemon continues to listen for new requests.

Clients communicate with *lpd* using a simple transaction oriented protocol. Authentication of remote clients is done based on the ''privilege port'' scheme employed by *rshd*(8C) and *rcmd*(3X). The following table shows the requests understood by *lpd*. In each request the first byte indicates the ''meaning'' of the request, followed by the name of the printer to which it should be applied. Additional qualifiers may follow, depending on the request.

Request	Interpretation
^Aprinter\n	check the queue for jobs and print any found
^Bprinter\n	receive and queue a job from another machine
^Cprinter [users ...] [jobs ...]\n	return short list of current queue state
^Dprinter [users ...] [jobs ...]\n	return long list of current queue state
^Eprinter person [users ...] [jobs ...]\n	remove jobs from a queue

The *lpr*(1) command is used by users to enter a print job in a local queue and to notify the local *lpd* that there are new jobs in the spooling area. *Lpd* either schedules the job to be printed locally, or if printing remotely, attempts to forward the job to the appropriate machine. If the printer cannot be opened or the destination machine is unreachable, the job will remain queued until it is possible to complete the work.

2.2. lpq – show line printer queue

The *lpq*(1) program works recursively backwards displaying the queue of the machine with the printer and then the queue(s) of the machine(s) that lead to it. *Lpq* has two forms of output: in the default, short, format it gives a single line of output per queued job; in the long format it shows the list of files, and their sizes, that comprise a job.

2.3. lprm – remove jobs from a queue

The *lprm*(1) command deletes jobs from a spooling queue. If necessary, *lprm* will first kill off a running daemon that is servicing the queue and restart it after the required files are removed. When removing jobs destined for a remote printer, *lprm* acts similarly to *lpq* except it first checks locally for jobs to remove and then tries to remove files in queues off-machine.

2.4. lpc – line printer control program

The *lpc*(8) program is used by the system administrator to control the operation of the line printer system. For each line printer configured in /etc/printcap, *lpc* may be used to:

- disable or enable a printer,
- disable or enable a printer's spooling queue,
- rearrange the order of jobs in a spooling queue,
- find the status of printers, and their associated spooling queues and printer daemons.

3. Access control

The printer system maintains protected spooling areas so that users cannot circumvent printer accounting or remove files other than their own. The strategy used to maintain protected spooling areas is as follows:

- The spooling area is writable only by a *daemon* user and *daemon* group.
- The *lpr* program runs set-user-id to *root* and set-group-id to group *daemon*. The *root* access permits reading any file required. Accessibility is verified with an *access*(2) call. The group ID is used in setting up proper ownership of files in the spooling area for *lprm*.
- Control files in a spooling area are made with *daemon* ownership and group ownership *daemon*. Their mode is 0660. This insures control files are not modified by a user and that no user can remove files except through *lprm*.
- The spooling programs, *lpd*, *lpq*, and *lprm* run set-user-id to *root* and set-group-id to group *daemon* to access spool files and printers.
- The printer server, *lpd*, uses the same verification procedures as *rshd*(8C) in authenticating remote clients. The host on which a client resides must be present in the file /etc/hosts.equiv or /etc/hosts.lpd and the request message must come from a reserved port number.

In practice, none of *lpd*, *lpq*, or *lprm* would have to run as user *root* if remote spooling were not supported. In previous incarnations of the printer system *lpd* ran set-user-id to *daemon*, set-group-id to group *spooling*, and *lpq* and *lprm* ran set-group-id to group *spooling*.

4. Setting up

The 4.3BSD release comes with the necessary programs installed and with the default line printer queue created. If the system must be modified, the makefile in the directory /usr/src/usr.lib/lpr should be used in recompiling and reinstalling the necessary programs.

The real work in setting up is to create the *printcap* file and any printer filters for printers not supported in the distribution system.

4.1. Creating a printcap file

The *printcap* database contains one or more entries per printer. A printer should have a separate spooling directory; otherwise, jobs will be printed on different printers depending on which printer daemon starts first. This section describes how to create entries for printers that do not conform to the default printer description (an LP-11 style interface to a standard, band printer).

4.1.1. Printers on serial lines

When a printer is connected via a serial communication line it must have the proper baud rate and terminal modes set. The following example is for a DecWriter III printer connected locally via a 1200 baud serial line.

```
lp|LA-180 DecWriter III:\
        :lp=/dev/lp:br#1200:fs#06320:\
        :tr=\f:of=/usr/lib/lpf:lf=/usr/adm/lpd-errs:
```

The **lp** entry specifies the file name to open for output. Here it could be left out since "/dev/lp" is the default. The **br** entry sets the baud rate for the tty line and the **fs** entry sets CRMOD, no parity, and XTABS (see *tty*(4)). The **tr** entry indicates that a form-feed should be printed when the queue empties so the paper can be torn off without turning the printer off-line and pressing form feed. The **of** entry specifies the filter program *lpf* should be used for printing the files; more will be said about filters later. The last entry causes errors to be written to the file "/usr/adm/lpd-errs" instead of the console. Most errors from *lpd* are logged using *syslogd*(8) and will not be logged in the specified file. The filters should use *syslogd* to report errors; only those that write to standard error output will end up with errors in the **lf** file. (Occasionally errors sent to standard error output have not appeared in the log file; the use of *syslogd* is highly recommended.)

4.1.2. Remote printers

Printers that reside on remote hosts should have an empty **lp** entry. For example, the following printcap entry would send output to the printer named ''lp'' on the machine ''ucbvax''.

```
lp|default line printer:\
        :lp=:rm=ucbvax:rp=lp:sd=/usr/spool/vaxlpd:
```

The **rm** entry is the name of the remote machine to connect to; this name must be a known host name for a machine on the network. The **rp** capability indicates the name of the printer on the remote machine is ''lp''; here it could be left out since this is the default value. The **sd** entry specifies ''/usr/spool/vaxlpd'' as the spooling directory instead of the default value of ''/usr/spool/lpd''.

4.2. Output filters

Filters are used to handle device dependencies and to do accounting functions. The output filtering of **of** is used when accounting is not being done or when all text data must be passed through a filter. It is not intended to do accounting since it is started only once, all text files are filtered through it, and no provision is made for passing owners' login name, identifying the beginning and ending of jobs, etc. The other filters (if specified) are started for each file printed and do accounting if there is an **af** entry. If entries for both **of** and other filters are specified, the output filter is used only to print the banner page; it is then stopped to allow other filters access to the printer. An example of a printer that requires output filters is the Benson-Varian.

```
va|varian|Benson-Varian:\
        :lp=/dev/va0:sd=/usr/spool/vad:of=/usr/lib/vpf:\
        :tf=/usr/lib/rvcat:mx#2000:pl#58:px=2112:py=1700:tr=\f:
```

The **tf** entry specifies ''/usr/lib/rvcat'' as the filter to be used in printing *troff*(1) output. This filter is needed to set the device into print mode for text, and plot mode for printing *troff* files and raster images (see *va*(4V)). Note that the page length is set to 58 lines by the **pl** entry for 8.5" by 11" fan-fold paper. To enable accounting, the varian entry would be augmented with an **af** filter as shown below.

```
va|varian|Benson-Varian:\
        :lp=/dev/va0:sd=/usr/spool/vad:of=/usr/lib/vpf:\
        :if=/usr/lib/vpf:tf=/usr/lib/rvcat:af=/usr/adm/vaacct:\
        :mx#2000:pl#58:px=2112:py=1700:tr=\f:
```

4.3. Access Control

Local access to printer queues is controlled with the **rg** printcap entry.

```
        :rg=lprgroup:
```

Users must be in the group *lprgroup* to submit jobs to the specified printer. The default is to allow all users access. Note that once the files are in the local queue, they can be printed locally or forwarded to another host depending on the configuration.

Remote access is controlled by listing the hosts in either the file /etc/hosts.equiv or /etc/hosts.lpd, one host per line. Note that *rsh*(1) and *rlogin*(1) use /etc/hosts.equiv to determine which hosts are equivalent for allowing logins without passwords. The file /etc/hosts.lpd is only used to control which hosts have line printer access. Remote access can be further restricted to only allow remote users with accounts on the local host to print jobs by using the **rs** printcap entry.

```
        :rs:
```

5. Output filter specifications

The filters supplied with 4.3BSD handle printing and accounting for most common line printers, the Benson-Varian, the wide (36") and narrow (11") Versatec printer/plotters. For other devices or accounting methods, it may be necessary to create a new filter.

Filters are spawned by *lpd* with their standard input the data to be printed, and standard output the printer. The standard error is attached to the **lf** file for logging errors or *syslogd* may be used for logging errors. A filter must return a 0 exit code if there were no errors, 1 if the job should be reprinted, and 2 if the job should be thrown away. When *lprm* sends a kill signal to the *lpd* process controlling printing, it sends a SIGINT signal to all filters and descendents of filters. This signal can be trapped by filters that need to do cleanup operations such as deleting temporary files.

Arguments passed to a filter depend on its type. The **of** filter is called with the following arguments.

filter –**w**width –**l**length

The *width* and *length* values come from the **pw** and **pl** entries in the printcap database. The **if** filter is passed the following parameters.

filter [–**c**] –**w**width –**l**length –**i**indent –**n** login –**h** host accounting_file

The –**c** flag is optional, and only supplied when control characters are to be passed uninterpreted to the printer (when using the –**l** option of *lpr* to print the file). The –**w** and –**l** parameters are the same as for the **of** filter. The –**n** and –**h** parameters specify the login name and host name of the job owner. The last argument is the name of the accounting file from *printcap*.

All other filters are called with the following arguments:

filter –**x**width –**y**length –**n** login –**h** host accounting_file

The –**x** and –**y** options specify the horizontal and vertical page size in pixels (from the **px** and **py** entries in the printcap file). The rest of the arguments are the same as for the **if** filter.

6. Line printer Administration

The *lpc* program provides local control over line printer activity. The major commands and their intended use will be described. The command format and remaining commands are described in *lpc*(8).

abort and **start**

Abort terminates an active spooling daemon on the local host immediately and then disables printing (preventing new daemons from being started by *lpr*). This is normally used to forcibly restart a hung line printer daemon (i.e., *lpq* reports that there is a daemon present but nothing is happening). It does not remove any jobs from the queue (use the *lprm* command instead). *Start* enables printing and requests *lpd* to start printing jobs.

enable and **disable**

Enable and *disable* allow spooling in the local queue to be turned on/off. This will allow/prevent *lpr* from putting new jobs in the spool queue. It is frequently convenient to turn spooling off while testing new line printer filters since the *root* user can still use *lpr* to put jobs in the queue but no one else can. The other main use is to prevent users from putting jobs in the queue when the printer is expected to be unavailable for a long time.

restart

Restart allows ordinary users to restart printer daemons when *lpq* reports that there is no daemon present.

stop

Stop halts a spooling daemon after the current job completes; this also disables printing. This is a clean way to shutdown a printer to do maintenance, etc. Note that users can still enter jobs in a spool queue while a printer is *stopped.*

topq

Topq places jobs at the top of a printer queue. This can be used to reorder high priority jobs since *lpr* only provides first-come-first-serve ordering of jobs.

7. Troubleshooting

There are several messages that may be generated by the the line printer system. This section categorizes the most common and explains the cause for their generation. Where the message implies a failure, directions are given to remedy the problem.

In the examples below, the name *printer* is the name of the printer from the *printcap* database.

7.1. LPR

lpr: *printer* **: unknown printer**

The *printer* was not found in the *printcap* database. Usually this is a typing mistake; however, it may indicate a missing or incorrect entry in the /etc/printcap file.

lpr: *printer* **: jobs queued, but cannot start daemon.**

The connection to *lpd* on the local machine failed. This usually means the printer server started at boot time has died or is hung. Check the local socket /dev/printer to be sure it still exists (if it does not exist, there is no *lpd* process running). Usually it is enough to get a super-user to type the following to restart *lpd*.

```
% /usr/lib/lpd
```

You can also check the state of the master printer daemon with the following.

```
% ps l`cat /usr/spool/lpd.lock`
```

Another possibility is that the *lpr* program is not set-user-id to *root*, set-group-id to group *daemon*. This can be checked with

```
% ls –lg /usr/ucb/lpr
```

lpr: *printer* **: printer queue is disabled**

This means the queue was turned off with

% lpc disable *printer*

to prevent *lpr* from putting files in the queue. This is normally done by the system manager when a printer is going to be down for a long time. The printer can be turned back on by a super-user with *lpc*.

7.2. LPQ

waiting for *printer* **to become ready (offline ?)**

The printer device could not be opened by the daemon. This can happen for several reasons, the most common is that the printer is turned off-line. This message can also be generated if the printer is out of paper, the paper is jammed, etc. The actual reason is dependent on the meaning of error codes returned by system device driver. Not all printers supply enough information to distinguish when a printer is off-line or having trouble (e.g. a printer connected through a serial line). Another possible cause of this message is some other process, such as an output filter, has an exclusive open on the device. Your only recourse here is to kill off the offending program(s) and restart the printer with *lpc*.

printer **is ready and printing**

The *lpq* program checks to see if a daemon process exists for *printer* and prints the file *status* located in the spooling directory. If the daemon is hung, a super user can use *lpc* to abort the current daemon and start a new one.

waiting for *host* to come up

This implies there is a daemon trying to connect to the remote machine named *host* to send the files in the local queue. If the remote machine is up, *lpd* on the remote machine is probably dead or hung and should be restarted as mentioned for *lpr*.

sending to *host*

The files should be in the process of being transferred to the remote *host*. If not, the local daemon should be aborted and started with *lpc*.

Warning: *printer* is down

The printer has been marked as being unavailable with *lpc*.

Warning: no daemon present

The *lpd* process overseeing the spooling queue, as specified in the ''lock'' file in that directory, does not exist. This normally occurs only when the daemon has unexpectedly died. The error log file for the printer and the *syslogd* logs should be checked for a diagnostic from the deceased process. To restart an *lpd*, use

% lpc restart *printer*

no space on remote; waiting for queue to drain

This implies that there is insufficient disk space on the remote. If the file is large enough, there will never be enough space on the remote (even after the queue on the remote is empty). The solution here is to move the spooling queue or make more free space on the remote.

7.3. LPRM

lprm: *printer*: cannot restart printer daemon

This case is the same as when *lpr* prints that the daemon cannot be started.

7.4. LPD

The *lpd* program can log many different messages using *syslogd*(8). Most of these messages are about files that can not be opened and usually imply that the *printcap* file or the protection modes of the files are incorrect. Files may also be inaccessible if people manually manipulate the line printer system (i.e. they bypass the *lpr* program).

In addition to messages generated by *lpd*, any of the filters that *lpd* spawns may log messages using *syslogd* or to the error log file (the file specified in the **lf** entry in *printcap*).

7.5. LPC

couldn't start printer

This case is the same as when *lpr* reports that the daemon cannot be started.

cannot examine spool directory

Error messages beginning with ''cannot ...'' are usually because of incorrect ownership or protection mode of the lock file, spooling directory or the *lpc* program.

7

8

SENDMAIL

INSTALLATION AND OPERATION GUIDE

Eric Allman
University of California, Berkeley
Mammoth Project
eric@CS.Berkeley.EDU

Version 8.37

For Sendmail Version 8.6

Sendmail implements a general purpose internetwork mail routing facility under the UNIX* operating system. It is not tied to any one transport protocol — its function may be likened to a crossbar switch, relaying messages from one domain into another. In the process, it can do a limited amount of message header editing to put the message into a format that is appropriate for the receiving domain. All of this is done under the control of a configuration file.

Due to the requirements of flexibility for *sendmail,* the configuration file can seem somewhat unapproachable. However, there are only a few basic configurations for most sites, for which standard configuration files have been supplied. Most other configurations can be built by adjusting an existing configuration files incrementally.

Sendmail is based on RFC822 (Internet Mail Format Protocol), RFC821 (Simple Mail Transport Protocol), RFC1123 (Internet Host Requirements), and RFC1425 (SMTP Service Extensions). However, since *sendmail* is designed to work in a wider world, in many cases it can be configured to exceed these protocols. These cases are described herein.

Although *sendmail* is intended to run without the need for monitoring, it has a number of features that may be used to monitor or adjust the operation under unusual circumstances. These features are described.

Section one describes how to do a basic *sendmail* installation. Section two explains the day-to-day information you should know to maintain your mail system. If you have a relatively normal site, these two sections should contain sufficient information for you to install *sendmail* and keep it happy. Section three describes some parameters that may be safely tweaked. Section four has information regarding the command line arguments. Section five contains the nitty-gritty information about the configuration file. This section is for masochists and people who must write their own configuration file. Section six describes configuration that can be done at compile time. Section seven gives a brief description of differences in this version of *sendmail.* The appendixes give a brief but detailed explanation of a number of features not described in the rest of the paper.

---

*UNIX is a trademark of Unix Systems Laboratories.

TABLE OF CONTENTS

1. BASIC INSTALLATION

There are two basic steps to installing *sendmail*. The hard part is to build the configuration table. This is a file that *sendmail* reads when it starts up that describes the mailers it knows about, how to parse addresses, how to rewrite the message header, and the settings of various options. Although the configuration table is quite complex, a configuration can usually be built by adjusting an existing off-the-shelf configuration. The second part is actually doing the installation, i.e., creating the necessary files, etc.

The remainder of this section will describe the installation of *sendmail* assuming you can use one of the existing configurations and that the standard installation parameters are acceptable. All pathnames and examples are given from the root of the *sendmail* subtree, normally */usr/src/usr.sbin/sendmail* on 4.4BSD.

If you are loading this off the tape, continue with the next section. If you have a running binary already on your system, you should probably skip to section 1.2.

1.1. Compiling Sendmail

All *sendmail* source is in the *src* subdirectory. If you are running on a 4.4BSD system, compile by typing ''make''. On other systems, you may have to make some other adjustments.

1.1.1. Old versions of make

If you are not running the new version of **make** you will probably have to use

```
make –f Makefile.dist
```

This file does not assume several new syntaxes, including the ''+='' syntax in macro definition and the ''.include'' syntax.

1.1.2. Compilation flags

Sendmail supports two different formats for the *aliases* database. These formats are:

NDBM — The ''new DBM'' format, available on nearly all systems around today. This was the preferred format prior to 4.4BSD. It allows such complex things as multiple databases and closing a currently open database.

NEWDB — The new database package from Berkeley. If you have this, use it. It allows long records, multiple open databases, real in-memory caching, and so forth. You can define this in conjunction with one of the other two; if you do, old databases are read, but when a new database is created it will be in NEWDB format. As a nasty hack, if you have NEWDB, NDBM, and NIS defined, and if the file */var/yp/Makefile* exists and is readable, *sendmail* will create both new and old versions of the alias file during a *newalias* command. This is required because the Sun NIS/YP system reads the DBM version of the alias file. It's ugly as sin, but it works.

If neither of these are defined, *sendmail* reads the alias file into memory on every invocation. This can be slow and should be avoided.

System V based systems can define SYSTEM5 to make several small adjustments. This changes the handling of timezones and uses the much less efficient *lockf* call in preference to *flock*. These can be specified separately using the compilation flags SYS5TZ and LOCKF respectively.

If you don't have the *unsetenv* routine in your system library, define the UNSETENV compilation flag.

You may also have to define the compilation variable LA_TYPE to describe how your load average is computed. This and other flags are detailed in section 6.1.

8

1.1.3. Compilation and installation

After making the local system configuration described above, You should be able to compile and install the system. Compilation can be performed using "make[1]" in the **sendmail/src** directory. You may be able to install using

make install

This should install the binary in /usr/sbin and create links from /usr/bin/newaliases and /usr/bin/mailq to /usr/sbin/sendmail. On 4.4BSD systems it will also format and install man pages.

1.2. Configuration Files

Sendmail cannot operate without a configuration file. The configuration defines the mail systems understood at this site, how to access them, how to forward email to remote mail systems, and a number of tuning parameters. This configuration file is detailed in the later portion of this document.

The *sendmail* configuration can be daunting at first. The world is complex, and the mail configuration reflects that. The distribution includes an m4-based configuration package that hides a lot of the complexity.

These configuration files are simpler than old versions largely because the world has become simpler; in particular, text-based host files are officially eliminated, obviating the need to "hide" hosts behind a registered internet gateway.

These files also assume that most of your neighbors use domain-based UUCP addressing; that is, instead of naming hosts as "host!user" they will use "host.domain!user". The configuration files can be customized to work around this, but it is more complex.

I haven't tested these yet on an isolated LAN environment with a single UUCP connection to the outside world. If you are in such an environment, please send comments to sendmail@CS.Berkeley.EDU.

Our configuration files are processed by *m4* to facilitate local customization; the directory *cf* of the *sendmail* distribution directory contains the source files. This directory contains several subdirectories:

cf — Both site-dependent and site-independent descriptions of hosts. These can be literal host names (e.g., "ucbvax.mc") when the hosts are gateways or more general descriptions (such as "tcpproto.mc" as a general description of an SMTP-connected host or "uucpproto.mc" as a general description of a UUCP-connected host). Files ending **.mc** ("Master Configuration") are the input descriptions; the output is in the corresponding **.cf** file. The general structure of these files is described below.

domain — Site-dependent subdomain descriptions. These are tied to the way your organization wants to do addressing. For example, **domain/cs.exposed.m4** is our description for hosts in the CS.Berkeley.EDU subdomain that want their individual hostname to be externally visible; **domain/cs.hidden.m4** is the same except that the hostname is hidden (everything looks like it comes from CS.Berkeley.EDU). These are referenced using the DOMAIN **m4** macro in the **.mc** file.

feature — Definitions of specific features that some particular host in your site might want. These are referenced using the FEATURE **m4** macro. An example feature is use_cw_file (which tells *sendmail* to read an /etc/sendmail.cw file on startup to find the set of local names).

hack — Local hacks, referenced using the HACK **m4** macro. Try to avoid these. The point of having them here is to make it clear that they smell.

---

[1]where you may have to replace "make" with "make –f Makefile.dist" as appropriate.

m4 — Site-independent *m4*(1) include files that have information common to all configuration files. This can be thought of as a "#include" directory.

mailer — Definitions of mailers, referenced using the MAILER **m4** macro. Defined mailer types in this distribution are fax, local, smtp, uucp, and usenet.

ostype — Definitions describing various operating system environments (such as the location of support files). These are referenced using the OSTYPE **m4** macro.

sh — Shell files used by the **m4** build process. You shouldn't have to mess with these.

siteconfig — Local site configuration information, such as UUCP connectivity. They normally contain lists of site information, for example:

```
SITE(contessa)
SITE(hoptoad)
SITE(nkainc)
SITE(well)
```

They are referenced using the SITECONFIG macro:

```
SITECONFIG(site.config.file, name_of_site, X)
```

where *X* is the macro/class name to use. It can be U (indicating locally connected hosts) or one of W, X, or Y for up to three remote UUCP hubs.

If you are in a new domain (e.g., a company), you will probably want to create a cf/domain file for your domain. This consists primarily of relay definitions: for example, Berkeley's domain definition defines relays for BitNET, CSNET, and UUCP. Of these, only the UUCP relay is particularly specific to Berkeley. All of these are internet-style domain names. Please check to make certain they are reasonable for your domain.

Subdomains at Berkeley are also represented in the cf/domain directory. For example, the domain cs-exposed is the Computer Science subdomain with the local hostname shown to other users; cs-hidden makes users appear to be from the CS.Berkeley.EDU subdomain (with no local host information included). You will probably have to update this directory to be appropriate for your domain.

You will have to use or create **.mc** files in the *cf/cf* subdirectory for your hosts. This is detailed in the cf/README file.

1.3. Details of Installation Files

This subsection describes the files that comprise the *sendmail* installation.

1.3.1. /usr/sbin/sendmail

The binary for *sendmail* is located in /usr/sbin[2]. It should be setuid root. For security reasons, /, /usr, and /usr/sbin should be owned by root, mode 755[3].

1.3.2. /etc/sendmail.cf

This is the configuration file for *sendmail*. This is the only non-library file name compiled into *sendmail*[4]. Some older systems install it in **/usr/lib/sendmail.cf.**

If you want to move this file, change *src/pathnames.h.*

---

[2]This is usually /usr/sbin on 4.4BSD and newer systems; many systems install it in /usr/lib. I understand it is in /usr/ucblib on System V Release 4.

[3]Some vendors ship them owned by bin; this creates a security hole that is not actually related to *sendmail*. Other important directories that should have restrictive ownerships and permissions are /bin, /usr/bin, /etc, /usr/etc, /lib, and /usr/lib.

[4]The system libraries can reference other files; in particular, system library subroutines that *sendmail* calls probably reference */etc/passwd* and */etc/resolv.conf.*

The configuration file is normally created using the distribution files described above. If you have a particularly unusual system configuration you may need to create a special version. The format of this file is detailed in later sections of this document.

1.3.3. /usr/bin/newaliases

The *newaliases* command should just be a link to *sendmail*:

```
rm –f /usr/bin/newaliases
ln –s /usr/sbin/sendmail /usr/bin/newaliases
```

This can be installed in whatever search path you prefer for your system.

1.3.4. /var/spool/mqueue

The directory */var/spool/mqueue* should be created to hold the mail queue. This directory should be mode 700 and owned by root.

The actual path of this directory is defined in the **Q** option of the *sendmail.cf* file.

1.3.5. /etc/aliases*

The system aliases are held in ''/etc/aliases''. A sample is given in ''lib/aliases'' which includes some aliases which *must* be defined:

```
cp lib/aliases /etc/aliases
edit /etc/aliases
```

You should extend this file with any aliases that are apropos to your system.

Normally *sendmail* looks at a version of these files maintained by the *dbm*(3) or *db*(3) routines. These are stored either in ''/etc/aliases.dir'' and ''/etc/aliases.pag'' or ''/etc/aliases.db'' depending on which database package you are using. These can initially be created as empty files, but they will have to be initialized promptly. These should be mode 644:

```
cp /dev/null /etc/aliases.dir
cp /dev/null /etc/aliases.pag
chmod 644 /etc/aliases.*
newaliases
```

The *db* routines preset the mode reasonably, so this step can be skipped. The actual path of this file is defined in the **A** option of the *sendmail.cf* file.

1.3.6. /etc/rc

It will be necessary to start up the *sendmail* daemon when your system reboots. This daemon performs two functions: it listens on the SMTP socket for connections (to receive mail from a remote system) and it processes the queue periodically to insure that mail gets delivered when hosts come up.

Add the following lines to ''/etc/rc'' (or ''/etc/rc.local'' as appropriate) in the area where it is starting up the daemons:

```
if [ –f /usr/sbin/sendmail –a –f /etc/sendmail.cf ]; then
        (cd /var/spool/mqueue; rm –f [lnx]f*)
        /usr/sbin/sendmail –bd –q30m &
        echo –n ' sendmail' >/dev/console
fi
```

The ''cd'' and ''rm'' commands insure that all lock files have been removed; extraneous lock files may be left around if the system goes down in the middle of processing a message. The line that actually invokes *sendmail* has two flags: ''–bd'' causes it to listen on the SMTP port, and ''–q30m'' causes it to run the queue every half hour.

Some people use a more complex startup script, removing zero length qf files and df files for which there is no qf file. For example:

```
# remove zero length qf files
for qffile in qf*
do
	if [ -r $qffile ]
	then
		if [ ! -s $qffile ]
		then
			echo -n " <zero: $qffile>" > /dev/console
			rm -f $qffile
		fi
	fi
done
# rename tf files to be qf if the qf does not exist
for tffile in tf*
do
	qffile=`echo $tffile | sed 's/t/q/'`
	if [ -r $tffile -a ! -f $qffile ]
	then
		echo -n " <recovering: $tffile>" > /dev/console
		mv $tffile $qffile
	else
		echo -n " <extra: $tffile>" > /dev/console
		rm -f $tffile
	fi
done
# remove df files with no corresponding qf files
for dffile in df*
do
	qffile=`echo $dffile | sed 's/d/q/'`
	if [ -r $dffile -a ! -f $qffile ]
	then
		echo -n " <incomplete: $dffile>" > /dev/console
		mv $dffile `echo $dffile | sed 's/d/D/'`
	fi
done
# announce files that have been saved during disaster recovery
for xffile in [A-Z]f*
do
	echo -n " <panic: $xffile>" > /dev/console
done
```

If you are not running a version of UNIX that supports Berkeley TCP/IP, do not include the **–bd** flag.

1.3.7. /usr/lib/sendmail.hf

This is the help file used by the SMTP **HELP** command. It should be copied from "lib/sendmail.hf":

```
cp lib/sendmail.hf /usr/lib
```

The actual path of this file is defined in the **H** option of the *sendmail.cf* file.

1.3.8. /etc/sendmail.st

If you wish to collect statistics about your mail traffic, you should create the file "/etc/sendmail.st":

```
cp /dev/null /etc/sendmail.st
chmod 666 /etc/sendmail.st
```

This file does not grow. It is printed with the program "mailstats/mailstats.c." The actual path of this file is defined in the **S** option of the *sendmail.cf* file.

1.3.9. /usr/bin/newaliases

If *sendmail* is invoked as "newaliases," it will simulate the **–bi** flag (i.e., will rebuild the alias database; see below). This should be a link to /usr/sbin/sendmail.

1.3.10. /usr/bin/mailq

If *sendmail* is invoked as "mailq," it will simulate the **–bp** flag (i.e., *sendmail* will print the contents of the mail queue; see below). This should be a link to /usr/sbin/sendmail.

2. NORMAL OPERATIONS

2.1. The System Log

The system log is supported by the *syslogd*(8) program. All messages from *sendmail* are logged under the LOG_MAIL facility.

2.1.1. Format

Each line in the system log consists of a timestamp, the name of the machine that generated it (for logging from several machines over the local area network), the word "sendmail:", and a message.

2.1.2. Levels

If you have *syslogd*(8) or an equivalent installed, you will be able to do logging. There is a large amount of information that can be logged. The log is arranged as a succession of levels. At the lowest level only extremely strange situations are logged. At the highest level, even the most mundane and uninteresting events are recorded for posterity. As a convention, log levels under ten are considered generally "useful;" log levels above 64 are reserved for debugging purposes. Levels from 11–64 are reserved for verbose information that some sites might want.

A complete description of the log levels is given in section 4.6.

2.2. The Mail Queue

The mail queue should be processed transparently. However, you may find that manual intervention is sometimes necessary. For example, if a major host is down for a period of time the queue may become clogged. Although *sendmail* ought to recover gracefully when the host comes up, you may find performance unacceptably bad in the meantime.

2.2.1. Printing the queue

The contents of the queue can be printed using the *mailq* command (or by specifying the **–bp** flag to *sendmail*):

```
mailq
```

This will produce a listing of the queue id's, the size of the message, the date the message entered the queue, and the sender and recipients.

2.2.2. Forcing the queue

Sendmail should run the queue automatically at intervals. The algorithm is to read and sort the queue, and then to attempt to process all jobs in order. When it attempts to run the job, *sendmail* first checks to see if the job is locked. If so, it ignores the job.

There is no attempt to insure that only one queue processor exists at any time, since there is no guarantee that a job cannot take forever to process (however, *sendmail* does include heuristics to try to abort jobs that are taking absurd amounts of time; technically, this violates RFC 821, but is blessed by RFC 1123). Due to the locking algorithm, it is impossible for one job to freeze the entire queue. However, an uncooperative recipient host or a program recipient that never returns can accumulate many processes in your system. Unfortunately, there is no completely general way to solve this.

In some cases, you may find that a major host going down for a couple of days may create a prohibitively large queue. This will result in *sendmail* spending an inordinate amount of time sorting the queue. This situation can be fixed by moving the queue to a temporary place and creating a new queue. The old queue can be run later when the offending host returns to service.

To do this, it is acceptable to move the entire queue directory:

```
cd /var/spool
mv mqueue omqueue; mkdir mqueue; chmod 700 mqueue
```

You should then kill the existing daemon (since it will still be processing in the old queue directory) and create a new daemon.

To run the old mail queue, run the following command:

```
/usr/sbin/sendmail –oQ/var/spool/omqueue –q
```

The **–oQ** flag specifies an alternate queue directory and the **–q** flag says to just run every job in the queue. If you have a tendency toward voyeurism, you can use the **–v** flag to watch what is going on.

When the queue is finally emptied, you can remove the directory:

```
rmdir /var/spool/omqueue
```

2.3. The Alias Database

The alias database exists in two forms. One is a text form, maintained in the file */etc/aliases.* The aliases are of the form

```
name: name1, name2, ...
```

Only local names may be aliased; e.g.,

```
eric@prep.ai.MIT.EDU: eric@CS.Berkeley.EDU
```

will not have the desired effect. Aliases may be continued by starting any continuation lines with a space or a tab. Blank lines and lines beginning with a sharp sign (“#”) are comments.

The second form is processed by the *dbm*(3) (or *db*(3)) library. This form is in the files */etc/aliases.dir* and */etc/aliases.pag*. This is the form that *sendmail* actually uses to resolve aliases. This technique is used to improve performance.

You can also use NIS-based alias files. For example, the specification:

```
OA/etc/aliases
OAnis:mail.aliases@my.nis.domain
```

will first search the /etc/aliases file and then the map named “mail.aliases” in “my.nis.domain”. Warning: if you build your own NIS-based alias files, be sure to provide the **–l** flag to *makedbm*(8) to map upper case letters in the keys to lower case; otherwise, aliases with upper case letters in their names won’t match incoming addresses.

Additional flags can be added after the colon exactly like a **K** line — for example:

```
OAnis:-N mail.aliases@my.nis.domain
```

will search the appropriate NIS map and always include null bytes in the key.

2.3.1. Rebuilding the alias database

The DB or DBM version of the database may be rebuilt explicitly by executing the command

newaliases

This is equivalent to giving *sendmail* the **–bi** flag:

/usr/sbin/sendmail –bi

If the "D" option is specified in the configuration, *sendmail* will rebuild the alias database automatically if possible when it is out of date. Auto-rebuild can be dangerous on heavily loaded machines with large alias files; if it might take more than five minutes to rebuild the database, there is a chance that several processes will start the rebuild process simultaneously.

If you have multiple aliases databases specified, the **–bi** flag rebuilds all the database types it understands (for example, it can rebuild dbm databases but not nis databases).

2.3.2. Potential problems

There are a number of problems that can occur with the alias database. They all result from a *sendmail* process accessing the DBM version while it is only partially built. This can happen under two circumstances: One process accesses the database while another process is rebuilding it, or the process rebuilding the database dies (due to being killed or a system crash) before completing the rebuild.

Sendmail has two techniques to try to relieve these problems. First, it ignores interrupts while rebuilding the database; this avoids the problem of someone aborting the process leaving a partially rebuilt database. Second, at the end of the rebuild it adds an alias of the form

@: @

(which is not normally legal). Before *sendmail* will access the database, it checks to insure that this entry exists[5].

2.3.3. List owners

If an error occurs on sending to a certain address, say "*x*", *sendmail* will look for an alias of the form "owner-*x*" to receive the errors. This is typically useful for a mailing list where the submitter of the list has no control over the maintenance of the list itself; in this case the list maintainer would be the owner of the list. For example:

```
unix-wizards: eric@ucbarpa, wnj@monet, nosuchuser,
        sam@matisse
owner-unix-wizards: eric@ucbarpa
```

would cause "eric@ucbarpa" to get the error that will occur when someone sends to unix-wizards due to the inclusion of "nosuchuser" on the list.

List owners also cause the envelope sender address to be modified. The contents of the owner alias are used if they point to a single user, otherwise the name of the alias itself is used. For this reason, and to obey Internet conventions, a typical scheme would be:

```
list:          some, set, of, addresses
list-request:  list-admin-1, list-admin-2, ...
owner-list:    list-request
```

2.4. User Information Database

If you have a version of *sendmail* with the user information database compiled in, and you have specified one or more databases using the **U** option, the databases will be searched for a

[5]The "a" option is required in the configuration for this action to occur. This should normally be specified.

user:maildrop entry. If found, the mail will be sent to the specified address.

If the first token passed to user part of the "local" mailer is an at sign, the at sign will be stripped off and this step will be skipped.

2.5. Per-User Forwarding (.forward Files)

As an alternative to the alias database, any user may put a file with the name ".forward" in his or her home directory. If this file exists, *sendmail* redirects mail for that user to the list of addresses listed in the .forward file. For example, if the home directory for user "mckusick" has a .forward file with contents:

```
mckusick@ernie
kirk@calder
```

then any mail arriving for "mckusick" will be redirected to the specified accounts.

Actually, the configuration file defines a sequence of filenames to check. By default, this is the user's .forward file, but can be defined to be more generally using the **J** option. If you change this, you will have to inform your user base of the change; .forward is pretty well incorporated into the collective subconscious.

2.6. Special Header Lines

Several header lines have special interpretations defined by the configuration file. Others have interpretations built into *sendmail* that cannot be changed without changing the code. These builtins are described here.

2.6.1. Return-Receipt-To:

If this header is sent, a message will be sent to any specified addresses when the final delivery is complete, that is, when successfully delivered to a mailer with the **l** flag (local delivery) set in the mailer descriptor[6]. This header can be disabled with the "noreceipts" privacy flag.

2.6.2. Errors-To:

If errors occur anywhere during processing, this header will cause error messages to go to the listed addresses. This is intended for mailing lists.

The Errors-To: header was created in the bad old days when UUCP didn't understand the distinction between an envelope and a header; this was a hack to provide what should now be passed as the envelope sender address. It should go away. It is only used if the **l** option is set.

2.6.3. Apparently-To:

If a message comes in with no recipients listed in the message (in a To:, Cc:, or Bcc: line) then *sendmail* will add an "Apparently-To:" header line for any recipients it is aware of. This is not put in as a standard recipient line to warn any recipients that the list is not complete.

At least one recipient line is required under RFC 822.

2.7. IDENT Protocol Support

Sendmail supports the IDENT protocol as defined in RFC 1413. Although this enhances identification of the author of an email message by doing a "call back" to the originating system to include the owner of a particular TCP connection in the audit trail it is in no sense perfect; a

[6]Some sites disable this header, and other (non-*sendmail*) systems do not implement it. Do not assume that a failure to get a return receipt means that the mail did not arrive. Also, do not assume that getting a return receipt means that the mail has been read; it just means that the message has been delivered to the recipient's mailbox.

determined forger can easily spoof the IDENT protocol. The following description is excerpted from RFC 1413:

> 6. Security Considerations
>
> The information returned by this protocol is at most as trustworthy as the host providing it OR the organization operating the host. For example, a PC in an open lab has few if any controls on it to prevent a user from having this protocol return any identifier the user wants. Likewise, if the host has been compromised the information returned may be completely erroneous and misleading.
>
> The Identification Protocol is not intended as an authorization or access control protocol. At best, it provides some additional auditing information with respect to TCP connections. At worst, it can provide misleading, incorrect, or maliciously incorrect information.
>
> The use of the information returned by this protocol for other than auditing is strongly discouraged. Specifically, using Identification Protocol information to make access control decisions - either as the primary method (i.e., no other checks) or as an adjunct to other methods may result in a weakening of normal host security.
>
> An Identification server may reveal information about users, entities, objects or processes which might normally be considered private. An Identification server provides service which is a rough analog of the CallerID services provided by some phone companies and many of the same privacy considerations and arguments that apply to the CallerID service apply to Identification. If you wouldn't run a "finger" server due to privacy considerations you may not want to run this protocol.

3. ARGUMENTS

The complete list of arguments to *sendmail* is described in detail in Appendix A. Some important arguments are described here.

3.1. Queue Interval

The amount of time between forking a process to run through the queue is defined by the **–q** flag. If you run in mode **f** or **a** this can be relatively large, since it will only be relevant when a host that was down comes back up. If you run in **q** mode it should be relatively short, since it defines the maximum amount of time that a message may sit in the queue.

RFC 1123 section 5.3.1.1 says that this value should be at least 30 minutes (although that probably doesn't make sense if you use ''queue-only'' mode).

3.2. Daemon Mode

If you allow incoming mail over an IPC connection, you should have a daemon running. This should be set by your */etc/rc* file using the **–bd** flag. The **–bd** flag and the **–q** flag may be combined in one call:

```
/usr/sbin/sendmail –bd –q30m
```

3.3. Forcing the Queue

In some cases you may find that the queue has gotten clogged for some reason. You can force a queue run using the **–q** flag (with no value). It is entertaining to use the **–v** flag (verbose) when this is done to watch what happens:

```
/usr/sbin/sendmail –q –v
```

You can also limit the jobs to those with a particular queue identifier, sender, or recipient using one of the queue modifiers. For example, ''–qRberkeley'' restricts the queue run to jobs that have the string ''berkeley'' somewhere in one of the recipient addresses. Similarly, ''–qSstring'' limits the run to particular senders and ''–qIstring'' limits it to particular identifiers.

3.4. Debugging

There are a fairly large number of debug flags built into *sendmail*. Each debug flag has a number and a level, where higher levels means to print out more information. The convention is that levels greater than nine are ''absurd,'' i.e., they print out so much information that you wouldn't normally want to see them except for debugging that particular piece of code. Debug flags are set using the **–d** option; the syntax is:

```
debug-flag:   –d debug-list
debug-list:   debug-option [ , debug-option ]
debug-option: debug-range [ . debug-level ]
debug-range:  integer | integer – integer
debug-level:  integer
```

where spaces are for reading ease only. For example,

–d12	Set flag 12 to level 1
–d12.3	Set flag 12 to level 3
–d3-17	Set flags 3 through 17 to level 1
–d3-17.4	Set flags 3 through 17 to level 4

For a complete list of the available debug flags you will have to look at the code (they are too dynamic to keep this documentation up to date).

3.5. Trying a Different Configuration File

An alternative configuration file can be specified using the **–C** flag; for example,

/usr/sbin/sendmail –Ctest.cf

uses the configuration file *test.cf* instead of the default */etc/sendmail.cf.* If the **–C** flag has no value it defaults to *sendmail.cf* in the current directory.

3.6. Changing the Values of Options

Options can be overridden using the **–o** flag. For example,

/usr/sbin/sendmail –oT2m

sets the **T** (timeout) option to two minutes for this run only.

Some options have security implications. Sendmail allows you to set these, but refuses to run as root thereafter.

3.7. Logging Traffic

Many SMTP implementations do not fully implement the protocol. For example, some personal computer based SMTPs do not understand continuation lines in reply codes. These can be very hard to trace. If you suspect such a problem, you can set traffic logging using the **–X** flag. For example,

/usr/sbin/sendmail –X /tmp/traffic -bd

will log all traffic in the file */tmp/traffic.*

This logs a lot of data very quickly and should never be used during normal operations. After starting up such a daemon, force the errant implementation to send a message to your host. All message traffic in and out of *sendmail*, including the incoming SMTP traffic, will be logged in this file.

3.8. Dumping State

You can ask *sendmail* to log a dump of the open files and the connection cache by sending it a SIGUSR1 signal. The results are logged at LOG_DEBUG priority.

8

4. TUNING

There are a number of configuration parameters you may want to change, depending on the requirements of your site. Most of these are set using an option in the configuration file. For example, the line ''OT5d'' sets option ''T'' to the value ''5d'' (five days).

Most of these options have appropriate defaults for most sites. However, sites having very high mail loads may find they need to tune them as appropriate for their mail load. In particular, sites experiencing a large number of small messages, many of which are delivered to many recipients, may find that they need to adjust the parameters dealing with queue priorities.

4.1. Timeouts

All time intervals are set using a scaled syntax. For example, ''10m'' represents ten minutes, whereas ''2h30m'' represents two and a half hours. The full set of scales is:

s	seconds
m	minutes
h	hours
d	days
w	weeks

4.1.1. Queue interval

The argument to the **−q** flag specifies how often a sub-daemon will run the queue. This is typically set to between fifteen minutes and one hour. RFC 1123 section 5.3.1.1 recommends that this be at least 30 minutes.

4.1.2. Read timeouts

It is possible to time out when reading the standard input or when reading from a remote SMTP server. These timeouts are set using the **r** option in the configuration file. The argument is a list of *keyword=value* pairs. The recognized keywords, their default values, and the minimum values allowed by RFC 1123 section 5.3.2 are:

initial	The wait for the initial 220 greeting message [5m, 5m].
helo	The wait for a reply from a HELO or EHLO command [5m, unspecified]. This may require a host name lookup, so five minutes is probably a reasonable minimum.
mail†	The wait for a reply from a MAIL command [10m, 5m].
rcpt†	The wait for a reply from a RCPT command [1h, 5m]. This should be long because it could be pointing at a list that takes a long time to expand.
datainit†	The wait for a reply from a DATA command [5m, 2m].
datablock†	The wait for reading a data block (that is, the body of the message). [1h, 3m]. This should be long because it also applies to programs piping input to *sendmail* which have no guarantee of promptness.
datafinal†	The wait for a reply from the dot terminating a message. [1h, 10m]. If this is shorter than the time actually needed for the receiver to deliver the message, duplicates will be generated. This is discussed in RFC 1047.
rset	The wait for a reply from a RSET command [5m, unspecified].
quit	The wait for a reply from a QUIT command [2m, unspecified].
misc	The wait for a reply from miscellaneous (but short) commands such as NOOP (no-operation) and VERB (go into verbose mode). [2m, unspecified].
command†	In server SMTP, the time to wait for another command. [1h, 5m].
ident	The timeout waiting for a reply to an IDENT query [30s, unspecified].

For compatibility with old configuration files, if no ''keyword='' is specified, all the timeouts marked with † are set to the indicated value.

Many of the RFC 1123 minimum values may well be too short. *Sendmail* was designed to the RFC 822 protocols, which did not specify read timeouts; hence, *sendmail* does not guarantee to reply to messages promptly. In particular, a ''RCPT'' command specifying a mailing list will expand and verify the entire list; a large list on a slow system may take more than five minutes[7]. I recommend a one hour timeout — since this failure is rare, a long timeout is not onerous and may ultimately help reduce network load.

For example, the line:

Orcommand=25m,datablock=3h

sets the server SMTP command timeout to 25 minutes and the input data block timeout to three hours.

4.1.3. Message timeouts

After sitting in the queue for a few days, a message will time out. This is to insure that at least the sender is aware of the inability to send a message. The timeout is typically set to three days. This timeout is set using the **T** option in the configuration file.

The time of submission is set in the queue, rather than the amount of time left until timeout. As a result, you can flush messages that have been hanging for a short period by running the queue with a short message timeout. For example,

/usr/sbin/sendmail –oT1d –q

will run the queue and flush anything that is one day old.

Since this option is global, and since you can not *a priori* know how long another host outside your domain will be down, a five day timeout is recommended. This allows a recipient to fix the problem even if it occurs at the beginning of a long weekend. RFC 1123 section 5.3.1.1 says that this parameter should be ''at least 4–5 days''.

The **T** option can also take a second timeout indicating a time after which a warning message should be sent; the two timeouts are separated by a slash. For example, the value

5d/4h

causes email to fail after five days, but a warning message will be sent after four hours. This should be large enough that the message will have been tried several times.

4.2. Forking During Queue Runs

By setting the **Y** option, *sendmail* will fork before each individual message while running the queue. This will prevent *sendmail* from consuming large amounts of memory, so it may be useful in memory-poor environments. However, if the **Y** option is not set, *sendmail* will keep track of hosts that are down during a queue run, which can improve performance dramatically.

If the **Y** option is set, *sendmail* can not use connection caching.

4.3. Queue Priorities

Every message is assigned a priority when it is first instantiated, consisting of the message size (in bytes) offset by the message class times the ''work class factor'' and the number of recipients times the ''work recipient factor.'' The priority is used to order the queue. Higher numbers for the priority mean that the message will be processed later when running the queue.

The message size is included so that large messages are penalized relative to small messages. The message class allows users to send ''high priority'' messages by including a ''Precedence:''

[7]This verification includes looking up every address with the name server; this involves network delays, and can in some cases can be considerable.

field in their message; the value of this field is looked up in the **P** lines of the configuration file. Since the number of recipients affects the amount of load a message presents to the system, this is also included into the priority.

The recipient and class factors can be set in the configuration file using the **y** and **z** options respectively. They default to 30000 (for the recipient factor) and 1800 (for the class factor). The initial priority is:

$$pri = msgsize - (class \times \mathbf{z}) + (nrcpt \times \mathbf{y})$$

(Remember, higher values for this parameter actually mean that the job will be treated with lower priority.)

The priority of a job can also be adjusted each time it is processed (that is, each time an attempt is made to deliver it) using the "work time factor," set by the **Z** option. This is added to the priority, so it normally decreases the precedence of the job, on the grounds that jobs that have failed many times will tend to fail again in the future. The **Z** option defaults to 90000.

4.4. Load Limiting

Sendmail can be asked to queue (but not deliver) mail if the system load average gets too high using the **x** option. When the load average exceeds the value of the **x** option, the delivery mode is set to **q** (queue only) if the *Queue Factor* (**q** option) divided by the difference in the current load average and the **x** option plus one exceeds the priority of the message — that is, the message is queued iff:

$$pri > \frac{\mathbf{q}}{LA - \mathbf{x} + 1}$$

The **q** option defaults to 600000, so each point of load average is worth 600000 priority points (as described above).

For drastic cases, the **X** option defines a load average at which *sendmail* will refuse to accept network connections. Locally generated mail (including incoming UUCP mail) is still accepted.

4.5. Delivery Mode

There are a number of delivery modes that *sendmail* can operate in, set by the "d" configuration option. These modes specify how quickly mail will be delivered. Legal modes are:

- i deliver interactively (synchronously)
- b deliver in background (asynchronously)
- q queue only (don't deliver)

There are tradeoffs. Mode "i" passes the maximum amount of information to the sender, but is hardly ever necessary. Mode "q" puts the minimum load on your machine, but means that delivery may be delayed for up to the queue interval. Mode "b" is probably a good compromise. However, this mode can cause large numbers of processes if you have a mailer that takes a long time to deliver a message.

If you run in mode "q" (queue only) or "b" (deliver in background) *sendmail* will not expand aliases and follow .forward files upon initial receipt of the mail. This speeds up the response to RCPT commands.

4.6. Log Level

The level of logging can be set for *sendmail*. The default using a standard configuration table is level 9. The levels are as follows:

0 No logging.

1 Serious system failures and potential security problems.

2 Lost communications (network problems) and protocol failures.

3 Other serious failures.

4	Minor failures.
5	Message collection statistics.
6	Creation of error messages, VRFY and EXPN commands.
7	Delivery failures (host or user unknown, etc.).
8	Successful deliveries.
9	Messages being deferred (due to a host being down, etc.).
10	Database expansion (alias, forward, and userdb lookups).
15	Automatic alias database rebuilds.
20	Logs attempts to run locked queue files. These are not errors, but can be useful to note if your queue appears to be clogged.
30	Lost locks (only if using lockf instead of flock).

Additionally, values above 64 are reserved for extremely verbose debuggging output. No normal site would ever set these.

4.7. File Modes

There are a number of files that may have a number of modes. The modes depend on what functionality you want and the level of security you require.

4.7.1. To suid or not to suid?

Sendmail can safely be made setuid to root. At the point where it is about to *exec* (2) a mailer, it checks to see if the userid is zero; if so, it resets the userid and groupid to a default (set by the **u** and **g** options). (This can be overridden by setting the **S** flag to the mailer for mailers that are trusted and must be called as root.) However, this will cause mail processing to be accounted (using *sa* (8)) to root rather than to the user sending the mail.

4.7.2. Should my alias database be writable?

At Berkeley we have the alias database (/etc/aliases*) mode 644. While this is not as flexible as if the database were more 666, it avoids potential security problems with a globally writable database.

The database that *sendmail* actually used is represented by the two files *aliases.dir* and *aliases.pag* (both in /etc) (or *aliases.db* if you are running with the new Berkeley database primitives). The mode on these files should match the mode on /etc/aliases. If *aliases* is writable and the DBM files (*aliases.dir* and *aliases.pag*) are not, users will be unable to reflect their desired changes through to the actual database. However, if *aliases* is read-only and the DBM files are writable, a slightly sophisticated user can arrange to steal mail anyway.

If your DBM files are not writable by the world or you do not have auto-rebuild enabled (with the ''D'' option), then you must be careful to reconstruct the alias database each time you change the text version:

```
newaliases
```

If this step is ignored or forgotten any intended changes will also be ignored or forgotten.

4.8. Connection Caching

When processing the queue, *sendmail* will try to keep the last few open connections open to avoid startup and shutdown costs. This only applies to IPC connections.

When trying to open a connection the cache is first searched. If an open connection is found, it is probed to see if it is still active by sending a NOOP command. It is not an error if this fails; instead, the connection is closed and reopened.

Two parameters control the connection cache. The **k** option defines the number of simultaneous open connections that will be permitted. If it is set to zero, connections will be closed as quickly as possible. The default is one. This should be set as appropriate for your system size; it will limit the amount of system resources that *sendmail* will use during queue runs.

The **K** option specifies the maximum time that any cached connection will be permitted to idle. When the idle time exceeds this value the connection is closed. This number should be small (under ten minutes) to prevent you from grabbing too many resources from other hosts. The default is five minutes.

4.9. Name Server Access

If your system supports the name server, then the probability is that *sendmail* will be using it regardless of how you configure *sendmail*. In particular, the system routine *gethostbyname*(3) is used to look up host names, and most vendor versions try some combination of DNS, NIS, and file lookup in /etc/hosts.

However, if you do not have a nameserver configured at all, such as at a UUCP-only site, *sendmail* will get a "connection refused" message when it tries to connect to the name server (either indirectly by calling *gethostbyname* or directly by looking up MX records). If the **I** option is set, *sendmail* will interpret this to mean a temporary failure and will queue the mail for later processing; otherwise, it ignores the name server data. If your name server is running properly, the setting of this option is not relevant; however, it is important that it be set properly to make error handling work properly.

This option also allows you to tweak name server options. The command line takes a series of flags as documented in *resolver*(3) (with the leading "RES_" deleted). Each can be preceded by an optional '+' or '–'. For example, the line

```
OITrue +AAONLY –DNSRCH
```

turns on the AAONLY (accept authoritative answers only) and turns off the DNSRCH (search the domain path) options. Most resolver libraries default DNSRCH, DEFNAMES, and RECURSE flags on and all others off. Note the use of the initial "True" — this is for compatibility with previous versions of *sendmail*, but is not otherwise necessary.

Version level 1 configurations turn DNSRCH and DEFNAMES off when doing delivery lookups, but leave them on everywhere else. Version 8 of *sendmail* ignores them when doing canonification lookups (that is, when using $[... $]), and always does the search. If you don't want to do automatic name extension, don't call $[... $].

The search rules for $[... $] are somewhat different than usual. If the name (that is, the "...") has at least one dot, it always tries the unmodified name first. If that fails, it tries the reduced search path, and lastly tries the unmodified name (but only for names without a dot, since names with a dot have already been tried). This allows names such as "utc.CS" to match the site in Czechoslovakia rather than the site in your local Computer Science department. It also prefers A and CNAME records over MX records — that is, if it finds an MX record it makes note of it, but keeps looking. This way, if you have a wildcard MX record matching your domain, it will not assume that all names match.

4.10. Moving the Per-User Forward Files

Some sites mount each user's home directory from a local disk on their workstation, so that local access is fast. However, the result is that .forward file lookups are slow. In some cases, mail can even be delivered on machines inappropriately because of a file server being down. The performance can be especially bad if you run the automounter.

The **J** option allows you to set a path of forward files. For example, the config file line

```
OJ/var/forward/$u:$z/.forward
```

would first look for a file with the same name as the user's login in /var/forward; if that is not found (or is inaccessible) the file ".forward" in the user's home directory is searched. A truly perverse site could also search by sender by using $r, $s, or $f.

If you create a directory such as /var/forward, it should be mode 1777 (that is, the sticky bit should be set). Users should create the files mode 644.

4.11. Free Space

On systems that have the *statfs*(2) system call, you can specify a minimum number of free blocks on the queue filesystem using the **b** option. If there are fewer than the indicated number of blocks free on the filesystem on which the queue is mounted the SMTP server will reject mail with the 452 error code. This invites the SMTP client to try again later.

Beware of setting this option too high; it can cause rejection of email when that mail would be processed without difficulty.

This option can also specify an advertised ''maximum message size'' for hosts that speak ESMTP.

4.12. Privacy Flags

The **p** option allows you to set certain ''privacy'' flags. Actually, many of them don't give you any extra privacy, rather just insisting that client SMTP servers use the HELO command before using certain commands.

The option takes a series of flag names; the final privacy is the inclusive or of those flags. For example:

```
Op needmailhelo, noexpn
```

insists that the HELO or EHLO command be used before a MAIL command is accepted and disables the EXPN command.

The ''restrictmailq'' option restricts printing the queue to the group that owns the queue directory. It is absurd to set this if you don't also protect the logs.

The ''restrictqrun'' option restricts people running the queue (that is, using the **–q** command line flag) to root and the owner of the queue directory.

4.13. Send to Me Too

Normally, *sendmail* deletes the (envelope) sender from any list expansions. For example, if ''matt'' sends to a list that contains ''matt'' as one of the members he won't get a copy of the message. If the **–m** (me too) command line flag, or if the **m** option is set in the configuration file, this behaviour is supressed. Some sites like to run the SMTP daemon with **–m**.

5. THE WHOLE SCOOP ON THE CONFIGURATION FILE

This section describes the configuration file in detail, including hints on how to write one of your own if you have to.

There is one point that should be made clear immediately: the syntax of the configuration file is designed to be reasonably easy to parse, since this is done every time *sendmail* starts up, rather than easy for a human to read or write. On the ''future project'' list is a configuration-file compiler.

An overview of the configuration file is given first, followed by details of the semantics.

5.1. Configuration File Lines

The configuration file is organized as a series of lines, each of which begins with a single character defining the semantics for the rest of the line. Lines beginning with a space or a tab are continuation lines (although the semantics are not well defined in many places). Blank lines and lines beginning with a sharp symbol ('#') are comments.

5.1.1. R and S — rewriting rules

The core of address parsing are the rewriting rules. These are an ordered production system. *Sendmail* scans through the set of rewriting rules looking for a match on the left hand side (LHS) of the rule. When a rule matches, the address is replaced by the right hand side (RHS) of the rule.

There are several sets of rewriting rules. Some of the rewriting sets are used internally and must have specific semantics. Other rewriting sets do not have specifically assigned semantics, and may be referenced by the mailer definitions or by other rewriting sets.

The syntax of these two commands are:

S*n*

Sets the current ruleset being collected to *n*. If you begin a ruleset more than once it deletes the old definition.

R*lhs rhs comments*

The fields must be separated by at least one tab character; there may be embedded spaces in the fields. The *lhs* is a pattern that is applied to the input. If it matches, the input is rewritten to the *rhs*. The *comments* are ignored.

Macro expansions of the form **$***x* are performed when the configuration file is read. Expansions of the form **$&***x* are performed at run time using a somewhat less general algorithm. This for is intended only for referencing internally defined macros such as **$h** that are changed at runtime.

5.1.1.1. The left hand side

The left hand side of rewriting rules contains a pattern. Normal words are simply matched directly. Metasyntax is introduced using a dollar sign. The metasymbols are:

$*	Match zero or more tokens
$+	Match one or more tokens
$–	Match exactly one token
$=*x*	Match any phrase in class *x*
$~*x*	Match any word not in class *x*

If any of these match, they are assigned to the symbol **$***n* for replacement on the right hand side, where *n* is the index in the LHS. For example, if the LHS:

$–:$+

is applied to the input:

UCBARPA:eric

the rule will match, and the values passed to the RHS will be:

$1	UCBARPA
$2	eric

Additionally, the LHS can include **$@** to match zero tokens. This is *not* bound to a **$***N* on the RHS, and is normally only used when it stands alone in order to match the null input.

5.1.1.2. The right hand side

When the left hand side of a rewriting rule matches, the input is deleted and replaced by the right hand side. Tokens are copied directly from the RHS unless they begin with a dollar sign. Metasymbols are:

$*n*	Substitute indefinite token *n* from LHS
$[***name***$]	Canonicalize *name*
$(*map key* **$@***arguments* **$:***default* **$)**	Generalized keyed mapping function
$>*n*	''Call'' ruleset *n*
$#*mailer*	Resolve to *mailer*
$@*host*	Specify *host*
$:*user*	Specify *user*

The **$*n*** syntax substitutes the corresponding value from a **$+**, **$–**, **$***, **$=**, or **$~** match on the LHS. It may be used anywhere.

A host name enclosed between **$[** and **$]** is looked up using the *gethostent*(3) routines and replaced by the canonical name[8]. For example, ''$[csam$]'' might become ''lbl-csam.arpa'' and ''$[[128.32.130.2]$]'' would become ''vangogh.CS.Berkeley.EDU.'' *Sendmail* recognizes it's numeric IP address without calling the name server and replaces it with it's canonical name.

The **$(... $)** syntax is a more general form of lookup; it uses a named map instead of an implicit map. If no lookup is found, the indicated *default* is inserted; if no default is specified and no lookup matches, the value is left unchanged.

The **$>*n*** syntax causes the remainder of the line to be substituted as usual and then passed as the argument to ruleset *n*. The final value of ruleset *n* then becomes the substitution for this rule.

The **$#** syntax should *only* be used in ruleset zero or a subroutine of ruleset zero. It causes evaluation of the ruleset to terminate immediately, and signals to *sendmail* that the address has completely resolved. The complete syntax is:

> **$#*mailer*** **$@*host*** **$:*user***

This specifies the {mailer, host, user} 3-tuple necessary to direct the mailer. If the mailer is local the host part may be omitted[9]. The *mailer* must be a single word, but the *host* and *user* may be multi-part. If the *mailer* is the builtin IPC mailer, the *host* may be a colon-separated list of hosts that are searched in order for the first working address (exactly like MX records). The *user* is later rewritten by the mailer-specific envelope rewriting set and assigned to the **$u** macro. As a special case, if the value to **$#** is ''local'' and the first character of the **$:** value is ''@'', the ''@'' is stripped off, and a flag is set in the address descriptor that causes sendmail to not do ruleset 5 processing.

Normally, a rule that matches is retried, that is, the rule loops until it fails. A RHS may also be preceded by a **$@** or a **$:** to change this behavior. A **$@** prefix causes the ruleset to return with the remainder of the RHS as the value. A **$:** prefix causes the rule to terminate immediately, but the ruleset to continue; this can be used to avoid continued application of a rule. The prefix is stripped before continuing.

The **$@** and **$:** prefixes may precede a **$>** spec; for example:

```
R$+        $: $>7 $1
```

matches anything, passes that to ruleset seven, and continues; the **$:** is necessary to avoid an infinite loop.

Substitution occurs in the order described, that is, parameters from the LHS are substituted, hostnames are canonicalized, ''subroutines'' are called, and finally **$#**, **$@**, and **$:** are processed.

5.1.1.3. Semantics of rewriting rule sets

There are five rewriting sets that have specific semantics. These are related as depicted by figure 1.

Ruleset three should turn the address into ''canonical form.'' This form should have the basic syntax:

> local-part@host-domain-spec

If no ''@'' sign is specified, then the host-domain-spec *may* be appended from the sender

[8]This is actually completely equivalent to $(host *hostname*$). In particular, a **$:** default can be used.

[9]You may want to use it for special ''per user'' extensions. For example, at CMU you can send email to ''jgm+foo''; the part after the plus sign is not part of the user name, and is passed to the local mailer for local use.

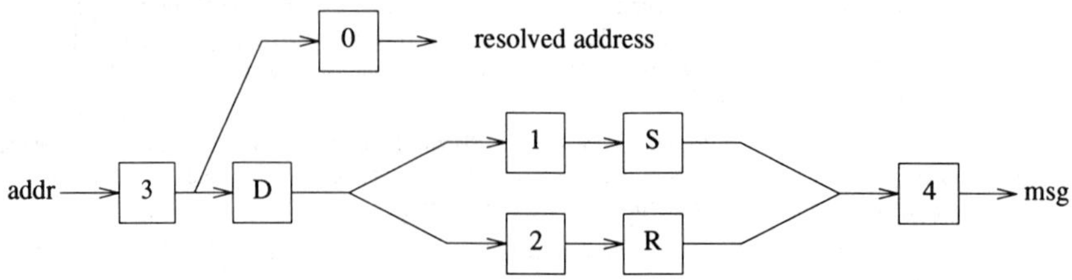

Figure 1 — Rewriting set semantics
D — sender domain addition
S — mailer-specific sender rewriting
R — mailer-specific recipient rewriting

address (if the **C** flag is set in the mailer definition corresponding to the *sending* mailer). Ruleset three is applied by *sendmail* before doing anything with any address.

Ruleset zero is applied after ruleset three to addresses that are going to actually specify recipients. It must resolve to a *{mailer, host, user}* triple. The *mailer* must be defined in the mailer definitions from the configuration file. The *host* is defined into the **$h** macro for use in the argv expansion of the specified mailer.

Rulesets one and two are applied to all sender and recipient addresses respectively. They are applied before any specification in the mailer definition. They must never resolve.

Ruleset four is applied to all addresses in the message. It is typically used to translate internal to external form.

5.1.1.4. IPC mailers

Some special processing occurs if the ruleset zero resolves to an IPC mailer (that is, a mailer that has ''[IPC]'' listed as the Path in the **M** configuration line. The host name passed after ''$@'' has MX expansion performed; this looks the name up in DNS to find alternate delivery sites.

The host name can also be provided as a dotted quad in square brackets; for example:

    [128.32.149.78]

This causes direct conversion of the numeric value to a TCP/IP host address.

The host name passed in after the ''$@'' may also be a colon-separated list of hosts. Each is separately MX expanded and the results are concatenated to make (essentially) one long MX list. The intent here is to create ''fake'' MX records that are not published in DNS for private internal networks.

As a final special case, the host name can be passed in as a text string in square brackets:

    [ucbvax.berkeley.edu]

This form avoids the MX mapping. **N.B.:** This is intended only for situations where you have a network firewall, so that your MX record points to a gateway machine; this machine could then do direct delivery to machines within your local domain. Use of this feature directly violates RFC 1123 section 5.3.5: it should not be used lightly.

5.1.2. D — define macro

Macros are named with a single character. These may be selected from the entire ASCII set, but user-defined macros should be selected from the set of upper case letters only. Lower case letters and special symbols are used internally.

The syntax for macro definitions is:

D*x val*

where *x* is the name of the macro and *val* is the value it should have.

Macros are interpolated using the construct **$***x*, where *x* is the name of the macro to be interpolated. This interpolation is done when the configuration file is read, except in **M** lines. The special construct **$&***x* can be used in **R** lines to get deferred interpolation.

Conditionals can be specified using the syntax:

$?x text1 $| text2 $.

This interpolates *text1* if the macro **$x** is set, and *text2* otherwise. The ''else'' (**$|**) clause may be omitted.

Lower case macro names are reserved to have special semantics, used to pass information in or out of *sendmail*, and special characters are reserved to provide conditionals, etc. Upper case names (that is, **$A** through **$Z**) are specifically reserved for configuration file authors.

The following macros are defined and/or used internally by *sendmail* for interpolation into argv's for mailers or for other contexts. The ones marked † are information passed into sendmail[10], the ones marked ‡ are information passed both in and out of sendmail, and the unmarked macros are passed out of sendmail but are not otherwise used internally. These macros are:

$a **The origination date in RFC 822 format.**

$b **The current date in RFC 822 format.**

$c **The hop count.**

$d **The current date in UNIX (ctime) format.**

$e† **The SMTP entry message.** This is printed out when SMTP starts up. The first word must be the **$j** macro as specified by RFC821. Defaults to ''$j Sendmail $v ready at $b''. Commonly redefined to include the configuration version number, e.g., ''$j Sendmail $v/$Z ready at $b''

$f **The sender (from) address.**

$g **The sender address relative to the recipient.**

$h **The recipient host.**

$i **The queue id.**

$j‡ **The ''official'' domain name for this site.** This is fully qualified if the full qualification can be found. It *must* be redefined to be the fully qualified domain name if your system is not configured so that information can find it automatically.

$k **The UUCP node name (from the uname system call).**

$l† **The format of the UNIX from line.** Unless you have changed the UNIX mailbox format, you should not change the default, which is ''From $g $d''.

$m **The domain part of the *gethostname* return value.** Under normal circumstances, **$j** is equivalent to **$w.$m**.

$n† **The name of the daemon (for error messages).** Defaults to ''MAILER-DAEMON''.

---

[10]As of version 8.6, all of these macros have reasonable defaults. Previous versions required that they be defined.

$o† **The set of "operators" in addresses.** A list of characters which will be considered tokens and which will separate tokens when doing parsing. For example, if "@" were in the **$o** macro, then the input "a@b" would be scanned as three tokens: "a," "@," and "b." Defaults to ".:@[]", which is the minimum set necessary to do RFC 822 parsing; a richer set of operators is ".:%@!/[]", which adds support for UUCP, the %-hack, and X.400 addresses.

$p **Sendmail's process id.**

$q† **Default format of sender address.** The **$q** macro specifies how an address should appear in a message when it is defaulted. Defaults to "<$g>". It is commonly redefined to be "$?x$x <$g>$|g." or "g?x ($x)$.", corresponding to the following two formats:

> Eric Allman <eric@CS.Berkeley.EDU>
> eric@CS.Berkeley.EDU (Eric Allman)

Sendmail properly quotes names that have special characters if the first form is used.

$r **Protocol used to receive the message.**

$s **Sender's host name.**

$t **A numeric representation of the current time.**

$u **The recipient user.**

$v **The version number of *sendmail*.**

$w‡ **The hostname of this site.**

The **$w** macro is set to the root name of this host (but see below for caveats).

$x **The full name of the sender.**

$z **The home directory of the recipient.**

$_ **The validated sender address.**

There are three types of dates that can be used. The **$a** and **$b** macros are in RFC 822 format; **$a** is the time as extracted from the "Date:" line of the message (if there was one), and **$b** is the current date and time (used for postmarks). If no "Date:" line is found in the incoming message, **$a** is set to the current time also. The **$d** macro is equivalent to the **$b** macro in UNIX (ctime) format.

The macros **$w**, **$j**, and **$m** are set to the identity of this host. *Sendmail* tries to find the fully qualified name of the host if at all possible; it does this by calling *gethostname*(2) to get the current hostname and then passing that to *gethostbyname*(3) which is supposed to return the canonical version of that host name.[11] Assuming this is successful, **$j** is set to the fully qualified name and **$m** is set to the domain part of the name (everything after the first dot). The **$w** macro is set to the first word (everything before the first dot) if you have a level 5 or higher configuration file; otherwise, it is set to the same value as **$j**. If the canonification is not successful, it is imperative that the config file set **$j** to the fully qualified domain name[12].

The **$f** macro is the id of the sender as originally determined; when mailing to a specific host the **$g** macro is set to the address of the sender *relative to the recipient.* For example, if I send to "bollard@matisse.CS.Berkeley.EDU" from the machine "vangogh.CS.Berkeley.EDU" the **$f** macro will be "eric" and the **$g** macro will be "eric@vangogh.CS.Berkeley.EDU."

The **$x** macro is set to the full name of the sender. This can be determined in several ways. It can be passed as flag to *sendmail.* The second choice is the value of the "Full-name:"

---

[11]For example, on some systems *gethostname* might return "foo" which would be mapped to "foo.bar.com" by *gethostbyname.*

[12]Older versions of sendmail didn't pre-define **$j** at all, so up until 8.6, config files *always* had to define **$j**.

line in the header if it exists, and the third choice is the comment field of a "From:" line. If all of these fail, and if the message is being originated locally, the full name is looked up in the */etc/passwd* file.

When sending, the **$h**, **$u**, and **$z** macros get set to the host, user, and home directory (if local) of the recipient. The first two are set from the **$@** and **$:** part of the rewriting rules, respectively.

The **$p** and **$t** macros are used to create unique strings (e.g., for the "Message-Id:" field). The **$i** macro is set to the queue id on this host; if put into the timestamp line it can be extremely useful for tracking messages. The **$v** macro is set to be the version number of *sendmail*; this is normally put in timestamps and has been proven extremely useful for debugging.

The **$c** field is set to the "hop count," i.e., the number of times this message has been processed. This can be determined by the **–h** flag on the command line or by counting the timestamps in the message.

The **$r** and **$s** fields are set to the protocol used to communicate with *sendmail* and the sending hostname.

The **$_** is set to a validated sender host name. If the sender is running an RFC 1413 compliant IDENT server, it will include the user name on that host.

5.1.3. C and F — define classes

Classes of phrases may be defined to match on the left hand side of rewriting rules, where a "phrase" is a sequence of characters that do not contain space characters. For example a class of all local names for this site might be created so that attempts to send to oneself can be eliminated. These can either be defined directly in the configuration file or read in from another file. Classes may be given names from the set of upper case letters. Lower case letters and special characters are reserved for system use.

The syntax is:

> **C***c phrase1 phrase2...*
> **F***c file*

The first form defines the class *c* to match any of the named words. It is permissible to split them among multiple lines; for example, the two forms:

```
CHmonet ucbmonet
```

and

```
CHmonet
CHucbmonet
```

are equivalent. The second form reads the elements of the class *c* from the named *file*.

The **$~** (match entries not in class) only matches a single word; multi-word entries in the class are ignored in this context.

The class **$=w** is set to be the set of all names this host is known by. This can be used to match local hostnames.

The class **$=k** is set to be the same as **$k**, that is, the UUCP node name.

The class **$=m** is set to the set of domains by which this host is known, initially just **$m**.

Sendmail can be compiled to allow a *scanf*(3) string on the **F** line. This lets you do simplistic parsing of text files. For example, to read all the user names in your system */etc/passwd* file into a class, use

```
FL/etc/passwd %[^:]
```

which reads every line up to the first colon.

5.1.4. M — define mailer

Programs and interfaces to mailers are defined in this line. The format is:

M*name*, *{field=value }**

where *name* is the name of the mailer (used internally only) and the "field=name" pairs define attributes of the mailer. Fields are:

Path	The pathname of the mailer
Flags	Special flags for this mailer
Sender	A rewriting set for sender addresses
Recipient	A rewriting set for recipient addresses
Argv	An argument vector to pass to this mailer
Eol	The end-of-line string for this mailer
Maxsize	The maximum message length to this mailer
Linelimit	The maximum line length in the message body
Directory	The working directory for the mailer

Only the first character of the field name is checked.

The following flags may be set in the mailer description. Any other flags may be used freely to conditionally assign headers to messages destined for particular mailers.

a Run Extended SMTP (ESMTP) protocol (defined in RFCs 1425, 1426, and 1427).

b Force a blank line on the end of a message. This is intended to work around some stupid versions of /bin/mail that require a blank line, but do not provide it themselves. It would not normally be used on network mail.

c Do not include comments in addresses. This should only be used if you have to work around a remote mailer that gets confused by comments.

C If mail is *received* from a mailer with this flag set, any addresses in the header that do not have an at sign ("@") after being rewritten by ruleset three will have the "@domain" clause from the sender tacked on. This allows mail with headers of the form:

From: usera@hosta
To: userb@hostb, userc

to be rewritten as:

From: usera@hosta
To: userb@hostb, userc@hosta

automatically.

D This mailer wants a "Date:" header line.

e This mailer is expensive to connect to, so try to avoid connecting normally; any necessary connection will occur during a queue run.

E Escape lines beginning with "From" in the message with a '>' sign.

f The mailer wants a **–f** *from* flag, but only if this is a network forward operation (i.e., the mailer will give an error if the executing user does not have special permissions).

F This mailer wants a "From:" header line.

g Normally, *sendmail* sends internally generated email (e.g., error messages) using the null return address[13] as required by RFC 1123. However, some mailers don't accept a null return address. If necessary, you can set the **g** flag to prevent *sendmail* from obeying the standards; error messages will be sent as from the MAILER-DAEMON (actually, the value of the **$n** macro).

[13]Actually, this only applies to SMTP, which uses the "MAIL FROM:<>" command.

h Upper case should be preserved in host names for this mailer.

I This mailer will be speaking SMTP to another *sendmail* — as such it can use special protocol features. This option is not required (i.e., if this option is omitted the transmission will still operate successfully, although perhaps not as efficiently as possible).

l This mailer is local (i.e., final delivery will be performed).

L Limit the line lengths as specified in RFC821. This deprecated option should be replaced by the **L=** mail declaration. For historic reasons, the **L** flag also sets the **7** flag.

m This mailer can send to multiple users on the same host in one transaction. When a **$u** macro occurs in the *argv* part of the mailer definition, that field will be repeated as necessary for all qualifying users.

M This mailer wants a ''Message-Id:'' header line.

n Do not insert a UNIX-style ''From'' line on the front of the message.

p Use the route-addr style reverse-path in the SMTP ''MAIL FROM:'' command rather than just the return address; although this is required in RFC821 section 3.1, many hosts do not process reverse-paths properly. Reverse-paths are officially discouraged by RFC 1123.

P This mailer wants a ''Return-Path:'' line.

r Same as **f**, but sends a **–r** flag.

s Strip quote characters off of the address before calling the mailer.

S Don't reset the userid before calling the mailer. This would be used in a secure environment where *sendmail* ran as root. This could be used to avoid forged addresses. This flag is suppressed if given from an ''unsafe'' environment (e.g, a user's mail.cf file).

u Upper case should be preserved in user names for this mailer.

U This mailer wants Unix-style ''From'' lines with the ugly UUCP-style ''remote from <host>'' on the end.

x This mailer wants a ''Full-Name:'' header line.

X This mailer want to use the hidden dot algorithm as specified in RFC821; basically, any line beginning with a dot will have an extra dot prepended (to be stripped at the other end). This insures that lines in the message containing a dot will not terminate the message prematurely.

7 Strip all output to seven bits. This is the default if the **L** flag is set. Note that clearing this option is not sufficient to get full eight bit data passed through *sendmail.* If the **7** option is set, this is essentially always set, since the eighth bit was stripped on input.

The mailer with the special name ''error'' can be used to generate a user error. The (optional) host field is an exit status to be returned, and the user field is a message to be printed. The exit status may be numeric or one of the values USAGE, NOUSER, NOHOST, UNAVAILABLE, SOFTWARE, TEMPFAIL, PROTOCOL, or CONFIG to return the corresponding EX_ exit code. For example, the entry:

```
$#error $@ NOHOST $: Host unknown in this domain
```

on the RHS of a rule will cause the specified error to be generated and the ''Host unknown'' exit status to be returned if the LHS matches. This mailer is only functional in ruleset zero.

The mailer named ''local'' *must* be defined in every configuration file. This is used to deliver local mail, and is treated specially in several ways. Additionally, three other mailers named ''prog'', ''*file*'', and ''*include*'' may be defined to tune the delivery of messages to programs, files, and :include: lists respectively. They default to:

```
Mprog, P=/bin/sh, F=lsD, A=sh –c $u
M*file*, P=/dev/null, F=lsDFMPEu, A=FILE
M*include*, P=/dev/null, F=su, A=INCLUDE
```

The Sender and Recipient rewriting sets may either be a simple integer or may be two integers separated by a slash; if so, the first rewriting set is applied to envelope addresses and the second is applied to headers.

The Directory is actually a colon-separated path of directories to try. For example, the definition "D=$z:/" first tries to execute in the recipient's home directory; if that is not available, it tries to execute in the root of the filesystem. This is intended to be used only on the "prog" mailer, since some shells (such as *csh*) refuse to execute if they cannot read the home directory. Since the queue directory is not normally readable by normal users *csh* scripts as recipients can fail.

5.1.5. H — define header

The format of the header lines that *sendmail* inserts into the message are defined by the **H** line. The syntax of this line is:

H[?*mflags***?]***hname***:** *htemplate*

Continuation lines in this spec are reflected directly into the outgoing message. The *htemplate* is macro expanded before insertion into the message. If the *mflags* (surrounded by question marks) are specified, at least one of the specified flags must be stated in the mailer definition for this header to be automatically output. If one of these headers is in the input it is reflected to the output regardless of these flags.

Some headers have special semantics that will be described below.

5.1.6. O — set option

There are a number of "random" options that can be set from a configuration file. Options are represented by single characters. The syntax of this line is:

O*o value*

This sets option *o* to be *value*. Depending on the option, *value* may be a string, an integer, a boolean (with legal values "t", "T", "f", or "F"; the default is TRUE), or a time interval.

The options supported are:

a*N* — If set, wait up to *N* minutes for an "@:@" entry to exist in the alias database before starting up. If it does not appear in *N* minutes, rebuild the database (if the **D** option is also set) or issue a warning.

A*spec, spec, ...* — Specify possible alias file(s). Each *spec* should be in the format "*class***:** *file*" where *class***:** is optional and defaults to "implicit". Depending on how *sendmail* is compiled, valid classes are "implicit" (search through a compiled-in list of alias file types, for back compatibility), "hash" (if NEWDB is specified), "dbm" (if NDBM is specified), "stab" (internal symbol table — not normally used unless you have no other database lookup), or "nis" (if NIS is specified). If a list of *spec*s are provided, *sendmail* searches them in order.

b*N*/*M* — Insist on at least *N* blocks free on the filesystem that holds the queue files before accepting email via SMTP. If there is insufficient space *sendmail* gives a 452 response to the MAIL command. This invites the sender to try again later. The optional *M* is a maximum message size advertised in the ESMTP EHLO response. It is currently otherwise unused.

B*c* — Set the blank substitution character to *c*. Unquoted spaces in addresses are replaced by this character. Defaults to space (i.e., no change is made).

c — If an outgoing mailer is marked as being expensive, don't connect immediately. This requires that queueing be compiled in, since it will depend on a queue run process to actually send the mail.

C*N* — Checkpoints the queue every *N* (default 10) addresses sent. If your system crashes during delivery to a large list, this prevents retransmission to any but the last recipients.

d*x* Deliver in mode *x*. Legal modes are:

- i Deliver interactively (synchronously)
- b Deliver in background (asynchronously)
- q Just queue the message (deliver during queue run)

Defaults to ''b'' if no option is specified, ''i'' if it is specified but given no argument (i.e., ''Od'' is equivalent to ''Odi'').

D If set, rebuild the alias database if necessary and possible. If this option is not set, *sendmail* will never rebuild the alias database unless explicitly requested using **–bi**.

e*x* Dispose of errors using mode *x*. The values for *x* are:

- p Print error messages (default)
- q No messages, just give exit status
- m Mail back errors
- w Write back errors (mail if user not logged in)
- e Mail back errors and give zero exit stat always

E*file/message* Prepend error messages with the indicated message. If it begins with a slash, it is assumed to be the pathname of a file containing a message (this is the recommended setting). Otherwise, it is a literal message. The error file might contain the name, email address, and/or phone number of a local postmaster who could provide assistance in to end users. If the option is missing or null, or if it names a file which does not exist or which is not readable, no message is printed.

f Save Unix-style ''From'' lines at the front of headers. Normally they are assumed redundant and discarded.

F*mode* The file mode for queue files.

g*n* Set the default group id for mailers to run in to *n*. Defaults to 1. The value can also be given as a symbolic group name.

G Allow fuzzy matching on the GECOS field. If this flag is set, and the usual user name lookups fail (that is, there is no alias with this name and a *getpwnam* fails), sequentially search the password file for a matching entry in the GECOS field. This also requires that MATCHGECOS be turned on during compilation. This option is not recommended.

h*N* The maximum hop count. Messages that have been processed more than *N* times are assumed to be in a loop and are rejected. Defaults to 25.

H*file* Specify the help file for SMTP.

i Ignore dots in incoming messages. This is always disabled (that is, dots are always accepted) when reading SMTP mail.

I Insist that the BIND name server be running to resolve host names. If this is not set and the name server is not running, the */etc/hosts* file will be considered complete. In general, you do want to set this option if your */etc/hosts* file does not include all hosts known to you or if you are using the MX (mail forwarding) feature of the BIND name server. The name server will still be consulted even if this option is not set, but *sendmail* will feel free to resort to reading */etc/hosts* if the name server is not available. Thus, you should *never* set this option if you do not run the name server.

j If set, send error messages in MIME format (see RFC1341 and RFC1344 for details).

J*path* Set the path for searching for users' .forward files. The default is ''$z/.forward''. Some sites that use the automounter may prefer to change this to ''/var/forward/$u'' to search a file with the same name as the user in a system directory. It can also be set to a sequence of paths separated by colons; *sendmail* stops at the first file it can successfully and safely open. For example, ''/var/forward/$u:$z/.forward'' will search first in /var/forward/*username* and then in ˜*username*/.forward (but only if the first file does not exist).

k*N* — The maximum number of open connections that will be cached at a time. The default is one. This delays closing the current connection until either this invocation of *sendmail* needs to connect to another host or it terminates. Setting it to zero defaults to the old behavior, that is, connections are closed immediately.

K*timeout* — The maximum amount of time a cached connection will be permitted to idle without activity. If this time is exceeded, the connection is immediately closed. This value should be small (on the order of ten minutes). Before *sendmail* uses a cached connection, it always sends a NOOP (no operation) command to check the connection; if this fails, it reopens the connection. This keeps your end from failing if the other end times out. The point of this option is to be a good network neighbor and avoid using up excessive resources on the other end. The default is five minutes.

l — If there is an ''Errors-To:'' header, send error messages to the addresses listed there. They normally go to the envelope sender. Use of this option causes *sendmail* to violate RFC 1123.

L*n* — Set the default log level to *n*. Defaults to 9.

m — Send to me too, even if I am in an alias expansion.

M*x value* — Set the macro *x* to *value*. This is intended only for use from the command line.

n — Validate the RHS of aliases when rebuilding the alias database.

o — Assume that the headers may be in old format, i.e., spaces delimit names. This actually turns on an adaptive algorithm: if any recipient address contains a comma, parenthesis, or angle bracket, it will be assumed that commas already exist. If this flag is not on, only commas delimit names. Headers are always output with commas between the names.

O*options* — Set server SMTP options. The options are *key=value* pairs. Known keys are:

Port	Name/number of listening port (defaults to "smtp")
Addr	Address mask (defaults INADDR_ANY)
Family	Address family (defaults to INET)
Listen	Size of listen queue (defaults to 10)

The *Addr*ess mask may be a numeric address in dot notation or a network name.

p *opt,opt,...* — Set the privacy *opt*ions. ''Privacy'' is really a misnomer; many of these are just a way of insisting on stricter adherence to the SMTP protocol. The *opt*ions can be selected from:

public	Allow open access
needmailhelo	Insist on HELO or EHLO command before MAIL
needexpnhelo	Insist on HELO or EHLO command before EXPN
noexpn	Disallow EXPN entirely
needvrfyhelo	Insist on HELO or EHLO command before VRFY
novrfy	Disallow VRFY entirely
restrictmailq	Restrict mailq command
restrictqrun	Restrict –q command line flag
noreceipts	Ignore Return-Receipt-To: header
goaway	Disallow essentially all SMTP status queries
authwarnings	Put X-Authentication-Warning: headers in messages

The ''goaway'' pseudo-flag sets all flags except ''restrictmailq'' and ''restrictqrun''. If mailq is restricted, only people in the same group as the queue directory can print the queue. If queue runs are restricted, only root and the owner of the queue directory can run the queue. Authentication Warnings add warnings about various conditions that may indicate attempts to spoof the mail system, such as using an non-standard queue directory.

P*postmaster* If set, copies of error messages will be sent to the named *postmaster*. Only the header of the failed message is sent. Since most errors are user problems, this is probably not a good idea on large sites, and arguably contains all sorts of privacy violations, but it seems to be popular with certain operating systems vendors.

q*factor* Use *factor* as the multiplier in the map function to decide when to just queue up jobs rather than run them. This value is divided by the difference between the current load average and the load average limit (**x** flag) to determine the maximum message priority that will be sent. Defaults to 600000.

Q*dir* Use the named *dir* as the queue directory.

r *timeouts* Timeout reads after *time* interval. The *timeouts* argument is a list of *keyword=value* pairs. The recognized timeouts and their default values, and their minimum values specified in RFC 1123 section 5.3.2 are:

initial	wait for initial greeting message [5m, 5m]
helo	reply to HELO or EHLO command [5m, none]
mail	reply to MAIL command [10m, 5m]
rcpt	reply to RCPT command [1h, 5m]
datainit	reply to DATA command [5m, 2m]
datablock	data block read [1h, 3m]
datafinal	reply to final ''.'' in data [1h, 10m]
rset	reply to RSET command [5m, none]
quit	reply to QUIT command [2m, none]
misc	reply to NOOP and VERB commands [2m, none]
command	command read [1h, 5m]
ident	IDENT protocol timeout [30s, none]

All but ''command'' apply to client SMTP. For back compatibility, a timeout with no ''keyword='' part will set all of the longer values.

R Normally, *sendmail* tries to eliminate any unnecessary explicit routes when sending an error message (as discussed in RFC 1123 § 5.2.6). For example, when sending an error message to

<@known1,@known2,@unknown:user@known3>

sendmail will strip off the ''@known1'' in order to make the route as direct as possible. However, if the **R** option is set, this will be disabled, and the mail will be sent to the first address in the route, even if later addresses are known. This may be useful if you are caught behind a firewall.

s — Be super-safe when running things, i.e., always instantiate the queue file, even if you are going to attempt immediate delivery. *Sendmail* always instantiates the queue file before returning control the client under any circumstances.

S*file* — Log statistics in the named *file*.

t*tzinfo* — Set the local time zone info to *tzinfo* — for example, "PST8PDT". Actually, if this is not set, the TZ environment variable is cleared (so the system default is used); if set but null, the user's TZ variable is used, and if set and non-null the TZ variable is set to this value.

T*rtime/wtime* — Set the queue timeout to *rtime*. After this interval, messages that have not been successfully sent will be returned to the sender. Defaults to five days. The optional *wtime* is the time after which a warning message is sent. If it is missing or zero then no warning messages are sent.

u*n* — Set the default userid for mailers to *n*. Mailers without the *S* flag in the mailer definition will run as this user. Defaults to 1. The value can also be given as a symbolic user name.

U*udbspec* — The user database specification.

v — Run in verbose mode. If this is set, *sendmail* adjusts options **c** (don't connect to expensive mailers) and **d** (delivery mode) so that all mail is delivered completely in a single job so that you can see the entire delivery process. Option **v** should *never* be set in the configuration file; it is intended for command line use only.

V*fallbackhost* — If specified, the *fallbackhost* acts like a very low priority MX on every host. This is intended to be used by sites with poor network connectivity.

w — If you are the "best" (that is, lowest preference) MX for a given host, you should normally detect this situation and treat that condition specially, by forwarding the mail to a UUCP feed, treating it as local, or whatever. However, in some cases (such as Internet firewalls) you may want to try to connect directly to that host as though it had no MX records at all. Setting this option causes *sendmail* to try this. The downside is that errors in your configuration are likely to be diagnosed as "host unknown" or "message timed out" instead of something more meaningful. This option is disrecommended.

x*LA* — When the system load average exceeds *LA*, just queue messages (i.e., don't try to send them). Defaults to 8.

X*LA* — When the system load average exceeds *LA*, refuse incoming SMTP connections. Defaults to 12.

y*fact* — The indicated *fact*or is added to the priority (thus *lowering* the priority of the job) for each recipient, i.e., this value penalizes jobs with large numbers of recipients. Defaults to 30000.

Y — If set, deliver each job that is run from the queue in a separate process. Use this option if you are short of memory, since the default tends to consume considerable amounts of memory while the queue is being processed.

z*fact* — The indicated *fact*or is multiplied by the message class (determined by the Precedence: field in the user header and the **P** lines in the configuration file) and subtracted from the priority. Thus, messages with a higher Priority: will be favored. Defaults to 1800.

Z*fact* — The *fact*or is added to the priority every time a job is processed. Thus, each time a job is processed, its priority will be decreased by the indicated value. In most environments this should be positive, since hosts that are down are all too often down for a long time. Defaults to 90000.

7 — Strip input to seven bits for compatibility with old systems. This shouldn't be necessary.

All options can be specified on the command line using the –o flag, but most will cause *sendmail* to relinquish its setuid permissions. The options that will not cause this are b, d, e, i, L, m, o, p, r, s, v, C, and 7. Also, M (define macro) when defining the r or s macros is also considered ''safe''.

5.1.7. P — precedence definitions

Values for the ''Precedence:'' field may be defined using the **P** control line. The syntax of this field is:

P*name*=*num*

When the *name* is found in a ''Precedence:'' field, the message class is set to *num*. Higher numbers mean higher precedence. Numbers less than zero have the special property that if an error occurs during processing the body of the message will not be returned; this is expected to be used for ''bulk'' mail such as through mailing lists. The default precedence is zero. For example, our list of precedences is:

```
Pfirst-class=0
Pspecial-delivery=100
Plist=–30
Pbulk=–60
Pjunk=–100
```

People writing mailing list exploders are encouraged to use ''Precedence: list''. Older versions of *sendmail* (which discarded all error returns for negative precedences) didn't recognize this name, giving it a default precedence of zero. This allows list maintainers to see error returns on both old and new versions of *sendmail.*

5.1.8. V — configuration version level

To provide compatibility with old configuration files, the **V** line has been added to define some very basic semantics of the configuration file. These are not intended to be long term supports; rather, they describe compatibility features which will probably be removed in future releases.

N.B.: these version *levels* have nothing to do with the version *number* on the files. For example, as of this writing version 8 config files (specifically, 8.6) used version level 5 configurations.

''Old'' configuration files are defined as version level one. Version level two files make the following changes:

(1) Host name canonification ($[... $]) appends a dot if the name is recognized; this gives the config file a way of finding out if anything matched. (Actually, this just initializes the ''host'' map with the ''–a.'' flag — you can reset it to anything you prefer by declaring the map explicitly.)

(2) Default host name extension is consistent throughout processing; version level one configurations turned off domain extension (that is, adding the local domain name) during certain points in processing. Version level two configurations are expected to include a trailing dot to indicate that the name is already canonical.

(3) Local names that are not aliases are passed through a new distinguished ruleset five; this can be used to append a local relay. This behaviour can be prevented by resolving the local name with an initial '@'. That is, something that resolves to a local mailer and a user name of ''vikki'' will be passed through ruleset five, but a user name of ''@vikki'' will have the '@' stripped, will not be passed through ruleset five, but will otherwise be treated the same as the prior example. The expectation is that this might be used to implement a policy where mail sent to ''vikki'' was handled by a central hub, but mail sent to ''vikki@localhost'' was delivered directly.

Version level three files allow # initiated comments on all lines. Exceptions are backslash escaped # marks and the $# syntax.

Version level four configurations are completely equivalent to level three for historical reasons.

Version level five configuration files change the default definition of **$w** to be just the first component of the hostname.

The **V** line may have an optional */vendor* to indicate that this configuration file uses modifications specific to a particular vendor[14].

5.1.9. K — key file declaration

Special maps can be defined using the line:

Kmapname mapclass arguments

The *mapname* is the handle by which this map is referenced in the rewriting rules. The *mapclass* is the name of a type of map; these are compiled in to *sendmail.* The *arguments* are interpreted depending on the class; typically, there would be a single argument naming the file containing the map.

Maps are referenced using the syntax:

$(*map key* $@ *arguments* $: *default* $)

where either or both of the *arguments* or *default* portion may be omitted. The *arguments* may appear more than once. The indicated *key* and *arguments* are passed to the appropriate mapping function. If it returns a value, it replaces the input. If it does not return a value and the *default* is specified, the *default* replaces the input. Otherwise, the input is unchanged.

During replacement of either a map value or default the string ''%*n*'' (where *n* is a digit) is replaced by the corresponding *argument.* Argument zero is always the database key. For example, the rule

```
R$- ! $+                $: $(uucp $1 $@ $2 $: %1 @ %0 . UUCP $)
```

Looks up the UUCP name in a (user defined) UUCP map; if not found it turns it into ''.UUCP'' form. The database might contain records like:

```
decvax                  %1@%0.DEC.COM
research                %1@%0.ATT.COM
```

The built in map with both name and class ''host'' is the host name canonicalization lookup. Thus, the syntax:

$(host *hostname*$)

is equivalent to:

$[*hostname*$]

There are four predefined database lookup classes: ''dbm'', ''btree'', ''hash'', and ''nis''. The first requires that *sendmail* be compiled with the **ndbm** library; the second two require the **db** library, and the third requires that *sendmail* be compiled with NIS support. All four accept as arguments the same optional flags and a filename (or a mapname for NIS; the filename is the root of the database path, so that ''.db'' or some other extension appropriate for the database type will be added to get the actual database name). Known flags are:

–o — Indicates that this map is optional — that is, if it cannot be opened, no error is produced, and *sendmail* will behave as if the map existed but was empty.

–N — Normally when maps are written, the trailing null byte is not included as part of the key. If this flag is indicated it will be included. During lookups, only the null-byte-included form will be searched. See also **–O.**

[14]And of course, vendors are encouraged to add themselves to the list of recognized vendors by editing the routine *setvendor* in *conf.c.*

–O If neither **–N** or **–O** are specified, *sendmail* uses an adaptive algorithm to decide whether or not to look for null bytes on the end of keys. It starts by trying both; if it finds any key with a null byte it never tries again without a null byte and vice versa. If this flag is specified, it never tries with a null byte; this can speed matches but is never necessary. If both **–N** and **–O** are specified, *sendmail* will never try any matches at all — that is, everything will appear to fail.

–a*x* Append the string *x* on successful matches. For example, the default *host* map appends a dot on successful matches.

–f Do not fold upper to lower case before looking up the key.

–m Match only (without replacing the value). If you only care about the existence of a key and not the value (as you might when searching the NIS map ''hosts.byname'' for example), this flag prevents the map from substituting the value. However, The –a argument is still appended on a match, and the default is still taken if the match fails.

The *dbm* map appends the strings ''.pag'' and ''.dir'' to the given filename; the two *db*-based maps append ''.db''. For example, the map specification

Kuucp dbm –o –N /usr/lib/uucpmap

specifies an optional map named ''uucp'' of class ''dbm''; it always has null bytes at the end of every string, and the data is located in /usr/lib/uucpmap.{dir,pag}.

The program *makemap*(8) can be used to build any of the three database-oriented maps. It takes the following flags:

–f Fold upper to lower case in the map.

–N Include null bytes in keys.

–o Append to an existing (old) file.

–r Allow replacement of existing keys; normally, re-inserting an existing key is an error.

–v Print what is happening.

The *sendmail* daemon does not have to be restarted to read the new maps as long as you change them in place; file locking is used so that the maps won't be read while they are being updated.[15]

There are also two builtin maps that are, strictly speaking, not database lookups.

The ''host'' map does host domain canonification; given a host name it calls the name server to find the canonical name for that host.

The ''dequote'' map strips double quotes (") from a name. It does not strip backslashes. It will not strip quotes if the resulting string would contain unscannable syntax (that is, basic errors like unbalanced angle brackets; more sophisticated errors such as unknown hosts are not checked). The intent is for use when trying to accept mail from systems such as DECnet that routinely quote odd syntax such as

"49ers::ubell"

[15] That is, don't create new maps and then use *mv*(1) to move them into place. I consider this a shortfall (a.k.a. bug) in *sendmail* which should be fixed in a future release.

A typical usage is probably something like:

```
Kdequote dequote

...

R$-                    $: $(dequote $1 $)
R$- $+                 $: $>3 $1 $2
```

Care must be taken to prevent unexpected results; for example,

```
"|someprogram < input > output"
```

will have quotes stripped, but the result is probably not what you had in mind. Fortunately these cases are rare.

New classes can be added in the routine **setupmaps** in file **conf.c**.

5.2. Building a Configuration File From Scratch

Building a configuration table from scratch is an extremely difficult job. Fortunately, it is almost never necessary to do so; nearly every situation that may come up may be resolved by changing an existing table. In any case, it is critical that you understand what it is that you are trying to do and come up with a philosophy for the configuration table. This section is intended to explain what the real purpose of a configuration table is and to give you some ideas for what your philosophy might be.

Do not even consider writing your own configuration file without carefully studying RFC 821, 822, and 1123. You should also read RFC 976 if you are doing UUCP exchange.

5.2.1. What you are trying to do

The configuration table has three major purposes. The first and simplest is to set up the environment for *sendmail.* This involves setting the options, defining a few critical macros, etc. Since these are described in other places, we will not go into more detail here.

The second purpose is to rewrite addresses in the message. This should typically be done in two phases. The first phase maps addresses in any format into a canonical form. This should be done in ruleset three. The second phase maps this canonical form into the syntax appropriate for the receiving mailer. *Sendmail* does this in three subphases. Rulesets one and two are applied to all sender and recipient addresses respectively. After this, you may specify per-mailer rulesets for both sender and recipient addresses; this allows mailer-specific customization. Finally, ruleset four is applied to do any default conversion to external form.

The third purpose is to map addresses into the actual set of instructions necessary to get the message delivered. Ruleset zero must resolve to the internal form, which is in turn used as a pointer to a mailer descriptor. The mailer descriptor describes the interface requirements of the mailer.

5.2.2. Philosophy

The particular philosophy you choose will depend heavily on the size and structure of your organization. I will present a few possible philosophies here. There are as many philosophies as there are config designers; feel free to develop your own.

One general point applies to all of these philosophies: it is almost always a mistake to try to do full host route resolution. For example, if you are on a UUCP-only site and you are trying to get names of the form ''user@host'' to the Internet, it does not pay to route them to ''xyzvax!decvax!ucbvax!c70!user@host'' since you then depend on several links not under your control, some of which are likely to misparse it anyway. The best approach to this problem is to simply forward the message for ''user@host'' to ''xyzvax'' and let xyzvax worry about it from there. In summary, just get the message closer to the destination, rather than determining the full path.

5.2.2.1. Large site, many hosts — minimum information

Berkeley is an example of a large site, i.e., more than two or three hosts and multiple mail connections. We have decided that the only reasonable philosophy in our environment is to designate one host as the guru for our site. It must be able to resolve any piece of mail it receives. The other sites should have the minimum amount of information they can get away with. In addition, any information they do have should be hints rather than solid information.

For example, a typical site on our local ether network is ''monet'' (actually ''monet.CS.Berkeley.EDU''). When monet receives mail for delivery, it checks whether it knows that the destination host is directly reachable; if so, mail is sent to that host. If it receives mail for any unknown host, it just passes it directly to ''ucbvax.CS.Berkeley.EDU'', our master host. Ucbvax may determine that the host name is illegal and reject the message, or may be able to do delivery. However, it is important to note that when a new mail connection is added, the only host that *must* have its tables updated is ucbvax; the others *may* be updated if convenient, but this is not critical.

This picture is slightly muddied due to network connections that are not actually located on ucbvax. For example, some UUCP connections are currently on ''ucbarpa.'' However, monet *does not* know about this; the information is hidden totally between ucbvax and ucbarpa. Mail going from monet to a UUCP host is transferred via the ethernet from monet to ucbvax, then via the ethernet from ucbvax to ucbarpa, and then is submitted to UUCP. Although this involves some extra hops, we feel this is an acceptable tradeoff.

An interesting point is that it would be possible to update monet to send appropriate UUCP mail directly to ucbarpa if the load got too high; if monet failed to note a host as connected to ucbarpa it would go via ucbvax as before, and if monet incorrectly sent a message to ucbarpa it would still be sent by ucbarpa to ucbvax as before. The only problem that can occur is loops, for example, if ucbarpa thought that ucbvax had the UUCP connection and vice versa. For this reason, updates should *always* happen to the master host first.

This philosophy results as much from the need to have a single source for the configuration files (typically built using *m4*(1) or some similar tool) as any logical need. Maintaining more than three separate tables by hand is essentially an impossible job.

5.2.2.2. Small site — complete information

A small site (two or three hosts and few external connections) may find it more reasonable to have complete information at each host. This would require that each host know exactly where each network connection is, possibly including the names of each host on that network. As long as the site remains small and the configuration remains relatively static, the update problem will probably not be too great.

5.2.2.3. Single host

This is in some sense the trivial case. The only major issue is trying to insure that you don't have to know too much about your environment. For example, if you have a UUCP connection you might find it useful to know about the names of hosts connected directly to you, but this is really not necessary since this may be determined from the syntax.

5.2.2.4. A completely different philosophy

This is adapted from Bruce Lilly. Any errors in interpretation are mine.

Do minimal changes in ruleset 3: fix some common but unambiguous errors (e.g. trailing dot on domains) and hide bang paths foo!bar into bar@foo.UUCP. The resulting "canonical" form is any valid RFC822/RFC1123/RFC976 address.

Ruleset 0 does the bulk of the work. It removes the trailing "@.UUCP" that hides bang paths, strips anything not needed to resolve, e.g. the phrase from phrase <route-addr> and from named groups, rejects unparseable addresses using $#error, and finally resolves to a mailer/host/user triple. Ruleset 0 is rather lengthy as it has to handle 3 basic address forms: RFC976 bang paths, RFC1123 %-hacks (including vanilla RFC822 local-part@domain), and RFC822 source routes. It's also complicated by having to handle named lists.

The header rewriting rulesets 1 and 2 remove the trailing "@.UUCP" that hides bang paths. Ruleset 2 also strips the $# mailer $@ host (for test mode).

Ruleset 4 does absolutely nothing.

The per-mailer rewriting rulesets conform the envelope and header addresses to the requirements of the specific mailer.

Lots of rulesets-as-subroutines are used.

As a result, header addresses are subject to minimal munging (per RFC1123), and the general plan is per RFC822 sect. 3.4.10.

5.2.3. Relevant issues

The canonical form you use should almost certainly be as specified in the Internet protocols RFC819 and RFC822. Copies of these RFC's are included on the *sendmail* tape as *doc/rfc819.lpr* and *doc/rfc822.lpr.*

RFC822 describes the format of the mail message itself. *Sendmail* follows this RFC closely, to the extent that many of the standards described in this document can not be changed without changing the code. In particular, the following characters have special interpretations:

< > ( ) " \

Any attempt to use these characters for other than their RFC822 purpose in addresses is probably doomed to disaster.

RFC819 describes the specifics of the domain-based addressing. This is touched on in RFC822 as well. Essentially each host is given a name which is a right-to-left dot qualified pseudo-path from a distinguished root. The elements of the path need not be physical hosts; the domain is logical rather than physical. For example, at Berkeley one legal host might be "a.CC.Berkeley.EDU"; reading from right to left, "EDU" is a top level domain comprising educational institutions, "Berkeley" is a logical domain name, "CC" represents the Computer Center, (in this case a strictly logical entity), and "a" is a host in the Computer Center.

Beware when reading RFC819 that there are a number of errors in it.

5.2.4. How to proceed

Once you have decided on a philosophy, it is worth examining the available configuration tables to decide if any of them are close enough to steal major parts of. Even under the worst of conditions, there is a fair amount of boiler plate that can be collected safely.

The next step is to build ruleset three. This will be the hardest part of the job. Beware of doing too much to the address in this ruleset, since anything you do will reflect through to the message. In particular, stripping of local domains is best deferred, since this can leave you with addresses with no domain spec at all. Since *sendmail* likes to append the sending domain to addresses with no domain, this can change the semantics of addresses. Also try to avoid fully qualifying domains in this ruleset. Although technically legal, this can lead to unpleasantly and unnecessarily long addresses reflected into messages. The Berkeley configuration files define ruleset nine to qualify domain names and strip local domains. This is called from ruleset zero to get all addresses into a cleaner form.

Once you have ruleset three finished, the other rulesets should be relatively trivial. If you need hints, examine the supplied configuration tables.

5.2.5. Testing the rewriting rules — the –bt flag

When you build a configuration table, you can do a certain amount of testing using the "test mode" of *sendmail*. For example, you could invoke *sendmail* as:

sendmail –bt –Ctest.cf

which would read the configuration file ''test.cf'' and enter test mode. In this mode, you enter lines of the form:

rwset address

where *rwset* is the rewriting set you want to use and *address* is an address to apply the set to. Test mode shows you the steps it takes as it proceeds, finally showing you the address it ends up with. You may use a comma separated list of rwsets for sequential application of rules to an input. For example:

3,1,21,4 monet:bollard

first applies ruleset three to the input ''monet:bollard.'' Ruleset one is then applied to the output of ruleset three, followed similarly by rulesets twenty-one and four.

If you need more detail, you can also use the ''–d21'' flag to turn on more debugging. For example,

sendmail –bt –d21.99

turns on an incredible amount of information; a single word address is probably going to print out several pages worth of information.

You should be warned that internally, *sendmail* applies ruleset 3 to all addresses. In this version of *sendmail,* you will have to do that manually. For example, older versions allowed you to use

0 bruce@broadcast.sony.com

This version requires that you use:

3,0 bruce@broadcast.sony.com

5.2.6. Building mailer descriptions

To add an outgoing mailer to your mail system, you will have to define the characteristics of the mailer.

Each mailer must have an internal name. This can be arbitrary, except that the names ''local'' and ''prog'' must be defined.

The pathname of the mailer must be given in the P field. If this mailer should be accessed via an IPC connection, use the string ''[IPC]'' instead.

The F field defines the mailer flags. You should specify an ''f'' or ''r'' flag to pass the name of the sender as a **–f** or **–r** flag respectively. These flags are only passed if they were passed to *sendmail,* so that mailers that give errors under some circumstances can be placated. If the mailer is not picky you can just specify ''–f $g'' in the argv template. If the mailer must be called as **root** the ''S'' flag should be given; this will not reset the userid before calling the mailer[16]. If this mailer is local (i.e., will perform final delivery rather than another network hop) the ''l'' flag should be given. Quote characters (backslashes and " marks) can be stripped from addresses if the ''s'' flag is specified; if this is not given they are passed through. If the mailer is capable of sending to more than one user on the same host in a single transaction the ''m'' flag should be stated. If this flag is on, then the argv template containing **$u** will be repeated for each unique user on a given host. The ''e'' flag will mark the mailer as being ''expensive,'' which will cause *sendmail* to defer connection until a queue run[17].

An unusual case is the ''C'' flag. This flag applies to the mailer that the message is received from, rather than the mailer being sent to; if set, the domain spec of the sender (i.e., the ''@host.domain'' part) is saved and is appended to any addresses in the message that do not

[16] *Sendmail* must be running setuid to root for this to work.

[17] The ''c'' configuration option must be given for this to be effective.

already contain a domain spec. For example, a message of the form:

From: eric@vangogh.CS.Berkeley.EDU
To: wnj@monet.CS.Berkeley.EDU, mckusick

will be modified to:

From: eric@vangogh.CS.Berkeley.EDU
To: wnj@monet.CS.Berkeley.EDU, mckusick@vangogh.CS.Berkeley.EDU

if and only if the "C" flag is defined in the mailer resolved to by running "eric@vangogh.CS.Berkeley.EDU" through rulesets 3 and 0.

Other flags are described in Appendix C.

The S and R fields in the mailer description are per-mailer rewriting sets to be applied to sender and recipient addresses respectively. These are applied after the sending domain is appended and the general rewriting sets (numbers one and two) are applied, but before the output rewrite (ruleset four) is applied. A typical use is to append the current domain to addresses that do not already have a domain. For example, a header of the form:

From: eric

might be changed to be:

From: eric@vangogh.CS.Berkeley.EDU

or

From: ucbvax!eric

depending on the domain it is being shipped into. These sets can also be used to do special purpose output rewriting in cooperation with ruleset four.

The S and R fields can be specified as two numbers separated by a slash (e.g., "S=10/11"), meaning that all envelope addresses will be processed through ruleset 10 and all header addresses will be processed through ruleset 11. With only one number specified, both envelope and header rewriting sets are set to the indicated ruleset.

The E field defines the string to use as an end-of-line indication. A string containing only newline is the default. The usual backslash escapes (\r, \n, \f, \b) may be used.

Finally, an argv template is given as the A field. It may have embedded spaces. If there is no argv with a **$u** macro in it, *sendmail* will speak SMTP to the mailer. If the pathname for this mailer is "[IPC]," the argv should be

IPC $h [*port*]

where *port* is the optional port number to connect to.

For example, the specifications:

```
Mlocal, P=/bin/mail, F=rlsm  S=10, R=20, A=mail –d $u
Mether, P=[IPC],     F=meC, S=11, R=21, A=IPC $h, M=100000
```

specifies a mailer to do local delivery and a mailer for ethernet delivery. The first is called "local," is located in the file "/bin/mail," takes a picky **–r** flag, does local delivery, quotes should be stripped from addresses, and multiple users can be delivered at once; ruleset ten should be applied to sender addresses in the message and ruleset twenty should be applied to recipient addresses; the argv to send to a message will be the word "mail," the word "–d," and words containing the name of the receiving user. If a **–r** flag is inserted it will be between the words "mail" and "–d." The second mailer is called "ether," it should be connected to via an IPC connection, it can handle multiple users at once, connections should be deferred, and any domain from the sender address should be appended to any receiver name without a domain; sender addresses should be processed by ruleset eleven and recipient addresses by ruleset twenty-one. There is a 100,000 byte limit on messages passed through this mailer.

5.3. The User Database

If you have a version of *sendmail* with the user database package compiled in, the handling of sender and recipient addresses is modified.

The location of this database is controlled with the **U** option.

5.3.1. Structure of the user database

The database is a sorted (BTree-based) structure. User records are stored with the key:

user-name:*field-name*

The sorted database format ensures that user records are clustered together. Meta-information is always stored with a leading colon.

Field names define both the syntax and semantics of the value. Defined fields include:

maildrop	The delivery address for this user. There may be multiple values of this record. In particular, mailing lists will have one *maildrop* record for each user on the list.
mailname	The outgoing mailname for this user. For each outgoing name, there should be an appropriate *maildrop* record for that name to allow return mail. See also *:default:mailname*.
mailsender	Changes any mail sent to this address to have the indicated envelope sender. This is intended for mailing lists, and will normally be the name of an appropriate -request address. It is very similar to the owner-*list* syntax in the alias file.
fullname	The full name of the user.
office-address	The office address for this user.
office-phone	The office phone number for this user.
office-fax	The office FAX number for this user.
home-address	The home address for this user.
home-phone	The home phone number for this user.
home-fax	The home FAX number for this user.
project	A (short) description of the project this person is affiliated with. In the University this is often just the name of their graduate advisor.
plan	A pointer to a file from which plan information can be gathered.

As of this writing, only a few of these fields are actually being used by *sendmail*: *maildrop* and *mailname*. A *finger* program that uses the other fields is planned.

5.3.2. User database semantics

When the rewriting rules submit an address to the local mailer, the user name is passed through the alias file. If no alias is found (or if the alias points back to the same address), the name (with '':maildrop'' appended) is then used as a key in the user database. If no match occurs (or if the maildrop points at the same address), forwarding is tried.

If the first token of the user name returned by ruleset 0 is an ''@'' sign, the user database lookup is skipped. The intent is that the user database will act as a set of defaults for a cluster (in our case, the Computer Science Division); mail sent to a specific machine should ignore these defaults.

When mail is sent, the name of the sending user is looked up in the database. If that user has a ''mailname'' record, the value of that record is used as their outgoing name. For example, I might have a record:

```
eric:mailname        Eric.Allman@CS.Berkeley.EDU
```

This would cause my outgoing mail to be sent as Eric.Allman.

If a ''maildrop'' is found for the user, but no corresponding ''mailname'' record exists, the record '':default:mailname'' is consulted. If present, this is the name of a host to override the local host. For example, in our case we would set it to ''CS.Berkeley.EDU''. The effect is that anyone known in the database gets their outgoing mail stamped as ''user@CS.Berkeley.EDU'', but people not listed in the database use the local hostname.

5.3.3. Creating the database[18]

The user database is built from a text file using the *makemap* utility (in the distribution in the makemap subdirectory). The text file is a series of lines corresponding to userdb records; each line has a key and a value separated by white space. The key is always in the format described above — for example:

```
eric:maildrop
```

This file is normally installed in a system directory; for example, it might be called */etc/userdb*. To make the database version of the map, run the program:

```
makemap btree /etc/userdb.db < /etc/userdb
```

Then create a config file that uses this. For example, using the V8 M4 configuration, include the following line in your .mc file:

```
define(`confUSERDB_SPEC´, /etc/userdb.db)
```

6. OTHER CONFIGURATION

There are some configuration changes that can be made by recompiling *sendmail*. This section describes what changes can be made and what has to be modified to make them.

6.1. Parameters in src/Makefile

These parameters are intended to describe the compilation environment, not site policy, and should normally be defined in src/Makefile.

NDBM — If set, the new version of the DBM library that allows multiple databases will be used. If neither NDBM nor NEWDB are set, a much less efficient method of alias lookup is used.

NEWDB — If set, use the new database package from Berkeley (from 4.4BSD). This package is substantially faster than DBM or NDBM. If NEWDB and NDBM are both set, *sendmail* will read DBM files, but will create and use NEWDB files.

NIS — Include support for NIS. If set together with *both* NEWDB and NDBM, *sendmail* will create both DBM and NEWDB files if and only if the file /var/yp/Makefile exists and is readable. This is intended for compatibility with Sun Microsystems' *mkalias* program used on YP masters.

SYSTEM5 — Set all of the compilation parameters appropriate for System V.

LOCKF — Use System V **lockf** instead of Berkeley **flock**. Due to the highly unusual semantics of locks across forks in **lockf**, this should never be used unless absolutely necessary. Set by default if SYSTEM5 is set.

SYS5TZ — Use System V time zone semantics.

HASINITGROUPS — Set this if your system has the *initgroups()* call (if you have multiple group support). This is the default if SYSTEM5 is *not* defined or if you are on HPUX.

[18]These instructions are known to be incomplete. A future version of the user database is planned including things such as finger service — and good documentation.

HASUNAME Set this if you have the *uname*(2) system call (or corresponding library routine). Set by default if SYSTEM5 is set.

HASSTATFS Set this if you have the *statfs*(2) system call. This will allow you to give a temporary failure message to incoming SMTP email when you are low on disk space. It is set by default on 4.4BSD and OSF/1 systems.

HASUSTAT Set if you have the *ustat*(2) system call. This is an alternative implementation of disk space control. You should only set one of HASSTATFS or HASUSTAT; the first is preferred.

_PATH_SENDMAILCF
The pathname of the sendmail.cf file.

_PATH_SENDMAILPID
The pathname of the sendmail.pid file.

LA_TYPE The load average type. Details are described below.

The are several built-in ways of computing the load average. *Sendmail* tries to auto-configure them based on imperfect guesses; you can select one using the *cc* option **–DLA_TYPE=***type*, where *type* is:

LA_INT The kernel stores the load average in the kernel as an array of long integers. The actual values are scaled by a factor FSCALE (default 256).

LA_SHORT The kernel stores the load average in the kernel as an array of short integers. The actual values are scaled by a factor FSCALE (default 256).

LA_FLOAT The kernel stores the load average in the kernel as an array of double precision floats.

LA_MACH Use MACH-style load averages.

LA_SUBR Call the *getloadavg* routine to get the load average as an array of doubles.

LA_ZERO Always return zero as the load average. This is the fallback case.

If type LA_INT, LA_SHORT, or LA_FLOAT is specified, you may also need to specify _PATH_UNIX (the path to your system binary) and LA_AVENRUN (the name of the variable containing the load average in the kernel; usually ‘‘_avenrun’’ or ‘‘avenrun’’).

There are also several compilation flags to indicate the environment such as ‘‘_AIX3’’ and ‘‘_SCO_unix_’’. See the READ_ME file for the latest scoop on these flags.

6.2. Parameters in src/conf.h

Parameters and compilation options are defined in conf.h. Most of these need not normally be tweaked; common parameters are all in sendmail.cf. However, the sizes of certain primitive vectors, etc., are included in this file. The numbers following the parameters are their default value.

MAXLINE [1024] The maximum line length of any input line. If message lines exceed this length they will still be processed correctly; however, header lines, configuration file lines, alias lines, etc., must fit within this limit.

MAXNAME [256] The maximum length of any name, such as a host or a user name.

MAXPV [40] The maximum number of parameters to any mailer. This limits the number of recipients that may be passed in one transaction. It can be set to any arbitrary number above about 10, since *sendmail* will break up a delivery into smaller batches as needed. A higher number may reduce load on your system, however.

MAXATOM [100] The maximum number of atoms (tokens) in a single address. For example, the address ‘‘eric@CS.Berkeley.EDU’’ is seven atoms.

MAXMAILERS [25]
The maximum number of mailers that may be defined in the configuration file.

MAXRWSETS [100]
The maximum number of rewriting sets that may be defined.

MAXPRIORITIES [25]
The maximum number of values for the "Precedence:" field that may be defined (using the **P** line in sendmail.cf).

MAXUSERENVIRON [40]
The maximum number of items in the user environment that will be passed to subordinate mailers.

QUEUESIZE [1000] The maximum number of entries that will be processed in a single queue run.

MAXMXHOSTS [20]
The maximum number of MX records we will accept for any single host.

A number of other compilation options exist. These specify whether or not specific code should be compiled in.

DEBUG
If set, debugging information is compiled in. To actually get the debugging output, the **–d** flag must be used. **WE STRONGLY RECOMMEND THAT THIS BE LEFT ON.** Some people, believing that it was a security hole (it was, once) have turned it off and thus crippled debuggers.

NETINET
If set, support for Internet protocol networking is compiled in. Previous versions of *sendmail* referred to this as DAEMON; this old usage is now incorrect.

NETISO
If set, support for ISO protocol networking is compiled in (it may be appropriate to #define this in the Makefile instead of conf.h).

LOG
If set, the *syslog* routine in use at some sites is used. This makes an informational log record for each message processed, and makes a higher priority log record for internal system errors.

MATCHGECOS
Compile in the code to do "fuzzy matching" on the GECOS field in /etc/passwd. This also requires that option G be turned on.

NAMED_BIND
Compile in code to use the Berkeley Internet Name Domain (BIND) server to resolve TCP/IP host names.

NOTUNIX
If you are using a non-UNIX mail format, you can set this flag to turn off special processing of UNIX-style "From " lines.

QUEUE
This flag should be set to compile in the queueing code. If this is not set, mailers must accept the mail immediately or it will be returned to the sender.

SETPROCTITLE
If defined, *sendmail* will change its *argv* array to indicate its current status. This can be used in conjunction with the *ps* command to find out just what it's up to.

SMTP
If set, the code to handle user and server SMTP will be compiled in. This is only necessary if your machine has some mailer that speaks SMTP (this means most machines everywhere).

UGLYUUCP
If you have a UUCP host adjacent to you which is not running a reasonable version of *rmail,* you will have to set this flag to include the "remote from sysname" info on the from line. Otherwise, UUCP gets confused about where the mail came from.

USERDB
Include the **experimental** Berkeley user information database package. This adds a new level of local name expansion between aliasing and forwarding. It also uses the NEWDB package. This may change in future releases.

IDENTPROTO
Compile in the IDENT protocol as defined in RFC 1413. This defaults on for all systems except Ultrix, which apparently has the interesting "feature" that when it receives a "host unreachable" message it closes all open connections to that host. Since some firewall gateways send this error code when you access an unauthorized port (such as 113, used by IDENT), Ultrix cannot

receive email from such hosts.

6.3. Configuration in src/conf.c

The following changes can be made in conf.c.

6.3.1. Built-in Header Semantics

Not all header semantics are defined in the configuration file. Header lines that should only be included by certain mailers (as well as other more obscure semantics) must be specified in the *HdrInfo* table in *conf.c*. This table contains the header name (which should be in all lower case) and a set of header control flags (described below), The flags are:

H_ACHECK Normally when the check is made to see if a header line is compatible with a mailer, *sendmail* will not delete an existing line. If this flag is set, *sendmail* will delete even existing header lines. That is, if this bit is set and the mailer does not have flag bits set that intersect with the required mailer flags in the header definition in sendmail.cf, the header line is *always* deleted.

H_EOH If this header field is set, treat it like a blank line, i.e., it will signal the end of the header and the beginning of the message text.

H_FORCE Add this header entry even if one existed in the message before. If a header entry does not have this bit set, *sendmail* will not add another header line if a header line of this name already existed. This would normally be used to stamp the message by everyone who handled it.

H_TRACE If set, this is a timestamp (trace) field. If the number of trace fields in a message exceeds a preset amount the message is returned on the assumption that it has an aliasing loop.

H_RCPT If set, this field contains recipient addresses. This is used by the **–t** flag to determine who to send to when it is collecting recipients from the message.

H_FROM This flag indicates that this field specifies a sender. The order of these fields in the *HdrInfo* table specifies *sendmail*'s preference for which field to return error messages to.

Let's look at a sample *HdrInfo* specification:

```
struct hdrinfo          HdrInfo[] =
{
        /* originator fields, most to least significant */
    "resent-sender",    H_FROM,
    "resent-from",      H_FROM,
    "sender",           H_FROM,
    "from",             H_FROM,
    "full-name",        H_ACHECK,
        /* destination fields */
    "to",               H_RCPT,
    "resent-to",        H_RCPT,
    "cc",               H_RCPT,
        /* message identification and control */
    "message",          H_EOH,
    "text",             H_EOH,
        /* trace fields */
    "received",         H_TRACE|H_FORCE,

    NULL,               0,
};
```

This structure indicates that the "To:", "Resent-To:", and "Cc:" fields all specify recipient addresses. Any "Full-Name:" field will be deleted unless the required mailer flag (indicated in the configuration file) is specified. The "Message:" and "Text:" fields will terminate the header; these are used by random dissenters around the network world. The "Received:" field will always be added, and can be used to trace messages.

There are a number of important points here. First, header fields are not added automatically just because they are in the *HdrInfo* structure; they must be specified in the configuration file in order to be added to the message. Any header fields mentioned in the configuration file but not mentioned in the *HdrInfo* structure have default processing performed; that is, they are added unless they were in the message already. Second, the *HdrInfo* structure only specifies cliched processing; certain headers are processed specially by ad hoc code regardless of the status specified in *HdrInfo*. For example, the "Sender:" and "From:" fields are always scanned on ARPANET mail to determine the sender[19]; this is used to perform the "return to sender" function. The "From:" and "Full-Name:" fields are used to determine the full name of the sender if possible; this is stored in the macro **$x** and used in a number of ways.

6.3.2. Restricting Use of Email

If it is necessary to restrict mail through a relay, the *checkcompat* routine can be modified. This routine is called for every recipient address. It returns an exit status indicating the status of the message. The status EX_OK accepts the address, EX_TEMPFAIL queues the message for a later try, and other values (commonly EX_UNAVAILABLE) reject the message. It is up to *checkcompat* to print an error message (using *usrerr*) if the message is rejected. For example, *checkcompat* could read:

```
int
checkcompat(to, e)
        register ADDRESS *to;
        register ENVELOPE *e;
{
        register STAB *s;

        s = stab("private", ST_MAILER, ST_FIND);
        if (s != NULL && e->e_from.q_mailer != LocalMailer &&
            to->q_mailer == s->s_mailer)
        {
                usrerr("No private net mail allowed through this machine");
                return (EX_UNAVAILABLE);
        }
        if (MsgSize > 50000 && to->q_mailer != LocalMailer)
        {
                usrerr("Message too large for non-local delivery");
                NoReturn = TRUE;
                return (EX_UNAVAILABLE);
        }
        return (EX_OK);
}
```

This would reject messages greater than 50000 bytes unless they were local. The *NoReturn* flag can be sent to suppress the return of the actual body of the message in the error return. The actual use of this routine is highly dependent on the implementation, and use should be limited.

6.3.3. Load Average Computation

The routine *getla* should return an approximation of the current system load average as an integer. There are four versions included on compilation flags as described above.

---

[19]Actually, this is no longer true in SMTP; this information is contained in the envelope. The older ARPANET protocols did not completely distinguish envelope from header.

6.3.4. New Database Map Classes

New key maps can be added by creating a class initialization function and a lookup function. These are then added to the routine *setupmaps*.

The initialization function is called as

*xxx*_map_init(MAP *map, char *mapname, char *args)

The *map* is an internal data structure. The *mapname* is the name of the map (used for error messages). The *args* is a pointer to the rest of the configuration file line; flags and filenames can be extracted from this line. The initialization function must return TRUE if it successfully opened the map, FALSE otherwise.

The lookup function is called as

*xxx*_map_lookup(MAP *map, char buf[], int bufsize, char **av, int *statp)

The *map* defines the map internally. The parameters *buf* and *bufsize* have the input key. This may be (and often is) used destructively. The *av* is a list of arguments passed in from the rewrite line. The lookup function should return a pointer to the new value. IF the map lookup fails, **statp* should be set to an exit status code; in particular, it should be set to EX_TEMPFAIL if recovery is to be attempted by the higher level code.

6.3.5. Queueing Function

The routine *shouldqueue* is called to decide if a message should be queued or processed immediately. Typically this compares the message priority to the current load average. The default definition is:

```
bool
shouldqueue(pri, ctime)
    long pri;
    time_t ctime;
{
    if (CurrentLA < QueueLA)
        return (FALSE);
    if (CurrentLA >= RefuseLA)
        return (TRUE);
    return (pri > (QueueFactor / (CurrentLA – QueueLA + 1)));
}
```

If the current load average (global variable *CurrentLA*, which is set before this function is called) is less than the low threshold load average (option **x**, variable *QueueLA*), *shouldqueue* returns FALSE immediately (that is, it should *not* queue). If the current load average exceeds the high threshold load average (option **X**, variable *RefuseLA*), *shouldqueue* returns TRUE immediately. Otherwise, it computes the function based on the message priority, the queue factor (option **q**, global variable *QueueFactor*), and the current and threshold load averages.

An implementation wishing to take the actual age of the message into account can also use the *ctime* parameter, which is the time that the message was first submitted to *sendmail*. Note that the *pri* parameter is already weighted by the number of times the message has been tried (although this tends to lower the priority of the message with time); the expectation is that the *ctime* would be used as an ''escape clause'' to ensure that messages are eventually processed.

6.3.6. Refusing Incoming SMTP Connections

The function *refuseconnections* returns TRUE if incoming SMTP connections should be refused. The current implementation is based exclusively on the current load average and the refuse load average option (option **X**, global variable *RefuseLA*):

```
bool
refuseconnections()
{
    return (CurrentLA >= RefuseLA);
}
```

A more clever implementation could look at more system resources.

6.3.7. Load Average Computation

The routine *getla* returns the current load average (as a rounded integer). The distribution includes several possible implementations.

6.4. Configuration in src/daemon.c

The file *src/daemon.c* contains a number of routines that are dependent on the local networking environment. The version supplied assumes you have BSD style sockets.

In previous releases, we recommended that you modify the routine *maphostname* if you wanted to generalize **$[... $]** lookups. We now recommend that you create a new keyed map instead.

7. CHANGES IN VERSION 8

The following summarizes changes since the last commonly available version of *sendmail* (5.67):

7.1. Connection Caching

Instead of closing SMTP connections immediately, those connections are cached for possible future use. The advent of MX records made this effective for mailing lists; in addition, substantial performance improvements can be expected for queue processing.

7.2. MX Piggybacking

If two hosts with different names in a single message happen to have the same set of MX hosts, they can be sent in the same transaction. Version 8 notices this and tries to batch the messages.

7.3. RFC 1123 Compliance

A number of changes have been made to make *sendmail* ''conditionally compliant'' (that is, *sendmail* satisfies all of the ''MUST'' clauses and most but not all of the ''SHOULD'' clauses in RFC 1123).

The major areas of change are (numbers are RFC 1123 section numbers):

5.2.7 Response to RCPT command is fast.

5.2.8 Numeric IP addresses are logged in Received: lines.

5.2.17 Self domain literal is properly handled.

5.3.2 Better control over individual timeouts.

5.3.3 Error messages are sent as ''From:<>''.

5.3.3 Error messages are never sent to ''<>''.

5.3.3 Route-addrs are pruned.

The areas in which *sendmail* is not ''unconditionally compliant'' are:

5.2.6 *Sendmail* does do header munging.

5.2.10 *Sendmail* doesn't always use the exact SMTP message text as listed in RFC 821.

5.3.1.1 *Sendmail* doesn't guarantee only one connect for each host in queue runs.

5.3.1.1 *Sendmail* doesn't always provide adequate concurrency limits.

7.4. Extended SMTP Support

Version 8 includes both sending and receiving support for Extended SMTP support as defined by RFC 1425 (basic) and RFC 1427 (SIZE); and limited support for RFC 1426 (BODY).

7.5. Eight-Bit Clean

Previous versions of *sendmail* used the 0200 bit for quoting. This version avoids that use. However, for compatibility with RFC 822, you can set option '7' to get seven bit stripping.

Individual mailers can still produce seven bit output using the '7' mailer flag.

7.6. User Database

The user database is an as-yet experimental attempt to provide unified large-site name support. We are installing it at Berkeley; future versions may show significant modifications.

7.7. Improved BIND Support

The BIND support, particularly for MX records, had a number of annoying "features" which have been removed in this release. In particular, these more tightly bind (pun intended) the name server to *sendmail*, so that the name server resolution rules are incorporated directly into **sendmail.**

7.8. Keyed Files

Generalized keyed files is an idea taken directly from IDA *sendmail* (albeit with a completely different implementation). They can be useful on large sites.

Version 8 also understands YP.

7.9. Multi-Word Classes

Classes can now be multiple words. For example,

    CShofmann.CS.Berkeley.EDU

allows you to match the entire string "hofmann.CS.Berkeley.EDU" using the single construct "$=S".

7.10. Deferred Macro Expansion

The **$&***x* construct has been adopted from IDA.

7.11. IDENT Protocol Support

The IDENT protocol as defined in RFC 1413 is supported.

7.12. Parsing Bug Fixes

A number of small bugs having to do with things like backslash-escaped quotes inside of comments have been fixed.

7.13. Separate Envelope/Header Processing

Since the From: line is passed in separately from the envelope sender, these have both been made visible; the **$g** macro is set to the envelope sender during processing of mailer argument vectors and the header sender during processing of headers.

It is also possible to specify separate per-mailer envelope and header processing. The SenderRWSet and RecipientRWset arguments for mailers can be specified as *envelope/header* to give different rewritings for envelope versus header addresses.

8

7.14. Owner-List Propagates to Envelope

When an alias has an associated owner–list name, that alias is used to change the envelope sender address. This will cause downstream errors to be returned to that owner.

7.15. Dynamic Header Allocation

The fixed size limit on header lines has been eliminated.

7.16. New Command Line Flags

The **–B** flag has been added to pass in body type information.

The **–p** flag has been added to pass in protocol information.

The **–X** flag has been added to allow logging of all protocol in and out of *sendmail* for debugging.

7.17. Enhanced Command Line Flags

The **–q** flag can limit limit a queue run to specific recipients, senders, or queue ids using **–qR***substring*, **–qS***substring*, **or –qI***substring* **respectively.**

7.18. New and Old Configuration Line Types

The **T** (Trusted users) configuration line has been deleted. It will still be accepted but will be ignored.

The **K** line has been added to declare database maps.

The **V** line has been added to declare the configuration version level.

The **M** line has a ''D='' field that lets you change into a temporary directory while that mailer is running.

7.19. New Options

Several new options have been added, many to support new features, others to allow tuning that was previously available only by recompiling. They are described in detail in Section 5.1.5. Briefly,

b	Insist on a minimum number of disk blocks.
C	Set checkpoint interval.
E	Default error message.
G	Enable GECOS matching.
h	Maximum hop count.
j	Send errors in MIME-encapsulated format.
J	Forward file path.
k	Connection cache size
K	Connection cache lifetime.
l	Enable Errors-To: header. These headers violate RFC 1123; this option is included to provide back compatibility with old versions of *sendmail.*
O	Set incoming SMTP daemon options, such as an alternate SMTP port.
p	Privacy options.
R	Don't prune route-addrs.
U	User database spec.
V	Fallback ''MX'' host.

w ''Best MX'' handling technique.

7 Do not run eight bit clean.

7.20. Extended Options

The **r** (read timeout), **I** (use BIND), and **T** (queue timeout) options have been extended to pass in more information.

7.21. New Mailer Flags

Several new mailer flags have been added.

a Try to use ESMTP when creating a connection. If this is not set, *sendmail* will still try if the other end hints that it knows about ESMTP in its greeting message; this flag says to try even if it doesn't hint. If the EHLO (extended hello) command fails, *sendmail* falls back to old SMTP.

b Ensure that there is a blank line at the end of all messages.

c Strip all comments from addresses; this should only be used as a last resort when dealing with cranky mailers.

g Never use the null sender as the envelope sender, even when running SMTP. Although this violates RFC 1123, it may be necessary when you must deal with some obnoxious old hosts.

7 Strip all output to 7 bits.

7.22. New Pre-Defined Macros

The following macros are pre-defined:

$k The UUCP node name, nominally from *uname*(2) call.

$m The domain part of our full hostname.

$_ The RFC 1413-provided sender address.

7.23. New LHS Token

Version 8 allows **$@** on the Left Hand Side of an ''R'' line to match zero tokens. This is intended to be used to match the null input.

7.24. Bigger Defaults

Version 8 allows up to 100 rulesets instead of 30. It is recommended that rulesets 0–9 be reserved for *sendmail*'s dedicated use in future releases.

The total number of MX records that can be used has been raised to 20.

The number of queued messages that can be handled at one time has been raised from 600 to 1000.

7.25. Different Default Tuning Parameters

Version 8 has changed the default parameters for tuning queue costs to make the number of recipients more important than the size of the message (for small messages). This is reasonable if you are connected with reasonably fast links.

7.26. Auto-Quoting in Addresses

Previously, the ''Full Name <email address>'' syntax would generate incorrect protocol output if ''Full Name'' had special characters such as dot. This version puts quotes around such names.

7.27. Symbolic Names On Error Mailer

Several names have been built in to the $@ portion of the $#error mailer.

7.28. SMTP VRFY Doesn't Expand

Previous versions of *sendmail* treated VRFY and EXPN the same. In this version, VRFY doesn't expand aliases or follow .forward files. EXPN still does.

As an optimization, if you run with your default delivery mode being queue-only or deliver-in-background, the RCPT command will also not chase aliases and .forward files. It will chase them when it processes the queue.

7.29. [IPC] Mailers Allow Multiple Hosts

When an address resolves to a mailer that has ''[IPC]'' as its ''Path'', the $@ part (host name) can be a colon-separated list of hosts instead of a single hostname. This asks *sendmail* to search the list for the first entry that is available exactly as though it were an MX record. The intent is to route internal traffic through internal networks without publishing an MX record to the net. MX expansion is still done on the individual items.

7.30. Aliases Extended

The implementation has been merged with maps. Among other things, this supports NIS-based aliases.

7.31. Portability and Security Enhancements

A number of internal changes have been made to enhance portability.

Several fixes have been made to increase the paranoia factor.

7.32. Miscellaneous Changes

Sendmail writes a */etc/sendmail.pid* file with the current process id of the SMTP daemon.

Two people using the same program in their .forward file are considered different so that duplicate elimination doesn't delete one of them.

The *mailstats* program prints mailer names and gets the location of the *sendmail.st* file from */etc/sendmail.cf.*

Many minor bugs have been fixed, such as handling of backslashes inside of quotes.

A hook (ruleset 5) has been added to allow rewriting of local addresses after aliasing.

8. ACKNOWLEDGEMENTS

I've worked on *sendmail* for many years, and many employers have been remarkably patient about letting me work on a large project that was not part of my official job. This includes time on the INGRES Project at Berkeley, at Britton Lee, and again on the Mammoth Project at Berkeley.

Much of the second wave of improvements should be credited to Bryan Costales of ICSI. As he passed me drafts of his book on *sendmail* I was inspired to start working on things again. Bryan was also available to bounce ideas off of.

Many, many people contributed chunks of code and ideas to *sendmail.* It has proven to be a group network effort. Version 8 in particular was a group project. The following people made notable contributions:

Keith Bostic, CSRG, University of California, Berkeley
Michael J. Corrigan, University of California, San Diego
Bryan Costales, International Computer Science Institute
Pär (Pell) Emanuelsson
Craig Everhart, Transarc Corporation
Tom Ivar Helbekkmo, Norwegian School of Economics

Allan E. Johannesen, WPI
Jonathan Kamens, OpenVision Technologies, Inc.
Takahiro Kanbe, Fuji Xerox Information Systems Co., Ltd.
Brian Kantor, University of California, San Diego
Murray S. Kucherawy, HookUp Communication Corp.
Bruce Lilly, Sony U.S.
Karl London
Nakamura Motonori, Kyoto University
John Gardiner Myers, Carnegie Mellon University
Neil Rickert, Northern Illinois University
Eric Schnoebelen, Convex Computer Corp.
Eric Wassenaar, National Institute for Nuclear and High Energy Physics, Amsterdam
Christophe Wolfhugel, Herve Schauer Consultants (Paris)

I apologize for anyone I have omitted, misspelled, misattributed, or otherwise missed. Many other people have contributed ideas, comments, and encouragement. I appreciate their contribution as well.

APPENDIX A

COMMAND LINE FLAGS

Arguments must be presented with flags before addresses. The flags are:

–b*x* Set operation mode to *x*. Operation modes are:

- m Deliver mail (default)
- s Speak SMTP on input side
- d Run as a daemon
- t Run in test mode
- v Just verify addresses, don't collect or deliver
- i Initialize the alias database
- p Print the mail queue

–B*type* Indicate body type.

–C*file* Use a different configuration file. *Sendmail* runs as the invoking user (rather than root) when this flag is specified.

–d*level* Set debugging level.

–f *addr* The sender's machine address is *addr*.

–F*name* Sets the full name of this user to *name*.

–h *cnt* Sets the ''hop count'' to *cnt*. This represents the number of times this message has been processed by *sendmail* (to the extent that it is supported by the underlying networks). *Cnt* is incremented during processing, and if it reaches MAXHOP (currently 30) *sendmail* throws away the message with an error.

–n Don't do aliasing or forwarding.

–r *addr* An obsolete form of –**f**.

–o*x value* Set option *x* to the specified *value*. These options are described in Appendix B.

–p*protocol* Set the sending protocol. Programs are encouraged to set this. The protocol field can be in the form *protocol***:***host* to set both the sending protocol and sending host. For example, ''–pUUCP:uunet'' sets the sending protocol to UUCP and the sending host to uunet. (Some existing programs use –oM to set the r and s macros; this is equivalent to using –p.)

–q*time* Try to process the queued up mail. If the time is given, a *sendmail* will run through the queue at the specified interval to deliver queued mail; otherwise, it only runs once.

–q*Xstring* Run the queue once, limiting the jobs to those matching *Xstring*. The key letter *X* can be **I** to limit based on queue identifier, **R** to limit based on recipient, or **S** to limit based on sender. A particular queued job is accepted if one of the corresponding addresses contains the indicated *string*.

–t Read the header for ''To:'', ''Cc:'', and ''Bcc:'' lines, and send to everyone listed in those lists. The ''Bcc:'' line will be deleted before sending. Any addresses in the argument vector will be deleted from the send list.

–X *logfile* Log all traffic in and out of *sendmail* in the indicated *logfile* for debugging mailer problems. This produces a lot of data very quickly and should be used sparingly.

There are a number of options that may be specified as primitive flags. These are the e, i, m, and v options. Also, the f option may be specified as the –**s** flag.

8

APPENDIX B

QUEUE FILE FORMATS

This appendix describes the format of the queue files. These files live in the directory defined by the **Q** option in the *sendmail.cf* file, usually */var/spool/mqueue* or */usr/spool/mqueue.*

All queue files have the name *x* **f***AAA99999* where *AAA99999* is the *id* for this message and the *x* is a type. The first letter of the id encodes the hour of the day that the message was received by the system (with A being the hour between midnight and 1:00AM). All files with the same id collectively define one message.

The types are:

d The data file. The message body (excluding the header) is kept in this file.

l The lock file. If this file exists, the job is currently being processed, and a queue run will not process the file. For that reason, an extraneous **lf** file can cause a job to apparently disappear (it will not even time out!). [Actually, this file is obsolete on most systems that support the **flock** or **lockf** system calls.]

n This file is created when an id is being created. It is a separate file to insure that no mail can ever be destroyed due to a race condition. It should exist for no more than a few milliseconds at any given time. [This is only used on old versions of *sendmail*; it is not used on newer versions.]

q The queue control file. This file contains the information necessary to process the job.

t A temporary file. These are an image of the **qf** file when it is being rebuilt. It should be renamed to a **qf** file very quickly.

x A transcript file, existing during the life of a session showing everything that happens during that session.

The **qf** file is structured as a series of lines each beginning with a code letter. The lines are as follows:

D The name of the data file. There may only be one of these lines.

H A header definition. There may be any number of these lines. The order is important: they represent the order in the final message. These use the same syntax as header definitions in the configuration file.

C The controlling address. The syntax is ''localuser:aliasname''. Recipient addresses following this line will be flagged so that deliveries will be run as the *localuser* (a user name from the /etc/passwd file); *aliasname* is the name of the alias that expanded to this address (used for printing messages).

R A recipient address. This will normally be completely aliased, but is actually realiased when the job is processed. There will be one line for each recipient.

S The sender address. There may only be one of these lines.

E An error address. If any such lines exist, they represent the addresses that should receive error messages.

T The job creation time. This is used to compute when to time out the job.

P The current message priority. This is used to order the queue. Higher numbers mean lower priorities. The priority changes as the message sits in the queue. The initial priority depends on the message class and the size of the message.

M A message. This line is printed by the *mailq* command, and is generally used to store status information. It can contain any text.

F Flag bits, represented as one letter per flag. Defined flag bits are **r** indicating that this is a response message and **w** indicating that a warning message has been sent announcing that the mail has been delayed.

$ A macro definition. The values of certain macros (as of this writing, only **$r** and **$s**) are passed through to the queue run phase.

B The body type. The remainder of the line is a text string defining the body type. If this field is missing, the body type is assumed to be ``undefined'' and no special processing is attempted. Legal values are ``7BIT'' and ``8BITMIME''.

As an example, the following is a queue file sent to ``eric@mammoth.Berkeley.EDU'' and ``bostic@okeeffe.CS.Berkeley.EDU''[1]:

```
P835771
T404261372
DdfAAA13557
Seric
Eowner-sendmail@vangogh.CS.Berkeley.EDU
Ceric:sendmail@vangogh.CS.Berkeley.EDU
Reric@mammoth.Berkeley.EDU
Rbostic@okeeffe.CS.Berkeley.EDU
H?P?return-path: <owner-sendmail@vangogh.CS.Berkeley.EDU>
Hreceived: by vangogh.CS.Berkeley.EDU (5.108/2.7) id AAA06703;
     Fri, 17 Jul 92 00:28:55 -0700
Hreceived: from mail.CS.Berkeley.EDU by vangogh.CS.Berkeley.EDU (5.108/2.7)
     id AAA06698; Fri, 17 Jul 92 00:28:54 -0700
Hreceived: from [128.32.31.21] by mail.CS.Berkeley.EDU (5.96/2.5)
     id AA22777; Fri, 17 Jul 92 03:29:14 -0400
Hreceived: by foo.bar.baz.de (5.57/Ultrix3.0-C)
     id AA22757; Fri, 17 Jul 92 09:31:25 GMT
H?F?from: eric@foo.bar.baz.de (Eric Allman)
H?x?full-name: Eric Allman
Hmessage-id: <9207170931.AA22757@foo.bar.baz.de>
HTo: sendmail@vangogh.CS.Berkeley.EDU
Hsubject: this is an example message
```

This shows the name of the data file, the person who sent the message, the submission time (in seconds since January 1, 1970), the message priority, the message class, the recipients, and the headers for the message.

[1]This example is contrived and probably inaccurate for your environment. Glance over it to get an idea; nothing can replace looking at what your own system generates.

8

APPENDIX C

SUMMARY OF SUPPORT FILES

This is a summary of the support files that *sendmail* creates or generates. Many of these can be changed by editing the sendmail.cf file; check there to find the actual pathnames.

/usr/sbin/sendmail
: The binary of *sendmail.*

/usr/bin/newaliases
: A link to /usr/sbin/sendmail; causes the alias database to be rebuilt. Running this program is completely equivalent to giving *sendmail* the **–bi** flag.

/usr/bin/mailq
: Prints a listing of the mail queue. This program is equivalent to using the **–bp** flag to *sendmail.*

/etc/sendmail.cf
: The configuration file, in textual form.

/usr/lib/sendmail.hf
: The SMTP help file.

/etc/sendmail.st
: A statistics file; need not be present.

/etc/sendmail.pid
: Created in daemon mode; it contains the process id of the current SMTP daemon. If you use this in scripts; use ''head –1'' to get just the first line; later versions of *sendmail* may add information to subsequent lines.

/etc/aliases
: The textual version of the alias file.

/etc/aliases.{pag,dir}
: The alias file in *dbm*(3) format.

/var/spool/mqueue
: The directory in which the mail queue and temporary files reside.

/var/spool/mqueue/qf*
: Control (queue) files for messages.

/var/spool/mqueue/df*
: Data files.

/var/spool/mqueue/tf*
: Temporary versions of the qf files, used during queue file rebuild.

/var/spool/mqueue/xf*
: A transcript of the current session.

SENDMAIL — An Internetwork Mail Router

Eric Allman*

University of California, Berkeley
Mammoth Project

9

ABSTRACT

Routing mail through a heterogenous internet presents many new problems. Among the worst of these is that of address mapping. Historically, this has been handled on an *ad hoc* basis. However, this approach has become unmanageable as internets grow.

Sendmail acts a unified "post office" to which all mail can be submitted. Address interpretation is controlled by a production system, which can parse both domain-based addressing and old-style *ad hoc* addresses. The production system is powerful enough to rewrite addresses in the message header to conform to the standards of a number of common target networks, including old (NCP/RFC733) Arpanet, new (TCP/RFC822) Arpanet, UUCP, and Phonenet. Sendmail also implements an SMTP server, message queueing, and aliasing.

Sendmail implements a general internetwork mail routing facility, featuring aliasing and forwarding, automatic routing to network gateways, and flexible configuration.

In a simple network, each node has an address, and resources can be identified with a host-resource pair; in particular, the mail system can refer to users using a host-username pair. Host names and numbers have to be administered by a central authority, but usernames can be assigned locally to each host.

In an internet, multiple networks with different characterstics and managements must communicate. In particular, the syntax and semantics of resource identification change. Certain special cases can be handled trivially by *ad hoc* techniques, such as providing network names that appear local to hosts on other networks, as with the Ethernet at Xerox PARC. However, the general case is extremely complex. For example, some networks require point-to-point routing, which simplifies the database update problem since only adjacent hosts must be entered into the system tables, while others use end-to-end addressing. Some networks use a left-associative syntax and others use a right-associative syntax, causing ambiguity in mixed addresses.

Internet standards seek to eliminate these problems. Initially, these proposed expanding the address pairs to address triples, consisting of {network, host, resource} triples. Network numbers must be universally agreed upon, and hosts can be assigned locally on each network. The user-level presentation was quickly expanded to address domains, comprised of a local resource identification and a hierarchical domain specification with a common static root. The domain technique separates the issue of physical versus logical addressing. For example, an address of the form ''eric@a.cc.berkeley.arpa'' describes only the logical organization of the address space.

Sendmail is intended to help bridge the gap between the totally *ad hoc* world of networks that know nothing of each other and the clean, tightly-coupled world of unique network numbers. It can accept old arbitrary address syntaxes, resolving ambiguities using heuristics specified by the system administrator, as well as domain-based addressing. It helps guide the conversion of message formats between disparate

*A considerable part of this work was done while under the employ of the INGRES Project at the University of California at Berkeley and at Britton Lee.

networks. In short, *sendmail* is designed to assist a graceful transition to consistent internetwork addressing schemes.

Section 1 discusses the design goals for *sendmail.* Section 2 gives an overview of the basic functions of the system. In section 3, details of usage are discussed. Section 4 compares *sendmail* to other internet mail routers, and an evaluation of *sendmail* is given in section 5, including future plans.

1. DESIGN GOALS

Design goals for *sendmail* include:

(1) Compatibility with the existing mail programs, including Bell version 6 mail, Bell version 7 mail [UNIX83], Berkeley *Mail* [Shoens79], BerkNet mail [Schmidt79], and hopefully UUCP mail [Nowitz78a, Nowitz78b]. ARPANET mail [Crocker77a, Postel77] was also required.

(2) Reliability, in the sense of guaranteeing that every message is correctly delivered or at least brought to the attention of a human for correct disposal; no message should ever be completely lost. This goal was considered essential because of the emphasis on mail in our environment. It has turned out to be one of the hardest goals to satisfy, especially in the face of the many anomalous message formats produced by various ARPANET sites. For example, certain sites generate improperly formated addresses, occasionally causing error-message loops. Some hosts use blanks in names, causing problems with UNIX mail programs that assume that an address is one word. The semantics of some fields are interpreted slightly differently by different sites. In summary, the obscure features of the ARPANET mail protocol really *are* used and are difficult to support, but must be supported.

(3) Existing software to do actual delivery should be used whenever possible. This goal derives as much from political and practical considerations as technical.

(4) Easy expansion to fairly complex environments, including multiple connections to a single network type (such as with multiple UUCP or Ether nets [Metcalfe76]). This goal requires consideration of the contents of an address as well as its syntax in order to determine which gateway to use. For example, the ARPANET is bringing up the TCP protocol to replace the old NCP protocol. No host at Berkeley runs both TCP and NCP, so it is necessary to look at the ARPANET host name to determine whether to route mail to an NCP gateway or a TCP gateway.

(5) Configuration should not be compiled into the code. A single compiled program should be able to run as is at any site (barring such basic changes as the CPU type or the operating system). We have found this seemingly unimportant goal to be critical in real life. Besides the simple problems that occur when any program gets recompiled in a different environment, many sites like to ''fiddle'' with anything that they will be recompiling anyway.

(6) *Sendmail* must be able to let various groups maintain their own mailing lists, and let individuals specify their own forwarding, without modifying the system alias file.

(7) Each user should be able to specify which mailer to execute to process mail being delivered for him. This feature allows users who are using specialized mailers that use a different format to build their environment without changing the system, and facilitates specialized functions (such as returning an ''I am on vacation'' message).

(8) Network traffic should be minimized by batching addresses to a single host where possible, without assistance from the user.

These goals motivated the architecture illustrated in figure 1. The user interacts with a mail generating and sending program. When the mail is created, the generator calls *sendmail,* which routes the message to the correct mailer(s). Since some of the senders may be network servers and some of the mailers may be network clients, *sendmail* may be used as an internet mail gateway.

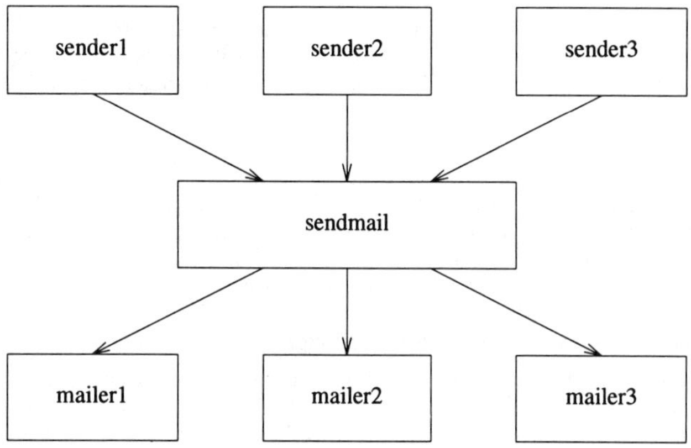

Figure 1 — Sendmail System Structure.

2. OVERVIEW

2.1. System Organization

Sendmail neither interfaces with the user nor does actual mail delivery. Rather, it collects a message generated by a user interface program (UIP) such as Berkeley *Mail*, MS [Crocker77b], or MH [Borden79], edits the message as required by the destination network, and calls appropriate mailers to do mail delivery or queueing for network transmission[1]. This discipline allows the insertion of new mailers at minimum cost. In this sense *sendmail* resembles the Message Processing Module (MPM) of [Postel79b].

2.2. Interfaces to the Outside World

There are three ways *sendmail* can communicate with the outside world, both in receiving and in sending mail. These are using the conventional UNIX argument vector/return status, speaking SMTP over a pair of UNIX pipes, and speaking SMTP over an interprocess(or) channel.

2.2.1. Argument vector/exit status

This technique is the standard UNIX method for communicating with the process. A list of recipients is sent in the argument vector, and the message body is sent on the standard input. Anything that the mailer prints is simply collected and sent back to the sender if there were any problems. The exit status from the mailer is collected after the message is sent, and a diagnostic is printed if appropriate.

2.2.2. SMTP over pipes

The SMTP protocol [Postel82] can be used to run an interactive lock-step interface with the mailer. A subprocess is still created, but no recipient addresses are passed to the mailer via

[1]except when mailing to a file, when *sendmail* does the delivery directly.

the argument list. Instead, they are passed one at a time in commands sent to the processes standard input. Anything appearing on the standard output must be a reply code in a special format.

2.2.3. SMTP over an IPC connection

This technique is similar to the previous technique, except that it uses a 4.2bsd IPC channel [UNIX83]. This method is exceptionally flexible in that the mailer need not reside on the same machine. It is normally used to connect to a sendmail process on another machine.

2.3. Operational Description

When a sender wants to send a message, it issues a request to *sendmail* using one of the three methods described above. *Sendmail* operates in two distinct phases. In the first phase, it collects and stores the message. In the second phase, message delivery occurs. If there were errors during processing during the second phase, *sendmail* creates and returns a new message describing the error and/or returns an status code telling what went wrong.

2.3.1. Argument processing and address parsing

If *sendmail* is called using one of the two subprocess techniques, the arguments are first scanned and option specifications are processed. Recipient addresses are then collected, either from the command line or from the SMTP RCPT command, and a list of recipients is created. Aliases are expanded at this step, including mailing lists. As much validation as possible of the addresses is done at this step: syntax is checked, and local addresses are verified, but detailed checking of host names and addresses is deferred until delivery. Forwarding is also performed as the local addresses are verified.

Sendmail appends each address to the recipient list after parsing. When a name is aliased or forwarded, the old name is retained in the list, and a flag is set that tells the delivery phase to ignore this recipient. This list is kept free from duplicates, preventing alias loops and duplicate messages deliverd to the same recipient, as might occur if a person is in two groups.

2.3.2. Message collection

Sendmail then collects the message. The message should have a header at the beginning. No formatting requirements are imposed on the message except that they must be lines of text (i.e., binary data is not allowed). The header is parsed and stored in memory, and the body of the message is saved in a temporary file.

To simplify the program interface, the message is collected even if no addresses were valid. The message will be returned with an error.

2.3.3. Message delivery

For each unique mailer and host in the recipient list, *sendmail* calls the appropriate mailer. Each mailer invocation sends to all users receiving the message on one host. Mailers that only accept one recipient at a time are handled properly.

The message is sent to the mailer using one of the same three interfaces used to submit a message to sendmail. Each copy of the message is prepended by a customized header. The mailer status code is caught and checked, and a suitable error message given as appropriate. The exit code must conform to a system standard or a generic message (''Service unavailable'') is given.

2.3.4. Queueing for retransmission

If the mailer returned an status that indicated that it might be able to handle the mail later, *sendmail* will queue the mail and try again later.

2.3.5. Return to sender

If errors occur during processing, *sendmail* returns the message to the sender for retransmission. The letter can be mailed back or written in the file "dead.letter" in the sender's home directory[2].

2.4. Message Header Editing

Certain editing of the message header occurs automatically. Header lines can be inserted under control of the configuration file. Some lines can be merged; for example, a "From:" line and a "Full-name:" line can be merged under certain circumstances.

2.5. Configuration File

Almost all configuration information is read at runtime from an ASCII file, encoding macro definitions (defining the value of macros used internally), header declarations (telling sendmail the format of header lines that it will process specially, i.e., lines that it will add or reformat), mailer definitions (giving information such as the location and characteristics of each mailer), and address rewriting rules (a limited production system to rewrite addresses which is used to parse and rewrite the addresses).

To improve performance when reading the configuration file, a memory image can be provided. This provides a "compiled" form of the configuration file.

3. USAGE AND IMPLEMENTATION

3.1. Arguments

Arguments may be flags and addresses. Flags set various processing options. Following flag arguments, address arguments may be given, unless we are running in SMTP mode. Addresses follow the syntax in RFC822 [Crocker82] for ARPANET address formats. In brief, the format is:

(1) Anything in parentheses is thrown away (as a comment).

(2) Anything in angle brackets ("<>") is preferred over anything else. This rule implements the ARPANET standard that addresses of the form

user name <machine-address>

will send to the electronic "machine-address" rather than the human "user name."

(3) Double quotes (") quote phrases; backslashes quote characters. Backslashes are more powerful in that they will cause otherwise equivalent phrases to compare differently — for example, *user* and *"user"* are equivalent, but *\user* is different from either of them.

Parentheses, angle brackets, and double quotes must be properly balanced and nested. The rewriting rules control remaining parsing[3].

3.2. Mail to Files and Programs

Files and programs are legitimate message recipients. Files provide archival storage of messages, useful for project administration and history. Programs are useful as recipients in a variety of situations, for example, to maintain a public repository of systems messages (such as the Berkeley *msgs* program, or the MARS system [Sattley78]).

Any address passing through the initial parsing algorithm as a local address (i.e, not appearing to be a valid address for another mailer) is scanned for two special cases. If prefixed by a vertical bar ("|") the rest of the address is processed as a shell command. If the user name begins with

---

[2]Obviously, if the site giving the error is not the originating site, the only reasonable option is to mail back to the sender. Also, there are many more error disposition options, but they only effect the error message — the "return to sender" function is always handled in one of these two ways.

[3]Disclaimer: Some special processing is done after rewriting local names; see below.

a slash mark ("/") the name is used as a file name, instead of a login name.

Files that have setuid or setgid bits set but no execute bits set have those bits honored if *sendmail* is running as root.

3.3. Aliasing, Forwarding, Inclusion

Sendmail reroutes mail three ways. Aliasing applies system wide. Forwarding allows each user to reroute incoming mail destined for that account. Inclusion directs *sendmail* to read a file for a list of addresses, and is normally used in conjunction with aliasing.

3.3.1. Aliasing

Aliasing maps names to address lists using a system-wide file. This file is indexed to speed access. Only names that parse as local are allowed as aliases; this guarantees a unique key (since there are no nicknames for the local host).

3.3.2. Forwarding

After aliasing, recipients that are local and valid are checked for the existence of a ".forward" file in their home directory. If it exists, the message is *not* sent to that user, but rather to the list of users in that file. Often this list will contain only one address, and the feature will be used for network mail forwarding.

Forwarding also permits a user to specify a private incoming mailer. For example, forwarding to:

"| /usr/local/newmail myname"

will use a different incoming mailer.

3.3.3. Inclusion

Inclusion is specified in RFC 733 [Crocker77a] syntax:

:Include: pathname

An address of this form reads the file specified by *pathname* and sends to all users listed in that file.

The intent is *not* to support direct use of this feature, but rather to use this as a subset of aliasing. For example, an alias of the form:

project: :include:/usr/project/userlist

is a method of letting a project maintain a mailing list without interaction with the system administration, even if the alias file is protected.

It is not necessary to rebuild the index on the alias database when a :include: list is changed.

3.4. Message Collection

Once all recipient addresses are parsed and verified, the message is collected. The message comes in two parts: a message header and a message body, separated by a blank line.

The header is formatted as a series of lines of the form

field-name: field-value

Field-value can be split across lines by starting the following lines with a space or a tab. Some header fields have special internal meaning, and have appropriate special processing. Other headers are simply passed through. Some header fields may be added automatically, such as time stamps.

The body is a series of text lines. It is completely uninterpreted and untouched, except that lines beginning with a dot have the dot doubled when transmitted over an SMTP channel. This extra dot is stripped by the receiver.

3.5. Message Delivery

The send queue is ordered by receiving host before transmission to implement message batching. Each address is marked as it is sent so rescanning the list is safe. An argument list is built as the scan proceeds. Mail to files is detected during the scan of the send list. The interface to the mailer is performed using one of the techniques described in section 2.2.

After a connection is established, *sendmail* makes the per-mailer changes to the header and sends the result to the mailer. If any mail is rejected by the mailer, a flag is set to invoke the return-to-sender function after all delivery completes.

3.6. Queued Messages

If the mailer returns a ''temporary failure'' exit status, the message is queued. A control file is used to describe the recipients to be sent to and various other parameters. This control file is formatted as a series of lines, each describing a sender, a recipient, the time of submission, or some other salient parameter of the message. The header of the message is stored in the control file, so that the associated data file in the queue is just the temporary file that was originally collected.

3.7. Configuration

Configuration is controlled primarily by a configuration file read at startup. *Sendmail* should not need to be recomplied except

(1) To change operating systems (V6, V7/32V, 4BSD).

(2) To remove or insert the DBM (UNIX database) library.

(3) To change ARPANET reply codes.

(4) To add headers fields requiring special processing.

Adding mailers or changing parsing (i.e., rewriting) or routing information does not require recompilation.

If the mail is being sent by a local user, and the file ''.mailcf'' exists in the sender's home directory, that file is read as a configuration file after the system configuration file. The primary use of this feature is to add header lines.

The configuration file encodes macro definitions, header definitions, mailer definitions, rewriting rules, and options.

3.7.1. Macros

Macros can be used in three ways. Certain macros transmit unstructured textual information into the mail system, such as the name *sendmail* will use to identify itself in error messages. Other macros transmit information from *sendmail* to the configuration file for use in creating other fields (such as argument vectors to mailers); e.g., the name of the sender, and the host and user of the recipient. Other macros are unused internally, and can be used as shorthand in the configuration file.

3.7.2. Header declarations

Header declarations inform *sendmail* of the format of known header lines. Knowledge of a few header lines is built into *sendmail*, such as the ''From:'' and ''Date:'' lines.

Most configured headers will be automatically inserted in the outgoing message if they don't exist in the incoming message. Certain headers are suppressed by some mailers.

3.7.3. Mailer declarations

Mailer declarations tell *sendmail* of the various mailers available to it. The definition specifies the internal name of the mailer, the pathname of the program to call, some flags associated with the mailer, and an argument vector to be used on the call; this vector is macro-expanded before use.

3.7.4. Address rewriting rules

The heart of address parsing in *sendmail* is a set of rewriting rules. These are an ordered list of pattern-replacement rules, (somewhat like a production system, except that order is critical), which are applied to each address. The address is rewritten textually until it is either rewritten into a special canonical form (i.e., a (mailer, host, user) 3-tuple, such as {arpanet, usc-isif, postel} representing the address "postel@usc-isif"), or it falls off the end. When a pattern matches, the rule is reapplied until it fails.

The configuration file also supports the editing of addresses into different formats. For example, an address of the form:

ucsfcgl!tef

might be mapped into:

tef@ucsfcgl.UUCP

to conform to the domain syntax. Translations can also be done in the other direction.

3.7.5. Option setting

There are several options that can be set from the configuration file. These include the pathnames of various support files, timeouts, default modes, etc.

4. COMPARISON WITH OTHER MAILERS

4.1. Delivermail

Sendmail is an outgrowth of *delivermail*. The primary differences are:

(1) Configuration information is not compiled in. This change simplifies many of the problems of moving to other machines. It also allows easy debugging of new mailers.

(2) Address parsing is more flexible. For example, *delivermail* only supported one gateway to any network, whereas *sendmail* can be sensitive to host names and reroute to different gateways.

(3) Forwarding and :include: features eliminate the requirement that the system alias file be writable by any user (or that an update program be written, or that the system administration make all changes).

(4) *Sendmail* supports message batching across networks when a message is being sent to multiple recipients.

(5) A mail queue is provided in *sendmail*. Mail that cannot be delivered immediately but can potentially be delivered later is stored in this queue for a later retry. The queue also provides a buffer against system crashes; after the message has been collected it may be reliably redelivered even if the system crashes during the initial delivery.

(6) *Sendmail* uses the networking support provided by 4.2BSD to provide a direct interface networks such as the ARPANET and/or Ethernet using SMTP (the Simple Mail Transfer Protocol) over a TCP/IP connection.

4.2. MMDF

MMDF [Crocker79] spans a wider problem set than *sendmail*. For example, the domain of MMDF includes a "phone network" mailer, whereas *sendmail* calls on preexisting mailers in most cases.

MMDF and *sendmail* both support aliasing, customized mailers, message batching, automatic forwarding to gateways, queueing, and retransmission. MMDF supports two-stage timeout, which *sendmail* does not support.

The configuration for MMDF is compiled into the code[4].

---

[4]Dynamic configuration tables are currently being considered for MMDF; allowing the installer to select either compiled or

Since MMDF does not consider backwards compatibility as a design goal, the address parsing is simpler but much less flexible.

It is somewhat harder to integrate a new channel[5] into MMDF. In particular, MMDF must know the location and format of host tables for all channels, and the channel must speak a special protocol. This allows MMDF to do additional verification (such as verifying host names) at submission time.

MMDF strictly separates the submission and delivery phases. Although *sendmail* has the concept of each of these stages, they are integrated into one program, whereas in MMDF they are split into two programs.

4.3. Message Processing Module

The Message Processing Module (MPM) discussed by Postel [Postel79b] matches *sendmail* closely in terms of its basic architecture. However, like MMDF, the MPM includes the network interface software as part of its domain.

MPM also postulates a duplex channel to the receiver, as does MMDF, thus allowing simpler handling of errors by the mailer than is possible in *sendmail*. When a message queued by *sendmail* is sent, any errors must be returned to the sender by the mailer itself. Both MPM and MMDF mailers can return an immediate error response, and a single error processor can create an appropriate response.

MPM prefers passing the message as a structured object, with type-length-value tuples[6]. Such a convention requires a much higher degree of cooperation between mailers than is required by *sendmail*. MPM also assumes a universally agreed upon internet name space (with each address in the form of a net-host-user tuple), which *sendmail* does not.

5. EVALUATIONS AND FUTURE PLANS

Sendmail is designed to work in a nonhomogeneous environment. Every attempt is made to avoid imposing unnecessary constraints on the underlying mailers. This goal has driven much of the design. One of the major problems has been the lack of a uniform address space, as postulated in [Postel79a] and [Postel79b].

A nonuniform address space implies that a path will be specified in all addresses, either explicitly (as part of the address) or implicitly (as with implied forwarding to gateways). This restriction has the unpleasant effect of making replying to messages exceedingly difficult, since there is no one ''address'' for any person, but only a way to get there from wherever you are.

Interfacing to mail programs that were not initially intended to be applied in an internet environment has been amazingly successful, and has reduced the job to a manageable task.

Sendmail has knowledge of a few difficult environments built in. It generates ARPANET FTP/SMTP compatible error messages (prepended with three-digit numbers [Neigus73, Postel74, Postel82]) as necessary, optionally generates UNIX-style ''From'' lines on the front of messages for some mailers, and knows how to parse the same lines on input. Also, error handling has an option customized for BerkNet.

The decision to avoid doing any type of delivery where possible (even, or perhaps especially, local delivery) has turned out to be a good idea. Even with local delivery, there are issues of the location of the mailbox, the format of the mailbox, the locking protocol used, etc., that are best decided by other programs. One surprisingly major annoyance in many internet mailers is that the location and format of local mail is built in. The feeling seems to be that local mail is so common that it should be efficient. This feeling is not born out by our experience; on the contrary, the location and format of

dynamic tables.

[5]The MMDF equivalent of a *sendmail* ''mailer.''

[6]This is similar to the NBS standard.

mailboxes seems to vary widely from system to system.

The ability to automatically generate a response to incoming mail (by forwarding mail to a program) seems useful (''I am on vacation until late August....'') but can create problems such as forwarding loops (two people on vacation whose programs send notes back and forth, for instance) if these programs are not well written. A program could be written to do standard tasks correctly, but this would solve the general case.

It might be desirable to implement some form of load limiting. I am unaware of any mail system that addresses this problem, nor am I aware of any reasonable solution at this time.

The configuration file is currently practically inscrutable; considerable convenience could be realized with a higher-level format.

It seems clear that common protocols will be changing soon to accommodate changing requirements and environments. These changes will include modifications to the message header (e.g., [NBS80]) or to the body of the message itself (such as for multimedia messages [Postel80]). Experience indicates that these changes should be relatively trivial to integrate into the existing system.

In tightly coupled environments, it would be nice to have a name server such as Grapvine [Birrell82] integrated into the mail system. This would allow a site such as ''Berkeley'' to appear as a single host, rather than as a collection of hosts, and would allow people to move transparently among machines without having to change their addresses. Such a facility would require an automatically updated database and some method of resolving conflicts. Ideally this would be effective even without all hosts being under a single management. However, it is not clear whether this feature should be integrated into the aliasing facility or should be considered a ''value added'' feature outside *sendmail* itself.

As a more interesting case, the CSNET name server [Solomon81] provides an facility that goes beyond a single tightly-coupled environment. Such a facility would normally exist outside of *sendmail* however.

ACKNOWLEDGEMENTS

Thanks are due to Kurt Shoens for his continual cheerful assistance and good advice, Bill Joy for pointing me in the correct direction (over and over), and Mark Horton for more advice, prodding, and many of the good ideas. Kurt and Eric Schmidt are to be credited for using *delivermail* as a server for their programs (*Mail* and BerkNet respectively) before any sane person should have, and making the necessary modifications promptly and happily. Eric gave me considerable advice about the perils of network software which saved me an unknown amount of work and grief. Mark did the original implementation of the DBM version of aliasing, installed the VFORK code, wrote the current version of *rmail*, and was the person who really convinced me to put the work into *delivermail* to turn it into *sendmail*. Kurt deserves accolades for using *sendmail* when I was myself afraid to take the risk; how a person can continue to be so enthusiastic in the face of so much bitter reality is beyond me.

Kurt, Mark, Kirk McKusick, Marvin Solomon, and many others have reviewed this paper, giving considerable useful advice.

Special thanks are reserved for Mike Stonebraker at Berkeley and Bob Epstein at Britton-Lee, who both knowingly allowed me to put so much work into this project when there were so many other things I really should have been working on.

9

REFERENCES

[Birrell82] Birrell, A. D., Levin, R., Needham, R. M., and Schroeder, M. D., ''Grapevine: An Exercise in Distributed Computing.'' In *Comm. A.C.M. 25,* 4, April 82.

[Borden79] Borden, S., Gaines, R. S., and Shapiro, N. Z., *The MH Message Handling System: Users' Manual.* R-2367-PAF. Rand Corporation. October 1979.

[Crocker77a] Crocker, D. H., Vittal, J. J., Pogran, K. T., and Henderson, D. A. Jr., *Standard for the Format of ARPA Network Text Messages.* RFC 733, NIC 41952. In [Feinler78]. November 1977.

[Crocker77b] Crocker, D. H., *Framework and Functions of the MS Personal Message System.* R-2134-ARPA, Rand Corporation, Santa Monica, California. 1977.

[Crocker79] Crocker, D. H., Szurkowski, E. S., and Farber, D. J., *An Internetwork Memo Distribution Facility — MMDF.* 6th Data Communication Symposium, Asilomar. November 1979.

[Crocker82] Crocker, D. H., *Standard for the Format of Arpa Internet Text Messages.* RFC 822. Network Information Center, SRI International, Menlo Park, California. August 1982.

[Metcalfe76] Metcalfe, R., and Boggs, D., ''Ethernet: Distributed Packet Switching for Local Computer Networks'', *Communications of the ACM 19,* 7. July 1976.

[Feinler78] Feinler, E., and Postel, J. (eds.), *ARPANET Protocol Handbook.* NIC 7104. Network Information Center, SRI International, Menlo Park, California. 1978.

[NBS80] National Bureau of Standards, *Specification of a Draft Message Format Standard.* Report No. ICST/CBOS 80-2. October 1980.

[Neigus73] Neigus, N., *File Transfer Protocol for the ARPA Network.* RFC 542, NIC 17759. In [Feinler78]. August, 1973.

[Nowitz78a] Nowitz, D. A., and Lesk, M. E., *A Dial-Up Network of UNIX Systems.* Bell Laboratories. In UNIX Programmer's Manual, Seventh Edition, Volume 2. August, 1978.

[Nowitz78b] Nowitz, D. A., *Uucp Implementation Description.* Bell Laboratories. In UNIX Programmer's Manual, Seventh Edition, Volume 2. October, 1978.

[Postel74] Postel, J., and Neigus, N., Revised FTP Reply Codes. RFC 640, NIC 30843. In [Feinler78]. June, 1974.

[Postel77] Postel, J., *Mail Protocol.* NIC 29588. In [Feinler78]. November 1977.

[Postel79a] Postel, J., *Internet Message Protocol.* RFC 753, IEN 85. Network Information Center, SRI International, Menlo Park, California. March 1979.

[Postel79b] Postel, J. B., *An Internetwork Message Structure.* In *Proceedings of the Sixth Data Communications Symposium,* IEEE. New York. November 1979.

[Postel80] Postel, J. B., *A Structured Format for Transmission of Multi-Media Documents.* RFC 767. Network Information Center, SRI International, Menlo Park, California. August 1980.

[Postel82] Postel, J. B., *Simple Mail Transfer Protocol.* RFC821 (obsoleting RFC788). Network Information Center, SRI International, Menlo Park, California. August 1982.

[Schmidt79] Schmidt, E., *An Introduction to the Berkeley Network.* University of California, Berkeley California. 1979.

[Shoens79] Shoens, K., *Mail Reference Manual.* University of California, Berkeley. In UNIX Programmer's Manual, Seventh Edition, Volume 2C. December 1979.

9

[Sluizer81] Sluizer, S., and Postel, J. B., *Mail Transfer Protocol.* RFC 780. Network Information Center, SRI International, Menlo Park, California. May 1981.

[Solomon81] Solomon, M., Landweber, L., and Neuhengen, D., ''The Design of the CSNET Name Server.'' CS-DN-2, University of Wisconsin, Madison. November 1981.

[Su82] Su, Zaw-Sing, and Postel, Jon, *The Domain Naming Convention for Internet User Applications.* RFC819. Network Information Center, SRI International, Menlo Park, California. August 1982.

[UNIX83] *The UNIX Programmer's Manual, Seventh Edition,* Virtual VAX-11 Version, Volume 1. Bell Laboratories, modified by the University of California, Berkeley, California. March, 1983.

Name Server Operations Guide for BIND

Release 4.9.2

Releases from 4.9
Paul Vixie[1]
<paul@vix.com>
Vixie Enterprises
Redwood City, CA

Releases through 4.8.3
Kevin J. Dunlap[2]
Michael J. Karels
Computer Systems Research Group
Computer Science Division
Department of Electrical Engineering and Computer Sciences
University of California
Berkeley CA 94720

10

1. Introduction

The Berkeley Internet Name Domain (BIND) implements an Internet name server for the UNIX† operating system. The BIND consists of a server (or "daemon") and a *resolver* library. A name server is a network service that enables clients to name resources or objects and share this information with other objects in the network. This in effect is a distributed data base system for objects in a computer network. BIND is fully integrated into BSD (4.3 and later releases) network programs for use in storing and retrieving host names and address. The system administrator can configure the system to use BIND as a replacement to the older host table lookup of information in the network hosts file */etc/hosts*. The default configuration for BSD uses BIND.

2. Building A System with a Name Server

BIND is composed of two parts. One is the user interface called the *resolver* which consists of a group of routines that reside in the C library */lib/libc.a*. Second is the actual server called *named*. This is a daemon that runs in the background and services queries on a given network port. The standard port for UDP and TCP is specified in */etc/services*.

---

[1] This author was employed by Digital Equipment Corporation's Network Systems Laboratory during the development and release of BIND 4.9. Releases from 4.9.2 were sponsored by Vixie Enterprises.

[2] This author was an employee of Digital Equipment Corporation's Ultrix Engineering Advanced Development Group and was on loan to CSRG when this work was done. Ultrix is a trademark of Digital Equipment Corporation.

†UNIX is a Trademark of AT&T Bell Laboratories

2.1. Resolver Routines in libc

When building your 4.3BSD system you may either build the C library to use the name server resolver routines or use the host table lookup routines to do host name and address resolution. The default resolver for 4.3BSD uses the name server. Newer BSD systems include both name server and host table functionality with preference given to the name server if there is one or if there is a */etc/resolv.conf* file.

Building the C library to use the name server changes the way *gethostbyname* (3N), *gethostbyaddr* (3N), and *sethostent* (3N) do their functions. The name server renders *gethostent* (3N) obsolete, since it has no concept of a next line in the database. These library calls are built with the resolver routines needed to query the name server.

The *resolver* contains functions that build query packets and exchange them with name servers.

Before building the 4.3BSD C library, set the variable *HOSTLOOKUP* equal to *named* in */usr/src/lib/libc/Makefile*. You then make and install the C library and compiler and then compile the rest of the 4.3BSD system. For more information see section 6.6 of ''Installing and Operating 4.3BSD on the VAX‡''.

If your operating system isn't VAX‡ 4.3BSD, it is probably the case that your vendor has included *resolver* support in the supplied C Library. You should consult your vendor's documentation to find out what has to be done to enable *resolver* support. Note that your vendor's *resolver* may be out of date with respect to the one shipped with BIND, and that you might want to build BIND's resolver library and install it, and its include files, into your system's compile/link path so that your own network applications will be able to use the newer features.

2.2. The Name Service

The basic function of the name server is to provide information about network objects by answering queries. The specifications for this name server are defined in RFC1034, RFC1035 and RFC974. These documents can be found in */usr/src/etc/named/doc* in 4.3BSD or *ftp*ed from **ftp.rs.internic.net**. It is also recommended that you read the related manual pages, *named* (8), *resolver* (3), and *resolver* (5).

The advantage of using a name server over the host table lookup for host name resolution is to avoid the need for a single centralized clearinghouse for all names. The authority for this information can be delegated to the different organizations on the network responsible for it.

The host table lookup routines require that the master file for the entire network be maintained at a central location by a few people. This works fine for small networks where there are only a few machines and the different organizations responsible for them cooperate. But this does not work well for large networks where machines cross organizational boundaries.

With the name server, the network can be broken into a hierarchy of domains. The name space is organized as a tree according to organizational or administrative boundaries. Each node, called a *domain*, is given a label, and the name of the domain is the concatenation of all the labels of the domains from the root to the current domain, listed from right to left separated by dots. A label need only be unique within its domain. The whole space is partitioned into several areas called *zones*, each starting at a domain and extending down to the leaf domains or to domains where other zones start. Zones usually represent administrative boundaries. An example of a host address for a host at the University of California, Berkeley would look as follows:

monet.Berkeley.EDU

The top level domain for educational organizations is EDU; Berkeley is a subdomain of EDU and monet is the name of the host.

‡VAX is a Trademark of Digital Equipment Corporation

2.3. About Hesiod, and HS-class Resource Records

Hesiod, developed by MIT Project Athena, is an information service built upon BIND. Its intent is similar to that of Sun's NIS: to furnish information about users, groups, network-accessible file systems, printcaps, and mail service throughout an installation. Aside from its use of BIND rather than separate server code another important difference between Hesiod and NIS is that Hesiod is not intended to deal with passwords and authentication, but only with data that are not security sensitive. Hesiod servers can be implemented by adding resource records to BIND servers; or they can be implemented as separate servers separately administered.

To learn about and obtain Hesiod make an anonymous FTP connection to host ATHENA-DIST.MIT.EDU and retrieve the compressed tar file **pub/hesiod.tar.Z.** You will not need the named and resolver library portions of the distribution because their functionality has already been integrated into BIND 4.9. To learn how Hesiod functions as part of the Athena computing environment obtain the paper **pub/usenix/athena-changes.PS** from the above FTP server host. There is also a tar file of sample Hesiod resource files.

Whether one should use Hesiod class is open to question, since the same services can probably be provided with class IN, type TXT and type CNAME records. In either case, the code and documents for Hesiod will suggest how to set up and use the service.

Note that while BIND includes support for *HS*-class queries, the zone transfer logic for non-*IN*-class zones is still experimental.

2.4. About "secure zones"

Secure zones implement named security on a zone by zone basis. It is designed to use a permission list of networks or hosts which may obtain particular information from the zone.

In order to use zone security, named must be compiled with SECURE_ZONES defined and you must have at least one secure_zone TXT RR. Unless a secure_zone record exists for a given zone, no restrictions will be applied to the data in that zone. The format of the secure_zone TXT RR is:

```
secure_zone        addr-class        TXT        string
```

The addr-class may be either HS or IN. The syntax for the TXT string is either "network address:netmask" or "host IP address:H".

"network address:netmask" allows queries from an entire network. If the netmask is omitted, named will use the default netmask for the network address specified.

"host IP address:H" allows queries from a host. The "H" after the ":" is required to differentiate the host address from a network address. Multiple secure_zone TXT RRs are allowed in the same zone file.

For example, you can set up a zone to only answer hesiod requests from the masked class B network 130.215.0.0 and from host 128.23.10.56 by adding the following two TXT RR's:

```
secure_zone        HS        TXT        "130.215.0.0:255.255.0.0"
secure_zone        HS        TXT        "128.23.10.56:H"
```

This feature can be used to restrict access to a Hesiod password map or to seperate internal and external internet address resolution on a firewall machine without needing to run a seperate named for internal and external address resolution.

3. Types of Zones

A "zone" is a point of delegation in the DNS tree. It contains all names from a certain point "downward" except those which are delegated to other servers. A "delegation point" has one or more *NS* records in the "parent zone", which should be matched by equivalent *NS* records at the root of the "delegated zone" (i.e., the "@" name in the zone file).

Understanding the difference between a ''zone'' and a ''domain'' is crucial to the proper operation of a name server. As an example, consider the DEC.COM *domain*, which includes names such as POBOX1.PA.DEC.COM and QUABBIN.CRL.DEC.COM even though the DEC.COM *zone* includes only *delegations* for the PA.DEC.COM and CRL.DEC.COM zones. A zone can map exactly to a single domain, but could also include only part of a domain (the rest of which could be delegated to other name servers). Technically speaking, every name in the DNS tree is a ''domain'', even if it is ''terminal'', that is, has no ''subdomains''. Technically speaking, every subdomain is a domain and every domain except the root is also a subdomain. The terminology is not intuitive and you would do well to read RFC's 1033, 1034, and 1035 to gain a complete understanding of this difficult and subtle topic.

Though BIND is a *Domain* Name Server, it deals primarily in terms of *zones*. The *primary* and *secondary* declarations in the *named.boot* file specify *zones*, not *domains*. When you ask someone if they are willing to be a secondary server for your ''domain'', you are actually asking for secondary service for some collection of *zones*.

Each zone will have one ''primary'' server, which loads the zone contents from some local file which is edited by humans or perhaps generated mechanically from some other local file which is edited by humans. Then there will be some number of ''secondary'' servers, which load the zone contents using the IP/DNS protocol (that is, the secondary servers will contact the primary and fetch the zone using IP/TCP). This set of servers (the primary and all of the secondaries) should be listed in the *NS* records in the parent zone, which will constitute a ''delegation''. This set of servers must also be listed in the zone file itself, usually under the ''@'' name which is a magic cookie that means the ''top level'' or ''root'' of current $ORIGIN. You can list servers in the zone's top-level ''@'' *NS* records that are not in the parent's *NS* delegation, but you cannot list servers in the parent's delegation that are not present in the zone's ''@''. (This latter condition is one form of what is called a ''lame delegation''.)

10

4. Types of Servers

Servers do not really have ''types''. A server can be a primary for some zones and a secondary for others, or it can be only a primary, or only a secondary, or it can serve no zones and just answer queries via its ''cache''. Previous versions of this document referred to servers as ''master'' and ''slave'' but we now feel that those distinctions — and the assignment of a ''type'' to a name server — are not useful.

4.1. Caching Only Server

All servers are caching servers. This means that the server caches the information that it receives for use until the data expires. A *Caching Only Server* is a server that is not authoritative for any domain. This server services queries and asks other servers, who have the authority, for the information needed. All servers keep data in their cache until the data expires, based on a *TTL* (''Time To Live'') field which is maintained for all resource records.

4.2. Remote Server

A Remote Server is an option given to people who would like to use a name server from their workstation or on a machine that has a limited amount of memory and CPU cycles. With this option you can run all of the networking programs that use the name server without the name server running on the local machine. All of the queries are serviced by a name server that is running on another machine on the network. This kind of host is technically not a ''server'', since it has no cache and does not answer queries. A host which has an */etc/resolv.conf* file listing only remote hosts, and which does not run a name server of its own, is sometimes called a Remote Server but more often it is called simply a DNS Client.

4.3. Slave Server

A Slave Server is a server that always forwards queries it cannot satisfy from its cache, to a fixed list of *forwarding* servers instead of interacting with the master nameservers for the root and other domains. The queries to the *forwarding servers* are recursive queries. There may be one or more forwarding servers, and they are tried in turn until the list is exhausted. A Slave and forwarder configuration is typically used when you do not wish all the servers at a given site to be interacting with the rest of the Internet servers. A typical scenario would involve a number of workstations and a departmental timesharing machine with Internet access. The workstations might be administratively prohibited from having Internet access. To give the workstations the appearance of access to the Internet domain system, the workstations could be Slave servers to the timesharing machine which would forward the queries and interact with other nameservers to resolve the query before returning the answer. An added benefit of using the forwarding feature is that the central machine develops a much more complete cache of information that all the workstations can take advantage of. The use of Slave mode and forwarding is discussed further under the description of the named bootfile commands.

There is no prohibition against declaring a server to be a *slave* even though it has *primary* and/or *secondary* zones as well; the effect will still be that anything in the local server's cache or zones will be answered, and anything else will be forwarded using the *forwarders* list.

5. Setting up Your Own Domain

When setting up a domain that is going to be on a public network the site administrator should contact the organization in charge of the network and request the appropriate domain registration form. An organization that belongs to multiple networks (such as the *Internet* and *BITNET*) should register with only one network.

The contacts are as follows:

5.1. Internet

Sites on the Internet who need information on setting up a domain should contact the registrar for their network, which is one of the following:

MILnet HOSTMASTER@NIC.DDN.MIL
other HOSTMASTER@RS.INTERNIC.NET

You may also want to be placed on the BIND mailing list, which is a mail group for people on the Internet who run BIND. The group discusses future design decisions, operational problems, and other related topic. The address to request being placed on this mailing list is:

bind-request@uunet.uu.net

5.2. BITNET

If you are on the BITNET and need to set up a domain, contact INFO@BITNIC.

5.3. Subdomains of Existing Domains

If you want a subdomain of some existing domain, you should find the contact point for the parent domain rather than asking one of the above top-level registrars. There should be a convention that **registrar@***domain* or **hostmaster@***domain* for any given domain will always be an alias for that domain's registrar (somewhat analogous to **postmaster**), but there is no such convention. Try it as a last resort, but first you should examine the *SOA* record for the domain and send mail to the ''responsible person'' shown therein.

6. Files

The name server uses several files to load its data base. This section covers the files and their formats needed for *named.*

6.1. Boot File

This is the file that is first read when *named* starts up. This tells the server what type of server it is, which zones it has authority over and where to get its initial data. The default location for this file is */etc/named.boot*. However this can be changed by setting the *BOOTFILE* variable when you compile *named* or by specifying the location on the command line when *named* is started up.

6.1.1. Domain

A default domain may be specified for the nameserver using a line such as

domain Berkeley.Edu

Older name servers use this information when they receive a query for a name without a "." that is not known. Newer designs assume that the resolver library will append its own idea of a "default domain" to any unqualified names. Though the name server can still be compiled with support for the *domain* directive in the boot file, the default is to leave it out and we strenuously recommend against its use. If you use this feature, clients outside your local domain which send you requests about unqualified names will have the implicit qualification of your domain rather than theirs. The proper place for this function is on the client, in their **/etc/resolv.conf** (or equivalent) file. Use of the *domain* directive in your boot file is strongly discouraged.

6.1.2. Directory

The *directory* directive specifies the directory in which the nameserver should run, allowing the other file names in the boot file to use relative path names. There can be only one *directory* directive and it should be given before any other directives that specify file names.

directory */var/named*

If you have more than a couple of named files to be maintained, you may wish to place the named files in a directory such as /var/named and adjust the directory command properly. The main purposes of this command are to make sure named is in the proper directory when trying to include files by relative path names with $Include and to allow named to run in a location that is reasonable to dump core if it feels the urge.

6.1.3. Primary Service

The line in the boot file that designates the server as a primary server for a zone looks as follows:

primary *Berkeley.Edu ucbhosts*

The first field specifies that the server is a primary one for the zone stated in the second field. The third field is the name of the file from which the data is read.

The above assumes that the zone you are specifying is a class *IN* zone. If you wish to designate a different class you can append */class* to the first field, where *class* is either the integer value or the standard mnemonic for the class. For example the line for a primary server for a hesiod class zone looks as follows:

primary/HS *Berkeley.Edu* *hesiod.data*

Note that this support for specifying other than class *IN* zones is a compile-time option which your vendor may not have enabled when they built your operating system.

6.1.4. Secondary Service

The line for a secondary server is similar to the primary except that it lists addresses of other servers (usually primary servers) from which the zone data will be obtained.

secondary *Berkeley.Edu 128.32.0.10 128.32.0.4 ucbhosts.bak*

The first field specifies that the server is a secondary master server for the zone stated in the second field. The two network addresses specify the name servers which have data for the zone. Note that at least one of these will be a *primary*, and, unless you are using some protocol other than IP/DNS for your zone transfer mechanism, the others will all be other *secondary* servers. Having your secondary server pull data from other secondary servers is usually unwise, since you can add delay to the propagation of zone updates if your network's connectivity varies in pathological but common ways. The intended use for multiple addresses on a *secondary* declaration is when the *primary* server has multiple network interfaces and therefore multiple host addresses. The secondary server gets its data across the network from one of the listed servers. The server addresses are tried in the order listed. If a filename is present after the list of primary servers, data for the zone will be dumped into that file as a backup. When the server is first started, the data is loaded from the backup file if possible, and a primary server is then consulted to check that the zone is still up-to-date. Note that listing your server as a *secondary* server does not neccessarily make it one — the parent zone must *delegate* authority to your server as well as the primary and the other secondaries, or you will be transferring a zone over for no reason; no other server will have a reason to query you for that zone unless the parent zone lists you as a server for the zone.

10

As with primary you may specify a secondary server for a class other than *IN* by appending */class* to the *secondary* keyword, e.g., *secondary/HS*.

6.1.5. Stub Service

The line for a stub server is similar to a secondary.

stub *Berkeley.Edu* *128.32.0.10 128.32.0.4 ucbhosts.bak*

The first field specifies that the server is a stub server for the zone stated in the second field.

Stub zones are intened to ensure that a primary for a zone always has the correct nameserver records for children of that zone. If the primary is not a secondary for a child zone it should be configured with stub zones for all its children. Stub zones provide a mechanism to allow nameserver records for a zone to be specified in only one place.

```
primary CSIRO.AU          csiro.dat
stub    dms.CSIRO.AU      130.155.16.1 dms.stub
stub    dap.CSIRO.AU      130.155.98.1 dap.stub
```

6.1.6. Caching Server

You do not need a special line to designate that a server is a caching server. What denotes a ''caching only'' server is the absence of authority lines, such as *secondary* or *primary* in the boot file.

All servers, including ''caching only'' servers, should have a line as follows in the boot file to prime the name servers cache:

cache . *root.cache*

All cache files listed will be read in at named boot time and any values still valid will be reinstated in the cache and the root nameserver information in the cache files will be used until a root query is actually answered by one of the name servers in your cache file, at which time that answer will be used until it times out and your cache file will be ignored.

As with *primary* and *secondary*, you may specify a secondary server for a class other than *IN* by appending */class* to the *cache* keyword, e.g., *class/HS*.

Do not put anything into your *cache* files other than root server information.

10

6.1.7. Forwarders

Any server can make use of *forwarders*. A *forwarder* is another server capable of processing recursive queries that is willing to try resolving queries on behalf of other systems. The *forwarders* command specifies forwarders by internet address as follows:

forwarders *128.32.0.10 128.32.0.4*

There are two main reasons for wanting to do so. First, some systems may not have full network access and may be prevented from sending any IP packets into the rest of the Internet and therefore must rely on a forwarder which does have access to the full net. The second reason is that the forwarder sees a union of all queries as they pass through his server and therefore it builds up a very rich cache of data compared to the cache in a typical workstation nameserver. In effect, the *forwarder* becomes a meta-cache that all hosts can benefit from, thereby reducing the total number of queries from that site to the rest of the net.

The effect of "forwarders" is to prepend some fixed addresses to the list of name servers to be tried for every query. Normally that list is made up only of higher-authority servers discovered via *NS* record lookups for the relevant domain. If the forwarders do not answer, then unless the *slave* directive was given, the appropriate servers for the domains will be queried directly.

6.1.8. Slave Servers

Slave mode is used if the use of forwarders is the only possible way to resolve queries due to lack of full net access or if you wish to prevent the nameserver from using other than the listed forwarders. Slave mode is activated by placing the simple command

slave

in the bootfile. If *slave* is used, then you must specify forwarders. When in slave mode, the server will forward each query to each of the the forwarders until an answer is found or the list of forwarders is exhausted. The server will not try to contact any remote name server other than those named in the *forwarders* list.

So while *forwarders* adds to the end of the "server list" for each query, *slave* causes the "server list" to contain *only* those addresses listed in the *forwarders* declarations. Careless use of the *slave* directive can cause really horrible forwarding loops, since you could end up forwarding queries only to some set of hosts which are also slaves, and one or several of them could be forwarding queries back to you.

Use of the *slave* directive should be considered very carefully.

6.1.9. Zone Transfer Restrictions

It may be the case that your organization does not wish to give complete lists of your hosts to anyone on the Internet who can reach your name servers. While it is still possible for people to "iterate" through your address range, looking for *PTR* records, and build a list of your hosts the "slow" way, it is still considered reasonable to restrict your export of zones via the zone transfer protocol. To limit the list of neighbors who can transfer zones from your server, use the

xfrnets

directive. This directive has the same syntax as *forwarders* except that you can list network numbers in addition to host addresses. For example, you could add the directive *xfrnets 16.0.0.0* if you wanted to permit only hosts on Class A network number 16 to transfer zones from your server. This is not nearly granular enough, and a future version of BIND will permit such access-control to be specified on a per-zone basis rather than the current "global" basis.

The *xfrnets* directive may also be given as *tcplist* for compatibility with interim releases of BIND 4.9.

Note that *xfrnets* support is a compile-time option which your vendor may not have enabled when they built your operating system.

6.1.10. Sorting Addresses

If there are multiple addresses available for a name server which BIND wants to contact, BIND will try the ones it believes are "closest" first. "Closeness" is defined in terms of similarity-of-address; that is, if one address is on the same *subnet* as some interface of the local host, then that address will be tried first. Failing that, an address which is on the same *network* will be tried first. Failing that, they will be tried in a more-or-less random order unless the *sortlist* directive was given in the *named.boot* file. *sortlist* has a syntax similar to *forwarders* and *xfrnets*; you give it a list of networks and it uses these to "prefer" some remote name server addresses over others. If you are on a Class C net which has a Class B net between you and the rest of the Internet, you could try to improve the name server's luck in getting answers by listing the Class B network's number in a *sortlist* directive. This should have the effect of trying "closer" servers before the more "distant" ones. Note that this behaviour is new in BIND 4.9.

The other and older effect of the *sortlist* directive is to cause BIND to sort the *A* records in any response it generates, so as to put those which appear on the *sortlist* earlier than those which do not. This is not as helpful as you might think, since many clients will reorder the *A* records either at random or using LIFO.

In actual practice, noone uses this directive since it hardwires information which changes rapidly; a network which is "close" today may be "distant" next month. Since BIND builds up a cache of the remote name servers' response times, it will quickly converge on "reasonable" behaviour, which isn't the same as "optimal" but it's close enough. Future directions for BIND include choosing addresses based on local interface metrics (on hosts which have more than one) and perhaps on routing table information. We do not intend to solve the generalized "multi-homed host" problem, but we should be able to do a little better than we're doing now. Likewise, we hope to see a higher-level resolver library that sorts responses using topology information that only exists on the client's host.

6.1.11. Bogus Name Servers

It happens occasionally that some remote name server goes "bad". You can tell your name server to refuse to listen to or ask questions of certain other name servers by listing them in a *bogusns* directive in your *named.boot* file. Its syntax is the same as *forwarders* — you just give it a list of dotted-quad Internet addresses.

Note that *bogusns* support is a compile-time option which your vendor may not have enabled when they built your operating system.

6.1.12. Segmented Boot Files

If you are secondary for a lot of zones, you may find it convenient to split your *named.boot* file into a static portion which hardly ever changes (directives such as *directory*, *sortlist*, *xfrnets* and *cache* could go here), and dynamic portions that change frequently (all of your *primary* directives might go in one file, and all of your *secondary* directives might go in another file — and either or both of these might be fetched automatically from some neighbor so that they can change your list of secondary zones without requiring your active intervention). You can accomplish this via the *include* directive, which takes just a single file name as its argument. No quotes are needed around the file name. The file name will be evaluated after the name server has changed its working directory to that specified in the *directory* directive, so you can use relative pathnames if your system supports them.

6.2. Resolver Configuration

The resolver will try to contact a nameserver on the localhost if it cannot find its configuration file. You should install the configuration file on every host anyway, since you can list the local host's address if the localhost runs a nameserver, and there is no other recommended way to specify a system-level default domain. Note that if you wish to list the local host in your resolver configuration file, you should probably use its primary Internet address rather than a localhost alias such as 127.0.0.1 or 0.0.0.0. This is due to a bug in the handling of connected SOCK_DGRAM sockets in some versions of the BSD networking code. If you must use an address-alias, you should prefer 0.0.0.0 (or simply ''0'') over 127.0.0.1, though be warned that depending on the vintage of your BSD-derived networking code, both of them are capable of failing in their own ways.

The configuration file's name is */etc/resolv.conf*. This file designates the name servers on the network that should be sent queries. It is considered reasonable to create this file even if you run a local server, since its contents will be cached by each client of the resolver library when the client makes its first call to a resolver routine. If you run a name server locally, list it in your *resolv.conf* file.

The *resolv.conf* file contains directives, one per line, of the following forms:

; comment
another comment
domain *local-domain*
search *search-list*
nameserver *server-address*
sortlist *sort-list*
options *option-list*

10

Exactly one of the *domain* or *search* directives should be given, exactly once. If the *search* directive is given, the first item in the given *search-list* will override any previously-specified *local-domain*. The *nameserver* directive may be given up to three times; additional *nameserver* directives will be ignored. Comments may be given by starting a line with a '';'' or ''#''; note that comments were not permitted in versions of the resolver earlier than the one included with BIND 4.9 — so if your vendor's resolver supports comments, you know they are really on the ball.

The *local-domain* will be appended to any query-name that does not contain a ''.''. *local-domain* can be overridden on a per-process basis by setting the LOCALDOMAIN environment variable. Note that *local-domain* processing can be disabled by setting an option in the resolver.

The *search-list* is a list of domains which are tried, in order, as qualifying domains for query-names which do not contain a ''.''. Note that *search-list* processing can be disabled by setting an option in the resolver. Also note that the environment variable ''LOCALDOMAIN'' can override this *search-list* on a per-process basis.

The *server-address*'s are aggregated and then used as the default destination of queries generated through the resolver. This is, in other words, the way you tell the resolver which name servers it should use. It is possible for a given client application to override this list, and this is often done inside the name server (which is itself a *resolver* client) and in test programs such as *nslookup*.

The *sort-list* is a list of IP address, netmask pairs. Addresses returned by gethostbyname are sorted to the order specifed by this list. Any addresses that do not match the address netmask pair will returned after those that do. The netmask is optional and the natural netmask will be used if not specified.

The *option-list* is a list of options which each override some internal resolver variable. Supported options at this time are:

debug
sets the RES_DEBUG bit in **_res.options.**

ndots:*n*
sets the lower threshold (measured in ''number of dots'') on names given to *res_query*() such that names with more than this number of dots will be tried as absolute names before any *local-domain* or *search-list* processing is done. The default for this internal variable is ''1''.

Finally, if the environment variable HOSTALIASES is set, it is taken to contain the name of a file which in turn contains resolver-level aliases. These aliases are applied only to names which do not contain any ''.'' characters, and they are applied to query-names before the query is generated. Note that the resolver options governing the operation of *local-domain* and *search-list* do not apply to HOSTALIASES.

6.3. Cache Initialization

6.3.1. root.cache

The name server needs to know the servers that are the authoritative name servers for the root domain of the network. To do this we have to prime the name server's cache with the addresses of these higher authorities. The location of this file is specified in the boot file. This file uses the Standard Resource Record Format (aka. Masterfile Format) covered further on in this paper.

6.3.2. named.local

This file specifies the *PTR* record for the local loopback interface, better known as *localhost*, whose network address is 127.0.0.1. The location of this file is specified in the boot file. It is vitally important to the proper operation of every name server that the 127.0.0.1 address have a *PTR* record pointing back to the name "**localhost.***my.dom.ain*". The name of this *PTR* record is always "**1.0.0.127.IN-ADDR.ARPA**". This is neccessary if you want your users to be able to use hostname-authentication (*hosts.equiv* or *~/.rhosts*) on the name "**localhost**". As implied by this *PTR* record, there should be an *A* record in your domain specifying that "**localhost.***my.dom.ain*" has the Internet address 127.0.0.1.

6.4. Domain Data Files

There are two standard files for specifying the data for a domain. These are *hosts* and *host.rev*. These files use the Standard Resource Record Format covered later in this paper. Note that the file names are arbitrary; many network administrators prefer to name their zone files after the domains they contain, especially in the average case which is where a given server is primary and/or secondary for many different zones.

6.4.1. hosts

This file contains all the data about the machines in this zone. The location of this file is specified in the boot file.

6.4.2. hosts.rev

This file specifies the IN-ADDR.ARPA domain. This is a special domain for allowing address to name mapping. As internet host addresses do not fall within domain boundaries, this special domain was formed to allow inverse mapping. The IN-ADDR.ARPA domain has four labels preceding it. These labels correspond to the 4 octets of an Internet address. All four octets must be specified even if an octets is zero. The Internet address 128.32.0.4 is located in the domain 4.0.32.128.IN-ADDR.ARPA. This reversal of the address is awkward to read but allows for the natural grouping of hosts in a network.

6.5. Standard Resource Record Format

The records in the name server data files are called resource records. The Standard Resource Record Format (RR) is specified in RFC1035. The following is a general description of these records:

{name} *{ttl}* *addr-class* *Record Type* *Record Specific data*

Resource records have a standard format shown above. The first field is always the name of the domain record and it must always start in column 1. For all RR's other than the first in a file, the name may be left blank; in that case it takes on the name of the previous RR. The second field is an optional time to live field. This specifies how long this data will be stored in the data base. By leaving this field blank the default time to live is specified in the *Start Of Authority* resource record (see below). The third field is the address class; currently, only one class is supported: *IN* for internet addresses and other internet information. Limited support is included for the *HS* class, which is for MIT/Athena ''Hesiod'' information. The fourth field states the type of the resource record. The fields after that are dependent on the type of the RR. Case is preserved in names and data fields when loaded into the name server. All comparisons and lookups in the name server data base are case insensitive.

The following characters have special meanings:

''.'' A free standing dot in the name field refers to the current domain.

''@'' A free standing @ in the name field denotes the current origin.

''..'' Two free standing dots represent the null domain name of the root when used in the name field.

''\X'' Where X is any character other than a digit (0-9), quotes that character so that its special meaning does not apply. For example, ''\.'' can be used to place a dot character in a label.

''\DDD''
Where each D is a digit, is the octet corresponding to the decimal number described by DDD. The resulting octet is assumed to be text and is not checked for special meaning.

''( )'' Parentheses are used to group data that crosses a line. In effect, line terminations are not recognized within parentheses.

'';'' Semicolon starts a comment; the remainder of the line is ignored.

''*'' An asterisk signifies wildcarding. Note that this is just another data character whose special meaning comes about only during internal name server search operations. Wildcarding is only meaningful for some RR types (notably *MX*), and then only in the name field — not in the data fields.

Anywhere a name appears — either in the name field or in some data field defined to contain names — the current origin will be appended if the name does not end in a ''.''. This is useful for appending the current domain name to the data, such as machine names, but may cause problems where you do not want this to happen. A good rule of thumb is that, if the name is not in the domain for which you are creating the data file, end the name with a ''.''.

6.5.1. $INCLUDE

An include line begins with $INCLUDE, starting in column 1, and is followed by a file name, and, optionally, by a new temporary $ORIGIN to be used while reading this file. This feature is particularly useful for separating different types of data into multiple files. An example would be:

$INCLUDE /usr/local/adm/named/data/mail-exchangers

The line would be interpreted as a request to load the file */usr/named/data/mail-exchangers*. The $INCLUDE command does not cause data to be loaded into a different zone or tree. This is simply a way to allow data for a given primary zone to be organized in separate files. Not even the ''temporary $ORIGIN'' feature described above is sufficient to cause your data to branch out into some other zone — zone boundaries can only be introduced in the boot file.

6.5.2. "$ORIGIN"

The origin is a way of changing the origin in a data file. The line starts in column 1, and is followed by a domain origin. This seems like it could be useful for putting more then one zone into a data file, but that's not how it works. The name server fundamentally requires that a given zone map entirely to some specific file. You should therefore be very careful to use $ORIGIN only once at the top of a file, or, within a file, to change to a ''lower'' domain in the zone — never to some other zone altogether.

6.5.3. SOA - Start Of Authority

name	*{ttl}*	*addr-class*	*SOA*	*Origin*	*Person in charge*
@		IN	SOA	ucbvax.Berkeley.Edu.	kjd.ucbvax.Berkeley.Edu
			1993041403	; Serial	
			10800	; Refresh	
			1800	; Retry	
			3600000	; Expire	
			259200)	; Minimum	

The *Start of Authority, SOA,* record designates the start of a zone. The name is the name of the zone. Origin is the name of the host on which this data file resides. Person in charge is the mailing address for the person responsible for the name server. The serial number is the version number of this data file; this number should be incremented whenever a change is made to the data. Older servers permitted the use of a phantom ''.'' in this and other numbers in a zone file; the meaning of n.m was ''n000m'' rather than the more intuitive ''n*1000+m'' (such that 1.234 translated to 1000234 rather than to 1234). This feature has been deprecated due to its obscurity, unpredictability, and lack of neccessity. Note that using a ''YYYYMMDDNN'' notation you can still make 100 changes per day until the year 4294. You should choose a notation that works for you. If you're a clever *perl* programmer you could even use *RCS* version numbers to help generate your zone serial numbers. The refresh indicates how often, in seconds, the secondary name servers are to check with the primary name server to see if an update is needed. The retry indicates how long, in seconds, a secondary server should wait before retrying a failed zone transfer. Expire is the upper limit, in seconds, that a secondary name server is to use the data before it expires for lack of getting a refresh. Minimum is the default number of seconds to be used for the Time To Live field on resource records which do not specify one in the zone file. It is also an enforced minimum on Time To Live if it is specified on an RR. There should only be one *SOA* record per zone.

6.5.4. NS - Name Server

{name}	*{ttl}*	*addr-class*	*NS*	*Name servers name*
		IN	NS	ucbarpa.Berkeley.Edu.

The *Name Server* record, *NS,* lists a name server responsible for a given domain. The first name field lists the domain that is serviced by the listed name server. There should be one *NS* record for each name server for the domain, and every domain should have at least two nameservers.

6.5.5. A - Address

{name}	*{ttl}*	*addr-class*	*A*	*address*
ucbarpa		IN	A	128.32.0.4
		IN	A	10.0.0.78

The *Address* record, *A*, lists the address for a given machine. The name field is the machine name and the address is the network address. There should be one *A* record for each address of the machine.

6.5.6. HINFO - Host Information

{name}	*{ttl}*	*addr-class*	*HINFO*	*Hardware*	*OS*
		IN	HINFO	VAX-11/780	UNIX

Host Information resource record, *HINFO*, is for host specific data. This lists the hardware and operating system that are running at the listed host. If you want to include a space in the machine name you must quote the name. There could be one *HINFO* record for each host, though for security reasons most domains don't have any *HINFO* records at all. No application depends on them.

6.5.7. WKS - Well Known Services

{name}	*{ttl}*	*addr-class*	*WKS*	*address*	*protocol*	*list of services*
		IN	WKS	128.32.0.10	UDP	who route timed domain
		IN	WKS	128.32.0.10	TCP	(echo telnet discard sunrpc sftp uucp-path systat daytime netstat qotd nntp link chargen ftp auth time whois mtp pop rje finger smtp supdup hostnames domain nameserver)

The *Well Known Services* record, *WKS*, describes the well known services supported by a particular protocol at a specified address. The list of services and port numbers come from the list of services specified in */etc/services*. There should be only one *WKS* record per protocol per address. Note that RFC 1123 says of *WKS* records:

```
2.2  Using Domain Name Service
...
  An application SHOULD NOT rely on the ability to locate a WKS
  record containing an accurate listing of all services at a
  particular host address, since the WKS RR type is not often used
  by Internet sites.  To confirm that a service is present, simply
  attempt to use it.
...
  5.2.12  WKS Use in MX Processing: RFC-974, p. 5

    RFC-974 [SMTP:3] recommended that the domain system be queried
    for WKS ("Well-Known Service") records, to verify that each
    proposed mail target does support SMTP.  Later experience has
    shown that WKS is not widely supported, so the WKS step in MX
    processing SHOULD NOT be used.
...
    6.1.3.6  Status of RR Types
...
         The TXT and WKS RR types have not been widely used by
         Internet sites; as a result, an application cannot rely
         on the the existence of a TXT or WKS RR in most
         domains.
```

6.5.8. CNAME - Canonical Name

aliases	*{ttl}*	*addr-class*	*CNAME*	*Canonical name*
ucbmonet		IN	CNAME	monet

The *Canonical Name* resource record, *CNAME*, specifies an alias or nickname for the official, or canonical, host name. This record should be the only one associated with the alias name. All other resource records should be associated with the canonical name, not with the nickname. Any resource records that include a domain name as their value (e.g., NS or MX) *must* list the canonical name, not the nickname.

Nicknames are also useful when a host changes its name. In that case, it is usually a good idea to have a *CNAME* record so that people still using the old name will get to the right place.

6.5.9. PTR - Domain Name Pointer

name	*{ttl}*	*addr-class*	*PTR*	*real name*
7.0		IN	PTR	monet.Berkeley.Edu.

A *Domain Name Pointer* record, *PTR*, allows special names to point to some other location in the domain. The above example of a *PTR* record is used in setting up reverse pointers for the special *IN-ADDR.ARPA* domain. This line is from the example *hosts.rev* file. *PTR* records are needed by the *gethostbyaddr* function. Note the trailing ''.'' which prevents BIND from appending the current $ORIGIN.

6.5.10. MX - Mail Exchanger

name	*{ttl}*	*addr-class*	*MX*	*preference value*	*mail exchanger*
Munnari.OZ.AU.		IN	MX	0	Seismo.CSS.GOV.
*.IL.		IN	MX	0	RELAY.CS.NET.

Mail eXchanger records, *MX*, are used to specify a list of hosts which are configured to receive mail sent to this domain name. Every name which receives mail should have an *MX* since if one is not found at the time mail is being delivered, an *MX* will be ''imputed'' with a cost of 0 and a destination of the host itself. If you want a host to receive its own mail, you should create an *MX* for your host's name, pointing at your host's name. It is better to have this be explicit than to let it be imputed by remote mailers. In the first example, above, Seismo.CSS.GOV. is a mail gateway that knows how to deliver mail to Munnari.OZ.AU.. These two machines may have a private connection or use a different transport medium. The preference value is the order that a mailer should follow when there is more then one way to deliver mail to a single machine. Note that lower numbers indicate higher precedence, and that mailers are supposed to randomize same-valued *MX* hosts so as to distribute the load evenly if the costs are equal. See RFC 974 for more detailed information.

Wildcard names containing the character ''*'' may be used for mail routing with *MX* records. There are likely to be servers on the network that simply state that any mail to a domain is to be routed through a relay. Second example, above, all mail to hosts in the domain IL is routed through RELAY.CS.NET. This is done by creating a wildcard resource record, which states that *.IL has an *MX* of RELAY.CS.NET. Wildcard *MX* records are not very useful in practice, though, since once a mail message gets to the gateway for a given domain it still has to be routed *within* that domain and it is not currently possible to have an apparently-different set of *MX* records inside and outside of a domain. If you won't be needing any Mail Exchangers inside your domain, go ahead and use a wildcard. If you want to use both wildcard ''top-level'' and specific ''interior'' *MX* records, note that each specific record will have to ''end with'' a complete recitation of the same data that is carried in the top-level record. This is because the specific *MX* records will take precedence over the top-level wildcard records, and must be able to perform the top-level's if a given interior domain is to be able to receive mail from outside the gateway. Wildcard *MX* records are very subtle and you should be careful with them.

6.5.11. TXT - Text

name	*{ttl}*	*addr-class*	*TXT*	*string*
Munnari.OZ.AU.		IN	TXT	"foo"

A *TXT* record contains free-form textual data. The syntax of the text depends on the domain where it is found; several systems use *TXT* records to encode the local user database (*/etc/passwd*) and other administrative data. MIT Hesiod is one such system, which, though it uses an addr-class of *HS* rather than *IN*, implements its database with *TXT* records in the DNS.

10

6.5.12. RP - Responsible Person

owner	*{ttl}*	*addr-class*	*RP*	*mbox-domain-name*	*TXT-domain-name*
franklin		IN	RP	ben.franklin.berkeley.edu.	sysadmins.berkeley.edu.

The Responsible Person record, *RP*, identifies the name or group name of the responsible person for a host. Often it is desirable to be able to identify the responsible entity for a particular host. When that host is down or malfunctioning, you would want to contact those parties who might be able to repair the host.

The first field, *mbox-domain-name*, is a domain name that specifies the mailbox for the responsible person. Its format in master files uses the DNS convention for mailbox encoding, identical to that used for the *Person-in-charge* mailbox field in the SOA record. In the example above, the mbox domain name shows the encoding for ``**<ben@franklin.berkeley.edu>**''. The root domain name (just ``.'') may be specified to indicate that no mailbox is available.

The second field, *TXT-domain-name*, is a domain name for which *TXT* records exist. A subsequent query can be performed to retrieve the associated *TXT* resource records at *TXT* domain name. This provides a level of indirection so that the entity can be referred to from multiple places in the DNS. The root domain name (just ``.'') may be specified for TXT domain name to indicate that no associated *TXT* RR exists. In the example above, ``**sysadmins.berkeley.edu.**'' is the name of a TXT record that might contain some text with names and phone numbers.

The format of the *RP* record is class-insensitive. Multiple *RP* records at a single name may be present in the database, though they should have identical TTLs.

The *RP* record is still experimental; not all name servers implement or recognize it.

6.5.13. AFSDB - DCE or AFS Server

name	*{ttl}*	*addr-class*	*AFSDB*	*subtype*	*mail exchanger*
toaster.com.		IN	AFSDB	1	jack.toaster.com
toaster.com.		IN	AFSDB	1	jill.toaster.com.
toaster.com.		IN	AFSDB	2	tracker.toaster.com.

AFSDB records are used to specify the hosts that provide a style of distributed service advertised under this domain name. A subtype value (analogous to the ``preference'' value in the *MX* record) indicates which style of distributed service is provided with the given name. Subtype 1 indicates that the named host is an AFS (R) database server for the AFS cell of the given domain name. Subtype 2 indicates that the named host provides intra-cell name service for the DCE (R) cell named by the given domain name. In the example above, jack.toaster.com and jill.toaster.com are declared to be AFS database servers for the toaster.com AFS cell, so that AFS clients wishing service from tracker.com are directed to those two hosts for further information. The third record declares that tracker.toaster.com houses a directory server for the root of the DCE cell toaster.com, so that DCE clients that wish to refer to DCE services should consult with the host tracker.toaster.com for further information. The DCE sub-type of record is usually accompanied by a *TXTP record for other information specifying other details to be used in accessing the DCE cell. RFC 1183 contains more detailed information on the use of this record type.*

The *AFSDB* record is still experimental; not all name servers implement or recognize it.

6.6. Discussion about the TTL

The Time To Live assigned to the records and to the zone via the Minimum field in the SOA record is very important. High values will lead to lower BIND network traffic and faster response time. Lower values will tend to generate lots of requests but will allow faster propagation of changes.

Only changes and deletions from the zone are affected by the TTLs. Additions propagate according to the Refresh value in the SOA.

Experience has shown that sites use default TTLs for their zones varying from around 0.5 day to around 7 days. You may wish to consider boosting the default TTL shown in former versions of this guide from one day (86400 seconds) to three days (259200 seconds). This will drastically reduce the number of requests made to your name servers.

If you need fast propagation of changes and deletions, it might be wise to reduce the Minimum field a few days before the change, then do the modification itself and augment the TTL to its former value.

If you know that your zone is pretty stable (you mainly add new records without changing regularly old ones) then you may even wish to consider a TTL higher than three days.

Note that in any case, it makes no sense to have records with a TTL below the SOA Refresh delay, as Delay is the time required for secondaries to get a copy of the newly modified zone.

6.7. Sample Files

The following section contains sample files for the name server. This covers example boot files for the different types of servers and example domain data base files.

10

6.7.1. Boot Files

6.7.1.1. Primary Server

```
;
; Boot file for Primary Name Server
;

; type        domain                  source file or host
;
directory     /usr/local/adm/named
primary       Berkeley.Edu            ucbhosts
primary       32.128.in-addr.arpa     ucbhosts.rev
primary       0.0.127.in-addr.arpa    named.local
cache         .                       root.cache
```

6.7.1.2. Secondary Server

```
;
; Boot file for Secondary Name Server
;

; type        domain                  source file or host
;
directory     /usr/local/adm/named
secondary     Berkeley.Edu            128.32.0.4 128.32.0.10 ucbhosts.bak
secondary     32.128.in-addr.arpa     128.32.0.4 128.32.0.10 ucbhosts.rev.bak
primary       0.0.127.in-addr.arpa    named.local
cache         .                       root.cache
```

6.7.1.3. Caching Only Server

```
;
; Boot file for Caching Only Name Server
;

; type        domain                   source file or host
;
directory     /usr/local/adm/named
cache         .                        root.cache
primary       0.0.127.in-addr.arpa     named.local
```


6.7.2. Remote Server / DNS Client

6.7.2.1. /etc/resolv.conf

```
domain Berkeley.Edu
nameserver 128.32.0.4
nameserver 128.32.0.10
sortlist 130.155.160.0/255.255.240.0 130.155.0.0
```

6.7.3. root.cache

```
;
; Initial cache data for root domain servers.
;
; This data was current as of April 15, 1993.  The official and current
; version is always available from via anonymous FTP from RS.INTERNIC.NET
; as /domain/named.cache.
;
; Thanks to Long-Morrow@CS.Yale.EDU for providing this update.
;

.                      99999999   IN   NS    NS.NIC.DDN.MIL.
                       99999999   IN   NS    NS.NASA.GOV.
                       99999999   IN   NS    KAVA.NISC.SRI.COM.
                       99999999   IN   NS    TERP.UMD.EDU.
                       99999999   IN   NS    AOS.ARL.ARMY.MIL.
                       99999999   IN   NS    C.NYSER.NET.
                       99999999   IN   NS    NIC.NORDU.NET.
                       99999999   IN   NS    NS.INTERNIC.NET.

;  Prep the cache (hotwire the addresses).
NS.NIC.DDN.MIL.        99999999   IN   A     192.112.36.4
NS.NASA.GOV.           99999999   IN   A     128.102.16.10
NS.NASA.GOV.           99999999   IN   A     192.52.195.10
KAVA.NISC.SRI.COM.     99999999   IN   A     192.33.33.24
AOS.ARL.ARMY.MIL.      99999999   IN   A     128.63.4.82
AOS.ARL.ARMY.MIL.      99999999   IN   A     192.5.25.82
C.NYSER.NET.           99999999   IN   A     192.33.4.12
TERP.UMD.EDU.          99999999   IN   A     128.8.10.90
NIC.NORDU.NET.         99999999   IN   A     192.36.148.17
NS.INTERNIC.NET.       99999999   IN   A     198.41.0.4
```

6.7.4. named.local

```
@    IN    SOA    ucbvax.Berkeley.Edu.      kjd.ucbvax.Berkeley.Edu. (
                  1993050201                ; Serial
                  10800                     ; Refresh
                  1800                      ; Retry
                  3600000                   ; Expire
                  259200 )                  ; Minimum
     IN    NS     ucbvax.Berkeley.Edu.      ; pedantic
1    IN    PTR    localhost.Berkeley.Edu.
```

10

6.7.5. Hosts

```
;
;   @(#)ucb-hosts   1.2   (berkeley)   88/02/05
;
@               IN   SOA      ucbvax.Berkeley.Edu.    kjd.monet.Berkeley.Edu. (
                              1988020501              ; Serial
                              10800                   ; Refresh
                              1800                    ; Retry
                              3600000                 ; Expire
                              259200 )                ; Minimum
                IN   NS       ucbarpa.Berkeley.Edu.
                IN   NS       ucbvax.Berkeley.Edu.
localhost       IN   A        127.1
                              ; note that 127.1 is the same as 127.0.0.1; see inet(3n)
ucbarpa         IN   A        128.32.4
                IN   A        10.0.0.78
                IN   HINFO    VAX-11/780 UNIX
arpa            IN   CNAME    ucbarpa
ernie           IN   A        128.32.6
                IN   HINFO    VAX-11/780 UNIX
ucbernie        IN   CNAME    ernie
monet           IN   A        128.32.7
                IN   A        128.32.130.6
                IN   HINFO    VAX-11/750 UNIX
ucbmonet        IN   CNAME    monet
ucbvax          IN   A        10.2.0.78
                              ; 128.32.10 means 128.32.0.10; see inet(3n)
                IN   A        128.32.10
                              ; HINFO and WKS are widely unused,
                              ; but we'll show them as examples.
                IN   HINFO    VAX-11/750 UNIX
                IN   WKS      128.32.0.10 TCP ( echo telnet
                              discard sunrpc sftp
                              uucp-path systat daytime
                              netstat qotd nntp
                              link chargen ftp
                              auth time whhois mtp
                              pop rje finger smtp
                              supdup hostnames
                              domain
                              nameserver )
vax             IN   CNAME    ucbvax
toybox          IN   A        128.32.131.119
                IN   HINFO    Pro350 RT11
toybox          IN   MX       0  monet.Berkeley.Edu.
csrg            IN   MX       0 Ralph.CS
                IN   MX       0 Zhou.CS
                IN   MX       0 Painter.CS
                IN   MX       0 Riggle.CS
                IN   MX       0 Terry.CS
                IN   MX       0 Kevin.CS
```

6.7.6. host.rev

```
;
;   @(#)ucb-hosts.rev   1.1   (Berkeley)   86/02/05
;
@       IN   SOA   ucbvax.Berkeley.Edu.    kjd.monet.Berkeley.Edu. (
                   1986020501              ; Serial
                   10800                   ; Refresh
                   1800                    ; Retry
                   3600000                 ; Expire
                   259200 )                ; Minimum
        IN   NS    ucbarpa.Berkeley.Edu.
        IN   NS    ucbvax.Berkeley.Edu.
0.0     IN   PTR   Berkeley-net.Berkeley.EDU.
        IN   A     255.255.255.0
0.130   IN   PTR   csdiv-net.Berkeley.EDU.
4.0     IN   PTR   ucbarpa.Berkeley.Edu.
6.0     IN   PTR   ernie.Berkeley.Edu.
7.0     IN   PTR   monet.Berkeley.Edu.
10.0    IN   PTR   ucbvax.Berkeley.Edu.
6.130   IN   PTR   monet.Berkeley.Edu.
```


7. Domain Management

This section contains information for starting, controlling and debugging *named.*

7.1. /etc/rc.local

The hostname should be set to the full domain style name in */etc/rc.local* using *hostname (1).* The following entry should be added to */etc/rc.local* to start up *named* at system boot time:

```
if [ -f /etc/named ]; then
        /etc/named [options] & echo -n ' named'     >/dev/console
fi
```

This usually directly follows the lines that start *syslogd.* **Do Not** attempt to run *named* from *inetd.* This will continuously restart the name server and defeat the purpose of the cache.

7.2. /etc/named.pid

When *named* is successfully started up it writes its process id into the file */etc/named.pid.* This is useful to programs that want to send signals to *named.* The name of this file may be changed by defining *PIDFILE* to the new name when compiling *named.*

7.3. /etc/hosts

The *gethostbyname()* library call can detect if *named* is running. If it is determined that *named* is not running it will look in */etc/hosts* to resolve an address. This option was added to allow *ifconfig (8C)* to configure the machines local interfaces and to enable a system manager to access the network while the system is in single user mode. It is advisable to put the local machines interface addresses and a couple of machine names and address in */etc/hosts* so the system manager can rcp files from another machine when the system is in single user mode. The format of */etc/hosts* has not changed. See *hosts (5)* for more information. Since the process of reading */etc/hosts* is slow, it is not advisable to use this option when the system is in multi user mode.

10

7.4. Signals

There are several signals that can be sent to the *named* process to have it do tasks without restarting the process.

7.4.1. Reload

SIGHUP - Causes *named* to read *named.boot* and reload the database. This is useful when you have made a change to a "primary" data file and you want *named*'s internal database to reflect the change. If you build BIND with the FORCED_RELOAD option, then SIGHUP also has the effect of scheduling all "secondary" zones for serial-number checks, which could lead to zone transfers ahead of the usual schedule. Normally serial-number compares are done only at the intervals specified in the zone's SOA record.

7.4.2. Debugging

When *named* is running incorrectly, look first in */var/log/messages* and check for any messages logged by *syslog*. Next send it a signal to see what is happening. Unless you run it with the "-d" option, *named* has very little to say on its standard output or standard error. Everything *named* has to say, it says to *syslog*.

SIGINT - Dumps the current data base and cache to */var/tmp/named_dump.db* This should give you an indication to whether the data base was loaded correctly. The name of the dump file may be changed by defining *DUMPFILE* to the new name when compiling *named*.

Note: the following two signals only work when *named* is built with *DEBUG* defined.

SIGUSR1 - Turns on debugging. Each following USR1 increments the debug level. The output goes to */var/tmp/named.run* The name of this debug file may be changed by defining *DEBUGFILE* to the new name before compiling *named*.

SIGUSR2 - Turns off debugging completely.

For more detailed debugging, define DEBUG when compiling the resolver routines into */lib/libc.a*.

SIGWINCH - Toggles tracing of all incoming queries if *named* has been compiled with *QRYLOG* defined. The trace is sent to syslog, and is huge, but it is very useful for tracking down problems.

To run with tracing of all queries specify the *-q* flag on the command line. If you routinely log queries you will probably want to analyze the results using the dnsstats stats script in the contrib directory.

ACKNOWLEDGEMENTS

Many thanks to the users at U.C. Berkeley for falling into many of the holes involved with integrating BIND into the system so that others would be spared the trauma. I would also like to extend gratitude to Jim McGinness and Digital Equipment Corporation for permitting me to spend most of my time on this project.

Ralph Campbell, Doug Kingston, Craig Partridge, Smoot Carl-Mitchell, Mike Muuss and everyone else on the DARPA Internet who has contributed to the development of BIND. To the members of the original BIND project, Douglas Terry, Mark Painter, David Riggle and Songnian Zhou.

Anne Hughes, Jim Bloom and Kirk McKusick and the many others who have reviewed this paper giving considerable advice.

This work was sponsored by the Defense Advanced Research Projects Agency (DoD), Arpa Order No. 4871 monitored by the Naval Electronics Systems Command under contract No. N00039-84-C-0089. The views and conclusions contained in this document are those of the authors and should not be interpreted as representing official policies, either expressed or implied, of the Defense Research Projects

Agency, of the US Government, or of Digital Equipment Corporation.

Update for the 4.9 release: the alpha-test group was extremely helpful in furnishing improvements, finding and repairing bugs, and being patient. I would like to express special thanks to Brian Reid for funding this work. Robert Elz, Alan Barrett, Paul Albitz, Bryan Beecher, Andrew Partan, Andy Cherenson, Tom Limoncelli, Berthold Paffrath, Fuat Baran, Anant Kumar, Art Harkin, Win Treese, Don Lewis, Christophe Wolfhugel, and a cast of dozens all helped out above and beyond the call of duty. Special thanks to Phil Almquist, who got the project started and contributed a lot of the code and fixed several of the worst bugs. [*Paul Vixie, DECWRL and DECNSL, April '93*].

REFERENCES

[Birrell] Birrell, A. D., Levin, R., Needham, R. M., and Schroeder, M.D., "Grapevine: An Exercise in Distributed Computing." In *Comm. A.C.M. 25,* 4:260-274 April 1982.

[RFC819] Su, Z. Postel, J., "The Domain Naming Convention for Internet User Applications." *Internet Request For Comment 819* Network Information Center, SRI International, Menlo Park, California. August 1982.

[RFC974] Partridge, C., "Mail Routing and The Domain System." *Internet Request For Comment 974* Network Information Center, SRI International, Menlo Park, California. February 1986.

[RFC1032] Stahl, M., "Domain Administrators Guide" *Internet Request For Comment 1032* Network Information Center, SRI International, Menlo Park, California. November 1987.

[RFC1033] Lottor, M., "Domain Administrators Guide" *Internet Request For Comment 1033* Network Information Center, SRI International, Menlo Park, California. November 1987.

[RFC1034] Mockapetris, P., "Domain Names - Concept and Facilities." *Internet Request For Comment 1034* Network Information Center, SRI International, Menlo Park, California. November 1987.

[RFC1035] Mockapetris, P., "Domain Names - Implementation and Specification." *Internet Request For Comment 1035* Network Information Center, SRI International, Menlo Park, California. November 1987.

[RFC1101] Mockapetris, P., "DNS Encoding of Network Names and Other Types." *Internet Request For Comment 1101* Network Information Center, SRI International, Menlo Park, California. April 1989.

[RFC1123] R. Braden, Editor, "Requirements for Internet Hosts -- Application and Support" *Internet Request For Comment 1123* Network Information Center, SRI International, Menlo Park, California. October 1989.

[RFC1183] Everhart, C., Mamakos, L., Ullmann, R., and Mockapetris, P., "New DNS RR Definitions" *Internet Request For Comment 1183* Network Information Center, SRI International, Menlo Park, California. October 1990.

[Terry] Terry, D. B., Painter, M., Riggle, D. W., and Zhou, S., *The Berkeley Internet Name Domain Server.* Proceedings USENIX Summer Conference, Salt Lake City, Utah. June 1984, pages 23-31.

[Zhou] Zhou, S., *The Design and Implementation of the Berkeley Internet Name Domain (BIND) Servers.* UCB/CSD 84/177. University of California, Berkeley, Computer Science Division. May 1984.

[Mockapetris] Mockapetris, P., Dunlap, K, *Development of the Domain Name System* ACM Computer Communications Review 18, 4:123-133. Proceedings ACM SIGCOMM '88 Symposium, August 1988.

[Liu] Liu, C., Albitz, P., *DNS and BIND* O'Reilly & Associates, Sebastopol, CA, 502 pages, ISBN 0-937175-82-X 1992

Timed Installation and Operation Guide

Riccardo Gusella, Stefano Zatti, James M. Bloom

Computer Systems Research Group
Computer Science Division
Department of Electrical Engineering and Computer Science
University of California, Berkeley
Berkeley, CA 94720

Kirk Smith

Engineering Computer Network
Department of Electrical Engineering
Purdue University
West Lafayette, IN 47906

11

Introduction

The clock synchronization service for the UNIX 4.3BSD operating system is composed of a collection of time daemons (*timed*) running on the machines in a local area network. The algorithms implemented by the service is based on a master-slave scheme. The time daemons communicate with each other using the *Time Synchronization Protocol* (TSP) which is built on the DARPA UDP protocol and described in detail in [4].

A time daemon has a twofold function. First, it supports the synchronization of the clocks of the various hosts in a local area network. Second, it starts (or takes part in) the election that occurs among slave time daemons when, for any reason, the master disappears. The synchronization mechanism and the election procedure employed by the program *timed* are described in other documents [1,2,3]. The next paragraphs are a brief overview of how the time daemon works. This document is mainly concerned with the administrative and technical issues of running *timed* at a particular site.

A *master time daemon* measures the time differences between the clock of the machine on which it is running and those of all other machines. The master computes the *network time* as the average of the times provided by nonfaulty clocks.[1] It then sends to each *slave time daemon* the correction that should be performed on the clock of its machine. This process is repeated periodically. Since the correction is expressed as a time difference rather than an absolute time, transmission delays do not interfere with the accuracy of the synchronization. When a machine comes up and joins the network, it starts a slave time daemon which will ask the master for the correct time and will reset the machine's clock before any user activity can begin. The time daemons are able to maintain a single network time in spite of the drift of clocks away from each other. The present implementation keeps processor clocks synchronized within 20 milliseconds.

To ensure that the service provided is continuous and reliable, it is necessary to implement an election algorithm to elect a new master should the machine running the current master crash, the master

This work was sponsored by the Defense Advanced Research Projects Agency (DoD), monitored by the Naval Electronics Systems Command under contract No. N00039-84-C-0089, and by the CSELT Corporation of Italy. The views and conclusions contained in this document are those of the authors and should not be interpreted as representing official policies, either expressed or implied, of the Defense Research Projects Agency, of the US Government, or of CSELT.

[1] A clock is considered to be faulty when its value is more than a small specified interval apart from the majority of the clocks of the other machines [1,2].

terminate (for example, because of a run-time error), or the network be partitioned. Under our algorithm, slaves are able to realize when the master has stopped functioning and to elect a new master from among themselves. It is important to note that, since the failure of the master results only in a gradual divergence of clock values, the election need not occur immediately.

The machines that are gateways between distinct local area networks require particular care. A time daemon on such machines may act as a *submaster*. This artifact depends on the current inability of transmission protocols to broadcast a message on a network other than the one to which the broadcasting machine is connected. The submaster appears as a slave on one network, and as a master on one or more of the other networks to which it is connected.

A submaster classifies each network as one of three types. A *slave network* is a network on which the submaster acts as a slave. There can only be one slave network. A *master network* is a network on which the submaster acts as a master. An *ignored network* is any other network which already has a valid master. The submaster tries periodically to become master on an ignored network, but gives up immediately if a master already exists.

Guidelines

While the synchronization algorithm is quite general, the election one, requiring a broadcast mechanism, puts constraints on the kind of network on which time daemons can run. The time daemon will only work on networks with broadcast capability augmented with point-to-point links. Machines that are only connected to point-to-point, non-broadcast networks may not use the time daemon.

If we exclude submasters, there will normally be, at most, one master time daemon in a local area internetwork. During an election, only one of the slave time daemons will become the new master. However, because of the characteristics of its machine, a slave can be prevented from becoming the master. Therefore, a subset of machines must be designated as potential master time daemons. A master time daemon will require CPU resources proportional to the number of slaves, in general, more than a slave time daemon, so it may be advisable to limit master time daemons to machines with more powerful processors or lighter loads. Also, machines with inaccurate clocks should not be used as masters. This is a purely administrative decision: an organization may well allow all of its machines to run master time daemons.

At the administrative level, a time daemon on a machine with multiple network interfaces, may be told to ignore all but one network or to ignore one network. This is done with the *–n network* and *–i network* options respectively at start-up time. Typically, the time daemon would be instructed to ignore all but the networks belonging to the local administrative control.

There are some limitations to the current implementation of the time daemon. It is expected that these limitations will be removed in future releases. The constant NHOSTS in /usr/src/etc/timed/globals.h limits the maximum number of machines that may be directly controlled by one master time daemon. The current maximum is 29 (NHOSTS – 1). The constant must be changed and the program recompiled if a site wishes to run *timed* on a larger (inter)network.

In addition, there is a *pathological situation* to be avoided at all costs, that might occur when time daemons run on multiply-connected local area networks. In this case, as we have seen, time daemons running on gateway machines will be submasters and they will act on some of those networks as master time daemons. Consider machines A and B that are both gateways between networks X and Y. If time daemons were started on both A and B without constraints, it would be possible for submaster time daemon A to be a slave on network X and the master on network Y, while submaster time daemon B is a slave on network Y and the master on network X. This *loop* of master time daemons will not function properly or guarantee a unique time on both networks, and will cause the submasters to use large amounts of system resources in the form of network bandwidth and CPU time. In fact, this kind of *loop* can also be generated with more than two master time daemons, when several local area networks are interconnected.

Installation

In order to start the time daemon on a given machine, the following lines should be added to the *local daemons* section in the file */etc/rc.local*:

```
if [ -f /etc/timed ]; then
        /etc/timed flags & echo -n ' timed' >/dev/console
fi
```

In any case, they must appear after the network is configured via ifconfig(8).

Also, the file */etc/services* should contain the following line:

```
timed       525/udp          timeserver
```

The *flags* are:

-n network to consider the named network.

-i network to ignore the named network.

-t to place tracing information in */usr/adm/timed.log.*

-M to allow this time daemon to become a master. A time daemon run without this option will be forced in the state of slave during an election.

Daily Operation

Timedc(8) is used to control the operation of the time daemon. It may be used to:

- measure the differences between machines' clocks,
- find the location where the master *timed* is running,
- cause election timers on several machines to expire at the same time,
- enable or disable tracing of messages received by *timed.*

See the manual page on *timed* (8) and *timedc* (8) for more detailed information.

The *date(1)* command can be used to set the network date. In order to set the time on a single machine, the *-n* flag can be given to date(1).

11

References

1. R. Gusella and S. Zatti, *TEMPO: A Network Time Controller for Distributed Berkeley UNIX System*, USENIX Summer Conference Proceedings, Salt Lake City, June 1984.

2. R. Gusella and S. Zatti, *Clock Synchronization in a Local Area Network*, University of California, Berkeley, Technical Report, *to appear*.

3. R. Gusella and S. Zatti, *An Election Algorithm for a Distributed Clock Synchronization Program*, University of California, Berkeley, CS Technical Report #275, Dec. 1985.

4. R. Gusella and S. Zatti, *The Berkeley UNIX 4.3BSD Time Synchronization Protocol*, UNIX Programmer's Manual, 4.3 Berkeley Software Distribution, Volume 2c.

The Berkeley UNIX† Time Synchronization Protocol

Riccardo Gusella, Stefano Zatti, and James M. Bloom

Computer Systems Research Group
Computer Science Division
Department of Electrical Engineering and Computer Science
University of California, Berkeley
Berkeley, CA 94720

Introduction

The Time Synchronization Protocol (TSP) has been designed for specific use by the program *timed*, a local area network clock synchronizer for the UNIX 4.3BSD operating system. Timed is built on the DARPA UDP protocol [4] and is based on a master slave scheme.

TSP serves a dual purpose. First, it supports messages for the synchronization of the clocks of the various hosts in a local area network. Second, it supports messages for the election that occurs among slave time daemons when, for any reason, the master disappears. The synchronization mechanism and the election procedure employed by the program timed are described in other documents [1,2,3].

Briefly, the synchronization software, which works in a local area network, consists of a collection of *time daemons* (one per machine) and is based on a master-slave structure. The present implementation keeps processor clocks synchronized within 20 milliseconds. A *master time daemon* measures the time difference between the clock of the machine on which it is running and those of all other machines. The current implementation uses ICMP *Time Stamp Requests* [5] to measure the clock difference between machines. The master computes the *network time* as the average of the times provided by nonfaulty clocks.[1] It then sends to each *slave time daemon* the correction that should be performed on the clock of its machine. This process is repeated periodically. Since the correction is expressed as a time difference rather than an absolute time, transmission delays do not interfere with synchronization. When a machine comes up and joins the network, it starts a slave time daemon, which will ask the master for the correct time and will reset the machine's clock before any user activity can begin. The time daemons therefore maintain a single network time in spite of the drift of clocks away from each other.

Additionally, a time daemon on gateway machines may run as a *submaster*. A submaster time daemon functions as a slave on one network that already has a master and as master on other networks. In addition, a submaster is responsible for propagating broadcast packets from one network to the other.

To ensure that service provided is continuous and reliable, it is necessary to implement an election algorithm that will elect a new master should the machine running the current master crash, the master terminate (for example, because of a run-time error), or the network be partitioned. Under our algorithm, slaves are able to realize when the master has stopped functioning and to elect a new master from among themselves. It is important to note that since the failure of the master results only in a gradual divergence

---

† UNIX is a registered trademark of AT&T Bell Laboratories in the USA and other countries.

This work was sponsored by the Defense Advanced Research Projects Agency (DoD), monitored by the Naval Electronics Systems Command under contract No. N00039-84-C-0089, and by the Italian CSELT Corporation. The views and conclusions contained in this document are those of the authors and should not be interpreted as representing official policies, either expressed or implied, of the Defense Research Projects Agency, of the US Government, or of CSELT.

[1] A clock is considered to be faulty when its value is more than a small specified interval apart from the majority of the clocks of the machines on the same network. See [1,2] for more details.

of clock values, the election need not occur immediately.

All the communication occurring among time daemons uses the TSP protocol. While some messages need not be sent in a reliable way, most communication in TSP requires reliability not provided by the underlying protocol. Reliability is achieved by the use of acknowledgements, sequence numbers, and retransmission when message losses occur. When a message that requires acknowledgment is not acknowledged after multiple attempts, the time daemon that has sent the message will assume that the addressee is down. This document will not describe the details of how reliability is implemented, but will only point out when a message type requires a reliable transport mechanism.

The message format in TSP is the same for all message types; however, in some instances, one or more fields are not used. The next section describes the message format. The following sections describe in detail the different message types, their use and the contents of each field. NOTE: The message format is likely to change in future versions of timed.

Message Format

All fields are based upon 8-bit bytes. Fields should be sent in network byte order if they are more than one byte long. The structure of a TSP message is the following:

1) A one byte message type.

2) A one byte version number, specifying the protocol version which the message uses.

3) A two byte sequence number to be used for recognizing duplicate messages that occur when messages are retransmitted.

4) Eight bytes of packet specific data. This field contains two 4 byte time values, a one byte hop count, or may be unused depending on the type of the packet.

5) A zero-terminated string of up to 256 ASCII characters with the name of the machine sending the message.

The following charts describe the message types, show their fields, and explain their usages. For the purpose of the following discussion, a time daemon can be considered to be in one of three states: slave, master, or candidate for election to master. Also, the term *broadcast* refers to the sending of a message to all active time daemons.

Adjtime Message

Byte 1	Byte 2	Byte 3	Byte 4
Type	Version No.	Sequence No.	
Seconds of Adjustment			
Microseconds of Adjustment			
Machine Name			
...			

Type: TSP_ADJTIME (1)

The master sends this message to a slave to communicate the difference between the clock of the slave and the network time the master has just computed. The slave will accordingly adjust the time of its machine. This message requires an acknowledgment.

Acknowledgment Message

Byte 1	Byte 2	Byte 3	Byte 4
Type	Version No.	Sequence No.	
(unused)			
(unused)			
Machine Name			
. . .			

Type: TSP_ACK (2)

Both the master and the slaves use this message for acknowledgment only. It is used in several different contexts, for example in reply to an Adjtime message.

Master Request Message

Byte 1	Byte 2	Byte 3	Byte 4
Type	Version No.	Sequence No.	
(unused)			
(unused)			
Machine Name			
. . .			

Type: TSP_MASTERREQ (3)

A newly-started time daemon broadcasts this message to locate a master. No other action is implied by this packet. It requires a Master Acknowledgment.

Master Acknowledgement

Byte 1	Byte 2	Byte 3	Byte 4
Type	Version No.	Sequence No.	
(unused)			
(unused)			
Machine Name			
. . .			

Type: TSP_MASTERACK (4)

The master sends this message to acknowledge the Master Request message and the Conflict Resolution Message.

Set Network Time Message

Byte 1	Byte 2	Byte 3	Byte 4
Type	Version No.	Sequence No.	
Seconds of Time to Set			
Microseconds of Time to Set			
Machine Name			
...			

Type: TSP_SETTIME (5)

The master sends this message to slave time daemons to set their time. This packet is sent to newly started time daemons and when the network date is changed. It contains the master's time as an approximation of the network time. It requires an acknowledgment. The next synchronization round will eliminate the small time difference caused by the random delay in the communication channel.

Master Active Message

Byte 1	Byte 2	Byte 3	Byte 4
Type	Version No.	Sequence No.	
(unused)			
(unused)			
Machine Name			
...			

Type: TSP_MASTERUP (6)

The master broadcasts this message to solicit the names of the active slaves. Slaves will reply with a Slave Active message.

Slave Active Message

Byte 1	Byte 2	Byte 3	Byte 4
Type	Version No.	Sequence No.	
(unused)			
(unused)			
Machine Name			
...			

Type: TSP_SLAVEUP (7)

A slave sends this message to the master in answer to a Master Active message. This message is also sent when a new slave starts up to inform the master that it wants to be synchronized.

Master Candidature Message

Byte 1	Byte 2	Byte 3	Byte 4
Type	Version No.	Sequence No.	
(unused)			
(unused)			
Machine Name			
. . .			

Type: TSP_ELECTION (8)

A slave eligible to become a master broadcasts this message when its election timer expires. The message declares that the slave wishes to become the new master.

Candidature Acceptance Message

Byte 1	Byte 2	Byte 3	Byte 4
Type	Version No.	Sequence No.	
(unused)			
(unused)			
Machine Name			
. . .			

Type: TSP_ACCEPT (9)

A slave sends this message to accept the candidature of the time daemon that has broadcast an Election message. The candidate will add the slave's name to the list of machines that it will control should it become the master.

12

Candidature Rejection Message

Byte 1	Byte 2	Byte 3	Byte 4
Type	Version No.	Sequence No.	
(unused)			
(unused)			
Machine Name			
. . .			

Type: TSP_REFUSE (10)

After a slave accepts the candidature of a time daemon, it will reply to any election messages from other slaves with this message. This rejects any candidature other than the first received.

Multiple Master Notification Message

Byte 1	Byte 2	Byte 3	Byte 4
Type	Version No.	Sequence No.	
(unused)			
(unused)			
Machine Name			
...			

Type: TSP_CONFLICT (11)

When two or more masters reply to a Master Request message, the slave uses this message to inform one of them that more than one master exists.

Conflict Resolution Message

Byte 1	Byte 2	Byte 3	Byte 4
Type	Version No.	Sequence No.	
(unused)			
(unused)			
Machine Name			
...			

Type: TSP_RESOLVE (12)

A master which has been informed of the existence of other masters broadcasts this message to determine who the other masters are.

Quit Message

Byte 1	Byte 2	Byte 3	Byte 4
Type	Version No.	Sequence No.	
(unused)			
(unused)			
Machine Name			
...			

Type: TSP_QUIT (13)

This message is sent by the master in three different contexts: 1) to a candidate that broadcasts an Master Candidature message, 2) to another master when notified of its existence, 3) to another master if a loop is detected. In all cases, the recipient time daemon will become a slave. This message requires an acknowledgement.

Set Date Message

Byte 1	Byte 2	Byte 3	Byte 4
Type	Version No.	Sequence No.	
Seconds of Time to Set			
Microseconds of Time to Set			
Machine Name			
...			

Type: TSP_SETDATE (22)

The program *date* (1) sends this message to the local time daemon when a super-user wants to set the network date. If the local time daemon is the master, it will set the date; if it is a slave, it will communicate the desired date to the master.

Set Date Request Message

Byte 1	Byte 2	Byte 3	Byte 4
Type	Version No.	Sequence No.	
Seconds of Time to Set			
Microseconds of Time to Set			
Machine Name			
...			

Type: TSP_SETDATEREQ (23)

A slave that has received a Set Date message will communicate the desired date to the master using this message.

Set Date Acknowledgment Message

Byte 1	Byte 2	Byte 3	Byte 4
Type	Version No.	Sequence No.	
(unused)			
(unused)			
Machine Name			
...			

Type: TSP_DATEACK (16)

The master sends this message to a slave in acknowledgment of a Set Date Request Message. The same message is sent by the local time daemon to the program *date(1)* to confirm that the network date has been set by the master.

Start Tracing Message

Byte 1	Byte 2	Byte 3	Byte 4
Type	Version No.	Sequence No.	
(unused)			
(unused)			
Machine Name			
...			

Type: TSP_TRACEON (17)

The controlling program *timedc* sends this message to the local time daemon to start the recording in a system file of all messages received.

Stop Tracing Message

Byte 1	Byte 2	Byte 3	Byte 4
Type	Version No.	Sequence No.	
(unused)			
(unused)			
Machine Name			
...			

Type: TSP_TRACEOFF (18)

Timedc sends this message to the local time daemon to stop the recording of messages received.

Master Site Message

Byte 1	Byte 2	Byte 3	Byte 4
Type	Version No.	Sequence No.	
(unused)			
(unused)			
Machine Name			
...			

Type: TSP_MSITE (19)

Timedc sends this message to the local time daemon to find out where the master is running.

Remote Master Site Message

Byte 1	Byte 2	Byte 3	Byte 4
Type	Version No.	Sequence No.	
(unused)			
(unused)			
Machine Name			
...			

Type: TSP_MSITEREQ (20)

A local time daemon broadcasts this message to find the location of the master. It then uses the Acknowledgement message to communicate this location to *timedc*.

Test Message

Byte 1	Byte 2	Byte 3	Byte 4
Type	Version No.	Sequence No.	
(unused)			
(unused)			
Machine Name			
...			

Type: TSP_TEST (21)

For testing purposes, *timedc* sends this message to a slave to cause its election timer to expire. NOTE: *timed* is not normally compiled to support this.

Loop Detection Message

Byte 1	Byte 2	Byte 3	Byte 4
Type	Version No.	Sequence No.	
Hop Count	(unused)		
(unused)			
Machine Name			
...			

Type: TSP_LOOP (24)

This packet is initiated by all masters occasionally to attempt to detect loops. All submasters forward this packet onto the networks over which they are master. If a master receives a packet it sent out initially, it knows that a loop exists and tries to correct the problem.

References

1. R. Gusella and S. Zatti, *TEMPO: A Network Time Controller for Distributed Berkeley UNIX System*, USENIX Summer Conference Proceedings, Salt Lake City, June 1984.

2. R. Gusella and S. Zatti, *Clock Synchronization in a Local Area Network*, University of California, Berkeley, Technical Report, *to appear*.

3. R. Gusella and S. Zatti, *An Election Algorithm for a Distributed Clock Synchronization Program*, University of California, Berkeley, CS Technical Report #275, Dec. 1985.

4. Postel, J., *User Datagram Protocol*, RFC 768. Network Information Center, SRI International, Menlo Park, California, August 1980.

5. Postel, J., *Internet Control Message Protocol*, RFC 792. Network Information Center, SRI International, Menlo Park, California, September 1981.

Amd

The 4.4 BSD Automounter

Reference Manual

Jan-Simon Pendry

and

Nick Williams

13

Last updated March 1991
Documentation for software revision 5.3 Alpha

13

Table of Contents

13

13

13

13

Preface

This manual documents the use of the 4.4 BSD automounter—*Amd*. This is primarily a reference manual. Unfortunately, no tutorial exists.

This manual comes in two forms: the published form and the Info form. The Info form is for on-line perusal with the INFO program which is distributed along with GNU Emacs. Both forms contain substantially the same text and are generated from a common source file, which is distributed with the *Amd* source.

License

Amd is not in the public domain; it is copyrighted and there are restrictions on its distribution.

Redistribution and use in source and binary forms are permitted provided that: (1) source distributions retain this entire copyright notice and comment, and (2) distributions including binaries display the following acknowledgement: "This product includes software developed by The University of California, Berkeley and its Contributors" in the documentation or other materials provided with the distribution and in all advertising materials mentioning features or use of this software. neither the name of the University nor the names of its Contributors may be used to endorse or promote products derived from this software without specific prior written permission.

THIS SOFTWARE IS PROVIDED "AS IS" AND WITHOUT ANY EXPRESS OR IMPLIED WARRANTIES, INCLUDING, WITHOUT LIMITATION, THE IMPLIED WARRANTIES OF MERCHANTABILITY AND FITNESS FOR A PARTICULAR PURPOSE.

Source Distribution

If you have access to the Internet, you can get the latest distribution version of *Amd* from host '`usc.edu`' using anonymous FTP. Move to the directory '`/pub/amd`' on that host and fetch the file '`amd.tar.Z`'.

If you are in the UK, you can get the latest distribution version of *Amd* from the UKnet info-server. Start by sending email to '`info-server@doc.ic.ac.uk`'.

Sites on the UK JANET network can get the latest distribution by using anonymous NIFTP to fetch the file '`<AMD>amd.tar.Z`' from host '`uk.ac.imperial.doc.src`'.

Revision 5.2 was part of the 4.3 BSD Reno distribution.

Revision 5.3bsdnet, a late alpha version of 5.3, was part of the BSD network version 2 distribution

Bug Reports

Send all bug reports to '`jsp@doc.ic.ac.uk`' quoting the details of the release and your configuration. These can be obtained by running the command '`amd -v`'.

Mailing List

There is a mailing list for people interested in keeping uptodate with developments. To subscribe, send a note to '`amd-workers-request@acl.lanl.gov`'.

Introduction

An *automounter* maintains a cache of mounted filesystems. Filesystems are mounted on demand when they are first referenced, and unmounted after a period of inactivity.

Amd may be used as a replacement for Sun's automounter. The choice of which filesystem to mount can be controlled dynamically with *selectors*. Selectors allow decisions of the form "hostname is *this*," or "architecture is not *that*." Selectors may be combined arbitrarily. *Amd* also supports a variety of filesystem types, including NFS, UFS and the novel *program* filesystem. The combination of selectors and multiple filesystem types allows identical configuration files to be used on all machines so reducing the administrative overhead.

Amd ensures that it will not hang if a remote server goes down. Moreover, *Amd* can determine when a remote server has become inaccessible and then mount replacement filesystems as and when they become available.

Amd contains no proprietary source code and has been ported to numerous flavours of Unix.

1 Overview

Amd maintains a cache of mounted filesystems. Filesystems are *demand-mounted* when they are first referenced, and unmounted after a period of inactivity. *Amd* may be used as a replacement for Sun's **automount**(8) program. It contains no proprietary source code and has been ported to numerous flavours of Unix. See Section 2.1 [Supported Operating Systems], page SMM:13-6.

Amd was designed as the basis for experimenting with filesystem layout and management. Although *Amd* has many direct applications it is loaded with additional features which have little practical use. At some point the infrequently used components may be removed to streamline the production system.

1.1 Fundamentals

The fundamental concept behind *Amd* is the ability to separate the name used to refer to a file from the name used to refer to its physical storage location. This allows the same files to be accessed with the same name regardless of where in the network the name is used. This is very different from placing '`/n/hostname`' in front of the pathname since that includes location dependent information which may change if files are moved to another machine.

By placing the required mappings in a centrally administered database, filesystems can be re-organised without requiring changes to configuration files, shell scripts and so on.

1.2 Filesystems and Volumes

Amd views the world as a set of fileservers, each containg one or more filesystems where each filesystem contains one or more *volumes*. Here the term *volume* is used to refer to a coherent set of files such as a user's home directory or a TeX distribution.

In order to access the contents of a volume, *Amd* must be told in which filesystem the volume resides and which host owns the filesystem. By default the host is assumed to be local and the volume is assumed to be the entire filesystem. If a filesystem contains more than one volume, then a *sublink* is used to refer to the sub-directory within the filesystem where the volume can be found.

1.3 Volume Naming

Volume names are defined to be unique across the entire network. A volume name is the pathname to the volume's root as known by the users of that volume. Since this name uniquely identifies the volume contents, all volumes can be named and accessed from each host, subject to administrative controls.

Volumes may be replicated or duplicated. Replicated volumes contain identical copies of the same data and reside at two or more locations in the network. Each of the replicated volumes can be used interchangeably. Duplicated volumes each have the same name but contain different, though functionally identical, data. For example, '`/vol/tex`' might be the name of a TeX distribution which varied for each machine architecture.

Amd provides facilities to take advantage of both replicated and duplicated volumes. Configuration options allow a single set of configuration data to be shared across an entire network by taking advantage of replicated and duplicated volumes.

Amd can take advantage of replacement volumes by mounting them as required should an active fileserver become unavailable.

1.4 Volume Binding

Unix implements a namespace of hierarchically mounted filesystems. Two forms of binding between names and files are provided. A *hard link* completes the binding when the name is added to the filesystem. A *soft link* delays the binding until the name is accessed. An *automounter* adds a further form in which the binding of name to filesystem is delayed until the name is accessed.

The target volume, in its general form, is a tuple (host, filesystem, sublink) which can be used to name the physical location of any volume in the network.

When a target is referenced, *Amd* ignores the sublink element and determines whether the required filesystem is already mounted. This is done by computing the local mount point for the filesystem and checking for an existing filesystem mounted at the same place. If such a filesystem already exists then it is assumed to be functionally identical to the target filesystem. By default there is a one-to-one mapping between the pair (host, filesystem) and the local mount point so this assumption is valid.

1.5 Operational Principles

Amd operates by introducing new mount points into the namespace. These are called *automount* points. The kernel sees these automount points as NFS filesystems being served by *Amd*. Having attached itself to the namespace, *Amd* is now able to control the view the rest of the system has of those mount points. RPC calls are received from the kernel one at a time.

When a *lookup* call is received *Amd* checks whether the name is already known. If it is not, the required volume is mounted. A symbolic link pointing to the volume root is then returned. Once the symbolic link is returned, the kernel will send all other requests direct to the mounted filesystem.

If a volume is not yet mounted, *Amd* consults a configuration *mount-map* corresponding to the automount point. *Amd* then makes a runtime decision on what and where to mount a filesystem based on the information obtained from the map.

Amd does not implement all the NFS requests; only those relevant to name binding such as *lookup*, *readlink* and *readdir*. Some other calls are also implemented but most simply return an error code; for example *mkdir* always returns "read-only filesystem".

1.6 Mounting a Volume

Each automount point has a corresponding mount map. The mount map contains a list of key–value pairs. The key is the name of the volume to be mounted. The value is a list of locations describing where the filesystem is stored in the network. In the source for the map the value would look like

    location1 location2 ... locationN

Amd examines each location in turn. Each location may contain *selectors* which control whether *Amd* can use that location. For example, the location may be restricted to use by certain hosts. Those locations which cannot be used are ignored.

Amd attempts to mount the filesystem described by each remaining location until a mount succeeds or *Amd* can no longer proceed. The latter can occur in three ways:

- If none of the locations could be used, or if all of the locations caused an error, then the last error is returned.
- If a location could be used but was being mounted in the background then *Amd* marks that mount as being "in progress" and continues with the next request; no reply is sent to the kernel.
- Lastly, one or more of the mounts may have been *deferred*. A mount is deferred if extra information is required before the mount can proceed. When the information becomes available the mount will take place, but in the mean time no reply is sent to the kernel. If the mount is deferred, *Amd* continues to try any remaining locations.

Once a volume has been mounted, *Amd* establishes a *volume mapping* which is used to satisfy subsequent requests.

1.7 Automatic Unmounting

To avoid an ever increasing number of filesystem mounts, *Amd* removes volume mappings which have not been used recently. A time-to-live interval is associated with each mapping and when that expires the mapping is removed. When the last reference to a filesystem is removed, that filesystem is unmounted. If the unmount fails, for example the filesystem is still busy, the mapping is re-instated and its time-to-live interval is extended. The global default for this grace period is controlled by the "-w" command-line option (see Section 4.11 [-w Option], page SMM:13-19). It is also possible to set this value on a per-mount basis (see Section 3.3.4.3 [opts], page SMM:13-15).

Filesystems can be forcefully timed out using the *Amq* command. See Chapter 6 [Run-time Administration], page SMM:13-27.

1.8 Keep-alives

Use of some filesystem types requires the presence of a server on another machine. If a machine crashes then it is of no concern to processes on that machine that the filesystem is unavailable. However, to processes on a remote host using that machine as a fileserver this event is important. This situation is most widely recognised when an NFS server crashes and the behaviour observed on client machines is that more and more processes hang. In order to provide the possibility of recovery, *Amd* implements a *keep-alive* interval timer for some filesystem types. Currently only NFS makes use of this service.

The basis of the NFS keep-alive implementation is the observation that most sites maintain replicated copies of common system data such as manual pages, most or all programs, system source code and so on. If one of those servers goes down it would be reasonable to mount one of the others as a replacement.

The first part of the process is to keep track of which fileservers are up and which are down. *Amd* does this by sending RPC requests to the servers' NFS `NullProc` and checking whether a reply is returned. While the server state is uncertain the requests are re-transmitted at three second intervals and if no reply is received after four attempts the server is marked down. If a reply is received the fileserver is marked up and stays in that state for 30 seconds at which time another NFS ping is sent.

Once a fileserver is marked down, requests continue to be sent every 30 seconds in order to determine when the fileserver comes back up. During this time any reference through *Amd* to the filesystems on that server fail with the error "Operation would block". If a replacement volume is available then it will be mounted, otherwise the error is returned to the user.

Although this action does not protect user files, which are unique on the network, or processes which do not access files via *Amd* or already have open files on the hung filesystem, it can prevent most new processes from hanging.

By default, fileserver state is not maintained for NFS/TCP mounts. The remote fileserver is always assumed to be up.

1.9 Non-blocking Operation

Since there is only one instance of *Amd* for each automount point, and usually only one instance on each machine, it is important that it is always available to service kernel calls. *Amd* goes to great lengths to ensure that it does not block in a system call. As a last resort *Amd* will fork before it attempts a system call that may block indefinitely, such as mounting an NFS filesystem. Other tasks such as obtaining filehandle information for an NFS filesystem, are done using a purpose built non-blocking RPC library which is integrated with *Amd*'s task scheduler. This library is also used to implement NFS keep-alives (see Section 1.8 [Keep-alives], page SMM:13-5).

Whenever a mount is deferred or backgrounded, *Amd* must wait for it to complete before replying to the kernel. However, this would cause *Amd* to block waiting for a reply to be constructed. Rather than do this, *Amd* simply *drops* the call under the assumption that the kernel RPC mechanism will automatically retry the request.

2 Supported Platforms

Amd has been ported to a wide variety of machines and operating systems. The table below lists those platforms supported by the current release.

2.1 Supported Operating Systems

The following operating systems are currently supported by *Amd*. *Amd*'s conventional name for each system is given.

`acis43` 4.3 BSD for IBM RT. Contributed by Jan-Simon Pendry `<jsp@doc.ic.ac.uk>`

`aix3` AIX 3.1. Contributed by Jan-Simon Pendry `<jsp@doc.ic.ac.uk>`

`aux` System V for Mac-II. Contributed by Julian Onions `<jpo@cs.nott.ac.uk>`

`bsd44` 4.4 BSD. Contributed by Jan-Simon Pendry `<jsp@doc.ic.ac.uk>`

`concentrix`
Concentrix 5.0. Contributed by Sjoerd Mullender `<sjoerd@cwi.nl>`

`convex` Convex OS 7.1. Contributed by Eitan Mizrotsky `<eitan@shumuji.ac.il>`

`dgux` Data General DG/UX. Contributed by Mark Davies `<mark@comp.vuw.ac.nz>`

`fpx4` Celerity FPX 4.1/2. Contributed by Stephen Pope `<scp@grizzly.acl.lanl.gov>`

`hcx` Harris HCX/UX. Contributed by Chris Metcalf `<metcalf@masala.lcs.mit.edu>`

`hlh42` HLH OTS 1.*x* (4.2 BSD). Contributed by Jan-Simon Pendry `<jsp@doc.ic.ac.uk>`

`hpux` HP-UX 6.*x* or 7.0. Contributed by Jan-Simon Pendry `<jsp@doc.ic.ac.uk>`

`irix` SGI Irix. Contributed by Scott R. Presnell `<srp@cgl.ucsf.edu>`

`next` Mach for NeXT. Contributed by Bill Trost `<trost%reed@cse.ogi.edu>`

`pyrOSx` Pyramid OSx. Contributed by Stefan Petri `<petri@tubsibr.UUCP>`

`riscix` Acorn RISC iX. Contributed by Piete Brooks `<pb@cam.cl.ac.uk>`

`sos3` SunOS 3.4 & 3.5. Contributed by Jan-Simon Pendry `<jsp@doc.ic.ac.uk>`

`sos4` SunOS 4.*x*. Contributed by Jan-Simon Pendry `<jsp@doc.ic.ac.uk>`

`u2_2` Ultrix 2.2. Contributed by Piete Brooks `<pb@cam.cl.ac.uk>`

`u3_0` Ultrix 3. Contributed by Piete Brooks `<pb@cam.cl.ac.uk>`

`u4_0` Ultrix 4.0. Contributed by Chris Lindblad `<cjl@ai.mit.edu>`

`umax43` Umax 4.3 BSD. Contributed by Sjoerd Mullender `<sjoerd@cwi.nl>`

`utek` Utek 4.0. Contributed by Bill Trost `<trost%reed@cse.ogi.edu>`

`xinu43` mt Xinu MORE/bsd. Contributed by Jan-Simon Pendry `<jsp@doc.ic.ac.uk>`

2.2 Supported Machine Architectures

`alliant`	Alliant FX/4
`arm`	Acorn ARM
`aviion`	Data General AViiON
`encore`	Encore
`fps500`	FPS Model 500
`hp9000`	HP 9000/300 family
`hp9k8`	HP 9000/800 family
`ibm032`	IBM RT
`ibm6000`	IBM RISC System/6000
`iris4d`	SGI Iris 4D
`macII`	Apple Mac II
`mips`	MIPS RISC
`multimax`	Encore Multimax
`orion105`	HLH Orion 1/05
`sun3`	Sun-3 family
`sun4`	Sun-4 family
`tahoe`	Tahoe family
`vax`	DEC Vax

3 Mount Maps

Amd has no built-in knowledge of machines or filesystems. External *mount-maps* are used to provide the required information. Specifically, *Amd* needs to know when and under what conditions it should mount filesystems.

The map entry corresponding to the requested name contains a list of possible locations from which to resolve the request. Each location specifies filesystem type, information required by that filesystem (for example the block special device in the case of UFS), and some information describing where to mount the filesystem (see Section 3.3.4.2 [fs Option], page SMM:13-14). A location may also contain *selectors* (see Section 3.3.3 [Selectors], page SMM:13-13).

13

3.1 Map Types

A mount-map provides the run-time configuration information to *Amd*. Maps can be implemented in many ways. Some of the forms supported by *Amd* are regular files, ndbm databases, NIS maps the *Hesiod* name server and even the password file.

A mount-map *name* is a sequence of characters. When an automount point is created a handle on the mount-map is obtained. For each map type configured *Amd* attempts to reference the a map of the appropriate type. If a map is found, *Amd* notes the type for future use and deletes the reference, for example closing any open file descriptors. The available maps are configure when *Amd* is built and can be displayed by running the command '`amd -v`'.

By default, *Amd* caches data in a mode dependent on the type of map. This is the same as specifying '`cache:=mapdefault`' and selects a suitable default cache mode depending on the map type. The individual defaults are described below. The *cache* option can be specified on automount points to alter the caching behaviour (see Section 5.8 [Automount Filesystem], page SMM:13-24).

The following map types have been implemented, though some are not available on all machines. Run the command '`amd -v`' to obtain a list of map types configured on your machine.

3.1.1 File maps

When *Amd* searches a file for a map entry it does a simple scan of the file and supports both comments and continuation lines.

Continuation lines are indicated by a backslash character ('\') as the last character of a line in the file. The backslash, newline character *and any leading white space on the following line* are discarded. A maximum line length of 2047 characters is enforced after continuation lines are read but before comments are stripped. Each line must end with a newline character; that is newlines are terminators, not separators. The following examples illustrate this:

```
key     valA   valB;   \
          valC
```

specifies *three* locations, and is identical to

```
key     valA   valB;   valC
```

However,

```
key     valA   valB;\
          valC
```

specifies only *two* locations, and is identical to

```
key     valA   valB;valC
```

After a complete line has been read from the file, including continuations, *Amd* determines whether there is a comment on the line. A comment begins with a hash ("`#`") character and continues to the end of the line. There is no way to escape or change the comment lead-in character.

Note that continuation lines and comment support *only* apply to file maps, or ndbm maps built with the `mk-amd-map` program.

When caching is enabled, file maps have a default cache mode of `all` (see Section 5.8 [Automount Filesystem], page SMM:13-24).

3.1.2 ndbm maps

An ndbm map may be used as a fast access form of a file map. The program, `mk-amd-map`, converts a normal map file into an ndbm database. This program supports the same continuation and comment conventions that are provided for file maps. Note that ndbm format files may *not* be sharable across machine architectures. The notion of speed generally only applies to large maps; a small map, less than a single disk block, is almost certainly better implemented as a file map.

ndbm maps do not support cache mode '`all`' and, when caching is enabled, have a default cache mode of '`inc`' (see Section 5.8 [Automount Filesystem], page SMM:13-24).

3.1.3 NIS maps

When using NIS (formerly YP), an *Amd* map is implemented directly by the underlying NIS map. Comments and continuation lines are *not* supported in the automounter and must be stripped when constructing the NIS server's database.

NIS maps do not support cache mode `all` and, when caching is enabled, have a default cache mode of `inc` (see Section 5.8 [Automount Filesystem], page SMM:13-24).

The following rule illustrates what could be added to your NIS '`Makefile`', in this case causing the '`amd.home`' map to be rebuilt:

```
$(YPTSDIR)/amd.home.time: $(ETCDIR)/amd.home
        -@sed -e "s/#.*$$//" -e "/^$$/d" $(ETCDIR)/amd.home | \
          awk '{  \
                 for (i = 1; i <= NF; i++) \
                     if (i == NF) { \
                         if (substr($$i, length($$i), 1) == "\\") \
                             printf("%s", substr($$i, 1, length($$i) - 1));
\
                         else \
                             printf("%s\n", $$i); \
                     } \
                     else \
                         printf("%s ", $$i); \
             }' | \
        $(MAKEDBM) - $(YPDBDIR)/amd.home; \
        touch $(YPTSDIR)/amd.home.time; \
        echo "updated amd.home"; \
        if [ ! $(NOPUSH) ]; then \
                $(YPPUSH) amd.home; \
                echo "pushed amd.home"; \
        else \
                : ; \
        fi
```

Here `$(YPTSDIR)` contains the time stamp files, and `$(YPDBDIR)` contains the dbm format NIS files.

13

3.1.4 Hesiod maps

When the map name begins with the string '`hesiod.`' lookups are made using the *Hesiod* name server. The string following the dot is used as a name qualifier and is prepended with the key being located. The entire string is then resolved in the `automount` context. For example, if the the key is '`jsp`' and map name is '`hesiod.homes`' then *Hesiod* is asked to resolve '`jsp.homes.automount`'.

Hesiod maps do not support cache mode '`all`' and, when caching is enabled, have a default cache mode of '`inc`' (see Section 5.8 [Automount Filesystem], page SMM:13-24).

The following is an example of a *Hesiod* map entry:

```
jsp.homes.automount HS TXT "rfs:=/home/charm;rhost:=charm;sublink:=jsp"
njw.homes.automount HS TXT "rfs:=/home/dylan/dk2;rhost:=dylan;sublink:=njw"
```

3.1.5 Password maps

The password map support is unlike the four previous map types. When the map name is the string '/etc/passwd' *Amd* can lookup a user name in the password file and re-arrange the home directory field to produce a usable map entry.

Amd assumes the home directory has the format '*/anydir/dom1/../domN/login*'. It breaks this string into a map entry where `${rfs}` has the value '*/anydir/domN*', `${rhost}` has the value '*domN.....dom1*', and `${sublink}` has the value 'login'.

Thus if the password file entry was

```
/home/achilles/jsp
```

the map entry used by *Amd* would be

```
rfs:=/home/achilles;rhost:=achilles;sublink:=jsp
```

Similarly, if the password file entry was

```
/home/cc/sugar/mjh
```

the map entry used by *Amd* would be

```
rfs:=/home/sugar;rhost:=sugar.cc;sublink:=jsp
```

3.1.6 Union maps

The union map support is provided specifically for use with the union filesystem, see Section 5.10 [Union Filesystem], page SMM:13-25.

It is identified by the string 'union:' which is followed by a colon separated list of directories. The directories are read in order, and the names of all entries are recorded in the map cache. Later directories take precedence over earlier ones. The union filesystem type then uses the map cache to determine the union of the names in all the directories.

3.2 How keys are looked up

13

The key is located in the map whose type was determined when the automount point was first created. In general the key is a pathname component. In some circumstances this may be modified by variable expansion (see Section 3.3.2 [Variable Expansion], page SMM:13-12) and prefixing. If the automount point has a prefix, specified by the *pref* option, then that is prepended to the search key before the map is searched.

If the map cache is a 'regexp' cache then the key is treated as an egrep-style regular expression, otherwise a normal string comparison is made.

If the key cannot be found then a *wildcard* match is attempted. *Amd* repeatedly strips the basename from the key, appends '/*' and attempts a lookup. Finally, *Amd* attempts to locate the special key '*'.

For example, the following sequence would be checked if 'home/dylan/dk2' was being located:

```
home/dylan/dk2
home/dylan/*
home/*
*
```

At any point when a wildcard is found, *Amd* proceeds as if an exact match had been found and the value field is then used to resolve the mount request, otherwise an error code is propagated back to the kernel. (see Chapter 5 [Filesystem Types], page SMM:13-20).

3.3 Location Format

The value field from the lookup provides the information required to mount a filesystem. The information is parsed according to the syntax shown below.

location-list:
: *location-selection*
: *location-list white-space* `||` *white-space location-selection*

location-selection:
: *location*
: *location-selection white-space location*

location:
: *location-info*
: `-`*location-info*
: `-`

location-info:
: *sel-or-opt*
: *location-info*`;`*sel-or-opt*
: `;`

sel-or-opt:
: *selection*
: *opt-ass*

selection:
: selector`==`*value*
: selector`!=`*value*

opt-ass:
: option`:=`*value*

white-space:
: space
: tab

Note that unquoted whitespace is not allowed in a location description. White space is only allowed, and is mandatory, where shown with non-terminal '`white-space`'.

A *location-selection* is a list of possible volumes with which to satisfy the request. *location-selections* are separated by the '`||`' operator. The effect of this operator is to prevent use of location-selections to its right if any of the location-selections on its left were selected whether or not any of them were successfully mounted (see Section 3.3.3 [Selectors], page SMM:13-13).

The location-selection, and singleton *location-list*, '`type:=ufs;dev:=/dev/xd1g`' would inform *Amd* to mount a UFS filesystem from the block special device '`/dev/xd1g`'.

The *sel-or-opt* component is either the name of an option required by a specific filesystem, or it is the name of a built-in, predefined selector such as the architecture type. The value may be quoted with double quotes '`"`', for example '`type:="ufs";dev:="/dev/xd1g"`'. These quotes are stripped when the value is parsed and there is no way to get a double quote into a value field. Double quotes are used to get white space into a value field, which is needed for the program filesystem (see Section 5.5 [Program Filesystem], page SMM:13-23).

13

3.3.1 Map Defaults

A location beginning with a dash '-' is used to specify default values for subsequent locations. Any previously specified defaults in the location-list are discarded. The default string can be empty in which case no defaults apply.

The location '-fs:=/mnt;opts:=ro' would set the local mount point to '/mnt' and cause mounts to be read-only by default. Defaults specified this way are appended to, and so override, any global map defaults given with '/defaults').

3.3.2 Variable Expansion

To allow generic location specifications *Amd* does variable expansion on each location and also on some of the option strings. Any option or selector appearing in the form $*var* is replaced by the current value of that option or selector. For example, if the value of ${key} was 'bin', ${autodir} was '/a' and ${fs} was '${autodir}/local/${key}' then after expansion ${fs} would have the value '/a/local/bin'. Any environment variable can be accessed in a similar way.

Two pathname operators are available when expanding a variable. If the variable name begins with '/' then only the last component of then pathname is substituted. For example, if ${path} was '/foo/bar' then ${/path} would be expanded to 'bar'. Similarly, if the variable name ends with '/' then all but the last component of the pathname is substituted. In the previous example, ${path/} would be expanded to '/foo'.

Two domain name operators are also provided. If the variable name begins with '.' then only the domain part of the name is substituted. For example, if ${rhost} was 'swan.doc.ic.ac.uk' then ${.rhost} would be expanded to 'doc.ic.ac.uk'. Similarly, if the variable name ends with '.' then only the host component is substituted. In the previous example, ${rhost.} would be expanded to 'swan'.

Variable expansion is a two phase process. Before a location is parsed, all references to selectors, *eg* ${path}, are expanded. The location is then parsed, selections are evaluated and option assignments recorded. If there were no selections or they all succeeded the location is used and the values of the following options are expanded in the order given: *sublink*, *rfs*, *fs*, *opts*, *remopts*, *mount* and *unmount*.

13

Note that expansion of option values is done after *all* assignments have been completed and not in a purely left to right order as is done by the shell. This generally has the desired effect but care must be taken if one of the options references another, in which case the ordering can become significant.

There are two special cases concerning variable expansion:

1. before a map is consulted, any selectors in the name received from the kernel are expanded. For example, if the request from the kernel was for '${arch}.bin' and the machine architecture was 'vax', the value given to ${key} would be 'vax.bin'.

2. the value of ${rhost} is expanded and normalized before the other options are expanded. The normalization process strips any local sub-domain components. For example, if ${domain} was 'Berkeley.EDU' and ${rhost} was initially 'snow.Berkeley.EDU', after the normalization it would simply be 'snow'. Hostname normalization is currently done in a *case-dependent* manner.

3.3.3 Selectors

Selectors are used to control the use of a location. It is possible to share a mount map between many machines in such a way that filesystem location, architecture and operating system differences are hidden from the users. A selector of the form '`arch==sun3;os==sos4`' would only apply on Sun-3s running SunOS 4.x.

Selectors are evaluated left to right. If a selector fails then that location is ignored. Thus the selectors form a conjunction and the locations form a disjunction. If all the locations are ignored or otherwise fail then *Amd* uses the *error* filesystem (see Section 5.11 [Error Filesystem], page SMM:13-26). This is equivalent to having a location '`type:=error`' at the end of each mount-map entry.

The selectors currently implemented are:

'`arch`' the machine architecture which was automatically determined at compile time. The architecture type can be displayed by running the command '`amd -v`'. See Section 2.2 [Supported Machine Architectures], page SMM:13-7.

'`autodir`' the default directory under which to mount filesystems. This may be changed by the "-a" command line option. See the *fs* option.

'`byte`' the machine's byte ordering. This is either '`little`', indicating little-endian, or '`big`', indicating big-endian. One possible use is to share '`rwho`' databases (see Section 8.5 [rwho servers], page SMM:13-49). Another is to share ndbm databases, however this use can be considered a courageous juggling act.

'`cluster`' is provided as a hook for the name of the local cluster. This can be used to decide which servers to use for copies of replicated filesystems. `${cluster}` defaults to the value of `${domain}` unless a different value is set with the "-C" command line option.

'`domain`' the local domain name as specified by the "-d" command line option. See '`host`'.

'`host`' the local hostname as determined by **gethostname**(2). If no domain name was specified on the command line and the hostname contains a period '`.`' then the string before the period is used as the host name, and the string after the period is assigned to `${domain}`. For example, if the hostname is '`styx.doc.ic.ac.uk`' then `host` would be '`styx`' and `domain` would be '`doc.ic.ac.uk`'. `hostd` would be '`styx.doc.ic.ac.uk`'.

'`hostd`' is `${host}` and `${domain}` concatenated with a '`.`' inserted between them if required. If `${domain}` is an empty string then `${host}` and `${hostd}` will be identical.

'`karch`' is provided as a hook for the kernel architecture. This is used on SunOS 4, for example, to distinguish between different '`/usr/kvm`' volumes. `${karch}` defaults to the value of `${arch}` unless a different value is set with the "-k" command line option.

'`os`' the operating system. Like the machine architecture, this is automatically determined at compile time. The operating system name can be displayed by running the command '`amd -v`'. See Section 2.1 [Supported Operating Systems], page SMM:13-6.

The following selectors are also provided. Unlike the other selectors, they vary for each lookup. Note that when the name from the kernel is expanded prior to a map lookup, these selectors are all defined as empty strings.

'`key`' the name being resolved. For example, if '`/home`' is an automount point, then accessing '`/home/foo`' would set `${key}` to the string '`foo`'. The key is prefixed by the *pref* option set in the parent mount point. The default prefix is an empty string. If the prefix was '`blah/`' then `${key}` would be set to '`blah/foo`'.

'`map`' the name of the mount map being used.

'path' the full pathname of the name being resolved. For example '/home/foo' in the example above.

'wire' the name of the network to which the primary network interface is attached. If a symbolic name cannot be found in the networks or hosts database then dotted IP address format is used. This value is also output by the "-v" option.

Selectors can be negated by using '!=' instead of '=='. For example to select a location on all non-Vax machines the selector 'arch!=vax' would be used.

3.3.4 Map Options

Options are parsed concurrently with selectors. The difference is that when an option is seen the string following the ':=' is recorded for later use. As a minimum the *type* option must be specified. Each filesystem type has other options which must also be specified. See Chapter 5 [Filesystem Types], page SMM:13-20, for details on the filesystem specific options.

Superfluous option specifications are ignored and are not reported as errors.

The following options apply to more than one filesystem type.

3.3.4.1 delay Option

The delay, in seconds, before an attempt will be made to mount from the current location. Auxilliary data, such as network address, file handles and so on are computed regardless of this value.

A delay can be used to implement the notion of primary and secondary file servers. The secondary servers would have a delay of a few seconds, thus giving the primary servers a chance to respond first.

3.3.4.2 fs Option

13

The local mount point. The semantics of this option vary between filesystems.

For NFS and UFS filesystems the value of **${fs}** is used as the local mount point. For other filesystem types it has other meanings which are described in the section describing the respective filesystem type. It is important that this string uniquely identifies the filesystem being mounted. To satisfy this requirement, it should contain the name of the host on which the filesystem is resident and the pathname of the filesystem on the local or remote host.

The reason for requiring the hostname is clear if replicated filesystems are considered. If a fileserver goes down and a replacement filesystem is mounted then the *local* mount point *must* be different from that of the filesystem which is hung. Some encoding of the filesystem name is required if more than one filesystem is to be mounted from any given host.

If the hostname is first in the path then all mounts from a particular host will be gathered below a single directory. If that server goes down then the hung mount points are less likely to be accidentally referenced, for example when **getwd**(3) traverses the namespace to find the pathname of the current directory.

The 'fs' option defaults to **${autodir}/${rhost}${rfs}**. In addition, 'rhost' defaults to the local host name (**${host}**) and 'rfs' defaults to the value of **${path}**, which is the full path of the requested file; '/home/foo' in the example above (see Section 3.3.3 [Selectors], page SMM:13-13). **${autodir}** defaults to '/a' but may be changed with the "-a" command line option. Sun's automounter defaults to '/tmp_mnt'. Note that there is no '/' between the **${rhost}** and **${rfs}** since **${rfs}** begins with a '/'.

3.3.4.3 opts Option

The options to pass to the mount system call. A leading '-' is silently ignored. The mount options supported generally correspond to those used by **mount**(8) and are listed below. Some additional pseudo-options are interpreted by *Amd* and are also listed.

Unless specifically overridden, each of the system default mount options applies. Any options not recognised are ignored. If no options list is supplied the string '**rw,defaults**' is used and all the system default mount options apply. Options which are not applicable for a particular operating system are silently ignored. For example, only 4.4 BSD is known to implement the **compress** and **spongy** options.

compress Use NFS compression protocol.

grpid Use BSD directory group-id semantics.

intr Allow keyboard interrupts on hard mounts.

noconn Don't make a connection on datagram transports.

nocto No close-to-open consistency.

nodevs Don't allow local special devices on this filesystem.

nosuid Don't allow set-uid or set-gid executables on this filesystem.

quota Enable quota checking on this mount.

retrans=*n*
: The number of NFS retransmits made before a user error is generated by a '**soft**' mounted filesystem, and before a '**hard**' mounted filesystem reports '**NFS server** *yoyo* **not responding still trying**'.

ro Mount this filesystem readonly.

rsize=*n* The NFS read packet size. You may need to set this if you are using NFS/UDP through a gateway.

soft Give up after *retrans* retransmissions.

spongy Like '**soft**' for status requests, and '**hard**' for data transfers.

tcp Use TCP/IP instead of UDP/IP, ignored if the NFS implementation does not support TCP/IP mounts.

timeo=*n* The NFS timeout, in tenth-seconds, before a request is retransmitted.

wsize=*n* The NFS write packet size. You may need to set this if you are using NFS/UDP through a gateway.

The following options are implemented by *Amd*, rather than being passed to the kernel.

nounmount
: Configures the mount so that its time-to-live will never expire. This is also the default for some filesystem types.

ping=*n* The interval, in seconds, between keep-alive pings. When four consecutive pings have failed the mount point is marked as hung. This interval defaults to 30 seconds. If the ping interval is less than zero, no pings are sent and the host is assumed to be always up. By default, pings are not sent for an NFS/TCP mount.

13

`retry=`*n* The number of times to retry the mount system call.

`utimeout=`*n*
: The interval, in seconds, by which the mount's time-to-live is extended after an unmount attempt has failed. In fact the interval is extended before the unmount is attempted to avoid thrashing. The default value is 120 seconds (two minutes) or as set by the "-w" command line option.

3.3.4.4 remopts Option

This option has the same use as `${opts}` but applies only when the remote host is on a non-local network. For example, when using NFS across a gateway it is often necessary to use smaller values for the data read and write sizes. This can simply be done by specifying the small values in *remopts*. When a non-local host is accessed, the smaller sizes will automatically be used.

Amd determines whether a host is local by examining the network interface configuration at startup. Any interface changes made after *Amd* has been started will not be noticed. The likely effect will be that a host may incorrectly be declared non-local.

Unless otherwise set, the value of `${rem}` is the same as the value of `${opts}`.

3.3.4.5 sublink Option

The subdirectory within the mounted filesystem to which the reference should point. This can be used to prevent duplicate mounts in cases where multiple directories in the same mounted filesystem are used.

3.3.4.6 type Option

The filesystem type to be used. See Chapter 5 [Filesystem Types], page SMM:13-20, for a full description of each type.

13

4 *Amd* Command Line Options

Many of *Amd*'s parameters can be set from the command line. The command line is also used to specify automount points and maps.

The general format of a command line is

`amd [`*options*`] { `*directory map-name* `[-`*map-options*`] } ...`

For each directory and map-name given, *Amd* establishes an automount point. The *map-options* may be any sequence of options or selectors—see Section 3.3 [Location Format], page SMM:13-11. The *map-options* apply only to *Amd*'s mount point.

'`type:=toplvl;cache:=mapdefault;fs:=${map}`' is the default value for the map options. Default options for a map are read from a special entry in the map whose key is the string '`/defaults`'. When default options are given they are prepended to any options specified in the mount-map locations as explained in. See Section 3.3.1 [Map Defaults], page SMM:13-12, for more details.

The *options* are any combination of those listed below.

Once the command line has been parsed, the automount points are mounted. The mount points are created if they do not already exist, in which case they will be removed when *Amd* exits. Finally, *Amd* disassociates itself from its controlling terminal and forks into the background.

Note: Even if *Amd* has been built with '`-DDEBUG`' it will still background itself and disassociate itself from the controlling terminal. To use a debugger it is necessary to specify '`-D nodaemon`' on the command line.

4.1 -a *directory*

Specifies the default mount directory. This option changes the variable `${autodir}` which otherwise defaults to '`/a`'. For example, some sites prefer '`/amd`'.

```
amd -a /amd ...
```

4.2 -c *cache-interval*

Selects the period, in seconds, for which a name is cached by *Amd*. If no reference is made to the volume in this period, *Amd* discards the volume name to filesystem mapping.

Once the last reference to a filesystem has been removed, *Amd* attempts to unmount the filesystem. If the unmount fails the interval is extended by a further period as specified by the '`-w`' command line option or by the '`utimeout`' mount option.

The default *cache-interval* is 300 seconds (five minutes).

4.3 -d *domain*

Specifies the host's domain. This sets the internal variable `${domain}` and affects the `${hostd}` variable.

If this option is not specified and the hostname already contains the local domain then that is used, otherwise the default value of `${domain}` is '`unknown.domain`'.

For example, if the local domain was '`doc.ic.ac.uk`', *Amd* could be started as follows:

```
amd -d doc.ic.ac.uk ...
```

4.4 -k *kernel-architecture*

Specifies the kernel architecture of the system. This is usually the output of '`arch -k`' and its only effect is to set the variable `${karch}`. If this option is not given, `${karch}` has the same value as `${arch}`.

This would be used as follows:

```
amd -k `arch -k` ...
```

13

4.5 `-l` *log-option*

Selects the form of logging to be made. Two special *log-options* are recognised.

1. If *log-option* is the string '`syslog`', *Amd* will use the **syslog**(3) mechanism.
2. If *log-option* is the string '`/dev/stderr`', *Amd* will use standard error, which is also the default target for log messages. To implement this, *Amd* simulates the effect of the '`/dev/fd`' driver.

Any other string is taken as a filename to use for logging. Log messages are appended to the file if it already exists, otherwise a new file is created. The file is opened once and then held open, rather than being re-opened for each message.

If the '`syslog`' option is specified but the system does not support syslog or if the named file cannot be opened or created, *Amd* will use standard error. Error messages generated before *Amd* has finished parsing the command line are printed on standard error.

Using '`syslog`' is usually best, in which case *Amd* would be started as follows:

```
amd -l syslog ...
```

4.6 `-n`

Normalises the remote hostname before using it. Normalisation is done by replacing the value of `${rhost}` with the primary name returned by a hostname lookup.

This option should be used if several names are used to refer to a single host in a mount map.

4.7 `-p`

Causes *Amd*'s process id to be printed on standard output. This can be redirected to a suitable file for use with kill:

```
amd -p > /var/run/amd.pid ...
```

This option only has an affect if *Amd* is running in daemon mode. If *Amd* is started with the `-D nodaemon` debug flag, this option is ignored.

13

4.8 `-r`

Tells *Amd* to restart existing mounts (see Section 5.14 [Inheritance Filesystem], page SMM:13-26).

4.9 `-t` *timeout.retransmit*

Specifies the RPC *timeout* and *retransmit* intervals used by the kernel to communicate to *Amd*. These are used to set the '`timeo`' and '`retrans`' mount options.

Amd relies on the kernel RPC retransmit mechanism to trigger mount retries. The value of this parameter changes the retry interval. Too long an interval gives poor interactive response, too short an interval causes excessive retries.

4.10 -v

Print version information on standard error and then exit. The output is of the form:

```
amd 5.2.1.11 of 91/03/17 18:04:05 5.3Alpha11 #0: Sun Mar 17 18:07:28 GMT 1991
Built by pendry@vangogh.Berkeley.EDU for a hp300 running bsd44 (big-endian).
Map support for: root, passwd, union, file, error.
FS: ufs, nfs, nfsx, host, link, program, union, auto, direct, toplvl, error.
Primary network is 128.32.130.0.
```

The information includes the version number, release date and name of the release. The architecture (see Section 2.2 [Supported Machine Architectures], page SMM:13-7), operating system (see Section 2.1 [Supported Operating Systems], page SMM:13-6) and byte ordering are also printed as they appear in the **${os}**, **${arch}** and **${byte}** variables.

4.11 -w *wait-timeout*

Selects the interval in seconds between unmount attempts after the initial time-to-live has expired.

This defaults to 120 seconds (two minutes).

4.12 -x *opts*

Specifies the type and verbosity of log messages. *opts* is a comma separated list selected from the following options:

`fatal`	Fatal errors
`error`	Non-fatal errors
`user`	Non-fatal user errors
`warn`	Recoverable errors
`warning`	Alias for `warn`
`info`	Information messages
`map`	Mount map usage
`stats`	Additional statistics
`all`	All of the above

Initially a set of default logging flags is enabled. This is as if '**-x all,nomap,nostats**' had been selected. The command line is parsed and logging is controlled by the "-x" option. The very first set of logging flags is saved and can not be subsequently disabled using *Amq*. This default set of options is useful for general production use.

The '**info**' messages include details of what is mounted and unmounted and when filesystems have timed out. If you want to have the default set of messages without the '**info**' messages then you simply need '**-x noinfo**'. The messages given by '**user**' relate to errors in the mount maps, so these are useful when new maps are installed. The following table lists the syslog priorites used for each of the message types.

`fatal`	LOG_CRIT
`error`	LOG_ERR

13

`user`	LOG_WARNING
`warning`	LOG_WARNING
`info`	LOG_INFO
`debug`	LOG_DEBUG
`map`	LOG_DEBUG
`stats`	LOG_INFO

The options can be prefixed by the string '`no`' to indicate that this option should be turned off. For example, to obtain all but '`info`' messages the option '`-x all,noinfo`' would be used.

If *Amd* was built with debugging enabled the **debug** option is automatically enabled regardless of the command line options.

4.13 -y *NIS-domain*

Selects an alternate NIS domain. This is useful for debugging and cross-domain shared mounting. If this flag is specified, *Amd* immediately attempts to bind to a server for this domain.

4.14 -C *cluster-name*

Specifies the name of the cluster of which the local machine is a member. The only effect is to set the variable `${cluster}`. The *cluster-name* is will usually obtained by running another command which uses a database to map the local hostname into a cluster name. `${cluster}` can then be used as a selector to restrict mounting of replicated data. If this option is not given, `${cluster}` has the same value as `${domain}`. This would be used as follows:

```
amd -C `clustername` ...
```

4.15 -D *opts*

13

Controls the verbosity and coverage of the debugging trace; *opts* is a comma separated list of debugging options. The "-D" option is only available if *Amd* was compiled with '`-DDEBUG`'. The memory debugging facilities are only available if *Amd* was compiled with '`-DDEBUG_MEM`' (in addition to '`-DDEBUG`').

The most common options to use are '`-D trace`' and '`-D test`' (which turns on all the useful debug options). See the program source for a more detailed explanation of the available options.

5 Filesystem Types

To mount a volume, *Amd* must be told the type of filesystem to be used. Each filesystem type typically requires additional information such as the fileserver name for NFS.

From the point of view of *Amd*, a *filesystem* is anything that can resolve an incoming name lookup. An important feature is support for multiple filesystem types. Some of these filesystems are implemented in the local kernel and some on remote fileservers, whilst the others are implemented internally by *Amd*.

The two common filesystem types are UFS and NFS. Four other user accessible filesystems ('link', 'program', 'auto' and 'direct') are also implemented internally by *Amd* and these are described below. There are two additional filesystem types internal to *Amd* which are not directly accessible to the user ('inherit' and 'error'). Their use is described since they may still have an effect visible to the user.

5.1 Network Filesystem ('type:=nfs')

The *nfs* filesystem type provides access to Sun's NFS.

The following options must be specified:

rhost the remote fileserver. This must be an entry in the hosts database. IP addresses are not accepted. The default value is taken from the local host name (**${host}**) if no other value is specified.

rfs the remote filesystem. If no value is specified for this option, an internal default of **${path}** is used.

NFS mounts require a two stage process. First, the *file handle* of the remote file system must be obtained from the server. Then a mount system call must be done on the local system. *Amd* keeps a cache of file handles for remote file systems. The cache entries have a lifetime of a few minutes.

If a required file handle is not in the cache, *Amd* sends a request to the remote server to obtain it. *Amd does not* wait for a response; it notes that one of the locations needs retrying, but continues with any remaining locations. When the file handle becomes available, and assuming none of the other locations was successfully mounted, *Amd* will retry the mount. This mechanism allows several NFS filesystems to be mounted in parallel. The first one which responds with a valid file handle will be used.

An NFS entry might be:

```
jsp  host!=charm;type:=nfs;rhost:=charm;rfs:=/home/charm;sublink:=jsp
```

The mount system call and any unmount attempts are always done in a new task to avoid the possibilty of blocking *Amd*.

5.2 Network Host Filesystem ('type:=host')

13

The *host* filesystem allows access to the entire export tree of an NFS server. The implementation is layered above the 'nfs' implementation so keep-alives work in the same way. The only option which needs to specified is 'rhost' which is the name of the fileserver to mount.

The 'host' filesystem type works by querying the mount daemon on the given fileserver to obtain its export list. *Amd* then obtains filehandles for each of the exported filesystems. Any errors at this stage cause that particular filesystem to be ignored. Finally each filesystem is mounted. Again, errors are logged but ignored. One common reason for mounts to fail is that the mount point does not exist. Although *Amd* attempts to automatically create the mount point, it may be on a remote filesystem to which *Amd* does not have write permission.

When an attempt to unmount a 'host' filesystem mount fails, *Amd* remounts any filesystems which had succesfully been unmounted. To do this *Amd* queries the mount daemon again and obtains a fresh copy of the export list. *Amd* then tries to mount any exported filesystems which are not currently mounted.

Sun's automounter provides a special '`-hosts`' map. To achieve the same effect with *Amd* requires two steps. First a mount map must be created as follows:

```
/defaults  type:=host;fs:=${autodir}/${rhost}/root;rhost:=${key}
*          opts:=rw,nosuid,grpid
```

and then start *Amd* with the following command

```
amd /n net.map
```

where '`net.map`' is the name of map described above. Note that the value of `${fs}` is overridden in the map. This is done to avoid a clash between the mount tree and any other filesystem already mounted from the same fileserver.

If different mount options are needed for different hosts then additional entries can be added to the map, for example

```
host2        opts:=ro,nosuid,soft
```

would soft mount '`host2`' read-only.

5.3 Network Filesystem Group ('`type:=nfsx`')

The *nfsx* filesystem allows a group of filesystems to be mounted from a single NFS server. The implementation is layered above the '`nfs`' implementation so keep-alives work in the same way.

The options are the same as for the '`nfs`' filesystem with one difference.

The following options must be specified:

`rhost` the remote fileserver. This must be an entry in the hosts database. IP addresses are not accepted. The default value is taken from the local host name (`${host}`) if no other value is specified.

`rfs` as a list of filesystems to mount. The list is in the form of a comma separated strings.

For example:

```
pub       type:=nfsx;rhost:=gould;\
rfs:=/public,/,graphics,usenet;fs:=${autodir}/${rhost}/root
```

13

The first string defines the root of the tree, and is applied as a prefix to the remaining members of the list which define the individual filesystems. The first string is *not* used as a filesystem name. A parallel operation is used to determine the local mount points to ensure a consistent layout of a tree of mounts.

Here, the *three* filesystems, '`/public`', '`/public/graphics`' and '`/public/usenet`', would be mounted.

A local mount point, `${fs}`, *must* be specified. The default local mount point will not work correctly in the general case. A suggestion is to use '`fs:=${autodir}/${rhost}/root`'.

5.4 Unix Filesystem ('`type:=ufs`')

The *ufs* filesystem type provides access to the system's standard disk filesystem—usually a derivative of the Berkeley Fast Filesystem.

The following option must be specified:

`dev` the block special device to be mounted.

A UFS entry might be:

```
jsp   host==charm;type:=ufs;dev:=/dev/xd0g;sublink:=jsp
```

5.5 Program Filesystem ('type:=program')

The *program* filesystem type allows a program to be run whenever a mount or unmount is required. This allows easy addition of support for other filesystem types, such as MIT's Remote Virtual Disk (RVD) which has a programmatic interface via the commands '`rvdmount`' and '`rvdunmount`'.

The following options must be specified:

`mount` the program which will perform the mount.

`unmount` the program which will perform the unmount.

The exit code from these two programs is interpreted as a Unix error code. As usual, exit code zero indicates success. To execute the program *Amd* splits the string on whitespace to create an array of substrings. Single quotes `''` can be used to quote whitespace if that is required in an argument. There is no way to escape or change the quote character.

To run the program '`rvdmount`' with a host name and filesystem as arguments would be specified by '`mount:="/etc/rvdmount rvdmount fserver ${path}"`'.

The first element in the array is taken as the pathname of the program to execute. The other members of the array form the argument vector to be passed to the program, *including argument zero.* This means that the split string must have at least two elements. The program is directly executed by *Amd*, not via a shell. This means that scripts must begin with a `#!` interpreter specification.

If a filesystem type is to be heavily used, it may be worthwhile adding a new filesystem type into *Amd*, but for most uses the program filesystem should suffice.

When the program is run, standard input and standard error are inherited from the current values used by *Amd*. Standard output is a duplicate of standard error. The value specified with the "-l" command line option has no effect on standard error.

5.6 Symbolic Link Filesystem ('type:=link')

Each filesystem type creates a symbolic link to point from the volume name to the physical mount point. The '`link`' filesystem does the same without any other side effects. This allows any part of the machines name space to be accessed via *Amd*.

One common use for the symlink filesystem is '`/homes`' which can be made to contain an entry for each user which points to their (auto-mounted) home directory. Although this may seem rather expensive, it provides a great deal of administrative flexibility.

The following option must be defined:

`fs` The value of *fs* option specifies the destination of the link, as modified by the *sublink* option. If *sublink* is non-null, it is appended to `${fs}/` and the resulting string is used as the target.

The '`link`' filesystem can be though of as identical to the '`ufs`' filesystem but without actually mounting anything.

An example entry might be:

```
jsp    host==charm;type:=link;fs:=/home/charm;sublink:=jsp
```

which would return a symbolic link pointing to '`/home/charm/jsp`'.

5.7 Symbolic Link Filesystem II ('`type:=link`')

The '`linkx`' filesystem type is identical to '`link`' with the exception that the target of the link must exist. Existence is checked with the '`lstat`' system call.

The '`linkx`' filesystem type is particularly useful for wildcard map entries. In this case, a list of possible targets can be give and *Amd* will choose the first one which exists on the local machine.

5.8 Automount Filesystem ('`type:=auto`')

The *auto* filesystem type creates a new automount point below an existing automount point. Top-level automount points appear as system mount points. An automount mount point can also appear as a sub-directory of an existing automount point. This allows some additional structure to be added, for example to mimic the mount tree of another machine.

The following options may be specified:

`cache` specifies whether the data in this mount-map should be cached. The default value is '`none`', in which case no caching is done in order to conserve memory. However, better performance and reliability can be obtained by caching some or all of a mount-map.

If the cache option specifies '`all`', the entire map is enumerated when the mount point is created.

If the cache option specifies '`inc`', caching is done incrementally as and when data is required. Some map types do not support cache mode '`all`', in which case '`inc`' is used whenever '`all`' is requested.

Caching can be entirely disabled by using cache mode '`none`'.

If the cache option specifies '`regexp`' then the entire map will be enumerated and each key will be treated as an egrep-style regular expression. The order in which a cached map is searched does not correspond to the ordering in the source map so the regular expressions should be mutually exclusive to avoid confusion.

Each mount map type has a default cache type, usually '`inc`', which can be selected by specifying '`mapdefault`'.

The cache mode for a mount map can only be selected on the command line. Starting *Amd* with the command:

```
amd /homes hesiod.homes -cache:=inc
```

will cause '`/homes`' to be automounted using the *Hesiod* name server with local incremental caching of all succesfully resolved names.

13

All cached data is forgotten whenever *Amd* receives a '`SIGHUP`' signal and, if cache '`all`' mode was selected, the cache will be reloaded. This can be used to inform *Amd* that a map has been updated. In addition, whenever a cache lookup fails and *Amd* needs to examine a map, the map's modify time is examined. If the cache is out of date with respect to the map then it is flushed as if a '`SIGHUP`' had been received.

An additional option ('`sync`') may be specified to force *Amd* to check the map's modify time whenever a cached entry is being used. For example, an incremental, synchronised cache would be created by the following command:

```
amd /homes hesiod.homes -cache:=inc,sync
```

`fs` specifies the name of the mount map to use for the new mount point.

Arguably this should have been specified with the `${rfs}` option but we are now stuck with it due to historical accident.

`pref` alters the name that is looked up in the mount map. If `${pref}`, the *prefix*, is non-null then it is prepended to the name requested by the kernel *before* the map is searched.

The server '`dylan.doc.ic.ac.uk`' has two user disks: '`/dev/dsk/2s0`' and '`/dev/dsk/5s0`'. These are accessed as '`/home/dylan/dk2`' and '`/home/dylan/dk5`' respectively. Since '`/home`' is already an automount point, this naming is achieved with the following map entries:

```
dylan        type:=auto;fs:=${map};pref:=${key}/
dylan/dk2    type:=ufs;dev:=/dev/dsk/2s0
dylan/dk5    type:=ufs;dev:=/dev/dsk/5s0
```

5.9 Direct Automount Filesystem ('`type:=direct`')

The *direct* filesystem is almost identical to the automount filesystem. Instead of appearing to be a directory of mount points, it appears as a symbolic link to a mounted filesystem. The mount is done at the time the link is accessed. See Section 5.8 [Automount Filesystem], page SMM:13-24 for a list of required options.

Direct automount points are created by specifying the '`direct`' filesystem type on the command line:

```
amd ... /usr/man auto.direct -type:=direct
```

where '`auto.direct`' would contain an entry such as:

```
usr/man     -type:=nfs;rfs:=/usr/man \
            rhost:=man-server1  rhost:=man-server2
```

In this example, '`man-server1`' and '`man-server2`' are file servers which export copies of the manual pages. Note that the key which is looked up is the name of the automount point without the leading '`/`'.

5.10 Union Filesystem ('`type:=union`')

The *union* filesystem type allows the contents of several directories to be merged and made visible in a single directory. This can be used to overcome one of the major limitations of the Unix mount mechanism which only allows complete directories to be mounted.

For example, supposing '`/tmp`' and '`/var/tmp`' were to be merged into a new directory called '`/mtmp`', with files in '`/var/tmp`' taking precedence. The following command could be used to achieve this effect:

```
amd ... /mtmp union:/tmp:/var/tmp -type:=union
```

Currently, the unioned directories must *not* be automounted. That would cause a deadlock. This seriously limits the current usefulness of this filesystem type and the problem will be addressed in a future release of *Amd*.

Files created in the union directory are actually created in the last named directory. This is done by creating a wildcard entry which points to the correct directory. The wildcard entry is visible if the union directory is listed, so allowing you to see which directory has priority.

The files visible in the union directory are computed at the time *Amd* is started, and are not kept uptodate with respect to the underlying directories. Similarly, if a link is removed, for example with the '`rm`' command, it will be lost forever.

5.11 Error Filesystem ('`type:=error`')

The *error* filesystem type is used internally as a catch-all in the case where none of the other filesystems was selected, or some other error occurred. Lookups and mounts always fail with "No such file or directory". All other operations trivially succeed.

The error filesystem is not directly accessible.

5.12 Top-level Filesystem ('`type:=toplvl`')

The *toplvl* filesystems is derived from the '`auto`' filesystem and is used to mount the top-level automount nodes. Requests of this type are automatically generated from the command line arguments and can also be passed in by using the "-M" option of the *Amq* command.

13

5.13 Root Filesystem

The *root* ('`type:=root`') filesystem type acts as an internal placeholder onto which *Amd* can pin '`toplvl`' mounts. Only one node of this type need ever exist and one is created automatically during startup. The effect of creating a second root node is undefined.

5.14 Inheritance Filesystem

The *inheritance* ('`type:=inherit`') filesystem is not directly accessible. Instead, internal mount nodes of this type are automatically generated when *Amd* is started with the "-r" option. At this time the system mount table is scanned to locate any filesystems which are already mounted. If any reference to these filesystems is made through *Amd* then instead of attempting to mount it, *Amd* simulates the mount and *inherits* the filesystem. This allows a new version of *Amd* to be installed on a live system simply by killing the old daemon with `SIGTERM` and starting the new one.

This filesystem type is not generally visible externally, but it is possible that the output from '`amq -m`' may list '`inherit`' as the filesystem type. This happens when an inherit operation cannot be completed for some reason, usually because a fileserver is down.

6 Run-time Administration

6.1 Starting *Amd*

Amd is best started from '/etc/rc.local':

```
if [ -f /etc/amd.start ]; then
        sh /etc/amd.start; (echo -n ' amd')       >/dev/console
fi
```

The shell script, 'amd.start', contains:

```
#!/bin/sh -
PATH=/etc:/bin:/usr/bin:/usr/ucb:$PATH export PATH

#
# Either name of logfile or "syslog"
#
LOGFILE=syslog
#LOGFILE=/var/log/amd

#
# Figure out whether domain name is in host name
# If the hostname is just the machine name then
# pass in the name of the local domain so that the
# hostnames in the map are domain stripped correctly.
#
case `hostname` in
*.*) dmn= ;;
*) dmn='-d doc.ic.ac.uk'
esac

#
# Zap earlier log file
#
case "$LOGFILE" in
*/*)
        mv "$LOGFILE" "$LOGFILE"-
        > "$LOGFILE"
        ;;
syslog)
        : nothing
        ;;
esac

cd /usr/sbin
#
# -r            restart
# -d dmn        local domain
# -w wait       wait between unmount attempts
```

13

```
# -l log        logfile or "syslog"
#
eval ./amd -r $dmn -w 240 -l "$LOGFILE" \
        /homes amd.homes -cache:=inc \
        /home amd.home -cache:=inc \
        /vol amd.vol -cache:=inc \
        /n amd.net -cache:=inc
```

If the list of automount points and maps is contained in a file or NIS map it is easily incorporated onto the command line:

```
...
eval ./amd -r $dmn -w 240 -l "$LOGFILE" `ypcat -k auto.master`
```

6.2 Stopping *Amd*

Amd stops in response to two signals.

'`SIGTERM`' causes the top-level automount points to be unmounted and then *Amd* to exit. Any automounted filesystems are left mounted. They can be recovered by restarting *Amd* with the "-r" command line option.

'`SIGINT`' causes *Amd* to attempt to unmount any filesystems which it has automounted, in addition to the actions of '`SIGTERM`'. This signal is primarly used for debugging.

Actions taken for other signals are undefined.

6.3 Controlling *Amd*

It is sometimes desirable or necessary to exercise external control over some of *Amd*'s internal state. To support this requirement, *Amd* implements an RPC interface which is used by the *Amq* program. A variety of information is available.

13

Amq generally applies an operation, specified by a single letter option, to a list of mount points. The default operation is to obtain statistics about each mount point. This is similar to the output shown above but includes information about the number and type of accesses to each mount point.

6.3.1 *Amq* default information

With no arguments, *Amq* obtains a brief list of all existing mounts created by *Amd*. This is different from the list displayed by **df**(1) since the latter only includes system mount points.

The output from this option includes the following information:

- the automount point,
- the filesystem type,
- the mount map or mount information,
- the internal, or system mount point.

For example:

```
/            root    "root"                       sky:(pid75)
/homes       toplvl  /usr/local/etc/amd.homes     /homes
/home        toplvl  /usr/local/etc/amd.home      /home
/homes/jsp   nfs     charm:/home/charm            /a/charm/home/charm/jsp
/homes/phjk  nfs     toytown:/home/toytown        /a/toytown/home/toytown/ai/phjk
```

If an argument is given then statistics for that volume name will be output. For example:

```
What            Uid   Getattr Lookup RdDir    RdLnk    Statfs Mounted@
/homes          0     1196    512    22       0        30     90/09/14 12:32:55
/homes/jsp      0     0       0      0        1180     0      90/10/13 12:56:58
```

`What` the volume name.

`Uid` ignored.

`Getattr` the count of NFS *getattr* requests on this node. This should only be non-zero for directory nodes.

`Lookup` the count of NFS *lookup* requests on this node. This should only be non-zero for directory nodes.

`RdDir` the count of NFS *readdir* requests on this node. This should only be non-zero for directory nodes.

`RdLnk` the count of NFS *readlink* requests on this node. This should be zero for directory nodes.

`Statfs` the could of NFS *statfs* requests on this node. This should only be non-zero for top-level automount points.

`Mounted@` the date and time the volume name was first referenced.

6.3.2 *Amq* -f option

The "-f" option causes *Amd* to flush the internal mount map cache. This is useful for Hesiod maps since *Amd* will not automatically notice when they have been updated. The map cache can also be synchronised with the map source by using the '`sync`' option (see Section 5.8 [Automount Filesystem], page SMM:13-24).

13

6.3.3 *Amq* -h option

By default the local host is used. In an HP-UX cluster the root server is used since that is the only place in the cluster where *Amd* will be running. To query *Amd* on another host the "-h" option should be used.

6.3.4 *Amq* -m option

The "-m" option displays similar information about mounted filesystems, rather than automount points. The output includes the following information:

- the mount information,
- the mount point,
- the filesystem type,
- the number of references to this filesystem,

- the server hostname,
- the state of the file server,
- any error which has occured.

For example:

```
"root"           truth:(pid602)      root   1 localhost is up
hesiod.home      /home               toplvl 1 localhost is up
hesiod.vol       /vol                toplvl 1 localhost is up
hesiod.homes     /homes              toplvl 1 localhost is up
amy:/home/amy    /a/amy/home/amy     nfs    5 amy is up
swan:/home/swan  /a/swan/home/swan   nfs    0 swan is up (Permission denied)
ex:/home/ex      /a/ex/home/ex       nfs    0 ex is down
```

When the reference count is zero the filesystem is not mounted but the mount point and server information is still being maintained by *Amd*.

6.3.5 *Amq* -M option

The "-M" option passes a new map entry to *Amd* and waits for it to be evaluated, possibly causing a mount. For example, the following command would cause '**/home/toytown**' on host '`toytown`' to be mounted locally on '`/mnt/toytown`'.

```
amq -M '/mnt/toytown type:=nfs;rfs:=/home/toytown;rhost:=toytown;fs:=${key}'
```

Amd applies some simple security checks before allowing this operation. The check tests whether the incoming request is from a privileged UDP port on the local machine. "Permission denied" is returned if the check fails.

A future release of *Amd* will include code to allow the **mount**(8) command to mount automount points:

```
mount -t amd /vol hesiod.vol
```

This will then allow *Amd* to be controlled from the standard system filesystem mount list.

6.3.6 *Amq* -s option

The "-s" option displays global statistics. If any other options are specified or any filesystems named then this option is ignored. For example:

```
requests  stale     mount     mount     unmount
deferred  fhandles  ok        failed    failed
1054      1         487       290       7017
```

'`Deferred requests`'
: are those for which an immediate reply could not be constructed. For example, this would happen if a background mount was required.

'`Stale filehandles`'
: counts the number of times the kernel passes a stale filehandle to *Amd*. Large numbers indicate problems.

'`Mount ok`' counts the number of automounts which were successful.

'Mount failed'
: counts the number of automounts which failed.

'Unmount failed'
: counts the number of times a filesystem could not be unmounted. Very large numbers here indicate that the time between unmount attempts should be increased.

6.3.7 *Amq* -u option

The "-u" option causes the time-to-live interval of the named mount points to be expired, thus causing an unmount attempt. This is the only safe way to unmount an automounted filesystem. It is not possible to unmount a filesystem which has been mounted with the '`nounmount`' flag.

6.3.8 *Amq* -v option

The "-v" option displays the version of *Amd* in a similar way to *Amd*'s "-v" option.

6.3.9 Other *Amq* options

Three other operations are implemented. These modify the state of *Amd* as a whole, rather than any particular filesystem. The "-l", "-x" and "-D" options have exactly the same effect as *Amd*'s corresponding command line options. The "-l" option is rejected by *Amd* in the current version for obvious security reasons. When *Amd* receives a "-x"flag it limits the log options being modified to those which were not enabled at startup. This prevents a user turning *off* any logging option which was specified at startup, though any which have been turned off since then can still be turned off. The "-D" option has a similar behaviour.

7 FSinfo

7.1 *FSinfo* overview

FSinfo is a filesystem management tool. It has been designed to work with *Amd* to help system administrators keep track of the ever increasing filesystem namespace under their control.

The purpose of *FSinfo* is to generate all the important standard filesystem data files from a single set of input data. Starting with a single data source guarantees that all the generated files are self-consistent. One of the possible output data formats is a set of *Amd* maps which can be used amongst the set of hosts described in the input data.

FSinfo implements a declarative language. This language is specifically designed for describing filesystem namespace and physical layouts. The basic declaration defines a mounted filesystem including its device name, mount point, and all the volumes and access permissions. *FSinfo* reads this information and builds an internal map of the entire network of hosts. Using this map, many different data formats can be produced including '`/etc/fstab`', '`/etc/exports`', *Amd* mount maps and '`/etc/bootparams`'.

7.2 Using *FSinfo*

The basic strategy when using *FSinfo* is to gather all the information about all disks on all machines into one set of declarations. For each machine being managed, the following data is required:

- Hostname
- List of all filesystems and, optionally, their mount points.
- Names of volumes stored on each filesystem.
- NFS export information for each volume.
- The list of static filesystem mounts.

The following information can also be entered into the same configuration files so that all data can be kept in one place.

- List of network interfaces
- IP address of each interface
- Hardware address of each interface
- Dumpset to which each filesystem belongs
- and more ...

To generate *Amd* mount maps, the automount tree must also be defined (see Section 7.8 [FSinfo automount definitions], page SMM:13-39). This will have been designed at the time the volume names were allocated. Some volume names will not be automounted, so *FSinfo* needs an explicit list of which volumes should be automounted.

Hostnames are required at several places in the *FSinfo* language. It is important to stick to either fully qualified names or unqualified names. Using a mixture of the two will inevitably result in confusion.

Sometimes volumes need to be referenced which are not defined in the set of hosts being managed with *FSinfo*. The required action is to add a dummy set of definitions for the host and volume names required. Since the files generated for those particular hosts will not be used on them, the exact values used is not critical.

7.3 *FSinfo* grammar

FSinfo has a relatively simple grammar. Distinct syntactic constructs exist for each of the different types of data, though they share a common flavour. Several conventions are used in the grammar fragments below.

The notation, *list(***xxx***)*, indicates a list of zero or more **xxx**'s. The notation, *opt(***xxx***)*, indicates zero or one **xxx**. Items in double quotes, *eg* **"host"**, represent input tokens. Items in angle brackets, *eg* *<hostname>*, represent strings in the input. Strings need not be in double quotes, except to differentiate them from reserved words. Quoted strings may include the usual set of C "\" escape sequences with one exception: a backslash-newline-whitespace sequence is squashed into a single space character. To defeat this feature, put a further backslash at the start of the second line.

At the outermost level of the grammar, the input consists of a sequence of host and automount declarations. These declarations are all parsed before they are analyzed. This means they can appear in any order and cyclic host references are possible.

```
fsinfo      : list(fsinfo_attr) ;

fsinfo_attr : host | automount ;
```

7.4 *FSinfo* host definitions

A host declaration consists of three parts: a set of machine attribute data, a list of filesystems physically attached to the machine, and a list of additional statically mounted filesystems.

```
host        : "host" host_data list(filesystem) list(mount) ;
```

Each host must be declared in this way exactly once. Such things as the hardware address, the architecture and operating system types and the cluster name are all specified within the *host data*.

All the disks the machine has should then be described in the *list of filesystems*. When describing disks, you can specify what *volname* the disk/partition should have and all such entries are built up into a dictionary which can then be used for building the automounter maps.

The *list of mounts* specifies all the filesystems that should be statically mounted on the machine.

7.5 *FSinfo* host attributes

The host data, *host_data*, always includes the *hostname*. In addition, several other host attributes can be given.

```
host_data    : <hostname>
             | "{" list(host_attrs) "}" <hostname>
             ;

host_attrs   : host_attr "=" <string>
             | netif
             ;

host_attr    : "config"
             | "arch"
             | "os"
             | "cluster"
             ;
```


The *hostname* is, typically, the fully qualified hostname of the machine.

Examples:

```
host dylan.doc.ic.ac.uk

host {
    os = hpux
    arch = hp300
} dougal.doc.ic.ac.uk
```

The options that can be given as host attributes are shown below.

7.5.1 netif Option

This defines the set of network interfaces configured on the machine. The interface attributes collected by *FSinfo* are the IP address, subnet mask and hardware address. Multiple interfaces may be defined for hosts with several interfaces by an entry for each interface. The values given are sanity checked, but are currently unused for anything else.

```
netif       : "netif" <string> "{" list(netif_attrs) "}" ;

netif_attrs : netif_attr "=" <string> ;

netif_attr  : "inaddr" | "netmask" | "hwaddr" ;
```

Examples:

```
netif ie0 {
        inaddr  = 129.31.81.37
        netmask = 0xfffffe00
        hwaddr  = "08:00:20:01:a6:a5"
}

netif ec0 { }
```

7.5.2 config Option

This option allows you to specify configuration variables for the startup scripts ('`rc`' scripts). A simple string should immediately follow the keyword.

Example:

```
config "NFS_SERVER=true"
config "ZEPHYR=true"
```

This option is currently unsupported.

7.5.3 arch Option

This defines the architecture of the machine. For example:

```
arch = hp300
```

This is intended to be of use when building architecture specific mountmaps, however, the option is currently unsupported.

7.5.4 os Option

This defines the operating system type of the host. For example:

```
os = hpux
```

This information is used when creating the '`fstab`' files, for example in choosing which format to use for the '`fstab`' entries within the file.

7.5.5 cluster Option

This is used for specifying in which cluster the machine belongs. For example:

```
cluster = "theory"
```

The cluster is intended to be used when generating the automount maps, although it is currently unsupported.

7.6 *FSinfo* filesystems

The list of physically attached filesystems follows the machine attributes. These should define all the filesystems available from this machine, whether exported or not. In addition to the device name, filesystems have several attributes, such as filesystem type, mount options, and '**fsck**' pass number which are needed to generate '**fstab**' entries.

```
filesystem  : "fs" <device> "{" list(fs_data) "}" ;

fs_data     : fs_data_attr "=" <string>
            | mount
            ;

fs_data_attr
            : "fstype" | "opts" | "passno"
            | "freq" | "dumpset" | "log"
            ;
```

Here, *<device>* is the device name of the disk (for example, '**/dev/dsk/2s0**'). The device name is used for building the mount maps and for the '**fstab**' file. The attributes that can be specified are shown in the following section.

The *FSinfo* configuration file for **dylan.doc.ic.ac.uk** is listed below.

```
host dylan.doc.ic.ac.uk

fs /dev/dsk/0s0 {
fstype = swap
}

fs /dev/dsk/0s0 {
fstype = hfs
opts = rw,noquota,grpid
passno = 0;
freq = 1;
mount / { }
}

fs /dev/dsk/1s0 {
fstype = hfs
opts = defaults
passno = 1;
freq = 1;
```

```
mount /usr {
local {
exportfs "dougal eden dylan zebedee brian"
volname /nfs/hp300/local
}
}
}

fs /dev/dsk/2s0 {
fstype = hfs
opts = defaults
passno = 1;
freq = 1;
mount default {
exportfs "toytown_clients hangers_on"
volname /home/dylan/dk2
}
}

fs /dev/dsk/3s0 {
fstype = hfs
opts = defaults
passno = 1;
freq = 1;
mount default {
exportfs "toytown_clients hangers_on"
volname /home/dylan/dk3
}
}

fs /dev/dsk/5s0 {
fstype = hfs
opts = defaults
passno = 1;
freq = 1;
mount default {
exportfs "toytown_clients hangers_on"
volname /home/dylan/dk5
}
}
```


7.6.1 fstype Option

This specifies the type of filesystem being declared and will be placed into the '**fstab**' file as is. The value of this option will be handed to **mount** as the filesystem type—it should have such values as 4.2, nfs or **swap**. The value is not examined for correctness.

There is one special case. If the filesystem type is specified as '**export**' then the filesystem information will not be added to the host's '**fstab**' information, but it will still be visible on the network. This is useful for defining hosts which contain referenced volumes but which are not under full control of *FSinfo*.

Example:

```
fstype = swap
```

7.6.2 opts Option

This defines any options that should be given to **mount**(8) in the '`fstab`' file. For example:

```
opts = rw,nosuid,grpid
```

7.6.3 passno Option

This defines the **fsck**(8) pass number in which to check the filesystem. This value will be placed into the '`fstab`' file.

Example:

```
passno = 1
```

7.6.4 freq Option

This defines the interval (in days) between dumps. The value is placed as is into the '`fstab`' file.

Example:

```
freq = 3
```

7.6.5 mount Option

This defines the mountpoint at which to place the filesystem. If the mountpoint of the filesystem is specified as `default`, then the filesystem will be mounted in the automounter's tree under its volume name and the mount will automatically be inherited by the automounter.

Following the mountpoint, namespace information for the filesystem may be described. The options that can be given here are `exportfs`, `volname` and `sel`.

The format is:

```
mount         : "mount" vol_tree ;

vol_tree      : list(vol_tree_attr) ;

vol_tree_attr
              :  <string> "{" list(vol_tree_info) vol_tree "}" ;

vol_tree_info
              : "exportfs" <export-data>
              | "volname" <volname>
              | "sel" <selector-list>
              ;
```

Example:

```
mount default {
    exportfs "dylan dougal florence zebedee"
    volname /vol/andrew
}
```

In the above example, the filesystem currently being declared will have an entry placed into the '`exports`' file allowing the filesystem to be exported to the machines `dylan`, `dougal`, `florence` and `zebedee`. The volume name by which the filesystem will be referred to remotely, is '`/vol/andrew`'. By declaring the mountpoint to be `default`, the filesystem will be mounted on the local machine in the automounter tree, where *Amd* will automatically inherit the mount as '`/vol/andrew`'.

'`exportfs`'
: a string defining which machines the filesystem may be exported to. This is copied, as is, into the '`exports`' file—no sanity checking is performed on this string.

'`volname`'
: a string which declares the remote name by which to reference the filesystem. The string is entered into a dictionary and allows you to refer to this filesystem in other places by this volume name.

'`sel`'
: a string which is placed into the automounter maps as a selector for the filesystem.

7.6.6 dumpset Option

This provides support for Imperial College's local file backup tools and is not documented further here.

7.6.7 log Option

Specifies the log device for the current filesystem. This is ignored if not required by the particular filesystem type.

7.7 *FSinfo* static mounts

13

Each host may also have a number of statically mounted filesystems. For example, the host may be a diskless workstation in which case it will have no `fs` declarations. In this case the `mount` declaration is used to determine from where its filesystems will be mounted. In addition to being added to the '`fstab`' file, this information can also be used to generate a suitable '`bootparams`' file.

```
mount           : "mount" <volname> list(localinfo) ;

localinfo       : localinfo_attr <string> ;

localinfo_attr
                : "as"
                | "from"
                | "fstype"
                | "opts"
                ;
```

The filesystem specified to be mounted will be searched for in the dictionary of volume names built when scanning the list of hosts' definitions.

The attributes have the following semantics:

'`from` *machine*'
: mount the filesystem from the machine with the hostname of *machine*.

'`as` *mountpoint*'
: mount the filesystem locally as the name given, in case this is different from the advertised volume name of the filesystem.

'`opts` *options*'
: native **mount**(8) options.

'`fstype` *type*'
: type of filesystem to be mounted.

An example:

```
mount /export/exec/hp300/local as /usr/local
```

If the mountpoint specified is either '`/`' or '`swap`', the machine will be considered to be booting off the net and this will be noted for use in generating a '`bootparams`' file for the host which owns the filesystems.

7.8 Defining an *Amd* Mount Map in *FSinfo*

The maps used by *Amd* can be constructed from *FSinfo* by defining all the automount trees. *FSinfo* takes all the definitions found and builds one map for each top level tree.

The automount tree is usually defined last. A single automount configuration will usually apply to an entire management domain. One `automount` declaration is needed for each *Amd* automount point. *FSinfo* determines whether the automount point is *direct* (see Section 5.9 [Direct Automount Filesystem], page SMM:13-25) or *indirect* (see Section 5.12 [Top-level Filesystem], page SMM:13-26). Direct automount points are distinguished by the fact that there is no underlying *automount_tree*.

```
automount      : "automount" opt(auto_opts) automount_tree ;

auto_opts      : "opts" <mount-options> ;

automount_tree
               : list(automount_attr)
               ;

automount_attr
               : <string> "=" <volname>
               | <string> "->" <symlink>
               | <string> "{" automount_tree "}"
               ;
```

If <*mount-options*> is given, then it is the string to be placed in the maps for *Amd* for the `opts` option.

A *map* is typically a tree of filesystems, for example '`home`' normally contains a tree of filesystems representing other machines in the network.

A map can either be given as a name representing an already defined volume name, or it can be a tree. A tree is represented by placing braces after the name. For example, to define a tree '/vol', the following map would be defined:

```
automount /vol { }
```

Within a tree, the only items that can appear are more maps. For example:

```
automount /vol {
    andrew { }
    X11 { }
}
```

In this case, *FSinfo* will look for volumes named '/vol/andrew' and '/vol/X11' and a map entry will be generated for each. If the volumes are defined more than once, then *FSinfo* will generate a series of alternate entries for them in the maps.

Instead of a tree, either a link (*name* -> *destination*) or a reference can be specified (*name* = *destination*). A link creates a symbolic link to the string specified, without further processing the entry. A reference will examine the destination filesystem and optimise the reference. For example, to create an entry for njw in the '/homes' map, either of the two forms can be used:

```
automount /homes {
    njw -> /home/dylan/njw
}
```

or

```
automount /homes {
    njw = /home/dylan/njw
}
```

In the first example, when '/homes/njw' is referenced from *Amd*, a link will be created leading to '/home/dylan/njw' and the automounter will be referenced a second time to resolve this filename. The map entry would be:

```
njw type:=link;fs:=/home/dylan/njw
```

In the second example, the destination directory is analysed and found to be in the filesystem '/home/dylan' which has previously been defined in the maps. Hence the map entry will look like:

```
njw rhost:=dylan;rfs:=/home/dylan;sublink:=njw
```

Creating only one symbolic link, and one access to *Amd*.

13

7.9 *FSinfo* Command Line Options

FSinfo is started from the command line by using the command:

fsinfo [*options*] files ...

The input to *FSinfo* is a single set of definitions of machines and automount maps. If multiple files are given on the command-line, then the files are concatenated together to form the input source. The files are passed individually through the C pre-processor before being parsed.

Several options define a prefix for the name of an output file. If the prefix is not specified no output of that type is produced. The suffix used will correspond either to the hostname to which a file belongs, or to the type of output if only one file is produced. Dumpsets and the '`bootparams`' file are in the latter class. To put the output into a subdirectory simply put a '`/`' at the end of the prefix, making sure that the directory has already been made before running '`fsinfo`'.

7.9.1 `-a` *autodir*

Specifies the directory name in which to place the automounter's mountpoints. This defaults to '`/a`'. Some sites have the autodir set to be '`/amd`', and this would be achieved by:

```
fsinfo -a /amd ...
```

7.9.2 `-b` *bootparams*

This specifies the prefix for the '`bootparams`' filename. If it is not given, then the file will not be generated. The '`bootparams`' file will be constructed for the destination machine and will be placed into a file named '`bootparams`' and prefixed by this string. The file generated contains a list of entries describing each diskless client that can boot from the destination machine.

As an example, to create a '`bootparams`' file in the directory '`generic`', the following would be used:

```
fsinfo -b generic/ ...
```

7.9.3 `-d` *dumpsets*

This specifies the prefix for the '`dumpsets`' file. If it is not specified, then the file will not be generated. The file will be for the destination machine and will be placed into a filename '`dumpsets`', prefixed by this string. The '`dumpsets`' file is for use by Imperial College's local backup system.

For example, to create a dumpsets file in the directory '`generic`', then you would use the following:

```
fsinfo -d generic/ ...
```


7.9.4 `-e` *exportfs*

Defines the prefix for the '`exports`' files. If it is not given, then the file will not be generated. For each machine defined in the configuration files as having disks, an '`exports`' file is constructed and given a filename determined by the name of the machine, prefixed with this string. If a machine is defined as diskless, then no '`exports`' file will be created for it. The files contain entries for directories on the machine that may be exported to clients.

Example: To create the '`exports`' files for each diskful machine and place them into the directory '`exports`':

```
fsinfo -e exports/ ...
```

7.9.5 `-f` *fstab*

This defines the prefix for the '**`fstab`**' files. The files will only be created if this prefix is defined. For each machine defined in the configuration files, a '**`fstab`**' file is created with the filename determined by prefixing this string with the name of the machine. These files contain entries for filesystems and partitions to mount at boot time.

Example, to create the files in the directory '**`fstabs`**':

```
fsinfo -f fstabs/ ...
```

7.9.6 `-h` *hostname*

Defines the hostname of the destination machine to process for. If this is not specified, it defaults to the local machine name, as returned by **gethostname**(2).

Example:

```
fsinfo -h dylan.doc.ic.ac.uk ...
```

7.9.7 `-m` *mount-maps*

Defines the prefix for the automounter files. The maps will only be produced if this prefix is defined. The mount maps suitable for the network defined by the configuration files will be placed into files with names calculated by prefixing this string to the name of each map.

For example, to create the automounter maps and place them in the directory '**`automaps`**':

```
fsinfo -m automaps/ ...
```

7.9.8 `-q`

Selects quiet mode. *FSinfo* suppress the "running commentary" and only outputs any error messages which are generated.

13

7.9.9 `-v`

Selects verbose mode. When this is activated, the program will display more messages, and display all the information discovered when performing the semantic analysis phase. Each verbose message is output to '**`stdout`**' on a line starting with a '**`#`**' character.

7.9.10 `-D` *name[=defn]*

Defines a symbol *name* for the preprocessor when reading the configuration files. Equivalent to **`#define`** directive.

7.9.11 `-I` *directory*

This option is passed into the preprocessor for the configuration files. It specifies directories in which to find include files

7.9.12 `-U` *name*

Removes any initial definition of the symbol *name*. Inverse of the `-D` option.

7.10 Errors produced by *FSinfo*

The following table documents the errors and warnings which *FSinfo* may produce.

`can't open` *filename* `for writing`
: Occurs if any errors are encountered when opening an output file.

`unknown host attribute`
: Occurs if an unrecognised keyword is used when defining a host.

`unknown filesystem attribute`
: Occurs if an unrecognised keyword is used when defining a host's filesystems.

`not allowed '/' in a directory name`
: When reading the configuration input, if there is a filesystem definition which contains a pathname with multiple directories for any part of the mountpoint element, and it is not a single absolute path, then this message will be produced by the parser.

`unknown directory attribute`
: If an unknown keyword is found while reading the definition of a hosts's filesystem mount option.

`unknown mount attribute`
: Occurs if an unrecognised keyword is found while parsing the list of static mounts.

`" expected`
: Occurs if an unescaped newline is found in a quoted string.

`unknown \ sequence`
: Occurs if an unknown escape sequence is found inside a string. Within a string, you can give the standard C escape sequences for strings, such as newlines and tab characters.

filename`: cannot open for reading`
: If a file specified on the command line as containing configuration data could not be opened.

`end of file within comment`
: A comment was unterminated before the end of one of the configuration files.

`host field "`*field-name*`" already set`
: If duplicate definitions are given for any of the fields with a host definition.

`duplicate host` *hostname*`!`
: If a host has more than one definition.

`netif field` *field-name* `already set`
: Occurs if you attempt to define an attribute of an interface more than once.

`malformed IP dotted quad:` *address*
: If the Internet address of an interface is incorrectly specified. An Internet address definition is handled to **inet_addr**(3N) to see if it can cope. If not, then this message will be displayed.

`malformed netmask:` *netmask*

If the netmask cannot be decoded as though it were a hexadecimal number, then this message will be displayed. It will typically be caused by incorrect characters in the *netmask* value.

`fs field "`*field-name*`" already set`

Occurs when multiple definitions are given for one of the attributes of a host's filesystem.

`mount tree field "`*field-name*`" already set`

Occurs when the *field-name* is defined more than once during the definition of a filesystems mountpoint.

`mount field "`*field-name*`" already set`

Occurs when a static mount has multiple definitions of the same field.

`no disk mounts on` *hostname*

If there are no static mounts, nor local disk mounts specified for a machine, this message will be displayed.

host`:`*device* `needs field "`*field-name*`"`

Occurs when a filesystem is missing a required field. *field-name* could be one of `fstype`, `opts`, `passno` or `mount`.

filesystem `has a volname but no exportfs data`

Occurs when a volume name is declared for a file system, but the string specifying what machines the filesystem can be exported to is missing.

`sub-directory` *directory* `of` *directory-tree* `starts with '/'`

Within the filesystem specification for a host, if an element *directory* of the mountpoint begins with a '`/`' and it is not the start of the tree.

host`:`*device* `has no mount point`

Occurs if the '`mount`' option is not specified for a host's filesystem.

host`:`*device* `has more than one mount point`

Occurs if the mount option for a host's filesystem specifies multiple trees at which to place the mountpoint.

`no volname given for` *host*`:`*device*

Occurs when a filesystem is defined to be mounted on '`default`', but no volume name is given for the file system, then the mountpoint cannot be determined.

host`:mount field specified for swap partition`

Occurs if a mountpoint is given for a filesystem whose type is declared to be `swap`.

`ambiguous mount:` *volume* `is a replicated filesystem`

If several filesystems are declared as having the same volume name, they will be considered replicated filesystems. To mount a replicated filesystem statically, a specific host will need to be named, to say which particular copy to try and mount, else this error will result.

`cannot determine localname since volname` *volume* `is not uniquely defined`

If a volume is replicated and an attempt is made to mount the filesystem statically without specifying a local mountpoint, *FSinfo* cannot calculate a mountpoint, as the desired pathname would be ambiguous.

volname *volume* **is unknown**

Occurs if an attempt is made to mount or reference a volume name which has not been declared during the host filesystem definitions.

volname *volume* **not exported from** *machine*

Occurs if you attempt to mount the volume *volume* from a machine which has not declared itself to have such a filesystem available.

network booting requires both root and swap areas

Occurs if a machine has mount declarations for either the root partition or the swap area, but not both. You cannot define a machine to only partially boot via the network.

unknown volname *volume* **automounted** *[* **on <name>** *]*

Occurs if *volume* is used in a definition of an automount map but the volume name has not been declared during the host filesystem definitions.

not allowed '/' in a directory name

Occurs when a pathname with multiple directory elements is specified as the name for an automounter tree. A tree should only have one name at each level.

device **has duplicate exportfs data**

Produced if the '`exportfs`' option is used multiple times within the same branch of a filesytem definition. For example, if you attempt to set the '`exportfs`' data at different levels of the mountpoint directory tree.

sub-directory of *directory-tree* **is named "default"**

'`default`' is a keyword used to specify if a mountpoint should be automatically calculated by *FSinfo*. If you attempt to specify a directory name as this, it will use the filename of '`default`' but will produce this warning.

pass number for *host*:*device* **is non-zero**

Occurs if *device* has its '`fstype`' declared to be '`swap`' or '`export`' and the **fsck**(8) pass number is set. Swap devices should not be fsck'd. See Section 7.6.1 [FSinfo filesystems fstype], page SMM:13-36

dump frequency for *host*:*device* **is non-zero**

Occurs if *device* has its '`fstype`' declared to be '`swap`' or '`export`' and the '`dump`' option is set to a value greater than zero. Swap devices should not be dumped.

8 Examples

8.1 User Filesystems

With more than one fileserver, the directories most frequently cross-mounted are those containing user home directories. A common convention used at Imperial College is to mount the user disks under `/home/`*machine*.

Typically, the '`/etc/fstab`' file contained a long list of entries such as:

machine`:/home/`*machine* `/home/`*machine* `nfs ...`

for each fileserver on the network.

There are numerous problems with this system. The mount list can become quite large and some of the machines may be down when a system is booted. When a new fileserver is installed, '`/etc/fstab`' must be updated on every machine, the mount directory created and the filesystem mounted.

In many environments most people use the same few workstations, but it is convenient to go to a colleague's machine and access your own files. When a server goes down, it can cause a process on a client machine to hang. By minimising the mounted filesystems to only include those actively being used, there is less chance that a filesystem will be mounted when a server goes down.

The following is a short extract from a map taken from a research fileserver at Imperial College.

Note the entry for '`localhost`' which is used for users such as the operator ('`opr`') who have a home directory on most machine as '`/home/localhost/opr`'.

```
/defaults       opts:=rw,intr,grpid,nosuid
charm           host!=${key};type:=nfs;rhost:=${key};rfs:=/home/${key} \
                host==${key};type:=ufs;dev:=/dev/xd0g
#
...

#
localhost       type:=link;fs:=${host}
...
#
# dylan has two user disks so have a
# top directory in which to mount them.
#
dylan           type:=auto;fs:=${map};pref:=${key}/
#
dylan/dk2       host!=dylan;type:=nfs;rhost:=dylan;rfs:=/home/${key} \
                host==dylan;type:=ufs;dev:=/dev/dsk/2s0
#
dylan/dk5       host!=dylan;type:=nfs;rhost:=dylan;rfs:=/home/${key} \
                host==dylan;type:=ufs;dev:=/dev/dsk/5s0
...
#
toytown         host!=${key};type:=nfs;rhost:=${key};rfs:=/home/${key} \
                host==${key};type:=ufs;dev:=/dev/xy1g
...
#
zebedee         host!=${key};type:=nfs;rhost:=${key};rfs:=/home/${key} \
                host==${key};type:=ufs;dev:=/dev/dsk/1s0
#
# Just for access...
#
gould           type:=auto;fs:=${map};pref:=${key}/
gould/staff     host!=gould;type:=nfs;rhost:=gould;rfs:=/home/${key}
#
gummo           host!=${key};type:=nfs;rhost:=${key};rfs:=/home/${key}
...
```

This map is shared by most of the machines listed so on those systems any of the user disks is accessible via a consistent name. *Amd* is started with the following command

```
amd /home amd.home
```

Note that when mounting a remote filesystem, the *automounted* mount point is referenced, so that the filesystem will be mounted if it is not yet (at the time the remote '`mountd`' obtains the file handle).

8.2 Home Directories

One convention for home directories is to locate them in '`/homes`' so user '`jsp`''s home directory is '`/homes/jsp`'. With more than a single fileserver it is convenient to spread user files across several machines. All that is required is a mount-map which converts login names to an automounted directory.

Such a map might be started by the command:

```
amd /homes amd.homes
```

where the map '`amd.homes`' contained the entries:

```
/defaults   type:=link   # All the entries are of type:=link
jsp         fs:=/home/charm/jsp
njw         fs:=/home/dylan/dk5/njw
...
phjk        fs:=/home/toytown/ai/phjk
sjv         fs:=/home/ganymede/sjv
```

Whenever a login name is accessed in '`/homes`' a symbolic link appears pointing to the real location of that user's home directory. In this example, '`/homes/jsp`' would appear to be a symbolic link pointing to '`/home/charm/jsp`'. Of course, '`/home`' would also be an automount point.

This system causes an extra level of symbolic links to be used. Although that turns out to be relatively inexpensive, an alternative is to directly mount the required filesystems in the '`/homes`' map. The required map is simple, but long, and its creation is best automated. The entry for '`jsp`' could be:

```
jsp    -sublink:=${key};rfs:=/home/charm \
              host==charm;type:=ufs;dev:=/dev/xd0g \
              host!=charm;type:=nfs;rhost:=charm
```


This map can become quite big if it contains a large number of entries. By combining two other features of *Amd* it can be greatly simplified.

First the UFS partitions should be mounted under the control of '`/etc/fstab`', taking care that they are mounted in the same place that *Amd* would have automounted them. In most cases this would be something like '`/a/`*host*`/home/`*host*' and '`/etc/fstab`' on host '`charm`' would have a line:

```
/dev/xy0g /a/charm/home/charm 4.2 rw,nosuid,grpid 1 5
```

The map can then be changed to:

```
/defaults    type:=nfs;sublink:=${key};opts:=rw,intr,nosuid,grpid
jsp          rhost:=charm;rfs:=/home/charm
njw          rhost:=dylan;rfs:=/home/dylan/dk5
```

```
...
phjk          rhost:=toytown;rfs:=/home/toytown;sublink:=ai/${key}
sjv           rhost:=ganymede;rfs:=/home/ganymede
```

This map operates as usual on a remote machine (*ie* `${host}` not equal to `${rhost}`). On the machine where the filesystem is stored (*ie* `${host}` equal to `${rhost}`), *Amd* will construct a local filesystem mount point which corresponds to the name of the locally mounted UFS partition. If *Amd* is started with the "-r" option then instead of attempting an NFS mount, *Amd* will simply inherit the UFS mount (see Section 5.14 [Inheritance Filesystem], page SMM:13-26). If "-r" is not used then a loopback NFS mount will be made. This type of mount is known to cause a deadlock on many systems.

8.3 Architecture Sharing

Often a filesystem will be shared by machines of different architectures. Separate trees can be maintained for the executable images for each architecture, but it may be more convenient to have a shared tree, with distinct subdirectories.

A shared tree might have the following structure on the fileserver (called '`fserver`' in the example):

```
local/tex
local/tex/fonts
local/tex/lib
local/tex/bin
local/tex/bin/sun3
local/tex/bin/sun4
local/tex/bin/hp9000
...
```

In this example, the subdirectories of '`local/tex/bin`' should be hidden when accessed via the automount point (conventionally '`/vol`'). A mount-map for '`/vol`' to achieve this would look like:

```
/defaults     sublink:=${/key};rhost:=fserver;type:=link
tex           type:=auto;fs:=${map};pref:=${key}/
tex/fonts     host!=fserver;type:=nfs;rfs:=/vol/tex \
              host==fserver;fs:=/usr/local/tex
tex/lib       host!=fserver;type:=nfs;rfs:=/vol/tex \
              host==fserver;fs:=/usr/local/tex
tex/bin       -sublink:=${/key}/${arch} host!=fserver;type:=nfs;rfs:=/vol/tex
\
              host:=fserver;fs:=/usr/local/tex
```

When '`/vol/tex/bin`' is referenced, the current machine architecture is automatically appended to the path by the `${sublink}` variable. This means that users can have '`/vol/tex/bin`' in their '`PATH`' without concern for architecture dependencies.

8.4 Wildcard names & Replicated Servers

By using the wildcard facility, *Amd* can *overlay* an existing directory with additional entries. The system files are usually mounted under '`/usr`'. If instead *Amd* is mounted on '`/usr`', additional names can be overlayed to augment or replace names in the "master" '/usr'. A map to do this would have the form:

```
local  type:=auto;fs:=local-map
share  type:=auto;fs:=share-map
*      -type:=nfs;rfs:=/export/exec/${arch};sublink:="${key}" \
        rhost:=fserv1  rhost:=fserv2  rhost:=fserv3
```

Note that the assignment to `${sublink}` is surrounded by double quotes to prevent the incoming key from causing the map to be misinterpreted. This map has the effect of directing any access to '/usr/local' or '/usr/share' to another automount point.

In this example, it is assumed that the '/usr' files are replicated on three fileservers: 'fserv1', 'fserv2' and 'fserv3'. For any references other than to 'local' and 'share' one of the servers is used and a symbolic link to `${autodir}/${rhost}/export/exec/${arch}/`*whatever* is returned once an appropriate filesystem has been mounted.

8.5 'rwho' servers

The '/usr/spool/rwho' directory is a good candidate for automounting. For efficiency reasons it is best to capture the rwho data on a small number of machines and then mount that information onto a large number of clients. The data written into the rwho files is byte order dependent so only servers with the correct byte ordering can be used by a client:

```
/defaults          type:=nfs
usr/spool/rwho     -byte==little;rfs:=/usr/spool/rwho \
                       rhost:=vaxA  rhost:=vaxB \
                   || -rfs:=/usr/spool/rwho \
                       rhost:=sun4  rhost:=hp300
```

8.6 '/vol'

'/vol' is used as a catch-all for volumes which do not have other conventional names.

Below is part of the '/vol' map for the domain 'doc.ic.ac.uk'. The 'r+d' tree is used for new or experimental software that needs to be available everywhere without installing it on all the fileservers. Users wishing to try out the new software then simply include '/vol/r+d/{bin,ucb}' in their path.

The main tree resides on one host 'gould.doc.ic.ac.uk', which has different 'bin', 'etc', 'lib' and 'ucb' sub-directories for each machine architecture. For example, '/vol/r+d/bin' for a Sun-4 would be stored in the sub-directory 'bin/sun4' of the filesystem '/usr/r+d'. When it was accessed a symbolic link pointing to '/a/gould/usr/r+d/bin/sun4' would be returned.

```
/defaults     type:=nfs;opts:=rw,grpid,nosuid,intr,soft
wp            -opts:=rw,grpid,nosuid;rhost:=charm \
              host==charm;type:=link;fs:=/usr/local/wp \
              host!=charm;type:=nfs;rfs:=/vol/wp
...
#
src           -opts:=rw,grpid,nosuid;rhost:=charm \
              host==charm;type:=link;fs:=/usr/src \
```

13

```
                host!=charm;type:=nfs;rfs:=/vol/src
#
r+d             type:=auto;fs:=${map};pref:=r+d/
# per architecture bin,etc,lib&ucb...
r+d/bin         rhost:=gould.doc.ic.ac.uk;rfs:=/usr/r+d;sublink:=${/key}/${arch}
r+d/etc         rhost:=gould.doc.ic.ac.uk;rfs:=/usr/r+d;sublink:=${/key}/${arch}
r+d/include     rhost:=gould.doc.ic.ac.uk;rfs:=/usr/r+d;sublink:=${/key}
r+d/lib         rhost:=gould.doc.ic.ac.uk;rfs:=/usr/r+d;sublink:=${/key}/${arch}
r+d/man         rhost:=gould.doc.ic.ac.uk;rfs:=/usr/r+d;sublink:=${/key}
r+d/src         rhost:=gould.doc.ic.ac.uk;rfs:=/usr/r+d;sublink:=${/key}
r+d/ucb         rhost:=gould.doc.ic.ac.uk;rfs:=/usr/r+d;sublink:=${/key}/${arch}
# hades pictures
pictures        -opts:=rw,grpid,nosuid;rhost:=thpfs \
                host==thpfs;type:=link;fs:=/nbsd/pictures \
                host!=thpfs;type:=nfs;rfs:=/nbsd;sublink:=pictures
# hades tools
hades           -opts:=rw,grpid,nosuid;rhost:=thpfs \
                host==thpfs;type:=link;fs:=/nbsd/hades \
                host!=thpfs;type:=nfs;rfs:=/nbsd;sublink:=hades
# bsd tools for hp.
bsd             -opts:=rw,grpid,nosuid;arch==hp9000;rhost:=thpfs \
                host==thpfs;type:=link;fs:=/nbsd/bsd \
                host!=thpfs;type:=nfs;rfs:=/nbsd;sublink:=bsd
```

9 Internals

9.1 Log Messages

13

In the following sections a brief explanation is given of some of the log messages made by *Amd*. Where the message is in '`typewriter`' font, it corresponds exactly to the message produced by *Amd*. Words in *italic* are replaced by an appropriate string. Variables, `${var}`, indicate that the value of the appropriate variable is output.

Log messages are either sent direct to a file, or logged via the **syslog**(3) mechanism. Messages are logged with facility '`LOG_DAEMON`' when using **syslog**(3). In either case, entries in the file are of the form:

date-string *hostname* `amd[`*pid*`]` *message*

9.1.1 Fatal errors

Amd attempts to deal with unusual events. Whenever it is not possible to deal with such an error, *Amd* will log an appropriate message and, if it cannot possibly continue, will either exit or abort. These messages are selected by '`-x fatal`' on the command line. When **syslog**(3) is being used, they are logged with level '`LOG_FATAL`'. Even if *Amd* continues to operate it is likely to remain in a precarious state and should be restarted at the earliest opportunity.

`Attempting to inherit not-a-filesystem`
: The prototype mount point created during a filesystem restart did not contain a reference to the restarted filesystem. This erorr "should never happen".

`Can't bind to domain "`*NIS-domain*`"`
: A specific NIS domain was requested on the command line, but no server for that domain is available on the local net.

`Can't determine IP address of this host (`*hostname*`)`
: When *Amd* starts it determines its own IP address. If this lookup fails then *Amd* cannot continue. The hostname it looks up is that obtained returned by **gethostname**(2) system call.

`Can't find root file handle for` *automount point*
: *Amd* creates its own file handles for the automount points. When it mounts itself as a server, it must pass these file handles to the local kernel. If the filehandle is not obtainable the mount point is ignored. This error "should never happen".

`Must be root to mount filesystems (euid =` *euid*`)`
: To prevent embarrassment, *Amd* makes sure it has appropriate system privileges. This amounts to having an euid of 0. The check is made after argument processing complete to give non-root users a chance to access the "-v" option.

`No work to do - quitting`
: No automount points were given on the command line and so there is no work to do.

`Out of memory in realloc`
: While attempting to realloc some memory, the memory space available to *Amd* was exhausted. This is an unrecoverable error.

`Out of memory`
: While attempting to malloc some memory, the memory space available to *Amd* was exhausted. This is an unrecoverable error.

`cannot create rpc/udp service`
: Either the NFS or AMQ endpoint could not be created.

`gethostname:` *description*
: The **gethostname**(2) system call failed during startup.

`host name is not set`
: The **gethostname**(2) system call returned a zero length host name. This can happen if *Amd* is started in single user mode just after booting the system.

`ifs_match called!`
: An internal error occurred while restarting a pre-mounted filesystem. This error "should never happen".

`mount_afs:` *description*
: An error occured while *Amd* was mounting itself.

`run_rpc failed`
: Somehow the main NFS server loop failed. This error "should never happen".

`unable to free rpc arguments in amqprog_1`
: The incoming arguments to the AMQ server could not be free'ed.

`unable to free rpc arguments in nfs_program_1`
: The incoming arguments to the NFS server could not be free'ed.

13

`unable to register (AMQ_PROGRAM, AMQ_VERSION, udp)`
: The AMQ server could not be registered with the local portmapper or the internal RPC dispatcher.

`unable to register (NFS_PROGRAM, NFS_VERSION, 0)`
: The NFS server could not be registered with the internal RPC dispatcher.

9.1.2 Info messages

Amd generates information messages to record state changes. These messages are selected by '`-x info`' on the command line. When **syslog**(3) is being used, they are logged with level '`LOG_INFO`'.

The messages listed below can be generated and are in a format suitable for simple statistical analysis. *mount-info* is the string that is displayed by *Amq* in its mount information column and placed in the system mount table.

`mount of "${`*path*`}" on ${`*fs*`} timed out`
: Attempts to mount a filesystem for the given automount point have failed to complete within 30 seconds.

`"${`*path*`}" forcibly timed out`
: An automount point has been timed out by the *Amq* command.

`restarting` *mount-info* `on ${`*fs*`}`
: A pre-mounted file system has been noted.

`"${`*path*`}" has timed out`
: No access to the automount point has been made within the timeout period.

`file server ${`*rhost*`} is down - timeout of "${`*path*`}" ignored`
: An automount point has timed out, but the corresponding file server is known to be down. This message is only produced once for each mount point for which the server is down.

`Re-synchronizing cache for map ${`*map*`}`
: The named map has been modified and the internal cache is being re-synchronized.

`Filehandle denied for "${`*rhost*`}:${`*rfs*`}"`
: The mount daemon refused to return a file handle for the requested filesystem.

13

`Filehandle error for "${`*rhost*`}:${`*rfs*`}":` *description*
: The mount daemon gave some other error for the requested filesystem.

`file server ${`*rhost*`} type nfs starts up`
: A new NFS file server has been referenced and is known to be up.

`file server ${`*rhost*`} type nfs starts down`
: A new NFS file server has been referenced and is known to be down.

`file server ${`*rhost*`} type nfs is up`
: An NFS file server that was previously down is now up.

`file server ${`*rhost*`} type nfs is down`
: An NFS file server that was previously up is now down.

`Finishing with status` *exit-status*
: *Amd* is about to exit with the given exit status.

mount-info **`mounted fstype ${`*type*`} on ${`*fs*`}`**
A new file system has been mounted.

mount-info **`restarted fstype ${`*type*`} on ${`*fs*`}`**
Amd is using a pre-mounted filesystem to satisfy a mount request.

mount-info **`unmounted fstype ${`*type*`} from ${`*fs*`}`**
A file system has been unmounted.

mount-info **`unmounted fstype ${`*type*`} from ${`*fs*`} link ${`*fs*`}/${`*sublink*`}`**
A file system of which only a sub-directory was in use has been unmounted.

Acknowledgements & Trademarks

Thanks to the Formal Methods Group at Imperial College for suffering patiently while *Amd* was being developed on their machines.

Thanks to the many people who have helped with the development of *Amd*, especially Piete Brooks at the Cambridge University Computing Lab for many hours of testing, experimentation and discussion.

Index

13

Installation and Operation of UUCP
4.4BSD Edition

D. A. Nowitz

AT&T Bell Laboratories
Murray Hill, New Jersey 07974

Carl S. Gutekunst

Communications Software Research and Development
Pyramid Technology Corporation
Mountain View, California 94039

ABSTRACT

UUCP is a series of programs designed to permit communication between UNIX† systems using a variety of communications links. UUCP provides batched, error free file transfers and remote command execution. It is well suited for tasks such as electronic mail, public news networks, and software distribution, particularly when only slow, low-cost communication links are available (e.g., 1200 baud dial-up).

This document describes the 4.3BSD version of UUCP. This is a distant but direct descendent of the ''second implementation'' of UUCP developed by D. A. Nowitz at AT&T Bell Laboratories. A number of other UUCP versions are in common usage; these are discussed only to the extent that they affect administration of 4.3BSD systems.

Revised August 24, 1986

1. UUCP OVERVIEW

UUCP is a batch-type operation. Users issue commands that are queued in a spool directory for processing by background daemons.

Uucp (UNIX-to-UNIX Copy) and *uux* (UNIX-to-UNIX Execution) provide the user interface to UUCP. *Uucp* has syntax and semantics similar to the standard UNIX utility *cp*(1), with the added ability to prefix filenames with system names. Similarly, *uux* mimics the conventions of *sh*(1), and allows commands to be prefixed with system names.

Uucico (Copy-In, Copy-Out) is the primary UUCP daemon. It processes the requests queued by *uucp* and *uux*, initiates calls to remote systems, transfers files, and forks other daemons to execute *uux*-requested commands. *Uucico* also acts as the UUCP ''shell'' when remote systems call in to requests transfers.

Three types of files are used in UUCP operation. *Control files* describe the UUCP environment, including known remote hosts, available devices, and remote file access permissions. Control files are relatively static; they are generally changed only by the system administrator. *Spool files* (also called *Queue files*) contain transfer requests and data; they are created and deleted as necessary by *uucp*, *uux*, and *uucico*. *Log files* accumulate a history of UUCP activity; these tend to grow forever if not periodically cleaned up.

Spool files are further divided into three types: *Work files* contain directions for file transfers between systems. Every invocation of *uucp* or *uux* creates one or more work files. *Data files* contain data for transfer to or from remote systems. *Execution files* contain directions for UNIX command executions which involve

† UNIX is a registered trademark of AT&T Bell Laboratories in the USA and other countries.

the resources of one or more systems. Execution files are created only by *uux*.

2. USER UTILITIES

UUCP includes a total of ten ''primary'' utilities, that is, ten utilities for general users. All reside in the **/usr/bin** directory, where they are easily accessible. This section provides detailed implementation descriptions for the more important commands; see the corresponding *man* pages for additional information.

The following two commands queue transfer requests:

uucp(1C) UNIX-to-UNIX File Copy. One of more *control files* are created, containing names of files to be transferred. When necessary, local files are copied into *data files* for transmission.

uux(1C) Execute command. An *execute file* is created, containing a UNIX command to be executed and its arguments. A *control file* is created that includes all files that must be transferred to execute the command, including the *execute file* itself. When necessary, local files are copied into *data files* for transmission. Any output from the command will also be written to *data files*.

The following four commands provide UUCP status information:

uulog(1C) Display selected information from the UUCP log.

uuname(1C) Display the names of all remote hosts that are directly accessible via UUCP.

uusnap(8C) Provide a snapshot of the current queue, including the number of work files, data files, and execute files for each site.

uuq(1C) A variant of *uusnap*, lists files and *uux* commands queued for each site. *Uuq* also permits the UUCP administrator to delete jobs.

The following four commands provide miscellaneous support services:

uudecode(1C) The decoder for files created by *uuencode*, below.

uuencode(1C) A filter to convert binary files into printable ASCII. This is useful when transferring object files over communications links that do not support 8-bit transfers.

uupoll(8C) A user utility to conveniently fork the UUCP daemon, *uucico*.

uusend(1C) A utility to send files to remote sites more than one ''hop'' distant.

2.1. Uucp - UNIX to UNIX File Copy

The *uucp* command is the user's primary interface with the system. The *uucp* command was designed to look like *cp* to the user. The syntax is

uucp [option] ... source ... destination

where the source and destination may contain the prefix *system-name*! which indicates the system on which the file or files reside or where they will be copied.

The options interpreted by *uucp* are:

–f Don't make directories when copying the file. The default is to make the necessary directories.

–C Copy source files to the spool directory. The default is to use the specified source when the actual transfer takes place.

–g*grade* Put *grade* in as the grade in the name of the work file. This is a single character in the range **[0-9][A-Z][a-z]**. The *grade* will be used by *uucico* to establish the priority of requests. **0** is the highest (best) grade; **z** is the lowest (worst). The default *grade* for *uucp* is **n**.

–m Send mail on completion of the work.

–n*user* Notify *user* on the destination system that a file was sent.

The following options are used primarily for debugging, or when *uucp* is invoked from other programs:

–r Queue the job but do not start *uucico*. The assumption is that *uucico* will be started at a later time, perhaps by *cron*(8) or *uupoll*.

–s*dir* Use directory *dir* for the top level spool directory.

–x*num* *Num* is the level of debugging output desired. This option requires the user to have read permission to the UUCP control file *L.sys*.

The destination may be a directory name, in which case the file name is taken from the last part of the source's name. The source name may contain special shell characters such as "**?*[]**"; these and other shell characters such as "**!<>**" will need to be quoted or escaped. If a source argument has a *system-name*! prefix for a remote system, the file name expansion will be done on the remote system.

The command

```
uucp *.c usg!/usr/dan
```

will set up the transfer of all files whose names end with ".c" to the "/usr/dan" directory on the "usg" machine.

The source and/or destination names may also contain a ˜*user* prefix. This translates to the login directory on the specified system. A lone ˜ prefix is expanded to the name of the specified system's public access directory, usually **/usr/spool/uucppublic**. For names with partial path-names, the current directory is prepended to the file name. File names with ../ are not permitted.

The command

```
uucp usg!˜dan/*.h ˜dan
```

will set up the transfer of files whose names end with ".h" in dan's login directory on system "usg" to dan's local login directory.

For each source file, the program will check the source and destination file-names and the system-part of each to classify the work into one of five types:

[1] Copy source to destination on local system.

[2] Receive files from a remote system.

[3] Send files to a remote system.

[4] Send files from remote system to another remote system.

[5] Receive files from remote system when the source pathname contains special shell characters as mentioned above.

After the work has been set up in the spool directories, the UUCP daemon *uucico* is started to try to contact the other machine to execute the work (unless the –r option was specified).

Type 1

Uucp makes a copy of the file. The *–m* option is not honored in this case.

Type 2

A one line *work file* is created for each file requested and put in the **C.** spool directory with the following fields, each separated by a blank. (All *work files* and *execute files* use a blank as the field separator.)

[1] R

[2] The full path-name of the source or a ˜user/path-name. The ˜*user* part will be expanded on the remote system.

[3] The full path-name of the local destination file. If the ˜*user* notation is used, it will be immediately expanded to be the login directory for the user.

[4] The user's login name.

[5] A '–' followed by an option list.

14

For each source file, a *work file* is created. A **–C** option on the *uucp* command will cause the *data file* to be copied into the spool directory and the file to be transmitted from the copy; the copy is deleted when the transfer completes. The fields of each entry are given below.

[1] S

[2] The full-path name of the source file.

[3] The full-path name of the destination or ~user/file-name.

[4] The user's login name.

[5] A '–' followed by an option list.

[6] The full path-name of the local source file. If the *~user* notation is used, it will be immediately expanded to be the login directory for the user. If the **–C** option was used, this will be the name of a *data file* in the spool directory.

[7] The file mode bits of the source file in octal print format (e.g. 0666).

[8] The user to notify on the remote system that the transfer has completed.

Type 4 and Type 5

Uucp generates a *uucp* command and sends it to the remote machine; the remote *uucico* executes the *uucp* command.

2.2. Uux - UNIX To UNIX Execution

The *uux* command is used to set up the execution of a UNIX command where the execution machine and/or some of the files are remote. The syntax of the uux command is

uux [–] [option] ... command-string

where the command-string is made up of one or more arguments. All special shell characters such as "<>|*?!" must be quoted either by quoting the entire command-string or quoting the character as a separate argument. Within the command-string, the command and file names may contain a *system-name*! prefix. All arguments which do not contain a "!" will not be treated as files. (They will not be copied to the execution machine.) The '–' is used to indicate that the standard input for *command-string* should be inherited from the standard input of the *uux* command.

The options, used mostly for debugging and by other programs, are:

–a*name* Use *name* as the requestor of the *uux* command, instead of the real system and login names. Unlike most other UUCP arguments, *name* may consist of a chain of system names separated by '!' characters, as in:

uux – –r –aihnp4!decwrl!pyramid!csg seismo!rmail rick

–C Copy source files to the spool directory. Same as for *uucp*.

–g*grade* Put *grade* in as the grade in the name of the work file. Same as for *uucp*. The default *grade* for *uux* is **A**.

–n Do not mail an acknowledgement to the requestor of the command. Normally the execution daemon, *uuxqt*, will mail a message to the user who entered the *uux* command. This message includes the status return value that the program exited with. The **–n** option requests that this message not be sent.

–r Do not start the UUCPcp daemons *uucico*(8C) or *uuxqt*(8C) after queuing the job.

–x*num* Num is the level of debugging output desired.

–z Mail an acknowledgement to the requestor only if the command fails, that is, the command exits with a non-zero status.

The command

pr abc | uux – usg!lpr

will set up the output of ''pr abc'' as standard input to an lpr command to be executed on system ''usg''.

Uux generates an *execute file* which contains the names of the files required for execution (including standard input), the user's login name, the destination of the standard output, and the command to be executed. This file is either put in the **X.** spool directory for local execution, or in the **D.***hostname***X** directory for transfer to the remote system.

For required files which are not on the execution machine, *uux* will generate receive command files (type 2 above). These command-files will be put on the execution machine and executed by *uucico*. (This will work only if the local system has permission to put files in the remote spool directory as controlled by the remote *USERFILE.*)

The *execute file* will be processed by the *uuxqt*(8C) program on the execution machine. It is made up of several lines, each of which contains an identification character and one or more arguments. The order of the lines in the file is not relevant and some of the lines may not be present. Each line is described below.

User Line

U user system

where the *user* and *system* are the requestor's login name and system.

Required File Line

F file-name real-name

where the *file-name* is the generated name of a file for the execute machine and *real-name* is the last part of the actual file name (contains no path information). Zero or more of these lines may be present in the *execute file*. The *uuxqt* program will check for the existence of all required files before the command is executed.

Standard Input Line

I file-name

The standard input is either specified by a '<' in the command-string or inherited from the standard input of the *uux* command if the '–' option is used. If a standard input is not specified, **/dev/null** is used.

Standard Output Line

O file-name system-name

The standard output is specified by a '>' within the command-string. If a standard output is not specified, **/dev/null** is used. (Note – the use of ''>>'' is not implemented.)

Status Return Line

N

Normally *uuxqt* mails an acknowledgement message to the requestor after the command completes. The message includes the status return value that the program exited with. This line inhibits mailing of the acknowledgement message. It is generated by the **-n** option of *uux*; it is also quietly assumed by *uuxqt* on the command **rmail**.

Error Status Return Line

Z

A variant of the *Status Return* line, this line indicates that an acknowledgement should be mailed only if the command's status return is non-zero, i.e., the program exited with an error. This line is generated by the **-z** option of *uux*. It is also quietly assumed by *uuxqt* on the command **rnews**. If both the **Z** and **N** lines appear, the **Z** line has precedence.

Requestor Line

R requestor

where *requestor* is a complete return mailing address to the original requestor. This line is generated by the **-a** option of *uux*, and is used to override the mail return address implied by the *User* line. This is commonly used by mailers and programs like *uusend* that know how to ''hop'' a file from system to system.

Command Line

C command [arguments] ...

The arguments are those specified in the command-string. The standard input and standard output will not appear on this line. All *required files* will be moved to the execution directory (a subdirectory of the spool directory) and the UNIX command is executed using the Shell specified in the *uucp.h* header file (usually */bin/sh*). In addition, a shell ''PATH'' statement is prepended to the command line.

After execution, the temporary standard output file is copied to or set up to be sent to the proper place.

3. SYSTEM AND ADMINISTRATIVE UTILITIES

UUCP includes four system utilities; these are not normally referenced by users. All except *uucpd* reside in the UUCP administrative directory, **/usr/lib/uucp**. These include:

uucico(8C)	Copy In, Copy Out. This is the primary UUCP daemon.
uuclean(8C)	A handy utility to clean up the UUCP spool directories.
uucpd	The UUCP TCP/IP daemon. This daemon ''answers'' the connection request from a remote *uucico* to a TCP/IP socket. It is functionally a stripped-down version of *rlogind*(8) that provides full 8-bit communication. (Note: this utility does not have a *man* page.)
uuxqt(8C)	Execution Daemon. This is forked by *uucico* to interpret execution files transferred from a remote system.

3.1. Uucico - Copy In, Copy Out (UUCP Daemon)

Uucico is the ''heart'' of the UUCP system. The program performs the following major functions:

- Scan the spool directory for work.
- Place a call to a remote system.
- Negotiate a line protocol to be used.
- Execute all requests from both systems.
- Log work requests and work completions.

Uucico may be started in several ways;

a) by a system daemon (such as *cron*(8)),

b) by one of the *uucp, uux, uuxqt* or *uupoll* programs,

c) directly by the user (this is usually for testing),

d) by a remote system. (The *uucico* program should be specified as the ''shell'' field in the **/etc/passwd** file for the UUCP logins.)

When started by method a, b or c, the program is considered to be in *MASTER* mode. In this mode, a connection will be made to a remote system. If started by a remote system (method d), the program is considered to be in *SLAVE* mode.

The *MASTER* mode will operate in one of two ways. If no system name is specified (–s option not specified) the program will scan the spool directory for systems to call. If a system name is specified, that system will be called, and work will only be done for that system.

The *uucico* program is generally started by another program. There are several options used for execution:

–g*grade* Set the minimum grade of this *uucico* run to *grade*. Only files of this grade or better will be transferred.

–r1 Start the program in *MASTER* mode. This is used when *uucico* is started by a program or *cron* shell.

–s*sys* Do work only for system *sys*. If **–s** is specified, a call to the specified system will be made even if there is no work for system *sys* in the spool directory. This is useful for polling systems which do not have the hardware to initiate a connection.

The following options are used primarily for debugging:

–d*dir* Use directory *dir* for the top level spool directory.

–x*num* *Num* is the level of debugging output desired.

The next part of this section will describe the major steps within the *uucico* program.

Scan For Work

The names of the work related files in a spool subdirectory have format

type **.** system-name grade number

where:

Type is an upper case letter, (**C** - work (copy command) file, **D** - data file, **X** - execute file);

System-name is the remote system;

Grade is a character in the range **[0-9][A-Z][a-z];**

Number is a four digit, padded sequence number.

The file

C.res45n0031

would be a *work file* for a file transfer between the local machine and the "res45" machine.

The scan for work is done by looking through the appropriate spool directory for *work files* (files with prefix **C.**). A list is made of all systems to be called. *Uucico* will then call each system and process all *work files*.

Call Remote System

The call is made using information from the *control* files that reside in the **/usr/lib/uucp** directory. At the start of the call process, a lock is set to forbid multiple conversations between the same two systems.

The system name is found in the *L.sys* control file. The information contained for each system is;

[1] system name,

[2] times to call the system (days-of-week and times-of-day),

[3] the *caller*, that is, the type of device to be used for the call,

[4] the line speed or network number (as appropriate),

[5] telephone number or device name (as appropriate),

[6] login information (multiple fields).

The time field is checked against the present time to see if the call should be made.

The *phone number* may contain abbreviations (e.g. mh, py, boston) which get translated into dial sequences using the *L-dialcodes* file.

The *L-devices* file is scanned using fields [3] and [4] from the *L.sys* file to find an available device for the call. The program will try all devices which satisfy [3] and [4] until the call is made or no more devices can be tried. If a device is successfully opened, a lock file is created so that another copy of *uucico* will not try to use it. If the call is complete, the *login information* (field [6] of *L.sys*) is used to login.

The conversation between the two *uucico* programs begins with a handshake started by the called, *SLAVE*, system. The *SLAVE* sends a message to let the *MASTER* know it is ready to receive the system identification and conversation sequence number. The response from the *MASTER* is verified by the *SLAVE* and if acceptable, protocol selection begins. The *SLAVE* can also reply with a ''call-back required'' message in which case, the current conversation is terminated.

Line Protocol Selection

The remote system sends a message

P*proto-list*

where proto-list is a string of characters, each representing a line protocol.

The calling program checks the proto-list for a letter corresponding to an available line protocol and returns a *use-protocol* message. The *use-protocol* message is

U*code*

where *code* is either a one character protocol letter or **N** which means there is no common protocol.

The following protocols are implemented in 4.3BSD UUCP:

g General. Default for dialup or hardwired lines, supported by all versions of UUCP. This protocol employs small (64 byte) data packets with checksums and packet-by-packet retransmission. This ensures reliable and efficient transfers over slow and noisy links like 1200-baud dial-up lines. These same characteristics make the **g** protocol bulky and slow over error free links, and very expensive on public data-switched networks.

f Optimized for use on X.25 PAD public data-switched networks. The protocol employs larger (256 byte) data packets, passes no control characters except CR, and uses only a 7-bit data path. (Note that the files transferred may still contain full 8-bit data.) It assumes that the link is ''mostly'' error-free, calculating a checksum for the entire file only. When an error is detected, the entire file is retransmitted.

t Optimized for use on TCP/IP networks and other completely error free links. It employs large (1024 byte) packets, and uses the full 8-bit data path.

Note: AT&T System VR2 UUCP supports the **x** (*X.25*) and **e** (*Error Free*) protocols, which provide functionality similar to the 4.3BSD **f** and **t** protocols, respectively. They are incompatible, however. Thus when attempting to connect two systems via X.25 or an local area network, it is not adequate for both systems to simply ''support X.25'' or ''support error free transfers.'' Both must support the same UUCP protocols.

Work Processing

The initial roles (*MASTER* or *SLAVE*) for the work processing are the mode in which each program starts. (The *MASTER* has been specified by the **–r1** *uucico* option.) The *MASTER* program does a work search similar to the one used in the ''Scan For Work'' section.

There are five messages used during the work processing, each specified by the first character of the message. They are;

S send a file,

R receive a file,

C copy complete,

X execute a *uucp* command, and

H hangup.

The *MASTER* will send *R*, *S* or *X* messages until all work from the spool directory is complete, at which point an *H* message will be sent. The *SLAVE* will reply with *SY*, *SN*, *RY*, *RN*, *HY*, *HN*, *XY*, *XN*, corresponding to *yes* or *no* for each request.

The send and receive replies are based on permission to access the requested file/directory using *USERFILE* and read/write permissions of the file/directory. After each file is copied into the spool directory of the receiving system, a copy-complete message is sent by the receiver of the file. The message *CY* will be sent if the file has successfully been moved from the temporary spool file to the actual destination. Otherwise, a *CN* message is sent. (In the case of *CN*, the transferred file will be in the **TM.** spool subdirectory.) The requests and results are logged on both systems.

The hangup response is determined by the *SLAVE* program by a work scan of its spool directory. If work for the *MASTER* 's system exists in the *SLAVE* 's spool directory, an *HN* message is sent and the programs switch roles. If no work exists, an *HY* response is sent.

Conversation Termination

When a *HY* message is received by the *MASTER* it is echoed back to the *SLAVE* and the protocols are turned off. Each program sends a final ''OO'' message to the other. The original *SLAVE* program will clean up and terminate. The *MASTER* will proceed to call other systems and process work as long as possible or terminate if a **–s** option was specified.

3.2. Uuxqt - Uucp Command Execution

The *uuxqt* program is used to execute *execute files* generated by *uux.* The *uuxqt* program may be started by either the *uucico* or *uux* programs. The program scans the **X.** spool directory for *execute files.* Each one is checked to see if all the required files are available and if so, the command line or send line is executed.

The *execute file* is described in the *uux* section above.

Command Execution

The execution is accomplished by executing a *sh –c* of the command line after appropriate standard input and standard output have been opened. If a standard output is specified, the program will create a send command or copy the output file as appropriate.

3.3. Uuclean - Uucp Spool Directory Cleanup

This program is typically started by the *cron*(8) daemon, once a day. Its function is to remove files from the spool directories which are more than 3 days old. These are usually files for work which can not be completed.

The options available are:

–d*dir* The directory to be scanned is *dir*.

–m Send mail to the owner of each file being removed. (Note that most files put into the spool directory will be owned by the owner of the uucp programs since the setuid bit will be set on these programs. The mail will therefore most often go to the owner of the uucp programs.)

–n*hours* Change the aging time from 72 hours to *hours* hours.

–p*pre* Examine files with prefix *pre* for deletion. (Up to 10 file prefixes may be specified.)

–x*num* This is the level of debugging output desired.

4. SYSTEM CONTROL FILES

Seven *Control Files* are referenced by the UUCP utilities. All live in the UUCP administrative directory, **/usr/lib/uucp**. These are ASCII files, and can be modified using standard text editors such as *vi* and *ex*. Lines beginning with a '#' character are comments; lines ending with a '\' are continued on the next input line.

L-devices(5) Declares all devices that are available to *uucico* for calling out.

L-dialcodes(5)	Phone number prefixes. Used to map alphabetic prefixes on phone numbers from *L.sys* to real phone numbers. Also useful to keep a phone number database outside of *L.sys*.
L.sys(5)	Systems. Declares all "adjacent" UUCP hosts, with directions on how to reach them.
L.aliases(5)	Contains aliases used to map obsolete or truncated host names to the correct names.
L.cmds(5)	Commands Permissions. Declares those commands for which remote *uux* execution is permitted.
SQFILE	Sequence-number check file. (Optional)
USERFILE(5)	Directory Tree Permissions. Specifies the set of directory trees that a particular user or host may reference.

A general description of each file follows; see the *man* pages for complete information. Examples of the six standard files are included in the distribution in the **/usr/lib/uucp/UUAIDS** directory.

4.1. L-devices – UUCP Devices File

This file declares all devices that are available to *uucico* for calling out. The special device files are assumed to be in the */dev* directory. The format for each entry is

caller line call-unit class dialer [chat....]

where;

caller	is the caller mechanism, that is, the type of device to be used. This can be one of **ACU** (for Automatic Call Units (modem)), **DIR** (direct hardwired), **PAD** (X.25/PAD), and others.
line	is the device for the link. For example, **cul0** for a modem, **tty10** for a hardwired line.
call-unit	is the automatic call unit associated with *device*. This is used on autodialers such as the Racal-Vadic MACS and the DEC DN-11 that use one device for data, and a second device for dialing. If unused, this field must contain a placeholder such as "unused" or "0". Some modems use this field to specify tone or pulse dialing.
class	is the line speed, plus an optional alphabetic prefix. The prefix can be used to distinguish among different devices that have identical *caller* and line speed.
dialer	applies to **ACU** devices only; this is the type or brand name of the modem. Supported modems include **DN11** (DEC DN-11), **hayes** (Hayes Smartmodem), **vadic** (Racal-Vadic 3451), **ventel** (VenTel 212A), and others.
chat	refers to an *expect/send* script, similar to that provided in *L.sys*. The difference is that the script in *L-devices* is executed before the connection is established, while the script in *L.sys* is executed afterwards.

The line

ACU tty47 unused 1200 hayes

would be set up for a system which had device tty47 wired to a Hayes "Smartmodem 1200" for use at 1200 baud.

14

4.2. L-dialcodes – Phone Number Prefix File

This file contains entries with location abbreviations used in the *L.sys* file (e.g. py, mh, boston). The entry format is

abb dial-seq

where;

abb	is the abbreviation,

dial-seq is the dial sequence to call that location.

The line

py 165–

would be set up so that entry py7777 would send 165–7777 to the dial-unit.

4.3. L.aliases – Hostname Aliases File

This file defines mapping (aliasing) of remote host names. This is intended for compensating for systems that have changed names, or do not provide their entire machine name (like most USG systems). It is also useful when a machine's name is not obvious or commonly misspelled.

Each line is of the form

real-name alias-name

where *real-name* is the full, correct name for the host, and *alias-name* is the old or truncated name.

4.4. L.sys – UUCP Systems File

Each entry in this file represents one system which can be called by the local uucp programs. The format for each entry is

system times caller class device/phone-number [login]

where;

system
: is the hostname of the remote system.

times
: is a keyword-encoded string that indicates the days-of-the-week and times-of-day when the system may be called. For example **MoTuTh0800–1730** would denote Monday, Tuesday, and Thursday, between 8 a.m. and 5:30p.m.

: The day portion may be a list containing any of **Su**, **Mo**, **Tu**, **We**, **Th**, **Fr**, **Sa**, or **Wk** for any week-day or **Any** for any day.

: The time should be a range of times (as in **0800–1230**). If no time portion is specified, any time of day is assumed to be acceptable for the call.

caller
: is one of the caller device-types listed in *L-devices*.

class
: is the line speed for the call (e.g., 300, 1200, 9600), plus an optional alphabetic prefix. Network devices use this field for the network port number.

phone
: is the the phone number to call (for **ACU** devices) or the device filename. A phone number is made up of an optional alphabetic abbreviation and a numeric part. The abbreviation is one which appears in the *L-dialcodes* file (e.g. mh5900, boston995–9980).

login
: is a script describing how to log in to the remote host. It is expressed as a series of fields and subfields in the format

: expect send [expect send] ...

: where; *expect* is the string expected to be read and *send* is the string to be sent when the *expect* string is received. The *send* string is normally terminated with carriage-return; an empty *send* string will send only a carriage-return.

: The expect field may be made up of subfields of the form

: expect[–send–expect]...

: where the *send* is sent if the prior *expect* is not successfully read and the *expect* following the *send* is the next expected string.

A typical entry in the L.sys file would be

sys Any ACU 1200 mh7654 login:--login: uucp ssword: word

The expect algorithm looks at the last part of the string as illustrated in the password field.

4.5. L.cmds – Commands Permissions File

This file contains a list of commands, one per line, that are permitted for remote execution via *uux*. This list should be chosen with great care, since commands that take filenames as arguments will allow users to easily circumvent UUCP's security. For most sites, *L.cmds* should only include the lines:

```
rmail
ruusend
```

4.6. SQFILE – Sequence Check File (Optional)

This file contains an entry for each remote system with which this site agrees to perform conversation sequence checks. The initial entry is just the system name of the remote system. The first conversation will add two items to the line, the conversation count, and the date/time of the most resent conversation. These items will be updated with each conversation. If a sequence check fails, which could indicate that an unauthorized connection has been attempted, the entry will have to be adjusted.

This facility is technically no longer supported in 4.3BSD UUCP, since it was hardly ever used and consumed precious memory space on PDP-11 systems. The compile-time #define GNXSEQ can be set to enable sequence checking should it be needed.

4.7. USERFILE – Pathnames Permissions File

This file contains user accessibility information. It specifies four types of constraint;

[1] which files can be accessed by a normal user of the local machine,

[2] which files can be accessed from a remote computer,

[3] which login name is used by a particular remote computer,

[4] whether a remote computer should be called back in order to confirm its identity.

Each line in the file has the following format

```
login,sys  [ c ]  path-name  [ path-name ] ...
```

where;

login	is the login name for a user or the remote computer,
sys	is the system name for a remote computer,
c	is the optional *call-back required* flag,
path-name	is a path-name prefix that is acceptable for *user*.

The constraints are implemented as follows.

[1] When the program is obeying a command stored on the local machine, *MASTER* mode, the path-names allowed are those given for the first line in the *USERFILE* that has a login name that matches the login name of the user who entered the command. If no such line is found, the first line with a *null* login name is used.

[2] When the program is responding to a command from a remote machine, *SLAVE* mode, the path-names allowed are those given for the first line in the file that has the system name that matches the system name of the remote machine. If no such line is found, the first one with a *null* system name is used.

14

[3] When a remote computer logs in, the login name that it uses must appear in the *USERFILE*. There may be several lines with the same login name but one of them must either have the name of the remote system or must contain a *null* system name. **Note:** This constraint, although stated in the original Nowitz UUCP document, was not implemented in Version 7 UUCP. For all practical purposes, a remote computer's login was not validated by UUCP. This is still the case in 4.3BSD. Remote login checking *is* implemented in AT&T's System VR2.2 release, and in the UUCP provided with Digital Equipment Corporation's ULTRIX. HoneyDanBer analogously requires all remote logins to be listed in its *Permissions* file.

[4] If the line matched in ([3]) contains a "c", the remote machine is called back before any transactions take place.

The line

u,m /usr/xyz

allows machine *m* to login with name *u* and request the transfer of files whose names start with "/usr/xyz".

The line

dan, /usr/dan

allows the ordinary user *dan* to issue commands for files whose name starts with "/usr/dan".

The lines

u,m /usr/xyz /usr/spool
u, /usr/spool

allows any remote machine to login with name *u*, but if its system name is not *m*, it can only ask to transfer files whose names start with "/usr/spool".

The lines

root, /
, /usr

allows any user to transfer files beginning with "/usr" but the user with login *root* can transfer any file.

5. SPOOL FILES

Spool Files contain UUCP transfer requests and data. Most have been described in detail earlier in this document.

All spool files live in the **/usr/spool/uucp** directory tree. To keep the spool directory from becoming hopelessly cluttered, each type of spool file is kept in its own subdirectory. The name of the directory is the same as the common prefix of the filename. For example, *work files* (files beginning with **C.**) are kept in the **C.** directory; *execute files* (which begin with **X.**) are kept in the **X.** directory, and so on.

A total of ten spool subdirectories are used, one of which is optional:

C.	*Work* files.
CORRUPT	Corrupted *work* and *execute* files. *Uucico* and *uuxqt* will deposit **C.** and **X.** files here when they are unable to parse them. A notice will also be placed in the UUCP log.
D.	*Data files* received from remote hosts.
D.*hostname*	*Data files* to be sent to remote hosts.
D.*hostname*X	*Execution files* to be sent to remote hosts.
LCK	Per-device and per-site lock (**LCK.**) files. (Optional)
STST	Per-site system status files.
TM.	Temporary files used in data transfer. When the transfer is complete, the file is typically *mv*'ed to the **D.** or **X.** directory.
X.	*Execution files* received from remote sites.
XTMP	Temporary files and home directory for *uuxqt*.

The following sections describe only those spool files that were not discussed earlier.

5.1. LCK – lock files

Lock files are created for each device in use (except for TCP/IP sockets) and each system conversing. This prevents duplicate conversations and multiple attempts to use the same devices. The form of the lock file name is

LCK..str

where *str* is either a device or system name. The files may be left in the spool directory if *uucico* aborts. They will be ignored (reused) after 90 minutes. When runs abort and calls are desired before the time limit expires, the lock files should be removed. If the **LCK.** subdirectory is used, it's access mode can be set to 777, thus allowing normal users to remove dead lock files when necessary.

5.2. STST – system status files

These files are created in the **STST** subdirectory by *uucico*. They contain information of failures such as login, dialup, or sequence check, and will contain a *TALKING*, *RECEIVING*, or *SENDING* status when two machines are conversing. The file name is **STST/***system*, where *system* is the host name of the remote machine.

For ordinary failures (dialup, login), the file indicates the time of the last failure; this allows *uucico* to avoid retrying the failed call too soon. For sequence check failures, the file must be removed before any future attempts to converse with that remote system.

If the file is left due to an aborted run, it may contain a *TALKING* status. In this case, the file must be removed before a conversation is attempted. The easiest way to do this is to use the *uupoll* command to force *uucico* to start up.

5.3. TM – temporary data files

These files are created in the **/usr/spool/uucp/TM.** directory while files are being copied from a remote machine. Their names have the form

TM.pid.ddd

where *pid* is a process-id and *ddd* is a sequential three digit number starting at zero for each invocation of *uucico* and incremented for each file received. After the entire remote file is received, the **TM** file is moved to the requested destination, often the **X.** or **D.** directory. If processing is abnormally terminated or the move fails, the file will remain in the **TM.** directory.

The stranded files should be periodically removed; the *uuclean* program is useful in this regard. The command

uuclean -d/usr/spool/uucp/TM. –pTM.

will remove all **TM** files older than three days.

6. LOG FILES

The following files provide a history of UUCP activities. All live in the spool directory, **/usr/spool/uucp**. They grow forever, and must be periodically trimmed or deleted; this is usually done weekly (or daily) via *cron*.

AUDIT — This is a directory of audit trail files, one file per site. *Uucico* uses an audit file for debugging output whenever it is run with debug enabled (via the **-x** option or a **SIGFPE** signal), but the standard message output file **stderr** is not available.

ERRLOG — This is an oft-forgotten log of UUCP "Assert" errors. An Assert error is a catastrophic and unrecoverable failure of the UUCP system. These include spool directories or control files that cannot be opened, an unexpected error return from a system call, or an "impossible case" in a utility's control flow.

Utilities that abort with an Assert error return a status code of -1. If a user reports *uucp* or *uux* dying with a message like "uux failed, status -1," then the ERRLOG file should be checked.

LOGFILE — This is the primary UUCP log. All UUCP activity is recorded here, including queue requests from *uucp* and *uux*, attempted connections, file transfers, and communications failures.

SYSLOG — This is a log of file transfer statistics: number of bytes, time required, and number of packet retries. The effective data rate can be calculated simply by dividing the

14

number of bytes by the time; low data rates or a large number of retries implies that the communication link may marginal.

Optionally, one *LOGFILE* per site may be maintained in the **LOG** subdirectory. This option can be selected at UUCP compile time via the LOGBYSITE #define in **uucp.h.**

7. ADMINISTRATION AND SYSTEM SECURITY

7.1. UNIX System Files

/etc/passwd

UUCP requires a login in **/etc/passwd**; at its simplest the entry would be

```
uucp::66:1:UNIX-to-UNIX Copy:/usr/spool/uucppublic:/usr/lib/uucp/uucico
```

This user should own all the UUCP files and utilities. Remote sites wishing to call in for UUCP transfers would login to **uucp** (with the correct password, if any), and get *uucico* as their ''shell.'' Since *uucico* would be called without any options, it would run in *SLAVE* mode, thus responding correctly to the remote system, which would be in *MASTER* mode.

The directory **/usr/spool/uucppublic** should be created with 777 access modes, owned by **uucp**. In addition to serving as the home directory for UUCP remote logins, **uucppublic** provides a ''public-access'' directory where any user can read, write, or transfer files.

There are a number of security problems with using a single login, not the least of which is that superuser permission would be necessary to edit the *control* files. A better arrangement would be:

```
uucp::66:1:UUCP Administrator:/usr/lib/uucp:
nuucp::67:1:UNIX-to-UNIX Copy:/usr/spool/uucppublic:/usr/lib/uucp/uucico
```

This provides one login for the UUCP administrator (which must be kept secure!) and a second for remote machines to use for login. A still more elaborate setup would use a separate login for each remote site, and possibly provide the administrator with a choice of shells:

```
uucp::66:1:UUCP Administrator:/usr/lib/uucp:
UUCP::66:1:UUCP Administrator:/usr/lib/uucp:/bin/csh
Uhosta::6001:1:UNIX-to-UNIX Copy:/usr/spool/uucppublic:/usr/lib/uucp/uucico
Uhostb::6002:1:UNIX-to-UNIX Copy:/usr/spool/uucppublic:/usr/lib/uucp/uucico
Uhostc::6003:1:UNIX-to-UNIX Copy:/usr/spool/uucppublic:/usr/lib/uucp/uucico
```

It is assumed that the login name used by a remote computer to dial in is not the same as the login name of a normal user of the machine. However, several remote computers may employ the same login name.

Note that **uucppublic** is *not* used as the home directory for **uucp** when it logs into a regular shell. This would be an extreme security hazard, since anyone could slip a ''Trojan horse'' into a **.profile** or **.cshrc** file, which would be automatically executed when the UUCP administrator logged in.

/etc/rc

The system startup file, **/etc/rc**, should clean up any stray lock files with the line

```
rm -f /usr/spool/uucp/LCK.*
```

or, if the LCK subdirectory is being used,

```
rm -f /usr/spool/uucp/LCK/LCK.*
```

/etc/services

If UUCP is to be used over TCP/IP links, then an entry for UUCP's port number should be added to **/etc/services**:

```
uucp 540/tcp uucpd # UUCP TCP/IP
```

7.2. Shell Scripts For Periodic Cleanup

The UUCP system has a fairly large number of activities that must occur periodically. These include starting *uucico* to process queued requests, running *uuclean* to remove old spool files, and shuffling the boundlessly-growing log files. Some sites will also want to poll other sites periodically.

While it's possible to put all the necessary commands into *cron*'s control file **/usr/lib/crontab**, this would be extremely awkward. The usual technique is to use three separate shells scripts, one each for hourly, daily, and weekly operations. Examples are provided in the **UUAIDS** directory; the following sections provide some specific recommendations.

Hourly

Activities that should occur hourly include:

- Polling of selected sites. Sites that have no dial-out capability will need to be periodically polled. The *uupoll* command works well for this.
- Start *uucico* to complete all unfinished work. This can be as simple as:

```
uucico -r1 &
```

Daily

The daily script should be started by *cron* in the wee hours, around 4 a.m. Activities that should occur daily include:

- Call *uuclean* to remove old spool files. The preferred technique is something like the following:

```
cd /usr/lib/uucp
deadtime=`expr 24 * 7`
uuclean -d/usr/spool/uucp/AUDIT -n72
uuclean -d/usr/spool/uucp/LCK -pLCK. -pLTMP. -n24
uuclean -d/usr/spool/uucp/STST -n72
uuclean -d/usr/spool/uucp/TM. -pTM. -n72
uuclean -d/usr/spool/uucp/XTMP -n72
uuclean -d/usr/spool/uucp/X. -pX. -n$deadtime
uuclean -d/usr/spool/uucp/C. -pC. -n$deadtime
uuclean -d/usr/spool/uucp/D. -pD. -n$deadtime
uuclean -d/usr/spool/uucp/D.`uuname -l` -pD. -n$deadtime
uuclean -d/usr/spool/uucp/D.`uuname -l`X -pD. -n$deadtime
```

  In this example, Audit files, Lock files, System Status files, temp files, and *uuxqt* output files are cleaned up every 72 hours (3 days). (**LTMP.** files are temporary files created by the lock mechanism; they are rarely around for more than a few seconds. Note, the above assumes that the **LCK** subdirectory is being used.) All normal data files are cleaned up every 24 * 7 hours, or every 7 days.

- Shuffle the log files. At the very least, LOGFILE should be moved to LOGFILE.old, and SYSLOG moved to SYSLOG.old. Busy sites may want to use *compress*(1) to squeeze down the old files.
- Use *find*(1) to clean up the **/usr/spool/uucppublic** directory. If left unattended, garbage will gradually accumulate there until it fills the file system.

14

Weekly

Small sites with very little traffic may chose to shuffle the log files once per week, instead of once per day. The weekly script should, like the daily script, be run early in the morning.

7.3. Connecting new systems

When first connecting a new machine to a UUCP network, it is useful to try and establish a connection with *tip* or *cu* first. The UUCP administrator will quickly become aware of any special facilities that are going to be required, for example: What lines and modems are to be used? Is the connection through different hardware and carriers? Does the remote system care about parity? What speed lines are being used and do they cycle through several speeds? Is there a line switch front end that will require special login dialogue in **L.sys**?

Once a successful login is achieved "by hand," the administrator should have enough information to allow the correct setup of the *control* files in **/usr/lib/uucp.**

The UUCP administrator should then negotiate with the remote site's UUCP administrator as to who (if anyone) will do polling and when. Both administrators must set up the relevant accounts and passwords. The local administrator should decide on what permissions and security precautions are to be observed. Testing time and facilities will need to be arranged to complete initial connection testing between the systems.

7.4. Miscellaneous Security Issues

The UUCP system, left unrestricted, will let any outside user execute any commands and copy any files that are accessible to the **uucp** login user. It is up to the individual sites to be aware of this and apply the protections that they feel are necessary.

There are several security features available aside from the normal file mode protections. These must be set up by the installer of the UUCP system.

- The login for uucp does not get a standard shell. Instead, *uucico* is started. Therefore, the only work that can be done is through *uucico*.
- A path check is done on file names that are to be sent or received. *USERFILE* supplies the information for these checks. *USERFILE* can also be set up to require call-back for certain login-ids. (See the description of *USERFILE* above.)
- A conversation sequence count can be set up so that the called system can be more confident that the caller is who he says he is.
- *Uuxqt* is restricted via the *L.cmds* file to a small list of commands that it will execute. A "PATH" shell statement is prepended to the command line as specified in the *L.cmds* file. The administrator may modify the list or remove the restrictions as desired.
- All the UUCP utilities except *uudecode*, *uuencode*, and *uusend* should be owned by the **uucp** login with the "setuid" bit set and only execute permissions (e.g. mode 04111). This will prevent outsiders from modifying the programs to get at a standard shell with a **uucp** login. Optionally, the utilities may belong to group **daemon** and be given "setgid" permissions (mode 06111). *Uuxqt* should only permit other UUCP programs to execute it; its mode should be 04100 or 06110.
- The *control* files *L.sys*, *USERFILE*, and *SQFILE* contain highly sensitive information. They should be owned by the **uucp** login, with read and write permission granted only to the owner (mode 0600).

8. INSTALLING THE UUCP SYSTEM

The source for the UUCP system resides in the **/usr/src/usr.bin/uucp** directory. The README file includes complete instructions on how to rebuild the UUCP system from source.

For most environments, only two files will need to be modified: **uucp.h** includes a large number of tunable system-dependent parameters, including operating system type, devices to be supported, and a variety of optional features. The **Makefile** may also have to be modified, particularly if you chose to keep certain files in different directories from usual.

14

9. ACKNOWLEDGEMENTS

4.3BSD UUCP was a group development effort, involving the contributed work of over one hundred members of the USENET community. We're extremely grateful to them all.

Special thanks go to the following individuals, whose contributions were especially valuable:

- Rick Adams (Center for Seismic Studies) coordinated the 4.3BSD UUCP release, incorporating (and often correcting) hundreds of bug fixes that were posted on the USENET and mailed to him directly. Rick also managed to find time to add many enhancements and corrections of his own.
- Tom Truscott (Research Triangle Institute) and Bob Gray (then with PAR Tech Corp, now at Univ of Colorado) coordinated the 4.2BSD UUCP release, which was also a group effort. Tom has continued to provide enhancements and fixes in 4.3BSD.
- Guy Harris (then with Computer Consoles, Inc., now with Sun Microsystems) contributed many general bug fixes; in particular, he was the first to isolate the infamous 4.2BSD ''TIMEOUT'' bug.
- Lou Salkind (New York University) wrote the *uuq* utility.
- James Bloom (U.C. Berkeley) isolated a major day-one bug in the **g**-protocol driver that had eluded many people's attempts to squash it.
- Piet Beertema (Centrum voor Wiskunde en Informatica, Amsterdam) wrote the **f**-protocol to support ''mostly error-free links''; Robert Elz (University of Melbourne) modified the protocol specifically for X.25/PAD.
- Peter Honeyman (Princeton) assisted Rick by providing information on the facilities provided in HoneyDanBer UUCP; Rick then added many HDB-compatibility features and HDB-like extensions to 4.3BSD UUCP.
- Ross Green (U.C. Berkeley) produced the first revision of this chapter, updating the aging Nowitz document to more closely reflect reality.

Thanks again to everyone who contributed. Berkeley UUCP continues to be a product of its own users, and would not exist as it does today without them.

14

A Dial-Up Network of UNIX™ Systems

D. A. Nowitz

M. E. Lesk

AT&T Bell Laboratories
Murray Hill, NJ

ABSTRACT

A network of over eighty UNIX† computer systems has been established using the telephone system as its primary communication medium. The network was designed to meet the growing demands for software distribution and exchange. Some advantages of our design are:

- The startup cost is low. A system needs only a dial-up port, but systems with automatic calling units have much more flexibility.
- No operating system changes are required to install or use the system.
- The communication is basically over dial-up lines, however, hardwired communication lines can be used to increase speed.
- The command for sending/receiving files is simple to use.

Keywords: networks, communications, software distribution, software maintenance

1. Purpose

The widespread use of the UNIX system[1] within Bell Laboratories has produced problems of software distribution and maintenance. A conventional mechanism was set up to distribute the operating system and associated programs from a central site to the various users. However this mechanism alone does not meet all software distribution needs. Remote sites generate much software and must transmit it to other sites. Some UNIX systems are themselves central sites for redistribution of a particular specialized utility, such as the Switching Control Center System. Other sites have particular, often long-distance needs for software exchange; switching research, for example, is carried on in New Jersey, Illinois, Ohio, and Colorado. In addition, general purpose utility programs are written at all UNIX system sites. The UNIX system is modified and enhanced by many people in many places and it would be very constricting to deliver new software in a one-way stream without any alternative for the user sites to respond with changes of their own.

Straightforward software distribution is only part of the problem. A large project may exceed the capacity of a single computer and several machines may be used by the one group of people. It then becomes necessary for them to pass messages, data and other information back an forth between computers.

Several groups with similar problems, both inside and outside of Bell Laboratories, have constructed networks built of hardwired connections only.[2, 3] Our network, however, uses both dial-up and hardwired connections so that service can be provided to as many sites as possible.

---

† UNIX is a registered trademark of AT&T Bell Laboratories in the USA and other countries.

2. Design Goals

Although some of our machines are connected directly, others can only communicate over low-speed dial-up lines. Since the dial-up lines are often unavailable and file transfers may take considerable time, we spool all work and transmit in the background. We also had to adapt to a community of systems which are independently operated and resistant to suggestions that they should all buy particular hardware or install particular operating system modifications. Therefore, we make minimal demands on the local sites in the network. Our implementation requires no operating system changes; in fact, the transfer programs look like any other user entering the system through the normal dial-up login ports, and obeying all local protection rules.

We distinguish "active" and "passive" systems on the network. Active systems have an automatic calling unit or a hardwired line to another system, and can initiate a connection. Passive systems do not have the hardware to initiate a connection. However, an active system can be assigned the job of calling passive systems and executing work found there; this makes a passive system the functional equivalent of an active system, except for an additional delay while it waits to be polled. Also, people frequently log into active systems and request copying from one passive system to another. This requires two telephone calls, but even so, it is faster than mailing tapes.

Where convenient, we use hardwired communication lines. These permit much faster transmission and multiplexing of the communications link. Dial-up connections are made at either 300 or 1200 baud; hardwired connections are asynchronous up to 9600 baud and might run even faster on special-purpose communications hardware.[4, 5] Thus, systems typically join our network first as passive systems and when they find the service more important, they acquire automatic calling units and become active systems; eventually, they may install high-speed links to particular machines with which they handle a great deal of traffic. At no point, however, must users change their programs or procedures.

The basic operation of the network is very simple. Each participating system has a spool directory, in which work to be done (files to be moved, or commands to be executed remotely) is stored. A standard program, *uucico*, performs all transfers. This program starts by identifying a particular communication channel to a remote system with which it will hold a conversation. *Uucico* then selects a device and establishes the connection, logs onto the remote machine and starts the *uucico* program on the remote machine. Once two of these programs are connected, they first agree on a line protocol, and then start exchanging work. Each program in turn, beginning with the calling (active system) program, transmits everything it needs, and then asks the other what it wants done. Eventually neither has any more work, and both exit.

In this way, all services are available from all sites; passive sites, however, must wait until called. A variety of protocols may be used; this conforms to the real, non-standard world. As long as the caller and called programs have a protocol in common, they can communicate. Furthermore, each caller knows the hours when each destination system should be called. If a destination is unavailable, the data intended for it remain in the spool directory until the destination machine can be reached.

The implementation of this Bell Laboratories network between independent sites, all of which store proprietary programs and data, illustratives the pervasive need for security and administrative controls over file access. Each site, in configuring its programs and system files, limits and monitors transmission. In order to access a file a user needs access permission for the machine that contains the file and access permission for the file itself. This is achieved by first requiring the user to use his password to log into his local machine and then his local machine logs into the remote machine whose files are to be accessed. In addition, records are kept identifying all files that are moved into and out of the local system, and how the requestor of such accesses identified himself. Some sites may arrange to permit users only to call up and request work to be done; the calling users are then called back before the work is actually done. It is then possible to verify that the request is legitimate from the standpoint of the target system, as well as the originating system. Furthermore, because of the call-back, no site can masquerade as another even if it knows all the necessary passwords.

Each machine can optionally maintain a sequence count for conversations with other machines and require a verification of the count at the start of each conversation. Thus, even if call back is not in use, a successful masquerade requires the calling party to present the correct sequence number. A would-be impersonator must not just steal the correct phone number, user name, and password, but also the sequence count, and must call in sufficiently promptly to precede the next legitimate request from either side. Even a successful masquerade will be detected on the next correct conversation.

3. Processing

The user has two commands which set up communications, *uucp* to set up file copying, and *uux* to set up command execution where some of the required resources (system and/or files) are not on the local machine. Each of these commands will put work and data files into the spool directory for execution by *uucp* daemons. Figure 1 shows the major blocks of the file transfer process.

File Copy

The *uucico* program is used to perform all communications between the two systems. It performs the following functions:

- Scan the spool directory for work.
- Place a call to a remote system.
- Negotiate a line protocol to be used.
- Start program *uucico* on the remote system.
- Execute all requests from both systems.
- Log work requests and work completions.

Uucico may be started in several ways;

a) by a system daemon,

b) by one of the *uucp* or *uux* programs,

c) by a remote system.

Scan For Work

The file names in the spool directory are constructed to allow the daemon programs *(uucico, uuxqt)* to determine the files they should look at, the remote machines they should call and the order in which the files for a particular remote machine should be processed.

Call Remote System

The call is made using information from several files which reside in the uucp program directory. At the start of the call process, a lock is set on the system being called so that another call will not be attempted at the same time.

The system name is found in a ''systems'' file. The information contained for each system is:

[1] system name,

[2] times to call the system (days-of-week and times-of-day),

[3] device or device type to be used for call,

[4] line speed,

[5] phone number,

[6] login information (multiple fields).

The time field is checked against the present time to see if the call should be made. The *phone number* may contain abbreviations (e.g. ''nyc'', ''boston'') which get translated into dial sequences using a ''dial-codes'' file. This permits the same ''phone number'' to be stored at every site, despite local variations in telephone services and dialing conventions.

A ''devices'' file is scanned using fields [3] and [4] from the ''systems'' file to find an available device for the connection. The program will try all devices which satisfy [3] and [4] until a connection is made, or no more devices can be tried. If a non-multiplexable device is successfully opened, a lock file is created so that another copy of *uucico* will not try to use it. If the connection is complete, the *login information* is used to log into the remote system. Then a command is sent to the remote system to start the *uucico* program. The conversation between the two *uucico* programs begins with a handshake started by the called, *SLAVE*, system. The *SLAVE* sends a message to let the *MASTER* know it is ready to receive the system identification and conversation sequence number. The response from the *MASTER* is verified by the *SLAVE* and if acceptable, protocol selection begins.

Line Protocol Selection

The remote system sends a message

P*proto-list*

where *proto-list* is a string of characters, each representing a line protocol. The calling program checks the proto-list for a letter corresponding to an available line protocol and returns a *use-protocol* message. The *use-protocol* message is

U*code*

where code is either a one character protocol letter or a *N* which means there is no common protocol.

Greg Chesson designed and implemented the standard line protocol used by the uucp transmission program. Other protocols may be added by individual installations.

Work Processing

During processing, one program is the *MASTER* and the other is *SLAVE*. Initially, the calling program is the *MASTER*. These roles may switch one or more times during the conversation.

There are four messages used during the work processing, each specified by the first character of the message. They are

S send a file,
R receive a file,
C copy complete,
H hangup.

The *MASTER* will send *R* or *S* messages until all work from the spool directory is complete, at which point an *H* message will be sent. The *SLAVE* will reply with *SY*, *SN*, *RY*, *RN*, *HY*, *HN*, corresponding to *yes* or *no* for each request.

The send and receive replies are based on permission to access the requested file/directory. After each file is copied into the spool directory of the receiving system, a copy-complete message is sent by the receiver of the file. The message *CY* will be sent if the UNIX *cp* command, used to copy from the spool directory, is successful. Otherwise, a *CN* message is sent. The requests and results are logged on both systems, and, if requested, mail is sent to the user reporting completion (or the user can request status information from the log program at any time).

The hangup response is determined by the *SLAVE* program by a work scan of the spool directory. If work for the remote system exists in the *SLAVE's* spool directory, a *HN* message is sent and the programs switch roles. If no work exists, an *HY* response is sent.

A sample conversation is shown in Figure 2.

Conversation Termination

When a *HY* message is received by the *MASTER* it is echoed back to the *SLAVE* and the protocols are turned off. Each program sends a final "OO" message to the other.

4. Present Uses

One application of this software is remote mail. Normally, a UNIX system user writes ''mail dan'' to send mail to user ''dan''. By writing ''mail usg!dan'' the mail is sent to user ''dan'' on system ''usg''.

15

The primary uses of our network to date have been in software maintenance. Relatively few of the bytes passed between systems are intended for people to read. Instead, new programs (or new versions of programs) are sent to users, and potential bugs are returned to authors. Aaron Cohen has implemented a ''stockroom'' which allows remote users to call in and request software. He keeps a ''stock list'' of available programs, and new bug fixes and utilities are added regularly. In this way, users can always obtain the latest version of anything without bothering the authors of the programs. Although the stock list is maintained on a particular system, the items in the stockroom may be warehoused in many places; typically each program is distributed from the home site of its author. Where necessary, uucp does remote-to-remote copies.

We also routinely retrieve test cases from other systems to determine whether errors on remote systems are caused by local misconfigurations or old versions of software, or whether they are bugs that must be fixed at the home site. This helps identify errors rapidly. For one set of test programs maintained by us, over 70% of the bugs reported from remote sites were due to old software, and were fixed merely by distributing the current version.

Another application of the network for software maintenance is to compare files on two different machines. A very useful utility on one machine has been Doug McIlroy's ''diff'' program which compares two text files and indicates the differences, line by line, between them.[6] Only lines which are not identical are printed. Similarly, the program ''uudiff'' compares files (or directories) on two machines. One of these directories may be on a passive system. The ''uudiff'' program is set up to work similarly to the inter-system mail, but it is slightly more complicated.

To avoid moving large numbers of usually identical files, *uudiff* computes file checksums on each side, and only moves files that are different for detailed comparison. For large files, this process can be iterated; checksums can be computed for each line, and only those lines that are different actually moved.

The ''uux'' command has been useful for providing remote output. There are some machines which do not have hard-copy devices, but which are connected over 9600 baud communication lines to machines with printers. The *uux* command allows the formatting of the printout on the local machine and printing on the remote machine using standard UNIX command programs.

5. Performance

Throughput, of course, is primarily dependent on transmission speed. The table below shows the real throughput of characters on communication links of different speeds. These numbers represent actual data transferred; they do not include bytes used by the line protocol for data validation such as checksums and messages. At the higher speeds, contention for the processors on both ends prevents the network from driving the line full speed. The range of speeds represents the difference between light and heavy loads on the two systems. If desired, operating system modifications can be installed that permit full use of even very fast links.

Nominal speed	Characters/sec.
300 baud	27
1200 baud	100-110
9600 baud	200-850

In addition to the transfer time, there is some overhead for making the connection and logging in ranging from 15 seconds to 1 minute. Even at 300 baud, however, a typical 5,000 byte source program can be transferred in four minutes instead of the 2 days that might be required to mail a tape.

Traffic between systems is variable. Between two closely related systems, we observed 20 files moved and 5 remote commands executed in a typical day. A more normal traffic out of a single system would be around a dozen files per day.

The total number of sites at present in the main network is 82, which includes most of the Bell Laboratories full-size machines which run the UNIX operating system. Geographically, the machines range from Andover, Massachusetts to Denver, Colorado.

Uucp has also been used to set up another network which connects a group of systems in operational sites with the home site. The two networks touch at one Bell Labs computer.

6. Further Goals

Eventually, we would like to develop a full system of remote software maintenance. Conventional maintenance (a support group which mails tapes) has many well-known disadvantages.[7] There are distribution errors and delays, resulting in old software running at remote sites and old bugs continually reappearing. These difficulties are aggravated when there are 100 different small systems, instead of a few large ones.

The availability of file transfer on a network of compatible operating systems makes it possible just to send programs directly to the end user who wants them. This avoids the bottleneck of negotiation and packaging in the central support group. The "stockroom" serves this function for new utilities and fixes to old utilities. However, it is still likely that distributions will not be sent and installed as often as needed. Users are justifiably suspicious of the "latest version" that has just arrived; all too often it features the "latest bug." What is needed is to address both problems simultaneously:

1. Send distributions whenever programs change.
2. Have sufficient quality control so that users will install them.

To do this, we recommend systematic regression testing both on the distributing and receiving systems. Acceptance testing on the receiving systems can be automated and permits the local system to ensure that its essential work can continue despite the constant installation of changes sent from elsewhere. The work of writing the test sequences should be recovered in lower counseling and distribution costs.

Some slow-speed network services are also being implemented. We now have inter-system "mail" and "diff," plus the many implied commands represented by "uux." However, we still need inter-system "write" (real-time inter-user communication) and "who" (list of people logged in on different systems). A slow-speed network of this sort may be very useful for speeding up counseling and education, even if not fast enough for the distributed data base applications that attract many users to networks. Effective use of remote execution over slow-speed lines, however, must await the general installation of multiplexable channels so that long file transfers do not lock out short inquiries.

7. Lessons

The following is a summary of the lessons we learned in building these programs.

1. By starting your network in a way that requires no hardware or major operating system changes, you can get going quickly.
2. Support will follow use. Since the network existed and was being used, system maintainers were easily persuaded to help keep it operating, including purchasing additional hardware to speed traffic.
3. Make the network commands look like local commands. Our users have a resistance to learning anything new: all the inter-system commands look very similar to standard UNIX system commands so that little training cost is involved.
4. An initial error was not coordinating enough with existing communications projects: thus, the first version of this network was restricted to dial-up, since it did not support the various hardware links between systems. This has been fixed in the current system.

Acknowledgements

We thank G. L. Chesson for his design and implementation of the packet driver and protocol, and A. S. Cohen, J. Lions, and P. F. Long for their suggestions and assistance.

References

1. D. M. Ritchie and K. Thompson, "The UNIX Time-Sharing System," *Bell Sys. Tech. J.*, vol. 57, no. 6, pp. 1905-1929, 1978.
2. T. A. Dolotta, R. C. Haight, and J. R. Mashey, "UNIX Time-Sharing System: The Programmer's Workbench," *Bell Sys. Tech. J.*, vol. 57, no. 6, pp. 2177-2200, 1978.
3. G. L. Chesson, "The Network UNIX System," *Operating Systems Review*, vol. 9, no. 5, pp. 60-66, 1975. Also in *Proc. 5th Symp. on Operating Systems Principles.*

15

4. A. G. Fraser, ''Spider — An Experimental Data Communications System,'' *Proc. IEEE Conf. on Communications*, p. 21F, June 1974. IEEE Cat. No. 74CH0859-9-CSCB.

5. A. G. Fraser, ''A Virtual Channel Network,'' *Datamation*, pp. 51-56, February 1975.

6. J. W. Hunt and M. D. McIlroy, ''An Algorithm for Differential File Comparison,'' Comp. Sci. Tech. Rep. No. 41, Bell Laboratories, Murray Hill, New Jersey, June 1976 .].

7. F. P. Brooks, Jr., *The Mythical Man-Month,* Addison-Wesley, Reading, Mass., 1975.

16

On the Security of UNIX

Dennis M. Ritchie

AT&T Bell Laboratories
Murray Hill, NJ

Recently there has been much interest in the security aspects of operating systems and software. At issue is the ability to prevent undesired disclosure of information, destruction of information, and harm to the functioning of the system. This paper discusses the degree of security which can be provided under the UNIX† system and offers a number of hints on how to improve security.

The first fact to face is that UNIX was not developed with security, in any realistic sense, in mind; this fact alone guarantees a vast number of holes. (Actually the same statement can be made with respect to most systems.) The area of security in which UNIX is theoretically weakest is in protecting against crashing or at least crippling the operation of the system. The problem here is not mainly in uncritical acceptance of bad parameters to system calls— there may be bugs in this area, but none are known— but rather in lack of checks for excessive consumption of resources. Most notably, there is no limit on the amount of disk storage used, either in total space allocated or in the number of files or directories. Here is a particularly ghastly shell sequence guaranteed to stop the system:

```
while : ; do
        mkdir x
        cd x
done
```

Either a panic will occur because all the i-nodes on the device are used up, or all the disk blocks will be consumed, thus preventing anyone from writing files on the device.

In this version of the system, users are prevented from creating more than a set number of processes simultaneously, so unless users are in collusion it is unlikely that any one can stop the system altogether. However, creation of 20 or so CPU or disk-bound jobs leaves few resources available for others. Also, if many large jobs are run simultaneously, swap space may run out, causing a panic.

It should be evident that excessive consumption of disk space, files, swap space, and processes can easily occur accidentally in malfunctioning programs as well as at command level. In fact UNIX is essentially defenseless against this kind of abuse, nor is there any easy fix. The best that can be said is that it is generally fairly easy to detect what has happened when disaster strikes, to identify the user responsible, and take appropriate action. In practice, we have found that difficulties in this area are rather rare, but we have not been faced with malicious users, and enjoy a fairly generous supply of resources which have served to cushion us against accidental overconsumption.

The picture is considerably brighter in the area of protection of information from unauthorized perusal and destruction. Here the degree of security seems (almost) adequate theoretically, and the problems lie more in the necessity for care in the actual use of the system.

Each UNIX file has associated with it eleven bits of protection information together with a user identification number and a user-group identification number (UID and GID). Nine of the protection bits are used to specify independently permission to read, to write, and to execute the file to the user himself, to members of the user's group, and to all other users. Each process generated by or for a user has associated with it an effective UID and a real UID, and an effective and real GID. When an attempt is made to access the file for reading, writing, or execution, the user process's effective UID is compared against the file's

† UNIX is a registered trademark of AT&T Bell Laboratories in the USA and other countries.

UID; if a match is obtained, access is granted provided the read, write, or execute bit respectively for the user himself is present. If the UID for the file and for the process fail to match, but the GID's do match, the group bits are used; if the GID's do not match, the bits for other users are tested. The last two bits of each file's protection information, called the set-UID and set-GID bits, are used only when the file is executed as a program. If, in this case, the set-UID bit is on for the file, the effective UID for the process is changed to the UID associated with the file; the change persists until the process terminates or until the UID changed again by another execution of a set-UID file. Similarly the effective group ID of a process is changed to the GID associated with a file when that file is executed and has the set-GID bit set. The real UID and GID of a process do not change when any file is executed, but only as the result of a privileged system call.

The basic notion of the set-UID and set-GID bits is that one may write a program which is executable by others and which maintains files accessible to others only by that program. The classical example is the game-playing program which maintains records of the scores of its players. The program itself has to read and write the score file, but no one but the game's sponsor can be allowed unrestricted access to the file lest they manipulate the game to their own advantage. The solution is to turn on the set-UID bit of the game program. When, and only when, it is invoked by players of the game, it may update the score file but ordinary programs executed by others cannot access the score.

There are a number of special cases involved in determining access permissions. Since executing a directory as a program is a meaningless operation, the execute-permission bit, for directories, is taken instead to mean permission to search the directory for a given file during the scanning of a path name; thus if a directory has execute permission but no read permission for a given user, he may access files with known names in the directory, but may not read (list) the entire contents of the directory. Write permission on a directory is interpreted to mean that the user may create and delete files in that directory; it is impossible for any user to write directly into any directory.

Another, and from the point of view of security, much more serious special case is that there is a "super user" who is able to read any file and write any non-directory. The super-user is also able to change the protection mode and the owner UID and GID of any file and to invoke privileged system calls. It must be recognized that the mere notion of a super-user is a theoretical, and usually practical, blemish on any protection scheme.

The first necessity for a secure system is of course arranging that all files and directories have the proper protection modes. Traditionally, UNIX software has been exceedingly permissive in this regard; essentially all commands create files readable and writable by everyone. In the current version, this policy may be easily adjusted to suit the needs of the installation or the individual user. Associated with each process and its descendants is a mask, which is in effect *and*-ed with the mode of every file and directory created by that process. In this way, users can arrange that, by default, all their files are no more accessible than they wish. The standard mask, set by *login,* allows all permissions to the user himself and to his group, but disallows writing by others.

To maintain both data privacy and data integrity, it is necessary, and largely sufficient, to make one's files inaccessible to others. The lack of sufficiency could follow from the existence of set-UID programs created by the user and the possibility of total breach of system security in one of the ways discussed below (or one of the ways not discussed below). For greater protection, an encryption scheme is available. Since the editor is able to create encrypted documents, and the *crypt* command can be used to pipe such documents into the other text-processing programs, the length of time during which cleartext versions need be available is strictly limited. The encryption scheme used is not one of the strongest known, but it is judged adequate, in the sense that cryptanalysis is likely to require considerably more effort than more direct methods of reading the encrypted files. For example, a user who stores data that he regards as truly secret should be aware that he is implicitly trusting the system administrator not to install a version of the crypt command that stores every typed password in a file.

Needless to say, the system administrators must be at least as careful as their most demanding user to place the correct protection mode on the files under their control. In particular, it is necessary that special files be protected from writing, and probably reading, by ordinary users when they store sensitive files belonging to other users. It is easy to write programs that examine and change files by accessing the device on which the files live.

On the issue of password security, UNIX is probably better than most systems. Passwords are stored in an encrypted form which, in the absence of serious attention from specialists in the field, appears reasonably secure, provided its limitations are understood. In the current version, it is based on a slightly defective version of the Federal DES; it is purposely defective so that easily-available hardware is useless for attempts at exhaustive key-search. Since both the encryption algorithm and the encrypted passwords are available, exhaustive enumeration of potential passwords is still feasible up to a point. We have observed that users choose passwords that are easy to guess: they are short, or from a limited alphabet, or in a dictionary. Passwords should be at least six characters long and randomly chosen from an alphabet which includes digits and special characters.

Of course there also exist feasible non-cryptanalytic ways of finding out passwords. For example: write a program which types out ''login: '' on the typewriter and copies whatever is typed to a file of your own. Then invoke the command and go away until the victim arrives.

The set-UID (set-GID) notion must be used carefully if any security is to be maintained. The first thing to keep in mind is that a writable set-UID file can have another program copied onto it. For example, if the super-user *(su)* command is writable, anyone can copy the shell onto it and get a password-free version of *su.* A more subtle problem can come from set-UID programs which are not sufficiently careful of what is fed into them. To take an obsolete example, the previous version of the *mail* command was set-UID and owned by the super-user. This version sent mail to the recipient's own directory. The notion was that one should be able to send mail to anyone even if they want to protect their directories from writing. The trouble was that *mail* was rather dumb: anyone could mail someone else's private file to himself. Much more serious is the following scenario: make a file with a line like one in the password file which allows one to log in as the super-user. Then make a link named ''.mail'' to the password file in some writable directory on the same device as the password file (say /tmp). Finally mail the bogus login line to /tmp/.mail; You can then login as the super-user, clean up the incriminating evidence, and have your will.

The fact that users can mount their own disks and tapes as file systems can be another way of gaining super-user status. Once a disk pack is mounted, the system believes what is on it. Thus one can take a blank disk pack, put on it anything desired, and mount it. There are obvious and unfortunate consequences. For example: a mounted disk with garbage on it will crash the system; one of the files on the mounted disk can easily be a password-free version of *su;* other files can be unprotected entries for special files. The only easy fix for this problem is to forbid the use of *mount* to unprivileged users. A partial solution, not so restrictive, would be to have the *mount* command examine the special file for bad data, set-UID programs owned by others, and accessible special files, and balk at unprivileged invokers.

Password Security: A Case History

Robert Morris

Ken Thompson

AT&T Bell Laboratories
Murray Hill, NJ

17

ABSTRACT

This paper describes the history of the design of the password security scheme on a remotely accessed time-sharing system. The present design was the result of countering observed attempts to penetrate the system. The result is a compromise between extreme security and ease of use.

INTRODUCTION

Password security on the UNIX† time-sharing system [1] is provided by a collection of programs whose elaborate and strange design is the outgrowth of many years of experience with earlier versions. To help develop a secure system, we have had a continuing competition to devise new ways to attack the security of the system (the bad guy) and, at the same time, to devise new techniques to resist the new attacks (the good guy). This competition has been in the same vein as the competition of long standing between manufacturers of armor plate and those of armor-piercing shells. For this reason, the description that follows will trace the history of the password system rather than simply presenting the program in its current state. In this way, the reasons for the design will be made clearer, as the design cannot be understood without also understanding the potential attacks.

An underlying goal has been to provide password security at minimal inconvenience to the users of the system. For example, those who want to run a completely open system without passwords, or to have passwords only at the option of the individual users, are able to do so, while those who require all of their users to have passwords gain a high degree of security against penetration of the system by unauthorized users.

The password system must be able not only to prevent any access to the system by unauthorized users (i.e. prevent them from logging in at all), but it must also prevent users who are already logged in from doing things that they are not authorized to do. The so called ''super-user'' password, for example, is especially critical because the super-user has all sorts of permissions and has essentially unlimited access to all system resources.

Password security is of course only one component of overall system security, but it is an essential component. Experience has shown that attempts to penetrate remote-access systems have been astonishingly sophisticated.

Remote-access systems are peculiarly vulnerable to penetration by outsiders as there are threats at the remote terminal, along the communications link, as well as at the computer itself. Although the security of a password encryption algorithm is an interesting intellectual and mathematical problem, it is only one tiny facet of a very large problem. In practice, physical security of the computer, communications security of the communications link, and physical control of the computer itself loom as far more important issues. Perhaps most important of all is control over the actions of ex-employees, since they are not under any direct control and they may have intimate knowledge about the system, its resources, and methods of

† UNIX is a registered trademark of AT&T Bell Laboratories in the USA and other countries.

access. Good system security involves realistic evaluation of the risks not only of deliberate attacks but also of casual unauthorized access and accidental disclosure.

PROLOGUE

The UNIX system was first implemented with a password file that contained the actual passwords of all the users, and for that reason the password file had to be heavily protected against being either read or written. Although historically, this had been the technique used for remote-access systems, it was completely unsatisfactory for several reasons.

The technique is excessively vulnerable to lapses in security. Temporary loss of protection can occur when the password file is being edited or otherwise modified. There is no way to prevent the making of copies by privileged users. Experience with several earlier remote-access systems showed that such lapses occur with frightening frequency. Perhaps the most memorable such occasion occurred in the early 60's when a system administrator on the CTSS system at MIT was editing the password file and another system administrator was editing the daily message that is printed on everyone's terminal on login. Due to a software design error, the temporary editor files of the two users were interchanged and thus, for a time, the password file was printed on every terminal when it was logged in.

Once such a lapse in security has been discovered, everyone's password must be changed, usually simultaneously, at a considerable administrative cost. This is not a great matter, but far more serious is the high probability of such lapses going unnoticed by the system administrators.

Security against unauthorized disclosure of the passwords was, in the last analysis, impossible with this system because, for example, if the contents of the file system are put on to magnetic tape for backup, as they must be, then anyone who has physical access to the tape can read anything on it with no restriction.

Many programs must get information of various kinds about the users of the system, and these programs in general should have no special permission to read the password file. The information which should have been in the password file actually was distributed (or replicated) into a number of files, all of which had to be updated whenever a user was added to or dropped from the system.

THE FIRST SCHEME

The obvious solution is to arrange that the passwords not appear in the system at all, and it is not difficult to decide that this can be done by encrypting each user's password, putting only the encrypted form in the password file, and throwing away his original password (the one that he typed in). When the user later tries to log in to the system, the password that he types is encrypted and compared with the encrypted version in the password file. If the two match, his login attempt is accepted. Such a scheme was first described in [3, p.91ff.]. It also seemed advisable to devise a system in which neither the password file nor the password program itself needed to be protected against being read by anyone.

All that was needed to implement these ideas was to find a means of encryption that was very difficult to invert, even when the encryption program is available. Most of the standard encryption methods used (in the past) for encryption of messages are rather easy to invert. A convenient and rather good encryption program happened to exist on the system at the time; it simulated the M-209 cipher machine [4] used by the U.S. Army during World War II. It turned out that the M-209 program was usable, but with a given key, the ciphers produced by this program are trivial to invert. It is a much more difficult matter to find out the key given the cleartext input and the enciphered output of the program. Therefore, the password was used not as the text to be encrypted but as the key, and a constant was encrypted using this key. The encrypted result was entered into the password file.

ATTACKS ON THE FIRST APPROACH

Suppose that the bad guy has available the text of the password encryption program and the complete password file. Suppose also that he has substantial computing capacity at his disposal.

One obvious approach to penetrating the password mechanism is to attempt to find a general method of inverting the encryption algorithm. Very possibly this can be done, but few successful results have come to light, despite substantial efforts extending over a period of more than five years. The results have not proved to be very useful in penetrating systems.

Another approach to penetration is simply to keep trying potential passwords until one succeeds; this is a general cryptanalytic approach called *key search.* Human beings being what they are, there is a strong tendency for people to choose relatively short and simple passwords that they can remember. Given free choice, most people will choose their passwords from a restricted character set (e.g. all lower-case letters), and will often choose words or names. This human habit makes the key search job a great deal easier.

The critical factor involved in key search is the amount of time needed to encrypt a potential password and to check the result against an entry in the password file. The running time to encrypt one trial password and check the result turned out to be approximately 1.25 milliseconds on a PDP-11/70 when the encryption algorithm was recoded for maximum speed. It is takes essentially no more time to test the encrypted trial password against all the passwords in an entire password file, or for that matter, against any collection of encrypted passwords, perhaps collected from many installations.

If we want to check all passwords of length *n* that consist entirely of lower-case letters, the number of such passwords is 26^n. If we suppose that the password consists of printable characters only, then the number of possible passwords is somewhat less than 95^n. (The standard system ''character erase'' and ''line kill'' characters are, for example, not prime candidates.) We can immediately estimate the running time of a program that will test every password of a given length with all of its characters chosen from some set of characters. The following table gives estimates of the running time required on a PDP-11/70 to test all possible character strings of length *n* chosen from various sets of characters: namely, all lower-case letters, all lower-case letters plus digits, all alphanumeric characters, all 95 printable ASCII characters, and finally all 128 ASCII characters.

n	26 lower-case letters	36 lower-case letters and digits	62 alphanumeric characters	95 printable characters	all 128 ASCII characters
1	30 msec.	40 msec.	80 msec.	120 msec.	160 msec.
2	800 msec.	2 sec.	5 sec.	11 sec.	20 sec.
3	22 sec.	58 sec.	5 min.	17 min.	43 min.
4	10 min.	35 min.	5 hrs.	28 hrs.	93 hrs.
5	4 hrs.	21 hrs.	318 hrs.		
6	107 hrs.				

One has to conclude that it is no great matter for someone with access to a PDP-11 to test all lower-case alphabetic strings up to length five and, given access to the machine for, say, several weekends, to test all such strings up to six characters in length. By using such a program against a collection of actual encrypted passwords, a substantial fraction of all the passwords will be found.

Another profitable approach for the bad guy is to use the word list from a dictionary or to use a list of names. For example, a large commercial dictionary contains typicallly about 250,000 words; these words can be checked in about five minutes. Again, a noticeable fraction of any collection of passwords will be found. Improvements and extensions will be (and have been) found by a determined bad guy. Some ''good'' things to try are:

- The dictionary with the words spelled backwards.
- A list of first names (best obtained from some mailing list). Last names, street names, and city names also work well.
- The above with initial upper-case letters.
- All valid license plate numbers in your state. (This takes about five hours in New Jersey.)
- Room numbers, social security numbers, telephone numbers, and the like.

The authors have conducted experiments to try to determine typical users' habits in the choice of passwords when no constraint is put on their choice. The results were disappointing, except to the bad guy. In a collection of 3,289 passwords gathered from many users over a long period of time;

15 were a single ASCII character;

72 were strings of two ASCII characters;

464 were strings of three ASCII characters;

477 were string of four alphamerics;

706 were five letters, all upper-case or all lower-case;

605 were six letters, all lower-case.

An additional 492 passwords appeared in various available dictionaries, name lists, and the like. A total of 2,831, or 86% of this sample of passwords fell into one of these classes.

There was, of course, considerable overlap between the dictionary results and the character string searches. The dictionary search alone, which required only five minutes to run, produced about one third of the passwords.

Users could be urged (or forced) to use either longer passwords or passwords chosen from a larger character set, or the system could itself choose passwords for the users.

AN ANECDOTE

An entertaining and instructive example is the attempt made at one installation to force users to use less predictable passwords. The users did not choose their own passwords; the system supplied them. The supplied passwords were eight characters long and were taken from the character set consisting of lower-case letters and digits. They were generated by a pseudo-random number generator with only 2^{15} starting values. The time required to search (again on a PDP-11/70) through all character strings of length 8 from a 36-character alphabet is 112 years.

Unfortunately, only 2^{15} of them need be looked at, because that is the number of possible outputs of the random number generator. The bad guy did, in fact, generate and test each of these strings and found every one of the system-generated passwords using a total of only about one minute of machine time.

IMPROVEMENTS TO THE FIRST APPROACH

1. Slower Encryption

Obviously, the first algorithm used was far too fast. The announcement of the DES encryption algorithm [2] by the National Bureau of Standards was timely and fortunate. The DES is, by design, hard to invert, but equally valuable is the fact that it is extremely slow when implemented in software. The DES was implemented and used in the following way: The first eight characters of the user's password are used as a key for the DES; then the algorithm is used to encrypt a constant. Although this constant is zero at the moment, it is easily accessible and can be made installation-dependent. Then the DES algorithm is iterated 25 times and the resulting 64 bits are repacked to become a string of 11 printable characters.

2. Less Predictable Passwords

The password entry program was modified so as to urge the user to use more obscure passwords. If the user enters an alphabetic password (all upper-case or all lower-case) shorter than six characters, or a password from a larger character set shorter than five characters, then the program asks him to enter a longer password. This further reduces the efficacy of key search.

These improvements make it exceedingly difficult to find any individual password. The user is warned of the risks and if he cooperates, he is very safe indeed. On the other hand, he is not prevented from using his spouse's name if he wants to.

3. Salted Passwords

The key search technique is still likely to turn up a few passwords when it is used on a large collection of passwords, and it seemed wise to make this task as difficult as possible. To this end, when a password is first entered, the password program obtains a 12-bit random number (by reading the real-time clock) and appends this to the password typed in by the user. The concatenated string is encrypted and both the 12-bit random quantity (called the *salt*) and the 64-bit result of the encryption are entered into the password file.

When the user later logs in to the system, the 12-bit quantity is extracted from the password file and appended to the typed password. The encrypted result is required, as before, to be the same as the remaining 64 bits in the password file. This modification does not increase the task of finding any individual password, starting from scratch, but now the work of testing a given character string against a large collection of encrypted passwords has been multiplied by 4096 (2^{12}). The reason for this is that there are 4096 encrypted versions of each password and one of them has been picked more or less at random by the system.

With this modification, it is likely that the bad guy can spend days of computer time trying to find a password on a system with hundreds of passwords, and find none at all. More important is the fact that it becomes impractical to prepare an encrypted dictionary in advance. Such an encrypted dictionary could be used to crack new passwords in milliseconds when they appear.

There is a (not inadvertent) side effect of this modification. It becomes nearly impossible to find out whether a person with passwords on two or more systems has used the same password on all of them, unless you already know that.

4. The Threat of the DES Chip

Chips to perform the DES encryption are already commercially available and they are very fast. The use of such a chip speeds up the process of password hunting by three orders of magnitude. To avert this possibility, one of the internal tables of the DES algorithm (in particular, the so-called E-table) is changed in a way that depends on the 12-bit random number. The E-table is inseparably wired into the DES chip, so that the commercial chip cannot be used. Obviously, the bad guy could have his own chip designed and built, but the cost would be unthinkable.

5. A Subtle Point

To login successfully on the UNIX system, it is necessary after dialing in to type a valid user name, and then the correct password for that user name. It is poor design to write the login command in such a way that it tells an interloper when he has typed in a invalid user name. The response to an invalid name should be identical to that for a valid name.

When the slow encryption algorithm was first implemented, the encryption was done only if the user name was valid, because otherwise there was no encrypted password to compare with the supplied password. The result was that the response was delayed by about one-half second if the name was valid, but was immediate if invalid. The bad guy could find out whether a particular user name was valid. The routine was modified to do the encryption in either case.

CONCLUSIONS

On the issue of password security, UNIX is probably better than most systems. The use of encrypted passwords appears reasonably secure in the absence of serious attention of experts in the field.

It is also worth some effort to conceal even the encrypted passwords. Some UNIX systems have instituted what is called an "external security code" that must be typed when dialing into the system, but before logging in. If this code is changed periodically, then someone with an old password will likely be prevented from using it.

Whenever any security procedure is instituted that attempts to deny access to unauthorized persons, it is wise to keep a record of both successful and unsuccessful attempts to get at the secured resource. Just as an out-of-hours visitor to a computer center normally must not only identify himself, but a record is usually also kept of his entry. Just so, it is a wise precaution to make and keep a record of all attempts to log into a remote-access time-sharing system, and certainly all unsuccessful attempts.

Bad guys fall on a spectrum whose one end is someone with ordinary access to a system and whose goal is to find out a particular password (usually that of the super-user) and, at the other end, someone who wishes to collect as much password information as possible from as many systems as possible. Most of the work reported here serves to frustrate the latter type; our experience indicates that the former type of bad guy never was very successful.

We recognize that a time-sharing system must operate in a hostile environment. We did not attempt to hide the security aspects of the operating system, thereby playing the customary make-believe game in which weaknesses of the system are not discussed no matter how apparent. Rather we advertised the password algorithm and invited attack in the belief that this approach would minimize future trouble. The approach has been successful.

References

[1] Ritchie, D.M. and Thompson, K. The UNIX Time-Sharing System. *Comm. ACM* **17** (July 1974), pp. 365-375.

[2] *Proposed Federal Information Processing Data Encryption Standard.* Federal Register (40FR12134), March 17, 1975

[3] Wilkes, M. V. *Time-Sharing Computer Systems.* American Elsevier, New York, (1968).

[4] U. S. Patent Number 2,089,603.

Networking Implementation Notes
4.4BSD Edition

Samuel J. Leffler, William N. Joy, Robert S. Fabry, and Michael J. Karels

Computer Systems Research Group
Computer Science Division
Department of Electrical Engineering and Computer Science
University of California, Berkeley
Berkeley, CA 94720

18

ABSTRACT

This report describes the internal structure of the networking facilities developed for the 4.4BSD version of the UNIX* operating system for the VAX†. These facilities are based on several central abstractions which structure the external (user) view of network communication as well as the internal (system) implementation.

The report documents the internal structure of the networking system. The "Berkeley Software Architecture Manual, 4.4BSD Edition" (PSD:5) provides a description of the user interface to the networking facilities.

Revised June 10, 1993

* UNIX is a trademark of Bell Laboratories.

† DEC, VAX, DECnet, and UNIBUS are trademarks of Digital Equipment Corporation.

TABLE OF CONTENTS

1. Introduction

This report describes the internal structure of facilities added to the 4.2BSD version of the UNIX operating system for the VAX, as modified in the 4.4BSD release. The system facilities provide a uniform user interface to networking within UNIX. In addition, the implementation introduces a structure for network communications which may be used by system implementors in adding new networking facilities. The internal structure is not visible to the user, rather it is intended to aid implementors of communication protocols and network services by providing a framework which promotes code sharing and minimizes implementation effort.

The reader is expected to be familiar with the C programming language and system interface, as described in the *Berkeley Software Architecture Manual, 4.4BSD Edition* [Joy86]. Basic understanding of network communication concepts is assumed; where required any additional ideas are introduced.

The remainder of this document provides a description of the system internals, avoiding, when possible, those portions which are utilized only by the interprocess communication facilities.

2. Overview

If we consider the International Standards Organization's (ISO) Open System Interconnection (OSI) model of network communication [ISO81] [Zimmermann80], the networking facilities described here correspond to a portion of the session layer (layer 3) and all of the transport and network layers (layers 2 and 1, respectively).

The network layer provides possibly imperfect data transport services with minimal addressing structure. Addressing at this level is normally host to host, with implicit or explicit routing optionally supported by the communicating agents.

At the transport layer the notions of reliable transfer, data sequencing, flow control, and service addressing are normally included. Reliability is usually managed by explicit acknowledgement of data delivered. Failure to acknowledge a transfer results in retransmission of the data. Sequencing may be handled by tagging each message handed to the network layer by a *sequence number* and maintaining state at the endpoints of communication to utilize received sequence numbers in reordering data which arrives out of order.

The session layer facilities may provide forms of addressing which are mapped into formats required by the transport layer, service authentication and client authentication, etc. Various systems also provide services such as data encryption and address and protocol translation.

The following sections begin by describing some of the common data structures and utility routines, then examine the internal layering. The contents of each layer and its interface are considered. Certain of the interfaces are protocol implementation specific. For these cases examples have been drawn from the Internet [Cerf78] protocol family. Later sections cover routing issues, the design of the raw socket interface and other miscellaneous topics.

3. Goals

The networking system was designed with the goal of supporting multiple *protocol families* and addressing styles. This required information to be ''hidden'' in common data structures which could be manipulated by all the pieces of the system, but which required interpretation only by the protocols which ''controlled'' it. The system described here attempts to minimize the use of shared data structures to those kept by a suite of protocols (a *protocol family*), and those used for rendezvous between ''synchronous'' and ''asynchronous'' portions of the system (e.g. queues of data packets are filled at interrupt time and emptied based on user requests).

A major goal of the system was to provide a framework within which new protocols and hardware could be easily be supported. To this end, a great deal of effort has been extended to create utility routines which hide many of the more complex and/or hardware dependent chores of networking. Later sections describe the utility routines and the underlying data structures they manipulate.

4. Internal address representation

Common to all portions of the system are two data structures. These structures are used to represent addresses and various data objects. Addresses, internally are described by the *sockaddr* structure,

```
struct sockaddr {
        short       sa_family;        /* data format identifier */
        char        sa_data[14];      /* address */
};
```

All addresses belong to one or more *address families* which define their format and interpretation. The *sa_family* field indicates the address family to which the address belongs, and the *sa_data* field contains the actual data value. The size of the data field, 14 bytes, was selected based on a study of current address formats.* Specific address formats use private structure definitions that define the format of the data field. The system interface supports larger address structures, although address-family-independent support facilities, for example routing and raw socket interfaces, provide only 14 bytes for address storage. Protocols that do not use those facilities (e.g, the current Unix domain) may use larger data areas.

18

5. Memory management

A single mechanism is used for data storage: memory buffers, or *mbuf*'s. An mbuf is a structure of the form:

```
struct mbuf {
        struct      mbuf *m_next;     /* next buffer in chain */
        u_long      m_off;            /* offset of data */
        short       m_len;            /* amount of data in this mbuf */
        short       m_type;           /* mbuf type (accounting) */
        u_char      m_dat[MLEN];      /* data storage */
        struct      mbuf *m_act;      /* link in higher-level mbuf list */
};
```

The *m_next* field is used to chain mbufs together on linked lists, while the *m_act* field allows lists of mbuf chains to be accumulated. By convention, the mbufs common to a single object (for example, a packet) are chained together with the *m_next* field, while groups of objects are linked via the *m_act* field (possibly when in a queue).

Each mbuf has a small data area for storing information, *m_dat*. The *m_len* field indicates the amount of data, while the *m_off* field is an offset to the beginning of the data from the base of the mbuf. Thus, for example, the macro *mtod*, which converts a pointer to an mbuf to a pointer to the data stored in the mbuf, has the form

```
#define   mtod(x,t)          ((t)((int)(x) + (x)->m_off))
```

(note the *t* parameter, a C type cast, which is used to cast the resultant pointer for proper assignment).

In addition to storing data directly in the mbuf's data area, data of page size may be also be stored in a separate area of memory. The mbuf utility routines maintain a pool of pages for this purpose and manipulate a private page map for such pages. An mbuf with an external data area may be recognized by the larger offset to the data area; this is formalized by the macro M_HASCL(*m*), which is true if the mbuf whose address is *m* has an external page cluster. An array of reference counts on pages is also maintained so that copies of pages may be made without core to core copying (copies are created simply by duplicating the reference to the data and incrementing the associated reference counts for the pages). Separate data pages are currently used only when copying data from a user process into the kernel, and when bringing data in at the hardware level. Routines which manipulate mbufs are not normally aware whether data is stored directly in the mbuf data array, or if it is kept in separate pages.

---

* Later versions of the system may support variable length addresses.

The following may be used to allocate and free mbufs:

m = m_get(wait, type);
MGET(m, wait, type);

The subroutine *m_get* and the macro *MGET* each allocate an mbuf, placing its address in *m*. The argument *wait* is either M_WAIT or M_DONTWAIT according to whether allocation should block or fail if no mbuf is available. The *type* is one of the predefined mbuf types for use in accounting of mbuf allocation.

MCLGET(m);

This macro attempts to allocate an mbuf page cluster to associate with the mbuf *m*. If successful, the length of the mbuf is set to CLSIZE, the size of the page cluster.

n = m_free(m);
MFREE(m,n);

The routine *m_free* and the macro *MFREE* each free a single mbuf, *m*, and any associated external storage area, placing a pointer to its successor in the chain it heads, if any, in *n*.

m_freem(m);

This routine frees an mbuf chain headed by *m*.

The following utility routines are available for manipulating mbuf chains:

m = m_copy(m0, off, len);

The *m_copy* routine create a copy of all, or part, of a list of the mbufs in *m0*. *Len* bytes of data, starting *off* bytes from the front of the chain, are copied. Where possible, reference counts on pages are used instead of core to core copies. The original mbuf chain must have at least *off* + *len* bytes of data. If *len* is specified as M_COPYALL, all the data present, offset as before, is copied.

m_cat(m, n);

The mbuf chain, *n*, is appended to the end of *m*. Where possible, compaction is performed.

m_adj(m, diff);

The mbuf chain, *m* is adjusted in size by *diff* bytes. If *diff* is non-negative, *diff* bytes are shaved off the front of the mbuf chain. If *diff* is negative, the alteration is performed from back to front. No space is reclaimed in this operation; alterations are accomplished by changing the *m_len* and *m_off* fields of mbufs.

m = m_pullup(m0, size);

After a successful call to *m_pullup*, the mbuf at the head of the returned list, *m*, is guaranteed to have at least *size* bytes of data in contiguous memory within the data area of the mbuf (allowing access via a pointer, obtained using the *mtod* macro, and allowing the mbuf to be located from a pointer to the data area using *dtom*, defined below). If the original data was less than *size* bytes long, *len* was greater than the size of an mbuf data area (112 bytes), or required resources were unavailable, *m* is 0 and the original mbuf chain is deallocated.

This routine is particularly useful when verifying packet header lengths on reception. For example, if a packet is received and only 8 of the necessary 16 bytes required for a valid packet header are present at the head of the list of mbufs representing the packet, the remaining 8 bytes may be ''pulled up'' with a single *m_pullup* call. If the call fails the invalid packet will have been discarded.

By insuring that mbufs always reside on 128 byte boundaries, it is always possible to locate the mbuf associated with a data area by masking off the low bits of the virtual address. This allows modules to store data structures in mbufs and pass them around without concern for locating the original mbuf when it comes time to free the structure. Note that this works only with objects stored in the internal data buffer of the mbuf. The *dtom* macro is used to convert a pointer into an mbuf's data area to a pointer to the mbuf,

```
#define     dtom(x)     ((struct mbuf *)((int)x & ~(MSIZE-1)))
```

Mbufs are used for dynamically allocated data structures such as sockets as well as memory allocated for packets and headers. Statistics are maintained on mbuf usage and can be viewed by users using the *netstat*(1) program.

6. Internal layering

The internal structure of the network system is divided into three layers. These layers correspond to the services provided by the socket abstraction, those provided by the communication protocols, and those provided by the hardware interfaces. The communication protocols are normally layered into two or more individual cooperating layers, though they are collectively viewed in the system as one layer providing services supportive of the appropriate socket abstraction.

The following sections describe the properties of each layer in the system and the interfaces to which each must conform.

6.1. Socket layer

The socket layer deals with the interprocess communication facilities provided by the system. A socket is a bidirectional endpoint of communication which is ''typed'' by the semantics of communication it supports. The system calls described in the *Berkeley Software Architecture Manual* [Joy86] are used to manipulate sockets.

18

A socket consists of the following data structure:

```
struct socket {
        short       so_type;            /* generic type */
        short       so_options;         /* from socket call */
        short       so_linger;          /* time to linger while closing */
        short       so_state;           /* internal state flags */
        caddr_t     so_pcb;             /* protocol control block */
        struct      protosw *so_proto;  /* protocol handle */
        struct      socket *so_head;    /* back pointer to accept socket */
        struct      socket *so_q0;      /* queue of partial connections */
        short       so_q0len;           /* partials on so_q0 */
        struct      socket *so_q;       /* queue of incoming connections */
        short       so_qlen;            /* number of connections on so_q */
        short       so_qlimit;          /* max number queued connections */
        struct      sockbuf so_rcv;     /* receive queue */
        struct      sockbuf so_snd;     /* send queue */
        short       so_timeo;           /* connection timeout */
        u_short     so_error;           /* error affecting connection */
        u_short     so_oobmark;         /* chars to oob mark */
        short       so_pgrp;            /* pgrp for signals */
};
```

Each socket contains two data queues, *so_rcv* and *so_snd*, and a pointer to routines which provide supporting services. The type of the socket, *so_type* is defined at socket creation time and used in selecting those services which are appropriate to support it. The supporting protocol is selected at socket creation time and recorded in the socket data structure for later use. Protocols are defined by a table of procedures, the *protosw* structure, which will be described in detail later. A pointer to a protocol-specific data structure, the ''protocol control block,'' is also present in the socket structure. Protocols control this data structure, which normally includes a back pointer to the parent socket structure to allow easy lookup when returning information to a user (for example, placing an error number in the *so_error* field). The other entries in the socket structure are used in queuing connection requests, validating user requests, storing socket characteristics (e.g. options supplied at the time a socket is created), and maintaining a socket's state.

Processes ''rendezvous at a socket'' in many instances. For instance, when a process wishes to extract data from a socket's receive queue and it is empty, or lacks sufficient data to satisfy the request, the process blocks, supplying the address of the receive queue as a ''wait channel' to be used in notification. When data arrives for the process and is placed in the socket's queue, the blocked process is identified by the fact it is waiting ''on the queue.''

6.1.1. Socket state

A socket's state is defined from the following:

```
#define SS_NOFDREF          0x001   /* no file table ref any more */
#define SS_ISCONNECTED      0x002   /* socket connected to a peer */
#define SS_ISCONNECTING     0x004   /* in process of connecting to peer */
#define SS_ISDISCONNECTING  0x008   /* in process of disconnecting */
#define SS_CANTSENDMORE     0x010   /* can't send more data to peer */
#define SS_CANTRCVMORE      0x020   /* can't receive more data from peer */
#define SS_RCVATMARK        0x040   /* at mark on input */

#define SS_PRIV             0x080   /* privileged */
#define SS_NBIO             0x100   /* non-blocking ops */
#define SS_ASYNC            0x200   /* async i/o notify */
```


The state of a socket is manipulated both by the protocols and the user (through system calls). When a socket is created, the state is defined based on the type of socket. It may change as control actions are performed, for example connection establishment. It may also change according to the type of input/output the user wishes to perform, as indicated by options set with *fcntl*. ''Non-blocking'' I/O implies that a process should never be blocked to await resources. Instead, any call which would block returns prematurely with the error EWOULDBLOCK, or the service request may be partially fulfilled, e.g. a request for more data than is present.

If a process requested ''asynchronous'' notification of events related to the socket, the SIGIO signal is posted to the process when such events occur. An event is a change in the socket's state; examples of such occurrences are: space becoming available in the send queue, new data available in the receive queue, connection establishment or disestablishment, etc.

A socket may be marked ''privileged'' if it was created by the super-user. Only privileged sockets may bind addresses in privileged portions of an address space or use ''raw'' sockets to access lower levels of the network.

6.1.2. Socket data queues

A socket's data queue contains a pointer to the data stored in the queue and other entries related to the management of the data. The following structure defines a data queue:

```
struct sockbuf {
        u_short     sb_cc;              /* actual chars in buffer */
        u_short     sb_hiwat;           /* max actual char count */
        u_short     sb_mbcnt;           /* chars of mbufs used */
        u_short     sb_mbmax;           /* max chars of mbufs to use */
        u_short     sb_lowat;           /* low water mark */
        short       sb_timeo;           /* timeout */
        struct      mbuf *sb_mb;        /* the mbuf chain */
        struct      proc *sb_sel;       /* process selecting read/write */
        short       sb_flags;           /* flags, see below */
};
```

Data is stored in a queue as a chain of mbufs. The actual count of data characters as well as high and low water marks are used by the protocols in controlling the flow of data. The amount of buffer space (characters of mbufs and associated data pages) is also recorded along with the limit on buffer allocation. The socket routines cooperate in implementing the flow control policy by blocking a process when it requests to send data and the high water mark has been reached, or when it requests to receive data and less than the low water mark is present (assuming non-blocking I/O has not been specified).*

* The low-water mark is always presumed to be 0 in the current implementation.

When a socket is created, the supporting protocol ''reserves'' space for the send and receive queues of the socket. The limit on buffer allocation is set somewhat higher than the limit on data characters to account for the granularity of buffer allocation. The actual storage associated with a socket queue may fluctuate during a socket's lifetime, but it is assumed that this reservation will always allow a protocol to acquire enough memory to satisfy the high water marks.

The timeout and select values are manipulated by the socket routines in implementing various portions of the interprocess communications facilities and will not be described here.

Data queued at a socket is stored in one of two styles. Stream-oriented sockets queue data with no addresses, headers or record boundaries. The data are in mbufs linked through the *m_next* field. Buffers containing access rights may be present within the chain if the underlying protocol supports passage of access rights. Record-oriented sockets, including datagram sockets, queue data as a list of packets; the sections of packets are distinguished by the types of the mbufs containing them. The mbufs which comprise a record are linked through the *m_next* field; records are linked from the *m_act* field of the first mbuf of one packet to the first mbuf of the next. Each packet begins with an mbuf containing the ''from'' address if the protocol provides it, then any buffers containing access rights, and finally any buffers containing data. If a record contains no data, no data buffers are required unless neither address nor access rights are present.

A socket queue has a number of flags used in synchronizing access to the data and in acquiring resources:

```
#define   SB_LOCK      0x01   /* lock on data queue (so_rcv only) */
#define   SB_WANT      0x02   /* someone is waiting to lock */
#define   SB_WAIT      0x04   /* someone is waiting for data/space */
#define   SB_SEL       0x08   /* buffer is selected */
#define   SB_COLL      0x10   /* collision selecting */
```

The last two flags are manipulated by the system in implementing the select mechanism.

6.1.3. Socket connection queuing

In dealing with connection oriented sockets (e.g. SOCK_STREAM) the two ends are considered distinct. One end is termed *active*, and generates connection requests. The other end is called *passive* and accepts connection requests.

From the passive side, a socket is marked with SO_ACCEPTCONN when a *listen* call is made, creating two queues of sockets: *so_q0* for connections in progress and *so_q* for connections already made and awaiting user acceptance. As a protocol is preparing incoming connections, it creates a socket structure queued on *so_q0* by calling the routine *sonewconn*(). When the connection is established, the socket structure is then transferred to *so_q*, making it available for an *accept*.

If an SO_ACCEPTCONN socket is closed with sockets on either *so_q0* or *so_q*, these sockets are dropped, with notification to the peers as appropriate.

6.2. Protocol layer(s)

Each socket is created in a communications domain, which usually implies both an addressing structure (address family) and a set of protocols which implement various socket types within the domain (protocol family). Each domain is defined by the following structure:

```
struct  domain {
        int     dom_family;            /* PF_xxx */
        char    *dom_name;
        int     (*dom_init)();         /* initialize domain data structures */
        int     (*dom_externalize)();  /* externalize access rights */
        int     (*dom_dispose)();      /* dispose of internalized rights */
        struct  protosw *dom_protosw, *dom_protoswNPROTOSW;
        struct  domain *dom_next;
};
```

At boot time, each domain configured into the kernel is added to a linked list of domain. The initialization procedure of each domain is then called. After that time, the domain structure is used to locate protocols within the protocol family. It may also contain procedure references for externalization of access rights at the receiving socket and the disposal of access rights that are not received.

Protocols are described by a set of entry points and certain socket-visible characteristics, some of which are used in deciding which socket type(s) they may support.

An entry in the ''protocol switch'' table exists for each protocol module configured into the system. It has the following form:

```
struct protosw {
        short  pr_type;                /* socket type used for */
        struct domain *pr_domain;      /* domain protocol a member of */
        short  pr_protocol;            /* protocol number */
        short  pr_flags;               /* socket visible attributes */
/* protocol-protocol hooks */
        int    (*pr_input)();          /* input to protocol (from below) */
        int    (*pr_output)();         /* output to protocol (from above) */
        int    (*pr_ctlinput)();       /* control input (from below) */
        int    (*pr_ctloutput)();      /* control output (from above) */
/* user-protocol hook */
        int    (*pr_usrreq)();         /* user request */
/* utility hooks */
        int    (*pr_init)();           /* initialization routine */
        int    (*pr_fasttimo)();       /* fast timeout (200ms) */
        int    (*pr_slowtimo)();       /* slow timeout (500ms) */
        int    (*pr_drain)();          /* flush any excess space possible */
};
```

A protocol is called through the *pr_init* entry before any other. Thereafter it is called every 200 milliseconds through the *pr_fasttimo* entry and every 500 milliseconds through the *pr_slowtimo* for timer based actions. The system will call the *pr_drain* entry if it is low on space and this should throw away any non-critical data.

Protocols pass data between themselves as chains of mbufs using the *pr_input* and *pr_output* routines. *Pr_input* passes data up (towards the user) and *pr_output* passes it down (towards the network); control information passes up and down on *pr_ctlinput* and *pr_ctloutput*. The protocol is responsible for the space occupied by any of the arguments to these entries and must either pass it onward or dispose of it. (On output, the lowest level reached must free buffers storing the arguments; on input, the highest level is responsible for freeing buffers.)

The *pr_usrreq* routine interfaces protocols to the socket code and is described below.

The *pr_flags* field is constructed from the following values:

```
#define PR_ATOMIC         0x01   /* exchange atomic messages only */
#define PR_ADDR           0x02   /* addresses given with messages */
#define PR_CONNREQUIRED   0x04   /* connection required by protocol */
#define PR_WANTRCVD       0x08   /* want PRU_RCVD calls */
#define PR_RIGHTS         0x10   /* passes capabilities */
```

Protocols which are connection-based specify the PR_CONNREQUIRED flag so that the socket routines will never attempt to send data before a connection has been established. If the PR_WANTRCVD flag is set, the socket routines will notify the protocol when the user has removed data from the socket's receive queue. This allows the protocol to implement acknowledgement on user receipt, and also update windowing information based on the amount of space available in the receive queue. The PR_ADDR field indicates that any data placed in the socket's receive queue will be preceded by the address of the sender. The PR_ATOMIC flag specifies that each *user* request to send data must be performed in a single *protocol* send request; it is the protocol's responsibility to maintain record boundaries on data to be sent. The

PR_RIGHTS flag indicates that the protocol supports the passing of capabilities; this is currently used only by the protocols in the UNIX protocol family.

When a socket is created, the socket routines scan the protocol table for the domain looking for an appropriate protocol to support the type of socket being created. The *pr_type* field contains one of the possible socket types (e.g. SOCK_STREAM), while the *pr_domain* is a back pointer to the domain structure. The *pr_protocol* field contains the protocol number of the protocol, normally a well-known value.

6.3. Network-interface layer

18

Each network-interface configured into a system defines a path through which packets may be sent and received. Normally a hardware device is associated with this interface, though there is no requirement for this (for example, all systems have a software "loopback" interface used for debugging and performance analysis). In addition to manipulating the hardware device, an interface module is responsible for encapsulation and decapsulation of any link-layer header information required to deliver a message to its destination. The selection of which interface to use in delivering packets is a routing decision carried out at a higher level than the network-interface layer. An interface may have addresses in one or more address families. The address is set at boot time using an *ioctl* on a socket in the appropriate domain; this operation is implemented by the protocol family, after verifying the operation through the device *ioctl* entry.

An interface is defined by the following structure,

```
struct ifnet {
	char	*if_name;		/* name, e.g. ''en'' or ''lo'' */
	short	if_unit;		/* sub-unit for lower level driver */
	short	if_mtu;			/* maximum transmission unit */
	short	if_flags;		/* up/down, broadcast, etc. */
	short	if_timer;		/* time 'til if_watchdog called */
	struct	ifaddr *if_addrlist;	/* list of addresses of interface */
	struct	ifqueue if_snd;		/* output queue */
	int	(*if_init)();		/* init routine */
	int	(*if_output)();		/* output routine */
	int	(*if_ioctl)();		/* ioctl routine */
	int	(*if_reset)();		/* bus reset routine */
	int	(*if_watchdog)();	/* timer routine */
	int	if_ipackets;		/* packets received on interface */
	int	if_ierrors;		/* input errors on interface */
	int	if_opackets;		/* packets sent on interface */
	int	if_oerrors;		/* output errors on interface */
	int	if_collisions;		/* collisions on csma interfaces */
	struct	ifnet *if_next;
};
```

Each interface address has the following form:

```
struct ifaddr {
	struct	sockaddr ifa_addr;	/* address of interface */
	union {
		struct	sockaddr ifu_broadaddr;
		struct	sockaddr ifu_dstaddr;
	} ifa_ifu;
	struct	ifnet *ifa_ifp;		/* back-pointer to interface */
	struct	ifaddr *ifa_next;	/* next address for interface */
};
#define ifa_broadaddr	ifa_ifu.ifu_broadaddr	/* broadcast address */
#define ifa_dstaddr	ifa_ifu.ifu_dstaddr	/* other end of p-to-p link */
```

The protocol generally maintains this structure as part of a larger structure containing additional information concerning the address.

Each interface has a send queue and routines used for initialization, *if_init*, and output, *if_output*. If the interface resides on a system bus, the routine *if_reset* will be called after a bus reset has been performed. An interface may also specify a timer routine, *if_watchdog*; if *if_timer* is non-zero, it is decremented once per second until it reaches zero, at which time the watchdog routine is called.

The state of an interface and certain characteristics are stored in the *if_flags* field. The following values are possible:

```
#define  IFF_UP            0x1    /* interface is up */
#define  IFF_BROADCAST     0x2    /* broadcast is possible */
#define  IFF_DEBUG         0x4    /* turn on debugging */
#define  IFF_LOOPBACK      0x8    /* is a loopback net */
#define  IFF_POINTOPOINT   0x10   /* interface is point-to-point link */
#define  IFF_NOTRAILERS    0x20   /* avoid use of trailers */
#define  IFF_RUNNING       0x40   /* resources allocated */
#define  IFF_NOARP         0x80   /* no address resolution protocol */
```

If the interface is connected to a network which supports transmission of *broadcast* packets, the IFF_BROADCAST flag will be set and the *ifa_broadaddr* field will contain the address to be used in sending or accepting a broadcast packet. If the interface is associated with a point-to-point hardware link (for example, a DEC DMR-11), the IFF_POINTOPOINT flag will be set and *ifa_dstaddr* will contain the address of the host on the other side of the connection. These addresses and the local address of the interface, *if_addr*, are used in filtering incoming packets. The interface sets IFF_RUNNING after it has allocated system resources and posted an initial read on the device it manages. This state bit is used to avoid multiple allocation requests when an interface's address is changed. The IFF_NOTRAILERS flag indicates the interface should refrain from using a *trailer* encapsulation on outgoing packets, or (where per-host negotiation of trailers is possible) that trailer encapsulations should not be requested; *trailer* protocols are described in section 14. The IFF_NOARP flag indicates the interface should not use an ''address resolution protocol'' in mapping internetwork addresses to local network addresses.

Various statistics are also stored in the interface structure. These may be viewed by users using the *netstat*(1) program.

The interface address and flags may be set with the SIOCSIFADDR and SIOCSIFFLAGS *ioctls*. SIOCSIFADDR is used initially to define each interface's address; SIOGSIFFLAGS can be used to mark an interface down and perform site-specific configuration. The destination address of a point-to-point link is set with SIOCSIFDSTADDR. Corresponding operations exist to read each value. Protocol families may also support operations to set and read the broadcast address. In addition, the SIOCGIFCONF *ioctl* retrieves a list of interface names and addresses for all interfaces and protocols on the host.

6.3.1. UNIBUS interfaces

All hardware related interfaces currently reside on the UNIBUS. Consequently a common set of utility routines for dealing with the UNIBUS has been developed. Each UNIBUS interface utilizes a structure of the following form:

```
struct  ifubinfo {
        short     iff_uban;             /* uba number */
        short     iff_hlen;             /* local net header length */
        struct    uba_regs *iff_uba;    /* uba regs, in vm */
        short     iff_flags;            /* used during uballoc's */
};
```

Additional structures are associated with each receive and transmit buffer, normally one each per interface; for read,

```
struct  ifrw {
        caddr_t     ifrw_addr;                  /* virt addr of header */
        short       ifrw_bdp;                   /* unibus bdp */
        short       ifrw_flags;                 /* type, etc. */
#define IFRW_W      0x01                        /* is a transmit buffer */
        int         ifrw_info;                  /* value from ubaalloc */
        int         ifrw_proto;                 /* map register prototype */
        struct      pte *ifrw_mr;               /* base of map registers */
};
```

and for write,

```
struct  ifxmt {
        struct      ifrw ifrw;
        caddr_t     ifw_base;                   /* virt addr of buffer */
        struct      pte ifw_wmap[IF_MAXNUBAMR]; /* base pages for output */
        struct      mbuf *ifw_xtofree;          /* pages being dma'd out */
        short       ifw_xswapd;                 /* mask of clusters swapped */
        short       ifw_nmr;                    /* number of entries in wmap */
};
#define ifw_addr    ifrw.ifrw_addr
#define ifw_bdp     ifrw.ifrw_bdp
#define ifw_flags   ifrw.ifrw_flags
#define ifw_info    ifrw.ifrw_info
#define ifw_proto   ifrw.ifrw_proto
#define ifw_mr      ifrw.ifrw_mr
```

One of each of these structures is conveniently packaged for interfaces with single buffers for each direction, as follows:

```
struct  ifuba {
        struct      ifubinfo ifu_info;
        struct      ifrw ifu_r;
        struct      ifxmt ifu_xmt;
};
#define ifu_uban    ifu_info.iff_uban
#define ifu_hlen    ifu_info.iff_hlen
#define ifu_uba     ifu_info.iff_uba
#define ifu_flags   ifu_info.iff_flags
#define ifu_w       ifu_xmt.ifrw
#define ifu_xtofree ifu_xmt.ifw_xtofree
```

The *if_ubinfo* structure contains the general information needed to characterize the I/O-mapped buffers for the device. In addition, there is a structure describing each buffer, including UNIBUS resources held by the interface. Sufficient memory pages and bus map registers are allocated to each buffer upon initialization according to the maximum packet size and header length. The kernel virtual address of the buffer is held in *ifrw_addr*, and the map registers begin at *ifrw_mr*. UNIBUS map register *ifrw_mr*[−1] maps the local network header ending on a page boundary. UNIBUS data paths are reserved for read and for write, given by *ifrw_bdp*. The prototype of the map registers for read and for write is saved in *ifrw_proto*.

When write transfers are not at least half-full pages on page boundaries, the data are just copied into the pages mapped on the UNIBUS and the transfer is started. If a write transfer is at least half a page long and on a page boundary, UNIBUS page table entries are swapped to reference the pages, and then the initial pages are remapped from *ifw_wmap* when the transfer completes. The mbufs containing the mapped pages are placed on the *ifw_xtofree* queue to be freed after transmission.

When read transfers give at least half a page of data to be input, page frames are allocated from a network page list and traded with the pages already containing the data, mapping the allocated pages to replace the input pages for the next UNIBUS data input.

The following utility routines are available for use in writing network interface drivers; all use the structures described above.

if_ubaminit(ifubinfo, uban, hlen, nmr, ifr, nr, ifx, nx);
if_ubainit(ifuba, uban, hlen, nmr);

> *if_ubaminit* allocates resources on UNIBUS adapter *uban*, storing the information in the *ifubinfo*, *ifrw* and *ifxmt* structures referenced. The *ifr* and *ifx* parameters are pointers to arrays of *ifrw* and *ifxmt* structures whose dimensions are *nr* and *nx*, respectively. *if_ubainit* is a simpler, backwards-compatible interface used for hardware with single buffers of each type. They are called only at boot time or after a UNIBUS reset. One data path (buffered or unbuffered, depending on the *ifu_flags* field) is allocated for each buffer. The *nmr* parameter indicates the number of UNIBUS mapping registers required to map a maximal sized packet onto the UNIBUS, while *hlen* specifies the size of a local network header, if any, which should be mapped separately from the data (see the description of trailer protocols in chapter 14). Sufficient UNIBUS mapping registers and pages of memory are allocated to initialize the input data path for an initial read. For the output data path, mapping registers and pages of memory are also allocated and mapped onto the UNIBUS. The pages associated with the output data path are held in reserve in the event a write requires copying non-page-aligned data (see *if_wubaput* below). If *if_ubainit* is called with memory pages already allocated, they will be used instead of allocating new ones (this normally occurs after a UNIBUS reset). A 1 is returned when allocation and initialization are successful, 0 otherwise.

m = if_ubaget(ifubinfo, ifr, totlen, off0, ifp);
m = if_rubaget(ifuba, totlen, off0, ifp);

> *if_ubaget* and *if_rubaget* pull input data out of an interface receive buffer and into an mbuf chain. The first interface passes pointers to the *ifubinfo* structure for the interface and the *ifrw* structure for the receive buffer; the second call may be used for single-buffered devices. *totlen* specifies the length of data to be obtained, not counting the local network header. If *off0* is non-zero, it indicates a byte offset to a trailing local network header which should be copied into a separate mbuf and prepended to the front of the resultant mbuf chain. When the data amount to at least a half a page, the previously mapped data pages are remapped into the mbufs and swapped with fresh pages, thus avoiding any copy. The receiving interface is recorded as *ifp*, a pointer to an *ifnet* structure, for the use of the receiving network protocol. A 0 return value indicates a failure to allocate resources.

if_wubaput(ifubinfo, ifx, m);
if_wubaput(ifuba, m);

> *if_ubaput* and *if_wubaput* map a chain of mbufs onto a network interface in preparation for output. The first interface is used by devices with multiple transmit buffers. The chain includes any local network header, which is copied so that it resides in the mapped and aligned I/O space. Page-aligned data that are page-aligned in the output buffer are mapped to the UNIBUS in place of the normal buffer page, and the corresponding mbuf is placed on a queue to be freed after transmission. Any other mbufs which contained non-page-sized data portions are copied to the I/O space and then freed. Pages mapped from a previous output operation (no longer needed) are unmapped.

7. Socket/protocol interface

The interface between the socket routines and the communication protocols is through the *pr_usrreq* routine defined in the protocol switch table. The following requests to a protocol module are possible:

```
#define PRU_ATTACH        0   /* attach protocol */
#define PRU_DETACH        1   /* detach protocol */
#define PRU_BIND          2   /* bind socket to address */
#define PRU_LISTEN        3   /* listen for connection */
#define PRU_CONNECT       4   /* establish connection to peer */
#define PRU_ACCEPT        5   /* accept connection from peer */
#define PRU_DISCONNECT    6   /* disconnect from peer */
#define PRU_SHUTDOWN      7   /* won't send any more data */
#define PRU_RCVD          8   /* have taken data; more room now */
#define PRU_SEND          9   /* send this data */
#define PRU_ABORT         10  /* abort (fast DISCONNECT, DETATCH) */
#define PRU_CONTROL       11  /* control operations on protocol */
#define PRU_SENSE         12  /* return status into m */
#define PRU_RCVOOB        13  /* retrieve out of band data */
#define PRU_SENDOOB       14  /* send out of band data */
#define PRU_SOCKADDR      15  /* fetch socket's address */
#define PRU_PEERADDR      16  /* fetch peer's address */
#define PRU_CONNECT2      17  /* connect two sockets */
/* begin for protocols internal use */
#define PRU_FASTTIMO      18  /* 200ms timeout */
#define PRU_SLOWTIMO      19  /* 500ms timeout */
#define PRU_PROTORCV      20  /* receive from below */
#define PRU_PROTOSEND     21  /* send to below */
```

A call on the user request routine is of the form,

```
error = (*protosw[].pr_usrreq)(so, req, m, addr, rights);
int error; struct socket *so; int req; struct mbuf *m, *addr, *rights;
```

The mbuf data chain *m* is supplied for output operations and for certain other operations where it is to receive a result. The address *addr* is supplied for address-oriented requests such as PRU_BIND and PRU_CONNECT. The *rights* parameter is an optional pointer to an mbuf chain containing user-specified capabilities (see the *sendmsg* and *recvmsg* system calls). The protocol is responsible for disposal of the data mbuf chains on output operations. A non-zero return value gives a UNIX error number which should be passed to higher level software. The following paragraphs describe each of the requests possible.

PRU_ATTACH

When a protocol is bound to a socket (with the *socket* system call) the protocol module is called with this request. It is the responsibility of the protocol module to allocate any resources necessary. The ''attach'' request will always precede any of the other requests, and should not occur more than once.

PRU_DETACH

This is the antithesis of the attach request, and is used at the time a socket is deleted. The protocol module may deallocate any resources assigned to the socket.

PRU_BIND

When a socket is initially created it has no address bound to it. This request indicates that an address should be bound to an existing socket. The protocol module must verify that the requested address is valid and available for use.

PRU_LISTEN

The ''listen'' request indicates the user wishes to listen for incoming connection requests on the associated socket. The protocol module should perform any state changes needed to carry out this request (if possible). A ''listen'' request always precedes a request to accept a connection.

PRU_CONNECT

The ''connect'' request indicates the user wants to a establish an association. The *addr* parameter supplied describes the peer to be connected to. The effect of a connect request may vary depending on the protocol. Virtual circuit protocols, such as TCP [Postel81b], use this request to initiate establishment of a TCP connection. Datagram protocols, such as UDP [Postel80], simply record the peer's address in a private data structure and use it to tag all outgoing packets. There are no restrictions on how many times a connect request may be used after an attach. If a protocol supports the notion of *multi-casting*, it is possible to use multiple connects to establish a multi-cast group. Alternatively, an association may be broken by a PRU_DISCONNECT request, and a new association created with a subsequent connect request; all without destroying and creating a new socket.

PRU_ACCEPT

Following a successful PRU_LISTEN request and the arrival of one or more connections, this request is made to indicate the user has accepted the first connection on the queue of pending connections. The protocol module should fill in the supplied address buffer with the address of the connected party.

PRU_DISCONNECT

Eliminate an association created with a PRU_CONNECT request.

PRU_SHUTDOWN

This call is used to indicate no more data will be sent and/or received (the *addr* parameter indicates the direction of the shutdown, as encoded in the *soshutdown* system call). The protocol may, at its discretion, deallocate any data structures related to the shutdown and/or notify a connected peer of the shutdown.

PRU_RCVD

This request is made only if the protocol entry in the protocol switch table includes the PR_WANTRCVD flag. When a user removes data from the receive queue this request will be sent to the protocol module. It may be used to trigger acknowledgements, refresh windowing information, initiate data transfer, etc.

PRU_SEND

Each user request to send data is translated into one or more PRU_SEND requests (a protocol may indicate that a single user send request must be translated into a single PRU_SEND request by specifying the PR_ATOMIC flag in its protocol description). The data to be sent is presented to the protocol as a list of mbufs and an address is, optionally, supplied in the *addr* parameter. The protocol is responsible for preserving the data in the socket's send queue if it is not able to send it immediately, or if it may need it at some later time (e.g. for retransmission).

PRU_ABORT

This request indicates an abnormal termination of service. The protocol should delete any existing association(s).

PRU_CONTROL

The ''control'' request is generated when a user performs a UNIX *ioctl* system call on a socket (and the ioctl is not intercepted by the socket routines). It allows protocol-specific operations to be provided outside the scope of the common socket interface. The *addr* parameter contains a pointer to a static kernel data area where relevant information may be obtained or returned. The *m* parameter contains the actual *ioctl* request code (note the non-standard calling convention). The *rights* parameter contains a pointer to an *ifnet* structure if the *ioctl* operation pertains to a particular network interface.

PRU_SENSE

The ''sense'' request is generated when the user makes an *fstat* system call on a socket; it requests status of the associated socket. This currently returns a standard *stat* structure. It typically contains only the optimal transfer size for the connection (based on buffer size, windowing information and maximum packet size). The *m* parameter contains a pointer to a static kernel data area where the status buffer should be placed.

PRU_RCVOOB

Any ''out-of-band'' data presently available is to be returned. An mbuf is passed to the protocol module, and the protocol should either place data in the mbuf or attach new mbufs to the one supplied if there is insufficient space in the single mbuf. An error may be returned if out-of-band data is not (yet) available or has already been consumed. The *addr* parameter contains any options such as MSG_PEEK to examine data without consuming it.

PRU_SENDOOB

Like PRU_SEND, but for out-of-band data.

PRU_SOCKADDR

The local address of the socket is returned, if any is currently bound to it. The address (with protocol specific format) is returned in the *addr* parameter.

PRU_PEERADDR

The address of the peer to which the socket is connected is returned. The socket must be in a SS_ISCONNECTED state for this request to be made to the protocol. The address format (protocol specific) is returned in the *addr* parameter.

PRU_CONNECT2

The protocol module is supplied two sockets and requested to establish a connection between the two without binding any addresses, if possible. This call is used in implementing the *socketpair*(2) system call.

The following requests are used internally by the protocol modules and are never generated by the socket routines. In certain instances, they are handed to the *pr_usrreq* routine solely for convenience in tracing a protocol's operation (e.g. PRU_SLOWTIMO).

PRU_FASTTIMO

A ''fast timeout'' has occurred. This request is made when a timeout occurs in the protocol's *pr_fastimo* routine. The *addr* parameter indicates which timer expired.

PRU_SLOWTIMO

A ''slow timeout'' has occurred. This request is made when a timeout occurs in the protocol's *pr_slowtimo* routine. The *addr* parameter indicates which timer expired.

PRU_PROTORCV

This request is used in the protocol-protocol interface, not by the routines. It requests reception of data destined for the protocol and not the user. No protocols currently use this facility.

PRU_PROTOSEND

This request allows a protocol to send data destined for another protocol module, not a user. The details of how data is marked ''addressed to protocol'' instead of ''addressed to user'' are left to the protocol modules. No protocols currently use this facility.

8. Protocol/protocol interface

The interface between protocol modules is through the *pr_usrreq*, *pr_input*, *pr_output*, *pr_ctlinput*, and *pr_ctloutput* routines. The calling conventions for all but the *pr_usrreq* routine are expected to be specific to the protocol modules and are not guaranteed to be consistent across protocol families. We will examine the conventions used for some of the Internet protocols in this section as an example.

8.1. pr_output

The Internet protocol UDP uses the convention,

```
error = udp_output(inp, m);
int error; struct inpcb *inp; struct mbuf *m;
```

where the *inp*, ''*in*ternet *p*rotocol *c*ontrol *b*lock'', passed between modules conveys per connection state information, and the mbuf chain contains the data to be sent. UDP performs consistency checks, appends its header, calculates a checksum, etc. before passing the packet on. UDP is based on the Internet Protocol, IP [Postel81a], as its transport. UDP passes a packet to the IP module for output as follows:

```
error = ip_output(m, opt, ro, flags);
int error; struct mbuf *m, *opt; struct route *ro; int flags;
```

18

The call to IP's output routine is more complicated than that for UDP, as befits the additional work the IP module must do. The *m* parameter is the data to be sent, and the *opt* parameter is an optional list of IP options which should be placed in the IP packet header. The *ro* parameter is is used in making routing decisions (and passing them back to the caller for use in subsequent calls). The final parameter, *flags* contains flags indicating whether the user is allowed to transmit a broadcast packet and if routing is to be performed. The broadcast flag may be inconsequential if the underlying hardware does not support the notion of broadcasting.

All output routines return 0 on success and a UNIX error number if a failure occurred which could be detected immediately (no buffer space available, no route to destination, etc.).

8.2. pr_input

Both UDP and TCP use the following calling convention,

```
(void) (*protosw[].pr_input)(m, ifp);
struct mbuf *m; struct ifnet *ifp;
```

Each mbuf list passed is a single packet to be processed by the protocol module. The interface from which the packet was received is passed as the second parameter.

The IP input routine is a VAX software interrupt level routine, and so is not called with any parameters. It instead communicates with network interfaces through a queue, *ipintrq*, which is identical in structure to the queues used by the network interfaces for storing packets awaiting transmission. The software interrupt is enabled by the network interfaces when they place input data on the input queue.

8.3. pr_ctlinput

This routine is used to convey ''control'' information to a protocol module (i.e. information which might be passed to the user, but is not data).

The common calling convention for this routine is,

```
(void) (*protosw[].pr_ctlinput)(req, addr);
int req; struct sockaddr *addr;
```

The *req* parameter is one of the following,

```
#define PRC_IFDOWN                0    /* interface transition */
#define PRC_ROUTEDEAD             1    /* select new route if possible */
#define PRC_QUENCH                4    /* some said to slow down */
#define PRC_MSGSIZE               5    /* message size forced drop */
#define PRC_HOSTDEAD              6    /* normally from IMP */
#define PRC_HOSTUNREACH           7    /* ditto */
#define PRC_UNREACH_NET           8    /* no route to network */
#define PRC_UNREACH_HOST          9    /* no route to host */
#define PRC_UNREACH_PROTOCOL      10   /* dst says bad protocol */
#define PRC_UNREACH_PORT          11   /* bad port # */
#define PRC_UNREACH_NEEDFRAG      12   /* IP_DF caused drop */
#define PRC_UNREACH_SRCFAIL       13   /* source route failed */
#define PRC_REDIRECT_NET          14   /* net routing redirect */
#define PRC_REDIRECT_HOST         15   /* host routing redirect */
#define PRC_REDIRECT_TOSNET       14   /* redirect for type of service & net */
#define PRC_REDIRECT_TOSHOST      15   /* redirect for tos & host */
#define PRC_TIMXCEED_INTRANS      18   /* packet lifetime expired in transit */
#define PRC_TIMXCEED_REASS        19   /* lifetime expired on reass q */
#define PRC_PARAMPROB             20   /* header incorrect */
```

while the *addr* parameter is the address to which the condition applies. Many of the requests have obviously been derived from ICMP (the Internet Control Message Protocol [Postel81c]), and from error messages defined in the 1822 host/IMP convention [BBN78]. Mapping tables exist to convert control requests to UNIX error codes which are delivered to a user.

8.4. pr_ctloutput

This is the routine that implements per-socket options at the protocol level for *getsockopt* and *setsockopt*. The calling convention is,

```
error = (*protosw[].pr_ctloutput)(op, so, level, optname, mp);
int op; struct socket *so; int level, optname; struct mbuf **mp;
```

where *op* is one of PRCO_SETOPT or PRCO_GETOPT, *so* is the socket from whence the call originated, and *level* and *optname* are the protocol level and option name supplied by the user. The results of a PRCO_GETOPT call are returned in an mbuf whose address is placed in *mp* before return. On a PRCO_SETOPT call, *mp* contains the address of an mbuf containing the option data; the mbuf should be freed before return.

9. Protocol/network-interface interface

The lowest layer in the set of protocols which comprise a protocol family must interface itself to one or more network interfaces in order to transmit and receive packets. It is assumed that any routing decisions have been made before handing a packet to a network interface, in fact this is absolutely necessary in order to locate any interface at all (unless, of course, one uses a single ''hardwired'' interface). There are two cases with which to be concerned, transmission of a packet and receipt of a packet; each will be considered separately.

9.1. Packet transmission

Assuming a protocol has a handle on an interface, *ifp*, a (struct ifnet *), it transmits a fully formatted packet with the following call,

```
error = (*ifp->if_output)(ifp, m, dst)
int error; struct ifnet *ifp; struct mbuf *m; struct sockaddr *dst;
```

The output routine for the network interface transmits the packet *m* to the *dst* address, or returns an error indication (a UNIX error number). In reality transmission may not be immediate or successful; normally the output routine simply queues the packet on its send queue and primes an interrupt driven routine to actually transmit the packet. For unreliable media, such as the Ethernet, ''successful'' transmission simply means that the packet has been placed on the cable without a collision. On the other hand, an 1822 interface guarantees proper delivery or an error indication for each message transmitted. The model employed in the networking system attaches no promises of delivery to the packets handed to a network interface, and thus corresponds more closely to the Ethernet. Errors returned by the output routine are only those that can be detected immediately, and are normally trivial in nature (no buffer space, address format not handled, etc.). No indication is received if errors are detected after the call has returned.

9.2. Packet reception

Each protocol family must have one or more ''lowest level'' protocols. These protocols deal with internetwork addressing and are responsible for the delivery of incoming packets to the proper protocol processing modules. In the PUP model [Boggs78] these protocols are termed Level 1 protocols, in the ISO model, network layer protocols. In this system each such protocol module has an input packet queue assigned to it. Incoming packets received by a network interface are queued for the protocol module, and a VAX software interrupt is posted to initiate processing.

Three macros are available for queuing and dequeuing packets:

IF_ENQUEUE(ifq, m)
: This places the packet *m* at the tail of the queue *ifq*.

IF_DEQUEUE(ifq, m)
: This places a pointer to the packet at the head of queue *ifq* in *m* and removes the packet from the queue. A zero value will be returned in *m* if the queue is empty.

IF_DEQUEUEIF(ifq, m, ifp)
: Like IF_DEQUEUE, this removes the next packet from the head of a queue and returns it in *m*. A pointer to the interface on which the packet was received is placed in *ifp*, a (struct ifnet *).

IF_PREPEND(ifq, m)
: This places the packet *m* at the head of the queue *ifq*.

Each queue has a maximum length associated with it as a simple form of congestion control. The macro IF_QFULL(ifq) returns 1 if the queue is filled, in which case the macro IF_DROP(ifq) should be used to increment the count of the number of packets dropped, and the offending packet is dropped. For example, the following code fragment is commonly found in a network interface's input routine,

```
if (IF_QFULL(inq)) {
        IF_DROP(inq);
        m_freem(m);
} else
        IF_ENQUEUE(inq, m);
```

10. Gateways and routing issues

The system has been designed with the expectation that it will be used in an internetwork environment. The ''canonical'' environment was envisioned to be a collection of local area networks connected at one or more points through hosts with multiple network interfaces (one on each local area network), and possibly a connection to a long haul network (for example, the ARPANET). In such an environment, issues of gatewaying and packet routing become very important. Certain of these issues, such as congestion control, have been handled in a simplistic manner or specifically not addressed. Instead, where possible, the network system attempts to provide simple mechanisms upon which more involved policies may be implemented. As some of these problems become better understood, the solutions developed will be incorporated into the system.

This section will describe the facilities provided for packet routing. The simplistic mechanisms provided for congestion control are described in chapter 12.

10.1. Routing tables

The network system maintains a set of routing tables for selecting a network interface to use in delivering a packet to its destination. These tables are of the form:

```
struct rtentry {
        u_long  rt_hash;                /* hash key for lookups */
        struct  sockaddr rt_dst;        /* destination net or host */
        struct  sockaddr rt_gateway;    /* forwarding agent */
        short   rt_flags;               /* see below */
        short   rt_refcnt;              /* no. of references to structure */
        u_long  rt_use;                 /* packets sent using route */
        struct  ifnet *rt_ifp;          /* interface to give packet to */
};
```


The routing information is organized in two separate tables, one for routes to a host and one for routes to a network. The distinction between hosts and networks is necessary so that a single mechanism may be used for both broadcast and multi-drop type networks, and also for networks built from point-to-point links (e.g DECnet [DEC80]).

Each table is organized as a hashed set of linked lists. Two 32-bit hash values are calculated by routines defined for each address family; one based on the destination being a host, and one assuming the target is the network portion of the address. Each hash value is used to locate a hash chain to search (by taking the value modulo the hash table size) and the entire 32-bit value is then used as a key in scanning the list of routes. Lookups are applied first to the routing table for hosts, then to the routing table for networks. If both lookups fail, a final lookup is made for a ''wildcard'' route (by convention, network 0). The first appropriate route discovered is used. By doing this, routes to a specific host on a network may be present as well as routes to the network. This also allows a ''fall back'' network route to be defined to a ''smart'' gateway which may then perform more intelligent routing.

Each routing table entry contains a destination (the desired final destination), a gateway to which to send the packet, and various flags which indicate the route's status and type (host or network). A count of the number of packets sent using the route is kept, along with a count of ''held references'' to the dynamically allocated structure to insure that memory reclamation occurs only when the route is not in use. Finally, a pointer to the a network interface is kept; packets sent using the route should be handed to this interface.

Routes are typed in two ways: either as host or network, and as ''direct'' or ''indirect''. The host/network distinction determines how to compare the *rt_dst* field during lookup. If the route is to a network, only a packet's destination network is compared to the *rt_dst* entry stored in the table. If the route is to a host, the addresses must match bit for bit.

The distinction between ''direct'' and ''indirect'' routes indicates whether the destination is directly connected to the source. This is needed when performing local network encapsulation. If a packet is destined for a peer at a host or network which is not directly connected to the source, the internetwork packet header will contain the address of the eventual destination, while the local network header will address the intervening gateway. Should the destination be directly connected, these addresses are likely to be identical, or a mapping between the two exists. The RTF_GATEWAY flag indicates that the route is to an ''indirect'' gateway agent, and that the local network header should be filled in from the *rt_gateway* field instead of from the final internetwork destination address.

It is assumed that multiple routes to the same destination will not be present; only one of multiple routes, that most recently installed, will be used.

Routing redirect control messages are used to dynamically modify existing routing table entries as well as dynamically create new routing table entries. On hosts where exhaustive routing information is too expensive to maintain (e.g. work stations), the combination of wildcard routing entries and routing redirect messages can be used to provide a simple routing management scheme without the use of a higher level policy process. Current connections may be rerouted after notification of the protocols by means of their *pr_ctlinput* entries. Statistics are kept by the routing table routines on the use of routing redirect messages and their affect on the routing tables. These statistics may be viewed using *netstat*(1).

Status information other than routing redirect control messages may be used in the future, but at present they are ignored. Likewise, more intelligent ''metrics'' may be used to describe routes in the future, possibly based on bandwidth and monetary costs.

10.2. Routing table interface

A protocol accesses the routing tables through three routines, one to allocate a route, one to free a route, and one to process a routing redirect control message. The routine *rtalloc* performs route allocation; it is called with a pointer to the following structure containing the desired destination:

```
struct route {
        struct      rtentry *ro_rt;
        struct      sockaddr ro_dst;
};
```

The route returned is assumed ''held'' by the caller until released with an *rtfree* call. Protocols which implement virtual circuits, such as TCP, hold onto routes for the duration of the circuit's lifetime, while connection-less protocols, such as UDP, allocate and free routes whenever their destination address changes.

The routine *rtredirect* is called to process a routing redirect control message. It is called with a destination address, the new gateway to that destination, and the source of the redirect. Redirects are accepted only from the current router for the destination. If a non-wildcard route exists to the destination, the gateway entry in the route is modified to point at the new gateway supplied. Otherwise, a new routing table entry is inserted reflecting the information supplied. Routes to interfaces and routes to gateways which are not directly accessible from the host are ignored.

10.3. User level routing policies

Routing policies implemented in user processes manipulate the kernel routing tables through two *ioctl* calls. The commands SIOCADDRT and SIOCDELRT add and delete routing entries, respectively; the tables are read through the /dev/kmem device. The decision to place policy decisions in a user process implies that routing table updates may lag a bit behind the identification of new routes, or the failure of existing routes, but this period of instability is normally very small with proper implementation of the routing process. Advisory information, such as ICMP error messages and IMP diagnostic messages, may be read from raw sockets (described in the next section).

Several routing policy processes have already been implemented. The system standard ''routing daemon'' uses a variant of the Xerox NS Routing Information Protocol [Xerox82] to maintain up-to-date routing tables in our local environment. Interaction with other existing routing protocols, such as the Internet EGP (Exterior Gateway Protocol), has been accomplished using a similar process.

11. Raw sockets

A raw socket is an object which allows users direct access to a lower-level protocol. Raw sockets are intended for knowledgeable processes which wish to take advantage of some protocol feature not directly accessible through the normal interface, or for the development of new protocols built atop existing lower level protocols. For example, a new version of TCP might be developed at the user level by utilizing a raw IP socket for delivery of packets. The raw IP socket interface attempts to provide an identical interface to the one a protocol would have if it were resident in the kernel.

The raw socket support is built around a generic raw socket interface, (possibly) augmented by protocol-specific processing routines. This section will describe the core of the raw socket interface.

11.1. Control blocks

Every raw socket has a protocol control block of the following form:

```
struct rawcb {
        struct   rawcb *rcb_next;         /* doubly linked list */
        struct   rawcb *rcb_prev;
        struct   socket *rcb_socket;      /* back pointer to socket */
        struct   sockaddr rcb_faddr;      /* destination address */
        struct   sockaddr rcb_laddr;      /* socket's address */
        struct   sockproto rcb_proto;     /* protocol family, protocol */
        caddr_t  rcb_pcb;                 /* protocol specific stuff */
        struct   mbuf *rcb_options;       /* protocol specific options */
        struct   route rcb_route;         /* routing information */
        short    rcb_flags;
};
```


All the control blocks are kept on a doubly linked list for performing lookups during packet dispatch. Associations may be recorded in the control block and used by the output routine in preparing packets for transmission. The *rcb_proto* structure contains the protocol family and protocol number with which the raw socket is associated. The protocol, family and addresses are used to filter packets on input; this will be described in more detail shortly. If any protocol-specific information is required, it may be attached to the control block using the *rcb_pcb* field. Protocol-specific options for transmission in outgoing packets may be stored in *rcb_options*.

A raw socket interface is datagram oriented. That is, each send or receive on the socket requires a destination address. This address may be supplied by the user or stored in the control block and automatically installed in the outgoing packet by the output routine. Since it is not possible to determine whether an address is present or not in the control block, two flags, RAW_LADDR and RAW_FADDR, indicate if a local and foreign address are present. Routing is expected to be performed by the underlying protocol if necessary.

11.2. Input processing

Input packets are "assigned" to raw sockets based on a simple pattern matching scheme. Each network interface or protocol gives unassigned packets to the raw input routine with the call:

```
raw_input(m, proto, src, dst)
struct mbuf *m; struct sockproto *proto, struct sockaddr *src, *dst;
```

The data packet then has a generic header prepended to it of the form

```
struct raw_header {
        struct      sockproto raw_proto;
        struct      sockaddr raw_dst;
        struct      sockaddr raw_src;
};
```

and it is placed in a packet queue for the "raw input protocol" module. Packets taken from this queue are copied into any raw sockets that match the header according to the following rules,

1) The protocol family of the socket and header agree.

2) If the protocol number in the socket is non-zero, then it agrees with that found in the packet header.

3) If a local address is defined for the socket, the address format of the local address is the same as the destination address's and the two addresses agree bit for bit.

4) The rules of 3) are applied to the socket's foreign address and the packet's source address.

A basic assumption is that addresses present in the control block and packet header (as constructed by the network interface and any raw input protocol module) are in a canonical form which may be "block compared".

11.3. Output processing

On output the raw *pr_usrreq* routine passes the packet and a pointer to the raw control block to the raw protocol output routine for any processing required before it is delivered to the appropriate network interface. The output routine is normally the only code required to implement a raw socket interface.

12. Buffering and congestion control

One of the major factors in the performance of a protocol is the buffering policy used. Lack of a proper buffering policy can force packets to be dropped, cause falsified windowing information to be emitted by protocols, fragment host memory, degrade the overall host performance, etc. Due to problems such as these, most systems allocate a fixed pool of memory to the networking system and impose a policy optimized for ''normal'' network operation.

The networking system developed for UNIX is little different in this respect. At boot time a fixed amount of memory is allocated by the networking system. At later times more system memory may be requested as the need arises, but at no time is memory ever returned to the system. It is possible to garbage collect memory from the network, but difficult. In order to perform this garbage collection properly, some portion of the network will have to be ''turned off'' as data structures are updated. The interval over which this occurs must kept small compared to the average inter-packet arrival time, or too much traffic may be lost, impacting other hosts on the network, as well as increasing load on the interconnecting mediums. In our environment we have not experienced a need for such compaction, and thus have left the problem unresolved.

The mbuf structure was introduced in chapter 5. In this section a brief description will be given of the allocation mechanisms, and policies used by the protocols in performing connection level buffering.

12.1. Memory management

The basic memory allocation routines manage a private page map, the size of which determines the maximum amount of memory that may be allocated by the network. A small amount of memory is allocated at boot time to initialize the mbuf and mbuf page cluster free lists. When the free lists are exhausted, more memory is requested from the system memory allocator if space remains in the map. If memory cannot be allocated, callers may block awaiting free memory, or the failure may be reflected to the caller immediately. The allocator will not block awaiting free map entries, however, as exhaustion of the page map usually indicates that buffers have been lost due to a ''leak.'' The private page table is used by the network buffer management routines in remapping pages to be logically contiguous as the need arises. In addition, an array of reference counts parallels the page table and is used when multiple references to a page are present.

Mbufs are 128 byte structures, 8 fitting in a 1Kbyte page of memory. When data is placed in mbufs, it is copied or remapped into logically contiguous pages of memory from the network page pool if possible. Data smaller than half of the size of a page is copied into one or more 112 byte mbuf data areas.

12.2. Protocol buffering policies

Protocols reserve fixed amounts of buffering for send and receive queues at socket creation time. These amounts define the high and low water marks used by the socket routines in deciding when to block and unblock a process. The reservation of space does not currently result in any action by the memory management routines.

Protocols which provide connection level flow control do this based on the amount of space in the associated socket queues. That is, send windows are calculated based on the amount of free space in the socket's receive queue, while receive windows are adjusted based on the amount of data awaiting transmission in the send queue. Care has been taken to avoid the ''silly window syndrome'' described in [Clark82] at both the sending and receiving ends.

12.3. Queue limiting

Incoming packets from the network are always received unless memory allocation fails. However, each Level 1 protocol input queue has an upper bound on the queue's length, and any packets exceeding that bound are discarded. It is possible for a host to be overwhelmed by excessive network traffic (for instance a host acting as a gateway from a high bandwidth network to a low bandwidth network). As a ''defensive'' mechanism the queue limits may be adjusted to throttle network traffic load on a host. Consider a host willing to devote some percentage of its machine to handling network traffic. If the cost of handling an incoming packet can be calculated so that an acceptable ''packet handling rate'' can be determined, then input queue lengths may be dynamically adjusted based on a host's network load and the number of packets awaiting processing. Obviously, discarding packets is not a satisfactory solution to a problem such as this (simply dropping packets is likely to increase the load on a network); the queue lengths were incorporated mainly as a safeguard mechanism.

12.4. Packet forwarding

When packets can not be forwarded because of memory limitations, the system attempts to generate a ''source quench'' message. In addition, any other problems encountered during packet forwarding are also reflected back to the sender in the form of ICMP packets. This helps hosts avoid unneeded retransmissions.

Broadcast packets are never forwarded due to possible dire consequences. In an early stage of network development, broadcast packets were forwarded and a ''routing loop'' resulted in network saturation and every host on the network crashing.

13. Out of band data

Out of band data is a facility peculiar to the stream socket abstraction defined. Little agreement appears to exist as to what its semantics should be. TCP defines the notion of ''urgent data'' as in-line, while the NBS protocols [Burruss81] and numerous others provide a fully independent logical transmission channel along which out of band data is to be sent. In addition, the amount of the data which may be sent as an out of band message varies from protocol to protocol; everything from 1 bit to 16 bytes or more.

A stream socket's notion of out of band data has been defined as the lowest reasonable common denominator (at least reasonable in our minds); clearly this is subject to debate. Out of band data is expected to be transmitted out of the normal sequencing and flow control constraints of the data stream. A minimum of 1 byte of out of band data and one outstanding out of band message are expected to be supported by the protocol supporting a stream socket. It is a protocol's prerogative to support larger-sized messages, or more than one outstanding out of band message at a time.

Out of band data is maintained by the protocol and is usually not stored in the socket's receive queue. A socket-level option, SO_OOBINLINE, is provided to force out-of-band data to be placed in the normal receive queue when urgent data is received; this sometimes ameliorates problems due to loss of data when multiple out-of-band segments are received before the first has been passed to the user. The PRU_SENDOOB and PRU_RCVOOB requests to the *pr_usrreq* routine are used in sending and receiving data.

14. Trailer protocols

Core to core copies can be expensive. Consequently, a great deal of effort was spent in minimizing such operations. The VAX architecture provides virtual memory hardware organized in page units. To cut down on copy operations, data is kept in page-sized units on page-aligned boundaries whenever possible. This allows data to be moved in memory simply by remapping the page instead of copying. The mbuf and network interface routines perform page table manipulations where needed, hiding the complexities of the VAX virtual memory hardware from higher level code.

Data enters the system in two ways: from the user, or from the network (hardware interface). When data is copied from the user's address space into the system it is deposited in pages (if sufficient data is present). This encourages the user to transmit information in messages which are a multiple of the system page size.

Unfortunately, performing a similar operation when taking data from the network is very difficult. Consider the format of an incoming packet. A packet usually contains a local network header followed by one or more headers used by the high level protocols. Finally, the data, if any, follows these headers. Since the header information may be variable length, DMA'ing the eventual data for the user into a page aligned area of memory is impossible without *a priori* knowledge of the format (e.g., by supporting only a single protocol header format).

To allow variable length header information to be present and still ensure page alignment of data, a special local network encapsulation may be used. This encapsulation, termed a *trailer protocol* [Leffler84], places the variable length header information after the data. A fixed size local network header is then prepended to the resultant packet. The local network header contains the size of the data portion (in units of 512 bytes), and a new *trailer protocol header*, inserted before the variable length information, contains the size of the variable length header information. The following trailer protocol header is used to store information regarding the variable length protocol header:

```
struct {
        short       protocol;         /* original protocol no. */
        short       length;           /* length of trailer */
};
```

The processing of the trailer protocol is very simple. On output, the local network header indicates that a trailer encapsulation is being used. The header also includes an indication of the number of data pages present before the trailer protocol header. The trailer protocol header is initialized to contain the actual protocol identifier and the variable length header size, and is appended to the data along with the variable length header information.

On input, the interface routines identify the trailer encapsulation by the protocol type stored in the local network header, then calculate the number of pages of data to find the beginning of the trailer. The trailing information is copied into a separate mbuf and linked to the front of the resultant packet.

Clearly, trailer protocols require cooperation between source and destination. In addition, they are normally cost effective only when sizable packets are used. The current scheme works because the local network encapsulation header is a fixed size, allowing DMA operations to be performed at a known offset from the first data page being received. Should the local network header be variable length this scheme fails.

Statistics collected indicate that as much as 200Kb/s can be gained by using a trailer protocol with 1Kbyte packets. The average size of the variable length header was 40 bytes (the size of a minimal TCP/IP packet header). If hardware supports larger sized packets, even greater gains may be realized.

Acknowledgements

The internal structure of the system is patterned after the Xerox PUP architecture [Boggs79], while in certain places the Internet protocol family has had a great deal of influence in the design. The use of software interrupts for process invocation is based on similar facilities found in the VMS operating system. Many of the ideas related to protocol modularity, memory management, and network interfaces are based on Rob Gurwitz's TCP/IP implementation for the 4.1BSD version of UNIX on the VAX [Gurwitz81]. Greg Chesson explained his use of trailer encapsulations in Datakit, instigating their use in our system.

18

References

[Boggs79] Boggs, D. R., J. F. Shoch, E. A. Taft, and R. M. Metcalfe; *PUP: An Internetwork Architecture*. Report CSL-79-10. XEROX Palo Alto Research Center, July 1979.

[BBN78] Bolt Beranek and Newman; Specification for the Interconnection of Host and IMP. BBN Technical Report 1822. May 1978.

[Cerf78] Cerf, V. G.; The Catenet Model for Internetworking. Internet Working Group, IEN 48. July 1978.

[Clark82] Clark, D. D.; Window and Acknowledgement Strategy in TCP, RFC-813. Network Information Center, SRI International. July 1982.

[DEC80] Digital Equipment Corporation; *DECnet DIGITAL Network Architecture – General Description*. Order No. AA-K179A-TK. October 1980.

[Gurwitz81] Gurwitz, R. F.; VAX-UNIX Networking Support Project – Implementation Description. Internetwork Working Group, IEN 168. January 1981.

[ISO81] International Organization for Standardization. *ISO Open Systems Interconnection – Basic Reference Model*. ISO/TC 97/SC 16 N 719. August 1981.

[Joy86] Joy, W.; Fabry, R.; Leffler, S.; McKusick, M.; and Karels, M.; Berkeley Software Architecture Manual, 4.4BSD Edition. *UNIX Programmer's Supplementary Documents*, Vol. 1 (PSD:5). Computer Systems Research Group, University of California, Berkeley. May, 1986.

[Leffler84] Leffler, S.J. and Karels, M.J.; Trailer Encapsulations, RFC-893. Network Information Center, SRI International. April 1984.

[Postel80] Postel, J. User Datagram Protocol, RFC-768. Network Information Center, SRI International. May 1980.

[Postel81a] Postel, J., ed. Internet Protocol, RFC-791. Network Information Center, SRI International. September 1981.

[Postel81b] Postel, J., ed. Transmission Control Protocol, RFC-793. Network Information Center, SRI International. September 1981.

[Postel81c] Postel, J. Internet Control Message Protocol, RFC-792. Network Information Center, SRI International. September 1981.

[Xerox81] Xerox Corporation. *Internet Transport Protocols*. Xerox System Integration Standard 028112. December 1981.

[Zimmermann80] Zimmermann, H. OSI Reference Model – The ISO Model of Architecture for Open Systems Interconnection. *IEEE Transactions on Communications*. Com-28(4); 425-432. April 1980.

The PERL Programming Language

Larry Wall

<lwall@netlabs.com>

ABSTRACT

The Practical Extraction and Report Language (perl) is an interpreted language optimized for scanning arbitrary text files, extracting information from those text files, and printing reports based on that information. It is also a good language for many system management tasks. The language is intended to be practical (easy to use, efficient, complete) rather than beautiful (tiny, elegant, minimal). It combines (in the author's opinion, anyway) some of the best features of C, *sed*, *awk*, and *sh*, so people familiar with those languages should have little difficulty with it. (Language historians will also note some vestiges of *csh*, Pascal, and even BASIC-PLUS.) Expression syntax corresponds quite closely to C expression syntax. Unlike most Unix utilities, *perl* does not arbitrarily limit the size of your data—if you've got the memory, *perl* can slurp in your whole file as a single string. Recursion is of unlimited depth. And the hash tables used by associative arrays grow as necessary to prevent degraded performance. *Perl* uses sophisticated pattern matching techniques to scan large amounts of data very quickly. Although optimized for scanning text, *perl* can also deal with binary data, and can make dbm files look like associative arrays (where dbm is available). Setuid *perl* scripts are safer than C programs through a dataflow tracing mechanism which prevents many stupid security holes. If you have a problem that would ordinarily use *sed* or *awk* or *sh*, but it exceeds their capabilities or must run a little faster, and you don't want to write the silly thing in C, then *perl* may be for you. There are also translators to turn your *sed* and *awk* scripts into *perl* scripts.

1. Data Types and Objects

Perl has three data types: scalars, arrays of scalars, and associative arrays of scalars. Normal arrays are indexed by number, and associative arrays by string.

The interpretation of operations and values in perl sometimes depends on the requirements of the context around the operation or value. There are three major contexts: string, numeric and array. Certain operations return array values in contexts wanting an array, and scalar values otherwise. (If this is true of an operation it will be mentioned in the documentation for that operation.) Operations which return scalars don't care whether the context is looking for a string or a number, but scalar variables and values are interpreted as strings or numbers as appropriate to the context. A scalar is interpreted as TRUE in the boolean sense if it is not the null string or 0. Booleans returned by operators are 1 for true and 0 or '' (the null string) for false.

There are actually two varieties of null string: defined and undefined. Undefined null strings are returned when there is no real value for something, such as when there was an error, or at end of file, or when you refer to an uninitialized variable or element of an array. An undefined null string may become defined the first time you access it, but prior to that you can use the defined() operator to determine whether the value is defined or not.

References to scalar variables always begin with '$', even when referring to a scalar that is part of an array. Thus:

```
$days               # a simple scalar variable
$days[28]           # 29th element of array @days
$days{'Feb'}        # one value from an associative array
$#days              # last index of array @days
```

but entire arrays or array slices are denoted by '@':

```
@days               # ($days[0], $days[1],... $days[n])
@days[3,4,5]        # same as @days[3..5]
@days{'a','c'}      # same as ($days{'a'},$days{'c'})
```

and entire associative arrays are denoted by '%':

```
%days               # (key1, val1, key2, val2 ...)
```

Any of these eight constructs may serve as an lvalue, that is, may be assigned to. (It also turns out that an assignment is itself an lvalue in certain contexts—see examples under s, tr and chop.) Assignment to a scalar evaluates the righthand side in a scalar context, while assignment to an array or array slice evaluates the righthand side in an array context.

19

You may find the length of array @days by evaluating "$#days", as in *csh*. (Actually, it's not the length of the array, it's the subscript of the last element, since there is (ordinarily) a 0th element.) Assigning to $#days changes the length of the array. Shortening an array by this method does not actually destroy any values. Lengthening an array that was previously shortened recovers the values that were in those elements. You can also gain some measure of efficiency by preextending an array that is going to get big. (You can also extend an array by assigning to an element that is off the end of the array. This differs from assigning to $#whatever in that intervening values are set to null rather than recovered.) You can truncate an array down to nothing by assigning the null list () to it. The following are exactly equivalent

```
@whatever = ();
$#whatever = $[ - 1;
```

If you evaluate an array in a scalar context, it returns the length of the array. The following is always true:

```
scalar(@whatever) == $#whatever - $[ + 1;
```

If you evaluate an associative array in a scalar context, it returns a value which is true if and only if the array contains any elements. (If there are any elements, the value returned is a string consisting of the number of used buckets and the number of allocated buckets, separated by a slash.)

Multi-dimensional arrays are not directly supported, but see the discussion of the $; variable later for a means of emulating multiple subscripts with an associative array. You could also write a subroutine to turn multiple subscripts into a single subscript.

Every data type has its own namespace. You can, without fear of conflict, use the same name for a scalar variable, an array, an associative array, a filehandle, a subroutine name, and/or a label. Since variable and array references always start with '$', '@', or '%', the "reserved" words aren't in fact reserved with respect to variable names. (They ARE reserved with respect to labels and filehandles, however, which don't have an initial special character. Hint: you could say open(LOG,'logfile') rather than open(log,'logfile'). Using uppercase filehandles also improves readability and protects you from conflict with future reserved words.) Case IS significant—"FOO", "Foo" and "foo" are all different names. Names which start with a letter may also contain digits and underscores. Names which do not start with a letter are limited to one character, e.g. "$%" or "$$". (Most of the one character names have a predefined significance to *perl*. More later.)

Numeric literals are specified in any of the usual floating point or integer formats:

```
12345
12345.67
.23E-10
0xffff      # hex
0377        # octal
4_294_967_296
```

String literals are delimited by either single or double quotes. They work much like shell quotes: double-quoted string literals are subject to backslash and variable substitution; single-quoted strings are not (except for \' and \\). The usual backslash rules apply for making characters such as newline, tab, etc., as well as some more exotic forms:

\t	tab
\n	newline
\r	return
\f	form feed
\b	backspace
\a	alarm (bell)
\e	escape
\033	octal char
\x1b	hex char
\c[	control char
\l	lowercase next char
\u	uppercase next char
\L	lowercase till \E
\U	uppercase till \E
\E	end case modification

You can also embed newlines directly in your strings, i.e. they can end on a different line than they begin. This is nice, but if you forget your trailing quote, the error will not be reported until *perl* finds another line containing the quote character, which may be much further on in the script. Variable substitution inside strings is limited to scalar variables, normal array values, and array slices. (In other words, identifiers beginning with $ or @, followed by an optional bracketed expression as a subscript.) The following code segment prints out "The price is $100."

```
$Price = '$100';                          # not interpreted
print "The price is $Price.\n";           # interpreted
```

Note that you can put curly brackets around the identifier to delimit it from following alphanumerics. Also note that a single quoted string must be separated from a preceding word by a space, since single quote is a valid character in an identifier (see Packages).

Two special literals are __LINE__ and __FILE__, which represent the current line number and filename at that point in your program. They may only be used as separate tokens; they will not be interpolated into strings. In addition, the token __END__ may be used to indicate the logical end of the script before the actual end of file. Any following text is ignored, but may be read via the DATA filehandle. (The DATA filehandle may read data only from the main script, but not from any required file or evaluated string.) The two control characters ^D and ^Z are synonyms for __END__.

A word that doesn't have any other interpretation in the grammar will be treated as if it had single quotes around it. For this purpose, a word consists only of alphanumeric characters and underline, and must start with an alphabetic character. As with filehandles and labels, a bare word that consists entirely of

19

lowercase letters risks conflict with future reserved words, and if you use the **–w** switch, Perl will warn you about any such words.

Array values are interpolated into double-quoted strings by joining all the elements of the array with the delimiter specified in the $" variable, space by default. (Since in versions of perl prior to 3.0 the @ character was not a metacharacter in double-quoted strings, the interpolation of @array, $array[EXPR], @array[LIST], $array{EXPR}, or @array{LIST} only happens if array is referenced elsewhere in the program or is predefined.) The following are equivalent:

```
    $temp = join($",@ARGV);
    system "echo $temp";

    system "echo @ARGV";
```

Within search patterns (which also undergo double-quotish substitution) there is a bad ambiguity: Is /$foo[bar]/ to be interpreted as /${foo}[bar]/ (where [bar] is a character class for the regular expression) or as /${foo[bar]}/ (where [bar] is the subscript to array @foo)? If @foo doesn't otherwise exist, then it's obviously a character class. If @foo exists, perl takes a good guess about [bar], and is almost always right. If it does guess wrong, or if you're just plain paranoid, you can force the correct interpretation with curly brackets as above.

A line-oriented form of quoting is based on the shell here-is syntax. Following a << you specify a string to terminate the quoted material, and all lines following the current line down to the terminating string are the value of the item. The terminating string may be either an identifier (a word), or some quoted text. If quoted, the type of quotes you use determines the treatment of the text, just as in regular quoting. An unquoted identifier works like double quotes. There must be no space between the << and the identifier. (If you put a space it will be treated as a null identifier, which is valid, and matches the first blank line—see Merry Christmas example below.) The terminating string must appear by itself (unquoted and with no surrounding whitespace) on the terminating line.

```
    print <<EOF;            # same as above
The price is $Price.
EOF

    print <<"EOF";          # same as above
The price is $Price.
EOF

    print << x 10;          # null identifier is delimiter
Merry Christmas!

    print <<‘EOC‘;          # execute commands
echo hi there
echo lo there
EOC

    print <<foo, <<bar;     # you can stack them
I said foo.
foo
I said bar.
bar
```

Array literals are denoted by separating individual values by commas, and enclosing the list in parentheses:

```
    (LIST)
```

In a context not requiring an array value, the value of the array literal is the value of the final element, as in the C comma operator. For example,

```
@foo = ('cc', '-E', $bar);
```

assigns the entire array value to array foo, but

```
$foo = ('cc', '-E', $bar);
```

assigns the value of variable bar to variable foo. Note that the value of an actual array in a scalar context is the length of the array; the following assigns to $foo the value 3:

```
@foo = ('cc', '-E', $bar);
$foo = @foo;          # $foo gets 3
```

You may have an optional comma before the closing parenthesis of an array literal, so that you can say:

```
@foo = (
    1,
    2,
    3,
);
```

When a LIST is evaluated, each element of the list is evaluated in an array context, and the resulting array value is interpolated into LIST just as if each individual element were a member of LIST. Thus arrays lose their identity in a LIST—the list

```
(@foo,@bar,&SomeSub)
```

contains all the elements of @foo followed by all the elements of @bar, followed by all the elements returned by the subroutine named SomeSub.

A list value may also be subscripted like a normal array. Examples:

```
$time = (stat($file))[8];  # stat returns array value
$digit = ('a','b','c','d','e','f')[$digit-10];
return (pop(@foo),pop(@foo))[0];
```

Array lists may be assigned to if and only if each element of the list is an lvalue:

```
($a, $b, $c) = (1, 2, 3);

($map{'red'}, $map{'blue'}, $map{'green'}) = (0x00f, 0x0f0, 0xf00);
```

The final element may be an array or an associative array:

```
($a, $b, @rest) = split;
local($a, $b, %rest) = @_;
```

You can actually put an array anywhere in the list, but the first array in the list will soak up all the values, and anything after it will get a null value. This may be useful in a local().

An associative array literal contains pairs of values to be interpreted as a key and a value:

19

```
# same as map assignment above
%map = ('red',0x00f,'blue',0x0f0,'green',0xf00);
```

Array assignment in a scalar context returns the number of elements produced by the expression on the right side of the assignment:

```
$x = (($foo,$bar) = (3,2,1));     # set $x to 3, not 2
```

There are several other pseudo-literals that you should know about. If a string is enclosed by backticks (grave accents), it first undergoes variable substitution just like a double quoted string. It is then interpreted as a command, and the output of that command is the value of the pseudo-literal, like in a shell. In a scalar context, a single string consisting of all the output is returned. In an array context, an array of values is returned, one for each line of output. (You can set $/ to use a different line terminator.) The command is executed each time the pseudo-literal is evaluated. The status value of the command is returned in $? (see Predefined Names for the interpretation of $?). Unlike in *csh*, no translation is done on the return data—newlines remain newlines. Unlike in any of the shells, single quotes do not hide variable names in the command from interpretation. To pass a $ through to the shell you need to hide it with a backslash.

Evaluating a filehandle in angle brackets yields the next line from that file (newline included, so it's never false until EOF, at which time an undefined value is returned). Ordinarily you must assign that value to a variable, but there is one situation where an automatic assignment happens. If (and only if) the input symbol is the only thing inside the conditional of a *while* loop, the value is automatically assigned to the variable "$_". (This may seem like an odd thing to you, but you'll use the construct in almost every *perl* script you write.) Anyway, the following lines are equivalent to each other:


```
while ($_ = <STDIN>) { print; }
while (<STDIN>) { print; }
for (;<STDIN>;) { print; }
print while $_ = <STDIN>;
print while <STDIN>;
```

The filehandles *STDIN*, *STDOUT* and *STDERR* are predefined. (The filehandles *stdin*, *stdout* and *stderr* will also work except in packages, where they would be interpreted as local identifiers rather than global.) Additional filehandles may be created with the *open* function.

If a <FILEHANDLE> is used in a context that is looking for an array, an array consisting of all the input lines is returned, one line per array element. It's easy to make a LARGE data space this way, so use with care.

The null filehandle <> is special and can be used to emulate the behavior of *sed* and *awk*. Input from <> comes either from standard input, or from each file listed on the command line. Here's how it works: the first time <> is evaluated, the ARGV array is checked, and if it is null, $ARGV[0] is set to '-', which when opened gives you standard input. The ARGV array is then processed as a list of filenames. The loop

```
while (<>) {
        ...                 # code for each line
}
```

is equivalent to the following Perl-like pseudo code:

```
unshift(@ARGV, '-') if $#ARGV < $[;
while ($ARGV = shift) {
        open(ARGV, $ARGV);
        while (<ARGV>) {
                ...             # code for each line
        }
}
```

except that it isn't as cumbersome to say, and will actually work. It really does shift array ARGV and put the current filename into variable ARGV. It also uses filehandle ARGV internally—<> is just a synonym for <ARGV>, which is magical. (The pseudo code above doesn't work because it treats <ARGV> as non-magical.)

You can modify @ARGV before the first <> as long as the array ends up containing the list of filenames you really want. Line numbers ($.) continue as if the input was one big happy file. (But see example under eof for how to reset line numbers on each file.)

If you want to set @ARGV to your own list of files, go right ahead. If you want to pass switches into your script, you can put a loop on the front like this:

```
while ($_ = $ARGV[0], /^-/) {
        shift;
    last if /^--$/;
        /^-D(.*)/ && ($debug = $1);
        /^-v/ && $verbose++;
        ...             # other switches
}
while (<>) {
        ...             # code for each line
}
```

The <> symbol will return FALSE only once. If you call it again after this it will assume you are processing another @ARGV list, and if you haven't set @ARGV, will input from *STDIN*.

If the string inside the angle brackets is a reference to a scalar variable (e.g. <$foo>), then that variable contains the name of the filehandle to input from.

If the string inside angle brackets is not a filehandle, it is interpreted as a filename pattern to be globbed, and either an array of filenames or the next filename in the list is returned, depending on context. One level of $ interpretation is done first, but you can't say <$foo> because that's an indirect filehandle as explained in the previous paragraph. You could insert curly brackets to force interpretation as a filename glob: <${foo}>. Example:

```
while (<*.c>) {
        chmod 0644, $_;
}
```

is equivalent to

```
open(foo, "echo *.c | tr -s '\t\r\f' '\\012\\012\\012\\012' |");
while (<foo>) {
        chop;
        chmod 0644, $_;
}
```

19

In fact, it's currently implemented that way. (Which means it will not work on filenames with spaces in them unless you have /bin/csh on your machine.) Of course, the shortest way to do the above is:

```
chmod 0644, <*.c>;
```

2. Syntax

A *perl* script consists of a sequence of declarations and commands. The only things that need to be declared in *perl* are report formats and subroutines. See the sections below for more information on those declarations. All uninitialized user-created objects are assumed to start with a null or 0 value until they are defined by some explicit operation such as assignment. The sequence of commands is executed just once, unlike in *sed* and *awk* scripts, where the sequence of commands is executed for each input line. While this means that you must explicitly loop over the lines of your input file (or files), it also means you have much more control over which files and which lines you look at. (Actually, I'm lying—it is possible to do an implicit loop with either the **–n** or **–p** switch.)

A declaration can be put anywhere a command can, but has no effect on the execution of the primary sequence of commands—declarations all take effect at compile time. Typically all the declarations are put at the beginning or the end of the script.

Perl is, for the most part, a free-form language. (The only exception to this is format declarations, for fairly obvious reasons.) Comments are indicated by the # character, and extend to the end of the line. If you attempt to use /* */ C comments, it will be interpreted either as division or pattern matching, depending on the context. So don't do that.

3. Compound statements

In *perl*, a sequence of commands may be treated as one command by enclosing it in curly brackets. We will call this a BLOCK.

The following compound commands may be used to control flow:

```
if (EXPR) BLOCK
if (EXPR) BLOCK else BLOCK
if (EXPR) BLOCK elsif (EXPR) BLOCK ... else BLOCK
LABEL while (EXPR) BLOCK
LABEL while (EXPR) BLOCK continue BLOCK
LABEL for (EXPR; EXPR; EXPR) BLOCK
LABEL foreach VAR (ARRAY) BLOCK
LABEL BLOCK continue BLOCK
```

Note that, unlike C and Pascal, these are defined in terms of BLOCKs, not statements. This means that the curly brackets are *required*—no dangling statements allowed. If you want to write conditionals without curly brackets there are several other ways to do it. The following all do the same thing:

```
if (!open(foo)) { die "Can't open $foo: $!"; }
die "Can't open $foo: $!" unless open(foo);
open(foo) || die "Can't open $foo: $!";      # foo or bust!
open(foo) ? 'hi mom' : die "Can't open $foo: $!";
                    # a bit exotic, that last one
```

The *if* statement is straightforward. Since BLOCKs are always bounded by curly brackets, there is never any ambiguity about which *if* an *else* goes with. If you use *unless* in place of *if*, the sense of the test is reversed.

The *while* statement executes the block as long as the expression is true (does not evaluate to the null string or 0). The LABEL is optional, and if present, consists of an identifier followed by a colon. The

LABEL identifies the loop for the loop control statements *next*, *last*, and *redo* (see below). If there is a *continue* BLOCK, it is always executed just before the conditional is about to be evaluated again, similarly to the third part of a *for* loop in C. Thus it can be used to increment a loop variable, even when the loop has been continued via the *next* statement (similar to the C "continue" statement).

If the word *while* is replaced by the word *until*, the sense of the test is reversed, but the conditional is still tested before the first iteration.

In either the *if* or the *while* statement, you may replace "(EXPR)" with a BLOCK, and the conditional is true if the value of the last command in that block is true.

The *for* loop works exactly like the corresponding *while* loop:

```
for ($i = 1; $i < 10; $i++) {
        ...
}
```

is the same as

```
$i = 1;
while ($i < 10) {
        ...
} continue {
        $i++;
}
```

The foreach loop iterates over a normal array value and sets the variable VAR to be each element of the array in turn. The variable is implicitly local to the loop, and regains its former value upon exiting the loop. The "foreach" keyword is actually identical to the "for" keyword, so you can use "foreach" for readability or "for" for brevity. If VAR is omitted, $_ is set to each value. If ARRAY is an actual array (as opposed to an expression returning an array value), you can modify each element of the array by modifying VAR inside the loop. Examples:

```
for (@ary) { s/foo/bar/; }

foreach $elem (@elements) {
        $elem *= 2;
}

for ((10,9,8,7,6,5,4,3,2,1,'BOOM')) {
        print $_, "\n"; sleep(1);
}

for (1..15) { print "Merry Christmas\n"; }

foreach $item (split(/:[\\\n:]*/, $ENV{'TERMCAP'})) {
        print "Item: $item\n";
}
```

The BLOCK by itself (labeled or not) is equivalent to a loop that executes once. Thus you can use any of the loop control statements in it to leave or restart the block. The *continue* block is optional. This construct is particularly nice for doing case structures.

19

```
foo: {
        if (/^abc/) { $abc = 1; last foo; }
        if (/^def/) { $def = 1; last foo; }
        if (/^xyz/) { $xyz = 1; last foo; }
        $nothing = 1;
    }
```

There is no official switch statement in perl, because there are already several ways to write the equivalent. In addition to the above, you could write

```
    foo: {
        $abc = 1, last foo  if /^abc/;
        $def = 1, last foo  if /^def/;
        $xyz = 1, last foo  if /^xyz/;
        $nothing = 1;
    }
```

or

```
    foo: {
        /^abc/ && do { $abc = 1; last foo; };
        /^def/ && do { $def = 1; last foo; };
        /^xyz/ && do { $xyz = 1; last foo; };
        $nothing = 1;
    }
```

19

or

```
    foo: {
        /^abc/ && ($abc = 1, last foo);
        /^def/ && ($def = 1, last foo);
        /^xyz/ && ($xyz = 1, last foo);
        $nothing = 1;
    }
```

or even

```
    if (/^abc/)
        { $abc = 1; }
    elsif (/^def/)
        { $def = 1; }
    elsif (/^xyz/)
        { $xyz = 1; }
    else
        {$nothing = 1;}
```

As it happens, these are all optimized internally to a switch structure, so perl jumps directly to the desired statement, and you needn't worry about perl executing a lot of unnecessary statements when you have a string of 50 elsifs, as long as you are testing the same simple scalar variable using ==, eq, or pattern matching as above. (If you're curious as to whether the optimizer has done this for a particular case statement, you can use the –D1024 switch to list the syntax tree before execution.)

4. Simple statements

The only kind of simple statement is an expression evaluated for its side effects. Every simple statement must be terminated with a semicolon, unless it is the final statement in a block, in which case the semicolon is optional. (Semicolon is still encouraged there if the block takes up more than one line).

Any simple statement may optionally be followed by a single modifier, just before the terminating semicolon. The possible modifiers are:

```
if EXPR
unless EXPR
while EXPR
until EXPR
```

The *if* and *unless* modifiers have the expected semantics. The *while* and *until* modifiers also have the expected semantics (conditional evaluated first), except when applied to a do-BLOCK or a do-SUBROUTINE command, in which case the block executes once before the conditional is evaluated. This is so that you can write loops like:

```
do {
        $_ = <STDIN>;
        ...
} until $_ eq ".\n";
```

(See the *do* operator below. Note also that the loop control commands described later will NOT work in this construct, since modifiers don't take loop labels. Sorry.)

5. Expressions

Since *perl* expressions work almost exactly like C expressions, only the differences will be mentioned here.

Here's what *perl* has that C doesn't:

**	The exponentiation operator.

**=	The exponentiation assignment operator.

()	The null list, used to initialize an array to null.

.	Concatenation of two strings.

.=	The concatenation assignment operator.

eq	String equality (== is numeric equality). For a mnemonic just think of ''eq'' as a string. (If you are used to the *awk* behavior of using == for either string or numeric equality based on the current form of the comparands, beware! You must be explicit here.)

ne	String inequality (!= is numeric inequality).

lt	String less than.

gt	String greater than.

le	String less than or equal.

ge	String greater than or equal.

cmp	String comparison, returning -1, 0, or 1.

<=>	Numeric comparison, returning -1, 0, or 1.

=~	Certain operations search or modify the string ''$_'' by default. This operator makes that kind of operation work on some other string. The right argument is a search pattern, substitution, or translation. The left argument is what is supposed to be searched, substituted, or translated instead of the default ''$_''. The return value indicates the success of the operation. (If the right argument is an expression other than a search pattern, substitution, or translation, it is interpreted as a search pattern at run time. This is less efficient than an explicit search, since the pattern must be compiled every time the expression is evaluated.) The precedence of this operator is lower than unary minus and autoincrement/decrement, but higher than everything else.

!~ Just like =~ except the return value is negated.

x The repetition operator. Returns a string consisting of the left operand repeated the number of times specified by the right operand. In an array context, if the left operand is a list in parens, it repeats the list.

```
print '–' x 80;# print row of dashes
print '–' x80;# illegal, x80 is identifier

print "\t" x ($tab/8), ' ' x ($tab%8);# tab over

@ones = (1) x 80;# an array of 80 1's
@ones = (5) x @ones;# set all elements to 5
```

x= The repetition assignment operator. Only works on scalars.

.. The range operator, which is really two different operators depending on the context. In an array context, returns an array of values counting (by ones) from the left value to the right value. This is useful for writing "for (1..10)" loops and for doing slice operations on arrays.

In a scalar context, .. returns a boolean value. The operator is bistable, like a flip-flop, and emulates the line-range (comma) operator of sed, awk, and various editors. Each .. operator maintains its own boolean state. It is false as long as its left operand is false. Once the left operand is true, the range operator stays true until the right operand is true, AFTER which the range operator becomes false again. (It doesn't become false till the next time the range operator is evaluated. It can test the right operand and become false on the same evaluation it became true (as in awk), but it still returns true once. If you don't want it to test the right operand till the next evaluation (as in sed), use three dots (...) instead of two.) The right operand is not evaluated while the operator is in the "false" state, and the left operand is not evaluated while the operator is in the "true" state. The precedence is a little lower than || and &&. The value returned is either the null string for false, or a sequence number (beginning with 1) for true. The sequence number is reset for each range encountered. The final sequence number in a range has the string 'E0' appended to it, which doesn't affect its numeric value, but gives you something to search for if you want to exclude the endpoint. You can exclude the beginning point by waiting for the sequence number to be greater than 1. If either operand of scalar .. is static, that operand is implicitly compared to the $. variable, the current line number. Examples:

As a scalar operator:

```
if (101 .. 200) { print; }# print 2nd hundred lines

next line if (1 .. /^$/);# skip header lines

s/^/> / if (/^$/ .. eof());# quote body
```

As an array operator:

```
for (101 .. 200) { print; }# print $_ 100 times

@foo = @foo[$[ .. $#foo];# an expensive no-op
@foo = @foo[$#foo-4 .. $#foo];# slice last 5 items
```

–x A file test. This unary operator takes one argument, either a filename or a filehandle, and tests the associated file to see if something is true about it. If the argument is omitted, tests $_, except for –t, which tests *STDIN*. It returns 1 for true and ´´ for false, or the undefined value if the file doesn't exist. Precedence is higher than logical and relational operators, but lower than arithmetic operators. The operator may be any of:

–rFile is readable by effective uid/gid.
–wFile is writable by effective uid/gid.
–xFile is executable by effective uid/gid.
–oFile is owned by effective uid.
–RFile is readable by real uid/gid.
–WFile is writable by real uid/gid.
–XFile is executable by real uid/gid.
–OFile is owned by real uid.
–eFile exists.
–zFile has zero size.
–sFile has non-zero size (returns size).
–fFile is a plain file.
–dFile is a directory.
–lFile is a symbolic link.
–pFile is a named pipe (FIFO).
–SFile is a socket.
–bFile is a block special file.
–cFile is a character special file.
–uFile has setuid bit set.
–gFile has setgid bit set.
–kFile has sticky bit set.
–tFilehandle is opened to a tty.
–TFile is a text file.
–BFile is a binary file (opposite of –T).
–MAge of file in days when script started.
–ASame for access time.
–CSame for inode change time.

The interpretation of the file permission operators –r, –R, –w, –W, –x and –X is based solely on the mode of the file and the uids and gids of the user. There may be other reasons you can't actually read, write or execute the file. Also note that, for the superuser, –r, –R, –w and –W always return 1, and –x and –X return 1 if any execute bit is set in the mode. Scripts run by the superuser may thus need to do a stat() in order to determine the actual mode of the file, or temporarily set the uid to something else.

Example:

```
while (<>) {
chop;
next unless –f $_;# ignore specials
...
}
```

Note that –s/a/b/ does not do a negated substitution. Saying –exp($foo) still works as expected, however— only single letters following a minus are interpreted as file tests.

The –T and –B switches work as follows. The first block or so of the file is examined for odd characters such as strange control codes or metacharacters. If too many odd characters (>10%) are found, it's a –B file, otherwise it's a –T file. Also, any file containing null in the first block is considered a binary file. If –T or –B is used on a filehandle, the current stdio buffer is examined

19

rather than the first block. Both –T and –B return TRUE on a null file, or a file at EOF when testing a filehandle.

If any of the file tests (or either stat operator) are given the special filehandle consisting of a solitary underline, then the stat structure of the previous file test (or stat operator) is used, saving a system call. (This doesn't work with –t, and you need to remember that lstat and -l will leave values in the stat structure for the symbolic link, not the real file.) Example:

```
print "Can do.\n" if -r $a || -w _ || -x _;

stat($filename);
print "Readable\n" if -r _;
print "Writable\n" if -w _;
print "Executable\n" if -x _;
print "Setuid\n" if -u _;
print "Setgid\n" if -g _;
print "Sticky\n" if -k _;
print "Text\n" if -T _;
print "Binary\n" if -B _;
```

Here is what C has that *perl* doesn't:

unary &	Address-of operator.
unary *	Dereference-address operator.
(TYPE)	Type casting operator.

19

Like C, *perl* does a certain amount of expression evaluation at compile time, whenever it determines that all of the arguments to an operator are static and have no side effects. In particular, string concatenation happens at compile time between literals that don't do variable substitution. Backslash interpretation also happens at compile time. You can say

```
'Now is the time for all' . "\n" .
'good men to come to.'
```

and this all reduces to one string internally.

The autoincrement operator has a little extra built-in magic to it. If you increment a variable that is numeric, or that has ever been used in a numeric context, you get a normal increment. If, however, the variable has only been used in string contexts since it was set, and has a value that is not null and matches the pattern /^[a–zA–Z]*[0–9]*$/, the increment is done as a string, preserving each character within its range, with carry:

```
print ++($foo = '99');    # prints '100'
print ++($foo = 'a0');    # prints 'a1'
print ++($foo = 'Az');    # prints 'Ba'
print ++($foo = 'zz');    # prints 'aaa'
```

The autodecrement is not magical.

The range operator (in an array context) makes use of the magical autoincrement algorithm if the minimum and maximum are strings. You can say

```
@alphabet = ('A' .. 'Z');
```

to get all the letters of the alphabet, or

```
$hexdigit = (0 .. 9, 'a' .. 'f')[$num & 15];
```

to get a hexadecimal digit, or

```
@z2 = ('01' .. '31'); print @z2[$mday];
```

to get dates with leading zeros. (If the final value specified is not in the sequence that the magical increment would produce, the sequence goes until the next value would be longer than the final value specified.)

The || and && operators differ from C's in that, rather than returning 0 or 1, they return the last value evaluated. Thus, a portable way to find out the home directory might be:

```
$home = $ENV{'HOME'} || $ENV{'LOGDIR'} ||
  (getpwuid($<))[7] || die "You're homeless!\n";
```

Along with the literals and variables mentioned earlier, the operations in the following section can serve as terms in an expression. Some of these operations take a LIST as an argument. Such a list can consist of any combination of scalar arguments or array values; the array values will be included in the list as if each individual element were interpolated at that point in the list, forming a longer single-dimensional array value. Elements of the LIST should be separated by commas. If an operation is listed both with and without parentheses around its arguments, it means you can either use it as a unary operator or as a function call. To use it as a function call, the next token on the same line must be a left parenthesis. (There may be intervening white space.) Such a function then has highest precedence, as you would expect from a function. If any token other than a left parenthesis follows, then it is a unary operator, with a precedence depending only on whether it is a LIST operator or not. LIST operators have lowest precedence. All other unary operators have a precedence greater than relational operators but less than arithmetic operators. See the section on Precedence.

For operators that can be used in either a scalar or array context, failure is generally indicated in a scalar context by returning the undefined value, and in an array context by returning the null list. Remember though that THERE IS NO GENERAL RULE FOR CONVERTING A LIST INTO A SCALAR. Each operator decides which sort of scalar it would be most appropriate to return. Some operators return the length of the list that would have been returned in an array context. Some operators return the first value in the list. Some operators return the last value in the list. Some operators return a count of successful operations. In general, they do what you want, unless you want consistency.

/PATTERN/

See m/PATTERN/.

?PATTERN?

This is just like the /pattern/ search, except that it matches only once between calls to the *reset* operator. This is a useful optimization when you only want to see the first occurrence of something in each file of a set of files, for instance. Only ?? patterns local to the current package are reset.

accept(NEWSOCKET,GENERICSOCKET)

Does the same thing that the accept system call does. Returns true if it succeeded, false otherwise. See example in section on Interprocess Communication.

alarm(SECONDS)

alarm SECONDS

Arranges to have a SIGALRM delivered to this process after the specified number of seconds (minus 1, actually) have elapsed. Thus, alarm(15) will cause a SIGALRM at some point more than 14 seconds in the future. Only one timer may be counting at once. Each call disables the previous timer, and an argument of 0 may be supplied to cancel the previous timer without starting a new one. The returned value is the amount of time remaining on the previous timer.

atan2(Y,X)

Returns the arctangent of Y/X in the range $-\pi$ to π.

bind(SOCKET,NAME)

Does the same thing that the bind system call does. Returns true if it succeeded, false otherwise. NAME should be a packed address of the proper type for the socket. See example in section on Interprocess Communication.

binmode(FILEHANDLE)

binmode FILEHANDLE

Arranges for the file to be read in "binary" mode in operating systems that distinguish between binary and text files. Files that are not read in binary mode have CR LF sequences translated to LF on input and LF translated to CR LF on output. Binmode has no effect under Unix. If FILEHANDLE is an expression, the value is taken as the name of the filehandle.

caller(EXPR)

caller Returns the context of the current subroutine call:

```
($package,$filename,$line) = caller;
```

With EXPR, returns some extra information that the debugger uses to print a stack trace. The value of EXPR indicates how many call frames to go back before the current one.

chdir(EXPR)

chdir EXPR

Changes the working directory to EXPR, if possible. If EXPR is omitted, changes to home directory. Returns 1 upon success, 0 otherwise. See example under *die*.

chmod(LIST)

chmod LIST

Changes the permissions of a list of files. The first element of the list must be the numerical mode. Returns the number of files successfully changed.

```
$cnt = chmod 0755, 'foo', 'bar';
chmod 0755, @executables;
```

chop(LIST)

chop(VARIABLE)

chop VARIABLE

chop Chops off the last character of a string and returns the character chopped. It's used primarily to remove the newline from the end of an input record, but is much more efficient than s/\n// because it neither scans nor copies the string. If VARIABLE is omitted, chops $_. Example:

```
while (<>) {
chop;# avoid \n on last field
@array = split(/:/);
...
}
```

You can actually chop anything that's an lvalue, including an assignment:

```
chop($cwd = `pwd`);
chop($answer = <STDIN>);
```

If you chop a list, each element is chopped. Only the value of the last chop is returned.

chown(LIST)

chown LIST

Changes the owner (and group) of a list of files. The first two elements of the list must be the NUMERICAL uid and gid, in that order. Returns the number of files successfully changed.

```
$cnt = chown $uid, $gid, 'foo', 'bar';
chown $uid, $gid, @filenames;
```

Here's an example that looks up non-numeric uids in the passwd file:

```
print "User: ";
$user = <STDIN>;
chop($user);
print "Files: "
$pattern = <STDIN>;
chop($pattern);
open(pass, '/etc/passwd') || die "Can't open passwd: $!\n";
while (<pass>) {
($login,$pass,$uid,$gid) = split(/:/);
$uid{$login} = $uid;
$gid{$login} = $gid;
}
@ary = <${pattern}>;# get filenames
if ($uid{$user} eq '') {
die "$user not in passwd file";
}
else {
chown $uid{$user}, $gid{$user}, @ary;
}
```

chroot(FILENAME)

chroot FILENAME

Does the same as the system call of that name. If you don't know what it does, don't worry about it. If FILENAME is omitted, does chroot to $_.

close(FILEHANDLE)

close FILEHANDLE

Closes the file or pipe associated with the file handle. You don't have to close FILEHANDLE if you are immediately going to do another open on it, since open will close it for you. (See *open.*) However, an explicit close on an input file resets the line counter ($.), while the implicit close done by *open* does not. Also, closing a pipe will wait for the process executing on the pipe to complete, in case you want to look at the output of the pipe afterwards. Closing a pipe explicitly also puts the status value of the command into $?. Example:

```
open(OUTPUT, '| sort >foo');# pipe to sort
...# print stuff to output
close OUTPUT;# wait for sort to finish
open(INPUT, 'foo');# get sort's results
```

FILEHANDLE may be an expression whose value gives the real filehandle name.

19

closedir(DIRHANDLE)

closedir DIRHANDLE

Closes a directory opened by opendir().

connect(SOCKET,NAME)

Does the same thing that the connect system call does. Returns true if it succeeded, false otherwise. NAME should be a package address of the proper type for the socket. See example in section on Interprocess Communication.

cos(EXPR)

cos EXPRReturns the cosine of EXPR (expressed in radians). If EXPR is omitted takes cosine of $_.

crypt(PLAINTEXT,SALT)

Encrypts a string exactly like the crypt() function in the C library. Useful for checking the password file for lousy passwords. Only the guys wearing white hats should do this.

dbmclose(ASSOC_ARRAY)

dbmclose ASSOC_ARRAY

Breaks the binding between a dbm file and an associative array. The values remaining in the associative array are meaningless unless you happen to want to know what was in the cache for the dbm file. This function is only useful if you have ndbm.

dbmopen(ASSOC,DBNAME,MODE)

This binds a dbm or ndbm file to an associative array. ASSOC is the name of the associative array. (Unlike normal open, the first argument is NOT a filehandle, even though it looks like one). DBNAME is the name of the database (without the .dir or .pag extension). If the database does not exist, it is created with protection specified by MODE (as modified by the umask). If your system only supports the older dbm functions, you may perform only one dbmopen in your program. If your system has neither dbm nor ndbm, calling dbmopen produces a fatal error.

Values assigned to the associative array prior to the dbmopen are lost. A certain number of values from the dbm file are cached in memory. By default this number is 64, but you can increase it by preallocating that number of garbage entries in the associative array before the dbmopen. You can flush the cache if necessary with the reset command.

If you don't have write access to the dbm file, you can only read associative array variables, not set them. If you want to test whether you can write, either use file tests or try setting a dummy array entry inside an eval, which will trap the error.

Note that functions such as keys() and values() may return huge array values when used on large dbm files. You may prefer to use the each() function to iterate over large dbm files. Example:

```
# print out history file offsets
dbmopen(HIST,'/usr/lib/news/history',0666);
while (($key,$val) = each %HIST) {
print $key, ' = ', unpack('L',$val), "\n";
}
dbmclose(HIST);
```

defined(EXPR)

defined EXPR

Returns a boolean value saying whether the lvalue EXPR has a real value or not. Many operations return the undefined value under exceptional conditions, such as end of file, uninitialized variable, system error and such. This function allows you to distinguish between an undefined null string and a defined null string with operations that might return a real null string, in particular referencing elements of an array. You may also check to see if arrays or subroutines exist. Use on predefined variables is not guaranteed to produce intuitive results. Examples:

```
print if defined $switch{'D'};
    print "$val\n" while defined($val = pop(@ary));
    die "Can't readlink $sym: $!"
    unless defined($value = readlink $sym);
    eval '@foo = ()' if defined(@foo);
    die "No XYZ package defined" unless defined %_XYZ;
    sub foo { defined &$bar ? &$bar(@_) : die "No bar"; }
```

See also undef.

delete $ASSOC{KEY}

Deletes the specified value from the specified associative array. Returns the deleted value, or the undefined value if nothing was deleted. Deleting from $ENV{} modifies the environment. Deleting from an array bound to a dbm file deletes the entry from the dbm file.

The following deletes all the values of an associative array:

```
foreach $key (keys %ARRAY) {
delete $ARRAY{$key};
}
```

(But it would be faster to use the *reset* command. Saying undef %ARRAY is faster yet.)

die(LIST)

die LIST Outside of an eval, prints the value of LIST to *STDERR* and exits with the current value of $! (errno). If $! is 0, exits with the value of ($? >> 8) (`command` status). If ($? >> 8) is 0, exits with 255. Inside an eval, the error message is stuffed into $@ and the eval is terminated with the undefined value.

19

Equivalent examples:

```
die "Can't cd to spool: $!\n" unless chdir '/usr/spool/news';

chdir '/usr/spool/news' || die "Can't cd to spool: $!\n"
```

If the value of EXPR does not end in a newline, the current script line number and input line number (if any) are also printed, and a newline is supplied. Hint: sometimes appending ``, stopped'' to your message will cause it to make better sense when the string ``at foo line 123'' is appended. Suppose you are running script ``canasta''.

```
die "/etc/games is no good";
die "/etc/games is no good, stopped";
```

produce, respectively

```
/etc/games is no good at canasta line 123.
/etc/games is no good, stopped at canasta line 123.
```

See also *exit*.

do BLOCK

Returns the value of the last command in the sequence of commands indicated by BLOCK. When modified by a loop modifier, executes the BLOCK once before testing the loop condition. (On other statements the loop modifiers test the conditional first.)

do SUBROUTINE (LIST)

Executes a SUBROUTINE declared by a *sub* declaration, and returns the value of the last expression evaluated in SUBROUTINE. If there is no subroutine by that name, produces a fatal error. (You may use the ''defined'' operator to determine if a subroutine exists.) If you pass arrays as part of LIST you may wish to pass the length of the array in front of each array. (See the section on subroutines later on.) The parentheses are required to avoid confusion with the ''do EXPR'' form.

SUBROUTINE may also be a single scalar variable, in which case the name of the subroutine to execute is taken from the variable.

As an alternate (and preferred) form, you may call a subroutine by prefixing the name with an ampersand: &foo(@args). If you aren't passing any arguments, you don't have to use parentheses. If you omit the parentheses, no @_ array is passed to the subroutine. The & form is also used to specify subroutines to the defined and undef operators:

```
if (defined &$var) { &$var($parm); undef &$var; }
```

do EXPR Uses the value of EXPR as a filename and executes the contents of the file as a *perl* script. Its primary use is to include subroutines from a *perl* subroutine library.

```
do 'stat.pl';
```

19

is just like

```
eval `cat stat.pl`;
```

except that it's more efficient, more concise, keeps track of the current filename for error messages, and searches all the **–I** libraries if the file isn't in the current directory (see also the @INC array in Predefined Names). It's the same, however, in that it does reparse the file every time you call it, so if you are going to use the file inside a loop you might prefer to use –P and #include, at the expense of a little more startup time. (The main problem with #include is that cpp doesn't grok # comments—a workaround is to use '';#'' for standalone comments.) Note that the following are NOT equivalent:

```
do $foo;# eval a file
do $foo();# call a subroutine
```

Note that inclusion of library routines is better done with the ''require'' operator.

dump LABEL

This causes an immediate core dump. Primarily this is so that you can use the undump program to turn your core dump into an executable binary after having initialized all your variables at the beginning of the program. When the new binary is executed it will begin by executing a "goto LABEL" (with all the restrictions that goto suffers). Think of it as a goto with an intervening core dump and reincarnation. If LABEL is omitted, restarts the program from the top. WARNING: any files opened at the time of the dump will NOT be open any more when the program is reincarnated, with possible resulting confusion on the part of perl. See also –u.

Example:

```
#!/usr/bin/perl
    require 'getopt.pl';
    require 'stat.pl';
    %days = (
        'Sun',1,
        'Mon',2,
        'Tue',3,
        'Wed',4,
        'Thu',5,
        'Fri',6,
        'Sat',7);

    dump QUICKSTART if $ARGV[0] eq '-d';

QUICKSTART:
    do Getopt('f');
```

each(ASSOC_ARRAY)

each ASSOC_ARRAY

Returns a 2 element array consisting of the key and value for the next value of an associative array, so that you can iterate over it. Entries are returned in an apparently random order. When the array is entirely read, a null array is returned (which when assigned produces a FALSE (0) value). The next call to each() after that will start iterating again. The iterator can be reset only by reading all the elements from the array. You must not modify the array while iterating over it. There is a single iterator for each associative array, shared by all each(), keys() and values() function calls in the program. The following prints out your environment like the printenv program, only in a different order:

```
while (($key,$value) = each %ENV) {
print "$key=$value\n";
}
```

See also keys() and values().

eof(FILEHANDLE)

eof()

eof Returns 1 if the next read on FILEHANDLE will return end of file, or if FILEHANDLE is not open. FILEHANDLE may be an expression whose value gives the real filehandle name. (Note that this function actually reads a character and then ungetc's it, so it is not very useful in an interactive context.) An eof without an argument returns the eof status for the last file read. Empty parentheses () may be used to indicate the pseudo file formed of the files listed on the command line, i.e. eof() is reasonable to use inside a while (<>) loop to detect the end of only the last file. Use eof(ARGV) or eof without the parentheses to test EACH file in a while (<>) loop. Examples:

```
# insert dashes just before last line of last file
while (<>) {
if (eof()) {
print "--------------\n";
}
print;
}
```

19

```
# reset line numbering on each input file
while (<>) {
print "$.\t$_";
if (eof) {# Not eof().
close(ARGV);
}
}
```

eval(EXPR)

eval EXPR

eval BLOCK

EXPR is parsed and executed as if it were a little *perl* program. It is executed in the context of the current *perl* program, so that any variable settings, subroutine or format definitions remain afterwards. The value returned is the value of the last expression evaluated, just as with subroutines. If there is a syntax error or runtime error, or a die statement is executed, an undefined value is returned by eval, and $@ is set to the error message. If there was no error, $@ is guaranteed to be a null string. If EXPR is omitted, evaluates $_. The final semicolon, if any, may be omitted from the expression.

Note that, since eval traps otherwise-fatal errors, it is useful for determining whether a particular feature (such as dbmopen or symlink) is implemented. It is also Perl's exception trapping mechanism, where the die operator is used to raise exceptions.

19

If the code to be executed doesn't vary, you may use the eval-BLOCK form to trap run-time errors without incurring the penalty of recompiling each time. The error, if any, is still returned in $@. Evaluating a single-quoted string (as EXPR) has the same effect, except that the eval-EXPR form reports syntax errors at run time via $@, whereas the eval-BLOCK form reports syntax errors at compile time. The eval-EXPR form is optimized to eval-BLOCK the first time it succeeds. (Since the replacement side of a substitution is considered a single-quoted string when you use the e modifier, the same optimization occurs there.) Examples:

```
# make divide-by-zero non-fatal
eval { $answer = $a / $b; }; warn $@ if $@;

# optimized to same thing after first use
eval '$answer = $a / $b'; warn $@ if $@;

# a compile-time error
eval { $answer = };

# a run-time error
eval '$answer =';# sets $@
```

exec(LIST)

exec LISTIf there is more than one argument in LIST, or if LIST is an array with more than one value, calls execvp() with the arguments in LIST. If there is only one scalar argument, the argument is checked for shell metacharacters. If there are any, the entire argument is passed to "/bin/sh –c" for parsing. If there are none, the argument is split into words and passed directly to execvp(), which is more efficient. Note: exec (and system) do not flush your output buffer, so you may need to set $| to avoid lost output. Examples:

```
exec '/bin/echo', 'Your arguments are: ', @ARGV;
exec "sort $outfile | uniq";
```

If you don't really want to execute the first argument, but want to lie to the program you are executing about its own name, you can specify the program you actually want to run by assigning that to a variable and putting the name of the variable in front of the LIST without a comma. (This always forces interpretation of the LIST as a multi-valued list, even if there is only a single scalar in the list.) Example:

```
$shell = '/bin/csh';
exec $shell '-sh';# pretend it's a login shell
```

exit(EXPR)

exit EXPR Evaluates EXPR and exits immediately with that value. Example:

```
$ans = <STDIN>;
exit 0 if $ans =~ /^[Xx]/;
```

See also *die*. If EXPR is omitted, exits with 0 status.

exp(EXPR)

exp EXPR Returns *e* to the power of EXPR. If EXPR is omitted, gives exp($_).

fcntl(FILEHANDLE,FUNCTION,SCALAR)

Implements the fcntl(2) function. You'll probably have to say

```
require "fcntl.ph";# probably /usr/local/lib/perl/fcntl.ph
```

first to get the correct function definitions. If fcntl.ph doesn't exist or doesn't have the correct definitions you'll have to roll your own, based on your C header files such as <sys/fcntl.h>. (There is a perl script called h2ph that comes with the perl kit which may help you in this.) Argument processing and value return works just like ioctl below. Note that fcntl will produce a fatal error if used on a machine that doesn't implement fcntl(2).

fileno(FILEHANDLE)

fileno FILEHANDLE

Returns the file descriptor for a filehandle. Useful for constructing bitmaps for select(). If FILEHANDLE is an expression, the value is taken as the name of the filehandle.

flock(FILEHANDLE,OPERATION)

Calls flock(2) on FILEHANDLE. See manual page for flock(2) for definition of OPERATION. Returns true for success, false on failure. Will produce a fatal error if used on a machine that doesn't implement flock(2). Here's a mailbox appender for BSD systems.

```
$LOCK_SH = 1;
$LOCK_EX = 2;
$LOCK_NB = 4;
$LOCK_UN = 8;

sub lock {
   flock(MBOX,$LOCK_EX);
   # and, in case someone appended
   # while we were waiting...
   seek(MBOX, 0, 2);
}
```

19

```
sub unlock {
    flock(MBOX,$LOCK_UN);
}

open(MBOX, ">>/usr/spool/mail/$ENV{'USER'}")
|| die "Can't open mailbox: $!";

do lock();
print MBOX $msg,"\n\n";
do unlock();
```

fork Does a fork() call. Returns the child pid to the parent process and 0 to the child process. Note: unflushed buffers remain unflushed in both processes, which means you may need to set $| to avoid duplicate output.

getc(FILEHANDLE)

getc FILEHANDLE

getc Returns the next character from the input file attached to FILEHANDLE, or a null string at EOF. If FILEHANDLE is omitted, reads from STDIN.

getlogin Returns the current login from /etc/utmp, if any. If null, use getpwuid.

```
$login = getlogin || (getpwuid($<))[0] || "Somebody";
```


getpeername(SOCKET)
Returns the packed sockaddr address of other end of the SOCKET connection.

```
# An internet sockaddr
$sockaddr = 'S n a4 x8';
$hersockaddr = getpeername(S);
($family, $port, $heraddr) = unpack($sockaddr,$hersockaddr);
```

getpgrp(PID)

getpgrp PID
Returns the current process group for the specified PID, 0 for the current process. Will produce a fatal error if used on a machine that doesn't implement getpgrp(2). If EXPR is omitted, returns process group of current process.

getppid Returns the process id of the parent process.

getpriority(WHICH,WHO)
Returns the current priority for a process, a process group, or a user. (See getpriority(2).) Will produce a fatal error if used on a machine that doesn't implement getpriority(2).

getpwnam(NAME)

getgrnam(NAME)

gethostbyname(NAME)

getnetbyname(NAME)

getprotobyname(NAME)

getpwuid(UID)

getgrgid(GID)

getservbyname(NAME,PROTO)

gethostbyaddr(ADDR,ADDRTYPE)

getnetbyaddr(ADDR,ADDRTYPE)

getprotobynumber(NUMBER)

getservbyport(PORT,PROTO)

getpwent

getgrent

gethostent

getnetent

getprotoent

getservent

setpwent

setgrent

sethostent(STAYOPEN)

setnetent(STAYOPEN)

setprotoent(STAYOPEN)

setservent(STAYOPEN)

endpwent

endgrent

endhostent

endnetent

endprotoent

endserventThese routines perform the same functions as their counterparts in the system library. Within an array context, the return values from the various get routines are as follows:

```
($name,$passwd,$uid,$gid,
  $quota,$comment,$gcos,$dir,$shell) = getpw...
($name,$passwd,$gid,$members) = getgr...
($name,$aliases,$addrtype,$length,@addrs) = gethost...
($name,$aliases,$addrtype,$net) = getnet...
($name,$aliases,$proto) = getproto...
($name,$aliases,$port,$proto) = getserv...
```

(If the entry doesn't exist you get a null list.)

Within a scalar context, you get the name, unless the function was a lookup by name, in which case you get the other thing, whatever it is. (If the entry doesn't exist you get the undefined value.) For example:

```
$uid = getpwnam
$name = getpwuid
$name = getpwent
$gid = getgrnam
$name = getgrgid
$name = getgrent
etc.
```

The $members value returned by getgr... is a space separated list of the login names of the members of the group.

For the gethost... functions, if the h_errno variable is supported in C, it will be returned to you via $? if the function call fails. The @addrs value returned by a successful call is a list of the raw addresses returned by the corresponding system library call. In the Internet domain, each address is four bytes long and you can unpack it by saying something like:

```
($a,$b,$c,$d) = unpack('C4',$addr[0]);
```

getsockname(SOCKET)
: Returns the packed sockaddr address of this end of the SOCKET connection.

```
# An internet sockaddr
$sockaddr = 'S n a4 x8';
$mysockaddr = getsockname(S);
($family, $port, $myaddr) = unpack($sockaddr,$mysockaddr);
```

getsockopt(SOCKET,LEVEL,OPTNAME)
: Returns the socket option requested, or undefined if there is an error.

gmtime(EXPR)

gmtime EXPR
: Converts a time as returned by the time function to a 9-element array with the time analyzed for the Greenwich timezone. Typically used as follows:


```
($sec,$min,$hour,$mday,$mon,$year,$wday,$yday,$isdst) = gmtime(time);
```

All array elements are numeric, and come straight out of a struct tm. In particular this means that $mon has the range 0..11 and $wday has the range 0..6. If EXPR is omitted, does gmtime(time).

goto LABEL
: Finds the statement labeled with LABEL and resumes execution there. Currently you may only go to statements in the main body of the program that are not nested inside a do {} construct. This statement is not implemented very efficiently, and is here only to make the *sed*-to- translator easier. I may change its semantics at any time, consistent with support for translated *sed* scripts. Use it at your own risk. Better yet, don't use it at all.

grep(EXPR,LIST)
: Evaluates EXPR for each element of LIST (locally setting $_ to each element) and returns the array value consisting of those elements for which the expression evaluated to true. In a scalar context, returns the number of times the expression was true.

```
@foo = grep(!/^#/, @bar);    # weed out comments
```

Note that, since $_ is a reference into the array value, it can be used to modify the elements of the array. While this is useful and supported, it can cause bizarre results if the LIST is not a named array.

hex(EXPR)

hex EXPRReturns the decimal value of EXPR interpreted as an hex string. (To interpret strings that might start with 0 or 0x see oct().) If EXPR is omitted, uses $_.

index(STR,SUBSTR,POSITION)

index(STR,SUBSTR)
: Returns the position of the first occurrence of SUBSTR in STR at or after POSITION. If POSITION is omitted, starts searching from the beginning of the string. The return value is based at 0, or whatever you've set the $[variable to. If the substring is not found, returns one less than the base, ordinarily −1.

int(EXPR)

int EXPR Returns the integer portion of EXPR. If EXPR is omitted, uses $_.

ioctl(FILEHANDLE,FUNCTION,SCALAR)

Implements the ioctl(2) function. You'll probably have to say

```
require "ioctl.ph";# probably /usr/local/lib/perl/ioctl.ph
```

first to get the correct function definitions. If ioctl.ph doesn't exist or doesn't have the correct definitions you'll have to roll your own, based on your C header files such as <sys/ioctl.h>. (There is a perl script called h2ph that comes with the perl kit which may help you in this.) SCALAR will be read and/or written depending on the FUNCTION— a pointer to the string value of SCALAR will be passed as the third argument of the actual ioctl call. (If SCALAR has no string value but does have a numeric value, that value will be passed rather than a pointer to the string value. To guarantee this to be true, add a 0 to the scalar before using it.) The pack() and unpack() functions are useful for manipulating the values of structures used by ioctl(). The following example sets the erase character to DEL.

```
require 'ioctl.ph';
$sgttyb_t = "ccccs";# 4 chars and a short
if (ioctl(STDIN,$TIOCGETP,$sgttyb)) {
@ary = unpack($sgttyb_t,$sgttyb);
$ary[2] = 127;
$sgttyb = pack($sgttyb_t,@ary);
ioctl(STDIN,$TIOCSETP,$sgttyb)
|| die "Can't ioctl: $!";
}
```

The return value of ioctl (and fcntl) is as follows:

if OS returns:	perl returns:
-1	undefined value
0	string "0 but true"
anything else	that number

Thus perl returns true on success and false on failure, yet you can still easily determine the actual value returned by the operating system:

```
($retval = ioctl(...)) || ($retval = -1);
printf "System returned %d\n", $retval;
```

join(EXPR,LIST)

join(EXPR,ARRAY)

Joins the separate strings of LIST or ARRAY into a single string with fields separated by the value of EXPR, and returns the string. Example:

```
$_ = join(':', $login,$passwd,$uid,$gid,$gcos,$home,$shell);
```

See *split*.

19

keys(ASSOC_ARRAY)

keys ASSOC_ARRAY

Returns a normal array consisting of all the keys of the named associative array. The keys are returned in an apparently random order, but it is the same order as either the values() or each() function produces (given that the associative array has not been modified). Here is yet another way to print your environment:

```
@keys = keys %ENV;
@values = values %ENV;
while ($#keys >= 0) {
print pop(@keys), '=', pop(@values), "\n";
}
```

or how about sorted by key:

```
foreach $key (sort(keys %ENV)) {
print $key, '=', $ENV{$key}, "\n";
}
```

kill(LIST)

kill LIST Sends a signal to a list of processes. The first element of the list must be the signal to send. Returns the number of processes successfully signaled.

```
$cnt = kill 1, $child1, $child2;
kill 9, @goners;
```

If the signal is negative, kills process groups instead of processes. (On System V, a negative *process* number will also kill process groups, but that's not portable.) You may use a signal name in quotes.

last LABEL

last The *last* command is like the *break* statement in C (as used in loops); it immediately exits the loop in question. If the LABEL is omitted, the command refers to the innermost enclosing loop. The *continue* block, if any, is not executed:

```
line: while (<STDIN>) {
last line if /^$/;# exit when done with header
...
}
```

length(EXPR)

length EXPR

Returns the length in characters of the value of EXPR. If EXPR is omitted, returns length of $_.

link(OLDFILE,NEWFILE)

Creates a new filename linked to the old filename. Returns 1 for success, 0 otherwise.

listen(SOCKET,QUEUESIZE)

Does the same thing that the listen system call does. Returns true if it succeeded, false otherwise. See example in section on Interprocess Communication.

local(LIST)

Declares the listed variables to be local to the enclosing block, subroutine, eval or "do". All the listed elements must be legal lvalues. This operator works by saving the current values of those variables in LIST on a hidden stack and restoring them upon exiting the block, subroutine or eval. This means that called subroutines can also reference the local variable, but not the global one. The LIST may be assigned to if desired, which allows you to initialize your local variables. (If no initializer is given for a particular variable, it is created with an undefined value.) Commonly this is used to name the parameters to a subroutine. Examples:

```
sub RANGEVAL {
local($min, $max, $thunk) = @_;
local($result) = '';
local($i);

# Presumably $thunk makes reference to $i

for ($i = $min; $i < $max; $i++) {
$result .= eval $thunk;
}

$result;
}

if ($sw eq '-v') {
   # init local array with global array
   local(@ARGV) = @ARGV;
   unshift(@ARGV,'echo');
   system @ARGV;
}
# @ARGV restored

# temporarily add to digits associative array
if ($base12) {
# (NOTE: not claiming this is efficient!)
local(%digits) = (%digits,'t',10,'e',11);
do parse_num();
}
```

Note that local() is a run-time command, and so gets executed every time through a loop, using up more stack storage each time until it's all released at once when the loop is exited.

localtime(EXPR)

localtime EXPR

Converts a time as returned by the time function to a 9-element array with the time analyzed for the local timezone. Typically used as follows:

```
($sec,$min,$hour,$mday,$mon,$year,$wday,$yday,$isdst) = localtime(time);
```

All array elements are numeric, and come straight out of a struct tm. In particular this means that $mon has the range 0..11 and $wday has the range 0..6. If EXPR is omitted, does localtime(time).

log(EXPR)

log EXPRReturns logarithm (base *e*) of EXPR. If EXPR is omitted, returns log of $_.

19

lstat(FILEHANDLE)

lstat FILEHANDLE

lstat(EXPR)

lstat SCALARVARIABLE

Does the same thing as the stat() function, but stats a symbolic link instead of the file the symbolic link points to. If symbolic links are unimplemented on your system, a normal stat is done.

m/PATTERN/gio

/PATTERN/gio

Searches a string for a pattern match, and returns true (1) or false (´´). If no string is specified via the =˜ or !˜ operator, the $_ string is searched. (The string specified with =˜ need not be an lvalue—it may be the result of an expression evaluation, but remember the =˜ binds rather tightly.) See also the section on regular expressions.

If / is the delimiter then the initial ‘m’ is optional. With the ‘m’ you can use any pair of non-alphanumeric characters as delimiters. This is particularly useful for matching Unix path names that contain ‘/’. If the final delimiter is followed by the optional letter ‘i’, the matching is done in a case-insensitive manner. PATTERN may contain references to scalar variables, which will be interpolated (and the pattern recompiled) every time the pattern search is evaluated. (Note that $) and $| may not be interpolated because they look like end-of-string tests.) If you want such a pattern to be compiled only once, add an ‘‘o’’ after the trailing delimiter. This avoids expensive run-time recompilations, and is useful when the value you are interpolating won't change over the life of the script. If the PATTERN evaluates to a null string, the most recent successful regular expression is used instead.

If used in a context that requires an array value, a pattern match returns an array consisting of the subexpressions matched by the parentheses in the pattern, i.e. ($1, $2, $3...). It does NOT actually set $1, $2, etc. in this case, nor does it set $+, $‘, $& or $’. If the match fails, a null array is returned. If the match succeeds, but there were no parentheses, an array value of (1) is returned.

Examples:

```
open(tty, ´/dev/tty´);
<tty> =˜ /ˆy/i && do foo( );# do foo if desired

if (/Version: * ([0–9.]* ) / ) { $version = $1; }

next if m#ˆ/usr/spool/uucp#;

# poor man's grep
$arg = shift;
while (<>) {
        print if /$arg/o;# compile only once
}

if (($F1, $F2, $Etc) = ($foo =˜ /ˆ(\S+)\s+(\S+)\s*(.*)/))
```

This last example splits $foo into the first two words and the remainder of the line, and assigns those three fields to $F1, $F2 and $Etc. The conditional is true if any variables were assigned, i.e. if the pattern matched.

The ‘‘g’’ modifier specifies global pattern matching—that is, matching as many times as possible within the string. How it behaves depends on the context. In an array context, it returns a list of all the substrings matched by all the parentheses in the regular expression. If there are no parentheses, it returns a list of all the matched strings, as if there were parentheses around the whole pattern. In a scalar context, it iterates through the string, returning TRUE each time it matches, and FALSE when it eventually runs out of matches. (In other words, it remembers where it left off last time and restarts the search at that point.) It presumes that you have not modified the string since the last match. Modifying the string between matches may result in undefined behavior. (You can actually get away with in-place modifications via substr() that do not change the length of the entire string. In general, however, you should be using s///g for such modifications.) Examples:

```
# array context
($one,$five,$fifteen) = (`uptime` =~ /(\d+\.\d+)/g);

# scalar context
$/ = ""; $* = 1;
while ($paragraph = <>) {
   while ($paragraph =~ /[a-z]['")]*[.!?]+['")]*\s/g) {
$sentences++;
   }
}
print "$sentences\n";
```


mkdir(FILENAME,MODE)
: Creates the directory specified by FILENAME, with permissions specified by MODE (as modified by umask). If it succeeds it returns 1, otherwise it returns 0 and sets $! (errno).

msgctl(ID,CMD,ARG)
: Calls the System V IPC function msgctl. If CMD is &IPC_STAT, then ARG must be a variable which will hold the returned msqid_ds structure. Returns like ioctl: the undefined value for error, "0 but true" for zero, or the actual return value otherwise.

msgget(KEY,FLAGS)
: Calls the System V IPC function msgget. Returns the message queue id, or the undefined value if there is an error.

msgsnd(ID,MSG,FLAGS)
: Calls the System V IPC function msgsnd to send the message MSG to the message queue ID. MSG must begin with the long integer message type, which may be created with pack("L", $type). Returns true if successful, or false if there is an error.

msgrcv(ID,VAR,SIZE,TYPE,FLAGS)
: Calls the System V IPC function msgrcv to receive a message from message queue ID into variable VAR with a maximum message size of SIZE. Note that if a message is received, the message type will be the first thing in VAR, and the maximum length of VAR is SIZE plus the size of the message type. Returns true if successful, or false if there is an error.

next LABEL

next
: The *next* command is like the *continue* statement in C; it starts the next iteration of the loop:

```
line: while (<STDIN>) {
next line if /^#/;# discard comments
...
}
```

Note that if there were a *continue* block on the above, it would get executed even on discarded lines. If the LABEL is omitted, the command refers to the innermost enclosing loop.

oct(EXPR)

oct EXPRReturns the decimal value of EXPR interpreted as an octal string. (If EXPR happens to start off with 0x, interprets it as a hex string instead.) The following will handle decimal, octal and hex in the standard notation:

```
$val = oct($val) if $val =~ /^0/;
```

If EXPR is omitted, uses $_.

open(FILEHANDLE,EXPR)

open(FILEHANDLE)

open FILEHANDLE

Opens the file whose filename is given by EXPR, and associates it with FILEHANDLE. If FILEHANDLE is an expression, its value is used as the name of the real filehandle wanted. If EXPR is omitted, the scalar variable of the same name as the FILEHANDLE contains the filename. If the filename begins with ‘‘<’’ or nothing, the file is opened for input. If the filename begins with ‘‘>’’, the file is opened for output. If the filename begins with ‘‘>>’’, the file is opened for appending. (You can put a ´+´ in front of the ´>´ or ´<´ to indicate that you want both read and write access to the file.) If the filename begins with ‘‘| ’’, the filename is interpreted as a command to which output is to be piped, and if the filename ends with a ‘‘| ’’, the filename is interpreted as command which pipes input to us. (You may not have a command that pipes both in and out.) Opening ´–´ opens *STDIN* and opening ´>–´ opens *STDOUT*. Open returns non-zero upon success, the undefined value otherwise. If the open involved a pipe, the return value happens to be the pid of the subprocess. Examples:

```
$article = 100;
open article || die "Can't find article $article: $!\n";
while (<article>) {...

open(LOG, '>>/usr/spool/news/twitlog');# (log is reserved)

open(article, "caesar <$article | ");# decrypt article

open(extract, "| sort >/tmp/Tmp$$");# $$ is our process#

# process argument list of files along with any includes

foreach $file (@ARGV) {
do process($file, 'fh00');# no pun intended
}

sub process {
local($filename, $input) = @_;
$input++;# this is a string increment
unless (open($input, $filename)) {
print STDERR "Can't open $filename: $!\n";
return;
}
while (<$input>) {# note the use of indirection
if (/^#include "(.*)"/) {
do process($1, $input);
next;
}
```

```
        . . .# whatever
    }
}
```

You may also, in the Bourne shell tradition, specify an EXPR beginning with ‘‘>&’’, in which case the rest of the string is interpreted as the name of a filehandle (or file descriptor, if numeric) which is to be duped and opened. You may use & after >, >>, <, +>, +>> and +<. The mode you specify should match the mode of the original filehandle. Here is a script that saves, redirects, and restores *STDOUT* and *STDERR*:

```
#!/usr/bin/perl
open(SAVEOUT, ">&STDOUT");
open(SAVEERR, ">&STDERR");

open(STDOUT, ">foo.out") || die "Can't redirect stdout";
open(STDERR, ">&STDOUT") || die "Can't dup stdout";

select(STDERR); $| = 1;# make unbuffered
select(STDOUT); $| = 1;# make unbuffered

print STDOUT "stdout 1\n";# this works for
print STDERR "stderr 1\n"; # subprocesses too

close(STDOUT);
close(STDERR);

open(STDOUT, ">&SAVEOUT");
open(STDERR, ">&SAVEERR");

print STDOUT "stdout 2\n";
print STDERR "stderr 2\n";
```


If you open a pipe on the command ‘‘–’’, i.e. either ‘‘|–’’ or ‘‘–|’’, then there is an implicit fork done, and the return value of open is the pid of the child within the parent process, and 0 within the child process. (Use defined($pid) to determine if the open was successful.) The filehandle behaves normally for the parent, but i/o to that filehandle is piped from/to the *STDOUT/* of the child process. In the child process the filehandle isn't opened—i/o happens from/to the new *STDOUT* or *STDIN*. Typically this is used like the normal piped open when you want to exercise more control over just how the pipe command gets executed, such as when you are running setuid, and don't want to have to scan shell commands for metacharacters. The following pairs are more or less equivalent:

```
open(FOO, "| tr ´[a–z]´ ´[A–Z]´");
open(FOO, "|–") || exec ´tr´, ´[a–z]´, ´[A–Z]´;

open(FOO, "cat –n '$file'|");
open(FOO, "–|") || exec ´cat´, ´–n´, $file;
```

Explicitly closing any piped filehandle causes the parent process to wait for the child to finish, and returns the status value in $?. Note: on any operation which may do a fork, unflushed buffers remain unflushed in both processes, which means you may need to set $| to avoid duplicate output.

The filename that is passed to open will have leading and trailing whitespace deleted. In order to open a file with arbitrary weird characters in it, it's necessary to protect any leading and trailing whitespace thusly:

```
$file =~ s#^(\s)#./$1#;
open(FOO, "< $file\0");
```

opendir(DIRHANDLE,EXPR)

Opens a directory named EXPR for processing by readdir(), telldir(), seekdir(), rewinddir() and closedir(). Returns true if successful. DIRHANDLEs have their own namespace separate from FILEHANDLEs.

ord(EXPR)

ord EXPRReturns the numeric ascii value of the first character of EXPR. If EXPR is omitted, uses $_.

pack(TEMPLATE,LIST)

Takes an array or list of values and packs it into a binary structure, returning the string containing the structure. The TEMPLATE is a sequence of characters that give the order and type of values, as follows:

AAn ascii string, will be space padded.
aAn ascii string, will be null padded.
cA signed char value.
CAn unsigned char value.
sA signed short value.
SAn unsigned short value.
iA signed integer value.
IAn unsigned integer value.
lA signed long value.
LAn unsigned long value.
nA short in ''network'' order.
NA long in ''network'' order.
fA single-precision float in the native format.
dA double-precision float in the native format.
pA pointer to a string.
vA short in ''VAX'' (little-endian) order.
VA long in ''VAX'' (little-endian) order.
xA null byte.
XBack up a byte.
@Null fill to absolute position.
uA uuencoded string.
bA bit string (ascending bit order, like vec()).
BA bit string (descending bit order).
hA hex string (low nybble first).
HA hex string (high nybble first).

19

Each letter may optionally be followed by a number which gives a repeat count. With all types except "a", "A", "b", "B", "h" and "H", the pack function will gobble up that many values from the LIST. A * for the repeat count means to use however many items are left. The "a" and "A" types gobble just one value, but pack it as a string of length count, padding with nulls or spaces as necessary. (When unpacking, "A" strips trailing spaces and nulls, but "a" does not.) Likewise, the "b" and "B" fields pack a string that many bits long. The "h" and "H" fields pack a string that many nybbles long. Real numbers (floats and doubles) are in the native machine format only; due to the multiplicity of floating formats around, and the lack of a standard ''network'' representation, no facility for interchange has been made. This means that packed floating point

data written on one machine may not be readable on another - even if both use IEEE floating point arithmetic (as the endian-ness of the memory representation is not part of the IEEE spec). Note that perl uses doubles internally for all numeric calculation, and converting from double -> float -> double will lose precision (i.e. unpack("f", pack("f", $foo)) will not in general equal $foo).
Examples:

```
$foo = pack("cccc",65,66,67,68);
# foo eq "ABCD"
$foo = pack("c4",65,66,67,68);
# same thing

$foo = pack("ccxxcc",65,66,67,68);
# foo eq "AB\0\0CD"

$foo = pack("s2",1,2);
# "\1\0\2\0" on little-endian
# "\0\1\0\2" on big-endian

$foo = pack("a4","abcd","x","y","z");
# "abcd"

$foo = pack("aaaa","abcd","x","y","z");
# "axyz"

$foo = pack("a14","abcdefg");
# "abcdefg\0\0\0\0\0\0\0"

$foo = pack("i9pl", gmtime);
# a real struct tm (on my system anyway)

sub bintodec {
  unpack("N", pack("B32", substr("0" x 32 . shift, -32)));
}
```

The same template may generally also be used in the unpack function.

pipe(READHANDLE,WRITEHANDLE)

Opens a pair of connected pipes like the corresponding system call. Note that if you set up a loop of piped processes, deadlock can occur unless you are very careful. In addition, note that perl's pipes use stdio buffering, so you may need to set $| to flush your WRITEHANDLE after each command, depending on the application. [Requires version 3.0 patchlevel 9.]

pop(ARRAY)

pop ARRAY

Pops and returns the last value of the array, shortening the array by 1. Has the same effect as

```
$tmp = $ARRAY[$#ARRAY--];
```

If there are no elements in the array, returns the undefined value.

print(FILEHANDLE LIST)

print(LIST)

print FILEHANDLE LIST

print LIST

print
: Prints a string or a comma-separated list of strings. Returns non-zero if successful. FILEHANDLE may be a scalar variable name, in which case the variable contains the name of the filehandle, thus introducing one level of indirection. (NOTE: If FILEHANDLE is a variable and the next token is a term, it may be misinterpreted as an operator unless you interpose a + or put parens around the arguments.) If FILEHANDLE is omitted, prints by default to standard output (or to the last selected output channel—see select()). If LIST is also omitted, prints $_ to *STDOUT*. To set the default output channel to something other than *STDOUT* use the select operation. Note that, because print takes a LIST, anything in the LIST is evaluated in an array context, and any subroutine that you call will have one or more of its expressions evaluated in an array context. Also be careful not to follow the print keyword with a left parenthesis unless you want the corresponding right parenthesis to terminate the arguments to the print—interpose a + or put parens around all the arguments.

printf(FILEHANDLE LIST)

printf(LIST)

printf FILEHANDLE LIST

printf LIST

Equivalent to a ''print FILEHANDLE sprintf(LIST)''.

push(ARRAY,LIST)

Treats ARRAY (@ is optional) as a stack, and pushes the values of LIST onto the end of ARRAY. The length of ARRAY increases by the length of LIST. Has the same effect as

```
for $value (LIST) {
        $ARRAY[++$#ARRAY] = $value;
}
```

but is more efficient.

q/STRING/

qq/STRING/

qx/STRING/

These are not really functions, but simply syntactic sugar to let you avoid putting too many backslashes into quoted strings. The q operator is a generalized single quote, and the qq operator a generalized double quote. The qx operator is a generalized backquote. Any non-alphanumeric delimiter can be used in place of /, including newline. If the delimiter is an opening bracket or parenthesis, the final delimiter will be the corresponding closing bracket or parenthesis. (Embedded occurrences of the closing bracket need to be backslashed as usual.) Examples:

```
        $foo = q!I said, "You said, 'She said it.'"!;
        $bar = q('This is it.');
        $today = qx{ date };
        $_ .= qq
*** The previous line contains the naughty word "$&".\n
        if /(ibm|apple|awk)/;     # :-)
```

rand(EXPR)

rand EXPR

rand Returns a random fractional number between 0 and the value of EXPR. (EXPR should be positive.) If EXPR is omitted, returns a value between 0 and 1. See also srand().

read(FILEHANDLE,SCALAR,LENGTH,OFFSET)

read(FILEHANDLE,SCALAR,LENGTH)

Attempts to read LENGTH bytes of data into variable SCALAR from the specified FILEHANDLE. Returns the number of bytes actually read, or undef if there was an error. SCALAR will be grown or shrunk to the length actually read. An OFFSET may be specified to place the read data at some other place than the beginning of the string. This call is actually implemented in terms of stdio's fread call. To get a true read system call, see sysread.

readdir(DIRHANDLE)

readdir DIRHANDLE

Returns the next directory entry for a directory opened by opendir(). If used in an array context, returns all the rest of the entries in the directory. If there are no more entries, returns an undefined value in a scalar context or a null list in an array context.

readlink(EXPR)

readlink EXPR

Returns the value of a symbolic link, if symbolic links are implemented. If not, gives a fatal error. If there is some system error, returns the undefined value and sets $! (errno). If EXPR is omitted, uses $_.

recv(SOCKET,SCALAR,LEN,FLAGS)

Receives a message on a socket. Attempts to receive LENGTH bytes of data into variable SCALAR from the specified SOCKET filehandle. Returns the address of the sender, or the undefined value if there's an error. SCALAR will be grown or shrunk to the length actually read. Takes the same flags as the system call of the same name.

redo LABEL

redo The *redo* command restarts the loop block without evaluating the conditional again. The *continue* block, if any, is not executed. If the LABEL is omitted, the command refers to the innermost enclosing loop. This command is normally used by programs that want to lie to themselves about what was just input:

```
# a simpleminded Pascal comment stripper
# (warning: assumes no { or } in strings)
line: while (<STDIN>) {
while (s| ({.*}.*){.*}| $1 |) {}
s| {.*}| |;
if (s| {.*| |) {
$front = $_;
while (<STDIN>) {
if (/ }/) {# end of comment?
s| ^| $front{| ;
redo line;
}
}
}
print;
}
```

rename(OLDNAME,NEWNAME)
: Changes the name of a file. Returns 1 for success, 0 otherwise. Will not work across filesystem boundaries.

require(EXPR)

require EXPR

require
: Includes the library file specified by EXPR, or by $_ if EXPR is not supplied. Has semantics similar to the following subroutine:

```
sub require {
   local($filename) = @_;
   return 1 if $INC{$filename};
   local($realfilename,$result);
   ITER: {
foreach $prefix (@INC) {
   $realfilename = "$prefix/$filename";
   if (-f $realfilename) {
$result = do $realfilename;
last ITER;
   }
}
die "Can't find $filename in \@INC";
   }
   die $@ if $@;
   die "$filename did not return true value" unless $result;
   $INC{$filename} = $realfilename;
   $result;
}
```

Note that the file will not be included twice under the same specified name. The file must return true as the last statement to indicate successful execution of any initialization code, so it's customary to end such a file with "1;" unless you're sure it'll return true otherwise.

reset(EXPR)

reset EXPR

reset
: Generally used in a *continue* block at the end of a loop to clear variables and reset ?? searches so that they work again. The expression is interpreted as a list of single characters (hyphens allowed for ranges). All variables and arrays beginning with one of those letters are reset to their pristine state. If the expression is omitted, one-match searches (?pattern?) are reset to match again. Only resets variables or searches in the current package. Always returns 1. Examples:

```
reset 'X';          # reset all X variables
reset 'a–z';        # reset lower case variables
reset;              # just reset ?? searches
```

Note: resetting "A–Z" is not recommended since you'll wipe out your ARGV and ENV arrays.

The use of reset on dbm associative arrays does not change the dbm file. (It does, however, flush any entries cached by perl, which may be useful if you are sharing the dbm file. Then again, maybe not.)

return LIST
: Returns from a subroutine with the value specified. (Note that a subroutine can automatically return the value of the last expression evaluated. That's the preferred method—use of an explicit *return* is a bit slower.)

19

reverse(LIST)

reverse LIST

In an array context, returns an array value consisting of the elements of LIST in the opposite order. In a scalar context, returns a string value consisting of the bytes of the first element of LIST in the opposite order.

rewinddir(DIRHANDLE)

rewinddir DIRHANDLE

Sets the current position to the beginning of the directory for the readdir() routine on DIRHANDLE.

rindex(STR,SUBSTR,POSITION)

rindex(STR,SUBSTR)

Works just like index except that it returns the position of the LAST occurrence of SUBSTR in STR. If POSITION is specified, returns the last occurrence at or before that position.

rmdir(FILENAME)

rmdir FILENAME

Deletes the directory specified by FILENAME if it is empty. If it succeeds it returns 1, otherwise it returns 0 and sets $! (errno). If FILENAME is omitted, uses $_.

s/PATTERN/REPLACEMENT/gieo

Searches a string for a pattern, and if found, replaces that pattern with the replacement text and returns the number of substitutions made. Otherwise it returns false (0). The ''g'' is optional, and if present, indicates that all occurrences of the pattern are to be replaced. The ''i'' is also optional, and if present, indicates that matching is to be done in a case-insensitive manner. The ''e'' is likewise optional, and if present, indicates that the replacement string is to be evaluated as an expression rather than just as a double-quoted string. Any non-alphanumeric delimiter may replace the slashes; if single quotes are used, no interpretation is done on the replacement string (the e modifier overrides this, however); if backquotes are used, the replacement string is a command to execute whose output will be used as the actual replacement text. If the PATTERN is delimited by bracketing quotes, the REPLACEMENT has its own pair of quotes, which may or may not be bracketing quotes, e.g. s(foo)(bar) or s<foo>/bar/. If no string is specified via the =~ or !~ operator, the $_ string is searched and modified. (The string specified with =~ must be a scalar variable, an array element, or an assignment to one of those, i.e. an lvalue.) If the pattern contains a $ that looks like a variable rather than an end-of-string test, the variable will be interpolated into the pattern at run-time. If you only want the pattern compiled once the first time the variable is interpolated, add an ''o'' at the end. If the PATTERN evaluates to a null string, the most recent successful regular expression is used instead. See also the section on regular expressions. Examples:

```
s/\bgreen\b/mauve/g;# don't change wintergreen

$path =~ s| /usr/bin| /usr/local/bin| ;

s/Login: $foo/Login: $bar/; # run-time pattern

($foo = $bar) =~ s/bar/foo/;

$_ = 'abc123xyz';
s/\d+/$&*2/e;# yields 'abc246xyz'
s/\d+/sprintf("%5d",$&)/e;# yields 'abc  246xyz'
s/\w/$& x 2/eg;# yields 'aabbcc  224466xxyyzz'
```

```
s/ ([^ ]* ) * ([^ ]* )/ $2 $1/;# reverse 1st two fields
```

(Note the use of $ instead of \ in the last example. See section on regular expressions.)

scalar(EXPR)
: Forces EXPR to be interpreted in a scalar context and returns the value of EXPR.

seek(FILEHANDLE,POSITION,WHENCE)
: Randomly positions the file pointer for FILEHANDLE, just like the fseek() call of stdio. FILEHANDLE may be an expression whose value gives the name of the filehandle. Returns 1 upon success, 0 otherwise.

seekdir(DIRHANDLE,POS)
: Sets the current position for the readdir() routine on DIRHANDLE. POS must be a value returned by telldir(). Has the same caveats about possible directory compaction as the corresponding system library routine.

select(FILEHANDLE)

select
: Returns the currently selected filehandle. Sets the current default filehandle for output, if FILEHANDLE is supplied. This has two effects: first, a *write* or a *print* without a filehandle will default to this FILEHANDLE. Second, references to variables related to output will refer to this output channel. For example, if you have to set the top of form format for more than one output channel, you might do the following:

```
select(REPORT1);
$^ = ´report1_top´;
select(REPORT2);
$^ = ´report2_top´;
```

FILEHANDLE may be an expression whose value gives the name of the actual filehandle. Thus:

```
$oldfh = select(STDERR); $| = 1; select($oldfh);
```

select(RBITS,WBITS,EBITS,TIMEOUT)
: This calls the select system call with the bitmasks specified, which can be constructed using fileno() and vec(), along these lines:

```
$rin = $win = $ein = '';
vec($rin,fileno(STDIN),1) = 1;
vec($win,fileno(STDOUT),1) = 1;
$ein = $rin | $win;
```

If you want to select on many filehandles you might wish to write a subroutine:

```
sub fhbits {
   local(@fhlist) = split(' ',$_[0]);
   local($bits);
   for (@fhlist) {
vec($bits,fileno($_),1) = 1;
   }
   $bits;
}
$rin = &fhbits('STDIN TTY SOCK');
```

19

The usual idiom is:

```
($nfound,$timeleft) =
  select($rout=$rin, $wout=$win, $eout=$ein, $timeout);
```

or to block until something becomes ready:

```
$nfound = select($rout=$rin, $wout=$win, $eout=$ein, undef);
```

Any of the bitmasks can also be undef. The timeout, if specified, is in seconds, which may be fractional. NOTE: not all implementations are capable of returning the $timeleft. If not, they always return $timeleft equal to the supplied $timeout.

semctl(ID,SEMNUM,CMD,ARG)
: Calls the System V IPC function semctl. If CMD is &IPC_STAT or &GETALL, then ARG must be a variable which will hold the returned semid_ds structure or semaphore value array. Returns like ioctl: the undefined value for error, "0 but true" for zero, or the actual return value otherwise.

semget(KEY,NSEMS,SIZE,FLAGS)
: Calls the System V IPC function semget. Returns the semaphore id, or the undefined value if there is an error.

semop(KEY,OPSTRING)
: Calls the System V IPC function semop to perform semaphore operations such as signaling and waiting. OPSTRING must be a packed array of semop structures. Each semop structure can be generated with 'pack("sss", $semnum, $semop, $semflag)'. The number of semaphore operations is implied by the length of OPSTRING. Returns true if successful, or false if there is an error. As an example, the following code waits on semaphore $semnum of semaphore id $semid:

```
$semop = pack("sss", $semnum, -1, 0);
die "Semaphore trouble: $!\n" unless semop($semid, $semop);
```

To signal the semaphore, replace "-1" with "1".

send(SOCKET,MSG,FLAGS,TO)

send(SOCKET,MSG,FLAGS)
: Sends a message on a socket. Takes the same flags as the system call of the same name. On unconnected sockets you must specify a destination to send TO. Returns the number of characters sent, or the undefined value if there is an error.

setpgrp(PID,PGRP)
: Sets the current process group for the specified PID, 0 for the current process. Will produce a fatal error if used on a machine that doesn't implement setpgrp(2).

setpriority(WHICH,WHO,PRIORITY)
: Sets the current priority for a process, a process group, or a user. (See setpriority(2).) Will produce a fatal error if used on a machine that doesn't implement setpriority(2).

setsockopt(SOCKET,LEVEL,OPTNAME,OPTVAL)
: Sets the socket option requested. Returns undefined if there is an error. OPTVAL may be specified as undef if you don't want to pass an argument.

shift(ARRAY)

shift ARRAY

shift
: Shifts the first value of the array off and returns it, shortening the array by 1 and moving everything down. If there are no elements in the array, returns the undefined value. If ARRAY is omitted, shifts the @ARGV array in the main program, and the @_ array in subroutines. (This is determined lexically.) See also unshift(), push() and pop(). Shift() and unshift() do the same thing to the left end of an array that push() and pop() do to the right end.

shmctl(ID,CMD,ARG)
: Calls the System V IPC function shmctl. If CMD is &IPC_STAT, then ARG must be a variable which will hold the returned shmid_ds structure. Returns like ioctl: the undefined value for error, "0 but true" for zero, or the actual return value otherwise.

shmget(KEY,SIZE,FLAGS)
: Calls the System V IPC function shmget. Returns the shared memory segment id, or the undefined value if there is an error.

shmread(ID,VAR,POS,SIZE)

shmwrite(ID,STRING,POS,SIZE)
: Reads or writes the System V shared memory segment ID starting at position POS for size SIZE by attaching to it, copying in/out, and detaching from it. When reading, VAR must be a variable which will hold the data read. When writing, if STRING is too long, only SIZE bytes are used; if STRING is too short, nulls are written to fill out SIZE bytes. Return true if successful, or false if there is an error.

shutdown(SOCKET,HOW)
: Shuts down a socket connection in the manner indicated by HOW, which has the same interpretation as in the system call of the same name.

sin(EXPR)

sin EXPRReturns the sine of EXPR (expressed in radians). If EXPR is omitted, returns sine of $_.

sleep(EXPR)

sleep EXPR

sleep Causes the script to sleep for EXPR seconds, or forever if no EXPR. May be interrupted by sending the process a SIGALRM. Returns the number of seconds actually slept. You probably cannot mix alarm() and sleep() calls, since sleep() is often implemented using alarm().

socket(SOCKET,DOMAIN,TYPE,PROTOCOL)
: Opens a socket of the specified kind and attaches it to filehandle SOCKET. DOMAIN, TYPE and PROTOCOL are specified the same as for the system call of the same name. You may need to run h2ph on sys/socket.h to get the proper values handy in a perl library file. Return true if successful. See the example in the section on Interprocess Communication.

socketpair(SOCKET1,SOCKET2,DOMAIN,TYPE,PROTOCOL)
: Creates an unnamed pair of sockets in the specified domain, of the specified type. DOMAIN, TYPE and PROTOCOL are specified the same as for the system call of the same name. If unimplemented, yields a fatal error. Return true if successful.

sort(SUBROUTINE LIST)

sort(LIST)

sort SUBROUTINE LIST

sort BLOCK LIST

sort LIST Sorts the LIST and returns the sorted array value. Nonexistent values of arrays are stripped out. If SUBROUTINE or BLOCK is omitted, sorts in standard string comparison order. If SUBROUTINE is specified, gives the name of a subroutine that returns an integer less than, equal to, or greater than 0, depending on how the elements of the array are to be ordered. (The <=> and cmp operators are extremely useful in such routines.) SUBROUTINE may be a scalar variable name, in which case the value provides the name of the subroutine to use. In place of a SUBROUTINE name, you can provide a BLOCK as an anonymous, in-line sort subroutine.

In the interests of efficiency the normal calling code for subroutines is bypassed, with the following effects: the subroutine may not be a recursive subroutine, and the two elements to be compared are passed into the subroutine not via @_ but as $a and $b (see example below). They are passed by reference so don't modify $a and $b.

Examples:

```
# sort lexically
@articles = sort @files;

# same thing, but with explicit sort routine
@articles = sort {$a cmp $b} @files;

# same thing in reversed order
@articles = sort {$b cmp $a} @files;

# sort numerically ascending
@articles = sort {$a <=> $b} @files;

# sort numerically descending
@articles = sort {$b <=> $a} @files;

# sort using explicit subroutine name
sub byage {
   $age{$a} <=> $age{$b};# presuming integers
}
@sortedclass = sort byage @class;

sub reverse { $b cmp $a; }
@harry = ('dog','cat','x','Cain','Abel');
@george = ('gone','chased','yz','Punished','Axed');
print sort @harry;
# prints AbelCaincatdogx
print sort reverse @harry;
# prints xdogcatCainAbel
print sort @george, 'to', @harry;
# prints AbelAxedCainPunishedcatchaseddoggonetoxyz
```


splice(ARRAY,OFFSET,LENGTH,LIST)
splice(ARRAY,OFFSET,LENGTH)
splice(ARRAY,OFFSET)

Removes the elements designated by OFFSET and LENGTH from an array, and replaces them with the elements of LIST, if any. Returns the elements removed from the array. The array grows or shrinks as necessary. If LENGTH is omitted, removes everything from OFFSET onward. The following equivalencies hold (assuming $[== 0):

```
push(@a,$x,$y)          splice(@a,$#a+1,0,$x,$y)
pop(@a)                 splice(@a,-1)
shift(@a)               splice(@a,0,1)
unshift(@a,$x,$y)       splice(@a,0,0,$x,$y)
$a[$x] = $y             splice(@a,$x,1,$y);
```

Example, assuming array lengths are passed before arrays:

```
sub aeq {# compare two array values
local(@a) = splice(@_,0,shift);
local(@b) = splice(@_,0,shift);
return 0 unless @a == @b;# same len?
while (@a) {
```

```
        return 0 if pop(@a) ne pop(@b);
    }
    return 1;
}
if (&aeq($len,@foo[1..$len],0+@bar,@bar)) { ... }
```

split(/PATTERN/,EXPR,LIMIT)

split(/PATTERN/,EXPR)

split(/PATTERN/)

split Splits a string into an array of strings, and returns it. (If not in an array context, returns the number of fields found and splits into the @_ array. (In an array context, you can force the split into @_ by using ?? as the pattern delimiters, but it still returns the array value.)) If EXPR is omitted, splits the $_ string. If PATTERN is also omitted, splits on whitespace (/[\t\n]+/). Anything matching PATTERN is taken to be a delimiter separating the fields. (Note that the delimiter may be longer than one character.) If LIMIT is specified, splits into no more than that many fields (though it may split into fewer). If LIMIT is unspecified, trailing null fields are stripped (which potential users of pop() would do well to remember). A pattern matching the null string (not to be confused with a null pattern //, which is just one member of the set of patterns matching a null string) will split the value of EXPR into separate characters at each point it matches that way. For example:


```
print join(':', split(/ */, 'hi there'));
```

produces the output 'h:i:t:h:e:r:e'.

The LIMIT parameter can be used to partially split a line

```
($login, $passwd, $remainder) = split(/:/, $_, 3);
```

(When assigning to a list, if LIMIT is omitted, perl supplies a LIMIT one larger than the number of variables in the list, to avoid unnecessary work. For the list above LIMIT would have been 4 by default. In time critical applications it behooves you not to split into more fields than you really need.)

If the PATTERN contains parentheses, additional array elements are created from each matching substring in the delimiter.

```
split(/([,-])/,"1-10,20");
```

produces the array value

```
(1,'-',10,',',20)
```

The pattern /PATTERN/ may be replaced with an expression to specify patterns that vary at runtime. (To do runtime compilation only once, use /$variable/o.) As a special case, specifying a space (' ') will split on white space just as split with no arguments does, but leading white space does NOT produce a null first field. Thus, split(' ') can be used to emulate *awk*'s default behavior, whereas split(/ /) will give you as many null initial fields as there are leading spaces.

Example:

```
open(passwd, '/etc/passwd');
while (<passwd>) {
($login, $passwd, $uid, $gid, $gcos, $home, $shell) = split(/:/);
...
}
```

(Note that $shell above will still have a newline on it. See chop().) See also *join*.

sprintf(FORMAT,LIST)
: Returns a string formatted by the usual printf conventions. The * character is not supported.

sqrt(EXPR)

sqrt EXPRReturn the square root of EXPR. If EXPR is omitted, returns square root of $_.

srand(EXPR)

srand EXPR
: Sets the random number seed for the *rand* operator. If EXPR is omitted, does srand(time).

stat(FILEHANDLE)

stat FILEHANDLE

stat(EXPR)

stat SCALARVARIABLE
: Returns a 13-element array giving the statistics for a file, either the file opened via FILEHANDLE, or named by EXPR. Returns a null list if the stat fails. Typically used as follows:

```
($dev,$ino,$mode,$nlink,$uid,$gid,$rdev,$size,
  $atime,$mtime,$ctime,$blksize,$blocks)
    = stat($filename);
```

If stat is passed the special filehandle consisting of an underline, no stat is done, but the current contents of the stat structure from the last stat or filetest are returned. Example:

```
if (-x $file && (($d) = stat(_)) && $d < 0) {
print "$file is executable NFS file\n";
}
```

(This only works on machines for which the device number is negative under NFS.)

study(SCALAR)

study SCALAR

study
: Takes extra time to study SCALAR ($_ if unspecified) in anticipation of doing many pattern matches on the string before it is next modified. This may or may not save time, depending on the nature and number of patterns you are searching on, and on the distribution of character frequencies in the string to be searched— you probably want to compare runtimes with and without it to see which runs faster. Those loops which scan for many short constant strings (including the constant parts of more complex patterns) will benefit most. You may have only one study active at a time— if you study a different scalar the first is ''unstudied''. (The way study works is this: a linked list of every character in the string to be searched is made, so we know, for example, where all the 'k' characters are. From each search string, the rarest character is selected, based on some static frequency tables constructed from some C programs and English text. Only those places that contain this ''rarest'' character are examined.)

For example, here is a loop which inserts index producing entries before any line containing a certain pattern:

```
while (<>) {
study;
print ".IX foo\n" if /\bfoo\b/;
print ".IX bar\n" if /\bbar\b/;
print ".IX blurfl\n" if /\bblurfl\b/;
...
print;
}
```

In searching for /\bfoo\b/, only those locations in $_ that contain 'f' will be looked at, because 'f' is rarer than 'o'. In general, this is a big win except in pathological cases. The only question is whether it saves you more time than it took to build the linked list in the first place.

Note that if you have to look for strings that you don't know till runtime, you can build an entire loop as a string and eval that to avoid recompiling all your patterns all the time. Together with undefining $/ to input entire files as one record, this can be very fast, often faster than specialized programs like fgrep. The following scans a list of files (@files) for a list of words (@words), and prints out the names of those files that contain a match:

```
$search = 'while (<>) { study;';
foreach $word (@words) {
   $search .= "++\$seen{\$ARGV} if /\\b$word\\b/;\n";
}
$search .= "}";
@ARGV = @files;
undef $/;
eval $search;# this screams
$/ = "\n";# put back to normal input delim
foreach $file (sort keys(%seen)) {
   print $file, "\n";
}
```

19

substr(EXPR,OFFSET,LEN)

substr(EXPR,OFFSET)

Extracts a substring out of EXPR and returns it. First character is at offset 0, or whatever you've set $[to. If OFFSET is negative, starts that far from the end of the string. If LEN is omitted, returns everything to the end of the string. You can use the substr() function as an lvalue, in which case EXPR must be an lvalue. If you assign something shorter than LEN, the string will shrink, and if you assign something longer than LEN, the string will grow to accommodate it. To keep the string the same length you may need to pad or chop your value using sprintf().

symlink(OLDFILE,NEWFILE)

Creates a new filename symbolically linked to the old filename. Returns 1 for success, 0 otherwise. On systems that don't support symbolic links, produces a fatal error at run time. To check for that, use eval:

```
$symlink_exists = (eval 'symlink("","");', $@ eq '');
```

syscall(LIST)

syscall LIST

Calls the system call specified as the first element of the list, passing the remaining elements as arguments to the system call. If unimplemented, produces a fatal error. The arguments are interpreted as follows: if a given argument is numeric, the argument is passed as an int. If not, the pointer to the string value is passed. You are responsible to make sure a string is pre-extended long enough to receive any result that might be written into a string. If your integer arguments are not literals and have never been interpreted in a numeric context, you may need to add 0 to them to force them to look like numbers.

```
require 'syscall.ph';# may need to run h2ph
syscall(&SYS_write, fileno(STDOUT), "hi there\n", 9);
```

sysread(FILEHANDLE,SCALAR,LENGTH,OFFSET)

sysread(FILEHANDLE,SCALAR,LENGTH)

Attempts to read LENGTH bytes of data into variable SCALAR from the specified FILEHANDLE, using the system call read(2). It bypasses stdio, so mixing this with other kinds of reads may cause confusion. Returns the number of bytes actually read, or undef if there was an error. SCALAR will be grown or shrunk to the length actually read. An OFFSET may be specified to place the read data at some other place than the beginning of the string.

system(LIST)

system LIST

Does exactly the same thing as "exec LIST" except that a fork is done first, and the parent process waits for the child process to complete. Note that argument processing varies depending on the number of arguments. The return value is the exit status of the program as returned by the wait() call. To get the actual exit value divide by 256. See also *exec*.

syswrite(FILEHANDLE,SCALAR,LENGTH,OFFSET)

syswrite(FILEHANDLE,SCALAR,LENGTH)

Attempts to write LENGTH bytes of data from variable SCALAR to the specified FILEHANDLE, using the system call write(2). It bypasses stdio, so mixing this with prints may cause confusion. Returns the number of bytes actually written, or undef if there was an error. An OFFSET may be specified to place the read data at some other place than the beginning of the string.

tell(FILEHANDLE)

tell FILEHANDLE

tell Returns the current file position for FILEHANDLE. FILEHANDLE may be an expression whose value gives the name of the actual filehandle. If FILEHANDLE is omitted, assumes the file last read.

telldir(DIRHANDLE)

telldir DIRHANDLE

Returns the current position of the readdir() routines on DIRHANDLE. Value may be given to seekdir() to access a particular location in a directory. Has the same caveats about possible directory compaction as the corresponding system library routine.

time Returns the number of non-leap seconds since 00:00:00 UTC, January 1, 1970. Suitable for feeding to gmtime() and localtime().

times Returns a four-element array giving the user and system times, in seconds, for this process and the children of this process.

```
($user,$system,$cuser,$csystem) = times;
```

tr/SEARCHLIST/REPLACEMENTLIST/cds

y/SEARCHLIST/REPLACEMENTLIST/cds

Translates all occurrences of the characters found in the search list with the corresponding character in the replacement list. It returns the number of characters replaced or deleted. If no string is specified via the =~ or !~ operator, the $_ string is translated. (The string specified with =~ must be a scalar variable, an array element, or an assignment to one of those, i.e. an lvalue.) For *sed* devotees, *y* is provided as a synonym for *tr*. If the SEARCHLIST is delimited by bracketing quotes, the REPLACEMENTLIST has its own pair of quotes, which may or may not be bracketing quotes, e.g. tr[A-Z][a-z] or tr(+-*/)/ABCD/.

If the c modifier is specified, the SEARCHLIST character set is complemented. If the d modifier is specified, any characters specified by SEARCHLIST that are not found in REPLACEMENTLIST are deleted. (Note that this is slightly more flexible than the behavior of some *tr* programs, which delete anything they find in the SEARCHLIST, period.) If the s modifier is specified, sequences of characters that were translated to the same character are squashed down to 1 instance of the character.

If the d modifier was used, the REPLACEMENTLIST is always interpreted exactly as specified. Otherwise, if the REPLACEMENTLIST is shorter than the SEARCHLIST, the final character is replicated till it is long enough. If the REPLACEMENTLIST is null, the SEARCHLIST is replicated. This latter is useful for counting characters in a class, or for squashing character sequences in a class.

Examples:

```
$ARGV[1] =~ y/A-Z/a-z/;                # canonicalize to lower case

$cnt = tr/*/*/;                        # count the stars in $_

$cnt = tr/0-9//;                       # count the digits in $_

tr/a-zA-Z//s;                          # bookkeeper -> bokeper

($HOST = $host) =~ tr/a-z/A-Z/;

y/a-zA-Z/ /cs;                         # change non-alphas to single space

tr/\200-\377/\0-\177/;                 # delete 8th bit
```

truncate(FILEHANDLE,LENGTH)

truncate(EXPR,LENGTH)

Truncates the file opened on FILEHANDLE, or named by EXPR, to the specified length. Produces a fatal error if truncate isn't implemented on your system.

umask(EXPR)

umask EXPR

umask Sets the umask for the process and returns the old one. If EXPR is omitted, merely returns current umask.

undef(EXPR)

undef EXPR

undef Undefines the value of EXPR, which must be an lvalue. Use only on a scalar value, an entire array, or a subroutine name (using &). (Undef will probably not do what you expect on most predefined variables or dbm array values.) Always returns the undefined value. You can omit the EXPR, in which case nothing is undefined, but you still get an undefined value that you could, for instance, return from a subroutine. Examples:

```
undef $foo;
undef $bar{'blurfl'};
undef @ary;
undef %assoc;
undef &mysub;
return (wantarray ? () : undef) if $they_blew_it;
```

unlink(LIST)

unlink LIST

Deletes a list of files. Returns the number of files successfully deleted.

```
$cnt = unlink 'a', 'b', 'c';
unlink @goners;
unlink <*.bak>;
```

Note: unlink will not delete directories unless you are superuser and the **–U** flag is supplied to *perl*. Even if these conditions are met, be warned that unlinking a directory can inflict damage on your filesystem. Use rmdir instead.

unpack(TEMPLATE,EXPR)

Unpack does the reverse of pack: it takes a string representing a structure and expands it out into an array value, returning the array value. (In a scalar context, it merely returns the first value produced.) The TEMPLATE has the same format as in the pack function. Here's a subroutine that does substring:

```
sub substr {
local($what,$where,$howmuch) = @_;
unpack("x$where a$howmuch", $what);
}
```

and then there's

```
sub ord { unpack("c",$_[0]); }
```

In addition, you may prefix a field with a %<number> to indicate that you want a <number>-bit checksum of the items instead of the items themselves. Default is a 16-bit checksum. For example, the following computes the same number as the System V sum program:

```
while (<>) {
    $checksum += unpack("%16C*", $_);
}
$checksum %= 65536;
```

unshift(ARRAY,LIST)

Does the opposite of a *shift*. Or the opposite of a *push*, depending on how you look at it. Prepends list to the front of the array, and returns the number of elements in the new array.

```
unshift(ARGV, '-e') unless $ARGV[0] =~ /^-/;
```

utime(LIST)

utime LIST

Changes the access and modification times on each file of a list of files. The first two elements of the list must be the NUMERICAL access and modification times, in that order. Returns the number of files successfully changed. The inode modification time of each file is set to the current time. Example of a ''touch'' command:

```
#!/usr/bin/perl
$now = time;
utime $now, $now, @ARGV;
```

19

values(ASSOC_ARRAY)

values ASSOC_ARRAY

Returns a normal array consisting of all the values of the named associative array. The values are returned in an apparently random order, but it is the same order as either the keys() or each() function would produce on the same array. See also keys() and each().

vec(EXPR,OFFSET,BITS)

Treats a string as a vector of unsigned integers, and returns the value of the bitfield specified. May also be assigned to. BITS must be a power of two from 1 to 32.

Vectors created with vec() can also be manipulated with the logical operators |, & and ^, which will assume a bit vector operation is desired when both operands are strings. This interpretation is not enabled unless there is at least one vec() in your program, to protect older programs.

To transform a bit vector into a string or array of 0's and 1's, use these:

```
$bits = unpack("b*", $vector);
@bits = split(//, unpack("b*", $vector));
```

If you know the exact length in bits, it can be used in place of the *.

wait Waits for a child process to terminate and returns the pid of the deceased process, or -1 if there are no child processes. The status is returned in $?.

waitpid(PID,FLAGS)

Waits for a particular child process to terminate and returns the pid of the deceased process, or -1 if there is no such child process. The status is returned in $?. If you say

```
require "sys/wait.h";
...
waitpid(-1,&WNOHANG);
```

then you can do a non-blocking wait for any process. Non-blocking wait is only available on machines supporting either the *waitpid*(2) or *wait4*(2) system calls. However, waiting for a particular pid with FLAGS of 0 is implemented everywhere. (Perl emulates the system call by remembering the status values of processes that have exited but have not been harvested by the Perl script yet.)

wantarrayReturns true if the context of the currently executing subroutine is looking for an array value. Returns false if the context is looking for a scalar.

```
return wantarray ? () : undef;
```

warn(LIST)

warn LISTProduces a message on STDERR just like "die", but doesn't exit.

write(FILEHANDLE)

write(EXPR)

write Writes a formatted record (possibly multi-line) to the specified file, using the format associated with that file. By default the format for a file is the one having the same name is the filehandle, but the format for the current output channel (see *select*) may be set explicitly by assigning the name of the format to the $~ variable.

Top of form processing is handled automatically: if there is insufficient room on the current page for the formatted record, the page is advanced by writing a form feed, a special top-of-page format is used to format the new page header, and then the record is written. By default the top-of-page format is the name of the filehandle with "_TOP" appended, but it may be dynamicallly set to the format of your choice by assigning the name to the $^ variable while the filehandle is selected. The number of lines remaining on the current page is in variable $-, which can be set to 0 to force a new page.

If FILEHANDLE is unspecified, output goes to the current default output channel, which starts out as *STDOUT* but may be changed by the *select* operator. If the FILEHANDLE is an EXPR, then the expression is evaluated and the resulting string is used to look up the name of the FILEHANDLE at run time. For more on formats, see the section on formats later on.

Note that write is NOT the opposite of read.

6. Precedence

Perl operators have the following associativity and precedence:

```
nonassoc    print printf exec system sort reverse
                chmod chown kill unlink utime die return
left        ,
right       = += -= *= etc.
right       ?:
nonassoc    ..
left        ||
left        &&
left        | ^
left        &
nonassoc    == != <=> eq ne cmp
nonassoc    < > <= >= lt gt le ge
nonassoc    chdir exit eval reset sleep rand umask
nonassoc    -r -w -x etc.
left        << >>
left        + - .
left        * / % x
left        =~ !~
right       ! ~ and unary minus
right       **
nonassoc    ++ --
left        '('
```

As mentioned earlier, if any list operator (print, etc.) or any unary operator (chdir, etc.) is followed by a left parenthesis as the next token on the same line, the operator and arguments within parentheses are taken to be of highest precedence, just like a normal function call. Examples:

```
chdir $foo || die;          # (chdir $foo) || die
chdir($foo) || die;         # (chdir $foo) || die
chdir ($foo) || die;        # (chdir $foo) || die
chdir +($foo) || die;       # (chdir $foo) || die
```

but, because * is higher precedence than || :

```
chdir $foo * 20;            # chdir ($foo * 20)
chdir($foo) * 20;           # (chdir $foo) * 20
chdir ($foo) * 20;          # (chdir $foo) * 20
chdir +($foo) * 20;         # chdir ($foo * 20)

rand 10 * 20;               # rand (10 * 20)
rand(10) * 20;              # (rand 10) * 20
```

```
rand (10) * 20;                    # (rand 10) * 20
   rand +(10) * 20;                # rand (10 * 20)
```

In the absence of parentheses, the precedence of list operators such as print, sort or chmod is either very high or very low depending on whether you look at the left side of operator or the right side of it. For example, in

```
@ary = (1, 3, sort 4, 2);
print @ary;         # prints 1324
```

the commas on the right of the sort are evaluated before the sort, but the commas on the left are evaluated after. In other words, list operators tend to gobble up all the arguments that follow them, and then act like a simple term with regard to the preceding expression. Note that you have to be careful with parens:

```
# These evaluate exit before doing the print:
print($foo, exit);  # Obviously not what you want.
print $foo, exit;   # Nor is this.

# These do the print before evaluating exit:
(print $foo), exit; # This is what you want.
print($foo), exit;  # Or this.
print ($foo), exit; # Or even this.
```

Also note that

```
print ($foo & 255) + 1, "\n";
```

probably doesn't do what you expect at first glance.

7. Subroutines

A subroutine may be declared as follows:

```
sub NAME BLOCK
```

Any arguments passed to the routine come in as array @_, that is ($_[0], $_[1], . . .). The array @_ is a local array, but its values are references to the actual scalar parameters. The return value of the subroutine is the value of the last expression evaluated, and can be either an array value or a scalar value. Alternately, a return statement may be used to specify the returned value and exit the subroutine. To create local variables see the *local* operator.

A subroutine is called using the *do* operator or the & operator.

Example:

```
sub MAX {
        local($max) = pop(@_);
        foreach $foo (@_) {
                $max = $foo if $max < $foo;
        }
        $max;
}

. . .
$bestday = &MAX($mon,$tue,$wed,$thu,$fri);
```

Example:

```
# get a line, combining continuation lines
#  that start with whitespace
sub get_line {
        $thisline = $lookahead;
        line: while ($lookahead = <STDIN>) {
                if ($lookahead =~ /^[ \t]/) {
                        $thisline .= $lookahead;
                }
                else {
                        last line;
                }
        }
        $thisline;
}

$lookahead = <STDIN>;           # get first line
while ($_ = do get_line()) {
        ...
}
```

Use array assignment to a local list to name your formal arguments:

```
sub maybeset {
        local($key, $value) = @_;
        $foo{$key} = $value unless $foo{$key};
}
```

This also has the effect of turning call-by-reference into call-by-value, since the assignment copies the values.

Subroutines may be called recursively. If a subroutine is called using the & form, the argument list is optional. If omitted, no @_ array is set up for the subroutine; the @_ array at the time of the call is visible to subroutine instead.

```
do foo(1,2,3);          # pass three arguments
&foo(1,2,3);            # the same

do foo();       # pass a null list
&foo();                 # the same
&foo;           # pass no arguments—more efficient
```

8. Passing By Reference

Sometimes you don't want to pass the value of an array to a subroutine but rather the name of it, so that the subroutine can modify the global copy of it rather than working with a local copy. In perl you can refer to all the objects of a particular name by prefixing the name with a star: *foo. When evaluated, it produces a scalar value that represents all the objects of that name, including any filehandle, format or subroutine. When assigned to within a local() operation, it causes the name mentioned to refer to whatever * value was assigned to it. Example:

```
sub doubleary {
    local(*someary) = @_;
    foreach $elem (@someary) {
```

```
        $elem *= 2;
    }
}
do doubleary(*foo);
do doubleary(*bar);
```

Assignment to *name is currently recommended only inside a local(). You can actually assign to *name anywhere, but the previous referent of *name may be stranded forever. This may or may not bother you.

Note that scalars are already passed by reference, so you can modify scalar arguments without using this mechanism by referring explicitly to the $_[nnn] in question. You can modify all the elements of an array by passing all the elements as scalars, but you have to use the * mechanism to push, pop or change the size of an array. The * mechanism will probably be more efficient in any case.

Since a *name value contains unprintable binary data, if it is used as an argument in a print, or as a %s argument in a printf or sprintf, it then has the value '*name', just so it prints out pretty.

Even if you don't want to modify an array, this mechanism is useful for passing multiple arrays in a single LIST, since normally the LIST mechanism will merge all the array values so that you can't extract out the individual arrays.

9. Regular Expressions

The patterns used in pattern matching are regular expressions such as those supplied in the Version 8 regexp routines. (In fact, the routines are derived from Henry Spencer's freely redistributable reimplementation of the V8 routines.) In addition, \w matches an alphanumeric character (including "_") and \W a nonalphanumeric. Word boundaries may be matched by \b, and non-boundaries by \B. A whitespace character is matched by \s, non-whitespace by \S. A numeric character is matched by \d, non-numeric by \D. You may use \w, \s and \d within character classes. Also, \n, \r, \f, \t and \NNN have their normal interpretations. Within character classes \b represents backspace rather than a word boundary. Alternatives may be separated by |. The bracketing construct (...) may also be used, in which case \<digit> matches the digit'th substring. (Outside of the pattern, always use $ instead of \ in front of the digit. The scope of $<digit> (and $`, $& and $') extends to the end of the enclosing BLOCK or eval string, or to the next pattern match with subexpressions. The \<digit> notation sometimes works outside the current pattern, but should not be relied upon.) You may have as many parentheses as you wish. If you have more than 9 substrings, the variables $10, $11, ... refer to the corresponding substring. Within the pattern, \10, \11, etc. refer back to substrings if there have been at least that many left parens before the backreference. Otherwise (for backward compatibilty) \10 is the same as \010, a backspace, and \11 the same as \011, a tab. And so on. (\1 through \9 are always backreferences.)

$+ returns whatever the last bracket match matched. $& returns the entire matched string. ($0 used to return the same thing, but not any more.) $` returns everything before the matched string. $' returns everything after the matched string. Examples:

```
s/^([^ ]*) *([^ ]*)/$2 $1/;    # swap first two words

if (/Time: (..):(..):(..)/) {
        $hours = $1;
        $minutes = $2;
        $seconds = $3;
}
```

By default, the ^ character is only guaranteed to match at the beginning of the string, the $ character only at the end (or before the newline at the end) and *perl* does certain optimizations with the assumption that the string contains only one line. The behavior of ^ and $ on embedded newlines will be inconsistent. You may, however, wish to treat a string as a multi-line buffer, such that the ^ will match after any newline within the string, and $ will match before any newline. At the cost of a little more overhead, you can do this by setting the variable $* to 1. Setting it back to 0 makes *perl* revert to its old behavior.

To facilitate multi-line substitutions, the . character never matches a newline (even when $* is 0). In particular, the following leaves a newline on the $_ string:

```
$_ = <STDIN>;
s/.*(some_string).*/$1/;
```

If the newline is unwanted, try one of

```
s/.*(some_string).*\n/$1/;
s/.*(some_string)[^\000]*/$1/;
s/.*(some_string)(.|\n)*/$1/;
chop; s/.*(some_string).*/$1/;
/(some_string)/ && ($_ = $1);
```

Any item of a regular expression may be followed with digits in curly brackets of the form {n,m}, where n gives the minimum number of times to match the item and m gives the maximum. The form {n} is equivalent to {n,n} and matches exactly n times. The form {n,} matches n or more times. (If a curly bracket occurs in any other context, it is treated as a regular character.) The * modifier is equivalent to {0,}, the + modifier to {1,} and the ? modifier to {0,1}. There is no limit to the size of n or m, but large numbers will chew up more memory.

You will note that all backslashed metacharacters in *perl* are alphanumeric, such as \b, \w, \n. Unlike some other regular expression languages, there are no backslashed symbols that aren't alphanumeric. So anything that looks like \\, \(, \), \<, \>, \{, or \} is always interpreted as a literal character, not a metacharacter. This makes it simple to quote a string that you want to use for a pattern but that you are afraid might contain metacharacters. Simply quote all the non-alphanumeric characters:

```
$pattern =~ s/(\W)/\\$1/g;
```

10. Formats

Output record formats for use with the *write* operator may declared as follows:

```
format NAME =
FORMLIST
.
```

If name is omitted, format "STDOUT" is defined. FORMLIST consists of a sequence of lines, each of which may be of one of three types:

1. A comment.
2. A "picture" line giving the format for one output line.
3. An argument line supplying values to plug into a picture line.

Picture lines are printed exactly as they look, except for certain fields that substitute values into the line. Each picture field starts with either @ or ^. The @ field (not to be confused with the array marker @) is the normal case; ^ fields are used to do rudimentary multi-line text block filling. The length of the field is supplied by padding out the field with multiple <, >, or | characters to specify, respectively, left justification, right justification, or centering. As an alternate form of right justification, you may also use # characters (with an optional .) to specify a numeric field. (Use of ^ instead of @ causes the field to be blanked if undefined.) If any of the values supplied for these fields contains a newline, only the text up to the newline is printed. The special field @* can be used for printing multi-line values. It should appear by itself on a line.

The values are specified on the following line, in the same order as the picture fields. The values should be separated by commas.

Picture fields that begin with ^ rather than @ are treated specially. The value supplied must be a scalar variable name which contains a text string. *Perl* puts as much text as it can into the field, and then chops off the front of the string so that the next time the variable is referenced, more of the text can be printed. Normally you would use a sequence of fields in a vertical stack to print out a block of text. If you like, you can end the final field with ..., which will appear in the output if the text was too long to appear in its entirety. You can change which characters are legal to break on by changing the variable $: to a list of the desired characters.

Since use of ^ fields can produce variable length records if the text to be formatted is short, you can suppress blank lines by putting the tilde (~) character anywhere in the line. (Normally you should put it in the front if possible, for visibility.) The tilde will be translated to a space upon output. If you put a second tilde contiguous to the first, the line will be repeated until all the fields on the line are exhausted. (If you use a field of the @ variety, the expression you supply had better not give the same value every time forever!)

Examples:

```
# a report on the /etc/passwd file
format STDOUT_TOP =
                        Passwd File
Name                Login    Office   Uid   Gid Home
------------------------------------------------------------------
.
format STDOUT =
@<<<<<<<<<<<<<<<<<< @||||||| @<<<<<<@>>>> @>>>> @<<<<<<<<<<<<<<<<<
$name,              $login,  $office,$uid,$gid, $home
.

# a report from a bug report form
format STDOUT_TOP =
                        Bug Reports
@<<<<<<<<<<<<<<<<<<<<<<<     @||          @>>>>>>>>>>>>>>>>>>>>>>>
$system,                      $%,         $date
------------------------------------------------------------------
.
format STDOUT =
Subject: @<<<<<<<<<<<<<<<<<<<<<<<<<<<<<<<<<<<<<<<<<<<<<<<<<<<<<<<<<
         $subject
Index: @<<<<<<<<<<<<<<<<<<<<<<<<<<<< ^<<<<<<<<<<<<<<<<<<<<<<<<<<<<
       $index,                       $description
Priority: @<<<<<<<<<< Date: @<<<<<<< ^<<<<<<<<<<<<<<<<<<<<<<<<<<<<
          $priority,        $date,   $description
From: @<<<<<<<<<<<<<<<<<<<<<<<<<<<<< ^<<<<<<<<<<<<<<<<<<<<<<<<<<<<
      $from,                         $description
```

```
Assigned to: @<<<<<<<<<<<<<<<<<<<<<< ^<<<<<<<<<<<<<<<<<<<<<<<<<<<<
             $programmer,            $description
~                                    ^<<<<<<<<<<<<<<<<<<<<<<<<<<<<
                                     $description
~                                    ^<<<<<<<<<<<<<<<<<<<<<<<<<<<<
                                     $description
~                                    ^<<<<<<<<<<<<<<<<<<<<<<<<<<<<
                                     $description
~                                    ^<<<<<<<<<<<<<<<<<<<<<<<<<<<<
                                     $description
~                                    ^<<<<<<<<<<<<<<<<<<<<<<<<...
                                     $description
```

…ame output channel, but you'll have to handle $– (lines

…lly blank, you should consider using the reset operator …it can prevent the bug of adding another field and forget-

…rkeley socket mechanism. If you don't have sockets, you … names as the corresponding system calls, but the argu- … rl file handles work differently than C file descriptors. … gs, so you don't need to pass that information. Here is a

```
…ame('tcp');
…ne($port, 'tcp')

…) = gethostbyname($hostname);
…) = gethostbyname($them);

…, $thisaddr);
…port, $thataddr);

socket(S, &PF_INET, &SOCK_STREAM, $proto) || die "socket: $!";
bind(S, $this) || die "bind: $!";
connect(S, $that) || die "connect: $!";

select(S); $| = 1; select(stdout);
```

```
if ($child = fork) {
        while (<>) {
                print S;
        }
        sleep 3;
        do dokill();
}
else {
        while (<S>) {
                print;
        }
}
```

And here's a server:

```
($port) = @ARGV;
$port = 2345 unless $port;

require 'sys/socket.ph';

$sockaddr = 'S n a4 x8';

($name, $aliases, $proto) = getprotobyname('tcp');
($name, $aliases, $port) = getservbyname($port, 'tcp')
        unless $port =~ /^\d+$/;

$this = pack($sockaddr, &AF_INET, $port, "\0\0\0\0");

select(NS); $| = 1; select(stdout);

socket(S, &PF_INET, &SOCK_STREAM, $proto) || die "socket: $!";
bind(S, $this) || die "bind: $!";
listen(S, 5) || die "connect: $!";

select(S); $| = 1; select(stdout);

for (;;) {
        print "Listening again\n";
        ($addr = accept(NS,S)) || die $!;
        print "accept ok\n";

        ($af,$port,$inetaddr) = unpack($sockaddr,$addr);
        @inetaddr = unpack('C4',$inetaddr);
        print "$af $port @inetaddr\n";

        while (<NS>) {
                print;
                print NS;
        }
}
```

19

12. Predefined Names

The following names have special meaning to *perl.* I could have used alphabetic symbols for some of these, but I didn't want to take the chance that someone would say reset ''a–zA–Z'' and wipe them all out. You'll just have to suffer along with these silly symbols. Most of them have reasonable mnemonics, or analogues in one of the shells.

`$_` The default input and pattern-searching space. The following pairs are equivalent:

```
while (<>) {...# only equivalent in while!
while ($_ = <>) {...

/^Subject:/
$_ =~ /^Subject:/

y/a-z/A-Z/
$_ =~ y/a-z/A-Z/

chop
chop($_)
```

(Mnemonic: underline is understood in certain operations.)

`$.` The current input line number of the last filehandle that was read. Readonly. Remember that only an explicit close on the filehandle resets the line number. Since <> never does an explicit close, line numbers increase across ARGV files (but see examples under eof). (Mnemonic: many programs use . to mean the current line number.)

`$/` The input record separator, newline by default. Works like *awk*'s RS variable, including treating blank lines as delimiters if set to the null string. You may set it to a multicharacter string to match a multi-character delimiter. Note that setting it to "\n\n" means something slightly different than setting it to "", if the file contains consecutive blank lines. Setting it to "" will treat two or more consecutive blank lines as a single blank line. Setting it to "\n\n" will blindly assume that the next input character belongs to the next paragraph, even if it's a newline. (Mnemonic: / is used to delimit line boundaries when quoting poetry.)

`$,` The output field separator for the print operator. Ordinarily the print operator simply prints out the comma separated fields you specify. In order to get behavior more like *awk*, set this variable as you would set *awk*'s OFS variable to specify what is printed between fields. (Mnemonic: what is printed when there is a , in your print statement.)

`$"` This is like $, except that it applies to array values interpolated into a double-quoted string (or similar interpreted string). Default is a space. (Mnemonic: obvious, I think.)

`$\` The output record separator for the print operator. Ordinarily the print operator simply prints out the comma separated fields you specify, with no trailing newline or record separator assumed. In order to get behavior more like *awk*, set this variable as you would set *awk*'s ORS variable to specify what is printed at the end of the print. (Mnemonic: you set $\ instead of adding \n at the end of the print. Also, it's just like /, but it's what you get ''back'' from *perl*.)

`$#` The output format for printed numbers. This variable is a half-hearted attempt to emulate *awk*'s OFMT variable. There are times, however, when *awk* and *perl* have differing notions of what is in fact numeric. Also, the initial value is %.20g rather than %.6g, so you need to set $# explicitly to get *awk*'s value. (Mnemonic: # is the number sign.)

`$%` The current page number of the currently selected output channel. (Mnemonic: % is page number in nroff.)

`$=` The current page length (printable lines) of the currently selected output channel. Default is 60. (Mnemonic: = has horizontal lines.)

$– The number of lines left on the page of the currently selected output channel. (Mnemonic: lines_on_page – lines_printed.)

$~ The name of the current report format for the currently selected output channel. Default is name of the filehandle. (Mnemonic: brother to $^.)

$^ The name of the current top-of-page format for the currently selected output channel. Default is name of the filehandle with "_TOP" appended. (Mnemonic: points to top of page.)

$| If set to nonzero, forces a flush after every write or print on the currently selected output channel. Default is 0. Note that *STDOUT* will typically be line buffered if output is to the terminal and block buffered otherwise. Setting this variable is useful primarily when you are outputting to a pipe, such as when you are running a *perl* script under rsh and want to see the output as it's happening. (Mnemonic: when you want your pipes to be piping hot.)

$$ The process number of the *perl* running this script. (Mnemonic: same as shells.)

$? The status returned by the last pipe close, backtick (``) command or *system* operator. Note that this is the status word returned by the wait() system call, so the exit value of the subprocess is actually ($? >> 8). $? & 255 gives which signal, if any, the process died from, and whether there was a core dump. (Mnemonic: similar to sh and ksh.)

$& The string matched by the last successful pattern match (not counting any matches hidden within a BLOCK or eval enclosed by the current BLOCK). (Mnemonic: like & in some editors.)

$` The string preceding whatever was matched by the last successful pattern match (not counting any matches hidden within a BLOCK or eval enclosed by the current BLOCK). (Mnemonic: ` often precedes a quoted string.)

$´ The string following whatever was matched by the last successful pattern match (not counting any matches hidden within a BLOCK or eval enclosed by the current BLOCK). (Mnemonic: ´ often follows a quoted string.) Example:

```
$_ = ´abcdefghi´;
/def/;
print "$`:$&:$´\n"; # prints abc:def:ghi
```

$+ The last bracket matched by the last search pattern. This is useful if you don't know which of a set of alternative patterns matched. For example:

```
/Version: (.*)|Revision: (.*)/ && ($rev = $+);
```

(Mnemonic: be positive and forward looking.)

$* Set to 1 to do multiline matching within a string, 0 to tell *perl* that it can assume that strings contain a single line, for the purpose of optimizing pattern matches. Pattern matches on strings containing multiple newlines can produce confusing results when $* is 0. Default is 0. (Mnemonic: * matches multiple things.) Note that this variable only influences the interpretation of ^ and $. A literal newline can be searched for even when $* == 0.

$0 Contains the name of the file containing the *perl* script being executed. Assigning to $0 modifies the argument area that the ps(1) program sees. (Mnemonic: same as sh and ksh.)

$<digit> Contains the subpattern from the corresponding set of parentheses in the last pattern matched, not counting patterns matched in nested blocks that have been exited already. (Mnemonic: like \digit.)

$[The index of the first element in an array, and of the first character in a substring. Default is 0, but you could set it to 1 to make *perl* behave more like *awk* (or Fortran) when subscripting and when evaluating the index() and substr() functions. (Mnemonic: [begins subscripts.)

$] The string printed out when you say ''perl -v''. It can be used to determine at the beginning of a script whether the perl interpreter executing the script is in the right range of versions. If used in a numeric context, returns the version + patchlevel / 1000. Example:

```
        # see if getc is available
    ($version,$patchlevel) =
        $] =~ /(\d+\.\d+).*\nPatch level: (\d+)/;
    print STDERR "(No filename completion available.)\n"
        if $version * 1000 + $patchlevel < 2016;
```

or, used numerically,

```
warn "No checksumming!\n" if $] < 3.019;
```

(Mnemonic: Is this version of perl in the right bracket?)

$; The subscript separator for multi-dimensional array emulation. If you refer to an associative array element as

```
$foo{$a,$b,$c}
```

it really means

```
$foo{join($;, $a, $b, $c)}
```

But don't put

```
@foo{$a,$b,$c}# a slice—note the @
```

which means

```
($foo{$a},$foo{$b},$foo{$c})
```

Default is "\034", the same as SUBSEP in *awk*. Note that if your keys contain binary data there might not be any safe value for $;. (Mnemonic: comma (the syntactic subscript separator) is a semi-semicolon. Yeah, I know, it's pretty lame, but $, is already taken for something more important.)

$! If used in a numeric context, yields the current value of errno, with all the usual caveats. (This means that you shouldn't depend on the value of $! to be anything in particular unless you've gotten a specific error return indicating a system error.) If used in a string context, yields the corresponding system error string. You can assign to $! in order to set errno if, for instance, you want $! to return the string for error n, or you want to set the exit value for the die operator. (Mnemonic: What just went bang?)

$@ The perl syntax error message from the last eval command. If null, the last eval parsed and executed correctly (although the operations you invoked may have failed in the normal fashion). (Mnemonic: Where was the syntax error ''at''?)

$< The real uid of this process. (Mnemonic: it's the uid you came FROM, if you're running setuid.)

$> The effective uid of this process. Example:

```
$< = $>;# set real uid to the effective uid
($<,$>) = ($>,$<);# swap real and effective uid
```

(Mnemonic: it's the uid you went TO, if you're running setuid.) Note: $< and $> can only be swapped on machines supporting setreuid().

$(The real gid of this process. If you are on a machine that supports membership in multiple groups simultaneously, gives a space separated list of groups you are in. The first number is the one returned by getgid(), and the subsequent ones by getgroups(), one of which may be the same as the first number. (Mnemonic: parentheses are used to GROUP things. The real gid is the group you LEFT, if you're running setgid.)

$) The effective gid of this process. If you are on a machine that supports membership in multiple groups simultaneously, gives a space separated list of groups you are in. The first number is the one returned by getegid(), and the subsequent ones by getgroups(), one of which may be the same as the first number. (Mnemonic: parentheses are used to GROUP things. The effective gid is the group that's RIGHT for you, if you're running setgid.)

Note: $<, $>, $(and $) can only be set on machines that support the corresponding set[re][ug]id() routine. $(and $) can only be swapped on machines supporting setregid().

$: The current set of characters after which a string may be broken to fill continuation fields (starting with ^) in a format. Default is "\n-", to break on whitespace or hyphens. (Mnemonic: a "colon" in poetry is a part of a line.)

$^D The current value of the debugging flags. (Mnemonic: value of **–D** switch.)

$^F The maximum system file descriptor, ordinarily 2. System file descriptors are passed to subprocesses, while higher file descriptors are not. During an open, system file descriptors are preserved even if the open fails. Ordinary file descriptors are closed before the open is attempted.

19 $^I The current value of the inplace-edit extension. Use undef to disable inplace editing. (Mnemonic: value of **–i** switch.)

$^L What formats output to perform a formfeed. Default is \f.

$^P The internal flag that the debugger clears so that it doesn't debug itself. You could conceivable disable debugging yourself by clearing it.

$^T The time at which the script began running, in seconds since the epoch. The values returned by the **–M**, **–A** and **–C** filetests are based on this value.

$^W The current value of the warning switch. (Mnemonic: related to the **–w** switch.)

$^X The name that Perl itself was executed as, from argv[0].

$ARGV contains the name of the current file when reading from <>.

@ARGV The array ARGV contains the command line arguments intended for the script. Note that $#ARGV is the generally number of arguments minus one, since $ARGV[0] is the first argument, NOT the command name. See $0 for the command name.

@INC The array INC contains the list of places to look for *perl* scripts to be evaluated by the "do EXPR" command or the "require" command. It initially consists of the arguments to any **–I** command line switches, followed by the default *perl* library, probably "/usr/local/lib/perl", followed by ".", to represent the current directory.

%INC The associative array INC contains entries for each filename that has been included via "do" or "require". The key is the filename you specified, and the value is the location of the file actually found. The "require" command uses this array to determine whether a given file has already been included.

$ENV{expr}
The associative array ENV contains your current environment. Setting a value in ENV changes the environment for child processes.

$SIG{expr}

The associative array SIG is used to set signal handlers for various signals. Example:

```
sub handler {# 1st argument is signal name
local($sig) = @_;
print "Caught a SIG$sig--shutting down\n";
close(LOG);
exit(0);
}

$SIG{'INT'} = 'handler';
$SIG{'QUIT'} = 'handler';
...
$SIG{'INT'} = 'DEFAULT';# restore default action
$SIG{'QUIT'} = 'IGNORE';# ignore SIGQUIT
```

The SIG array only contains values for the signals actually set within the perl script.

13. Packages

Perl provides a mechanism for alternate namespaces to protect packages from stomping on each others variables. By default, a perl script starts compiling into the package known as "main". By use of the *package* declaration, you can switch namespaces. The scope of the package declaration is from the declaration itself to the end of the enclosing block (the same scope as the local() operator). Typically it would be the first declaration in a file to be included by the "require" operator. You can switch into a package in more than one place; it merely influences which symbol table is used by the compiler for the rest of that block. You can refer to variables and filehandles in other packages by prefixing the identifier with the package name and a single quote. If the package name is null, the "main" package as assumed.

Only identifiers starting with letters are stored in the packages symbol table. All other symbols are kept in package "main". In addition, the identifiers STDIN, STDOUT, STDERR, ARGV, ARGVOUT, ENV, INC and SIG are forced to be in package "main", even when used for other purposes than their built-in one. Note also that, if you have a package called "m", "s" or "y", the you can't use the qualified form of an identifier since it will be interpreted instead as a pattern match, a substitution or a translation.

Eval'ed strings are compiled in the package in which the eval was compiled in. (Assignments to $SIG{}, however, assume the signal handler specified is in the main package. Qualify the signal handler name if you wish to have a signal handler in a package.) For an example, examine perldb.pl in the perl library. It initially switches to the DB package so that the debugger doesn't interfere with variables in the script you are trying to debug. At various points, however, it temporarily switches back to the main package to evaluate various expressions in the context of the main package.

The symbol table for a package happens to be stored in the associative array of that name prepended with an underscore. The value in each entry of the associative array is what you are referring to when you use the *name notation. In fact, the following have the same effect (in package main, anyway), though the first is more efficient because it does the symbol table lookups at compile time:

```
local(*foo) = *bar;
local($_main{'foo'}) = $_main{'bar'};
```

You can use this to print out all the variables in a package, for instance. Here is dumpvar.pl from the perl library:

19

```
package dumpvar;

    sub main'dumpvar {
        ($package) = @_;
        local(*stab) = eval("*_$package");
        while (($key,$val) = each(%stab)) {
            {
                local(*entry) = $val;
                if (defined $entry) {
                    print "\$$key = '$entry'\n";
                }
                if (defined @entry) {
                    print "\@$key = (\n";
                    foreach $num ($[ .. $#entry) {
                        print "  $num\t'",$entry[$num],"'\n";
                    }
                    print ")\n";
                }
                if ($key ne "_$package" && defined %entry) {
                    print "\%$key = (\n";
                    foreach $key (sort keys(%entry)) {
                        print "  $key\t'",$entry{$key},"'\n";
                    }
                    print ")\n";
                }
            }
        }
    }
```


Note that, even though the subroutine is compiled in package dumpvar, the name of the subroutine is qualified so that its name is inserted into package ''main''.

14. Style

Each programmer will, of course, have his or her own preferences in regards to formatting, but there are some general guidelines that will make your programs easier to read.

1. Just because you CAN do something a particular way doesn't mean that you SHOULD do it that way. *Perl* is designed to give you several ways to do anything, so consider picking the most readable one. For instance

   ```
   open(FOO,$foo) || die "Can't open $foo: $!";
   ```

   is better than

   ```
   die "Can't open $foo: $!" unless open(FOO,$foo);
   ```

   because the second way hides the main point of the statement in a modifier. On the other hand

   ```
   print "Starting analysis\n" if $verbose;
   ```

   is better than

   ```
   $verbose && print "Starting analysis\n";
   ```

   since the main point isn't whether the user typed -v or not.

Similarly, just because an operator lets you assume default arguments doesn't mean that you have to make use of the defaults. The defaults are there for lazy systems programmers writing one-shot programs. If you want your program to be readable, consider supplying the argument.

Along the same lines, just because you *can* omit parentheses in many places doesn't mean that you ought to:

```
return print reverse sort num values array;
return print(reverse(sort num (values(%array))));
```

When in doubt, parenthesize. At the very least it will let some poor schmuck bounce on the % key in vi.

Even if you aren't in doubt, consider the mental welfare of the person who has to maintain the code after you, and who will probably put parens in the wrong place.

2. Don't go through silly contortions to exit a loop at the top or the bottom, when *perl* provides the "last" operator so you can exit in the middle. Just outdent it a little to make it more visible:

```
line:
    for (;;) {
        statements;
    last line if $foo;
        next line if /^#/;
        statements;
    }
```


3. Don't be afraid to use loop labels— they're there to enhance readability as well as to allow multi-level loop breaks. See last example.
4. For portability, when using features that may not be implemented on every machine, test the construct in an eval to see if it fails. If you know what version or patchlevel a particular feature was implemented, you can test $] to see if it will be there.
5. Choose mnemonic identifiers.
6. Be consistent.

15. Debugging

If you invoke *perl* with a **–d** switch, your script will be run under a debugging monitor. It will halt before the first executable statement and ask you for a command, such as:

h — Prints out a help message.

T — Stack trace.

s — Single step. Executes until it reaches the beginning of another statement.

n — Next. Executes over subroutine calls, until it reaches the beginning of the next statement.

f — Finish. Executes statements until it has finished the current subroutine.

c — Continue. Executes until the next breakpoint is reached.

c line — Continue to the specified line. Inserts a one-time-only breakpoint at the specified line.

<CR> — Repeat last n or s.

l min+incr — List incr+1 lines starting at min. If min is omitted, starts where last listing left off. If incr is omitted, previous value of incr is used.

l min-max List lines in the indicated range.

l line List just the indicated line.

l List next window.

\- List previous window.

w line List window around line.

l subname List subroutine. If it's a long subroutine it just lists the beginning. Use "l" to list more.

/pattern/ Regular expression search forward for pattern; the final / is optional.

?pattern? Regular expression search backward for pattern; the final ? is optional.

L List lines that have breakpoints or actions.

S Lists the names of all subroutines.

t Toggle trace mode on or off.

b line conditionSet a breakpoint. If line is omitted, sets a breakpoint on the line that is about to be executed. If a condition is specified, it is evaluated each time the statement is reached and a breakpoint is taken only if the condition is true. Breakpoints may only be set on lines that begin an executable statement.

b subname condition
Set breakpoint at first executable line of subroutine.

d line Delete breakpoint. If line is omitted, deletes the breakpoint on the line that is about to be executed.

D Delete all breakpoints.

a line commandSet an action for line. A multi-line command may be entered by backslashing the newlines.

A Delete all line actions.

< command Set an action to happen before every debugger prompt. A multi-line command may be entered by backslashing the newlines.

> command Set an action to happen after the prompt when you've just given a command to return to executing the script. A multi-line command may be entered by backslashing the newlines.

V package List all variables in package. Default is main package.

! number Redo a debugging command. If number is omitted, redoes the previous command.

! -number Redo the command that was that many commands ago.

H -number Display last n commands. Only commands longer than one character are listed. If number is omitted, lists them all.

q or ^D Quit.

command Execute command as a perl statement. A missing semicolon will be supplied.

p expr Same as "print DB'OUT expr". The DB'OUT filehandle is opened to /dev/tty, regardless of where STDOUT may be redirected to.

If you want to modify the debugger, copy perldb.pl from the perl library to your current directory and modify it as necessary. (You'll also have to put -I. on your command line.) You can do some customization by setting up a .perldb file which contains initialization code. For instance, you could make aliases like these:

```
$DB'alias{'len'} = 's/^len(.*)/p length($1)/';
$DB'alias{'stop'} = 's/^stop (at| in)/b/';
$DB'alias{'.'} =
  's/^\./p "\$DB\'sub(\$DB\'line):\t",\$DB\'line[\$DB\'line]/';
```

16. Setuid Scripts

Perl is designed to make it easy to write secure setuid and setgid scripts. Unlike shells, which are based on multiple substitution passes on each line of the script, *perl* uses a more conventional evaluation scheme with fewer hidden ''gotchas''. Additionally, since the language has more built-in functionality, it has to rely less upon external (and possibly untrustworthy) programs to accomplish its purposes.

In an unpatched 4.2 or 4.3bsd kernel, setuid scripts are intrinsically insecure, but this kernel feature can be disabled. If it is, *perl* can emulate the setuid and setgid mechanism when it notices the otherwise useless setuid/gid bits on perl scripts. If the kernel feature isn't disabled, *perl* will complain loudly that your setuid script is insecure. You'll need to either disable the kernel setuid script feature, or put a C wrapper around the script.

When perl is executing a setuid script, it takes special precautions to prevent you from falling into any obvious traps. (In some ways, a perl script is more secure than the corresponding C program.) Any command line argument, environment variable, or input is marked as ''tainted'', and may not be used, directly or indirectly, in any command that invokes a subshell, or in any command that modifies files, directories or processes. Any variable that is set within an expression that has previously referenced a tainted value also becomes tainted (even if it is logically impossible for the tainted value to influence the variable). For example:

```
$foo = shift;             # $foo is tainted
$bar = $foo,'bar';        # $bar is also tainted
$xxx = <>;                # Tainted
$path = $ENV{'PATH'};     # Tainted, but see below
$abc = 'abc';             # Not tainted

system "echo $foo";       # Insecure
system "/bin/echo", $foo; # Secure (doesn't use sh)
system "echo $bar";       # Insecure
system "echo $abc";       # Insecure until PATH set

$ENV{'PATH'} = '/bin:/usr/bin';
$ENV{'IFS'} = '' if $ENV{'IFS'} ne '';

$path = $ENV{'PATH'};     # Not tainted
system "echo $abc";       # Is secure now!

open(FOO,"$foo");         # OK
open(FOO,">$foo");        # Not OK

open(FOO,"echo $foo|");   # Not OK, but...
open(FOO,"-|") || exec 'echo', $foo;     # OK

$zzz = `echo $foo`;       # Insecure, zzz tainted

unlink $abc,$foo;         # Insecure
umask $foo;               # Insecure

exec "echo $foo";         # Insecure
exec "echo", $foo;        # Secure (doesn't use sh)
exec "sh", '-c', $foo;    # Considered secure, alas
```

The taintedness is associated with each scalar value, so some elements of an array can be tainted, and others not.

19

If you try to do something insecure, you will get a fatal error saying something like ''Insecure dependency'' or ''Insecure PATH''. Note that you can still write an insecure system call or exec, but only by explicitly doing something like the last example above. You can also bypass the tainting mechanism by referencing subpatterns—*perl* presumes that if you reference a substring using $1, $2, etc, you knew what you were doing when you wrote the pattern:

```
$ARGV[0] =~ /^-P(\w+)$/;
$printer = $1;              # Not tainted
```

This is fairly secure since \w+ doesn't match shell metacharacters. Use of .+ would have been insecure, but *perl* doesn't check for that, so you must be careful with your patterns. This is the ONLY mechanism for untainting user supplied filenames if you want to do file operations on them (unless you make $> equal to $<).

It's also possible to get into trouble with other operations that don't care whether they use tainted values. Make judicious use of the file tests in dealing with any user-supplied filenames. When possible, do opens and such after setting $> = $<. *Perl* doesn't prevent you from opening tainted filenames for reading, so be careful what you print out. The tainting mechanism is intended to prevent stupid mistakes, not to remove the need for thought.

17. Traps

Accustomed *awk* users should take special note of the following:

* Semicolons are required after all simple statements in *perl* (except at the end of a block). Newline is not a statement delimiter.
* Curly brackets are required on ifs and whiles.
* Variables begin with $ or @ in *perl.*
* Arrays index from 0 unless you set $[. Likewise string positions in substr() and index().
* You have to decide whether your array has numeric or string indices.
* Associative array values do not spring into existence upon mere reference.
* You have to decide whether you want to use string or numeric comparisons.
* Reading an input line does not split it for you. You get to split it yourself to an array. And the *split* operator has different arguments.
* The current input line is normally in $_, not $0. It generally does not have the newline stripped. ($0 is the name of the program executed.)
* $<digit> does not refer to fields—it refers to substrings matched by the last match pattern.
* The *print* statement does not add field and record separators unless you set $, and $\.
* You must open your files before you print to them.
* The range operator is ''..'', not comma. (The comma operator works as in C.)
* The match operator is ''=~'', not ''~''. (''~'' is the one's complement operator, as in C.)
* The exponentiation operator is ''**'', not ''^''. (''^'' is the XOR operator, as in C.)
* The concatenation operator is ''.'', not the null string. (Using the null string would render ''/pat/ /pat/'' unparsable, since the third slash would be interpreted as a division operator—the tokener is in fact slightly context sensitive for operators like /, ?, and <. And in fact, . itself can be the beginning of a number.)
* *Next, exit* and *continue* work differently.
* The following variables work differently

Awk	Perl
ARGC	$#ARGV
ARGV[0]	$0

FILENAME	$ARGV
FNR	$. – something
FS	(whatever you like)
NF	$#Fld, or some such
NR	$.
OFMT	$#
OFS	$,
ORS	$\
RLENGTH	length($&)
RS	$/
RSTART	length($`)
SUBSEP	$;

* When in doubt, run the *awk* construct through a2p and see what it gives you.

Cerebral C programmers should take note of the following:

* Curly brackets are required on ifs and whiles.
* You should use ''elsif'' rather than ''else if''
* *Break* and *continue* become *last* and *next*, respectively.
* There's no switch statement.
* Variables begin with $ or @ in *perl.*
* Printf does not implement *.
* Comments begin with #, not /*.
* You can't take the address of anything.
* ARGV must be capitalized.
* The ''system'' calls link, unlink, rename, etc. return nonzero for success, not 0.
* Signal handlers deal with signal names, not numbers.

Seasoned *sed* programmers should take note of the following:

* Backreferences in substitutions use $ rather than \.
* The pattern matching metacharacters (,), and | do not have backslashes in front.
* The range operator is .. rather than comma.

Sharp shell programmers should take note of the following:

* The backtick operator does variable interpretation without regard to the presence of single quotes in the command.
* The backtick operator does no translation of the return value, unlike csh.
* Shells (especially csh) do several levels of substitution on each command line. *Perl* does substitution only in certain constructs such as double quotes, backticks, angle brackets and search patterns.
* Shells interpret scripts a little bit at a time. *Perl* compiles the whole program before executing it.
* The arguments are available via @ARGV, not $1, $2, etc.
* The environment is not automatically made available as variables.

18. Errata and Addenda

The Perl book, *Programming Perl*, has the following omissions and goofs.

On page 5, the examples which read

```
eval "/usr/bin/perl
```

19

should read

```
eval "exec /usr/bin/perl
```

On page 195, the equivalent to the System V sum program only works for very small files. To do larger files, use

```
undef $/;
$checksum = unpack("%32C*",<>) % 32767;
```

The descriptions of alarm and sleep refer to signal SIGALARM. These should refer to SIGALRM.

The **–0** switch to set the initial value of $/ was added to Perl after the book went to press.

The **–l** switch now does automatic line ending processing.

The qx// construct is now a synonym for backticks.

$0 may now be assigned to set the argument displayed by *ps* (1).

The new @###.## format was omitted accidentally from the description on formats.

It wasn't known at press time that s///ee caused multiple evaluations of the replacement expression. This is to be construed as a feature.

(LIST) x $count now does array replication.

There is now no limit on the number of parentheses in a regular expression.

In double-quote context, more escapes are supported: \e, \a, \x1b, \c[, \l, \L, \u, \U, \E. The latter five control up/lower case translation.

The **$/** variable may now be set to a multi-character delimiter.

There is now a g modifier on ordinary pattern matching that causes it to iterate through a string finding multiple matches.

All of the $^X variables are new except for $^T.

The default top-of-form format for FILEHANDLE is now FILEHANDLE_TOP rather than top.

The eval {} and sort {} constructs were added in version 4.018.

The v and V (little-endian) template options for pack and unpack were added in 4.019.

Berkeley 4.4 Software Distribution

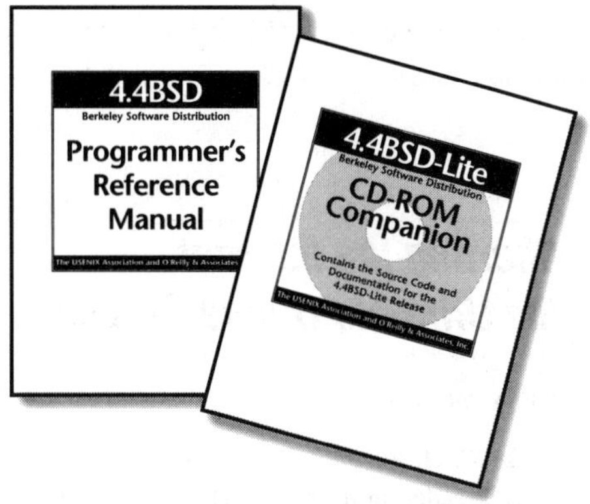

4.4BSD is the final release of what may be one of the most significant research projects in the history of computing. When Bell Labs originally released UNIX source code to the R&D community, brilliant researchers wrote their own software and added it to UNIX in a spree of creative anarchy that hasn't been equaled since. The Berkeley Software Distribution became the repository of much of that work.

In those years of creative ferment, source code was widely available, so programmers could build on the work of others. As UNIX became commercialized, access to source became increasingly curtailed and original development more difficult.

With this release of 4.4BSD-Lite, you need no longer work at a university or UNIX system development house to have access to UNIX source. The source code included on the 4.4BSD-Lite CD-ROM Companion will provide invaluable information on the design of any modern UNIX or UNIX-like system, and the source code for the utilities and support libraries will greatly enhance any programmer's toolkit. (Note that the 4.4BSD-Lite distribution does not include sources for the complete 4.4BSD system. The source code for a small number of utilities and files, including a few from the operating system, were removed so that the system could be freely distributed.)

In addition to source code, the CD includes the manual pages, other documentation, and research papers from the University of California, Berkeley's 4.4BSD-Lite distribution.

This documentation is also available in printed form as a five-volume set.

—Tim O'Reilly

4.4BSD-Lite CD Companion

112 pages plus CD-ROM
CD Domestic ISBN 1-56592-081-3
CD International ISBN 1-56592-092-9

This CD is a copy of the University of California, Berkeley's 4.4BSD-Lite release, with additional documentation and enhancements. Access to the source code included here will provide invaluable information on the design of a modern UNIX-like system, and the source code for the utilities and support libraries will greatly enhance any programmer's toolkit. The CD is a source distribution, and does not contain program binaries for any architecture. It will not be possible to compile or run this software without a pre-existing system that is already installed and running. The 4.4BSD-Lite distribution did not include sources for the complete 4.4BSD system. The source code for a small number of utilities and files (including a few from the operating system) were removed so that the system could be freely distributed.

4.4BSD System Manager's Manual

646(est.) pages, ISBN 1-56592-080-5

Man pages for system administration commands and files, plus papers on system administration.

4.4BSD User's Reference Manual

909 pages, ISBN 1-56592-075-9

The famous "man pages" for over 500 utilities.

4.4BSD User's Supplementary Documents

686(est.) pages, ISBN 1-56592-076-7

Papers providing in-depth documentation of complex programs such as the shell, editors, and word processing utilities.

4.4BSD Programmer's Reference Manual

884 pages, ISBN 1-56592-078-3

Man pages for system calls, libraries, and file formats.

4.4BSD Programmer's Supplementary Documents

606(est.) pages, ISBN 1-56592-079-1

The original Bell and BSD research papers providing in-depth documentation of the programming environment.

GLOBAL NETWORK NAVIGATOR

The Global Network Navigator™ (GNN) is a unique kind of information service that makes the Internet easy and enjoyable to use. We organize access to the vast information resources of the Internet so that you can find what you want. We also help you understand the Internet and the many ways you can explore it.

Charting the Internet, the Ultimate Online Service

In GNN you'll find:

- ***The Online Whole Internet Catalog***, an interactive card catalog for Internet resources that expands on the catalog in Ed Krol's bestselling book, *The Whole Internet User's Guide & Catalog.*

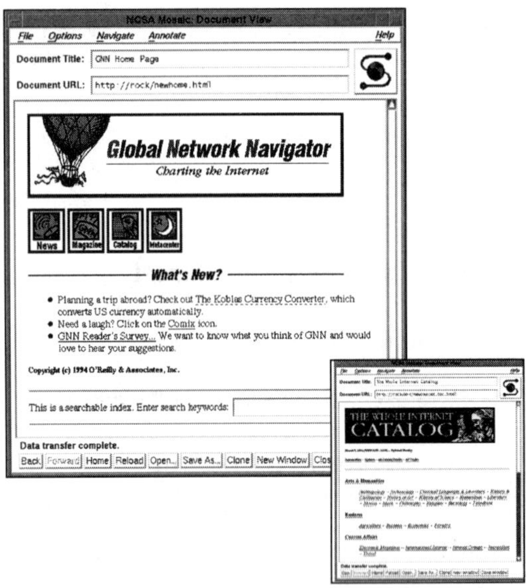

- ***Newsnet***, a news service that keeps you up to date on what's happening on the Net.
- ***The Netheads department***, which features profiles of interesting people on the Internet and commentary by Internet experts.
- ***GNN Metacenters***, special-interest online magazines aimed at serving the needs of particular audiences. GNN Metacenters not only gather the best Internet resources together in one convenient place, they also introduce new material from a variety of sources. Each Metacenter contains new feature articles, as well as columns, subject-oriented reference guides for using the Internet, and topic-oriented discussion groups. Travel, music, education, and computers are some of the areas that we cover.

All in all, GNN helps you get more value for the time you spend on the Internet.

Subscribe Today

GNN is available over the Internet as a subscription service. To get complete information about subscribing to GNN, send email to **info@gnn.com**. If you have access to a World Wide Web browser such as Mosaic or Lynx, you can use the following URL to register online: `http://gnn.com/`

If you use a browser that does not support online forms, you can retrieve an email version of the registration form automatically by sending email to **form@gnn.com**. Fill this form out and send it back to us by email, and we will confirm your registration.

FOR INFORMATION: ***800-998-9938****, 707-829-0515;* ***NUTS@ORA.COM***

BOOK INFORMATION AT YOUR FINGERTIPS

O'Reilly & Associates offers extensive online information through a Gopher server (*gopher.ora.com*). Here you can find detailed information on our entire catalog of books, tapes, and much more.

The O'Reilly Online Catalog

Gopher is basically a hierarchy of menus and files that can easily lead you to a wealth of information. Gopher is also easy to navigate; helpful instructions appear at the bottom of each screen (notice the three prompts in the sample screen below). Another nice feature is that Gopher files can be downloaded, saved, or printed out for future reference. You can also search Gopher files and even email them.

To give you an idea of our Gopher, here's a look at the top, or root, menu:

```
O'Reilly & Associates (The public gopher server)

      1.  News Flash! -- New Products and Projects/
      2.  Feature Articles/
      3.  Product Descriptions/
      4.  Ordering Information/
      5.  Complete Listing of Titles
      6.  Errata for "Learning Perl"
      7.  FTP Archive and Email Information/
      8.  Bibliographies/

Press ? for Help, q to Quit, u to go up a menu
```

The heart of the O'Reilly Gopher service is the extensive information provided on all ORA products in menu item three, "Product Descriptions." For most books this usually includes title information, a long description, a short author bio, the table of contents, quotes and reviews, a gif image of the book's cover, and even some interesting information about the animal featured on the cover (one of the benefits of a Gopher database is the ability to pack a lot of information in an organized, easy-to-find place).

How to Order

Another important listing is "Ordering Information," where we supply information to those interested in buying our books. Here, you'll find instructions and an application for ordering O'Reilly products online, a listing of distributors (local and international), a listing of bookstores that carry our titles, and much more.

The item that follows, "Complete Listing of Titles," is helpful when it's time to order. This single file, with short one-line listings of all ORA products, quickly provides the essentials for easy ordering: title, ISBN, and price.

And More

One of the most widely read areas of the O'Reilly Gopher is "News Flash!," which focuses on important new products and projects of ORA. Here, you'll find entries on newly published books and audiotapes; announcements of exciting new projects and product lines from ORA; upcoming tradeshows, conferences, and exhibitions of interest; author appearances; contest winners; job openings; and anything else that's timely and topical.

"Feature Articles" contains just that—many of the articles and interviews found here are excerpted from the O'Reilly magazine/catalog *ora.com*.

The "Bibliographies" entries are also very popular with readers, providing critical, objective reviews on the important literature in the field.

"FTP Archive and Email Information" contains helpful ORA email addresses, information about our "ora-news" listproc server, and detailed instructions on how to download ORA book examples via FTP.

Other menu listings are often available. "Errata for 'Learning Perl,'" for example, apprised readers of errata found in the first edition of our book, and responses to this file greatly aided our campaign to ferret out errors and typos for the upcoming corrected edition (a nice example of the mutual benefits of online interactivity).

Come and Explore

Our Gopher is vibrant and constantly in flux. By the time you actually log onto this Gopher, the root menu may well have changed. The goal is to always improve, and to that end we welcome your input (email: **gopher@ora.com**). We invite you to come and explore.

Here are four basic ways to call up our Gopher online.

1) If you have a local Gopher client, type:
   `gopher gopher.ora.com`
2) For Xgopher:
   `xgopher -xrm "xgopher.root\`
   `Server: gopher.ora.com"`
3) To use telnet (for those without a Gopher client):
   `telnet gopher.ora.com`
   login: **gopher** (no password)
4) For a World Wide Web browser, use this URL:
   `http://gopher.ora.com:70/`

COMPLETE LISTING OF TITLES

from O'Reilly & Associates, Inc.

Internet

The Whole Internet User's Guide & Catalog
Connecting to the Internet: An O'Reilly Buyer's Guide
!%@:: A Directory of Electronic Mail Addressing & Networks
Smileys

Using UNIX and X

UNIX Power Tools (with CD-ROM)
UNIX in a Nutshell: System V Edition
UNIX in a Nutshell: Berkeley Edition
SCO UNIX in a Nutshell
Learning the UNIX Operating System
Learning the vi Editor
Learning GNU Emacs
Learning the Korn Shell
Making TeX Work
sed & awk
MH & xmh: E-mail for Users & Programmers
Using UUCP and Usenet
X Window System User's Guide: Volume 3
X Window System User's Guide, Motif Edition: Volume 3M

System Administration

Essential System Administration
sendmail
Computer Security Basics
Practical UNIX Security
System Performance Tuning
TCP/IP Network Administration
Learning Perl
Programming perl
Managing NFS and NIS
Managing UUCP and Usenet
DNS and BIND
termcap & terminfo
X Window System Administrator's Guide: Volume 8
(available with or without CD-ROM)

UNIX and C Programming

ORACLE Performance Tuning
High Performance Computing
lex & yacc
POSIX Programmer's Guide
Power Programming with RPC
Programming with curses
Managing Projects with make
Software Portability with imake
Understanding and Using COFF
Migrating to Fortran 90
UNIX for FORTRAN Programmers
Using C on the UNIX System
Checking C Programs with lint
Practical C Programming
Understanding Japanese Information Processing

DCE (Distributed Computing Environment)

Distributing Applications Across DCE and Windows NT
Guide to Writing DCE Applications
Understanding DCE

Berkeley 4.4 Software Distribution

4.4BSD System Manager's Manual
4.4BSD User's Reference Manual
4.4BSD User's Supplementary Documents
4.4BSD Programmer's Reference Manual
4.4BSD Programmer's Supplementary Documents
4.4BSD-Lite CD Companion

X Programming

The X Window System in a Nutshell
X Protocol Reference Manual: Volume 0
Xlib Programming Manual: Volume 1
Xlib Reference Manual: Volume 2
X Toolkit Intrinsics Programming Manual: Volume 4
X Toolkit Intrinsics Programming Manual, Motif Edition: Volume 4M
X Toolkit Intrinsics Reference Manual: Volume 5
Motif Programming Manual: Volume 6A
Motif Reference Manual: Volume 6B
XView Programming Manual: Volume 7A
XView Reference Manual: Volume 7B
PEXlib Programming Manual
PEXlib Reference Manual
PHIGS Programming Manual (softcover or hardcover)
PHIGS Reference Manual
Programmer's Supplement for R5 of the X Window System

The X Resource

A quarterly working journal for X programmers
The X Resource: Issues 0 through 10

Other

Building a Successful Software Business
Love Your Job!

Travel

Travelers' Tales Thailand

Audiotapes

Internet Talk Radio's "Geek of the Week" Interviews

The Future of the Internet Protocol, 4 hours
Global Network Operations, 2 hours
Mobile IP Networking, 1 hour
Networked Information and Online Libraries, 1 hour
Security and Networks, 1 hour
European Networking, 1 hour

Notable Speeches of the Information Age

John Perry Barlow, 1.5 hours

INTERNATIONAL DISTRIBUTORS

Customers outside North America can now order O'Reilly & Associates' books through the following distributors. They offer our international customers faster order processing, more bookstores, increased representation at tradeshows worldwide, and the high-quality, responsive service our customers have come to expect.

Europe, Middle East, and Africa

except Germany, Switzerland, and Austria

INQUIRIES

International Thomson Publishing Europe
Berkshire House
168-173 High Holborn
London WC1V 7AA
United Kingdom
Telephone: 44-71-497-1422
Fax: 44-71-497-1426
Email: danni.dolbear@itpuk.co.uk

ORDERS

International Thomson Publishing Services, Ltd.
Cheriton House, North Way
Andover, Hampshire SP10 5BE
United Kingdom
Telephone: 44-264-342-832 (UK orders)
Telephone: 44-264-342-806 (outside UK)
Fax: 44-264-364418 (UK orders)
Fax: 44-264-342761 (outside UK)

Germany, Switzerland, and Austria

International Thomson Publishing GmbH
O'Reilly-International Thomson Verlag
Königswinterer Strasse 418
53227 Bonn
Germany
Telephone: 49-228-445171
Fax: 49-228-441342
Email (CompuServe): 100272,2422
Email (Internet): 100272.2422@compuserve.com

Asia

except Japan

INQUIRIES

International Thomson Publishing Asia
221 Henderson Road
#05 10 Henderson Building
Singapore 0315
Telephone: 65-272-6496
Fax: 65-272-6498

ORDERS

Telephone: 65-268-7867
Fax: 65-268-6727

Australia

WoodsLane Pty. Ltd.
Unit 8, 101 Darley Street (P.O. Box 935)
Mona Vale NSW 2103
Australia
Telephone: 61-2-9795944
Fax: 61-2-9973348
Email: woods@tmx.mhs.oz.au

New Zealand

WoodsLane New Zealand Ltd.
7 Purnell Street (P.O. Box 575)
Wanganui, New Zealand
Telephone: 64-6-3476543
Fax: 64-6-3454840
Email: woods@tmx.mhs.oz.au

The Americas, Japan, and Oceania

O'Reilly & Associates, Inc.
103A Morris Street
Sebastopol, CA 95472 U.S.A.
Telephone: 707-829-0515
Telephone: 800-998-9938 (U.S. & Canada)
Fax: 707-829-0104
Email: order@ora.com

USENIX

THE UNIX AND ADVANCED COMPUTING SYSTEMS
PROFESSIONAL AND TECHNICAL ASSOCIATION
2560 Ninth Street, Suite 215, Berkeley, CA USA 94710
Telephone 1-510-528-8649, FAX: 1-510-548-5738
Internet: office@usenix.org

NO POSTAGE NECESSARY IF MAILED IN THE UNITED STATES

BUSINESS REPLY MAIL

FIRST CLASS MAIL PERMIT NO. 80 SEBASTOPOL, CA

Postage will be paid by addressee

O'Reilly & Associates, Inc.
103A Morris Street
Sebastopol, CA 95472-9902

NO POSTAGE NECESSARY IF MAILED IN THE UNITED STATES

BUSINESS REPLY MAIL

FIRST CLASS MAIL PERMIT NO. 80 SEBASTOPOL, CA

Postage will be paid by addressee

O'Reilly & Associates, Inc.
103A Morris Street
Sebastopol, CA 95472-9902